DISTANCE IN INTERNATIONAL BUSINESS: CONCEPT, COST AND VALUE

PROGRESS IN INTERNATIONAL BUSINESS RESEARCH

Series Editors: The European International Business Academy (EIBA)

Recent Volumes:

Volume 1: Progress in International Business Research – Edited by Gabriel R.G. Benito and Henrich R. Greve

Volume 2: Foreign Direct Investment, Location and Competitiveness – Edited by John H. Dunning and Philippe Gugler

Volume 3: New Perspectives in International Business Research – Edited by Maryann P. Feldman and Grazia D. Santangelo

Volume 4: Research on Knowledge, Innovation and Internationalization – Edited by Jorma Larimo and Tia Vissak

Volume 5: Reshaping the Boundaries of the Firm in an Era of Global Interdependence – Edited by José Pla-Barber and Joaquín Alegre

Volume 6: Entrepreneurship in the Global Firm – Edited by Alain Verbeke, Ana Teresa Tavares-Lehmann and Rob van Tulder

Volume 7: New Policy Challenges for European MNEs – Edited by Rob van Tulder, Alain Verbeke and Liviu Voinea

Volume 8: International Business and Sustainable Development – Edited by Rob van Tulder, Alain Verbeke and Roger Strange

Volume 9: Multinational Enterprises, Markets and Institutional Diversity – Edited by Alain Verbeke, Rob Van Tulder and Sarianna Lundan

Voume 10: The Future of Global Organizing – Edited by Rob van Tulder, Alain Verbeke and Rian Drogendijk

Volume 11: The Challenge of BRIC Multinationals – Edited by Rob van Tulder, Alain Verbeke, Jorge Carneiro and Maria Alejandra Gonzalez-Perez

PROGRESS IN INTERNATIONAL BUSINESS RESEARCH
VOLUME 12

DISTANCE IN INTERNATIONAL BUSINESS: CONCEPT, COST AND VALUE

EDITED BY

ALAIN VERBEKE
Haskayne School of Business, University of Calgary, Alberta, Canada; and Henley Business School, University of Reading, UK; and Solvay Business School, University of Brussels (VUB), Belgium

JONAS PUCK
WU Vienna, Vienna, Austria

ROB VAN TULDER
Erasmus University Rotterdam, Rotterdam, The Netherlands

emerald PUBLISHING

United Kingdom – North America – Japan
India – Malaysia – China

Emerald Publishing Limited
Howard House, Wagon Lane, Bingley BD16 1WA, UK

First edition 2018

British Library Cataloguing in Publication Data
A catalogue record for this book is available from the British Library

ISBN: 978-1-78743-719-7 (Print)
ISBN: 978-1-78743-718-0 (Online)
ISBN: 978-1-78743-841-5 (Epub)

ISSN: 1745-8862 (Series)

Printed and bound by CPI Group (UK) Ltd, Croydon, CR0 4YY

ISOQAR
REGISTERED
Certificate Number 1985
ISO 14001

ISOQAR certified Management System, awarded to Emerald for adherence to Environmental standard ISO 14001:2004.

INVESTOR IN PEOPLE

CONTENTS

PART V
ALTERNATIVE LENSES FOR IB RESEARCH

LIST OF CONTRIBUTORS

Fariza Achcaoucaou	UB Business School, Barcelona, Spain
Ahmad Arslan	Business School, Edge Hill University, Ormskirk, UK
Gabriel R.G. Benito	BI Norwegian Business School, Oslo, Norway
Guido AJM Berens	Rotterdam School of Management, Erasmus University, Rotterdam, The Netherlands
Enrique Claver	Department of Management, University of Alicante, Alicante, Spain
Federica De Vanna	Università degli Studi del Sannio, Sannio, Italy
Desislava Dikova	Institute for International Business, Vienna, Austria; and University of Economics and Business Administration, Vienna, Austria
Douglas Dow	Melbourne Business School, Melbourne, Australia
Maria Elo	University of Turku, Turku, Finland
Igor Filatotchev	Cass Business School, University of London, London, UK
Azar Goudarz	Brunel University, London, UK
Tilo Halaszovich	Lehrstuhl und Institut für Internationales Management und Governance, Bremen University, Bremen, Germany
Guus Hendriks	Rotterdam School of Management, Erasmus University, Rotterdam, The Netherlands

Markus Hödl	Institute for International Business, WU Vienna, Vienna, Austria
Viacheslav Iurkov	BI Norwegian Business School, Oslo, Norway
Anne Jacqueminet	Department of Management and Technology, Bocconi University, Milan, Italy
Hortênsia Karl Barandas	Faculdade de Economia da Universidade do Porto, Porto, Portugal
Palitha Konara	University of Plymouth, Plymouth, UK
Giulia Lanzilli	Universita degli Studi del Sannio, Sannio, Italy
Jorma Larimo	Department of Marketing, University of Vaasa, Vaasa, Finland
Thomas Lindner	Institute for International Business, WU Vienna, Vienna, Austria
Nina Magomedova	University of Barcelona, Barcelona, Spain
Francisco Vitorino Martins	Faculdade de Economia da Universidade do Porto, Porto, Portugal
Robbert Maseland	University of Groningen, Groningen, The Netherlands
Michela Matarazzo	Università degli Studi del Sannio, Sannio, Italy
Paloma Miravitlles	University of Barcelona, Barcelona, Spain
Michael Mueller	Ryerson University, Toronto, Canada
Alessandra Perri	Università Ca' Foscari Venezia, Venice, Italy
Dorota Piaskowska	UCD Michael Smurfit Graduate Business School, University College Dublin, Dublin, Ireland
Ursula Pregernig	Institute for International Business, WU Vienna, Vienna, Austria

Jonas Puck	Institute for International Business, WU Vienna, Vienna, Austria
Diego Quer	Department of Management, University of Alicante, Alicante, Spain
Riccardo Resciniti	Università degli Studi del Sannio, Sannio, Italy
Drogendijk Rian	University of Groningen; Uppsala University, Uppsala, Sweden
Laura Rienda	Department of Management, University of Alicante, Alicante, Spain
Grazia D. Santangelo	Department of Political and Social Science, University of Catania, Catania, Italy
João Carvalho Santos	School of Technology and Management globADVANTAGE – Center of Research in International Business & Strategy, Polytechnic Institute of Leiria, Leiria, Portugal
Vikrant Shirodkar	University of Sussex, Brighton, UK
Susana Costa e Silva	Universidade Catolica Portuguesa, Lisbon, Portugal
Arjen Slangen	Rotterdam School of Management, Erasmus University, Rotterdam, The Netherlands
Sverre Tomassen	Department of Strategy, BI Norwegian Business School, Oslo, Norway
Silviu H Tierean	Dundee Business School, Abertay University, Dundee, UK
Rob Van Tulder	Rotterdam School of Management, Erasmus University, Rotterdam, The Netherlands
Rosalie Tung	Beedie School of Business, Simon Fraser University, British Columbia, Canada

Alain Verbeke Haskayne School of Business, University of Calgary, Alberta, Canada; and Henley Business School, University of Reading, UK; and Solvay Business School, University of Brussels (VUB), Belgium

Yi Wang University of Southern Denmark, Denmark; University of Vaasa, Vaasa, Finland

ABOUT THE EDITORS

Dr. Alain Verbeke is a Professor of International Business Strategy and holds the McCaig Research Chair in Management at the Haskayne School of Business, University of Calgary. He is also the Research Director of the Strategy and Organization Area at the Haskayne School of Business. In 2014, Dr. Verbeke was elected as the Inaugural Alan M. Rugman Memorial Fellow at the Henley Business School, University of Reading (UK). He is the Editor-in-Chief of *the Journal of International Business Studies* (2017–2019).

Earlier in his career, Dr. Verbeke served as the Director of the MBA programme, Solvay Business School, University of Brussels (VUB), where he remains an adjunct professor. He has been a Visiting Professor at Dalhousie University, the University of Toronto and the Universite Catholique de Louvain, as well as an Associate Fellow of Templeton College (University of Oxford). He has also been an Academic Associate of the Centre for International Business and management, Judge Business School (University of Cambridge) and was associated with Skolkovo Institute for Emerging Market Studies (SIEMS), as an affiliated researcher. In June 2016, he was appointed as a Non-Resident Fellow with the Center for Emerging Market Studies, China Europe International Business School (CEIBS), Shanghai, China. Dr. Verbeke is an elected Fellow of the Academy of International Business, and has served as Secretary and Treasurer of the Fellows.

Dr. Verbeke has been a member of the European Science and Technology Assembly (ESTA), the highest advisory body to the European Commission on the future of European scientific and innovation policy and has served on the board of directors of various educational and scientific research institutions. He is a leading thinker on complex project evaluation, the strategic management of multinational networks, as well as the governance and restructuring of complex organizations.

In the consulting sphere, Dr. Verbeke has personally directed over 100 strategic management projects, most of these with a focus on the interface between large-scale investment programmes and governance challenges. His academic research agenda consists of revisiting, rethinking and augmenting the core paradigms in strategic management and international business, especially internalization theory, which is a joint transaction cost economics and resource-based view of the firm, focused on the governance of new resource combinations. He has particular expertise in the management of headquarters – subsidiary relationships and broader governance challenges in large multinational enterprises.

Dr. Verbeke has authored or edited more than 30 books and more than 200 refereed publications, including many articles in leading scholarly journals such as *the Journal of International Business Studies*, the *Strategic Management Journal* and the *Journal of Management Studies*.

Jonas Puck is Head of the Institute for International Business and Full Professor at the WU Vienna University of Economics and Business. He has held visiting positions at the University of Southern California, USA; the University of New South Wales, Australia; Tsinghua University, China; and the Bradford University School of Management, UK. He earned a Dipl.-Kfm., a PhD in International Management and a postdoctoral qualification (Habilitation) from Nuremberg University.

Jonas is an experienced teacher and consultant and has provided consulting solutions, research expertise, or executive education for numerous firms and institutions, including ABB, AT Kearney, BMW, BP, Coca Cola Hellenic, L'Oreal, OPEC, OMV, Siemens, Shell, and UNIDO. He has received awards for outstanding teaching as well as outstanding research, e.g., the CEMS Best International Business Project Award 2015, EIBA Fellows Research Award 2008, Ludwig Erhard Award 2008, Schoeller Fellow Award 2009, Festo Fellow Award 2010, and Best Paper/Best Reviewer Awards from a large number of journals and conferences.

His current research interests are at the intersection of global strategy, finance, and political science. Jonas serves on the Editorial Boards of the *Journal of International Business Studies, Long Range Planning, European Management Journal, Journal of World Business* and the *Multinational Business Review*. His research has been published in journals such as the *Journal of International Business Studies, Journal of Management Studies, Journal of World Business, Long Range Planning, Management International Review*, and *Human Resource Management (US)*, among others. In addition, he is editor or author of six books and numerous book chapters.

Rob van Tulder is Full Professor of International Business-Society management at the Rotterdam School of Management/Erasmus University Rotterdam. He has been a visiting professor at a number of universities and a consultant to international organisations (such as the United Nations, the International Monetary Fund and the European ministries around the world. He is co-founder of the Department of Business-Society Management, one of the leading departments in the world studying and teaching about the contribution of business and society. He founded the SCOPE databank project, which in collaboration with UNCTAD complies the listings of the world's largest multinational enterprises from developed and developing countries (www.scope.nl). Dr. van Tulder is founder and academic director of the Partnerships Resource Centre (www.partnerships-resourcecentre.org), which studies the cross-sector partnerships between firms, NGOs and government for sustainable development. The Resource Centre itself is organised as a partnership among business schools, multinational enterprises, governments and NGOs. Over the past 25 years, Dr. van Tulder has published in particular across disciplinary boundaries (development, international business, political science, international relations, economics and innovation) on following topics: internationalization motives, European and global business, high-tech industries, corporate social responsibility, sustainability, codes of conduct, reputation management, skills, network strategies, cross-sector partnership strategies, smaller industrial countries (welfare states) and European Community/Union policies. His latest book publications include, *inter alia: Managing the Transition to a Sustainable Enterprise* (Routledge/Earthscan, 2014); *Doing Business in Africa* (2013, NABC); *Corporate Responsibilities in Turbulent Times*, Beijing (2010, 2012, China Economic Publishing House (in Chinese); *Skill Sheets: An Integrated Approach to Research, Study and Management* (Pearson International, 2012) (www.skillsheet.com). For more information, see: www.ib-sm.org. Forthcoming books include volumes on 'Business Models for the future', 'Global Business' (second edition of the widely heralded, 2006 book 'International Business-Society Management') and 'Wicked Problems'.

PROLOGUE – VOYAGES OF SELF-DISCOVERY: A REFLECTION ON FOUR DECADES OF RESEARCH ON EXPATRIATION AND CROSS-CULTURAL INTERACTIONS

Rosalie L. Tung

ABSTRACT

In this chapter, I reflect on my research on expatriation and cross-cultural interactions over the past four decades. I have characterized it as voyages of self-discovery, as my research questions have been framed by my own experiences in growing up in a bicultural environment in Hong Kong and subsequent relocation to North America. My research findings have helped me understand the what, why, and how of my encounters and observations in the context of international assignments and cross-cultural encounters. The chapter then focuses on my 1981 publication that presented a contingency paradigm of selection and training that generated substantial interest in expatriation. While the contingency paradigm is essentially valid today, I outline four developments that have taken place since then – war for talent, greying of the labor force, rise of emerging markets, and need

Distance in International Business: Concept, Cost and Value
Progress in International Business Research, Volume 12, 1–15

ISSN: 1745-8862/doi:10.1108/S1745-886220170000012026

for global orientation – that necessitate new perspectives in understanding human resource management in the global context. I then allude to how I would rewrite my 1981 paper differently in light of these changes.

Keywords: Expatriation; international assignments; cross-cultural encounters; biculturalism

One of my earliest and most cited publications, "Selection and training of personnel for overseas assignments" (Tung, 1981), represents a voyage of self-discovery. In fact, much of the research that I have undertaken throughout my career can be characterized as such, hence the use of "voyages" in the plural. This view of my research as voyages of self-discovery explains why I wrote in my 2009 paper that the topics I have pursued throughout my academic career "were guided by my first-hand experience … (and) new research finding(s) helped … to unravel a bit more of the puzzle surrounding some of the experiences that I have encountered and/or observed in my life" (Tung, 2009, pp. 10–11). In this chapter, I will provide a brief genesis of my 1981 paper and my ensuing research on expatriate assignments and cross-cultural interactions. Then I will retrospect on how I would write that piece differently today in light of the elapsed time since the publication of my 1981 paper.

In my 2009 paper, I briefly outlined how the environment I grew up in during the formative years of my life had helped shape my research interests for much of my professional career. There is indeed a lot of truth to the saying that "we are a product of our experiences." While the term, "product," connotes determinism that I do not subscribe to as it denies the existence of free will, I believe that we are *inspired* by the sum of our past experiences, both positive and negative. Our past experiences, coupled with genetics, make each of us truly distinct. From the research standpoint, by drawing upon one's own unique background and experiences, it is possible to discern phenomena that have hitherto been unexplored or, at least, have not yet been recognized as meritorious of research attention. In other words, all of us possess a distinct bundle of attributes that is analogous to what researchers on foreign direct investment (FDI; see, e.g., Dunning, 1979; Rugman & Verbeke, 2001) have labeled as country- and firm-specific advantages. Just as a country or a firm capitalizes on its specific advantages in the context of FDI, either outward or inward, as scholars, we too should leverage our own distinctive set of capabilities and competencies in our selection of research topics and methodologies.

In this chapter, I will first briefly illustrate how my research over the years, beginning with my contingency paradigm of selection and training of expatriates for international assignments based on a study of American expatriates abroad (Tung, 1981) that was followed by many publications on different aspects of international assignments, has been profoundly influenced by my past. My focus here is on my 1981 paper since it was instrumental in igniting an explosion of interest in expatriation. Harzing (1995, p. 458) wrote: "Over the last three decades it has become almost 'traditional' to open an article on expatriate management by stating that expatriate failure rates are (very) high" even though there are very few studies on this topic, except my 1981 paper. My 1981 paper, which was built upon by others (Harvey, 1985; Mendenhall & Oddou, 1985; to cite a few), has accounted for the exponential growth in research on international assignments that to date has shown no signs of abating. The growing mobility of people across international boundaries (discussed later), whether permanent or temporary, has cemented the significance and importance of international human resource management (IHRM) in our literature.

Even though IHRM is broader than expatriate assignments *per se*, the latter has remained a core topic in that field. This renders my 1981 paper as "the most crucial study in this field" (Harzing, 1995, p. 461). Other researchers, such as Dowling, Festing and Engle (2013), authors of a popular textbook on IHRM, have acknowledged the seminal contribution of my contingency paradigm on selection and training as it represents the first systematic study of the causes of expatriate failure that has informed the broader field of research pertaining to cross-cultural encounters.

Without unduly repeating what I have written in my 2009 paper, I made two personal revelations to show how my upbringing helped shaped my research interests. The first disclosure pertains to spending the formative years of my life in Hong Kong, a city that represents the confluence of East and West, where I grew up bilingual and bicultural. My classmates in a Catholic girls' school were local Chinese and non-Chinese students. My non-Chinese classmates were either children of expatriates, primarily from the UK and Portugal[1] or merchants from Persia and India. The former are expatriates in the traditional sense as they were sent by their respective home countries to work in Hong Kong for specified periods of time, while the merchants would fall into the category of self-initiated expatriates (SIEs), using the terminology in our current literature, who went to Hong Kong on their own initiative to take advantage of the opportunities there. As such, they typically stayed for indefinite periods of time. A second disclosure in my 2009 paper pertained to the fact that even though both of my parents are Chinese, my father is "very Western in his upbringing and education" (Tung, 2009, p. 10). My mother, on the other hand, espoused very traditional Chinese values and, at the same time, embraced Catholicism[2] (see Figs. 1 and 2).

My years in Hong Kong were instrumental in shaping the topics that have fascinated me later as a graduate student and, subsequently, as a researcher in the following four ways: first, because of my exposure from a very early age to studying and playing with people who are different from myself, race- and ethnicity-wise, to me, multiculturalism or multicultural teams (MCT) have always been a matter of course, not an out-of-the-ordinary phenomenon that has to be contended with somehow. Second, given Hong Kong's status as a British colony until 1997 and my experience with my classmates,

Fig. 1. My Mom, the Guiding Influence in My Life, and I at my Ph.D. Convocation.

Fig. 2. A Picture of Myself.

I was able to observe up close how differences could contribute to both functional and dysfunctional outcomes. In terms of functional outcomes, I saw that lasting friendships and bonds could develop despite the differences. As a child, I learned that differences could be assets. This observation is similar to the findings in our literature that diversity can lead to more creative solutions to problems (Cox & Tung, 1997; Ng & Tung, 1998; Stahl, Maznevski, Voigt, & Jonsen, 2010).

From the dysfunctional perspective, I witnessed that differences could lead to tension, conflicts, and separation, whether spatially (such as the formation of expatriate enclaves) and/or socially (such as the tendency for some expatriates to socialize only with other expatriates). Such tensions and separation typically stemmed from suspicions and/or misinterpretations of the other's intentions and actions.

Third, through exposure to the different sets of values espoused by my more-Western-oriented father and the emphasis that my mother placed on traditional values as well as Catholic principles and beliefs, I saw no contradiction in borrowing from the best of different worlds. In the acculturation model developed by Berry (1997), this would be characterized as "integration" – this mode has been found to be most effective in Berry's (1997) study of immigrants to Canada and in my study of expatriates who work abroad (Tung, 1998). In the bicultural identity (BII) literature, Benet-Martinez and Haritatos (2005) show that biculturals who are high on the BII index are not conflicted between opposing value systems whereas those who score low on the index are frequently troubled as to whether they are betraying one of their dual identities where the values systems of the two identity groups collide.

Fourth, differences exist across countries as well as within countries, even though Hong Kong is categorized as an economy and not a country per se. While I learned about cultural dimensions (such as Hofstede, 1980) and cultural distance (Kogut & Singh, 1988) later on, I derived two lessons from growing up in Hong Kong: one, intra-national diversity can be as significant as cross-national diversity, the theme of my 1993 paper and my ongoing interest in studying differences within countries (Tung, 1993; Tung & Baumann, 2009; Tung, Worm, & Fang, 2008). Two, cultural differences can yield both positive and negative outcomes depending upon the situation under consideration. As Stahl and Tung (2015) have revealed through their analysis of 21 years of publications in the *Journal of International Business Studies*, while articles that focus on the downside of cultural distance outnumber those that spotlight the positives associated with such differences by a ratio of 17:1, this imbalance in assumptions is not borne out in the actual findings of these studies. Whether cultural distance can engender positive or negative outcomes is very much contingent upon the situational factors under consideration.

Now that I have provided a brief genesis of my 1981 paper that paved the way for my subsequent research on other aspects of expatriation and cross-cultural interactions; I will turn to how I would rewrite that paper in light of the changes that have taken place in the 30 plus years since its publication.

WHAT STANDS?

Before I delve into the "what's new," I believe that the contingency paradigm of selection and training I presented in 1981 continues to be valid. While "contingency" has now been replaced by the current terms of "contextual" or "situational," they all carry the same meaning. My contingency paradigm asserts that: (a) where possible, the MNC should hire host country nationals (HCNs); however, (b) where expatriates have to be deployed, there is *no* one set of criteria *nor* one type of training program that is suitable for all categories of assignments to all countries. In other words, it depends upon the contextual or situational factors.

The reasons for advancing a contingency approach are several-fold: One, since the cultural distance between the home and host countries varies, this affects the magnitude of adjustment required. Two, because of the different types of assignments in question, the extent and nature of interactions, including length of stay in a foreign country, vary. As such, the emphasis on relational vis-à-vis task competencies and capabilities in the selection criteria should also vary. Three, because of the aforementioned differences, the nature and content of the training programs would also vary, with the most intensive training programs to be provided to those whose assignments involve intensive interactions with the host society and for extended periods of time.

Today, due to the localization policies of most host countries and the high cost of expatriation, HCNs are used more extensively in the overseas subsidiaries of MNCs. However, expatriation is still used as a strategic tool for the development of a global orientation among those with potentials for advancement to senior management (Caligiuri & Bonache, 2016; Tung, 1998). Furthermore, not all HCNs are the same. Most MNCs continue to define HCNs on the basis of ethnicity. This practice is increasingly being challenged however. In Tung (2016a), I drew attention to inverse resonance, defined as the "attraction of opposites" and the converse of homophily. Inverse resonance has also been referred to as "internalized racism." Carr, Rugimbana, Walkom, and Bolitho (2001) provided an example of internalized racism in selected African countries. I alluded to the hostility that persists between Hong Kong Chinese and Mainland Chinese (Tung, 2016a; also see Manolova, Eunni, & Gyoshev, 2008; Young, 2014). Furthermore, I have coined the term ex-host country nationals (EHCNs) to refer to those who originate from one country, then went to study, live, and/or work overseas and later return to their country of origin (Tung & Larazova, 2006). EHCNs account for a sizable portion of the brain circulation phenomenon described by Saxenian (2002) in her studies of high-tech entrepreneurs in Silicon Valley. These developments have led me to assert that "the phenomenon of brain circulation has challenged us to fundamentally rethink our definitions of who are expatriates (whether company-sponsored or self-initiated) and who are locals" (Tung, 2016a, p. 149).

With regard to the use of varying selection criteria and training programs for different categories of assignments to different countries, while the general premise still holds, the multiple categories of assignees described above have to be factored into these decisions. In addition, my contingency framework was intended for use on company-sponsored assignments. Back then, SIE was rare. The growing incidence of SIE may be attributed, in part at least, to the rising cost of expatriation, need for global orientation, and career opportunities in emerging markets discussed later in this chapter.

In terms of the findings of my 1981 study, the failure rates of American expatriates abroad have improved significantly as reported in Tung (1998). I attributed the decline in failure rates to the growing global orientation among Americans who are on assignment as well as the emergence of "boundaryless" careers where assignees value an international assignment because it can broaden their worldview even though their home organization may not necessarily reward them for their service abroad (Cerdin & Brewster, 2014; Tung, 1998). Unfortunately, my findings with regard to, one, "family considerations" as an important cause for early return (Lazarova, Westman, & Shaffer, 2010; Shaffer & Harrison, 2001); and, two, expatriates' concerns about their company's inattention to repatriation (Baruch, Altman, & Tung, 2016; Tharenou & Caulfield, 2010) remain.

WHAT'S NEW?

A lot of changes have occurred since 1981. In my 2016 paper (Tung, 2016a) to commemorate the 50th anniversary of the *Journal of World's Business*, I outlined four major developments that necessitate our adoption of new perspectives in studying IHRM. A summary of these four major developments is presented below with implications for research:

1. Talent Poaching

The term, war for talent, was coined by McKinsey's Chambers, Foulon, Handfield-Jones, Hankin, and Michaels (1998) to refer to the reality that because of the shortage of highly skilled labor among countries that pursue high economic growth, organizations (both private and public) are increasingly willing to forego the traditional practice of recruiting from within one's home country and instead opt to actively hire highly qualified people wherever they can be found. An outstanding example in this regard is the case of Mark Carney, a Canadian and the 2008–2013 Governor of the Bank of Canada. He resigned his Canadian post to become the Governor of the Bank of England. The growing mobility of people across international boundaries coupled with the greying of the workforce in many countries, discussed below, imply that our traditional way of measuring "nationality" by passport an individual holds or country of incorporation of a company is increasingly suspect.

The media recently reported on the case of an American-born businessman who holds passports from eight countries, from Belize to Britain (Young, 2017). In early February 2017, it was disclosed that Peter Thiel, co-founder of PayPal and a tech billionaire, had acquired New Zealand citizenship despite failing to meet standard residency requirements for that country (Brockett, 2017). It appears that the acquisition of citizenship from multiple countries has become common among the super rich with investments and residences that span the globe. Barclays Bank (Barclays, 2014) has dubbed the super rich as "global citizens" who pursue educational, career, and investment opportunities wherever they arise (for a more detailed discussion, see Tung, 2016a).

2. Greying of the Labor Force

A second development is the overall aging of the labor force in many industrialized countries as well as some emerging markets, most noticeably China (see Chand & Tung, 2014). Aside from encouraging an upturn in birth rates in countries with an aging population, the attraction of skilled immigrants to fill the void could help redress the situation. This contributes to intra-national diversity. According to the 2016 Canadian Census, over one-half of the population (51%) in Toronto were born outside of Canada with lingual diversity to match (140 languages and dialects). Similarly, the US census data suggest that Whites will become the minority (49.7%) in that country by 2044 (Frey, 2014). Intra-national diversity, FDI (both outward and inward), and the formation of cross-national strategic alliances have given rise to the pervasive presence of MCTs, whether work or nonwork related. Depending upon the situation, MCTs can yield challenges as well as opportunities for organizations that have to contend with them (see Stahl et al., 2010).

Aside from the issues of inverse resonance and internalized racism discussed earlier, Harrison and Klein (2007) suggest that there are different types of diversity, namely, separation (spatial or cultural distance), variety (gender, race, ethnicity, and religious traditions), and disparity (stage of economic and technological development). The bulk of International Business

(IB) research has focused primarily on one type of diversity, namely cultural distance. Variety on the basis of gender has received more attention while other bases for variety, such as race, ethnicity, and religious traditions have been less explored, with some exceptions. Tung (2008) and Tung and Haq (2012) have examined the interaction effects of race and gender in influencing the decision-maker's perception of a candidate's suitability for international assignments. The literature on disparity, such as status differential, is just emerging (see e.g., Kim & Tung, 2013; Sharkey, 2014; Yildiz & Fey, 2016). Leung and Morris' (2015, p. 1045) have alluded to this by highlighting the tendency among employees in industrialized countries to view their Chinese bosses as "low in expert power" since China is often perceived as less developed, both economically and technologically – China is still officially labeled as an emerging market and is considered to be less technologically advanced than the United States.

3. Rise of Emerging Markets

The third development is the rise of emerging markets – most notably China and India – and their growing role in the global economy. In this context, we witness the rise of emerging market multinationals (EMMNCs). At the time of my 1981 article, China was just recovering from the ruins of the decade-long Cultural Revolution (1966–1976) that brought its economy to the verge of collapse. China's transformation since then has been nothing short of miraculous and it is now the third largest foreign investor in the world.

Most of the literature on international assignments has focused on expatriates from industrialized countries, such as the United States and Western Europe. Research on Outward Foreign Direct Investment (OFDI) from EMMNCs has received attention only recently. The status differential hypothesis discussed in the preceding section suggests that the dynamics and patterns of interaction between expatriates from EMMNCs and HCNs could be very different from the experiences of MNCs from industrialized countries. These merit research attention.

4. Need for Global Orientation

A fourth development is the consensus among corporate leaders of the need for global orientation. While global orientation can be developed through a variety of ways (see, e.g., Bird & Mendenhall, 2016), a proven and effective method is expatriation, whether company-sponsored or self-initiated (Tung, 2014). The issues of passport as a surrogate for nationality, biculturalism, and boundaryless careers have been discussed earlier – all of these have important implications on what development of a global orientation entails and how we need to rethink selection criteria and redesign training programs for cross-cultural encounters.

CONCLUDING REMARKS

At the time when I wrote my 1981 paper, while I had hoped for more open borders, I could not have anticipated the extent of globalization that has taken place in the course of less than 40 years. The speed and magnitude of globalization has been accelerated, in part at least, by the internet revolution that has enabled small entrepreneurs from remote corners of the world to sell their products worldwide, the emergence of virtual MCTs, and instantaneous access to information and faster sharing of knowledge across the world.

While recent developments on both sides of the Atlantic, Brexit and Trump's presidency, appear to be major setbacks to globalization, as Tselichtchev (2017) argues, "globalization's not dead, it just has a new powerhouse," China. Thus far, 50 countries have signed onto the China-led "One Belt, One Road" initiative. After the widely reported "combative" phone call between Australian Prime Minister Turnbull and President Trump, Australia, one of the United States' staunchest allies, has engaged in soul-searching on the merits and pitfalls of strengthening its ties with China. Australia's first ambassador to China has asserted that "the world had reached the end of an era defined by European and American leadership" and urged Australia "to make China its primary focus of diplomacy and economic policy" (Cave, 2017).

Even before Brexit and Trump's election, Rolland (2015, p. 4) has alerted us to how China's "One Belt, One Road" initiative can alter the "global landscape" by re-orienting trade and geopolitical focus to the large Eurasian landmass that spans across Asia, Russia, Central Asia, Middle and Near East to Europe, also known as the "New Silk Road." "If Europe shifts attention eastward to Asia instead of retaining its westward focus across the Atlantic, then U.S. policymakers may be compelled to radically alter their traditional approaches to these regions and indeed the entire world" (see also Tung, 2016b). In end of 2016, the Asia Infrastructure Investment Bank (AIIB), the vehicle for financing the "One Belt, One Road" initiative, has already approved and disbursed its first loans for infrastructure projects in four countries. Even if the "One Belt, One Road" initiative does not succeed in resurrecting the "New Silk Road," it still represents a major departure from the current geopolitical situation that is centered around the United States.

In short, it appears that globalization will continue to march on, albeit to the beat of a different or multiple drummers. Furthermore, it is normal to encounter speed bumps that require realignment along the way. Assuming that this is so, expatriation, cross-cultural encounters, and IHRM will become even more important and significant in the future. In particular, there is a need to recast expatriation in the context of boundary-less careers, EHCNs, and the war for talent, including the definition of who are expatriates and who are locals (see Tung, 2016a). Furthermore, expatriation from emerging multinationals will continue to gather momentum, thus necessitating us to examine the dynamics of interaction between EMMNCs' expatriates with employees in industrialized countries. In short, research opportunities on international assignments and cross-cultural encounters will abound as the four new developments briefly discussed in this chapter continue to unfold before us.

NOTES

1. Hong Kong's neighboring city of Macau was a colony of Portugal until its return to China in 1999.
2. Even though religions are supposedly universal, some people in the East have considered Christianity as a "western" religion.

REFERENCES

Baruch, Y., Altman, Y., & Tung, R. L. 2016. Career mobility in a global era – Advances in managing expatriation and repatriation. *Academy of Management Annals*, *10*(1), 841–889.

Barclays (2014). *The rise of the global citizen?* London, U.K: Barclays plc. Retrieved from https://wealth.barclays.com/content/dam/bwpublic/global/documents/shared/wealth-inisghts-volume-18.pdf

Benet-Martinez, V., & Haritatos, J. (2005). Bicultural identity integration (BII): Components and psychological antecedents. *Journal of Personality*, *73*, 1015–1050.

Berry, J. W. (1997). Immigration, acculturation, and adaptation. *Applied Psychology*, *46*(1), 5–34.

Bird, A., & Mendenhall, M. E. (2016). From cross-cultural management to global leadership: Evolution and adaptation. *Journal of World Business*, *51*(1), 115–126.

Brockett, M. (2017, February 1). *Billionaire Peter Thiel sparks New Zealand passport-for-sale row.* Bloomberg.com. Retrieved from https://www.bloomberg.com/news/articles/2017-02-01/

billionaire-peter-thiel-sparks-new-zealand-passport-for-sale-row. Accessed on February 2 2017.

Caligiuri, P., & Bonache, J. (2016). Evolving and enduring challenges in global mobility. *Journal of World Business*, *51*(1), 127–141.

Carr, S. C., Rugimbana, R. O., Walkom, E., & Bolitho, F. H. (2001). Selecting expatriates in developing areas: "Country-of-origin" effects in Tanzania? *International Journal of Intercultural Relations*, *25*, 441–457.

Cave, D. (2017, March 16). In Australia, a call for closer ties to China gains support. *New York Times*. Retrieved from https://www.nytimes.com/2017/03/16/world/australia/trump-us-china-relations-fitzgerald.html?emc=edit_ae_20170316&nl=todaysheadlines-asia&nlid=53905524. Accessed on March 17, 2017.

Cerdin, J.-L., & Brewster, C. (2014). Talent management and expatriation: Bridging two streams of research and practice. *Journal of World Business*, *49*, 245–252.

Chambers, E. G., Foulon, M., Handfield-Jones, H., Hankin, S. M., & Michaels, E. G. (1998). The war for talent. *McKinsey Quarterly 3*, 44–57.

Chand, M., & Tung, R. L. (2014). The aging of the world's population and its effects on global business. *Academy of Management Perspectives*, *28*(3), 409–429.

Cox, T., Jr., & Tung, R. L. (1997). The multicultural organization revisited. In C. L. Cooper & S. E. Jackson (Eds.), *Creating tomorrow's organizations* (pp. 7–28). New York, NY: John Wiley & Sons.

Dowling, P. J., Festing, M., & Engle, A. D. (2013). *International human resource management* (6th ed.). Australia: Cengage Learning.

Dunning, J. (1979). Toward an eclectic theory of international production: Some empirical tests. *Journal of International Business Studies*, *11*(1), 9–31.

Frey, W. H. (2014, December 12). *New projections point to a majority minority nation in 2044*. Brookings Institute. Retrieved from https://www.brookings.edu/blog/the-avenue/2014/12/12/new-projections-point-to-a-majority-minority-nation-in-2044/. Accessed on January 4, 2015.

Harrison, D. A., & Klein, K. J. (2007). What's the difference? Diversity constructs as separation, variety, or disparity in organizations. *Academy of Management Review*, *32*(4), 1199–1228.

Harvey, M. G. (1985). The executive family: An overlooked variable in international assignments. *Columbia Journal of World Business*, *20*, 84–93.

Harzing, A. W. K. (1995). The persistent myth of high expatriate failure rates. *International Journal of Human Resource Management*, *6*, 457–474.

Hofstede, G. (1980). *Culture's consequences: International differences in work-related values*. Beverly Hills, CA: Sage.

Kim, H. D., & Tung, R. L. (2013). Opportunities and challenges for expatriates in emerging markets: An exploratory study of Korean expatriates in India. *International Journal of Human Resource Management*, *24*(5), 1029–1050.

Kogut, B., & Singh, H. (1988). The effect of national culture on the choice of entry mode *Journal of International Business Studies*, *19*(3), 411–432.

Lazarova, M., Westman, M., & Shaffer, M. A. (2010). Elucidating the positive side of the work-family interface on international assignments: A model of expatriate work and family performance. *Academy of Management Review*, *35*(1), 93–117.

Leung, K., & Morris, M. W. (2015). Values, schemas, and norms in the culture–behavior nexus: A situated dynamics framework. *Journal of International Business Studies*, *46*(9), 1028–1050.

Manolova, T. S., Eunni, R. V., & Gyoshev, B. S. 2008. Institutional environments for entrepreneurship: Evidence from emerging economies in Eastern Europe. *Entrepreneurship: Theory & Practice*, *32*(1), 203–218.

Mendenhall, M., & Oddou, G. (1985). The dimensions of expatriate acculturation. *Academy of Management Review*, *10*, 39–47.
Ng, E. S. W., & Tung, R. L. (1998). Ethno-cultural diversity and organizational effectiveness: A field study. *International Journal of Human Resource Management*, *9*(6), 980–995.
Rolland, N. (2015). *China's new silk road*. Washington, DC: The National Bureau of Asian Research.
Rugman, A. M., & Verbeke, A. (2001). Subsidiary-specific advantages in multinational enterprises. *Strategic Management Journal*, *22*(3), 237–250.
Saxenian, A. (2002). Brain circulation: How high-skill immigration makes everyone better off. *The Brookings Review*, *20*(1), 28–31.
Shaffer, M. A., & Harrison, D. A. (2001). Forgotten partners of international assignments: Development and test of a model of spouse adjustment. *Journal of Applied Psychology*, *86*(2), 238–254.
Sharkey, A. J. (2014). Categories and organizational status: The role of industry status in the response to organizational deviance. *American Journal of Sociology*, *119*(5), 1380–1433.
Stahl, G. K., & Tung, R. L. (2015). Towards a more balanced treatment of culture in international business studies: The need for positive cross-cultural scholarship. *Journal of International Business Studies*, *46*(4), 391–414.
Stahl, G. K., Maznevski, M. L., Voigt, A., & Jonsen, K. (2010). Unraveling the effects of cultural diversity in teams: A meta-analysis of research on multicultural work groups. *Journal of International Business Studies*, *41*, 690–709.
Tharenou, P., & Caulfield, N. (2010). Will I stay or will I go? Explaining repatriation by self-initiated expatriates. *Academy of Management Journal*, *53*(5), 1009–1028.
Tselichtchev, I. (2017, March 4). Globalization's not dead, it just has a new powerhouse – Asia. *South China Morning Post*. Retrieved from http://www.scmp.com/week-asia/opinion/article/2075503/globalisations-not-dead-it-just-has-new-powerhouse-asia. Accessed on March 4, 2017.
Tung, R. L. (1981). Selection and training of personnel for overseas assignments. *Columbia Journal of World Business*, *16*(1), 68–78.
Tung, R. L. (1993). Managing cross-national and intra-national diversity. *Human Resource Management Journal*, *32*(4), 461–477.
Tung, R. L. (1998). American expatriates abroad: From neophytes to cosmopolitans. *Journal of World Business*, *33*(2), 125–144.
Tung, R. L. (2008). Do race and gender matter in international assignments to/from Asia Pacific? An exploratory study of attitudes among Chinese and Korean executives. *Human Resource Management*, *47*(1), 91–110.
Tung, R. L. (2009). Cross-cultural research diary: A personal odyssey. *European Journal of Cross-cultural Competence and Management*, *1*(1), 9–13.
Tung, R. L. (2014). Requisites to and ways of developing a global mind-set: Implications for research on leadership and organizations. *Journal of Leadership & Organizational Studies*, *21*(4), 229–337.
Tung, R. L. (2016a). New perspectives on human resource management in a global context. *Journal of World Business*, *51*(1), 142–152.
Tung, R. L. (2016b). Opportunities and challenges ahead of China's 'New Normal.' *Long Range Planning*, *49*, 632–640.
Tung, R. L., & Baumann, C. (2009). Comparing the attitudes toward money, material possessions and savings of overseas Chinese vis-á-vis Chinese in China: Convergence, divergence

or cross-vergence, vis-á-vis 'one size fits all' human resource management policies and practices. *International Journal of Human Resource Management*, *20*(11),2382–2401.

Tung, R. L., & Haq, R. (2012). International assignments to/from India: Do race and gender matter? *International Journal of Human Resource Management*, *23*(2), 221–235.

Tung, R. L., & Larazova, M. B. (2006). Brain drain versus brain gain: An exploratory study of ex-host country nationals in Central and East Europe. *International Journal of Human Resource Management*, *17*(11), 1853–1872.

Tung, R. L., Worm, V., & Fang, T. (2008). Sino-western business negotiations revisited – 30 years after China's open door policy. *Organizational Dynamics*, *37*(1), 60–74.

Yildiz, H. E., & Fey, C. F. (2016). Are the extent and effect of psychic distance perceptions symmetrical in cross-border M&As? Evidence from a two-country study. *Journal of International Business Studies*, *47*(7), 830–857.

Young, Y. (2014, March 6). Hong Kong must have zero tolerance for anti-mainlander hate campaigns. *South China Morning Post*. Retrieved from http://www.scmp.com/comment/insight-opinion/article/1441654/hong-kong-must-have-zero-tolerance-anti-mainlander-hate?page=all. Accessed on March 7, 2014.

Young, I. (2017, March 10). The case of the Canadian with eight citizenships, and why the world's rich covet 'backup' passports. *South China Morning Post*. Retrieved from http://www.scmp.com/news/world/united-states-canada/article/2077576/case-canadian-eight-citizenships-and-why-worlds-rich?utm_source=edm&utm_medium=edm&utm_content=20170310&utm_campaign=scmp_international. Accessed on March 11, 2017.

CHAPTER 1

DISTANCE IN INTERNATIONAL BUSINESS STUDIES: CONCEPT, COST AND VALUE

Alain Verbeke, Rob van Tulder and Jonas Puck

Keywords: Cultural distance, institutional distance, psychic distance, distance value, institutional overlap, cultural compatibility, institutional compatibility

INTRODUCTION

Distance is a central theme in international business (IB) research. A simple search for the word "distance" in the abstracts and titles of papers published in five leading IB journals over the period 1990–2015 illustrates the importance of the topic: overall, 341 papers have addressed the phenomenon, either in their titles or abstracts (*International Business Review* – *IBR*: 89, *Journal of International Business Studies* – *JIBS*: 99, *Journal of International Management* – *JIM*: 44, *Journal of World Business* – *JWB*: 59, *Management International Review* – *MIR*: 50). In other words, two annual volumes of each of the above journals could be filled solely with papers on the topic of distance. However, our knowledge of distance, in terms of conceptual specification and consequences for IB practice, is incomplete and sometimes ambiguous.

Distance in International Business: Concept, Cost and Value
Progress in International Business Research, Volume 12, 17–43

ISSN: 1745-8862/doi:10.1108/S1745-886220170000012016

In this research volume, we therefore analyze the conceptualization and impacts of distance in IB research, through various complementary lenses, each of these contributing in a substantive fashion to fill present knowledge gaps.

To capture the phenomenon of distance, a large number of constructs has emerged. These constructs include approximations of spatial distance (Ragozzino & Reuer, 2011), psychic distance (Johanson & Vahlne, 1977), regulatory distance (e.g. La Porta, Lopez-de-Silanes, & Shleifer, 2006), institutional distance (Kostova, 1999), and cultural distance (Kogut & Singh, 1988). The IB literature has thereby covered many aspects of distance that firms and managers supposedly do – or should – take into account when making strategic decisions, for example, in the realm of foreign entry mode selection, intra-organizational design, structuring of the interface with external actors, so on. Here, a high-distance context typically increases the complexity of organizational arrangements to govern economic transactions. In recent years, scholars in IB have attempted to unbundle empirically cross-national distance (Berry, Guillén, & Nan, 2010; Dow & Karunaratna, 2006). At the same time, the concept of "compounded distance" was coined, which focuses on the overall, simultaneous impact of all individual distance dimensions on firm-level decision-making (Rugman, Verbeke, & Nguyen, 2011). However, two challenges are associated with current approaches, namely a measurement problem (i.e. related to quantification) and a conceptual problem (i.e. related to underlying assumptions). First, with regard to measurement, the tendency to increase the number of distance measures has led to a large number of constructs, all supposedly being components of overall, cross-national distance between two countries or regions. However, it remains somewhat unclear which dimension matters most in specific circumstances, how to weigh and aggregate these different dimensions in terms of relevance to a particular strategic decision, and how to ascertain that no important dimensions of distance related to such strategic decision have been missed. Second, most existing concepts, while supposedly representing "distance," have been criticized for not meeting the conditions that hold when assessing the impact of geometric distance (Shenkar, Luo, & Yeheskel, 2008). This, as scholars have argued, has led to "illusions" about distance's impacts and to challenges when formulating normative implications for multinational companies (Shenkar, 2001; Tung & Verbeke, 2010). In sum, while of strong relevance to IB, there is ample room for further research on the conceptual nature of distance and related empirical work, as shown in Part I of this book.

Most extant research has focused on the costs or negative consequences associated with increasing distance. For example, on the firm level, many scholars have argued that distance creates additional costs of doing business abroad (Hymer, 1960) and a liability of outsidership (Johanson & Vahlne, 2009). On the individual and team level, findings similarly suggest that distance leads to communication challenges and cross-cultural misunderstanding (Hofstede, 2001). There is ample opportunity for further research adopting this perspective, for example, on the "cost" effects of specific dimensions of distance in team- and individual-level research, and on underexplored negative consequences of distance on the firm level. These cost dimensions are explored further in Parts II and III of this volume.

The largely negative perspective on distance prevailing in most IB studies may be valid in many cases. Yet, a sole focus on liabilities and adverse outcomes associated with distance may hinder our understanding of the processes and conditions that help to leverage the "value of diversity" in a wide range of contexts (Rugman & Verbeke, 2001; Verbeke & Yuan, 2016). The "value of diversity" perspective, that is, the notion that distances or differences between interacting parties along specific dimensions can create value, has long been acknowledged in the team-diversity literature. Research in this domain suggests that diversity can improve team creativity (McLeod et al., 1996) and problem solving (Shaw, 1981) because of the broader knowledge base present in more diverse team configurations. Team diversity can also enhance learning (Stahl et al., 2010). At the firm level, the "benefits of diversification" argument is strongly related to the distance concept. The diversification logic implies that investments with uncorrelated returns have a risk-reducing effect on the underlying portfolio (Chkir & Cosset, 2001; Singh, Davidson, & Suchard, 2003). Since distance can be assumed inversely correlated with connectedness, increasing distance within a portfolio arguably has the potential to reduce the risk-related outcomes of this portfolio. However, research on positive consequences, while advocated by many scholars, is scarce, and ultimately it is "net added value" that matters, that is, added value minus added cost (Verbeke & Kenworthy, 2008). There are obvious benefits of distance, related to strategic asset seeking investment, development of strategic capabilities, cross-border knowledge sharing and learning, synergy creation in cross-border mergers and acquisitions, unleashing the creative potential of diverse teams, and promoting sustainable and responsible behavior in multinational enterprises (MNEs). The value of distance is explored in Part IV of this volume.

Advancing the practice of international management research through alternative lenses (meaning alternative to the mainstream) has always been a key goal of the PIBR book series. We have therefore also included papers adopting alternative lenses such as in Part V of this volume.

PART I: THE CONCEPT OF DISTANCE

How exactly distance should be defined, measured, and applied is a key challenge in IB research. Empirical results regarding the impact of cross-border distances on entry mode choice, affiliate performance, and other firm-level decisions are mixed. One possible reason is that some contentious conceptual and /or methodological properties of the distance constructs deployed in empirical work may have undermined these constructs' validity and effectiveness as research instruments (Shenkar, 2001).

Part I of this volume, covering Chapters 2–5, explores different ways to address this challenge, namely by revisiting the ways to conceptualize and measure distance, taking into account the problems raised by Shenkar (2001). Overall, the chapters included in Part I of this volume highlight the critical issues that have typically been neglected in the extant IB distance research, and they provide recommendations on how to address these issues conceptually and empirically.

Chapter 2, by Dow, identifies research opportunities that would allow addressing some questionable assumptions and practices in distance research. The other three chapters in this part of the book exemplify various attempts to address the issues identified in Chapter 2, conceptually and/or empirically. The following important elements were addressed: the asymmetry effect or direction of distance (Chapters 4 and 5), the illusion of discordance or synergy effect when significant differences are present (Chapters 3 and 4), the illusion of linearity (Chapters 3 and 4), and the assumption of equivalence (Chapter 4). The empirical work included in this part also showcases some new approaches to address some of the above issues, such as the direction of distance (Chapter 5) and the assumption of equivalence (Chapter 4).

Chapter 2 provides a comprehensive review of the history of the distance literature in IB and argues that: "the distance research in international business studies is at a turning point, not in terms of its popularity, nor the quantity of articles published; but rather, in terms of the types of issues that are explored." Using "a metaphor borrowed from the social psychology literature, *Coleman's Boat*," this chapter explains the key issues involved in this shift and the opportunities for future research.

From his review of the literature, Dow concludes that conceptual work and commentaries have drawn attention to requisite nuances in distance research, for example, on the issue of diversity within a country, the direction of distance or asymmetry of distance, and the measurement of distance at the individual level. However, the quantity of empirical work investigating these issues has been limited. The vast majority of extant, empirical IB studies concerning distance has focused on linking national-level differences with organizational outcomes. With this relationship generally confirmed, the author argues that contemporary distance research needs to shift "from exploring whether distance matters" to understanding "why and how it matters." In other words, a tipping point (in the author's words) has been reached.

Dow advocates in favor of more micro-level and multi-level research that would explore the underlying moderating and mediating relationships involved in linking national-level differences with organizational outcomes. One key question is how individuals' perceptions of distance are formed. Another one is how within-country diversity, ownership structures, conservation values, and managers' personality directly or indirectly shape individuals' perceptions of distance. A third question is how such perceptions of distance translate into particular courses of action at the individual level, but also, and especially, at the firm level. IB scholars can contribute to overall strategic management research by pushing the bounds embedded in the last question, for example, as the "headquarters – foreign subsidiary structure of MNEs may present a novel environment for examining issues such as the relative power of stakeholders in the decision making process."

The author also points out that the empirical research in IB needs to heed Shenkar's (2001) warnings, irrespective of the level of analysis chosen. In particular, researchers should be aware of the illusions and assumptions in operationalizing distance when using the Kogut and Singh (1988) index and should attempt to address these, namely the illusions of symmetry, linearity, discordance, and stability, as well as assumptions of equivalence, corporate homogeneity, and spatial homogeneity.

The great contribution of this chapter is that it highlights areas of challenges and potential new research for distance in IB, in a systematic fashion, by using a modified multi-level Coleman's boat metaphor. The challenges and research opportunities described in this chapter are much in line, in substantive terms, with many other chapters in this research volume.

Chapter 3, by Maseland, proposes an alternative metaphor, "institutional overlap," as sharply contrasting with the traditional distance perspective, to capture the effects of institutional diversity on IB transactions. *Institutional overlap* is defined as "the presence of institutional structures that are shared between (potential) partners." By adopting the institutional overlap perspective rather than the dominant institutional distance perspective in IB research, Maseland highlights the opportunities for firms to create commonality, rather than focusing on costs arising from differences. The overlap perspective implies an approach whereby the process of managers "constructing commonality" is critical.

The author then argues that "changing the institutional debate in IB from a distance to an overlap perspective has a number of important implications and advantages." First, the overlap perspective perceives "MNEs as institutional entrepreneurs, identifying, negotiating and constructing such overlap, thereby linking hitherto separated institutional settings and exploiting opportunities for arbitrage," much in line with the recombination skills described in Verbeke (2013). Second, "the non-additive nature of overlap highlights the potential for institutional entrepreneurship of MNEs, exploiting arbitrage opportunities by forming a missing link between otherwise separated institutional communities," in line with the argument that MNEs' competitive advantage is based on their unique ability to recombine resources or features characteristic of different communities (Teece, 2014; Verbeke, 2013). Third, the overlap perspective is able to explain why many MNEs successfully expand abroad in spite of institutional diversity. Paradoxically, institutional diversity is related to the extent of institutional overlap that is present, and thereby determines the density of transactions, but not necessarily their cost. This is in line with the argument that MNEs may be driven to create value by combining elements from different archetypes of administrative heritage (Verbeke, 2013).

Maseland's chapter is important, because it provides "a reconceptualization of the role of institutional differences in international management" and it highlights "the role of institutional diversity in the identification of opportunities for cooperation and arbitrage, rather than interpreting institutions as a source of constraints."

Chapter 5, by Halaszovich, proposes a holistic perspective to investigate how distance between home and host countries influences international activities. It develops the concept of institutional and cultural compatibility, whereby compatibility is defined as the "synergies created by compatible institutional and cultural patterns of the countries involved in FDI flows." Halaszovich proposes a new approach to operationalize institutional and cultural compatibility and investigates their impacts on FDI flows. The study contributes not only to our conceptual understanding of "compatibility," but also to a narrowing of the gap between such conceptual understanding and empirical operationalization, that is, the chapter is an effective response to the call for new types of research in Chapter 2.

The author points out that the illusion of discordance, which neglects potential gains from diversity in the form of a "positive synergetic effect on investment and performance" (Shenkar, 2001), is deeply rooted in the IB literature. By drawing from the strategic alliance literature, the author argues that firms can actually strongly benefit from particular dissimilarities. The compatibility between different institutional and cultural patterns might actually complement negative distance effects, and increase FDI flows between two countries. Both distance and compatibility effects unfold simultaneously.

Empirically, this chapter "compiled a dataset of bilateral FDI inflows between 127 host countries and 122 home countries, covering the years 2001 to 2012," and it investigates how institutional and cultural dimensions (dissimilarity and compatibility) affect FDI flows. It measures dissimilarity by calculating cultural distance, building upon the six Hofstede dimensions (expanded model), and institutional distance based on the Worldwide Governance Indicators of Kaufmann (yearly data). It uses hierarchical cluster analysis based on the similarity of patterns in country-specific institutional and cultural profiles.

The author demonstrates empirically that institutional clusters are incompatible rather than compatible, implying that "differences in institutional systems erect barriers that are not easy to overcome." In contrast, the findings also show that FDI flows can be associated with a high level of cultural compatibility resulting from differences (e.g., power distance, masculinity). The importance of directionality in both institutional and cultural dimensions (compatibility from cluster A to B, but incompatibility from cluster B to A) is also confirmed in this study. The differential compatibility for different cultural dimensions also provides empirical evidence that the assumption of equivalence, embedded in the Kogut and Singh (1988) index, needs to be reconsidered (Shenkar, 2001), in line with the suggestions of Chapter 2.

The above findings contribute greatly to understanding the nature and consequences of institutional and cultural differences in IB activities and demonstrate the empirical relevance of the benefits of compatibility. This chapter also extends received theory about the relevance of home and host country institutions and cultures, by explaining the benefits of dissimilarities for FDI. It develops an empirical measurement approach to operationalize the concepts of institutional and cultural compatibility. Here, countries are grouped into clusters of common patterns for institutions and culture.

Chapter 13, by Dikova, Arslan, and Larimo, being the last chapter in Part III of this research volume, addresses the illusion of discordance. This concept was highlighted earlier by Shenkar (2001) and was reviewed in Chapter 2. It requires researchers to separate the influence of different types of distance, rather than collapsing these into one composite index. Dikova, Arslan, and Larimo investigate the effect of political, economic, cultural, and spatial distance on MNEs' ownership decisions in cross-border acquisitions, namely the choice among full ownership, majority acquisitions, and minority acquisitions.

The authors argue that the presence of uncertainty, as measured by the four distinct types of distance between the home and host country, will increase information-processing and transaction costs and thus reduce the equity commitment by MNEs in cross-border acquisitions. However, the available tangible and intangible resources can be employed to reduce the negative effect of distance. Based on data from 1,041 cross-border acquisitions undertaken by Finnish MNEs in 58 countries during the time period 1990–2010, the findings support the overall negative impact of various distance dimensions on equity commitment. However, different types of distance tend to have differential impacts depending upon what kind of equity commitment is analyzed (e.g., full versus partial; majority versus minority). The findings also demonstrate that firm-specific resources, such as firm size, international and host country experience, can reduce distance's negative effects.

In a more exploratory fashion, the authors also test whether the distance-ownership relationship in cross-borders acquisitions is influenced by the direction of capital flows, from developed to developed economy versus from developed to emerging market. Their results show that for emerging economies as host countries, only the firm's target country experience rather than its general international experience reduces the distance's negative effect. It implies that the impact of firm-specific resources is different when entering emerging host countries versus developed ones. This finding highlights the importance of studying emerging economies separately and incorporating direction when examining the impact of distance, as also suggested by Dow in Chapter 2.

This chapter also advances the resource-based view (RBV) approach by assuming firm-level, distance-reducing factors that are resource-based.

Chapters 2–5, in Part I of this volume, demonstrate that assessing the possible impacts of distance is truly a difficult undertaking if IB research in this area is to be both rigorous and relevant (Verbeke, 2013): The impacts of distance appear much more complex and diverse than recognized in most extant empirical work.

PART II: THE COST OF CULTURAL AND PSYCHIC DISTANCE

Even though most distance-related IB research has focused on the costs or negative consequences associated with increasing distance, there is much room for a more nuanced understanding of this "cost" element. Part II of this volume, covering Chapters 7–9, contributes to a deeper understanding of the costs of cultural and psychic distance. Psychic distance involves factors that prevent or disturb the flow of information between firms and markets, with language, culture, institutions, country development, and industrial development being key factors that constitute psychic distance.

The chapters in Part II of this volume investigate the effects of cultural distance (Chapter 7) and psychic distance (Chapters 8 and 9), thereby covering a broad range of IB issues, ranging from the impact on performance (Chapter 8), on acquisition ownership strategy and foreign subsidiary survival (Chapter 7), and on buyer–supplier relationships (Chapter 9). Different perspectives are adopted to explore the negative impact of cultural distance and psychic distance. For instance, Chapter 7 highlights the role of cultural distance in increasing transaction costs, when dealing with stakeholders in target markets, in the context of the ownership–survival relationship. Chapter 8 investigates the effects of specific dimensions of psychic distance. Chapter 9 explores how and why negative consequences of psychic distance materialize in international buyer–supplier relationships.

Chapter 4 by Azar and Drogendijk tries to answer the question whether cultural distance should be conceptualized using objective or subjective measures, and whether perceptual indicators can provide us with a more valid and reliable measure of cultural distance.

Azar and Drogendijk introduce a novel conceptualization of cultural distance, namely cultural distance deviation, which refers to the "degree to which managers' perceptions of cultural distance correspond with 'objective reality.'" To answer the question "whether deviations of manager's perceptions of cultural distance from 'objective' cultural distance have a negative influence on firm performance," the authors administered a survey to 573 managers in small and medium-sized Swedish enterprises and received 158 responses. They calculated the objective cultural distance based on multidimensional measures from Hofstede (1980). As regards the managers' perceptions, they asked respondents to indicate the degree to which a foreign host country was similar to the home country (Sweden) on a seven-point scale for four dimensions based on Hofstede (1980). They then used the Euclidean distance to calculate the deviations between perceptual and "objective" measures for each dimension of cultural distance.

Based on the above operationalization of cultural distance deviation, the authors used structural equation modeling to explore the deviation's impact on sales and return on assets when firms decide to expand into foreign markets. Their exploratory study shows that a larger cultural distance deviation lowers sales in foreign operations. Bounded rationality and bounded reliability challenges (Verbeke, 2013) may reduce decision-makers' ability to perceive correctly – and to select – the best internationalization choice. This exploratory study thereby highlights the impact of individual perceptions and the link between the perceptual individual-level data and the objective country-level data, a challenge also raised by Dow in Chapter 2.

Chapter 7 by Wang and Larimo investigates a range of parent firm and host country boundary conditions that could influence how acquirers' ownership strategies affect foreign subsidiary survival. It is a response to the call for taking on board more contingency factors, so as to explain the inconclusive findings regarding the links between ownership strategy and subsidiary survival in cross-border acquisitions.

Wang and Larimo suggest that the "ownership-survival relationship in foreign acquisitions is subject to both parent firm and host country boundary conditions," such as international or regional experience, target country experience, cultural distance, and host country development. They also argue, since the differences between acquisitions and greenfield investments are quite significant, that it is more appropriate to distinguish clearly between full and partial acquisitions. Their sample includes 1,345 foreign acquisitions made by 174 Finnish manufacturing firms in 59 countries during 1980–2005.

Their results indicate that generally full acquisitions increase the probability of survival of foreign acquired units, as compared to partial acquisitions. The findings also provide evidence of greater levels of liability of foreignness in culturally distant markets: the impact of full acquisitions on the survival of foreign acquired units is contingent upon cultural distance and host country development. In this study, cultural distance is operationalized, by using the Kogut and Singh (1988) index, based on Hofstede's (1980) four dimensions. The authors also ran their analysis for host country-specific subsamples. The findings demonstrate that country-specific results may differ from those in the pooled sample. Drawing from transaction cost economics (TCE), the study then zooms in on how and why the ownership strategy of acquiring firms might influence the survival of foreign acquired units.

Chapter 8 by Santos, Karl-Barandas, and Martins uses the event study methodology, a commonly used approach in corporate finance, to explore the impact of overall psychic distance and separate dimensions of psychic distance on stock market performance of acquirers in cross-border acquisitions.

Santos, Karl-Barandas, and Martins first deploy the formative index, based on five key dimensions of psychic distance stimuli, to determine the overall psychic distance's impact on stock market performance. They then test the impact of these five dimensions separately, namely language, education, religion, political system, and industrial development. They use cumulative abnormal returns (CARs) to operationalize the wealth effects or market performance for acquirers. They use an 11-day time window CARs (–5, 5) to represent short-term market performance and a 41-day time window CARs (–20, 20) to represent long-term market performance.

Based on data from 415 cross-border acquisitions between 2005 and 2012, involving acquirers from the United States and targets in 26 countries, this exploratory study illustrates that psychic distance, as a whole, has a negative impact on short-term CARs' performance. However, different dimensions of the psychic distance construct also tell a different story. Only differences in language, education, and political systems appear to have a negative impact on long-term market performance for acquirers. The results provide evidence supporting the illusion of discordance when using a composite distance index that simply aggregates different dimensions (Shenkar, 2001). The authors take into account the asymmetry of psychic distance, as they operationalize the psychic distance hazards from one direction only.

Chapter 9, by Tierean and Berens, as the last chapter in Part II of this research volume, discusses "the effects of the psychic distance dimensions in the context of a firm faced with the situation of choosing an international supplier." Tierean and Berens explore "causal mechanisms through which the distance between the countries of the buyer and the supplier influences the extent to which the two will enter a business relationship."

In this conceptual paper, they "propose that the distance between the countries where the supplier and the organizational buyer reside has a negative effect on the intentions to buy from the supplier." They propose two causal pathways to explain this negative relationship. The first pathway is that higher distance results in lower trust in the supplier, thereby negatively influencing the expected relationship quality. As a result, they argue "that trust and expected relationship quality serially mediate the effect of distance dimensions on the buyer's intentions to buy from the supplier." The other mechanism is identification with the supplier. They argue that large psychic distance creates difficulties to identify a foreign supplier, since psychologically distant objects are not known from direct experience. Here, identification with the supplier mediates the effect of distance on the buyers' intentions to buy from the supplier.

"By highlighting the potential mediating roles of trust, expected relationship quality, and identification with the supplier," the proposed model in this chapter provides an explanation to the question why "international tradeflows are dependent on the psychic distance between countries."

PART III: THE COST OF INSTITUTIONAL DISTANCE

Emerging economies perform an increasingly important role in the world economy. Both institutional voids and institutional overkill, and various forms of market failure that usually occur in emerging economies rather than in developed economies, can shape the firm-specific advantage (FSAs) of emerging economy multinational enterprises (EMNEs) and create special challenges for MNEs internationalizing into emerging economies.

Part III, covering Chapters 10–13, involves emerging economies, either as home countries (Chapters 11 and 13) or host countries (Chapters 10 and 12) for international economic activity. The institutional differences between developed economies and emerging economies increase the liability of foreignness for MNEs in different ways. Chapters 10–12 explore the impact of institutional distance on entry-mode choices. Chapter 13 compares location choices by MNEs from India and China, respectively.

Chapter 11, by Puck, Hödl, Filatotchev, and Lindner, explores how the MNE's intended transfer of various resource types influences ownership choice when entering a foreign market, and how these links are influenced by institutional distance. By grounding the study within the RBV, the authors distinguish between two types of intended resource transfers – namely intangible and tangible ones – to occur between the parent and the subsidiary and highlight their opposite effect on entry-mode choice. Specifically, they argue that parent firms intending to transfer high levels of intangible resources tend to choose wholly owned subsidiaries (WOS), while firms that intend to transfer high levels of tangible resources tend to choose international joint ventures (IJV).

The authors administered questionnaires over a two-month period in 2012 to foreign companies located in China, and the final sample consists of 128 foreign subsidiaries operating in that country. The authors used instrumental variables in their two-step logistic regression procedure to control for endogeneity. Their results show "that intra-firm resource transfer intentions have a significant effect on the choice of entry mode (IJV/WOS). The results indicate that the entry mode choice does not solely depend on efficiency and cost minimization aspects, but also on the intentions concerning firm resources to be transferred to foreign markets, as these resources may be differently exploited in IJV and WOS. More importantly, the value that firms expect to generate with the resources they plan to transfer abroad is far from being universal, but is influenced by institutional differences between the firm's home and the host country. With increasing institutional distance, parent firms that intend to transfer high levels of intangible or tangible resources may increase the legitimacy of their business operations and thus the value of their resource endowments by cooperating with local IJV partners.

This study contributes to the IB literature by augmenting TCE-based entry mode research with elements from the RBV and insights from institutional theory. The study also shows that TCE and RBV thinking are compatible, which is one of the main foundation of contemporary internalization theory (Narula & Verbeke, 2015; Rugman et al., 2011).

Both Chapters 6 and 12 address one of the illusions prevailing in much distance research, as noted by Shenkar (2001), namely the illusion of asymmetry, which was also reviewed in Chapter 2. "Negative regulative distance" can be observed "when the regulatory development in the host-country is lower than that in the MNEs' home country," which is the case when developed country MNEs invest in emerging countries. "Positive regulative distance" can be observed "when the regulatory development in the host-country is greater than that in the MNEs' home country," which is the case when EMNEs invest in developed countries.

Chapter 12 by Mueller, Henriks, and Slangen investigates the role of formal institutional distance in EMNE foreign entry-mode choices, taking into account both establishment modes (acquisition versus greenfield) and ownership modes (full versus partial). To explore this question, Mueller, Henriks, and Slangen take an information economics perspective given that the "quality of a country's formal institutions determines the amount of information that buyers have at their disposal about the assets that they purchase." They argue that "foreign entrants' perceptions of how well host-country institutions reduce information asymmetries not only depend on the quality of a host country's institutions per se, but also on how that quality compares to the quality of home-country institutions, i.e., on the direction of the institutional distance." The magnitude of differences between the home and host sides "will shape the information asymmetry-related risks that managers perceive in both the market for corporate control and the markets for intermediary inputs." The authors add that "the greater the negative institutional distance, the higher the information asymmetries that the entrant will likely perceive and, hence, the higher its inclination to select entry modes that reduce the risks associated with information asymmetries." That is, EMNEs will prefer to "set up greenfields and hold partial ownership in both acquired and greenfield subsidiaries." Positive institutional distance on the contrary will alter this preference, and EMNEs will rather "enter via acquisitions and hold full ownership in acquired and greenfield subsidiaries."

The authors test their hypotheses based on a sample of 1,070 foreign entries made by 796 EMNEs originating from 14 countries. Their results indicate that "EMNEs prefer full over partial acquisitions when geographic distance increases, whereas earlier studies relying on a global sample have found a negative effect." They also uncovered that "the higher the negative institutional distance, the more likely an EMNE will chose a full acquisition."

However, "the host country's institutional quality is not significantly associated with any ownership mode preferences in greenfields." In addition, they found "economic distance and acquisition restrictions to be negatively related with full ownership."

Chapter 6 by Konara and Shirodkar investigates the possibility of institutional distance exerting an asymmetric effect on ownership mode selection in MNE entry strategies into emerging countries. Shirodkar and Konara argue that in the case of negative regulatory distance, MNEs are more likely to deal with institutional voids via greater ownership of the subsidiary, although emerging markets also present risks associated with institutional voids for developed-country-based MNEs. The benefits of full ownership are related to the greater need to control operations and to capitalize on arbitrage-related opportunities. In the case of positive regulatory distance, firms from relatively weaker regulatory environments may not perceive such comparatively greater benefits of exercising stronger control through higher commitment modes.

The authors tested their hypotheses using a sample of 17,457 subsidiaries of MNEs from 88 home countries and operating in 19 emerging market host countries. They deconstructed the institutional distance measure, taking into account the direction of the institutional distance observed. The results show that in the case of negative regulatory distance, institutionally distant MNEs are more likely to choose the full-ownership mode. In the case of positive regulatory distance, institutionally distant MNEs are more likely to choose the joint-ownership mode. The findings in the context of emerging markets in this chapter run contrary to those found in Hernández and Nieto's (2015) study, which only had small and medium-sized enterprises and European countries in their sample.

The differences with the findings of the Hernández and Nieto (2015) study indirectly illustrate that FSAs are shaped by home and host country characteristics (Rugman et al., 2011). Emerging market MNEs may have FSAs such as a home country determined capability of operating with external partners, in line with Verbeke and Kano (2015). In the context of emerging host countries with large institutional voids, and therefore a preference for full control entry modes, recombination skills do remain important for firms to capitalize on arbitrage-related opportunities (Verbeke, 2013).

Chapters 6 and 12 illustrate that "it is not only the sheer quality of host country institutions that impacts entry mode choices, but also the extent to which host country institutions are inferior or superior to the home country institutions." Both chapters demonstrate the importance of distinguishing institutional profile effects from institutional distance effects in future IB research. The differential findings in Chapters 6 and 12, and the contradictory findings between Chapter 6 and Hernández and Nieto (2015), illustrate the importance of sufficiently contextualizing IB research (Welch, Piekkari, Plakoyiannaki, & Paavilainen-Mäntymäki, 2011).

Chapter 10 by Quer, Claver, and Rienda, as the last chapter in Part III of this volume, investigates the influence of political risk and cultural distance on the likelihood of Chinese and Indian MNEs engaging in FDI. Quer, Claver, and Rienda argue that Chinese MNEs typically do not view political risk as a constraint, since they are used to the Chinese government playing an active role. In addition, Chinese firms have a rich experience of cooperating with – and learning from – foreign MNEs internationalizing into China. Since China attaches much importance to strategic asset seeking, Chinese MNEs are typically not affected much by cultural distance either when deciding whether or not to enter a foreign market.

The authors tested their hypotheses using a sample of 832 outward FDIs performed by Chinese and Indian MNEs, between 2005 and 2014. They operationalized cultural distance by using the Kogut and Singh (1988) index, based on Hofstede's (1980) four original dimensions. Their findings "suggest that the behavior of Chinese MNEs is less conventional than that of their Indian counterparts when facing institutional obstacles in host countries." Specifically, political risk and cultural distance negatively influence Indian MNE decisions to engage in outward FDI. However, outward FDI decisions by Chinese MNEs do not appear to be affected by political risk or cultural distance, as suggested above. This study thus shows that home country institutional factors affect the extent to which host country distance-related features will have much or little influence on foreign entry decisions.

The four chapters included in Part III as a whole demonstrate the importance of properly contextualizing IB research, rather than, for example, including many different countries in a single pool, as is often the case when constructing studies based on large secondary data sets (Verbeke & Kano, 2015; Welch et al., 2011).

PART IV: THE VALUE OF DISTANCE

Parts II and III zoomed in on the specific aspect of cross-country distance as a cost/friction generating variable. Yet, differences across countries enable firms to benefit from arbitrage opportunities, access to new markets and resources, and improved efficiency, creating "value of diversity" (Verbeke &

Kano, 2015; Zaheer, Schomaker, & Nachum, 2012). Irrespective of the level of analysis chosen, that is, the MNE, the subsidiary, or the team, the "value of diversity" has been acknowledged but has not been investigated extensively. In other words, it is still not entirely clear how exactly distance can contribute to creating value.

Part IV of this volume, covering Chapters 14–18, addresses the above challenge. In particular, geographical distance may contribute to knowledge sourcing by amplifying the novelty factor in the knowledge accessed and accumulated by the subsidiary (Chapter 14). Distance can increase the level of corporate social responsibility (CSR) implementation (Chapter 15). Faultline distance can create value through diversity, as differences may serve as an advantage for teams (Chapter 16). Internationally experienced and diverse top management teams could help firms realize the differentiation benefits and learning benefits associated with higher distance (Chapter 17). This part, when studied in its entirety, demonstrates the nuanced, value-creating aspect of distance that goes beyond portraying distance as a pure cost-generating variable.

Chapter 14 by Perri and Santangelo links the nuances of distance with one major MNE strategy, namely sourcing knowledge across borders, whereby research and development (R&D) activities are geographically dispersed to tap into novel ideas and capabilities. Based on a critical review of the literature, Perri and Santangelo highlight several possible avenues of research in the field of international knowledge learning.

In this chapter, the authors first review the extant research on knowledge sourcing in the IB field and point out two major problems in studying geographic distance and knowledge sourcing. The first problem is that IB scholars typically collapse two distinct constructs, namely discrete border effects and continuous distance effects, into one construct. The second problem is the subnational spatial heterogeneity, which "drives the establishment of foreign subsidiaries in particular agglomerations and not at random locations within a country," has been ignored.

Drawing on economic geography and innovation studies, the authors point out that "Geographical distance offers opportunities to source diverse knowledge, to the extent that countries develop idiosyncratic patterns of technological specialization." The cross-country variation in technological specialization between home and host countries creates incentives for MNEs to source knowledge inputs that are different from those available in the home country. In addition, the continuous nature of spatial distance and the discrete nature of cross-country borders have differential distance effects in the realm of knowledge spillovers.

The authors suggest three future directions that IB scholars could fruitfully explore in the study of subsidiary knowledge sourcing: (1) "Internalize the role of the continuous nature of geographical distance in combination with multiple intra-host country border effects." This would allow assessing "how subsidiaries vary in their ability to source knowledge depending on the geographical distance that separates them from knowledge sources that are heterogeneously located within the host country territorial boundaries, and on the different types of intra-host country borders that stand between them"; (2) Explore the missing link between "geographical distance and the heterogeneity of host country knowledge sources"; and (3) Investigate "knowledge sourcing from geographically distant/proximate diverse host-country sources located in different sub-national regions."

This chapter does a good job in advancing the "understanding of the role of geography and geographical distance in international knowledge sourcing."

Chapter 15 by Jacqueminet attempts to answer the question how distance influences CSR implementation strategies adopted by subsidiaries. Jacqueminet proposes that distance's influence on the CSR implementation level and the degree of focus in the implementation of CSR practices is "mediated by the prioritization of local versus internal demands, and moderated by the subsidiary's dependence on its parent firm and on the level of conflict among its local stakeholders." In particular, "more distant subsidiaries will prioritize local demands at the expense of the corporate mandate, and therefore implement more practices but less extensively. But for subsidiaries that depend more heavily on their parent MNE, as internal legitimacy is key, distance might in fact increase the attention to the headquarters and therefore have a smaller effect on local prioritization. As a result, dependence on the parent firm will reduce the overall negative relationship between distance and CSR implementation level and focus. And the effect of the prioritization of local demands on CSR implementation will be more prevalent if local demands are conflicting. Thus, in case of high local stakeholder consensus, the overall negative relationship between distance and CSR implementation level and focus will again be assuaged."

Drawing on attention-based theory, this chapter contributes to the IB literature by considering the joint allocation of attention to external versus internal demands. It thereby provides a more nuanced conceptualization of the impact of the legitimacy trade-off at play at the subsidiary level on the distance–CSR implementation relationship. From the study, we can also observe the value-creating initiatives in MNEs as a result of distance. For instance, "distance could increase the level of CSR implementation because subsidiaries suffer from a liability of foreignness and need to gain local legitimacy." This positive assessment is then qualified by the more critical observation that "subsidiaries that are further away from the headquarters might have a reduced ability to implement CSR." Consequently, the specific impact of distance on CSR is likely contingent upon the particular sub-areas of CSR that are investigated.

Chapter 16 by Pregernig addresses the value of diversity by using the "faultline" framework. This chapter is in line with the view expressed in Chapter 2 that research on diverse teams and faultlines in MNEs is an area where IB could contribute to strategic management research. Faultlines, defined as "hypothetical dividing lines that split a group into relatively homogeneous subgroups based on the group members' demographic alignment along multiple attributes," allow a more comprehensive approach to studying the effects of demographic diversity, as compared to approaches measuring diversity in terms of single features.

This study investigates "the links between faultline strength, relationship conflict, performance and faultline distance." It integrates relationship conflict as a relevant process linking faultlines and team performance. Faultline strength can be defined as the "extent of demographic alignment across members within a group," while faultline distance is the "difference between subgroups emerging from such an alignment." Pregernig argues that groups with strong faultlines tend to experience more relationship conflicts as subgroup identities become more salient. Adverse subgroup interaction, perceived gaps, and misunderstandings can increase with a large faultline distance, since faultline distance may trigger additional stereotyping and bias in groups. However, team members typically attribute particular expectations of other distant members to greater demographic differences, rather than engaging in personal attacks or exhibiting negative emotions. Consequently, the author hypothesizes that faultline distance could actually reduce the level of relationship conflicts and moderate the relationship between faultline strength and performance.

Based on data gathered in a laboratory setting with 267 graduate students, the study shows that "faultline strength has a negative effect on perceived performance, partially via relationship conflict, which is contingent on the level of faultline distance." However, faultline distance increases performance, partially mediated via relationship conflict. The findings in this chapter support the notion that faultlines affect performance via conflict and that faultline strength and faultline distance have distinct effects. Faultline distance actually creates value by reducing conflict levels.

Few scholars have explicitly tested the effect of faultlines on performance via relationship conflict. This chapter fills this gap. In particular, it contributes to the IB literature by incorporating both faultline strength and faultline distance and investigating their interaction.

Chapter 17 by Piaskowska addresses a key question often raised in managerial practice: "what sets apart the companies which can capitalize on opportunities in various distant locations from those which cannot?" Piaskowska answers this question by focusing on top management, that is, the locus of internationalization decisions in MNEs.

First, the author reviews the two overarching distance concepts that function as an umbrella for multiple subtypes of distance, namely institutional distance and psychic distance. The author points out that while "institutional distance is normally seen as a set of environmental factors, psychic distance is more appropriately conceptualized as perceptions of the environmental stimuli. Despite this conceptual distinction, both institutional distance and psychic distance have been measured at the country dyad level, often with the use of the same or similar empirical indicators."

The above inconsistency leads the author to propose a unifying framework, which combines insights from the IB literature and the upper echelons literature: "The key insight is that managerial cognitions and values are central to how institutional distance stimuli are received and interpreted to form managerial perceptions, i.e., psychic distance." The proposed framework synthesizes different types of distance and analyzes multifaceted and cross-level influences of distance on internationalization. It suggests that "distance influences internationalization at multiple levels and across levels, of which the organizational, managerial, and top management team levels are the most apparent." The framework suggests that "distance is good for companies whose executives possess relevant (international) knowledge, abilities, and attitudes, and whose top teams have a level of diversity they can capitalize on, even when their companies lack relevant organizational experience." Hence, having the right individuals at the helm enables firms to realize the investment and learning opportunities associated with distance. The framework suggests that psychic distance should be assessed at the individual level, which is consistent with its original conceptualization as a perception, and this is also in line with the framework developed in Chapter 2 by Dow.

The author illustrates this approach with the example of UK's Vodafone Group PLC. Under the leadership of Arun Sarin (during the 2003 and 2008 periods), Vodafone embarked on a major expansion drive in emerging markets, which were distant from the firm's portfolio and experience at the time. The success of this expansion strategy was possible in part due to Mr. Sarin's background and experience in emerging markets, combined with his understanding of developed markets, despite relatively limited organizational-level experience.

PART V: ALTERNATIVE LENSES FOR IB RESEARCH

Part V, as a whole, explores various facets associated with distance, whether the implicit negative consequences associated with increasing distance (Chapters 19, 20, and 21), the possible value created by distance (Chapter 18), or the possible governance structures to reduce distance (Chapter 18). These chapters adopt alternative lenses to explore these issues, such as case studies (Chapters 18 and 20), quasi experimental design (Chapter 21), and a focus on the indirect consequences of distance (Chapters 19 and 22).

Chapter 19 by Tomassen addresses "the relationship between MNE headquarters (HQ) and their foreign subsidiaries, and examines matters of governance and performance consequences in such relationships." Tomassen also discusses measurement issues in the realm of governance costs and subsidiary performance, both theoretically and empirically.

This chapter denotes both transaction costs and management costs as "governance costs." There are four facets of ex post governance costs: bargaining costs, monitoring costs, information costs, and bonding costs. The author argues that the four facets of governance costs are not independent and unique latent variables. Some of these are more endogenous than other ones. MNEs need to make trade-offs among different types of governance costs. For instance, a higher level of communication might also intensify bargaining and monitoring activities. Intensifying bonding, in an effort to build "trust," so as to reduce the needs for formal control, should – on the contrary – decrease subsequent bargaining costs and monitoring costs.

The author develops multi-item reflective scales for the different categories of governance costs and subsidiary performance and conducts a principal component analysis, as well as confirmatory factor analysis to validate the measurement models. As there were indications of interference among the various governance costs, the author used a structural equation modeling approach, instead of the usual OLS or 2SLS to test his hypotheses. Building upon survey data from 159 Norwegian MNEs, the study finds that governance costs explain a substantial proportion (36%) of the variance in subsidiary performance. The results demonstrate that "information costs affect subsidiary performance through bargaining costs and monitoring costs, rather than through a direct effect," and "bonding costs have both direct and indirect effects on the subsidiary performance." The author therefore concludes: "this exploratory study indicates that governance costs might interact and affect subsidiary performance in ways that have not been explored in former studies."

Several insights result from the present study: First, the four main categories of governance costs cannot be treated as independent variables. Second, there are trade-offs to be made between different governance approaches (in terms of differential and interacting effects on various types of governance costs), which can only be assessed with longitudinal research designs. Third, distance creates information cost fallacies, which appear to be an important driver of perceived, extra needs for monitoring and bargaining in MNEs. Fourth, bargaining costs, monitoring costs, and bonding costs represent governance costs that directly affect subsidiary performance. Five, information fallacies, not representing a direct negative effect on subsidiary performance, do affect performance through bargaining costs and monitoring costs.

Instead of just focusing on the negative impact of psychic distance, Chapter 20, by Magomedova, Achcaoucaou, and Miravitlles, explores how MNEs could use springboard subsidiaries to reduce the psychic distance between the MNE headquarters and a distant target region, especially when the heterogeneity among different countries in the target region is substantial.

Springboard subsidiaries are defined as organizational units "located in the intermediate position in terms of institutional distance and business knowledge between the MNC home country and a target region, and that have successfully incorporated the specific advantages of their location." Springboard subsidiaries are thus characterized by their "intermediate position," between the head office and other subsidiaries in a target region, which may give them the status of impartial or unbiased intermediary, as perceived by the other subsidiaries in the target region.

Magomedova, Achcaoucaou, and Miravitlles selected a German MNE headquartered in Munich that coordinates its publishing activities in Latin America through its Spanish springboard subsidiary in Barcelona, as the basis of their study. They conducted analysis of psychic distance, using both perceived psychic distance data (inside the MNE) and country-level psychic distance stimuli. They collected data on perceived psychic distance between the MNE head office and the target region, through in-depth, personal semi-structured interviewing of the Spanish subsidiary top manager who had worked in the MNE through all the organizational transformation processes. They triangulated the interview data by using secondary data. They used the Kogut and Singh (1988) approach to calculate the distance between Germany,

Spain, and each Latin American country for each major constituent of psychic distance, namely language, culture, institutions, country development, and migration.

The findings suggest that the Spanish springboard subsidiary helped the MNE to reduce the perceived psychic distance between the head office and the target region. The reasons for this outcome are twofold. First, the Spanish subsidiary had an intermediate psychic proximity in both directions (i.e., vis-à-vis the head office and the target region). Second, the subsidiary was located outside of the target region, making it somewhat "impartial" and not involved in intra-regional conflicts.

This single case study also shows that "the sum of psychic distance stimuli between HQ's home country – springboard subsidiary's country and springboard subsidiary's – Latin American countries is actually smaller than the direct psychic distance between HQ's home country and Latin American countries." This observation represents exploratory empirical evidence of the nonadditive nature of distance measurements.

Chapter 20 by Costa and Elo discusses how a born global firm can leverage the ethnic origin of its products and assets in its early stage of internationalization. In this case study, Costa and Elo examine the distinct elements that constitute the firm's internationalization strategy from a marketing perspective. The study addresses international market selection and entry modes, but also the need to adapt versus standardize the different elements that make up the marketing mix of the company.

The authors collected primary data through in-depth interviews and observations of Nata Pura, a relatively young Portuguese firm, which has built its internationalization strategy based on exporting a traditional product, namely *pastel de nata* (egg tart pastry), using innovative solutions. They also collected secondary data, such as company documents, and other public data.

Nata Pura adapts its product, promotion, and distribution strategies to reach distant host markets. It has developed partnerships with local economic actors to produce and promote *pastel de nata* as an organic pastry made with high-quality, locally adapted ingredients. The network partnerships have helped the firm in overcoming administrative distance and the foreignness of the product. From this case study, we can conclude that Nata Pura's bundling of its internationally transferrable FSAs with location-bound FSAs contributed by both upstream and downstream partners in the host country has allowed developing new products and adjusting its other marketing strategies (Verbeke, 2013). Nata Pura is a good example of the centralized exporter archetype in Verbeke (2013), as its products manufactured at home embody the firm's FSAs developed on the basis of its home country characteristics.

Rather than focusing on financial and organizational outcomes, Chapter 21, by Matarazzo, Federica De Vanna, Lanzilli, and Resciniti, investigates the impact of cultural distance on consumers' behavior after cross-border acquisitions. Specifically, the authors analyze "the reputation transferability from the local target to the acquirer both in case of large and small cultural distance." They posit that reputation transferability of a local target is stronger when the cultural distance between the local target and the acquirer is smaller.

Reputation transferability is defined as "the degree to which an acquiring firm may realize benefits from the positive perceptions of the target firm among its key constituents after the transaction." In the present study, it is operationalized as consumers' attitude and purchase intentions after the acquisition. The authors argue that "cultural differences are likely to further exacerbate problems with reputation transferability. Acquiring firms are less able to appreciate the relationships a target has with key stakeholders when its value structures differ significantly."

The authors conducted an experiment involving 424 Italian University students and using a questionnaire built on validated scales. The experiment compared the participants' responses to two scenarios, namely that of a Chinese firm (large cultural distance with Italy) acquiring an Italian food company, versus a Spanish firm (small cultural distance with Italy) doing the same. "The findings show that Italian consumers have more negative attitudes toward the acquired firm and lower intentions to repurchase its products if the acquirer has large cultural distance rather than when it has small cultural distance."

Chapter 22, by Iurkov and Benito, as the last chapter in this volume, examines the effect of domestic alliances on firms' foreign divestment decisions. Unlike prior studies of foreign divestment that focused either on the role of general, intra-firm characteristics, or on factors external to firms' control, Iurkov and Benito investigate strategic trade-offs in a firm's overall resource deployment strategy, a more behavioral and capability-related trigger, internal to the firm in this chapter.

The authors argue that since "new domestic alliances are often formed to acquire, create or augment higher order capabilities, their formation may trigger resource recombination." As foreign operations consume more resources, firms may choose to reduce them to allow increased domestic collaboration, when new business opportunities arise in domestic markets. As a result, domestic alliances can affect firms' propensity to divest foreign operations.

Using data from 159 firms in the electronic and electrical equipment industries in the United States, over the period 2001–2008, the authors deployed a matching technique approach to study the effect of domestic alliance formation on foreign operations divestment. Their findings indeed demonstrate that firms were more likely to divest foreign subsidiaries if they had engaged in new domestic collaboration one year earlier.

Although this chapter does not study distance directly, it has important implications for future research on the impacts of distance. The chapter convincingly demonstrates that researchers cannot simply take distance measures and hope to explain anything in the realm of strategic decision-making without proper contextualizing. This particular chapter suggests that any "higher country distance" operations may be divested if the firm engages in "zero country distance" investments but associated with the need to manage inter-firm distance. In other words, from a Penrosean perspective, the capacity of firms to absorb a particular, aggregate level of country-level distances is reduced by having more investments requiring management of inter-firm distances (even if these occur in a context of zero country-level distance). This chapter thereby extends the prior work by Hutzschenreuter, Voll, and Verbeke (2011) on the need to consider "added distance" in international strategic management studies.

CONCLUSION

This research volume provides a comprehensive overview of the challenges associated with distance research in IB, as well as the various approaches that can be deployed to address these challenges. It demonstrates that there is much more than meets the eye when assessing how firms address distance in their international strategic management decisions (Verbeke, 2013). The chapters address a wide range of IB issues, ranging from the very micro individual-level, to the very macro country-level, as well as cross-level phenomena.

For instance, no universal relationship should be expected for the impact of distance on any performance outcome variable. Such relationship is contingent on the type of decision considered, the industry-level context, the specific dimensions of distance addressed, the particular combinations of MNE FSAs and specific host country CSAs involved, the level(s) of analysis relevant to the study, so on. Even for similar types of decisions (e.g., entry-mode choices), the expectations as to the impact of a distance dimension such as culture can differ widely. The above reflects the need for a better contextualizing of IB research, especially against the backdrop of the increasing importance of emerging economies and the large heterogeneity among – and within – these emerging markets. Provided such better contextualizing, future empirical work should then explore the factors underlying distance effects. As one example, the micro-foundations of bounded rationality and bounded reliability (Verbeke, 2013) are likely functioning as mediators (and in some cases as moderators) with "respect to the link between perceptions of distance and preferences for a particular alternative or course of action."

In terms of operationalizing distance constructs, an increasing number of scholars is paying attention to the "direction" of distance, so as to address the illusion of symmetry in Shenkar (2001), as shown in Chapters 5, 12 and 13. However, the illusion of discordance and the assumption of equivalence have not yet received much attention in the literature. Cultural distance is mostly operationalized as the Kogut and Singh (1988) index, especially when cultural distance is a moderator. Zaheer et al. (2012) actually found that more scholars have adopted the Kogut and Singh's measure since Shenkar's (2001) critique, possibly because of its "user-friendliness," when used in a regression equation. As regards the future, we encourage more scholars to build into their empirical work the (correct) observation that some cultural (and also other) differences may have complementarity effects (or be value-creating), whereas other ones may cause friction, in line with prior thinking about the psychic distance paradox (O'Grady & Lane, 1996).

We hope that this volume will function as a significant step forward in motivating IB scholars to explore more nuances regarding the possible impact of distance on managerial decision-making and on the outcomes thereof. We encourage IB researchers to rethink the prevailing notions of distance dimensions, foreignness, "outsidership," and diversity in general, and to move far beyond the traditional distance concepts deployed so far in IB research (Stahl, Tung, Kostova, & Zellmer-Bruhn, 2016).

REFERENCES

Berry, H., Guillén, M. F., & Nan, Z. (2010). An institutional approach to cross-national distance. *Journal of International Business Studies*, *41*(9), 1460–1480.

Chkir, I. E., & Cosset, J. C. (2001). Diversification strategy and capital structure of multinational corporations. *Journal of Multinational Financial Management*, *11*(1), 17–37.

Dow, D., & Karunaratna, A. (2006). Developing a multidimensional instrument to measure psychic distance stimuli. *Journal of International Business Studies*, *37*(5), 578–602.

Hernández, V., & Nieto, M. J. (2015). The effect of the magnitude and direction of institutional distance on the choice of international entry modes. *Journal of World Business*, *50*(1), 122–132.

Hofstede, G. (1980). *Culture's consequences: National differences in thinking and organizing*. Beverly Hills, CA: Sage.

Hofstede, G. (2001). *Culture's consequences: Comparing values, behaviors, institutions and organizations across nations*. Beverly Hills, CA: Sage.

Hutzschenreuter, T., Voll, J. C., & Verbeke, A. (2011). The impact of added cultural distance and cultural diversity on international expansion patterns: A Penrosean perspective. *Journal of Management Studies*, *48*(2), 305–329.

Hymer, S. (1960). On multinational corporations and foreign direct investment. *The Theory of Transnational Corporations*. London: Routledge for the United Nations.

Hymer, S. H. (1960). The international operations of national firms, a study of direct foreign investment, Doctoral dissertation, Massachusetts Institute of Technology.

Johanson, J., & Vahlne, J. E. (1977). The internationalization process of the firm – A model of knowledge development and increasing foreign market commitments. *Journal of International Business Studies*, *8*(1), 23–32.

Johanson, J., & Vahlne, J. E. (2009). The Uppsala internationalization process model revisited: From liability of foreignness to liability of outsidership. *Journal of International Business Studies*, *40*(9), 1411–1431.

Kogut, B., & Singh, H. (1988). The effect of national culture on the choice of entry mode. *Journal of International Business Studies*, *19*(3), 411–432.

Kostova, T. (1999). Transnational transfer of strategic organizational practices: A contextual perspective. *Academy of Management Review*, *24*(2), 308–324.

La Porta, R., Lopez-de-Silanes, F., & Shleifer, A. (2006). What works in securities laws? *The Journal of Finance*, *61*(1), 1–32

McLeod, P. L., Lobel, S. A. & Cox Jr, T. H. (1996). Ethnic diversity and creativity in small groups. *Small Group Research, 27*(2), 248–264.

Narula, R., & Verbeke, A. (2015). Making internalization theory good for practice: The essence of Alan Rugman's contributions to international business. *Journal of World Business*, *50*(4), 612–622.

O'Grady, S., & Lane, H. W. (1996). The psychic distance paradox. *Journal of International Business Studies*, *27*(2), 309–333.

Ragozzino, R., & Reuer, J. J. (2011). Geographic distance and corporate acquisitions: Signals from IPO firms. *Strategic Management Journal*, *32*(8), 876–894.

Rugman, A. M., & Verbeke, A. (2001). Subsidiary-specific advantages in multinational enterprises. *Strategic Management Journal*, *22*(3), 237–250.

Rugman, A. M., Verbeke, A., & Nguyen, P. C. Q. T. (2011). Fifty years of international business theory and beyond. *Management International Review*, *51*(6), 755–786.

Shaw, M.E. (1981). *Group dynamics: The psychology of small group behavior. New York*: McGraw-Hill.

Shenkar, O. (2001). Cultural distance revisited: Towards a more rigorous conceptualization and measurement of cultural differences. *Journal of International Business Studies*, *32*(3), 519–535.

Shenkar, O., Luo, Y., & Yeheskel, O. (2008). From "distance" to "friction": Substituting metaphors and redirecting intercultural research. *Academy of Management Review*, *33*(4), 905–923.

Singh, M., Davidson, W. N., & Suchard, J. A. (2003). Corporate diversification strategies and capital structure. *The Quarterly Review of Economics and Finance*, *43*(1), 147–167.

Stahl, G. K., Tung, R. L., Kostova, T., & Zellmer-Bruhn, M. (2016). Widening the lens: Rethinking distance, diversity, and foreignness in international business research through positive organizational scholarship. *Journal of International Business Studies*, *47*(6), 621–630.

Stahl, G. K., Mäkelä, K., Zander, L. & Maznevski, M. L. (2010). A look at the bright side of multicultural team diversity. *Scandinavian Journal of Management*, *26*(4), 439–447.

Teece, D. J. (2014). A dynamic capabilities-based entrepreneurial theory of the multinational enterprise. *Journal of International Business Studies*, *45*(1), 8–37.

Tung, R. L., & Verbeke, A. (2010). Beyond Hofstede and GLOBE: Improving the quality of cross-cultural research. *Journal of International Business Studies*, *41*(8), 1259–1274.

Verbeke, A. (2013). *International business strategy* (2nd ed.). Cambridge: Cambridge University Press.

Verbeke, A., & Kano, L. (2015). The new internalization theory and multinational enterprises from emerging economies: A business history perspective. *Business History Review*, *89*(3), 415–445.

Verbeke, A., & Kenworthy, T. P. (2008). Multidivisional vs metanational governance of the multinational enterprise. *Journal of International Business Studies*, *39*(6), 940–956.

Verbeke, A., & Yuan W. (2016). The impact of "distance" on multinational enterprise subsidiary capabilities: A value chain perspective. *Multinational Business Review*, *24*(2), 168–190.

Welch, C., Piekkari, R., Plakoyiannaki, E., & Paavilainen-Mäntymäki, E. (2011). Theorising from case studies: Towards a pluralist future for international business research. *Journal of International Business Studies*, *42*(5), 740–762.

Zaheer, S., Schomaker, M. S., & Nachum, L. (2012). Distance without direction: Restoring credibility to a much-loved construct. *Journal of International Business Studies*, *43*(1), 18–27.

PART I
THE CONCEPT OF DISTANCE

CHAPTER 2

ARE WE AT A TURNING POINT FOR DISTANCE RESEARCH IN INTERNATIONAL BUSINESS STUDIES?

Douglas Dow

ABSTRACT

In this chapter I argue that the distance research in international business studies is at a turning point, not in terms of its popularity, nor the quantity of articles published, but rather, in terms of the types of issues that are explored. Past distance research has largely been conducted at the level of the firm and/or the market – that is, linking national-level measures of distance with specific firm behaviors and outcomes. However, the seminal paper by Shenkar (2001) represents a shift in focus that is only just beginning to gain traction. This shift involves stepping back and beginning to unpack the black box we call 'distance' by exploring the micro-level mechanisms involved. In essence, it is about digging deeper in multiple aspects, to understand when, why and how distance matters in the international business (IB) context. These are issues that until now have typically been neglected. A metaphor borrowed from the social psychology literature, known as Coleman's Boat, is used as a vehicle

Distance in International Business: Concept, Cost and Value
Progress in International Business Research, Volume 12, 47–68

ISSN: 1745-8862/doi:10.1108/S1745-886220170000012001

to explain the key issues involved in this shift and the opportunities for future research.

Keywords: Cultural distance; psychic distance; multi-level analysis; micro-foundations

INTRODUCTION

As has been chronicled many times over, the concept of distance as a metaphor for cross-national differences has been dramatically rising in popularity in the international business (IB) literature (e.g. Beugelsdijk & Mudambi, 2013; Cho & Padmanabhan, 2005; Dow, 2014; Em, 2011; Ghemawat, 2016; Zaheer, Schomaker, & Nachum, 2012). Indeed, Ghemawat (2016) goes so far as to argue that, based on article counts in the *Journal of International Business Studies*, distance may now outrank internalization and transaction cost theory in terms of being one of the dominant perspectives in IB research. However, in this chapter I argue that distance research may be at a critical turning point not in terms of the amount of attention it attracts, but rather in terms of the types of issues that are explored. In order to explain this thesis, I draw upon and adapt a metaphor from social psychology, sometimes colloquially known as 'Coleman's Boat' (Coleman, 1994). In the process, I hope to not only show how the strands of research relate to one another but to also highlight the existing research in these areas and comment on the potential for future research. However, first I will provide a brief overview of the history of the distance literature in IB over the past 60 years.

A BRIEF HISTORY OF DISTANCE RESEARCH IN IB

Phase 1: Gravity Models

The initial use of the concept of distance in IB research was first as a surrogate measure for transportation costs in the gravity models used to explain and predict bilateral trade flows (Anderson, 1979; e.g. Beckerman, 1956; Linnemann, 1966). In these models, mirroring the Newtonian equation for gravity (1686), the size of the economies exporting and importing the goods takes on the role of the 'mass' of the two bodies, with the distance between the two playing the same role in both the Newton's original formulation and the bilateral trade version of the model. As noted by Anderson (1979, p. 106), this adaptation of the gravity model to an IB context is 'probably the most successful empirical trade device of the last 25 years'. This research is what I refer to as the 'first phase of distance research in IB'. It involves the use of geographic distance as a surrogate measure of transportation costs to predict trade flows. Nevertheless, even in one of the earliest papers of this stream (Beckerman, 1956), the seeds were sown for the first turning point in the literature. Specifically, Beckerman (1956) speculated that an additional unmeasured factor, which he coined as psychic distance, appeared to be influencing a significant portion of the intra-European trade.

The 1st Turning Point

For the next two decades, with the exception of a brief mention in passing by Linnemann (1966), the concept of psychic distance remained dormant, and geographic distance as a surrogate for transportation dominated the literature. It was not until the confluence of three separate research agendas spanning a 13-year period that the first major turning point in distance research in IB occurred. The first of these research agendas was development of the Uppsala internationalization process model in Sweden (Johanson & Vahlne, 1977; Johanson & Wiedersheim-Paul, 1975). As part of the development of their model, the Uppsala researchers resurrected the concept of psychic distance, providing a formal definition, giving examples of some of the possible underlying dimensions, and taking the first steps in broadening its application to firm-specific decisions. Johanson and Wiedersheim-Paul (1975, p. 308) defined psychic distance as: 'the sum of factors preventing or disturbing the flow of information between firm and market. Examples of such factors are differences in language, culture, political systems, level of education, level of industrial development, etc.'

Nevertheless, while the Uppsala researchers are certainly responsible for resurrecting and popularizing the concept of psychic distance, their contributions with respect to the concept of distance did not begin to substantially influence the empirical literature until they intersected with two other research streams. The first of these was Hofstede's (1980) seminal work where he created and disseminated empirical measures of national culture. This provided a rich and easily accessible data set covering 54 countries and regions. Kogut and Singh (1988) were then able to take Uppsala theoretical contributions and marry them with Hofstede's data to create their now ubiquitous 'national cultural distance index'. It is the intersection of these three agendas that I would describe the first major turning point in distance research[1].

Phase 2: The Kogut and Singh Index

From this point onwards research concerning the role of distance in IB began to flourish, at least in terms of the sheer quantity of peer-reviewed articles (Em, 2011). However, there are also some fundamental differences in the nature of the post-1988 distance research. The first critical difference is a shift in what the term 'distance' conceptually represents. Thanks to the contributions of Johanson and Vahlne (1977) and Johanson and Wiedersheim-Paul (1975), the term distance conceptually now represented much subtler barriers to international activities, such as difficulties in different parties communicating with and understanding one another and began to include a much broader range of factors including differences in culture. However, at the empirical level the shift in focus was much simpler – the Kogut and Singh (1988) index essentially replaced geographic distance as the *de rigour* measure of distance in IB research (Harzing, 2003).

The other major defining aspect of this new stream of distance research was the dramatic expansion of its application to a broad range of firm-level issues. While Kogut and Singh (1988) began the flood by applying their index to entry-mode choices, many others soon followed applying the concept to explain preferences for joint ventures versus wholly owned subsidiaries (Chang & Rosenzweig, 2001; Erramilli & Rao, 1993; Hennart & Larimo, 1998) and preferences for acquisitions versus greenfield start-ups (Brouthers & Brouthers, 2000; Cho & Padmanabhan, 1995). Similarly, others applied it to firm-level entry decisions via exporting (Benito & Gripsrud, 1992; Erramilli, 1991), and via foreign direct investment (Flores & Aguilera, 2007; Grosse & Trevino, 1996). In a different direction, numerous researchers applied the Kogut and Singh index to the survival of foreign subsidiaries (Barkema, Bell, & Pennings, 1996; Li, 1995; Vermeulen & Barkema, 2001), the survival of international joint ventures (Barkema & Vermeulen, 1997; Lu & Hebert, 2005; Park & Ungson, 1997), as well as other forms of firm performance (Fey & Beamish, 2001; Pothukuchi, Damanpour, Choi, Chen, & Park, 2002). In addition to all that, the Kogut and Singh index has at times been applied to other management issues such as human resource management practices (Boyacigiller, 1990), the degree of adaptation in foreign markets (Dow, 2001) and the technology transfer issues (Minbaeva, Pedersen, Bjorkman, Fey, & Park, 2003).

The 2nd Turning Point

The next turning point in the distance literature is the one that I argue we are already in the middle of, although this is often hard to confirm except in hindsight. Like the first turning point, the second turning point may actually span over a relatively long period of time – but it clearly begins with the seminal conceptual paper by Shenkar (2001). Shenkar identifies eight 'illusions' or 'assumptions' relating to the existent distance research; however, the significance and implications of his paper can be examined at two different levels. The first level is the specific assumptions and illusions that Shenkar nominates; and I will briefly discuss them next with respect to the literature that has emerged over the last 15 years in response to them. However, using the *Coleman's Boat* framework, I also want to highlight a more broad-based underlying implication, that is common to many of the Shenkar's specific illusions and assumptions; and which I believe may become the common theme to the third phase of distance research.

In terms of the number of publications addressing the issue, one of the main responses to Shenkar's work is a stream of literature arguing that distance, or more specifically psychic distance, should be measured at the level of the individual. Although there are some scholars who emphasized this issue before the publication of Shenkar's (2001) paper – e.g. Dichtl, Leibold, Koeglmayr, and Mueller (1984), Evans, Treadgold, & Mavondo (2000), Holzmuller and Kasper (1990), Stöttinger and Schlegelmilch (1998) – this stream of literature is broadly consistent with Shenkar's assumptions of *corporate homogeneity* and *spatial homogeneity* and certainly gained momentum with the publication of Shenkar's (2001) paper. In particular, two sets of authors – Evans and Mavondo (2002) and Sousa and Bradley (2005, 2006, 2008) – have vigorously argued that given the high levels heterogeneity within each country, the best approach is to measure the perceptions of psychic distance at the level of the individual, rather than the country. Empirically this approach appears to yield larger effect sizes (Zhao, Luo, & Suh, 2004); however, it is substantially more labor intensive when investigating actual decisions by firms; and in such settings it is close to impossible to obtain a priori, and thus unbiased perceptions.

More directly related to Shenkar's assumptions of *corporate homogeneity* and *spatial homogeneity* is another stream of literature that has focused explicitly on the issue of 'within country diversity'. Unfortunately, to date, most of this literature has been at the level of broad commentary endorsing this importance of the issue of diversity (Beugelsdijk & Mudambi, 2013; Luiz, 2015; Tung, 2009; Tung & Verbeke, 2010; Zaheer et al., 2012), with only a handful of studies addressing it empirically (Beugelsdijk, Maseland, Onrust, van Hoorn, & Slangen, 2015; Dow, Cuypers, & Ertug, 2016).

The same broadly holds true for Shenkar's *illusion of symmetry* (i.e. that the distance from A to B may not be the same as the distance from B to A) and his *illusion of discordance* (i.e. the assumption that the effects of distance are always negative). While some commentators such as Tung and Verbeke (2010) and Ambos and Håkanson (2014) have echoed Shenkar's concerns about asymmetry, the quantity of actual investigation into the issue of asymmetry has been extremely sparse (Håkanson & Ambos, 2010; Håkanson, Ambos, Schuster, & Leicht-Deobald, 2016; Yildiz & Fey, 2016). Similarly, a number of commentators (Stahl & Tung, 2015; Tung & Verbeke, 2010) have endorsed Shenkar's concern about researchers assuming that distance always has a negative effect; however, even a JIBS special issue on the issue only generated three articles, and only two of those are empirical investigations (Lisak, Erez, Sui, & Lee, 2016; Nurmi & Hinds, 2016). Thus once again the literature seems to conceptually endorse Shenkar's concerns, but at the empirical level the moves to actually investigate them have been glacial.

On a more positive note, a fifth issue identified by Shenkar (2001) that has sparked at least a modest level of new research is his *illusion of causality*. Despite the slightly misleading label, this illusion mainly concerns the fact that, at least at the empirical level, the IB literature has focussed too heavily on cultural differences as measured by the Kogut and Singh index to the exclusion of other dimensions of distance such as those identified by Johanson and Wiedersheim-Paul (1975) and Johanson and Vahlne (1977). In response to this, a variety of authors such as Berry, Guillen, & Zhou (2010), Brewer (2007), Dow and Karunaratna (2006) and Xu, Pan, & Beamish (2004) have developed a much broader range of instruments. While it must be said that a disappointingly large number of authors still continue to rely exclusively on the Kogut and Singh index, at least on this issue there is a modest shift in behaviors of the empirical researchers, and the range of potential instruments has broadened sufficiently that the availability of appropriate measures is no longer the limiting factor.

A sixth issue raised by Shenkar is the *illusion of stability*. In many respects this is a conceptually simple issue – researchers need to be diligent in ensuring that the metrics they are using are up-to-date. For instruments drawn from secondary sources that are revised regularly, such as the economic and demographic statistics provided by the United Nations, the political stability metrics provided by various organizations such as Freedom House and the Economist, and perceptual dimensions drawn from sources such as the World Values Survey, this is no longer a concern. However, for issues such as national culture, obtaining such updates is in general problematic because the data collection process is extremely onerous – usually well beyond the means of a single group of researchers. Nevertheless, two notable efforts in this respect have been made. Most famous of these is the GLOBE effort to create an expanded and update set of culture dimensions (House, Hanges,

Dorfman, & Gupta, 2004). However, taking a different approach Taras, Steel, & Kirkman (2012), using meta-analysis techniques, provided a comprehensive update of the Hofstede dimensions for each of three decades (the 1980s, 1990s and 2000s). Sadly, despite the huge efforts made by both of these sets of authors, the vast majority of empirical work involving national cultural distance still relies exclusively on the Hofstede data collected in the 1970s.

The final two concerns put forward by Shenkar (2001) – specifically the *illusion of linearity* and the *assumption of equivalence* – are more straight forward methodological issues. One, researchers should always be cognizant that the relationships that they are investigating may not be linear; and two, when collapsing multiple dimensions into a single factor they should avoid blindly assigning equal weight to each dimension. On this later issue, a recent paper by Williams and Gregoire (2015) takes a novel approach and begins to provide a theoretical explanation as to why some dimensions may have a greater or lesser impact than others. However, in reality, researchers do not need any new tools or instruments in order to avoid these pitfalls; but, as I have noted with respect to several of the preceding issues, that does not guarantee that the uptake of the new approaches will be rapid.[2]

As foreshadowed earlier, I argue that the implications of Shenkar's seminal work (2001) can also be viewed in terms of a broad underlying theme that touches on most of the eight issues he raises – a desperate need to step back and begin unpacking the black box we call 'distance' by exploring the micro-level mechanisms involved. In one sense, this is already reflected in the move towards measuring an individual's perception of distance (Sousa & Bradley, 2006), and it has implications for the issues of asymmetry and diversity, but they only represent the tip of the iceberg. It is about digging deeper in multiple aspects to understand when, why and how distance matters in the IB context; issues that until now have typically been neglected.

APPLYING COLEMAN'S BOAT TO DISTANCE RESEARCH IN IB

In order to frame this discussion, I adapt a metaphor put forward by Coleman (1994), also known as *Coleman's Boat.*[3] In this framework there are two main dimensions. The vertical dimension concerns the unit of analysis and reflects the fact that quite often the issues we deal with in management are inherently multi-level. In the case of distance research in IB, the lower half of the boat concerns issues at the level of the individual, and the upper half concerns issues at the firm and/or the national level (Fig. 1).

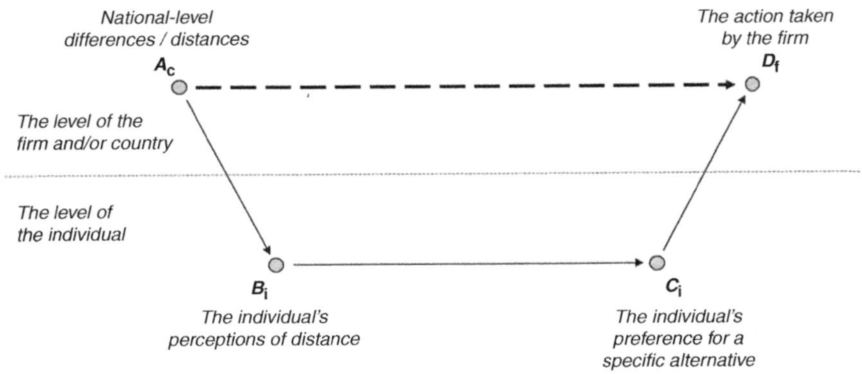

Fig. 1. Coleman's Boat Adapted to Distance Research in IB.

The importance of considering psychic distance at the level of the individual has been highlighted by numerous researchers such as Evans et al. (2000), and Sousa and Bradley (2006) and Stöttinger and Schlegelmilch (1998), and is a direct implication of Shenkar's (2001) concerns about the assumptions of *Corporate Homogeneity* and *Spatial Homogeneity*. Decisions are ultimately made by individuals, and even if a relative large top management team (TMT) is involved in a decision, to assume that they mirror the average characteristics of a country's population is at best contentious.

Nevertheless, for the majority of IB research issues, the ultimate action of interest is typically at the level of the firm or company subsidiary (e.g. market selection, entry mode, performance). It is also an unavoidable fact that large parts of the environment (e.g. legal and political systems, financial and monetary factors, and even language, religion) are either determined at the level of the nation or are heavily aligned at the national level. Thus, while we need to be cognizant of individual-level perceptions, we cannot ignore firm- and national-level factors. The vertical dimension of *Coleman's Boat* captures these aspects.

The horizontal dimension in *Coleman's Boat* reflects chronological cause and effect relationships. Specifically in the context of distance research, the environment and an individual's past experiences will shape their perceptions of other countries. Thus, while national-level differences between two countries (A_c) are not the sole determinant of an individual's perceptions of the distance (B_i), they are potentially a major factor stimulating those perceptions (Dow & Karunaratna, 2006). Similarly, an inherent assumption in essentially all distance research is that perceptions of distance (B_i) are likely to influence a person's preference for a specific alternative or course of action (C_i). And finally, as is true of virtually all management literature (e.g. Dean & Sharfman, 1996; Papadakis, Lioukas, & Chambers, 1998) and is more specifically debated in the consumer behavior literature (Armstrong, Morwitz, & Kumar, 2000; Juster, 1966; Morwitz & Schmittlein, 1992), an individual's preference for a specific alternative (C_i) is assumed to be ultimately related to the action taken (D_f). Although once again, we need to be clear, especially in the cases where decisions are jointly made by TMTs, that these espoused preferences may only be one of many factors influencing the final action. As a result the chain of cause and effect relationships that lead up to an IB decision are almost inescapably multi-level.

Now placing the existing IB distance literature in the context of Fig. 1, I would argue that the vast majority of distance research in the second phase – that is, the phase dominated by the Kogut and Singh index – can be best represented by the dotted line from A_c to D_f. Researchers essentially assume away three critical mediating relationships: A_c–B_i – how perceptions of distance are formed, B_i–C_i – how and why perceptions of distance influence preferences for particular courses of actions and C_i–D_f – how individual preferences for particular courses of action come together to determine what action a company actually takes. Now in saying this, I do not want to denigrate this substantial body of work. It is a necessary part of the progression of our field. Indeed, if the overall relationship A_c–D_f were not confirmed, one would have to question whether any deeper investigation of the mediating relationships is even necessary. However, I believe that for the most part, we have already reached that tipping point. While many researchers may have not yet fully embraced the newer techniques and approaches discussed above, by and large the tools necessary to do so are all available. Moreover, the multiple meta-analyses on the topic of distance (Magnusson, Baack, Zdravkovic, Staub, & Amine, 2008; Tihanyi, Griffith, & Russell, 2005; e.g. Zhao et al., 2004) would seem to indicate that there is a substantial body of exiting research confirming the A_c–D_f relationship on a variety of fronts. It is now time for a broad-based shift in focus to the underlying mediating and moderating relationships. In some cases this will imply a shift in the unit of analysis from the firm to the individual, and in other cases it may imply more multi-level analyses; however, the unifying issue is a shift from exploring whether distance matters, to unpacking the black box and understanding why and how it matters. In the next three sections I will discuss each of the three stages in the model presented in Fig. 1 – highlighting the early research that has been conducted in these areas and discussing the implications for future research.

How Perceptions of Distance Are Formed

What might be termed the 'bow' of *Coleman's Boat* (A_c–B_i) is essentially the issue of what factors and processes shape an individual's perceptions of distance, and most critically is whether national-level differences – or psychic distance stimuli (Dow & Karunaratna, 2006) – are appropriate indicators of individual-level perceptions of distance. Now despite my comments that I believe we are only partially through the 'second turning point', there have been several empirical papers that have explored the latter issue. The earliest of these is Sousa and Bradley (2006), who confirmed in a very simple model that, for their sample of Portuguese managers, the Kogut and Singh index is a statistically significant predictor of individual-level perceptions of the psychic distance of other countries. Working on a much larger data set of bilateral perceptions of psychic distance amongst 25 countries, Håkanson and Ambos (2010) and Dow, Håkanson, & Ambos (2014) have confirmed that the Kogut and Singh index is a statistically significant predictor of perceptions of psychic distance; however, they also find its effect size to be relatively small compared to other types of cross-national factors such as differences in language, religion, and industrial development[4]. In a subsequent investigation Håkanson et al. (2016) find that the predictive power of the Kogut and Singh index disappears once institutional distance is accounted for. Collectively these findings lend strong support to the concern Shenkar (2001) refers to as the *Illusion of Causality*. While the Kogut and Singh index might be a predictor of perceptions of distance, it is only one of many and is arguably one of the weaker metrics.

Nevertheless, the Håkanson and Ambos (2010) analysis also highlights an unexpected result – that geographic distance itself appears to be the single strongest predictor of perceptions of psychic distance. This result is itself somewhat ironic given that Beckerman (1956) coined the term psychic distance in order to explain patterns of trade that geographic distance could not account for. While it is not inconceivable that geographic distance does inhibit cross-national communication to some extent, in this day and age, with a plethora of advance telecommunication options and relatively easy international travel, it is surprizing that geographic distance would be the strongest factor. One alternative explanation for this result is that geographic distance and other cross-national differences are historically correlated due to migration patterns. However, more detailed analysis of the data (Dow et al., 2014) shows that even after accounting for any collinearity, geographic distance is still a statistically significant predictor of perceptions of distance. A third possible explanation for the importance of geographic distance is that the degree to which people are well informed about foreign markets. It may be the case that less internationally experienced individuals may be using geographic distance as a simple heuristic in the absence of better information (Dow & Pekerti, 2015). This possibility leads us into the realm of 'other factors' that might either directly influence people's perceptions of distance or moderate the impact of cross-national differences.

While direct empirical exploration of how factors other than cross-national differences may influence perceptions of distance has been quite limited until recently, for one dimension the issue has a long history in the distance literature. A core element of the original Uppsala model (Johanson & Vahlne, 1977) is that while psychic distance is one of the factors limiting entry into distance markets, international experience is a key-releasing mechanism. Indirectly this is reflected in the wide-spread practice of including international experience as a control variable whenever testing for the impact of distance (Tihanyi et al., 2005). In terms of more direct exploration of the issue, the results are both more limited and slightly ambiguous. Sousa and Bradley (2006) finds a direct negative relationship between general international experience and perceptions of distance; however, Evans, Mavondo, & Bridson (2008) find no such relationship, and Yildiz and Fey (2016) find that it holds for Swedish managers but not Chinese managers. In part these ambiguous results may be due to the fact that concept of experience is arguably ... multidimensional, and due to ... the nature of the relationship – for example, whether it is a direct effect or a moderating effect (Dow, 2008, 2009). This issue is illustrated in Fig. 2 with point A_j representing individual-level factors such as prior experience. A_j may directly influence $\boldsymbol{B}_i$, or it may be moderating the relationship A_c–B_i.

The idea that some factors (A_j) may be moderating the relationship A_c–B_i is in many ways one of the more fruitful areas for future distance research. One such paper is Baack, Dow, Parente, & Bacon (2015) which draws on the social psychology concept of confirmation bias (Klayman & Ha, 1987) and suggests that managers' prior experiences may bias their perceptions of foreign markets. The results indicate that if a manager already believes that a market is proximate to them, they are more prone to accepting and incorporating into their belief set information that confirms their prior beliefs. Similarly they will tend to reject information that disconfirms their prior beliefs. These findings imply that managers are very likely, over time, to underestimate the distance of proximate markets and overestimate the distance of distant markets. This prediction corresponds directly to the underlying assumptions of the *Psychic Distance Paradox* (Evans & Mavondo, 2002; O'Grady & Lane, 1996) and has implications for Shenkar's (2001) *Illusion of Linearity* in that the

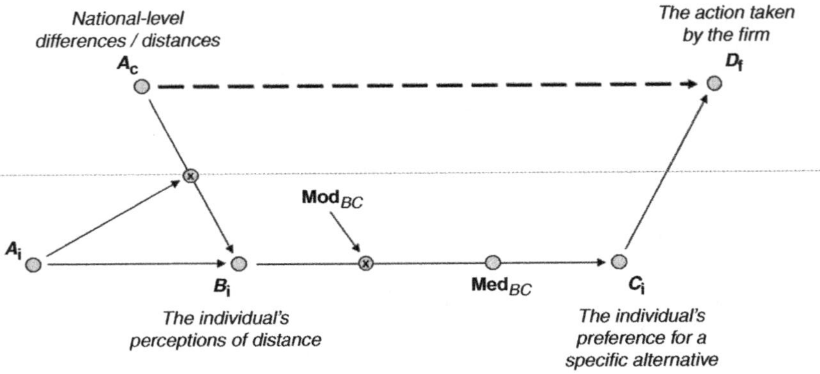

Fig. 2. Further Modifications to Coleman's Boat Adapted to Distance Research in IB.

relationship between exogenous cross-national differences and perceptions of psychic distance may be 'S' shaped, rather than linear.

Another recent paper in this area by Yildiz and Fey (2016) takes a slightly different tack and draws upon Approach Inhibition Theory (Anderson & Berdahl, 2002; Keltner, Gruenfeld, & Anderson, 2003) to explore when and why perceptions of psychic distance might be asymmetric. They argue, and demonstrate using a two country sample, that the relative status of the two countries tends to moderate the bilateral perceptions, with higher status countries perceiving lower status countries as relatively psychically closer than the converse (i.e. the perceptions of the higher status countries by the lower status countries). Interestingly Håkanson et al. (2016) tackle the same issue using a much larger population and focussing on reputation, rather than status and appear to find a slightly different relationship ('U' shaped). However, as will be discussed in the next section, Yildiz and Fey (2016) draw upon Social Identity Theory (Hogg & Terry, 2000) to argue that status also modifies the relationship between perceived distances and preferences for a specific course of action. Thus in the end, the two studies do predict broadly similar outcomes but differ in terms of which stage in the decision process they believe the moderators are operating.

While at this stage there do not appear to many other papers empirically exploring potential moderators (A_i) of the A_c–B_i relationship, there is no shortage of potential moderators. For example, Dow et al. (2016) explore how within-country diversity moderates the relationship between linguistic and religious distance and the ownership structures of cross-border ... acquisition. In many respects this is a classic A_c–D_f study; however ... the underlying logic of that moderating effect is that people from more diverse environments have a higher level of cognitive complexity (Bieri, 1955) with respect to the relevant dimension and that in turn may moderate their perceptions of the situation. Indeed, Håkanson and Ambos (2010)'s finding with respect to geographic distance, mentioned earlier, may be another example of this. Individuals with a lower level of cognitive complexity with respect to foreign markets seem to put more emphasis on simple heuristics, such as geographic distance, when they are forming their views about another country. Conversely, individuals with a higher level of cognitive complexity seem to take into account more dimensions, and subtler dimensions, when forming their views about a country. The preceding discussion also raises the issue of other related constructs: cultural intelligence (Thomas et al., 2008) and biculturalism (Benet-Martinez, Lee, & Leu, 2006; Brannen & Thomas, 2010). What role might they play in terms of moderating perceptions of distance?

Similarly, the third independent variable in Sousa and Bradley's (2006) early investigation into the antecedents of psychic distance – the other two being the Kogut and Singh index and international experience – was the manager's *Conservation Values* (Schwartz, 1992). This raises the issue of what other aspects of a manager's personality (Barrick, Stewart, & Piotrowski, 2002), such as their *Openness* and/or their *Neuroticism* may moderate their perceptions of distance.

How and Why Perceptions of Distance Influence Preferences for Particular Courses of Actions

What might be termed the 'bottom' of *Coleman's Boat* (B_i–C_i) is essentially the issue of how and why perceptions of distance influence preferences for particular courses of actions. This stage of the process can be broken into two distinct issues.

The first issue is characterized by the mediating variable – $\mathbf{Med}_{BC}$ – in Fig. 2 and raises the question: why does distance matter? In the case of the Uppsala model, Johanson and Vahlne (1977) quite explicitly argue that psychic distance is relevant because it increases the perceived risk of certain alternatives and that in turn will influence managers' preferences for particular alternatives. Subsequently, they have updated their model to acknowledge that distance may also influence a manager's awareness of alternatives (Johanson & Vahlne, 2006). Conversely, the institutional distance scholars (Kostova & Zaheer, 1999; Xu & Shenkar, 2002) typically draw upon Institutional Theory (Scott, 1995) and as a result are implicitly assuming that the key-mediating variable is legitimacy. In essence greater distances reduce a firm's potential legitimacy. And of course in some settings, authors such as Thomas (1999) draw on social psychology theories such as the *Similarity Attraction Paradigm* (Byrne, 1971) and *Social Identity Theory* (Tajfel, 1974) to explain the importance of various forms of distance; which in turn implies that constructs such as attraction, trust, a willingness to cooperate with and frequency of interaction may be key-mediating factors. The sad issue here is that despite the broad range of theoretical perspectives that authors have to draw upon, the issue of which ones actually underlie the effects we so often report is virtually unexplored within the IB literature.

The second issue with respect to the link between perceptions of distance and preferences for a particular alternative or course of action ($\boldsymbol{B}_i$–C_i) is the potential moderators in the process ($\mathbf{Mod}_{BC}$). As Maitland and Sammartino (2015) argue the 'boundedly rational decision-maker is underspecified in international business'. In some cases these moderators may parallel the ones discussed with respect to the A_c–B_i relationship, such as status. Indeed, one awkward issue that researchers will need to address here is: where in the process does a particular moderator intervene? And again, as Maitland and Sammartino (2015) highlight, differences in a manager's mental models and decision-making styles may heavily influence the outcomes. At this stage, that aspect of distance research is virtually untouched.

How Individual Preferences Determine What Action a Company Takes

What might be termed the 'stern' of *Coleman's Boat* ($\boldsymbol{C}_i$–D_f) is essentially the issue of how an individual's preference for a specific alternative (C_i) ultimately influences the action taken ($\boldsymbol{D}_f$). As with the previous section, this can be divided into two issues.

The first issue is one that researchers in marketing, and particularly consumer behavior and choice modeling have struggled with for many years (Armstrong et al., 2000): are professed preferences a reasonable predictor of how the individual will ultimately act? On this front one could ask whether there is any potential for a unique contribution from the IB perspective, but nevertheless we need to be cognizant of the assumptions and biases inherent in this stage. The good news is that while espoused preferences are never a perfect predictor of actual behavior, the link is well proven (Juster, 1966; McNeil, 1974; Morwitz & Schmittlein, 1992; Tobin, 1959).

Nevertheless, a second issue arises concerning the link between an individual's preferences and the ultimate action of the firm because major IB decisions are seldom made by one individual. It is far more common that a team of individuals will either collectively make the decision or advise the key decision-maker. It is here that our model begins to blend into the broader management literature about group decision-making, which has quite a long and diverse history (Black, 1948; Cannon-Bowers, Salas, & Converse, 1993; Gruenfeld, Mannix, Williams, & Neale, 1996). Once again one could ask whether there is any potential for a unique contribution from the international perspective; however, some IB scholars have already begun to push those bounds (Aharoni, Tihanyi, & Connelly, 2011; Barkema & Shvyrkov, 2007; Buckley, Devinney, & Louviere, 2007). In particular, for firms that are already multinational in nature (MNE), the degree of diversity in their TMTs may be higher than found elsewhere. As a result, research into the roles of fault lines (Lau & Murnighan, 1998; Van Knippenberg, Dawson, West, & Homan, 2011) and the impact of diversity on decision-making may be a fruitful area for further research. Similarly, the head office – foreign subsidiary structure of MNEs may present a novel environment for examining issues such as the relative power of stakeholders in the decision-making process (Baaij & Slangen, 2013; Mudambi, Pedersen, & Andersson, 2014).

CONCLUSIONS

In summary, I reiterate that I believe the IB literature concerning distance is at a turning point. Conceptually, the seminal paper by Shenkar (2001) has provided the initial spark, but in terms of actual change in the nature of the research topics investigated, we are only just beginning to gain traction. For the past three decades, the vast majority of the empirical IB research concerning distance has focussed on linking national-level differences with organizational outcomes. We, as a discipline, have certainly broadened the number of distance–outcome relationships investigated; and to a more limited extent we have begun (very slowly) to move away from an excessive reliance on the Kogut and Singh index. However, what is truly needed next is for us to step back and begin unpacking the black box we call 'distance' by exploring the micro-level mechanisms involved.

The shift to using individual-level perceptions of distance (e.g. Evans & Mavondo, 2002) is a tentative first step, but I believe we need to go much further. As illustrated through the adaptation of *Coleman's Boat*, we first need to begin looking at the factors and processes that shape a person's perceptions of a foreign market. What factors moderate those perceptions, and what factors introduce potential biases into those perceptions? This is a rich area for future research. In part these are critical issues because, as I have said before, actually being able to measure the *a priori* perceptions of the key decision-makers is a luxury we will rarely have – the events that are typically investigated in IB are just too infrequent, irregular and hard to predict in terms of their timing. As a result, the best and most realistic option available to us is to understand what are the key moderators and biases that influence a manager's perceptions of distance. We can then incorporate them into our analyses; thus allowing us to more accurately model what a manager's perceptions for distance might be.

A second key area that needs investigation is to better understand the factors that mediate the relationship between managers' perceptions of distance and their preferences for a particular course of action. In effect, we need to understand why distance is important. Is it primarily an indicator of potential disruptions and misunderstandings in the communication process, as argued by Johanson and Vahlne (1977)? What role does an organization's desire for legitimacy play here (Kostova & Zaheer, 1999)? Or is the impact of distance mainly a subconscious bias that managers should guard against (e.g. Byrne, 1961)? For too long the distance research in IB has glossed over the fact that we do not honestly know what are the underlying mechanisms. This research is critical to the field, but it will also be challenging to execute; particularly when one of the potential explanations is a subconscious bias.

The issues relating to the 'stern' of the boat – that is, the connection between one manager's preference for a course of action and the action that the firm actually takes – are undeniably important, but I argue that these issues are equally relevant to almost all branches of management literature. Thus, while there may be some opportunities for research from an IB perspective, it may be more a matter of IB researchers being cognizant of the relevant work in areas such as group decision-making processes (Papadakis et al., 1998) and fault line research (Lau & Murnighan, 2005).

Lastly, while the main point of this article is to highlight areas of potential new research for distance in IB and to be a rallying cry for more micro-level and multi-level research, I also want to encourage researchers who do continue to investigate the macro-level relationships (i.e. the impact of national-level distance on organizational outcomes) to heed Shenkar's (2001) warnings. Don't just blindly adopt the Kogut and Singh index as your sole metric of distance simply because so many before you made the same mistake, and be cognizant the degree to which Shenkar's other assumptions and illusions may be biasing your results.

NOTES

1. I do not want to trivialize Beckerman's (1956) contributions to distance research, but I would categorize it as being part of the origins of distance research in IB, rather than a turning point.

2. I should note here that two recent and important innovations in distance research are not discussed here. Specifically, Berry et al. (2010) use of Mahalanobis distance and Hutzschenreuter and Voll's (2008) concept of added distance. These innovations are certainly worthy contributions to the field but they are not direct responses to one of Shenkar's eight illusions and assumptions and do not directly relate to the subsequent discussions facilitated by the *Coleman's Boat* metaphor. As a result they are not discussed here.

3. I would like to thank here a colleague associate Professor Emre Yildiz of the University of Uppsala for making me aware of both the *Coleman's Boat* metaphor and the idea of applying it to distance research in IB.

4. Dow et al. (2014), Håkanson and Ambos (2010) and Håkanson et al. (2016) all rely on the same data set of perceptions of distance. Although they are exploring subtly different issues and using different techniques, their findings in this respect should be considered as one.

REFERENCES

Aharoni, Y., Tihanyi, L., & Connelly, B. L. (2011). Managerial decision-making in international business: A forty-five-year retrospective. *Journal of World Business*, *46*(2), 135–142.

Ambos, B., & Håkanson, L. (2014). The concept of distance in international management research. *Journal of International Management*, *20*(1), 1–7.

Anderson, J. E. (1979). A theoretical foundation for the gravity model. *American Economic Review*, *69*(1), 106–116.

Anderson, C., & Berdahl, J. L. (2002). The experience of power: Examining the effects of power on approach and inhibition tendencies. *Journal of Personality and Social Psychology*, *83*(6), 1362.

Armstrong, J. S., Morwitz, V. G., & Kumar, V. (2000). Sales forecasts for existing consumer products and services: Do purchase intentions contribute to accuracy? *International Journal of Forecasting*, *16*(3), 383–397.

Baack, D. W., Dow, D., Parente, R., & Bacon, D. (2015). Confirmation bias in individual-level perceptions of distance: An experimental investigation. *Journal of International Business Studies*, *46*(8), 938–959.

Baaij, M. G., & Slangen, A. (2013). The role of headquarters-subsidiary geographic distance in strategic decisions by spatially disaggregated headquarters. *Journal of International Business Studies*, *44*(9), 941–952.

Barkema, H. G., Bell, J., & Pennings, J. M. (1996). Foreign entry, cultural barriers, and learning. *Strategic Management Journal*, *17*, 151–166.

Barkema, H. G., & Shvyrkov, O. (2007). Does top management team diversity promote or hamper foreign expansion? *Strategic Management Journal*, *28*(7), 663–680.

Barkema, H. G., & Vermeulen, F. (1997). What differences in cultural backgrounds of partners are detrimental for international joint ventures? *Journal of International Business Studies*, *28*(4), 845–864.

Barrick, M. R., Stewart, G. L., & Piotrowski, M. (2002). Personality and job performance: Test of the mediating effects of motivation among sales representatives. *Journal of Applied Psychology*, *87*(1), 43–51.

Beckerman, W. (1956). Distance and the pattern of inter-European trade. *The Review of Economics and Statistics*, *38*(1), 31–40.

Benet-Martinez, V., Lee, F., & Leu, J. (2006). Biculturalism and cognitive complexity: Expertise in cultural representations. *Journal of Cross Cultural Psychology*, *37*(4), 386–407.

Benito, G. R. G., & Gripsrud, G. (1992). The expansion of foreign direct investments: Discrete rational location choices or a cultural learning process? *Journal of International Business Studies*, *23*(3), 461–476.

Berry, H., Guillen, M., & Zhou, A. (2010). An institutional approach to cross-national distance. *Journal of International Business Studies*, *41*(9), 1460–1480.

Beugelsdijk, S., Maseland, R., Onrust, M., van Hoorn, A., & Slangen, A. (2015). Cultural distance in international business and management: From mean-based to variance-based measures. *The International Journal of Human Resource Management*, *26*(2), 165–191.

Beugelsdijk, S., & Mudambi, R. (2013). MNEs as border-crossing multi-location enterprises: The role of discontinuities in geographic space. *Journal of International Business Studies*, *44*(5), 413–426.

Bieri, J. (1955). Cognitive complexity-simplicity and predictive behavior. *Journal of Abnormal Psychology*, *51*(2), 263–268.

Black, D. (1948). On the rationale of group decision-making. *Journal of Political Economy*, *56*(1), 23–34.

Boyacigiller, N. (1990). The role of expatriates in the management of interdependence, complexity and risk in multinational corporations. *Journal of International Business Studies*, *21*(3), 357–381.

Brannen, M. Y., & Thomas, D. C. (2010). Bicultural individuals in organizations implications and opportunity. *International Journal of Cross Cultural Management*, *10*(1), 5–16.

Brewer, P. (2007). Operationalizing psychic distance: A revised approach. *Journal of International Marketing*, *15*(1), 44–66.

Brouthers, K. D., & Brouthers, L. E. (2000). Acquisition or greenfield startup? Institutional, cultural and transaction cost influences. *Strategic Management Journal*, *21*(1), 89–97.

Buckley, P. J., Devinney, T. M., & Louviere, J. J. (2007). Do managers behave the way theory suggests? A choice-theoretic examination of foreign direct investment location decision-making. *Journal of International Business Studies*, *38*(7), 1069–1094.

Byrne, D. (1961). Interpersonal attraction and attitude similarities. *Journal of Abnormal and Social Psychology*, *62*(3), 713–715.

Byrne, D. (1971). *The attraction paradigm*. New York, NY: Academic Press.

Chang, S.-J., & Rosenzweig, P. M. (2001). The choice of entry mode in sequential foreign direct investment. *Strategic Management Journal*, *22*(8), 747–776.

Cho, K. R., & Padmanabhan, P. (1995). Acquisition versus new venture: The choice of foreign establishment mode by Japanese firms. *Journal of International Management*, *1*(3), 255–285.

Cho, K. R., & Padmanabhan, P. (2005). Revisiting the role of cultural distance in MNC's foreign ownership mode choice: The moderating effect of experience attributes. *International Business Review*, *14*(3), 307–324.

Coleman, J. S. (1994). *Foundations of social theory*. Cambridge, MA: Harvard University Press.

Cannon-Bowers, J. A., Salas, E., & Converse, S. (1993). Shared Mental Models in Expert Team Decision Making. In Castellan Jr., N. J., (Ed.), *Individual and Group Decision Making: Current Issues*. Chapter 12: 221–246, Hillsdale, NJ: Lawrence Erlbaum Associates Inc., Publishers.

Dean, J. W., & Sharfman, M. P. (1996). Does decision process matter? A study of strategic decision-making effectiveness. *Academy of Management Journal*, *39*(2), 368–392.

Dichtl, E., Leibold, M., Koeglmayr, H.-G., & Mueller, S. (1984). The export decision of small and medium-sized firms: A review. *Management International Review*, *24*(2), 49–60.

Dow, D. (2001). The adaptation of host market positioning strategies: Empirical evidence from Australia. *Journal of International Marketing*, *9*(3), 41–62.

Dow, D. (2008). *Factors influencing managerial perceptions of psychic distance*. Tallinn: European International Business Academy.

Dow, D. (2009). *Factors influencing perceptions of psychic distance*. San Diego, CA: Academy of International Business..

Dow, D. (2014). Distance in international business research: Are we really making any progress? In M. Laaksonen, A. Arslan, & M. Kontkanen (Eds.), *Contributions to international business: Essays in honour of Professor Jorma Larimo* (pp. 119–140). Vaasa: University of Vaasa.

Dow, D., Cuypers, I. R. P., & Ertug, G. (2016). The effects of within-country linguistic and religious diversity on foreign acquisitions. *Journal of International Business Studies*, *47*(3), 319–346.

Dow, D., Håkanson, L., & Ambos, B. (2014). Perceptions versus national-level differences: A mediating model of psychic distance. In A. Verbeke, R. Tulder, & S. M. Lundan (Eds.). *Progress in international business research: Multinational enterprises, markets and institutional diversity*. Bingham: Emerald Group Publishing Limited.

Dow, D., & Karunaratna, A. (2006). Developing a multidimensional instrument to measure psychic distance stimuli. *Journal of International Business Studies*, *37*(5), 575–577.

Dow, D., & Pekerti, A. A. (2015). *The impact of international experience on perceptions of distance: Role of cognitive complexity*. Bangalore: Academy of International Business (AIB).

Em, L. (2011). *Disentangling the different concepts of distance: A lexicographic exploration of the past 20 years of the Journal of International Business Studies*. Nagoya: Academy of International Business.

Erramilli, M. K. (1991). The experience factor in foreign market entry behavior of service firms. *Journal of International Business Studies*, *22*(3), 479–501.

Erramilli, M. K., & Rao, C. P. (1993). Service firms international entry mode choice: A modified transaction cost analysis approach. *Journal of Marketing*, *57*(3), 19–38.

Evans, J., & Mavondo, F. T. (2002). Psychic distance and organizational performance: An empirical examination of international retailing operations. *Journal of International Business Studies*, *33*(3), 515–532.

Evans, J., Mavondo, F. T., & Bridson, K. (2008). Psychic distance: Antecedents, retail strategy implications and performance outcomes. *Journal of International Marketing*, *16*(2), 32–63.

Evans, J., Treadgold, A., & Mavondo, F. T. (2000). Psychic distance and the performance of international retailers. *International Marketing Review*, *17*(4/5), 373–391.

Fey, C., & Beamish, P. (2001). Organisational climate similarity and performance: International joint ventures in Russia. *Organization Studies*, *22*(5), 853–882.

Flores, R. G., & Aguilera, R. V. (2007). Globalization and location choice: An analysis of US multinational firms in 1980 and 2000. *Journal of International Business Studies*, *38*(7), 1187–1210.

Ghemawat, P. (2016). *The laws of globalization and business applications*. Cambridge: Cambridge University Press.

Grosse, R., & Trevino, L. J. (1996). Foreign direct investment in the United States: An analysis by country of origin. *Journal of International Business Studies*, *27*(1), 139–155.

Gruenfeld, D. H., Mannix, E. A., Williams, K. Y., & Neale, M. A. (1996). Group composition and decision making: How member familiarity and information distribution affect process and performance. *Organizational Behavior and Human Decision Processes*, *67*(1), 1–15.

Håkanson, L., & Ambos, B. (2010). The antecedents of psychic distance. *Journal of International Management*, *16*(3), 195–210.

Håkanson, L., Ambos, B., Schuster, A., & Leicht-Deobald, U. (2016). The psychology of psychic distance: Antecedents of asymmetric perceptions. *Journal of World Business*, *51*(2), 308–318.

Harzing, A. W. (2003). The role of culture in entry mode studies: From neglect to Myopia. In J. Cheng & M. Hitt (Eds.), *Advances in international management*. Amsterdam/New York, NY: Elsevier/JAI.

Hennart, J. F., & Larimo, J. (1998). The impact of culture on the strategy of multinational enterprises: Does national origin affect ownership decisions? *Journal of International Business Studies*, *29*(3), 515–538.

Hofstede, G. (1980). *Cultural consequences: International differences in work related values*. Beverly Hills, CA: Sage Publications.

Hogg, M. A., & Terry, D. J. (2000). Social identity and self-categorization processes in organizational contexts. *Academy of Management Review*, *25*(1), 121–140.

Holzmuller, H. H., & Kasper, H. (1990). The decision-maker and export activity: A cross-national comparison of the foreign orientation of Austrian managers. *Management International Review*, *30*(3), 217–230.

House, R. J., Hanges, P. J., Dorfman, P. W., & Gupta, V. (2004). *Culture, leadership and organizations: The globe study of 62 nations*. Thousand Oaks, CA: Sage.

Hutzschenreuter, T., & Voll, J. C. (2008). Performance effects of "Added Cultural Distance" in the path of international expansion: The case of German multinational enterprises. *Journal of International Business Studies*, *39*(1), 53–70.

Johanson, J., & Vahlne, J.-E. (1977). The internationalization process of the firm-a model of knowledge development and increasing foreign commitments. *Journal of International Business Studies*, *8*(1), 23–32.

Johanson, J., & Vahlne, J.-E. (2006). Commitment and opportunity development in the internationalization process: A note on the Uppsala Internationalization Process Model. *Management International Review*, *46*(2), 1–14.

Johanson, J., & Wiedersheim-Paul, F. (1975). The internationalization of the firm: Four Swedish cases. *Journal of Management Studies*, *12*(October), 305–322.

Juster, F. T. (1966). Consumer buying intentions and purchase probability: An experiment in survey design. *Journal of the American Statistical Association*, *61*(315), 658–696.

Keltner, D., Gruenfeld, D. H., & Anderson, C. (2003). Power, approach, and inhibition. *Psychological Review*, *110*(2), 265.

Klayman, J., & Ha, Y.-W. (1987). Confirmation, disconfirmation, and information in hypothesis testing. *Psychological Review*, *94*(2), 211–228.

Kogut, B., & Singh, H. (1988). The effect of national culture on the choice of entry mode. *Journal of International Business Studies*, *19*(3), 411–432.

Kostova, T., & Zaheer, S. (1999). Organizational legitimacy under conditions of complexity: The case of the multinational enterprise. *Academy of Management Review*, *24*(1), 64–81.

Lau, D. C., & Murnighan, J. K. (1998). Demographic diversity and faultlines: The compositional dynamics of organizational groups. *Academy of Management Review*, *23*(2), 325–340.

Lau, D. C., & Murnighan, J. K. (2005) Interactions within groups and subgroups: The effects of demographic faultlines. *Academy of Management Journal*, *48*(4), 645–659.

Li, J. (1995). Foreign entry and survival: Effects of strategic choices on performance in international markets. *Strategic Management Journal*, *16*(5), 333–351.

Linnemann, H. (1966). *An econometric study of international trade flows*. Amsterdam: North Holland Press.

Lisak, A., Erez, M., Sui, Y., & Lee, C. (2016). The positive role of global leaders in enhancing multicultural team innovation. *Journal of International Business Studies*, *47*(6), 655–673.

Lu, J. W., & Hebert, L. (2005). Equity control and the survival of international joint ventures: A contingency approach. *Journal of Business Research*, *58*(6), 736–745.

Luiz, J. M. (2015). The impact of ethno-linguistic fractionalization on cultural measures: Dynamics, endogeneity and modernization. *Journal of International Business Studies*, *46*(9), 1080–1098.

Magnusson, P., Baack, D. W., Zdravkovic, S., Staub, K., & Amine, L. (2008). Meta-analysis of cultural differences: Another slice at the apple. *International Business Review*, *17*(5), 520–532.

Maitland, E., & Sammartino, A. (2015). Managerial cognition and internationalization. *Journal of International Business Studies*, *46*(7), 733–760.

McNeil, J. (1974). Federal programs to measure consumer purchase expectations, 1946–1973: A post-mortem. *Journal of Consumer Research*, *1*(3), 1–10.

Minbaeva, D., Pedersen, T., Bjorkman, I., Fey, C., & Park, H. J. (2003). MNC knowledge transfer, subsidiary absorptive capacity, and HRM. *Journal of International Business Studies*, *34*(6), 586–599.

Morwitz, V. G., & Schmittlein, D. (1992). Using segmentation to improve sales forecasts based on purchase intent: Which"Intenders" actually buy? *Journal of Marketing Research*, 391–405.

Mudambi, R., Pedersen, T., & Andersson, U. (2014). How subsidiaries gain power in multinational corporations. *Journal of World Business*, *49*(1), 101–113.

Newton, I. (1686). *Philosophiae naturalis principia mathematica* (First American Edition, 1846 ed.). New York, NY: Daniel Adee.

Nurmi, N., & Hinds, P. J. (2016). Job complexity and learning opportunities: A silver lining in the design of global virtual work. *Journal of International Business Studies*, *47*(6), 631–654.

O'Grady, S., & Lane, H. W. (1996). The psychic distance paradox. *Journal of International Business Studies*, *27*(2), 309–333.

Papadakis, V. M., Lioukas, S., & Chambers, D. (1998). Strategic decision-making processes: The role of management and context. *Strategic Management Journal*, *19*(2), 115–147.

Park, S. H., & Ungson, G. (1997). The effect of national culture, organisational complementarity and economic motivation on joint venture dissolution. *Academy of Management Journal*, *40*(2), 279–307.

Pothukuchi, V., Damanpour, F., Choi, J., Chen, C. C., & Park, S. H. (2002). National and organizational culture differences and international joint venture performance. *Journal of International Business Studies*, *33*(2), 243–265.

Schwartz, S. H. (1992). Universals in the content and structure of values: Theoretical advances and empirical tests in 20 countries. *Advances in Experimental Social Psychology*, *25*, 1–65.

Scott, R. (1995). *Institutions and organisations*. Thousand Oaks, CA: Sage.

Shenkar, O. (2001). Cultural distance revisited: Towards a more rigorous conceptualization and measurement of cultural differences. *Journal of International Business Studies*, *32*(3), 519–536.

Sousa, C. M. P., & Bradley, F. (2005). Global markets: Does psychic distance matter? *Journal of Strategic Marketing*, *13*(1), 43–59.

Sousa, C. M. P., & Bradley, F. (2006). Cultural distance and psychic distance: Two peas in a pod? *Journal of International Marketing*, *14*(1), 49–70.

Sousa, C. M. P., & Bradley, F. (2008). Cultural distance and psychic distance: Refinements in conceptualisation and measurement. *Journal of Marketing Management*, *24*(5/6), 467–488.

Stahl, G. K., & Tung, R. L. (2015). Towards a more balanced treatment of culture in international business studies: The need for positive cross-cultural scholarship. *Journal of International Business Studies*, *46*(4), 391–414.

Stöttinger, B., & Schlegelmilch, B. B. (1998). Explaining export development through psychic distance: Enlightening or elusive? *International Marketing Review*, *15*(5), 357–372.

Tajfel, H. (1974). Social identity and intergroup behaviour. *Social Science Information*, *13*(2), 65–93.

Taras, V., Steel, P., & Kirkman, B. I. (2012). Improving national cultural indices using a longitudinal meta-analysis of Hofstede's dimensions. *Journal of World Business*, *47*(3), 329–341.

Thomas, D. C. (1999). Cultural diversity and work group effectiveness: An experimental study. *Journal of Cross-Cultural Psychology*, *30*(2), 242–263.

Thomas, D. C., Elron, E., Stahl, G., Ekelund, B. Z., Ravlin, E. C., Cerdin, J. L., ..., Lazarova, M. B. (2008). Cultural intelligence: Domain and assessment. *International Journal of Cross Cultural Management*, *8*(2), 123–143.

Tihanyi, L., Griffith, D. A., & Russell, C. J. (2005). The effect of cultural distance on entry mode choice, international diversification, and MNE performance: A meta-analysis. *Journal of International Business Studies*, *36*(3), 270–283.

Tobin, J. (1959). On the predictive value of consumer intentions and attitudes. *The Review of Economics and Statistics*, *41*, 1–11.

Tung, R. L. (2009). The cross-cultural research imperative: The need to balance cross-national and intra-national diversity. *Journal of International Business Studies*, *39*(1), 41–46.

Tung, R. L., & Verbeke, A. (2010). Beyond Hofstede and GLOBE: Improving the quality of cross-cultural research. *Journal of International Business Studies*, *41*(8), 1259–1274.

Van Knippenberg, D., Dawson, J. F., West, M. A., & Homan, A. C. (2011). Diversity faultlines, shared objectives, and top management team performance. *Human Relations*, *64*(3), 307–336.

Vermeulen, F., & Barkema, H. G. (2001). Learning through acquisitions. *Academy of Management Journal*, *44*(3), 457–476.

Williams, D. W., & Gregoire, D. A. (2015). Seeking commonalities or avoiding differences? Re-conceptualizing distance and its effects on internationalization decisions. *Journal of International Business Studies*, *46*(3), 253–284.

Xu, D., Pan, Y., & Beamish, P. (2004). The effect of regulative and normative distances on MNE ownership and expatriate strategies. *Management International Review*, *44*(3), 285–307.

Xu, D., & Shenkar, O. (2002). Institutional distance and the multinational enterprise. *Academy of Management Review*, *27*(4), 608–618.

Yildiz, H. E., & Fey, C. F. (2016). Are the extent and effect of psychic distance perceptions symmetrical in cross-border M&As? Evidence from a two-country study. *Journal of International Business Studies*, *47*(7), 830–857.

Zaheer, S., Schomaker, M. S., & Nachum, L. (2012). Distance without direction: Restoring credibility to a much-loved construct. *Journal of International Business Studies*, *43*(1), 18–27.

Zhao, H., Luo, Y., & Suh, T. (2004). Transaction cost determinants and ownership-based entry mode choice: A meta-analytic review. *Journal of International Business Studies*, *35*(6), 524–544.

CHAPTER 3

INSTITUTIONAL OVERLAP AS BASIS FOR INTERNATIONAL BUSINESS

Robbert Maseland

ABSTRACT

This chapter investigates the theoretical support for the distance metaphor that is widely used to capture the effects of institutional diversity in international business (IB) and management studies. It argues that neither new institutional economics (NIE) nor in neo-institutional sociology (NIS) offers support for a focus on the degree of dissimilarity. Rather, both literatures emphasize discommonality as a problem for cooperation. In the NIE argument, common enforcement mechanisms are needed to reduce transaction costs. In the NIS argument, effective communication and cooperation is limited to meaning-giving structures common to all parties. In neither perspective, the degree of difference in structures that are not common is relevant. We propose an alternative metaphor, institutional overlap, to capture the effects of institutional diversity on IB transactions. We argue that such a concept differs from institutional distance in being agency-centered, sensitive to intra-country variation, non-additive, and driving the thickness rather than the costs of transactions.

Keywords: Institutions, distance, diversity, new institutional economics, neo-institutional sociology

Distance in International Business: Concept, Cost and Value
Progress in International Business Research, Volume 12, 69–90

ISSN: 1745-8862/doi:10.1108/S1745-886220170000012006

INTRODUCTION

It has been argued that international management is about managing distance (Zaheer, Schomaker, & Nachum, 2012). For a field defined by inter-nationality rather than inter-locality, this emphasis on distance is somewhat puzzling. After all, it is a crossing border that distinguishes international business (IB) from other business activities, not traversing distance. From the perspective of institutional theory, the focus on distance is all the more remarkable.

New institutional economics (NIE), associated with authors such as Greif (2006), North (1990, 2006), or Wallis (2011), highlights the importance of transparently and uniformly enforced rules as a prerequisite for functioning markets, focusing on the distinction between formal and informal enforcement. The neo-institutional sociology (NIS) tradition of authors such as Dimaggio and Powell (1983), Meyer and Rowan (1977), Meyer and Scott (1977) or Suchman (1995) is closely linked to the perspective of Giddens (1984), who highlights the importance of institutionalized, shared structuration within communities. Such shared structuration enables agents to act and communicate in effective and meaningful ways.

In both institutional traditions, as in their synthesis by Scott (2013), it is the sharing of structures that is of central importance for effective business interactions. Without shared institutional structures, communication and cooperation are problematic and costly. While international management is thus certainly complicated by the *existence* of different institutional settings, there seems little theoretical basis for a focus on the *degree* of differences, or distance, between these settings from an institutional perspective.

Yet, the focus on institutional distance and its negative repercussions is widespread and apparently empirically well established in IB studies (Brouthers, 2002; Flores & Aguilera, 2007; Gaur & Lu, 2007; Ghemawat, 2001; Jensen & Szulanski, 2004; López-Duarte & Vidal-Suárez, 2013; Salomon & Wu, 2012). This begs the question what is the theoretical rationale for observed diversity effects in IB and management. Is there an alternative way in which we can interpret the observed effects of diversity that is more grounded in institutional theory?

This chapter aims to provide such an alternative interpretation by proposing the concept of *institutional overlap*, defined as the presence of institutional structures that are shared between (potential) partners. On basis of a discussion of both NIE and the neo-institutional perspectives in organizational science and sociology, it highlights the need for commonality rather than similarity of institutional structures as basis for (international) transactions. Such commonality in the NIE perspective means one is able to rely on third-party enforcement mechanisms, removing room for opportunism and slashing prohibitive transaction costs. Sharing common structures in the neo-institutional perspective makes one's actions meaningful to the other, rendering behavior effective. Both types of institutional overlap are required for international interactions. Without them, either trust or understanding is lacking between partners.

The chapter goes on to discuss the implications of replacing the logic of distance with the logic of overlap. Rather than focusing on costs that affect all international transactions to some extent, an institutional overlap perspective highlights the opportunities for businesses connecting with individuals and communities on basis of shared institutions. Also, the overlap perspective implies an approach in which the process of construction of commonality by the manager stands central, rather than higher level, externally imposed constraints. Where overlap is not immediately evident, managers need to identify and negotiate such a common ground before embarking on any kind of exchange. International management is not about managing distance between contexts but about managing relations between partners (Granovetter, 1985).

This chapter contributes to international management studies by providing a reconceptualization of the role of institutional differences in international management that is better grounded in institutional theory, practically more relevant, and focuses less exclusively on the negative. It highlights the role of institutional diversity in the identification of opportunities for cooperation and arbitrage, rather than interpreting institutions as a source of constraints. Also, by attributing the effects of institutional differences to the presence of common institutions rather than to the (dis)similarity of institutions, the chapter indirectly contributes to current debates about the distinction and relation between border and distance effects (Beugelsdijk & Mudambi, 2013).

Our argument is made in three steps. The first section discusses the interpretation and importance of institutional diversity in NIE and sociological neo-institutionalism, the two perspectives underlying the dominant institutional paradigm in IB studies developed by Scott (2013). The second section investigates the theoretical basis for the concept of institutional distance in these institutional perspectives, introducing institutional overlap as a superior concept. The third section discusses the implications of moving from an institutional distance to an institutional overlap perspective.

INSTITUTIONAL DIVERSITY: THEORETICAL PERSPECTIVES

The concept of institutional distance was introduced in IB studies in the dissertation of Kostova (Kostova & Roth, 2002; Kostova & Zaheer, 1999), who defined it as the extent of (dis)similarity between the cognitive, normative, and regulative institutions of two countries. This definition mirrors the preceding, narrower concepts of psychic distance (Beckerman, 1956) and cultural distance (Kogut & Singh, 1988), which focus on dissimilarity in normative institutions.

All these concepts are based on the premise that the complexity of managing MNEs and the difficulty of establishing legitimacy in local contexts is argued to increase with the degree of differences in institutional profile (Kostova & Zaheer, 1999). Larger institutional differences make it harder to transfer strategic knowledge and routines between different parts of the firm or to local partners. Distance is argued to matter to MNEs because it is positively related to the challenges faced by firms when operating abroad (Eden & Miller, 2004; Xu & Shenkar, 2002).

The concept of institutional distance is strongly influenced by the work of Scott (2013). In Scott's view, institutional environments consist of three pillars: a regulative, normative, and cognitive pillar. These three pillars together make up a country's institutional profile (Kostova, 1997). The three-pillar framework rests upon two oppositions, rooted in two theoretical perspectives. The opposition between regulative and normative is inspired by NIE, which stresses the difference between formal institutions, enforced by an hierarchical authority, and informal institutions, enforced by communities or networks. The opposition between normative and regulative is inspired by sociological neo-institutionalism (Dimaggio & Powell, 1983; Meyer & Rowan, 1977; Meyer & Scott, 1983), which highlighted the importance of what people believe to be right (cognitive), in addition to what they are told to do by society (normative) or the state (regulative), for establishing structure in social behavior (Scott, 2013). Taken together, these two oppositions translate in a three-pillar framework. Scott (2013) is thus an explicit attempt to join NIE and NIS perspectives in a single perspective. In order to understand how differences in institutional profiles affect organizational behavior, we therefore need to discuss the role of institutional difference in each of these underlying theoretical perspectives.

New Institutional Economics

NIE is most closely associated with the work of North (1990, 1993, 2006). The central question in this work is how the existence of markets is possible. More specifically, North (1990) asks what kind of institutions is required for anonymous exchange to come about.

Building on neoclassical economics, NIE shares the assumptions of individuals being self-interested, autonomous, calculating agents. In contrast to the neoclassical paradigm, however, new institutional economists maintain that individuals expose bounded rather than full rationality and face uncertainty about the behavior of others. This uncertainty creates room for opportunism as it enables individuals to cheat or renege on contracts. In a setting in which agents know each other and transactions are repeated, such opportunism is checked by reciprocity. Once we move to societies larger than the small-scale communities in which everyone knows and repeatedly deals with everyone, though, trusting others enough to engage in exchange becomes problematic. With individuals having every incentive and opportunity to cheat, how can anonymous exchange come about?

The answer provided by North (1990, 1993, 2006) is that in a functioning society individuals are bound by institutions. Institutions, in this framework, are human-made constraints that serve to make society and the behavior of individual agents predictable. They are the "rules of the game" (North, 1990), and the constraints they create enable agents to trust one another to behave in expected ways. Institutions do so by grace of not only covering specific transactions but also applying to a broad range of similar exchanges; they are general, *institutionalized* rules transcending space and time. It is this institutionalization of behavior that sharply reduces the world's complexity and enables exchange on a wide scale (North, 2006).

Institutionalization is a function of third-party authorities capable and willing to enforce rules uniformly throughout a domain (Boisot & Child, 1996; North, 1990). Such an authority may be a formal state, but it might also be a kinship network or a local community enforcing rules informally through reciprocity or ostracization (Greif, 1993, 1994). It is the presence of such an organization enforcing institutions that solves the problem of trust within its jurisdiction (Williamson, 1985). Uniform rules make behavior of others predictable, but it is only the institutionalization of these rules by an enforcing authority that reduces the scope for opportunism for individual agents. Transaction costs do not fall when rules are just followed; they fall when one can count on the rules being followed because they are enforced. Any two individuals that are covered by the same enforcement system can turn to this system to get their right in case of a breach of contract. Thus backed up by external enforcers, individuals do not need to invest as much in getting information about a counterparty's reputation or in insuring themselves against opportunistic behavior before embarking on a transaction. Trust is possible because when rules are breached an external authority comes in to punish the deviant.

In the NIE perspective, therefore, for institutions to perform their function as enablers of anonymous exchange, what is important is that the same rules are applied to everyone in a domain equally (Wallis, 2011). It is being subject to the same enforcement system – sharing it – that allows individuals to trust and deal with each other.

NIE and International Management

The presence of institutions ensures that firms and managers engaging in transaction within a single legal environment or dealing with agents within their own network may be able to trust counterparties and enter in exchanges with them to an extent dependent on the quality of the institutions. When going abroad, however, a manager leaves the domain over which these enforcement systems have jurisdiction. As a consequence, international managers are dealing with agents that are not covered by the same authorities as they are (Ronen & Shenkar, 2013; Sundaram & Black, 1992). The conditions identified by North (1990) as necessary for anonymous exchange are not met in the international context. Since rules are not enforced uniformly to both parties of the transaction and parties have limited access to recourse in case of a breach, trust is likely to be low and transaction costs high. Note that this is even the case when both parties completely agree on the content of the rules; it is not lack of consensus about institutional rules that cause transaction costs but the possibility for cheating on those rules. If we define an institutional jurisdiction as the domain over which institutions are enforced by a third-party authority, this implies that *doing business over multiple jurisdictions implies not having recourse to a mutually accepted third party able to secure rules and enforce contracts. This results in uncertainty and high transaction costs, blocking anonymous exchange.*

Neo-Institutional Sociology

A basic tenet of NIS is that legitimacy, defined as the acceptance of an organization by its environment, is a prime concern for firms and other types of organizations (Kostova & Zaheer, 1999; Scott, 2013). Because of this need for legitimacy, firms face isomorphic pressures from their institutional environment (Dimaggio & Powell, 1983). Organizational survival depends on conformity to the rules and beliefs prevailing in an organization's setting (Dimaggio & Powell, 1983; Meyer & Rowan, 1977; Xu & Shenkar, 2002).

Why are legitimacy and fit so important? In the neo-institutional perspective, exchange and interaction require social structures (Giddens, 1984). Social structures are rules and guidelines linking certain behaviors to certain outcomes, which help agents make sense of their social environment and allow them to achieve goals. Without more or less fixed ideas of how one ought to behave in order to achieve a certain outcome, social action would be meaningless, if not impossible. Only because people within a linguistic community agree on certain grammatical structures and meanings of words, for example, they are able to communicate with each other. What is more, when speaking a language, agents confirm and reproduce these structural agreements that enable communication. This process of structuring one's behavior along the lines of agreed-upon structures is called structuration (Giddens, 1984). Every action thus has certain shared, structural properties which lend meaning to it (Scott, 2013). The most general of such structural properties is institutions. Institutions enable agents to function effectively (Giddens, 1984; Scott, 2013).

In order to perform this function, however, behavioral structures need to be shared and confirmed by others. Only if one's ideas about how to behave are agreed on by other people, they will respond to one's actions in the intended way. Actions that do not conform to the established structures within a society lack legitimacy and are ineffective; they simply do not make sense to others (Haugaard, 2002). This implies that agents face strong isomorphic pressures from the institutional environment to behave in accordance with accepted rules and principles (Dimaggio & Powell, 1983; Eden & Miller, 2004; Kostova & Zaheer, 1999).

Neo-Institutional Sociology and International Management

In the neo-institutional perspective, isomorphic pressures result in communities of agents that share similar ideas about how reality is constituted and about how people ought to behave. The rules, ideas, and values of these communities are likely to be distinctive from those in rival communities. Within communities, shared regulations, ideas, norms, and values facilitate social interaction and enable effective communication between agents. Between communities, however, conflicting beliefs will easily result in misunderstandings and present obstacles to knowledge exchange. Different norms and codes of conduct will make the behavior of outsiders appear as less meaningful and not legitimate. For this reason, the existence of distinctive institutional communities presents substantial challenges to international management.

Moving from one institutional environment to another implies moving to different systems of meaning, norms, and regulations. Behavior that makes sense in one's own community may not do so in others. Actions that are acceptable in one setting may be perceived as illegitimate in another (Kostova & Zaheer, 1999).

For MNEs acquiring external legitimacy is therefore a particularly complex challenge. MNEs are multi-leveled organizations, with each level operating in distinct institutional environments (Meyer, Mudambi, & Narula, 2011). Each individual subunit of the MNE faces isomorphic pressures from its local institutional environment (Kostova & Zaheer, 1999). For the MNE as a whole, managing institutional diversity is therefore an important and substantial challenge (Kostova, Roth, & Dacin, 2008). The difficulties of managing over institutionally different settings have received scant attention in the management literature. Institutional differences between an MNE's country of origin and a subsidiary's location have been associated with difficulties in attaining local legitimacy and transferring practices (Kostova, 1999; Kostova & Zaheer, 1999). They have been argued to increase transaction and communication costs (Albuquerque, Bronnenberg, & Corbett, 2007; Anderson & Gatignon, 1986; Giannetti & Yafeh, 2012), impede learning and acculturation (Barkema, Bell, & Pennings, 1996; Ojala & Tyrväinen, 2007; Weber, Shenkar, & Raveh, 1996), and – more generally – raise the liability of foreignness and the costs of doing business abroad (Nachum, 2003; Zaheer, 1995). If we define an institutional community as a group of actors sharing structuration, this implies that *doing business over various institutional communities implies not sharing a single system of meaning. This blocks communication, information transfer, and effective actions.*

WHY DIVERSITY IS ABOUT OVERLAP, NOT DISTANCE

Both the NIE and NIS literature provide ample reason why institutional diversity matters to organizations entering in transactions across different institutional settings. But do these arguments provide a basis for the argument that the degree of dissimilarity, or distance matters?

In both NIE and NIS literatures, effective cooperation is dependent on agents' ability to rely on institutions that provide a common structure to the behavior of all parties. In NIE, this common structure is the enforcement system: falling under the same jurisdiction, belonging to the same community, or being part of the same network that makes sure that rules – whatever they are – are followed so that actors can trust one another and engage in exchange. To be able to exchange in trust with a foreign partner, it does not matter whether contract law is identical or completely different between the two countries. It mainly matters whether both partners have access to the same court if they feel cheated. Likewise, social psychological research has shown that without differences in norms, values, and beliefs, rival communities may still emerge, treating each other's members as outsiders and creating obstacles for trust and exchange (Tajfel, 1970). Sharing enforcement of rules, not similarity in the content of those rules, is what facilitates exchange.

In NIS, it is the sharing of the institutional content that matters: agreement on the meaning of behaviors and agreement on the social consequences of certain actions so that actors can understand and accept each other. Cooperation emerges on basis of the structures that do overlap, as these provide a platform for communication and effective behavior. The degree of dissimilarity in the institutions on which cooperation is *not* based is not relevant. If a firm is able to communicate in English with its foreign partner, the linguistic distance between their native languages is not a factor in the success of their cooperation.

In short, although there are strong theoretical reasons to expect institutional diversity to be a challenge for MNEs, there seems very little basis for a focus on the *extent* of dissimilarity in institutional content. Institutional distance is an inaccurate metaphor. What makes internationalization possible is commonality or *institutional overlap* between two partners, that is, the presence of shared institutional structures governing the behavior of all parties toward each other. Overlap in enforcement mechanisms is required for exchange, as it mitigates the problems of opportunism, uncertainty, and distrust. Overlap in structures of meaning is a necessary condition for effective communication and organizational legitimacy. Overlap in both is required for any transaction to succeed. Agents need to be able to understand each other, and they need to be able to trust each other. This implies that *the ability to trust and exchange with one another depends on the presence of overlap in institutional enforcement mechanisms. The ability to communicate, understand, and accept each other depends on the presence of overlap in institutional content.*

AN INSTITUTIONAL OVERLAP PERSPECTIVE ON INTERNATIONAL BUSINESS

An overlap perspective on IB differs crucially from the traditional focus on institutional distance in a number of ways. Below we present several implications of an interpretation of institutional diversity in terms of overlap, and how they differ from the traditional interpretation in terms of institutional distance.

Constraints vs. Opportunities

First and foremost, viewing the task of managing institutional diversity in terms of seeking overlap rather than coping with distance highlights the active role of MNEs in the construction of international collaboration. MNEs' unique advantage comes from an ability to connect what other firms have left unconnected, transferring and combining knowledge across hitherto separated units (Grant, 1996; Gupta & Govindarajan, 2000). From a resource-based perspective (Barney, 1991), this ability to connect provides a unique advantage to a firm (Shenkar, 2001). Instead of viewing institutional diversity as a source of externally imposed constraints, an institutional overlap perspective focuses on opportunities fostered by MNEs to link different institutional environments. Any effective international collaboration requires overlap both in structures of enforcement and in structures of meaning. An overlap perspective approaches MNEs as institutional entrepreneurs, identifying, negotiating, and constructing such overlap, thereby linking hitherto separated institutional settings and exploiting opportunities for arbitrage. MNEs thus make markets "by creating exchanges where none previously existed" (Ellis, 2011).

In order to establish overlap in enforcement structures, MNEs pursue several strategies. IB by definition implies transactions that span borders of formal jurisdictions. Where neither state implied in the international transaction has jurisdiction in the other's territory, state enforcement of contracts cannot be automatically relied upon in IB. A first, common approach to deal with this problem is to identify and exploit existing alternative enforcement structures that do span state borders. The relative economic success of the Chinese diaspora is to some extent based on the exploitation of kinship-based trade and investment networks that allow members to engage in cross-border transactions at relatively low transaction costs (Rauch & Trindade, 2002; Tung & Chung, 2010), for example. Likewise, family links have regularly been used to enable firms to cross state borders (Ferguson, 1998). Ethnic and religious ties also may act as a substitute for overlap in formal enforcement structures (Greif, 1993, 1994).

A second approach to establish overlap in enforcement structures is to construct such overlap through relationship management. As noted by

Granovetter (1985), exchange is usually not of the anonymous kind North (1990) associates with modern markets, but is embedded in relationships. Before an MNE enters into contracts with partners, its managers usually invest in building personal relationships with their counterparts in the partner enterprise. Networks of personal ties form the basis for both national and international transactions (Uzzi, 1997). Likewise, firms such as McDonalds invest heavily in socialization of its staff, creating a network of managers bound by a shared identity and loyalty to the firm (Wathne & Heide, 2000). The purpose of these efforts is to ensure that, when being cheated, the personal connection can be employed to move the cheating enterprise to improve its behavior. Personal relationships and loyalties on the managerial level act as an overlapping enforcement structure, checking on the opportunistic behavior by the firms that employ the connected managers.

Where overlap can neither be identified nor satisfactorily constructed, a third strategy is to negotiate access to a third-party authority both partners agree on. This may take place simply by one party obtaining access to the other's enforcement zone by setting up a legal presence there, or both parties subjecting themselves to a third-party enforcement mechanism. The medieval Champagne fairs are a famous historical example of the latter: merchants from diverse origins came together to engage in trade, voluntarily utilizing collectively agreed upon legal institutions such as a fair court. Trade between agents from diverse jurisdictions was thus facilitated by the mutual acceptance of the jurisdiction of a dedicated third party. This innovation enabled merchants to link various hitherto unconnected enforcement zones and to make a profit by engaging in arbitrage between them (Ogilvie & Carus, 2013). In today's context, institutions of international commercial arbitration perform the same function (Dezalay & Garth, 1995).

Overlap in structures of meaning may similarly be established either through identification, construction, or negotiating access. When transfers of knowledge, practices, or symbols are complicated by differences in structures of meaning between two partners, firms commonly resort to identifying alternative structures both partners have in common and restrict communication to those structures. The development of a common corporate language is a clear example (Harzing & Pudelko, 2013). Thus, managers from a Russian and a Brazilian subsidiary of a firm may communicate with each other in English, when communication in either's first language turns out to be impossible.

Firms may also try to construct overlap where there is none. In international human resource management, it has long been recognized that developing a common organizational culture is an effective (though difficult) tool to provide cohesiveness and coherence to multinational enterprises spanning several, distinct institutional environments (Chan, Shaffer, & Snape, 2004; Schneider, 1988). By doing so, firms create overlap in structures of meaning that allows different parts of the firm to communicate better and effectively work together. Negotiating access in the context of structures of meaning implies employing "bridging mechanisms" (Shenkar, 2001). That may involve learning and adopting others' language, symbols, beliefs, and behavioral patterns. Often that is no realistic option, since the attribution of meanings and values to certain behavioral structures largely rests on preconscious, tacit understandings which are the consequence of long processes of socialization and hence are difficult to acquire for outsiders (Scott, 2013). Negotiating access therefore more commonly involves methods such as using alliances with local partners to target a market, or employing managers from certain population segments to acquire an entrance to a cultural community.

In all cases, focusing on overlap implies focusing on the active role of MNEs in fostering opportunities to link different institutional environments. This provides a sharp contrast with the traditional distance paradigm, which assumes the required content of any business relation to be given, so that the problem faced by MNEs is that their ability to effectively implement this relationship is limited by the constraints imposed by institutional diversity. An overlap perspective views the content of business relations, transactions, and cooperation as grounded in and limited to the available institutional common ground. The distance view is akin to having firms investing years in designing a complete contract for a preferred deal, only to find that there is no partner able or willing to take the deal. In an overlap scenario, firms talk to a number of potential partners, trying to gauge whether they have any mutual interests and ideas, and subsequently developing the content of any potential business relationship interactively from this initial basis for communication.

Difference 1.

Traditional distance perspective: managing institutional diversity is about optimizing firm behavior under the external constraints imposed by distance.

Overlap perspective: managing institutional diversity is about identifying, constructing, and negotiating areas of institutional common ground which provide opportunities for international expansion.

Countries vs. Transactions

A second important difference is the fact that whereas traditional institutional distance addresses differences between the institutional profiles of countries, overlap operates at the level of the transaction. Any exchange needs some kind of common ground both in structures of meaning and in structures of enforcement between all parties involved in the transaction. To obtain that, what matters to firms is the institutional embeddedness of the partners, employees, or customers they seek to work with. Firms target those members of a population with whom they share the structures relevant to the transaction at hand. The distance to society as a whole is at most indirectly relevant to this process, as it may be related to the likelihood of finding like-minded partners in a location (Beugelsdijk, Maseland, Onrust, van Hoorn, & Slangen, 2015; Beugelsdijk, Slangen, Maseland, & Onrust, 2014).

There is ample evidence supporting the thesis that firms target population segments with whom they share a common ground. Gerhart and Fang (2005) suggest that firms develop HRM policies aimed at attracting those members of a population that match their institutional background, rendering distance to the country as a whole irrelevant. This argument is supported by Florida and Kenney (1991), showing that Japanese automotive firms have been able to transplant organizational practices to their US subsidiaries by carefully selecting employees and regions that fit the firms' profile. When selecting local partners for joint ventures, Starbucks explicitly filters out companies that do not share Starbucks values and standards (Koehn, Besharov, & Miller, 2008). On the customer side, marketing research maintains that many firms simultaneously target segments of consumers with identical cultural–institutional backgrounds in various countries (Agarwal, Malhotra, & Bolton, 2010; Hassan & Craft, 2005; Okazaki et al., 2007). The Body Shop, for example, has successfully expanded internationally by focusing on the sub-section of environmentally conscious consumers present in almost any country (Hassan & Craft, 2005). Likewise, Starbucks is able to operate effectively in many diverse environments by not targeting countries as a whole but attracting the relatively homogenous group of younger, urban middle classes with lifestyles, and values that correspond to its own normative and cognitive profile (Koehn et al., 2008). Overlap on ethnic grounds may also serve as basis for successful expansion: The foreign activities of Jollibee, a large food chain from the Philippines, for example, mainly target Filipino migrants (Verbeke, 2013). Likewise, Miller, Thomas, Eden, and Hitt (2008) show that Latin American banks located in the United States enjoy an advantage in targeting those segments of the population that share the firms' cultural and ethnic backgrounds.

The overlap perspective thus highlights the fact that firms do business with other firms, customers, and workers, not with countries. Institutional environments matter through the fact that individual customers, partners, and workers are embedded in them. MNEs enter into transactions with actors with whom they share the institutional structures upon which the transaction is based. The size of such overlapping groups rather than distance to society as a whole determines business opportunities and attractiveness of a location. This conflicts with the idea of a country institutional profile (Busenitz, Gomez, & Spencer, 2000; Kostova, 1997). A country is a territorial unit, bounded by the formal enforcement structures of the state. There is no reason why the boundaries of other institutional structures would correspond to that unit. Structures of meaning and structures of enforcement are not attributes of countries but of the agents and organizations reproducing them. Different institutions do not constitute pillars of a single institutional profile. Rather, each institution is related to a different community of people that agree with, confirm, and reproduce this institution. Overlap is the amount of communities to which the two or more individuals engaging in a transaction collectively belong. This combination is potentially unique for each set of individuals. It is this combination that matters to firms seeking expansion.

Note that this is a different point from the familiar critique of country-based institutional studies which questions the appropriateness of taking country as a unit of analysis (McSweeney, 2002; Shenkar, 2001). Indeed, there is ample evidence that states act as homogenizing force, causing a degree of convergence of normative, regulative, and cognitive institutions in its realm (Cavusgil, Kiyak, & Yeniyurt, 2004; Gould & Grein, 2009; Hofstede, 1980, 2001; Javidan, Dorfman, De Luque, & House, 2006; Ronen & Shenkar, 1985, 2013; Tang & Koveos, 2008). There is little doubt about the correlations between institutional characteristics and country borders (Hofstede, 1980, 2001). However, cooperation depends on the presence of a group of agents with whom structures are shared, even if this is only a minority, not on similarity to the average institutional profile of a country's population. A German manager is not concerned with the fact that the French language is more similar to German than Russian is; she is concerned with whom she is able to speak English. The intra- and cross-societal distribution of ideas, beliefs, values, and other structures of meaning is hence of crucial importance.

Difference 2.

Traditional distance perspective: The legitimacy and effectiveness of firms abroad depend on their fit within the host environment's institutional profile. This institutional profile is an attribute of countries.

Overlap perspective: the legitimacy and effectiveness of firms abroad depend on the presence of population segments with whom the firm shares both structures of meaning and structures of enforcement. As each institution is related to a different community of agents sharing this institution, such overlap is a potentially unique attribute of sets of individual agents.

Additivity vs. Arbitrage

When interpreting institutional diversity in terms of distance, scholars frame the impact of diversity as being linear (Shenkar, 2001). Higher distance means bigger challenges for firms to gain legitimacy. One of the properties of linearity is additivity, implying that the distance from home toward an intermediate point and the distance from this intermediate point toward a final destination together make up the total distance between home and the final destination. This allows distance between two locations to be divided into smaller steps, each adding a little bit of distance to the total (Hutzschenreuter & Voll, 2008; Hutzschenreuter, Voll, & Verbeke, 2011). It also means that if distance toward two alternative locations is very low, the distance between these two locations cannot be very high either.

These properties contrast sharply with an overlap perspective. In such a perspective, cooperation and exchange may be based on common ground in various institutions. The overlap found with different partners may apply to different institutional structures, making overlap nonadditive. If a firm finds overlap with two alternative partners, it does not follow that these partners share any institutional structures with each other. A Dutch manager may effectively communicate with both her British and German counterparts because of her proficiency in both languages, but that does not mean that the German and British managers are able to speak to each other.

In fact, this nonadditive nature of overlap is precisely what allows firms to link various separate institutional communities, creating and exploiting opportunities for arbitrage. When different groups are not connected among themselves, MNEs can act as nodes, uniquely able to talk to and work with members of two communities and forming a bridge between them (Roth, Kostova, & Dakhli, 2011). This allows MNEs to shift otherwise non-transferable resources from one community to the other. For example, the basis for the relation between a firm like Apple and its customers or employees is a shared recognition of the value of "hip" design and constant innovation, while the basis of Apple's relationship with its suppliers and partners is a shared recognition of profit-seeking and cost-cutting as motives. Either relationship is developed around and limited to the overlap that is present in it. Apple's competitive advantage is based on its unique ability to connect these two communities, designing supply chains that allow it to swiftly offer cutting-edge, user-friendly design products (Bovet & Martha, 2000; Yoffie & Kim, 2011).

Difference 3.

Traditional distance perspective: distance is additive, implying that locations which are institutionally close to a firm are also close to each other.

Overlap perspective: distance is non-additive, implying that firms may exhibit overlap with communities lacking any overlap with each other, creating opportunities for arbitrage.

Transaction Costs vs. Transaction Thickness

A distance perspective presumes desirable transactions to be given, then adds costs originating in the challenges of distance to them. These costs drive firms to dismiss transactions in certain locations, adapt their entry modes, or simply perform worse (Shenkar, 2001). This conceptualization resembles the idea of iceberg transportation costs in international economics (Samuelson, 1954); some part of product shipments, information flows or practice transfers simply "melts away" passing from one institutional environment to the other.

In an overlap perspective, transactions are based on the amount of overlap that is present between two agents. In so far as there is overlap in structures of meaning or enforcement, no transaction costs apply to international transactions in addition to the ones affecting any kind of transaction. In so far as there is no overlap between partners, no exchange will occur between them. From this perspective, the difference between situations in which there is overlap on a lot of institutional structures and situations in which there is overlap on only a few is not so much that transactions are costlier in the latter case, but that transactions are thinner. Because they are based on a narrower shared basis, communications will be less complex and less comprehensive. Where agents share a large amount of structures of meaning, exchanges may be multi-dimensional and deep. This is the case of polycentric firms (Perlmutter, 1969), seeking to develop a close relation with local agents based on broad overlap in institutional structures. When a large part of tacit cognitive and normative structures go unshared, exchanges will be more superficial, and limited to simplified and codified information flows. If both partners are able to read such codified information, however, there is no reason why any of the knowledge that is transferred would go lost. Geocentrically oriented firms successfully operate on this principle, limiting themselves to a small set of relatively simple transactions, involving only those structures that all partners globally agree upon. In both cases, firms are successful in the transactions they actually conduct (cf. proposition 5 in Kostova & Zaheer, 1999). Lack of overlap results in thinner and fewer transactions, not costlier or more problematic ones.

Difference 4.

Traditional distance perspective: distance creates iceberg communication costs affecting a given set of desired transactions.

Overlap perspective: Transactions are built on those structures on which there is overlap. More overlapping structures enable firms to enter into more complex transactions and knowledge exchanges. Lack of overlap does not result in additional transaction costs, but in fewer and thinner transactions.

CONCLUSION

This chapter investigated the institutional theoretical foundations for the focus on distance in international management research. Discussion of the two dominant institutional perspectives in IB, NIE and NIS, revealed that in both perspectives institutional diversity is a source of frictions. Following the NIE perspective, a multiplicity of enforcement systems violates the conditions for anonymous exchange. Following NIS, absence of agreement on structures of meaning results in miscommunication, ineffective behavior, and lack of legitimacy. In both cases, however, the extent of dissimilarity of institutional structures is not a factor. What matters is whether institutions are shared or not, not how different they are. For this reason, I proposed a focus on *institutional overlap* rather than institutional distance. Not the extent of similarity, but the extent of commonality in the content and enforcement of institutions is what matters for effective cooperation.

Changing the institutional debate in IB from a distance to an overlap perspective has a number of important implications and advantages. First, as institutional overlap is an attribute of business relations or transactions rather than of country environments, it offers a theoretically informative way to align insights about the impact of institutional diversity on IB with the growing literature on intra-country variation (Beugelsdijk & Mudambi, 2013). Second, the nonadditive nature of overlap highlights the potential for institutional entrepreneurship of MNEs, exploiting arbitrage opportunities by forming a missing link between otherwise separated institutional communities. Third, the overlap perspective is able to explain why many MNEs successfully expand abroad in spite of institutional diversity; it is because institutional diversity, that is, the amount of institutional overlap, decides the thickness of transactions but not their cost. Most importantly, however, an overlap perspective leads to a much more dynamic perspective in which business opportunities fostered by the negotiation of shared structures stand central, rather than externally imposed distance constraints. The identification, production, and reproduction of common ground is a vital step for cooperation and exchange, allowing firms to link institutional environments and exploit opportunities for arbitrage between various institutional communities.

I conclude that the theoretical support for the way in which institutional distance has been understood in IB and management is tenuous and that important gains can be made by switching to the concept of institutional overlap. Echoing Granovetter's (1985) call to study transactions as embedded in social relations, I argue that studying overlap rightly stresses the opportunities offered by commonalities between agents joined in a business relations, rather than the costs generated by dissimilarities between macro-environments. IB and management are not about the management of distance between countries but about the management of the relations between managers and firms tied up in transactions.

REFERENCES

Agarwal, J., Malhotra, N. K., & Bolton, R. N. (2010). A cross-national and cross-cultural approach to global market segmentation: An application using consumers' perceived service quality. *Journal of International Marketing*, *18*(3), 18–40.

Albuquerque, P., Bronnenberg, B. J., & Corbett, C. J. (2007). A spatiotemporal analysis of the global diffusion of ISO 9000 and ISO 14000 certification. *Management Science*, *53*(3), 451–468.

Anderson, E., & Gatignon, H. (1986). Modes of foreign entry: A transaction cost analysis and propositions. *Journal of International Business Studies*, *17*(3), 1–26.

Barkema, H. G., Bell, J. H., & Pennings, J. M. (1996). Foreign entry, cultural barriers, and learning. *Strategic Management Journal*, *17*(1), 151–166.

Barney, J. (1991). Firm resources and sustained competitive advantage. *Journal of Management*, *17*(1), 99–120.

Beckerman, W. (1956). Distance and the pattern of intra-European trade. *The Review of Economics and Statistics*, *38*(1), 31–40.

Beugelsdijk, S., Maseland, R., Onrust, M., Van Hoorn, A., & Slangen, A. (2015). Cultural distance in international business and management: From mean-based to variance-based measures. *The International Journal of Human Resource Management*, *26*(2), 165–191.

Beugelsdijk, S., & Mudambi, R. (2013). MNEs as border-crossing multi-location enterprises: The role of discontinuities in geographic space. *Journal of International Business Studies*, *44*(5), 413–426.

Beugelsdijk, S., Slangen, A., Maseland, R., & Onrust, M. (2014). The impact of home–host cultural distance on foreign affiliate sales: The moderating role of cultural variation within host countries. *Journal of Business Research*, *67*(8), 1638–1646.

Boisot, M., & Child, J. (1996). From fiefs to clans and network capitalism: Explaining China's emerging economic order. *Administrative Science Quarterly*, *41*(4), 600–628.

Bovet, D., & Martha, J. (2000). Value nets: Reinventing the rusty supply chain for competitive advantage. *Strategy & Leadership*, *28*(4), 21–26.

Brouthers, K. D. (2002). Institutional, cultural and transaction cost influences on entry mode choice and performance. *Journal of International Business Studies*, *33*(2), 203–221.

Busenitz, L. W., Gomez, C., & Spencer, J. W. (2000). Country institutional profiles: Unlocking entrepreneurial phenomena. *Academy of Management Journal*, *43*(5), 994–1003.

Cavusgil, S. T., Kiyak, T., & Yeniyurt, S. (2004). Complementary approaches to preliminary foreign market opportunity assessment: Country clustering and country ranking. *Industrial Marketing Management*, *33*(7), 607–617.

Chan, L. L., Shaffer, M. A., & Snape, E. (2004). In search of sustained competitive advantage: The impact of organizational culture, competitive strategy and human resource management practices on firm performance. *The International Journal of Human Resource Management*, *15*(1), 17–35.

Dezalay, Y., & Garth, B. (1995). Merchants of law as moral entrepreneurs: Constructing international justice from the competition for transnational business disputes. *Law and Society Review*, *29*(1), 27–64.

Dimaggio, P., & Powell, W. W. (1983). The iron cage revisited: Collective rationality and institutional isomorphism in organizational fields. *American Sociological Review*, *48*(2), 147–160.

Eden, L., & Miller, S. R. (2004). Distance matters: Liability of foreignness, institutional distance and ownership strategy. In Michael A. Hitt, Joseph L. C. Cheng (Eds.), *Theories of the multinational enterprise: Diversity, complexity and relevance* (pp. 187–221). Bingley: Emerald Group Publishing Limited.

Ellis, P. D. (2011). Social ties and international entrepreneurship: Opportunities and constraints affecting firm internationalization. *Journal of International Business Studies*, *42*(1), 99–127.

Ferguson, N. (1998). *The world's banker: The history of the house of Rothschild*. London: Weidenfeld & Nicolson.

Flores, R. G., & Aguilera, R. V. (2007). Globalization and location choice: An analysis of US multinational firms in 1980 and 2000. *Journal of International Business Studies*, *38*(7), 1187–1210.

Florida, R., & Kenney, M. (1991). Transplanted organizations: The transfer of Japanese industrial organization to the US. *American Sociological Review*, *56*(3), 381–398.

Gaur, A. S., & Lu, J. W. (2007). Ownership strategies and survival of foreign subsidiaries: Impacts of institutional distance and experience. *Journal of Management*, *33*(1), 84–110.

Gerhart, B., & Fang, M. (2005) National culture and human resource management: Assumptions and evidence. *The International Journal of Human Resource Management*, *16*(6), 971–986.

Ghemawat, P. (2001). Distance still matters. *Harvard Business Review*, *79*(8), 137–147.

Giannetti, M., & Yafeh, Y. (2012). Do cultural differences between contracting parties matter? Evidence from syndicated bank loans. *Management Science*, *58*(2), 365–383.

Giddens, A. (1984). *The constitution of society: Outline of the theory of structuration*. Berkeley, CA: University of California Press.

Gould, S. J., & Grein, A. F. (2009). Think glocally, act glocally: A culture-centric comment on Leung, Bhagat, Buchan, Erez and Gibson (2005). *Journal of International Business Studies*, *40*(2), 237–254.

Granovetter, M. (1985). Economic action and social structure: The problem of embeddedness. *American Journal of Sociology*, *91*(3), 481–510.

Grant, R. M. (1996). Toward a knowledge-based theory of the firm. *Strategic Management Journal*, *17*(S2), 109–122.

Greif, A. (1993). Contract enforceability and economic institutions in early trade: The Maghribi traders' coalition. *The American Economic Review*, *83*(3), 525–548.

Greif, A. (1994). On the political foundations of the late medieval commercial revolution: Genoa during the twelfth and thirteenth centuries. *The Journal of Economic History*, *54*(02), 271–287.

Greif, A. (2006). *Institutions and the path to the modern economy: Lessons from medieval trade*. Cambridge: Cambridge University Press.

Gupta, A. K., & Govindarajan, V. (2000). Knowledge flows within multinational corporations. *Strategic Management Journal*, *21*(4), 473–496.

Harzing, A., & Pudelko, M. (2013). Language competencies, policies and practices in multinational corporations: A comprehensive review and comparison of Anglophone, Asian, Continental European and Nordic MNCs. *Journal of World Business*, *48*(1), 87–97.

Hassan, S. S., & Craft, S. H. (2005). Linking global market segmentation decisions with strategic positioning options. *Journal of Consumer Marketing*, *22*(2), 81–89.

Haugaard, M. (2002). *Power: A reader*. Manchester: Manchester University Press.

Hofstede, G. (1980). *Culture's consequences: National differences in thinking and organizing*. Beverly Hills, CA: Sage,

Hofstede, G. (2001). *Culture's consequences: Comparing values, behaviors, institutions and organizations across nations*. Beverly Hills, CA: Sage.

Hutzschenreuter, T., & Voll, J. C. (2008). Performance effects of "Added Cultural Distance" in the path of international expansion: The case of German multinational enterprises. *Journal of International Business Studies*, *39*(1), 53–70.

Hutzschenreuter, T., Voll, J. C., & Verbeke, A. (2011). The impact of added cultural distance and cultural diversity on international expansion patterns: A Penrosean perspective. *Journal of Management Studies*, *48*(2), 305–329.

Javidan, M., Dorfman, P. W., De Luque, M. S., & House, R. J. (2006). In the eye of the beholder: Cross cultural lessons in leadership from project GLOBE. *The Academy of Management Perspectives*, *20*(1), 67–90.

Jensen, R., & Szulanski, G. (2004). Stickiness and the adaptation of organizational practices in cross-border knowledge transfers. *Journal of International Business Studies*, *35*(6), 508–523.

Koehn, N. F., Besharov, M., & Miller, K. (2008). Starbucks coffee company in the 21st century. *Harvard Business School Case Study 808–019*, Harvard Business School.

Kogut, B., & Singh, H. (1988). The effect of national culture on the choice of entry mode. *Journal of International Business Studies*, *19*(3), 411–432.

Kostova, T. (1997). Country institutional profiles: Concept and measurement. *Academy of Management Proceedings*, *1997*(1) 180–184.

Kostova, T. (1999). Transnational transfer of strategic organizational practices: A contextual perspective. *Academy of Management Review*, *24*(2), 308–324.

Kostova, T., & Roth, K. (2002). Adoption of an organizational practice by subsidiaries of multinational corporations: Institutional and relational effects. *Academy of Management Journal*, *45*(1), 215–233.

Kostova, T., Roth, K., & Dacin, M. T. (2008). Institutional theory in the study of multinational corporations: A critique and new directions. *Academy of Management Review*, *33*(4), 994–1006.

Kostova, T., & Zaheer, S. (1999). Organizational legitimacy under conditions of complexity: The case of the multinational enterprise. *Academy of Management Review*, *24*(1), 64–81.

López-Duarte, C., & Vidal-Suárez, M. M. (2013). Cultural distance and the choice between wholly owned subsidiaries and joint ventures. *Journal of Business Research*, *66*(11), 2252–2261.

Mcsweeney, B. (2002). Hofstede's model of national cultural differences and their consequences: A triumph of faith-a failure of analysis. *Human Relations*, *55*(1), 89–118.

Meyer, K., Mudambi, R., & Narula, R. (2011). Multinational enterprises and local contexts: The opportunities and challenges of multiple embeddedness. *Journal of Management Studies*, *48*(2), 235–252.

Meyer, J. W., & Rowan, B. (1977). Institutionalized organizations: Formal structure as myth and ceremony. *American Journal of Sociology*, *83*(2), 340–363.

Meyer, J. W., & Scott, W. R. (1983). Centralization and the legitimacy problems of local government. *Organizational Environments: Ritual and Rationality*, *199*, 215.

Miller, S. R., Thomas, D. E., Eden, L., & Hitt, M. (2008). Knee deep in the big muddy: The survival of emerging market firms in developed markets. *Management International Review*, *48*(6), 645–666.

Nachum, L. (2003). Liability of foreignness in global competition? Financial service affiliates in the city of London. *Strategic Management Journal*, *24*(12), 1187–1208.

North, D. C. (1990). *Institutions, institutional change and economic performance*. Cambridge: Cambridge University Press.

North, D. C. (1993). Institutions and credible commitment. *Journal of Institutional and Theoretical Economics (JITE)/Zeitschrift Für Die Gesamte Staatswissenschaft*, *149*(1), 11–23.

North, D. C. (2006). *Understanding the process of economic change*. Princeton, NJ: Academic Foundation.

Ogilvie, S., & Carus, A. (2013). Institutions and economic growth in historical perspective. *Handbook of Economic Growth*, *2*, 403.

Ojala, A., & Tyrväinen, P. (2007). Market entry and priority of small and medium-sized enterprises in the software industry: An empirical analysis of cultural distance, geographic distance, and market size. *Journal of International Marketing*, *15*(3), 123–149.

Okazaki, S., Mueller, B., Ko, E., Kim, E., Taylor, C. R., Hoon Kim, K., & Jeong Kang, I. (2007). Cross-national market segmentation in the fashion industry: A study of European, Korean, and US consumers. *International Marketing Review*, *24*(5), 629–651.

Perlmutter, H. V. (1969). Some management problems in spaceship earth: The megafirm and the global industrial estate. *Academy of Management Proceedings*, *1969* (1) 59–87.

Rauch, J. E., & Trindade, V. (2002). Ethnic Chinese networks in international trade. *Review of Economics and Statistics*, *84*(1), 116–130.

Ronen, S., & Shenkar, O. (1985). Clustering countries on attitudinal dimensions: A review and synthesis. *Academy of Management Review*, *10*(3), 435–454.

Ronen, S., & Shenkar, O. (2013). Mapping world cultures: Cluster formation, sources and implications. *Journal of International Business Studies*, *44*(9), 867–897.

Roth, K., Kostova, T., & Dakhli, M. (2011). Exploring cultural misfit: Causes and consequences. *International Business Review*, *20*(1), 15–26.

Salomon, R., & Wu, Z. (2012). Institutional distance and local isomorphism strategy. *Journal of International Business Studies*, *43*(4), 343–367.

Samuelson, P. A. (1954). The transfer problem and transport costs, II: Analysis of effects of trade impediments. *The Economic Journal*, *64*(254), 264–289.

Schneider, S. C. (1988). National vs. corporate culture: Implications for human resource management. *Human Resource Management*, *27*(2), 231–246.

Scott, W. R. (2013). *Institutions and organizations: Ideas, interests, and identities*. Beverly Hills, CA: Sage Publications.

Shenkar, O. (2001). Cultural distance revisited: Towards a more rigorous conceptualization and measurement of cultural differences. *Journal of International Business Studies*, *32*(3), 519–535.

Suchman, M. C. (1995). Managing legitimacy: Strategic and institutional approaches. *Academy of Management Review*, *20*(3), 571–610.

Sundaram, A. K., & Black, J. S. (1992). The environment and internal organization of multinational enterprises. *Academy of Management Review*, *17*(4), 729–757.

Tajfel, H. (1970). Experiments in intergroup discrimination. *Scientific American*, *223*(5), 96–103.

Tang, L., & Koveos, P. E. (2008). A framework to update Hofstede's cultural value indices: Economic dynamics and institutional stability. *Journal of International Business Studies*, *39*(6), 1045–1063.

Tung, R. L., & Chung, H. F. (2010). Diaspora and trade facilitation: The case of ethnic Chinese in Australia. *Asia Pacific Journal of Management*, *27*(3), 371–392.

Uzzi, B. (1997). Social structure and competition in interfirm networks: The paradox of embeddedness. *Administrative Science Quarterly*, *42*(1), 35–67.

Verbeke, A. (2013). *International business strategy*. Cambridge: Cambridge University Press.

Wallis, J. J. (2011). Institutions, organizations, impersonality, and interests: The dynamics of institutions. *Journal of Economic Behavior & Organization*, *79*(1), 48–64.

Wathne, K. H., & Heide, J. B. (2000). Opportunism in interfirm relationships: Forms, outcomes, and solutions. *Journal of Marketing*, *64*(4), 36–51.

Weber, Y., Shenkar, O., & Raveh, A. (1996). National and corporate cultural fit in mergers/acquisitions: An exploratory study. *Management Science*, *42*(8), 1215–1227.

Williamson, O. E. (1985). *The economic institutions of capitalism*. New York, NY: Simon and Schuster.

Xu, D., & Shenkar, O. (2002). Note: Institutional distance and the multinational enterprise. *Academy of Management Review*, *27*(4), 608–618.

Yoffie, D. B., & Kim, R. (2011). *Apple Inc. in 2010*. Boston, MA: Harvard Business School.

Zaheer, S. (1995). Overcoming the liability of foreignness. *Academy of Management Journal*, *38*(2), 341–363.

Zaheer, S., Schomaker, M. S., & Nachum, L. (2012). Distance without direction: Restoring credibility to a much-loved construct. *Journal of International Business Studies*, *43*(1), 18–27.

CHAPTER 4

HOW DO MANAGERS' DEVIANT PERCEPTIONS OF "CULTURAL DISTANCE" RELATE TO THE PERFORMANCE OF INTERNATIONAL SMEs?

Goudarz Azar and Rian Drogendijk

ABSTRACT

Our study explores the performance implications of deviations in managers' perceptions of "cultural distance" – one of the most important concepts in International Business research – when expanding into foreign markets. Despite much research on "cultural distance," few researchers have paid attention to the effect of deviations in managers' perceptions of cultural distance on firm performance. This is important since managers formulate strategies for responding to the environment based on their perceptions of the firm's environment. These perceptions, however, do not always coincide with actual environmental characteristics. Therefore, formulating strategies based on inaccurate data may result in erroneous forecasts, missed opportunities and, ultimately, business failure. We explore this empirically by comparing managers' perceptions of cultural distance to export markets

Distance in International Business: Concept, Cost and Value
Progress in International Business Research, Volume 12, 91–106

ISSN: 1745-8862/doi:10.1108/S1745-886220170000012017

of Swedish SMEs to cultural distance measures based on secondary data and relate deviations of perceptions to the performance of these SMEs. Our results show that the larger the deviations of managers' perceptions of cultural differences from "actual differences" as expressed in Hofstede scores on cultural dimensions, the lower the performance expressed in firms' sales. The implications of the study are discussed.

Keywords: Cultural distance; firm performance; internationalization; perception

INTRODUCTION

The concept of "distance" (or differences between countries) is at the core of the domain of international business (IB; Zaheer, Schomaker, & Nachum, 2012). Firms engage in IB to find and exploit business opportunities outside the domestic market (Lu & Beamish, 2001). However, exploiting these opportunities entails costs and risks of doing business in a new foreign market, mainly resulting from barriers created by "distance" (Ghemawat, 2001). Distance may originate not only from geographic separations but also from administrative or political, economic, and cultural differences (Hutzschenreuter, Kleindienst, & Lange, 2016). "Cultural distance" is one of the most important explanatory factors in the field of IB (Shenkar, 2001). The concept of cultural distance typically refers to degrees of dissimilarity in norms, ideas, values, and beliefs between country pairs and is usually conceptualized using Kogut and Singh's (1988) index (Ambos & Håkanson, 2014). Despite its popularity the concept and measure have been questioned by extant research claiming that the original underlying assumptions and rationale behind the concept have been largely overlooked (Shenkar, 2001).

One of the fundamental questions with regard to the concept of "cultural distance" is whether it should be conceptualized using "objective" measures or whether subjective and perceptual indicators can provide us with a more valid and reliable measure of cultural distance (Håkanson & Ambos, 2010; Nebus & Chai, 2014). "Objective" measures at a national level have dominated the IB research (Hutzschenreuter et al., 2016). However, scholars suggest using perceptual data in assessing cultural distance because managers formulate strategies for responding to the environmental demands based on their *perceptions* of the firm's (external) environment (Child, Ng, & Wong, 2002; Evans, Mavondo, & Bridson, 2008; Harzing, 2003; Maitland & Sammartino,

2015b). Managerial perceptions of the firm's environment, however, do not always coincide with the actual environmental characteristics (Mezias & Starbuck, 2003; Taras, Rowney, & Steel, 2009). They are, for example, influenced by managers' personal characteristics, experience, and the time in which the environment is perceived (Starbuck & Milliken, 1988). Therefore, formulating strategies based on inaccurate data, namely perception-based judgments of the environment (e.g., country differences), may result in erroneous forecasts, missed opportunities, and, ultimately, business failure (O'Grady & Lane, 1996).

Despite much research on "cultural distance," little attention has been paid to the effect of deviations of managers' perceptions of distance and its implications on firm performance. According to Ambos and Håkanson (2014), one of the unexplored questions in IB research is related to the link between perceptual and "objective" measures of country differences and its influence on firm performance. Further, scholars state that one of the issues concerning measuring distance is the validity of data collected via self-report questionnaires – the most commonly used research design in cross-cultural research (Tsui, Nifadkar, & Ou, 2007). While, as Taras et al. (2009) argue "there may be a substantial difference between the perceptions of the respondents and reality" (p. 370), few studies have analyzed the validity of such data (Azar, 2014). Accordingly, we introduce a novel conceptualization of "cultural distance," that is, "cultural distance deviation." It refers to the degree to which managers' perceptions of cultural distance correspond with "objective reality," acting on the premise that business success relies on the accuracy of information acquired by managers and on their correct interpretation of this information (Mukherji, Mukherji, Dibrell, & Francis, 2013; Starbuck & Milliken, 1988). Our study is exploratory in nature and examines the performance implications of deviations in managers' perceptions of "cultural distance" when expanding into foreign markets.

"CULTURAL DISTANCE" IN INTERNATIONAL BUSINESS

The concept of cultural distance is one of the most widely researched concepts in IB research (Shenkar, 2001). It refers to the difference between countries in terms of norms, ideas, values, and beliefs. Research has shown cultural distance to be an important source of uncertainty for firms during their internationalization process (Johanson & Vahlne, 1977; Slangen & van

Tulder, 2009). Differences in norms, ideas, values, and beliefs in culturally distant markets increase the liability of foreignness and uncertainty that makes the firm see itself as lacking sufficient market information to accurately predict the challenges facing it in the new foreign market (Harzing, 2003; Yamin & Sinkovics, 2006). Consequenlty, cultural distance has been used to explain a variety of strategic decisions made in a firm's internationalization process, *inter alia*, foreign market selection (e.g., Dow & Ferencikova, 2010; Dow & Karunaratna, 2006), entry-mode choice (e.g., Drogendijk & Slangen, 2006; Wang & Schaan, 2008), and international marketing strategy (e.g., Calantone, Cavusgil, Schmidt, & Shin, 2004; Moon & Park, 2011). Based on a longitudinal analysis of bilateral trade between 25 major trading nations for the period 1962–2008, Håkanson and Dow (2012) revealed that cultural distance is related with declining trade flows between those countries. The underlying argument referred to the difficulty in obtaining and interpreting information in culturally distant markets. Further, Drogendijk and Slangen (2006) found that MNEs choose greenfield investments rather than acquisitions in culturally distant locations because substantial differences in organizational and managerial practices, as well as in communication styles, make it difficult for firms located in culturally distant markets to integrate into an MNE's corporate network after they have been acquired. Carlson (1974) argues that the cultural distance between countries represents a barrier to the international transfer of information, influencing the collection and interpretation costs of critical management information.

Objective vs. Perceptual Cultural Distance

Despite the dominance of objective country-level measures of cultural distance in IB research, scholars call for incorporating perceptual individual-level measures in those studies (Ambos & Håkanson, 2014). The main argument is that strategic decisions and organizational behavior rely on managerial perceptions of the firm's environment (Beyer et al., 1997; Child et al., 2002). However, as Harzing (2003) argues, most studies in the field of IB have succeeded in completely removing the managers who make the actual decisions from the equation. According to Maitland and Sammartino (2015b), IB research should incorporate managers' decision styles and biases into theoretical models of form, mode, and location choice.

Perception has been described as a critical process that helps people define their worlds and guides their behavior (Cook & Hunsaker, 2001). According to Robbins (1996, p. 39), "perception is a process by which individuals organize and interpret their sensory impressions in order to give meaning to their environment." Factors such as the perceiver's personal characteristics (e.g., attitudes, motives, interests, expectations, training, and past experience), characteristics of the target perceived (e.g., appearance and background), and the context in which the perceiver receives the stimuli (e.g., time and location) may affect an individual's perceptions. Therefore, different individuals in the same context or one individual in different contexts may perceive the same stimuli in different ways (Starbuck & Milliken, 1988).

A firm's environment is defined as "the totality of physical and social factors that are taken directly into consideration in the decision-making behavior of individuals in the organization" (Duncan, 1972, p. 314). Based on their perceptions of environmental properties, managers formulate strategies for responding to the environmental demands (Beyer et al., 1997; Evans et al., 2008). To do this, managers match their firm's organizational properties to its external environment (Lawrence & Lorsch, 1967; Maitland & Sammartino, 2015a). However, as already explained, different managers may perceive the same environment differently (Maitland & Sammartino, 2015a).

Deviations in Managers' Perceptions of Cultural Distance

The initial assumption in many organizational theories and practices is that managers accurately perceive their organizations' external environments (Mezias & Starbuck, 2003). However, previous research has reported errors and biases in managers' perceptions of their firms' external environment (Kahneman & Tversky, 1973; Lant, Milliken, & Batra, 1992; Starbuck & Mezias, 1996). This is critical since an organization performs best when managerial perceptions of environmental characteristics match reality (Bourgeois, 1985; Dess & Beard, 1984; Garg, Walters, & Priem, 2003; Simon, 1987). By empirically studying senior managers, Mezias and Starbuck (2003) found a prevalence of very large deviations between managers' perceptions of organizational and environmental properties and the corresponding objective data.

Firms are generally assumed to perform better in markets with a national culture that is similar to their domestic culture (Kogut & Singh, 1988). This is because similarity in culture leads to ease of critical communication (Carlson, 1974) and learning about the market environment and hence decreases the levels of decision uncertainty (Johanson & Vahlne, 1977). Also Evans and Mavondo (2002) state that managers who perceive larger cultural differences in foreign markets experience higher levels of uncertainty in these markets. Higher uncertainty is the result of a lack of sufficient market information to accurately predict the challenges facing the firm in the new foreign market (Maitland & Sammartino, 2015b; Yamin & Sinkovics, 2006). To reduce this uncertainty, managers may conduct extensive market research and planning which usually improves their strategic decision-making and hence performance (Evans et al., 2008). On the other hand, "perceived similarity can lead to carelessness and failure" (Evans et al., 2008). In other words, underestimating slight but important differences between the home market and a (perceived) culturally similar market may result in poor performance for the firms in those markets as well. O'Grady and Lane (1996), for example, concluded from their study of Canadian investors that the inaccuracy of the Canadian managers' perceptions of the US market as culturally similar to Canada was an underlying reason for their companies' failure in the United States. According to Mukherji et al. (2013), accurate knowledge of (cultural) differences between countries is crucial in making successful decisions in cross-border business. Powell, Lovallo, & Fox (2011, p. 1370) further state that "sound executive judgment … can enhance firm performance." Maitland and Sammartino (2015b) finally argue that differences in managers' experience, learning, and decision-making are important sources of heterogeneity in firm strategic decisions and performance. Therefore, the question is whether deviations of manager's perceptions of cultural distance from "objective" cultural distance have a negative influence on firm performance.

RESEARCH METHODOLOGY

Data Profile and Research Setting

To address our research question we conducted a survey of senior managers of Swedish SMEs in the forestry, fishing, food products, beverages, garment, and furniture industries that satisfied the following criteria: (1) exported products for at least three years and (2) exported to at least two foreign markets. The sample (573 SMEs) was selected randomly from a population of 963 companies using a stratified sampling method. Sweden is well suited to the subject of the study because it is a developed country with a very small domestic market, and its economy is extremely dependent on exporting into international markets. According to the World Bank's (2014) national accounts data, about 50 percent of Sweden's gross domestic product (GDP) comes from the export of goods and services to international markets.

Data Collection Procedure

Data were collected with help of a marketing research agency from Sweden, between February and April, 2012. The interviewers used a structured questionnaire that we designed for the study to collect data from senior managers in SMEs in the selected industries. The questionnaire was designed based on measures used and validated in previous research (Evans & Mavondo, 2002; Evans et al., 2008) and that we modified for our research context (Churchill, 1979). We received 158 responses from a total of 573 companies in the sample (approximately 28 percent) amounting potentially to 316 export ventures. Following Evans and Mavondo (2002) and Evans et al. (2008), the respondents were first asked to nominate two foreign markets to which their company had exported products during the previous 3 years. They were then asked to specify which of these foreign markets they perceived as "not so different" from their home market (Sweden) in terms of culture and which they perceived as "different" from Sweden. Accordingly, after removing the cases without specified export market, the effective responses corresponded to 294 export ventures in 34 countries.

In terms of the characteristics of the sample, most of the respondents were CEOs of firms with fewer than 50 full-time employees. Most of the firms in the sample had significant international experience and had engaged in export operations for an average of 20 years. The firms' average number of export markets was 8. The majority of the export ventures targeted other EU countries.

MEASURES

Cultural Distance Deviation

To do proper justice to the complexity of the concept of culture, we followed Evans and Mavondo (2002) and Evans et al. (2008) and employed their multidimensional measures of *perceived* cultural distance, adapting them to our context where necessary. These dimensions were measured based on Hofstede's (1980) definitions and descriptions of the four original dimensions of national culture: power distance, individualism, masculinity, and uncertainty avoidance. Following Evans and Mavondo (2002) and Evans et al. (2008), we asked respondents to indicate the degree to which the foreign market was similar to the home market (Sweden) on a seven-point scale (1 = totally the same, and 7 = totally different) with regard to each of these four dimensions.

According to Starbuck and Mezias (1996), one reason for the limited research to date into the validity of managers' perceptions relates to the difficulty of accessing suitable objective data. Consistent with previous studies (cf. Azar, 2014; Brock, Johnson, & Zhou, 2011; Moon & Park, 2011), in the present study Hofstede's (1980) scores for the four abovementioned dimensions of national culture were used as the basis for calculating "objective" measures of cultural distance. Despite increasing criticism regarding theoretical and methodological issues (McSweeney, 2002), Hofstede's framework is still among the most influential (Kirkman, Lowe, & Gibson, 2006). We applied Hofstede's framework, owing to – in addition to its appealing attributes (e.g., sample size, an emphasis on attitude in the workplace) – its comparability to the perceptual measures of cultural distance in the present study and also its large scope that covers all the foreign markets nominated by the respondents in this study.

To measure the cultural distance (both "objective" and perceptual) to the foreign markets, we calculated the Euclidean distance between the index for each dimension of each country (I_{ij}) and the corresponding index for Sweden (i.e., the home country, I_{is}; Barkema & Vermeulen, 1997; Brouthers & Brouthers, 2001; Drogendijk & Slangen, 2006). In calculating the Euclidean distance in the perceptual model, we created composite indices for each dimension by calculating the mean of the three indicators per dimension (see Appendix). In this model, the indices for all cultural dimensions for Sweden (I_{is}) were considered to be equal to 1 (Evans et al., 2008). The "distances" were then corrected for differences in the variance of each dimension (V_i). Algebraically, the following formula was used:

$$\mathrm{ED}_j = \sqrt{\left(I_{ij} - I_{is}\right)^2 / V_i}$$

where ED_j is the Euclidean distance in the ith cultural dimension of the jth foreign market from Sweden, I_{ij} represents the index of the ith cultural dimension and the jth market, s indicates Sweden, and V_i is the variance of the index of the ith dimension.

To calculate the deviations in managers' perceptions of cultural distance, first we standardized all distance variables for each dimension (in both "objective" and perceptual models). Then, using the Euclidean distance formula, the deviations between perceptual and "objective" measures in each dimension of cultural distance ($\mathrm{ED}_{j(\mathrm{dev})}$) were calculated. We conceptualized the construct "cultural distance deviation" as a reflective construct comprising the deviations in each cultural dimension of the foreign markets from Sweden ($\mathrm{ED}_{j(\mathrm{dev})}$) that are the manifestations of the overall construct

(Jarvis, MacKenzie, & Podsakoff, 2003). Unlike Kogut and Singh's (1988) formula for calculating cultural distance (treating cultural distance as an aggregated construct), this approach enables us to take into account the different effects and implications of different dimensions of cultural distance (Azar & Drogendijk, 2016; Shenkar, 2001).

Firm Performance

We measured firm performance using two objective financial indicators, Return on assets (ROA) and Sales (Morgan, Vorhies, & Mason, 2009). The underlying data for firm performance were extracted from firms' financial reports and supplemented to the survey data. We used LN transformed of a mean of data for 2013, 2014, and 2015.[1] We deliberately selected these financial years to be able to examine the ex-post effects of deviations in managers' perceptions of "distance" (calculated based on 2012 data) on firm performance.

We used the LN-transformed number of full-time employees as a proxy for firm size, and together with international experience measured as number of foreign markets to which the firm exports and number of years exporting (both LN-transformed) and entered them as control variables in the model. The size of a firm is suggested to enhance its performance (Wagner, 2001). Likewise, a firm's international experience is suggested as one of the key determinants of its performance (Sousa, Martínez-López, & Coelho, 2008).

Furthermore, following Tsui et al. (2007), to obtain a more valid analysis of the influence of cultural distance, we included additional national differentiators in the analysis as follows: legal and political environment, market structure, economic environment, and business practices.[2] We asked respondents to indicate the degree to which the foreign market was similar to the home market (Sweden) on a 7-point scale (1 = totally the same, and 7 = totally different; see Appendix). Based on the definitions and descriptions of these four dimensions (Evans & Mavondo, 2002), we extracted the corresponding objective measures for each dimension. We used the Economist political instability index for the period 2009/2010 as proxy for *legal and political environment* (Economist, 2016). Data for measuring dimensions market structure, economic environment, and business practices were extracted from the World Bank (2016).

To measure deviations in managers' perceptions of the four additional national difference dimensions we carried out the same procedures as for cultural distance and created the construct "business distance deviation" as a reflective construct comprising the deviations in each dimension.

DATA ANALYSIS

We assessed the underlying measurement model properties and analyzed the structural model using maximum likelihood estimation with LISREL (Jöreskog & Sörbom, 2006). We assessed all measures for convergent validity by performing a confirmatory factor analysis (CFA) and calculating average variance extracted (AVE; Fornell & Larcker, 1981) for all perceptual constructs (see Appendix). All the AVE values were greater than 0.5, indicating convergent validity. We assessed individual item reliability by examining the standardized loadings of items on their corresponding construct. All items exceeded the minimum accepted value which implies that all items converged on the common construct (Gerbing & Anderson, 1988). We determined the corresponding Cronbach's alpha values for all perceptual constructs. All values were greater than 0.8, indicating high reliability and consistency of the entire scale (Hair Jr., Black, Babin, & Anderson, 2010).

We used a path model to examine the influence of the construct "Cultural distance deviation" on firm performance. Initially, we performed a CFA with the measurement model (Anderson & Gerbing, 1988). All indices indicated that the measurement model had an adequate fit to the data ($\chi^2 = 97.94$ (53 d.f., $p = 0.00017$); RMSEA (root mean square of approximation) = 0.073; CFI (comparative fit index) = 0.89; IFI (incremental fit index) = 0.89; GFI (goodness of fit index) = 0.91; AGFI (adjusted goodness of fit index) = 0.85).

In the next stage we performed a CFA with the structural model to examine the relationships between cultural distance deviation and firm performance. The indices of the structural model were also satisfactory ($\chi^2 = 100.14$ (54 d.f., $p = 0.00014$); RMSEA (root mean square of approximation) = 0.073; CFI = 0.88; IFI = 0.89; GFI = 0.91; AGFI (adjusted goodness of fit index) = 0.85). Accordingly, the path coefficient between *cultural distance deviation* and sales was negative and significant ($\beta = -0.13$, $p < 0.05$). Regarding the control variables, as it was expected, both firm size and international experience positively and significantly influenced sales ($\beta = 0.79/0.18$, $p < 0.05$). We did not find a statistically significant path from *business distance deviation* to either sales or ROA.

DISCUSSION AND CONCLUDING REMARKS

Our exploratory study has shown that the larger the deviations of managers' perceptions of cultural differences from "actual differences" as expressed in Hofstede scores on national cultural dimensions, the lower the performance expressed in sales in foreign operations. In line with organization theory we find that firms perform better in terms of sales when their perceptions of the environment agree with reality (Garg et al., 2003; Maitland & Sammartino, 2015b; Mukherji et al., 2013; Powell et al., 2011). Our results imply that it is crucial to make proper judgments of differences between host and home country cultural aspects.

This study is important as Maitland and Sammartino (2015b, p. 755) argue that "incorporating boundedly rational decision makers' ability to identify and select the best option into explanations for differences in internationalization choice, design and performance is a critical theoretical and methodological step for IB." Furthermore, this study helps alleviate the scarcity of research analyzing the validity of perceptual data in organizational behavior studies. Studying perceptual accuracies will improve research methods, leading to the creation of a stronger foundation for theories about managerial behavior (Starbuck & Mezias, 1996). Our study is a first attempt to measure such accuracy and its effects on the performance of foreign operations of firms.

In this study we used Hofstede's country scores as "objective" measures for cultural distance. It can be argued that those scores are also based on the perceptions of individuals as they are derived from the survey instrument used by Hofstede to measure work preferences. Yet, the validity and reliability of Hofstede's national cultural scores may allow researchers to use them as "objective" or "hard" data in assessing cultural differences between countries (Brock et al., 2011). Furthermore, given the complexity and abstract nature of the concept culture we argue that no measure of culture could completely be considered as "objective." We compared the individual perceptions of cultural differences between host countries and Sweden made by our respondents to Hofstede's dimensions scores which are not only based on several indicators but also aggregated over large group of respondents to calculate "cultural distance deviation." Future studies may replicate this investigation using other frameworks to conceptualize cultural distance to establish or refute the validity of our approach. Moreover, Hofstede's (1980) cultural distance scores were collected between 1967 and 1973, while the scores for perceived cultural distance in the current study were based on a 2012 survey. Brown (1995) argues that culture develops continuously over time. However, Hofstede (2001) disputes this, claiming that "national cultures are extremely stable over time" (p. 34). He argues that "culture change basic enough to invalidate the county dimension index scores will need either a much longer period [...] or extremely dramatic outside events" (Hofstede, 2001, p. 36). For this study, we measured cultural distance constructs based on Hofstede's four original dimensions. We used those dimensions due to comparability with dimensions of perceived cultural distance and also availability of scores for the foreign markets covered by the study. However, we encourage future research incorporating other dimensions (e.g. long-/short-term orientation and indulgence/restriction) where appropriate. Likewise, future research could endeavor to explore which aspects or expressions of firm performance are influenced by *cultural distance deviation*, as our exploratory study suggests that differences may exist: our empirical study shows a significant relation between cultural distance deviation and sales performance but not ROA. This study focused on the implications of incongruities in managers' perceptions of cultural distance. An interesting avenue for future research is to include managers' limitations and cognitive biases into the analysis which would provide more insights into the determinants of such incongruities. Finally, the findings of this study are based on the perceptions of managers of Swedish companies in fishing, food products, beverages, garment, and furniture industries. This can limit the generalizability of our findings. Future studies should replicate this research in other regional and industrial contexts.

NOTES

1. For each dimension of business distance we selected the indicators for which we were able to find the corresponding objective measure(*s*).
2. We used data for 2012, 2013, and 2014 where applicable.

REFERENCES

Ambos, B., & Håkanson, L. (2014). The concept of distance in international management research. *Journal of International Management*, *20*(1), 1–7.

Anderson, J. C., & Gerbing, D. W. (1988). Structural equation modeling in practice: A review and recommended two-step approach. *Psychological Bulletin*, *103*(3), 411–423.

Azar, G. (2014). How congruent are managers' perceptions of cultural distance with objective reality? *Cross Cultural Management: An International Journal*, *21*(4), 400–421.

Azar, G., & Drogendijk, R. (2016). Cultural distance, innovation and export performance: An examination of perceived and objective cultural distance. *European Business Review*, *28*(2), 176–207.

Barkema, H. G., & Vermeulen, F. (1997). What differences in the cultural backgrounds of partners are detrimental for international joint ventures? *Journal of International Business Studies*, *28*(4), 845–864.

Beyer, J. M., Chattopadhyay, P., George, E., Glick, W. H., Ogilvie, D., & Pugliese, D. (1997). The selective perception of managers revisited. *Academy of Management Journal*, *40*(3), 716–737.

Bourgeois III, L. J. (1985). Strategic goals, perceived uncertainty, and economic performance in volatile environments. *Academy of Management Journal, 28*(3), 548–573.

Brock, J. K.-U., Johnson, J. E., & Zhou, J. Y. (2011). Does distance matter for internationally-oriented small firms? *Industrial Marketing Management, 40*(3), 384–394.

Brouthers, K. D., & Brouthers, L. E. (2001). Explaining the national cultural distance paradox. *Journal of International Business Studies, 32*(1), 177–189.

Brown, A. D. (1995). *Organisational culture*. London: Pitman.

Calantone, R. J., Cavusgil, S. T., Schmidt, J. B., & Shin, G. C. (2004). Internationalization and the dynamics of product adaptation – An empirical investigation. *Journal of Product Innovation Management, 21*(3), 185–198.

Carlson, S. (1974). International transmission of information and the business firm. *Annals of the American Academy of Political and Social Science, 412*, 55–63.

Child, J., Ng, S. H., & Wong, C. (2002). Psychic distance and internationalization: Evidence from Hong Kong firms. *International Studies of Management & Organization, 32*(1), 36–56.

Churchill, G. A., Jr. (1979). A paradigm for developing better measures of marketing constructs. *Journal of Marketing Research, 16*(1), 64–73.

Cook, C. W., & Hunsaker, P. L. (2001). *Management and organizational behavior*. Boston, MA: McGraw-Hill/Irwin.

Dess, G. G., & Beard, D. W. (1984). Dimensions of organizational task environments. *Administrative Science Quarterly, 29*(1), 52–73.

Dow, D., & Ferencikova, S. (2010). More than just national cultural distance: Testing new distance scales on FDI in Slovakia *International Business Review, 19*(1), 46–58.

Dow, D., & Karunaratna, A. (2006). Developing a multidimensional instrument to measure psychic distance stimuli. *Journal of International Business Studies, 37*(5), 578–602.

Drogendijk, R., & Slangen, A. (2006). Hofstede, Schwartz, or managerial perceptions? The effects of different cultural distance measures on establishment mode choices by multinational enterprises. *International Business Review, 15*(4), 361–380.

Duncan, R. B. (1972). Characteristics of organizational environments and perceived environmental uncertainty. *Administrative Science Quarterly, 17*(3), 313–327.

Economist. (2016). *The political instability index*. Retrieved from http://viewswire.eiu.com/site_info.asp?info_name=social_unrest_table&page=noads&rf=0. Accessed on April 26, 2016.

Evans, J., & Mavondo, F. T. (2002). Psychic distance and organizational performance: An empirical examination of international retailing operations. *Journal of International Business Studies, 33*(3), 515–532.

Evans, J., Mavondo, F. T., & Bridson, K. (2008). Psychic distance: Antecedents, retail strategy implications, and performance outcomes. *Journal of International Marketing, 16*(2), 32–63.

Fornell, C., & Larcker, D. F. (1981). Evaluating structural equation models with unobservable variables and measurement error. *Journal of Marketing Research, 18*(1), 39–50.

Garg, V. K., Walters, B. A., & Priem, R. L. (2003). Chief executive scanning emphases, environmental dynamism, and manufacturing firm performance. *Strategic Management Journal, 24*(8), 725–744.

Gerbing, D. W., & Anderson, J. C. (1988). An updated paradigm for scale development incorporating unidimensionality and its assessment. *Journal of Marketing Research, 25*(2), 186–192.

Ghemawat, P. (2001). Distance still matters. The hard reality of global expansion. *Harvard Business Review, 79*(8), 137–140, 142.

Hair, J. F., Jr. Black, W. C., Babin, B. J., & Anderson, R. E. (2010). *Multivariate data analysis: A global perspective*. Upper Saddle River, NJ: Pearson Education.

Håkanson, L., & Ambos, B. (2010). The antecedents of psychic distance. *Journal of International Management*, *16*(3), 195–210.

Håkanson, L., & Dow, D. (2012). Markets and networks in international trade: On the role of distances in globalization. *Management International Review*, *52*(6), 761–789.

Harzing, A. W. (2003). The role of culture in entry-mode studies: From neglect to myopia? *Advances in International Management*, *15*, 75–127.

Hofstede, G. (1980). *Culture's consequences: International differences in work-related values*. Beverly Hills, CA: Sage.

Hofstede, G. (2001). *Culture's consequences: Comparing values, behaviors, institutions, and organizations across nations*. Thousand Oaks, CA: Sage.

Hutzschenreuter, T., Kleindienst, I., & Lange, S. (2016). The concept of distance in international business research: A review and research agenda. *International Journal of Management Reviews*, *18*(2), 160–179.

Jarvis, C. B., MacKenzie, S. B., & Podsakoff, P. M. (2003). A critical review of construct indicators and measurement model misspecification in marketing and consumer research. *Journal of Consumer Research*, *30*(2), 199–218.

Johanson, J., & Vahlne, J. E. (1977). The internationalization process of the firm – A model of knowledge development and increasing foreign market commitments. *Journal of International Business Studies*, *8*(1), 23–32.

Jöreskog, K. G., & Sörbom, D. (2006). *LISREL 8.80 for Windows*. Lincolnwood, IL: Scientific Software International, Inc.

Kahneman, D., & Tversky, A. (1973). On the psychology of prediction. In D. Kahneman, P. Slovic, & A. Tversky (Eds.), *Judgement under uncertainty: Heuristics and biases* (pp. 48–68). Cambridge: Cambridge University Press.

Kirkman, B. L., Lowe, K. B., & Gibson, C. B. (2006). A quarter century of "Culture's Consequences": A review of empirical research incorporating Hofstede's cultural values framework. *Journal of International Business Studies*, *37*(3), 285–320.

Kogut, B., & Singh, H. (1988). The effect of national culture on the choice of entry mode. *Journal of International Business Studies*, *19*(3), 411–432.

Lant, T. K., Milliken, F. J., & Batra, B. (1992). The role of managerial learning and interpretation in strategic persistence and reorientation: An empirical exploration. *Strategic Management Journal*, *13*(8), 585–608.

Lawrence, P. R., & Lorsch, J. W. (1967). *Organization and environment: Managing differentiation and integration*. Homewood, IL: Irwin.

Lu, J. W., & Beamish, P. W. (2001). The internationalization and performance of SMEs. *Strategic Management Journal*, *22*(6–7), 565–586.

Maitland, E., & Sammartino, A. (2015a). Decision making and uncertainty: The role of heuristics and experience in assessing a politically hazardous environment. *Strategic Management Journal*, *36*(10), 1554–1578.

Maitland, E., & Sammartino, A. (2015b). Managerial cognition and internationalization. *Journal of International Business Studies*, *46*(7), 733–760.

McSweeney, B. (2002). Hofstede's model of national cultural differences and their consequences: A triumph of faith – A failure of analysis. *Human Relations*, *55*(1), 89–118.

Mezias, J. M., & Starbuck, W. H. (2003). Studying the accuracy of managers' perceptions: A research odyssey. *British Journal of Management*, *14*(1), 3–17.

Moon, T. W., & Park, S. I. (2011). The effect of cultural distance on international marketing strategy: A comparison of cultural distance and managerial perception measures. *Journal of Global Marketing*, *24*(1), 18–40.

Morgan, N. A., Vorhies, D. W., & Mason, C. H. (2009). Market orientation, marketing capabilities, and firm performance. *Strategic Management Journal, 30*(8), 909–920.

Mukherji, A., Mukherji, J., Dibrell, C., & Francis, J. D. (2013). Overbidding in cross-border acquisitions: Misperceptions in assessing and valuing knowledge. *Journal of World Business, 48*(1), 39–46.

Nebus, J., & Chai, K. H. (2014). Putting the "Psychic" back in psychic distance: Awareness, perceptions, and understanding as dimensions of psychic distance. *Journal of International Management, 20*(1), 8–24.

O'Grady, S., & Lane, H. (1996). The psychic distance paradox. *Journal of International Business Studies, 27*(2), 309–333.

Powell, T. C., Lovallo, D., & Fox, C. R. (2011). Behavioral strategy. *Strategic Management Journal, 32*(13), 1369–1386.

Robbins, S. P. (1996). *Essentials of organizational behavior*. Englewood Cliffs, NJ: Prentice Hall.

Shenkar, O. (2001). Cultural distance revisited: Towards a more rigorous conceptualization and measurement of cultural differences. *Journal of International Business Studies, 32*(3), 519–535.

Simon, H. A. (1987). Making management decisions: The role of intuition and emotion. *The Academy of Management Executive (1987–1989), 1*(1), 57–64.

Slangen, A. H. L., & van Tulder, R. J. M. (2009). Cultural distance, political risk, or governance quality? Towards a more accurate conceptualization and measurement of external uncertainty in foreign entry mode research. *International Business Review, 18*(3), 276–291.

Sousa, C. M. P., Martínez-López, F. J., & Coelho, F. (2008). The determinants of export performance: A review of the research in the literature between 1998 and 2005. *International Journal of Management Reviews, 10*(4), 343–374.

Starbuck, W. H., & Mezias, J. M. (1996). Opening pandora's box: Studying the accuracy of managers' perceptions. *Journal of Organizational Behavior, 17*(2), 99–117.

Starbuck, W. H., & Milliken, F. J. (1988). Executives' perceptual filters: What they notice and how they make sense. In D. C. Hambrick (Ed.), *The executive effect: Concepts and methods for studying top managers* (pp. 35–65). Greenwich, CT: JAI Press.

Taras, V., Rowney, J., & Steel, P. (2009). Half a century of measuring culture: Review of approaches, challenges, and limitations based on the analysis of 121 instruments for quantifying culture. *Journal of International Management, 15*(4), 357–373.

Tsui, A. S., Nifadkar, S. S., & Ou, A. Y. (2007). Cross-national, cross-cultural organizational behavior research: Advances, gaps, and recommendations. *Journal of Management, 33*(3), 426–478.

Wagner, J. (2001). A note on the firm size–export relationship. *Small Business Economics, 17*(4), 229–237.

Wang, H., & Schaan, J. L. (2008). How much distance do we need? Revisiting the "National Cultural Distance Paradox." *Management International Review, 48*(3), 263–277.

World Bank. (2014). *World development indicators*. Retrieved from http://data.worldbank.org/indicator/NE.EXP.GNFS.ZS/countries. Accessed on May 2, 2014.

World Bank. (2016). *World development indicators*. Retrieved from http://data.worldbank.org/indicator. Accessed on March/April 2016.

Yamin, M., & Sinkovics, R. R. (2006). Online internationalisation, psychic distance reduction and the virtuality trap. *International Business Review, 15*(4), 339–360.

Zaheer, S., Schomaker, M. S., & Nachum L. (2012). Distance without direction: Restoring credibility to a much-loved construct. *Journal of International Business Studies, 43*(1), 18–27.

APPENDIX: PERCEPTUAL CONSTRUCTS, ITEMS, RELIABILITY, AND CONVERGENT VALIDITY

Constructs and Items
Perceptual cultural distance
Power distance (AVE = 0.685/α = 0.853)
Degree of inequality among the people
Salary range between the highest and lowest paid in organizations
Importance of social status symbols
Individualism/collectivism (AVE = 0.644/α = 0.833)
Importance of loyalty to family and friends
Recognition of the right to privacy
Freedom of the press
Masculinity/femininity (AVE = 0.662/α = 0.843)
Importance of caring for others
Importance of material success
Degree to which women are expected to be assertive and ambitious
Uncertainty avoidance (AVE = 0.640/α = 0.838)
Openness to change and innovation
Tolerance of differences (i.e., religious, political, and ideological)
Reliance on rules to govern behavior
Perceptual business distance
Legal and political environment
Stability of political structure
Market structure
Physical distribution systems
Economic environment (AVE = 0.723/α = 0.866)
Gross domestic product (GDP) per capita
Capacity of the banking sector
Level of demands for goods and service
Business practices (AVE = 0.715/α = 0.821)
Terms of conditions of employment
Credits and financial arrangements with banking institutions

Notes: AVE = average variance extracted (Fornell & Larcker, 1981); α = Cronbach's coefficient alpha.

CHAPTER 5

THE CONCEPT OF INSTITUTIONAL AND CULTURAL COMPATIBILITY

Tilo Halaszovich

ABSTRACT

Institutions and culture as well as their distance between home and host countries matter for international business activities. Yet, the exact nature of this influence is still not fully understood. In this chapter, we develop the concept of institutional and cultural compatibility and propose empirical measures of both to contribute to our understanding in this regard. We argue that the institutional and cultural profiles of home and host countries can create synergies that facilitate bilateral foreign direct investment (FDI) flows (that is being compatible) even if they are characterized by high distances. We apply our measures of compatibility to a sample of bilateral FDI flows between 127 host and 122 home countries over 12 years.

Keywords: International business activities; institutions; culture; FDI flows

1. INTRODUCTION

The institutions and cultures of home and host countries matter for almost every kind of international business (IB) activity. Indeed, these effects have

Distance in International Business: Concept, Cost and Value
Progress in International Business Research, Volume 12, 107–133

ISSN: 1745-8862/doi:10.1108/S1745-886220170000012014

been discussed in IB studies for many years. In essence, two different concepts have become a standard in this field of research: profiles and distance (van Hoorn & Maseland, 2016). The profile describes the institutional or cultural environment in a given country. From the profile, challenges and opportunities arise for foreign and domestic firms doing business in that country (Halaszovich & Lundan, 2016). A country's profile can be considered as its unique institutional or cultural fingerprint. The extent of dissimilarity between the profiles of two countries equals the institutional or cultural distance a firm has to overcome when doing business from one country into the other. Thereby, distance creates additional challenges in terms of transfer of knowledge or routines, lack of legitimacy, or increasing uncertainty and risk.

While the existence and relevance of profiles and distances is widely acknowledged, especially the concept of distance has been frequently criticized in the literature (see, e.g., Shenkar, 2001). Yet, this critique is mostly concerned with the methods how distances are operationalized (e.g., ignoring the directionality of distance) and not with its relevance or effect as such. Concerning the effect of distance, it is noteworthy that "over the last 40 years, the unifying conclusion is that distance matters because it is associated with substantial drawbacks" (Hutzschenreuter, Kleindienst, & Lange, 2016, p. 167). Institutions that are different from a firm's home country, therefore, are perceived as a potential challenge or even threat.

In this chapter, we argue that the strongly negative perception of institutional and cultural dissimilarities, even though deeply rooted in IB studies, might be too one sided. Termed "the illusion of discordance" by Shenkar (2001, p. 524), it is most often assumed that distance always results in a lack of fit between two countries. Which in turn will hinder business transactions between both countries. This illusion, thereby, neglects potential gains from diversity in the form of a "positive synergetic effect on investment and performance" (Shenkar, 2001, p. 524). In fact, scholars in the field of strategic alliance research frequently pointed out that inter-firm relations can strongly benefit from certain dissimilarities. Dissimilarities in some characteristics and similarities in others between partner firms have been found to be essential drivers of value creation (Sarkar, Echambadi, Cavusgil, & Aulakh, 2001). In our theoretical discussion, we will follow this notion and develop the argument that some institutional and cultural profiles might differ in a sense that help to create synergies instead of substantial drawbacks. We call this concept institutional and cultural compatibility. The concept of institutional and cultural compatibility might complement negative distance effects by providing a more holistic perspective on the nature and consequences of institutional and cultural differences in IB activities.

Empirically, we develop an approach to cluster country-specific institutional and cultural profiles in terms of common patterns in their configuration. We show that foreign direct investment (FDI) flows differ significantly between these clusters, a finding that points toward the relevance of institutional and cultural compatibility as a complement to mere distance effects.

The main contribution of this study is twofold. First, we extend the theory about the relevance of home and host country institutions and cultures with the theoretical argument we develop about the benefits of dissimilarities for FDI. The resulting concept of institutional and cultural compatibility can be used in a variety of studies focusing on cross-border investments and helps to shed more light on the effects of institutions, culture, and resulting differences. Second, we develop an empirical measurement approach of the concept of institutional and cultural compatibility that allows to group countries into clusters of common patterns for both institutions and culture. These patterns, thereby, are not related to distances but focus on structural similarities.

The rest of this chapter is organized as follows: Next, we discuss the literature on profiles and distance as well as the implications of both for FDI. Thereafter, we extend the discussion toward the importance of partner characteristics for the success of alliances. Based on these streams of literature, we developed the concept of institutional and cultural compatibility. Afterwards, we show how we measured compatibility and proceed with our empirical study. The chapter ends with a discussion of our results and a conclusion.

2. INSTITUTIONAL AND CULTURAL PROFILES AND FOREIGN DIRECT INVESTMENTS

Institutions are the fundamental rules of a society (North, 1990). They shape how individuals interact with each other, including business practices, legal systems, and communication. The institutional environment of a country is considered to differ from the institutional environments of other countries (Dunning & Lundan, 2008). Foreign and domestic firms doing business in a country are embedded in its institutional environment (Halaszovich & Lundan, 2016).

Formal institutions (hereafter institutions) are concerned with policy, judiciary, bureaucracy of the government, definition and enforcement of property rights, and contract law (Dikova, Sahib, & van Witteloostuijn, 2010; Henisz & Williamson, 1999; Khoury, Cuervo-Cazurra, & Dau, 2014). Institutions influence the economic performance of a country and have been found to have a strong impact on FDI inflows as well (Globerman & Shapiro, 2002, 2003). The institutional environment of a country can be classified according to its quality (e.g., good/well-developed vs. flawed/undeveloped). Well-developed institutions increase the likelihood of FDI inflows in a country by reducing the risk of the investment (Lu, Liu, Wright, & Filatotchev, 2014). Several scholars presented evidence for the reversed effect of flawed institutions that hinder investments by reducing the attractiveness of a country as FDI destination.

This reduction of attractiveness is caused by the increasing uncertainty that results from flawed institutions. Delios and Henisz (2003), for example, showed that the entry-mode decision of Japanese investors is influenced by political uncertainty. For US investors, Globerman and Shapiro (2003) were able to demonstrate that governance infrastructure (i.e., "attributes of legislation, regulation, and legal systems that condition freedom of transacting, security of property rights, and transparency of government and legal processes"; Globerman & Shapiro, 2003, p. 19) moderates investments. Thereby, countries which fail to provide a certain threshold level of governance infrastructure receive no FDI at all. For those countries which receive FDI, the level of governance infrastructure moderates the amount of FDI. Corruption, an often observed outcome of weakly developed institutions, also reduces the extent of FDI a country receives (Cuervo-Cazurra, 2016; Habib & Zurawicki, 2010; Lambsdorff, 2003). Political risk and weak property rights protection increase transaction costs of firms and thereby reduce the economic attractiveness of investments (Coeurderoy & Murray, 2008; Khoury, Junkunc, & Mingo, 2015).

Culture describes the systems of norms and values shared among the people in a specific environment, such as a country or region. In contrast to institutions, culture cannot be classified as well developed or flawed. There is no good or bad culture in that sense. As a consequence, the influence of the cultural profile of a country on the amount of FDI inflows is less obvious. Scholarly work on this connection is also scarce. Makino and Neupert (2000), for instance, analyzed the effect of culture on modes of ownership of FDI. But they based their argument on the culture of the investor's home country and not on the situation in the receiving country. Yet, there are at least some cultural traits that might indirectly enhance or reduce the attractiveness of a country for FDI. Political scientist used the concept of social capital (Putman, Leonardi, & Nanetti, 1993) to analyze whether some cultural environments are more prone to promote economic growth than others (Woolcock, 1998). Using trust and civic norms as indicators Knack and Keefer (1997) demonstrated that social capital is associated with economic performance. According to the authors, trust is an element of every economic transaction as these transactions are based on the reliability of future actions of others. A lack of trust therefore imposes higher transaction costs due to the need for additional protection measures. Societies with high levels of trust have no need for these additional protection measures which in turn stimulates economic activities and growth. In the same vein, civic norms impose internal and external sanctions on the misbehavior of individuals. Hence, civic norms also increase the reliability of economic transactions and allow economic growth. Scholars from the field of IB studies established a well-tested positive influence of economic size on FDI inflows (see, e.g., Zwinkels & Beugelsdijk, 2010).

Up to this point, we discussed the influence of countries' institutional and cultural profiles on FDI. Next, we will turn to the concept of distance, the costs of distance, and the implications for FDI.

3. DISTANCE, COSTS OF DISTANCE, AND FOREIGN DIRECT INVESTMENTS

The extent of dissimilarity between the institutional or cultural profiles of a firm's home and host countries equals the distance a firm has to overcome when doing business abroad (Ghemawat, 2001; van Hoorn & Maseland, 2016). It is commonly accepted that overcoming these dissimilarities involves specific costs for companies that would not occur for a strictly national business.

The larger the distance between two countries, that is, the more the institutional or cultural environments of both countries differ, the larger are the costs for a firm to overcome the distance. To this extent, the concept of institutional and cultural distance mimics geographic distance where, for example, the costs of transportation or the difficulties of communication (e.g., because of different time zones) increase with an increasing spatial distance. Many of the costs of overcoming distances are related to transaction costs (Hernández & Nieto, 2015; Hutzschenreuter et al., 2016). Institutional or cultural distance increases the costs of communication, coordination, monitoring, and integration (Tan & Mahoney, 2006). Moreover, managing a multinational enterprise (MNE) with subsidiaries in different countries increases the management complexity (Hutzschenreuter & Voll, 2008). Distances have also found to negatively impact the flow of information and, as a result, decrease the learning abilities of foreign investors (Johanson & Vahlne, 1977).

Following Szulanski (1996), distance also hinders the application of existing knowledge and the absorption of new knowledge. This includes the transferability of business practices, innovations (Dellestrand & Kappen, 2012), and technology (Cui, Griffith, Cavusgil, & Dabic, 2006) from one country into a distant country. As a consequence, distance reduces the competitive advantage of the investing firm (Madhok, 1997) and increases the risk for the firm to lose its legitimacy (Li, Vertinsky, & Li, 2014).

More general, distance imposes uncertainty (Makino & Tsang, 2011). To compensate the increased uncertainty, MNEs need to invest in additional means of control. These means combine direct costs, costs due to delays in the decision-making processes, as well as costs arising from the resulting adjustments of management practices.

Differences between the institutions of countries can be based on two different reasons: First, they can differ in their completeness and enforcement efficiency (Oxley, 1997). This kind of difference is often present if the host country is an emerging market with an imperfect legal system, a high degree of political instability, or corruption issues. To some degree, these differences can be overcome by means of additional contractual mechanisms. But even then, the lack of legal reliability is a major source of non-ergodic uncertainty (Cantwell, Dunning, & Lundan, 2010). The second reason for differences in institutional profiles stems from differing interpretations of a legal situation, resulting in different obligations for the parties involved. National accounting standards or patent laws are examples of this kind of difference. These institutional rules can differ substantially between two countries even if the institutional environments of both countries are complete and efficient. To overcome this kind of difference, firms have to undertake additional efforts to comply with the legal frameworks they are exposed to even if the differences do not necessarily create uncertainty.

Cultural distance has also been intensively analyzed in the literature (Avloniti & Filippaios, 2014; Reus & Lamont, 2009; Sarala & Vaara, 2010; Shenkar, 2001; Zaheer, Schomaker, & Nachum, 2012). Following Drogendijk and Slangen (2006), cultural distance can be defined as "the extent to which the shared norms and values in one country differ from those in another" (Drogendijk & Slangen, 2006, p. 362). Cultural distance has been shown to influence country selection, mode of entry decisions, and also the extent of FDI a country is able to attract. The incompatibility between cultures is the main reason for inter-organizational failure (Cartwright & Cooper, 1993; Sirmon & Lane, 2004). A lack of shared norms, values, and codes of conduct prevents the building of relational capital, which in turn is essential for interfirm activities (Madhok & Tallman, 1998).

It is noteworthy to point out that the vast majority of IB scholars identified only negative consequences of distance (Hutzschenreuter et al., 2016), which in turn implies that differences between the institutional or cultural environment of two countries are strictly negative for transnational business activities. Despite the empirical robustness of these findings, the concept of distance has been criticized to overlook any potential gains from differences (Shenkar, 2001). As Shenkar (2001) pointed out in his seminal publication, IB activities involve the interaction of investors with focal business partners. These interactions can take many different forms including arm's length transactions, mergers, and acquisitions or strategic alliances. The mere focus on negative consequences of differences indeed contradicts many insights gained by scholars who researched characteristics of firms involved in interactions such as strategic alliances (Abdi & Aulakh, 2012; Hitt, Dacin, Levitas, Arregle, & Borza, 2000; Madhok, 1995; Parkhe, 1991; Sarkar et al., 2001; Saxton, 1997). To shed more light on the potential benefits of dissimilarities in inter-firm interactions, we continue with a discussion of the findings from research on strategic alliances.

4. PARTNER CHARACTERISTICS AND ALLIANCE SUCCESS

This stream of research postulates that "Value creation through alliances requires the simultaneous pursuit of partners with similar characteristics on certain dimensions and different characteristics on other dimensions" (Sarkar et al., 2001, p. 358). Hence, forming a partnership with either a company that shares exactly the same characteristics or a partner without any similarities is inferior to a partnership with a firm that is somewhat different in some crucial characteristics.

This brings forward the question which firm characteristics should be more similar between transnational alliance partners than others. A common notion in the literature is that successful alliances exhibit social compatibility that facilitates the achievement of joint objectives (Aulakh, Kotabe, & Sahay, 1996; Parkhe, 1993). This requires common social institutions (Cullen, Johnson, & Sakano, 2000; Heide & John, 1992) or common patterns of interactions (Cullen et al., 2000; Madhok & Tallman, 1998). Based on these common patterns relational capital builds up among the partner firms (Madhok & Tallman, 1998). Hence, these firms need to be compatible but not similar.

Against the background of different institutional and cultural environments in IB activities, the question here is how do both dimensions affect compatibility? We will first discuss this question through the lens of inter-firm relations. Thereafter, we will develop our arguments in the broader view of FDI.

Recently, Abdi and Aulakh (2012) showed that the governance of inter-firm relationships depends on the exogenous institutional environments and the endogenous administrative mechanisms developed by the firms' involved in the exchange. Thereby, the creation of internal mechanisms is strongly influenced by the institutional background of the firms, as "interfirm relationships occur in a context of surrounding institutional frameworks that shape and govern the economic behavior" (Abdi & Aulakh, 2012, p. 477). Similar institutions thereby support the creation of efficient mechanisms while a lack of support, that is, a lack of institutional similarity, hinders this process (Cartwright & Cooper, 1993; Park & Ungson, 1997). At the same time, the lack of institutional similarity can provide access to complementary resources (Gubbi, Aulakh, Ray, Sarkar, & Chittoor, 2010; Morosini, Shane, & Singh, 1998), support rather than hinder learning and capability development (Ghoshal & Bartlett, 1990), and is even able to reduce risks (Kim, Hwang, & Burgers, 1993).

Undisputable, the institutional and cultural environment shapes firm structures, governance mechanisms, and business practices (Dunning & Lundan, 2008). Moreover, familiarity with the environment helps to decipher its codes of conduct (North, 1990). Yet, dissimilar environments are not automatically incompatible. As Shenkar (2001) pointed out, it is possible that opposite values can create synergies instead of obstacle. In reference to Hofstede's cultural dimensions, Shenkar argued that concerns for performance of a firm (high masculinity score in its home country) can be supported in host countries driven by a high level of relationship building (low masculinity score). Yet, the differences in the dimension will create a high cultural distance between both countries.

5. SIMILARITY, COMPATIBILITY, AND FDI

Up to this point, our discussion about the effects of institutional similarity and compatibility was mostly based on the micro-level perspective of inter-firm relations. Every FDI project involves some degree of connection with local entities. These connections can include local recruitment of employees or workers, sourcing contracts, sales agents, government officials, competitors, or costumers to name but a few (Halaszovich & Lundan, 2016). Thereby, every connection between the investing MNE and local entities is subject to the effects of institutional and cultural similarity and compatibility.

Based on our discussion we assume that the occurrence of FDI from one country to another is subject to the effects of institutional or cultural (dis-) similarity and (in-)compatibility between both countries. Increasing institutional or cultural dissimilarity creates uncertainty and additional costs which jointly reduce the extent of FDI between both countries. At the same time, complementary characteristics offer additional benefits to exchange processes. Hence, institutional or cultural compatibility should increase the extent of FDI between two countries. Both effects, thereby, happen simultaneously as we expect them to complement rather than substitute each other. The resulting framework is visualized in Fig. 1. Based on the discussion above, we formulate the following propositions:

P1. Institutional and/or cultural compatibility of two countries should increase the amount of FDI from one country to the other.

P2. Institutional and/or cultural distance between two countries should decrease the amount of FDI from one country to the other.

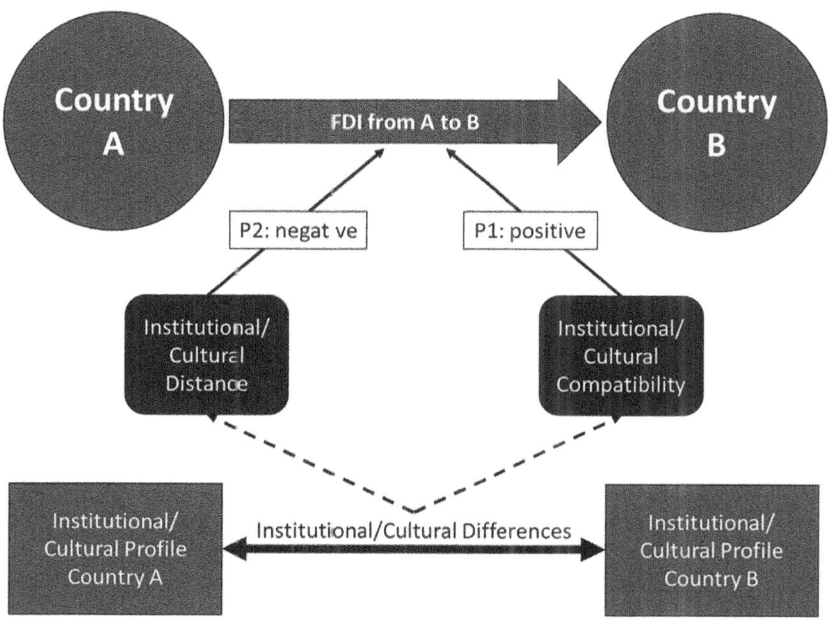

Fig. 1. Framework.

6. MEASURING SIMILARITY AND COMPATIBILITY

To analyze our propositions empirically, we compiled a data set of bilateral FDI inflows between 127 host and 122 home countries, covering the years 2001–2012. Our measures of similarity are the Kogut and Singh style measures of cultural distance (based on the six Hofstede dimensions; for those countries where Hofstede data are available) and institutional distance (based on Worldwide Governance Indicators [WGI] of Kaufmann). Institutional distance is measured on a yearly basis as the WGI index is published on a yearly basis. Cultural distance is static over the observation period.

Next, we describe how our measure of institutional and cultural compatibility is constructed. The core assumption of our compatibility concept is that compatibility as such is independent of the distance between two institutional environments. Therefore, a distance-free measure is required. Moreover, we follow Shenkar's argument (2001) that some dimensions of the institutional profiles of two countries create synergies if or even only if they differ. Yet, Shenkar's argument is only based on one dimension of Hofstede's cultural measurement. But institutions and cultures are complex and multi-dimensional. While one dissimilarity between the dimensions of two countries can create synergies, this effect might be mitigated by the configuration of the other dimensions. Hence, to measure compatibility between the institutional or cultural profiles of two countries we need a holistic representation of all dimensions involved.

To construct a measure that fulfills both requirements, we used hierarchical cluster analysis in the first step. Hierarchical cluster analysis have been used recently, for example, by Ronen and Shenkar (2013) to cluster countries by the extent of cultural similarity. In our case, clustering based on distance, the method Ronen and Shenkar used, violates the first requirement of our compatibility measure (compatibility is independent of distance). Instead, we used a cluster algorithm based on the similarity of patterns (average linkages algorithm). To illustrate the difference between both approaches, Fig. 2 shows the profiles of France, Jamaica, and Lithuania for the six WGI dimensions in the year 2012. A distance-based cluster algorithm would cluster France and Lithuania in one cluster and Jamaica in a separate one as the distance between France and Lithuania is rather small compared to Jamaica. The algorithm we used

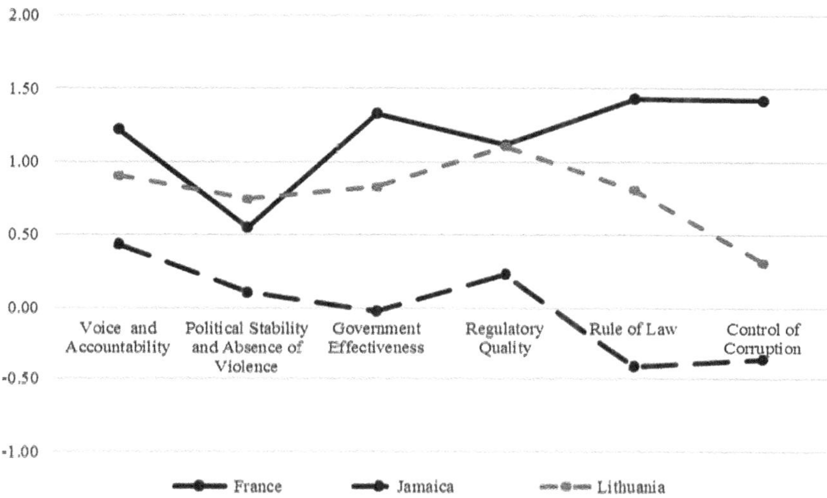

Fig. 2. WGI Profiles.

grouped Lithuania and Jamaica in one cluster, while France is grouped differently. This cluster solution is based on the similarity of the patterns Lithuania and Jamaica have in common (with the exception of "control of corruption" the profiles are almost parallel while the shape of the France profile strongly differs). We used this approach to cluster the countries in our data set based on the yearly WGI scores and separately on Hofstede's six cultural dimensions. The WGI cluster assignment of a country can vary over time depending on the yearly scores, a dynamic we observed several times in our results.

After removing outliers in a first step, our final cluster approach resulted in five clusters for the WGI scores and also five clusters for the Hofstede dimensions. To determine the optimal number of clusters we used the elbow criterion. Up to this point, each cluster contains countries that share similar profiles but differ in their scores. To compare the clusters more easily, we standardized the values of the individual scores (i.e., the six WGI dimensions and the six cultural dimensions) within each cluster so that the lowest value in each cluster equals zero and the highest value equals one. By doing so, we are able to compare the underlying patterns represented by the different clusters.

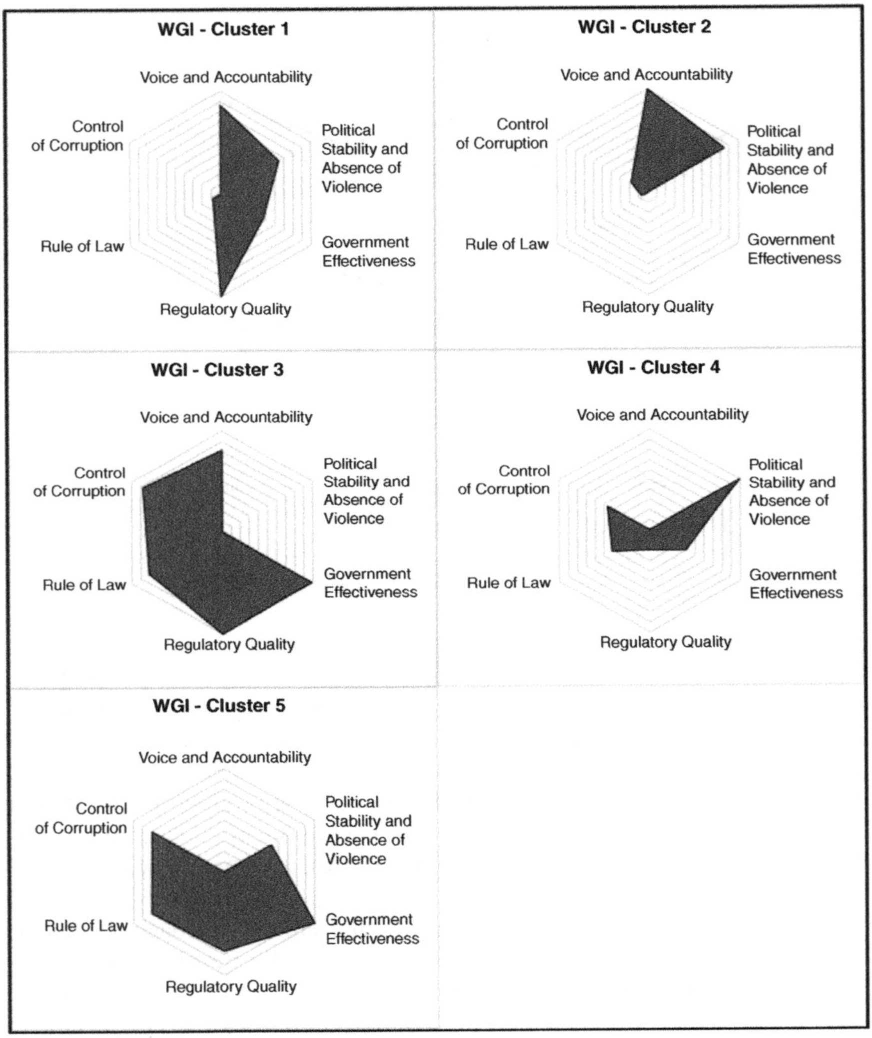

Fig. 3. Standardized Clusters – Institutions.

Figs. 3 and 4 show the spider graphs of the institutional clusters and cultural clusters, respectively. In Table 1, descriptive statistics about the clusters are presented. To save space, we do not report the dendrograms of our clustering procedure here.

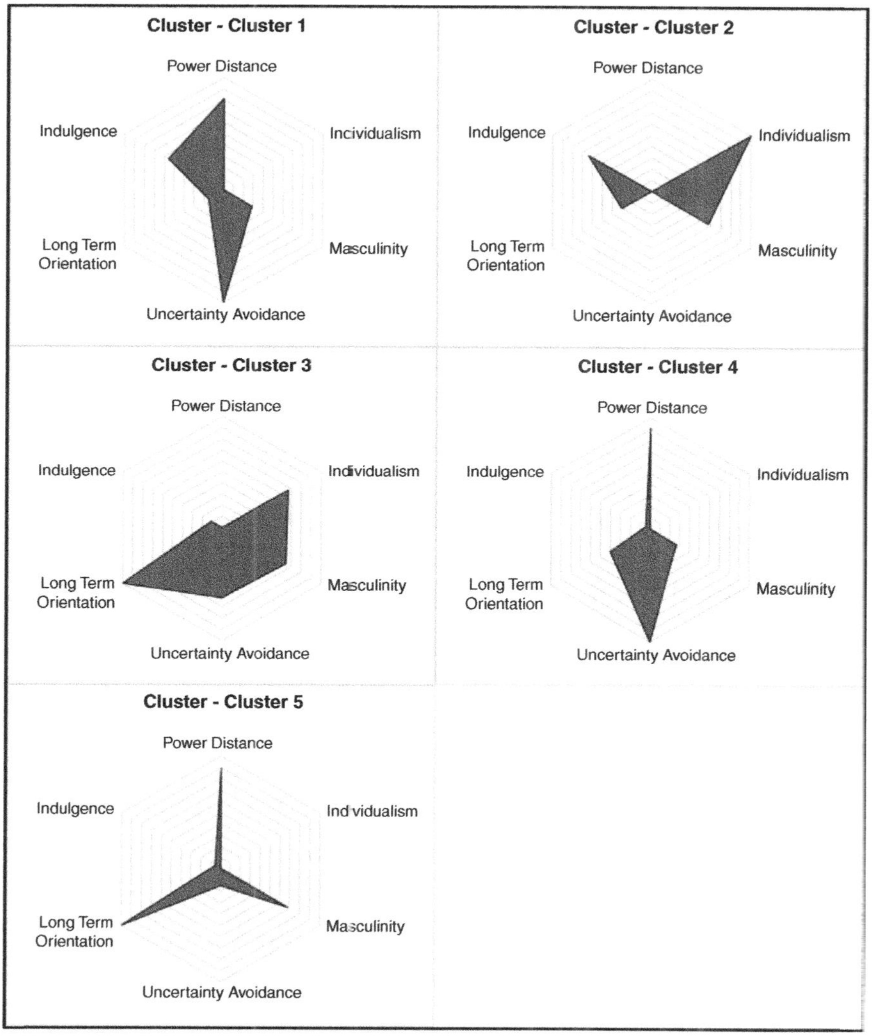

Fig. 4. Standardized Clusters – Culture.

In the final step of our procedure, we used gravity model regressions to estimate the influence of cluster memberships on FDI flows (Zwinkels & Beugelsdijk, 2010). Therefore, we used yearly bilateral log FDI inflows in constant US-$ as dependent measure.

Table 1. Mean Values and *N* per Cluster.

WGI – Cluster (2012)					
	1	2	3	4	5
N	27	20	58	13	10
Voice and Accountability (*Inst1*)	−0.03	−0.01	0.26	−1.18	−0.56
Pol. Stab./Abs. of Viol. (*Inst2*)	−0.07	0.04	−0.42	−0.06	−0.19
Government Effectiveness (*Inst3*)	−0.21	−0.49	0.37	−0.82	0.41
Regulatory Quality (*Inst4*)	0.09	−0.53	0.41	−1.03	0.27
Rule of Law (*Inst5*)	−0.40	−0.49	0.28	−0.81	0.24
Control of Corruption (*Inst6*)	−0.48	−0.41	0.27	−0.66	0.18
Cultural–Cluster					
N	25	11	7	15	7
Power Distance (*Cult1*)	68	32	39	65	78
Individualism (*Cult2*)	32	78	65	41	28
Masculinity (*Cult3*)	48	40	74	40	59
Uncertainty Avoidance (*Cult4*)	76	43	73	78	34
Long-Term Orientation (*Cult5*)	29	38	70	70	67
Indulgence (*Cult6*)	57	68	47	26	31

If some cluster pairs of institutions or cultures are compatible, we expect that this will create synergies which in turn will result in increased FDI inflows. It is also possible that certain cluster combinations are incompatible which should lead to reduced FDI inflows. To operationalize these effects, we used dummy measures indicating every possible cluster combination. For both institutional and cultural clusters 25 combinations are present. This procedure also accounts for the directionality of FDI flows, since we allow, for example, the effect from cluster 1 to cluster 2 to differ from the effect of cluster 2 to cluster 1. Moreover, we excluded all observations between countries within the same cluster (e.g., cluster 1 to cluster 1) as we are interested in the compatibility between clusters. Finally, we included 20 dummy variables (*CCI1–CCI20* for institutional cluster pairs and *CCC1–CCC20* for cultural cluster pairs). Table 2 shows all possible cluster combinations in our study.

Table 2. Cluster Combinations of Formal and Informal Institutional Clusters.

s	Cluster 1	Cluster 2	Cluster 3	Cluster 4	Cluster 5
Cluster 1		*CC1*: C2 → C1	*CC2*: C3 → C1	*CC3*: C4 → C1	*CC4*: C5 → C1
Cluster 2	*CC5:* C1 → C2		*CC6*: C3 → C2	*CC7*: C4 → C2	*CC8*: C5 → C2
Cluster 3	*CC9*: C1 → C3	*CC10*: C2 → C3		*CC11*: C4 → C3	*CC12*: C5 → C3
Cluster 4	*CC13*: C1 → C4	*CC14*: C2 → C4	*CC15*: C3 → C4		*CC16*: C5 → C4
Cluster 5	*CC17*: C1 → C5	*CC18*: C2 → C5	*CC19*: C3 → C5	*CC20*: C4 → C5	

Besides the cluster information, we also included bilateral Kogut and Singh style measures of cultural distance *CultDis* (based on the six Hofstede dimensions) and institutional distance *InstDist* (based on the six WGI dimensions). We also included the six Hofstede (*Cult1–Cult6*) and the six WGI dimensions (*Inst1–Inst6*) as measures of the profiles of the host countries.

In addition to these measures of main interest for our study, we also included a set of control variables, commonly used in gravity FDI models (see, e.g., Zwinkels & Beugelsdijk, 2010). First, we included whether country pairs were part of the same free trade agreement (FTA) in a specific year. Given that our sample includes countries from all over the world, we included information for a wide variety of FTAs (namely *CAN*, *AFTA*, *APTA*, *CARICOM*, *CACM*, *CEFTA*, *CEZ*, *COMESA*, *CIS*, *CAFTA*, *EAC*, *EC27*, *CEMAC*, *ECOWAS*, *ECO*, *EFTA*, *EAEC*, *GCC*, *LAIA*, *MERCOSUR*, *MSG*, *NAFTA*, *PICTA*, *PAFTA*, *PTN*, *SAFTA*, *SPARTECA*, *SACU*, *SADC*, *TPSEP*, and *WAEMU*) as dummy measures. Next, we controlled whether the host country is landlocked (*Landlocked*) or an island (*Island*) and if home and host countries share a common language (*ComLang*). We also included the log of the population size (*lnPop*) and the log of the GDP per capita in constant US-$ (*lnGDPPC*). Finally, we controlled for log geographic distance (*lnGeoDist*). Table 3 provides an overview of the different measures, their sources, and descriptive statistics.

7. RESULTS AND DISCUSSION

In Tables 4 and 5 the results of our gravity models are provided. For all models we used random effects GLS regressions with robust standard errors.

Table 3. Summary Measures.

Measure	Source	Static or Dynamic	Mean	Standard Deviation
LnFDIinflows	UNCTAD	Dynamic	3.28	2.44
CultDist	Hofstede	Static	1.97	1.09
InstDist	Kaufmann (WGI)	Dynamic	3.12	1.78
LnGeoDist	CEPII	Static	8.28	1.01
lnPop	World Bank	Dynamic	16.55	1.72
lnGDPPC	World Bank	Dynamic	9.49	1.06
Cult1	Hofstede	Static	57.841	20.583
Cult2	Hofstede	Static	49.359	23.749
Cult3	Hofstede	Static	49.088	20.165
Cult4	Hofstede	Static	70.865	20.768
Cult5	Hofstede	Static	53.130	22.975
Cult6	Hofstede	Static	44.774	21.798
Inst1	Kaufmann (WGI)	Dynamic	0.399	0.913
Inst2	Kaufmann (WGI)	Dynamic	0.091	0.921
Inst3	Kaufmann (WGI)	Dynamic	0.468	0.978
Inst4	Kaufmann (WGI)	Dynamic	0.475	0.921
Inst5	Kaufmann (WGI)	Dynamic	0.324	1.018
Inst6	Kaufmann (WGI)	Dynamic	0.317	1.073
Landlocked	CIA	Static	Dummy	Dummy
Island	CIA	Static	Dummy	Dummy
ComLang	CIA	Static	Dummy	Dummy
FTAs	WTO	Dynamic	Dummy	Dummy
CCI1–CCI20	Own Calculation	Dynamic	Dummy	Dummy
CCC1–CCC20	Own Calculation	Static	Dummy	Dummy

Model 1 contains only our control measures. In Model 2 we added *CCI1–CCI20*. Model 3 contains *CCC1–CCC20*. To save some space, we do not report the results of *Cult1–Cult6* and *Inst1–Inst6* here.

The results of model 1 (see Table 4) confirm that all control measures work as expected. All three distance measures included (*lnGeo*, *CultDist*, and *InstDist*) have negative signs and are significant. This is in line with our theoretical discussion and prior findings in the literature (see, e.g., Hutzschenreuter et al., 2016). Also, common languages among home and host countries increase FDI inflows (*ComLang*). Population size and economic performance of the host country exert a positive influence as well (*lnPop* and *lnGDPPC*). The last two host country characteristics, *Landlocked* and *Island*, are significant and negative.

In Table 5, the results of our models concerning institutional and cultural compatibility and distance are summarized. Model 2 extends the base model with the institutional cluster pairs (*CCI1–CCI20*). Out of the 20 cluster-pairs

Table 4. Results Control Measures.

Model 1		Model 1 c'ndt	
Coefficient (Std. Error)		Coefficient (Std. Error)	
Constant	−23.370 ***	*Island*	−1.237 ***
	(2.497)		(0.333)
FTA	0.524 *	*Landlocked*	−0.502 *
	(0.278)		(0.281)
lnPop	0.559 ***	*lnGeo*	−0.542 ***
	(0.072)		(0.120)
lnGDPPC	2.281 ***	*CultDist*	−0.369 ***
	(0.145)		(0.099)
ComLang	0.717 *	*FormDist*	−0.118 **
	(0.387)		(0.059)
N	3,100		
R^2	0.132		
Wald Chi^2	360.53		

Notes: ***$p < 0.01$; **$p < 0.05$; *$p < 0.1$.

in model 2, 10 combinations are significant. Yet, 9 of the 10 significant combinations show a negative sign. This result implies that 50 percent of the institutional cluster combinations indeed influence FDI flows in addition to institutional distance or the profile of the host country. At the same time, most of these effects are negative. Hence, our institutional clusters are rather incompatible than compatible. The one exception is *CCI6,* where investments from cluster 3 into cluster 2 seem to benefit from the compatibility. The other way around cluster 2 to cluster 3 (*CCI10*), we find a significant and negative result. This finding shows the importance of directionality. While institutional compatibility allows countries from clusters 3 to invest in countries from cluster 2 more easily, countries from cluster 2 are hindered by the incompatibility to invest in cluster 3.

In Fig. 5 we summarized the findings about the compatibility of the institutional clusters from model 2. From the figure, some additional patterns can be observed easier. WGI cluster 3 is a particularly difficult host cluster. All other clusters struggle to invest in WGI cluster 3. The situation is almost the same for WGI cluster 5. But both clusters a rather neutral home clusters, that is, both have mostly insignificant outgoing coefficients. WGI cluster 2 is a neutral to positive home cluster and a more negative host cluster. WGI cluster 4 works the other way around and is a neutral host and negative home cluster. WGI cluster 1 is negative to neutral in both ways. These classifications are summarized in Table 6.

Table 5. Results Institutional and Cultural Compatibility and Distance.

Model 2			Model 3		
Coefficient (SE)			Coefficient (SE)		
Constant	−16.802	***	Constant	−26.795	***
	(0.702)			(2.796)	
FTAs	0.552	***	FTA	−0.279	
	(0.109)			(0.309)	
lnPop	0.408	***	*lnPop*	0.542	***
	(0.025)			(0.099)	
lnGDPPC	1.578	***	*lnGDPPC*	3.268	***
	(0.049)			(0.182)	
ComLang	0.656	***	*ComLang*	0.819	*
	(0.126)			(0.495)	
Island	0.162		*Island*	−0.252	
	(0.119)			(0.46)	
Landlocked	0.387	***	*Landlocked*	0.414	
	(0.095)			(0.42)	
lnGeo	−0.213	***	*lnGeo*	−0.77	***
	(0.044)			(0.147)	
InstDist	−0.113	***	*InstDist*	−0.118	*
	(0.021)			(0.063)	
CCI1	−0.59	***	*CultDist*	−0.091	
	(0.181)			(0.106)	
CCI2	0.032		*CCC1*	2.387	***
	(0.059)			(0.504)	
CCI3	−0.481	*	*CCC2*	1.446	***
	(0.249)			(0.546)	
CCI4	−0.193		*CCC3*	1.51	***
	(0.132)			(0.515)	
CCI5	0.001		*CCC4*	−0.918	*
	(0.143)			(0.514)	
CCI6	0.649	***	*CCC5*	−2.831	***
	(0.086)			(0.596)	
CCI7	0.366		*CCC6*	−1.21	*
	(0.261)			(0.706)	
CCI8	0.127		*CCC7*	−0.907	
	(0.184)			(0.708)	
CCI9	−0.605	***	*CCC8*	−0.816	
	(0.084)			(0.858)	
CCI10	−0.61	***	*CCC9*	−1.926	***
	(0.123)			(0.449)	
CCI11	−0.847	***	*CCC10*	0.938	
	(0.172)			(0.698)	
CCI12	−0.156	*	*CCC11*	−0.323	
	(0.082)			(0.694)	

CCI13	−0.358 (0.536)	*CCC12*	−1.829 *** (0.475)
CCI14	−1.033 (0.915)	*CCC13*	−0.709 (0.432)
CCI15	0.153 (0.146)	*CCC14*	2.189 *** (0.588)
CCI16	−0.028 (0.272)	*CCC15*	1.136 ** (0.499)
CCI17	−0.771 *** (0.241)	*CCC16*	−0.809 (0.496)
CCI18	−0.125 (0.415)	*CCC17*	2.072 *** (0.716)
CCI19	−0.356 *** (0.09)	*CCC18*	3.844 ** (1.525)
CCI20	−0.771 ** (0.384)	*CCC19*	2.73 *** (0.678)
		CCC20	3.222 *** (1.172)
N	19,060	*N*	2,606
R^2	0.180	R^2	0.336

Notes: ***$p < 0.01$; **$p < 0.05$; *$p < 0.1$.

Table 6. Classification of Institutional Clusters.

WGI Cluster	As Host	As Home
1	Neutral/negative	Neutral/negative
2	Neutral/positive	Negative/neutral
3	Negative	Neutral/positive
4	Neutral	Negative
5	Negative	Neutral/positive

Combining the information on cluster compatibility and the patterns of the clusters, some careful inference of the effect of the individual WGI dimensions can be made. Low levels of "Control of Corruption," "Rule of Law," and "Government Effectiveness" seem to facilitate FDI inflows. High levels of "Regulatory Quality," on the other hand, seems to hinder FDI inflows. "Voice and Accountability" and "Political Stability and Absence of Violence" do not show any observable effects on FDI flows.

Model 3 in Table 5 shows the results of our model for culture. Out of the 20 cultural cluster pairs included in model 3, 14 are significant. Nine out of these have a positive sign and five a negative sign. Hence, the empirical results tend to support our first proposition for cultural in-/compatibility as well.

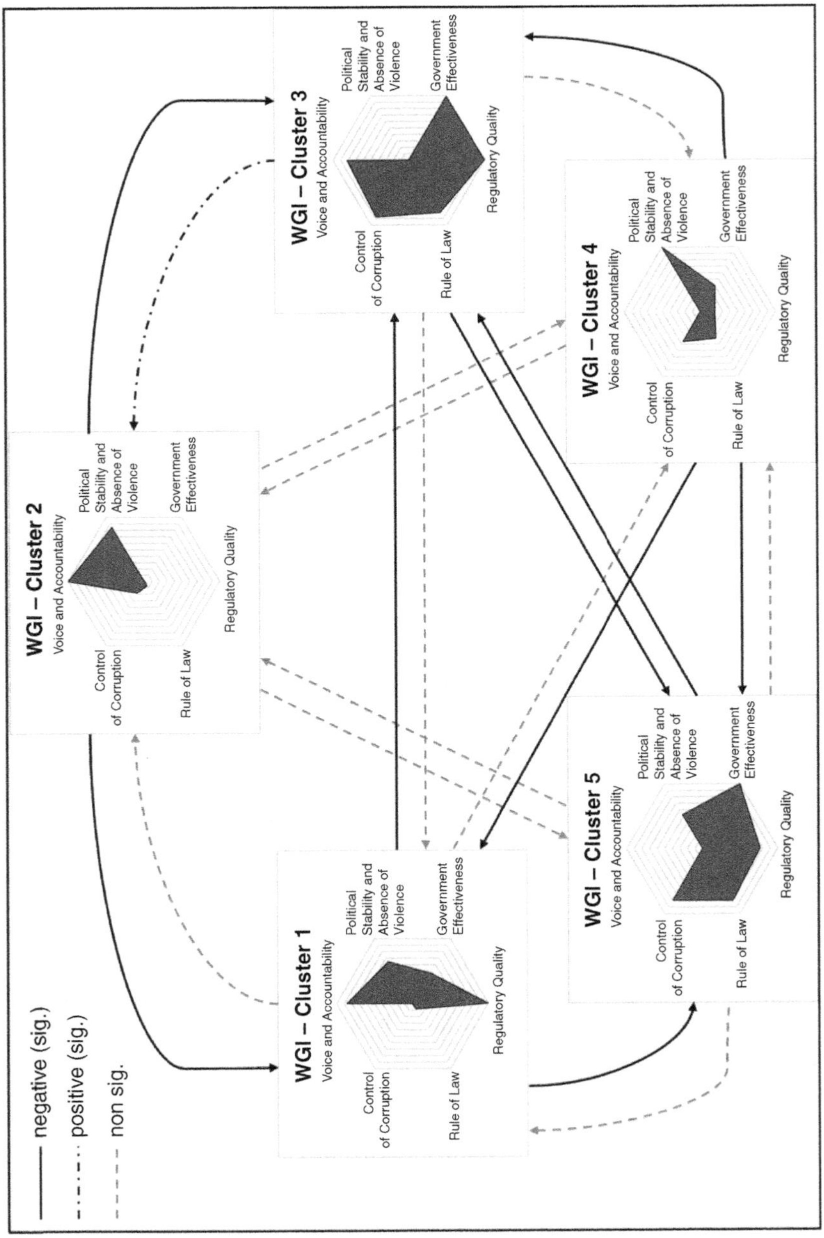

Fig. 5. Compatibility of Institutional Clusters.

Table 7. Classification of Cultural Clusters.

Cult. Cluster	As Host	As Home
1	Positive	Negative
2	Negative/neutral	Positive
3	Negative/neutral	Positive
4	Positive/neutral	Positive/neutral
5	Positive	Negative/neutral

We summarized the findings about the compatibility of the cultural clusters from model 3 in Fig. 6. From the results, we can describe the host and home characteristics of the clusters individually. Cluster 1 is a mostly compatible host cluster and a mostly incompatible home cluster. The only exceptions from this pattern are the exchanges with cluster 5. Here, signs are reversed. This highlights the importance of directionality again. While most FDI inflows are supported by cluster 1's compatibility, most FDI outflows are hindered by a lack of compatibility in that direction. Cluster 2 can be characterized as negative to neutral host cluster but is a highly compatible home cluster. The same classification holds for cluster 3. Interestingly, cluster 3 and cluster 2 are not compatible in terms of FDI outflows. Cluster 4 is positive to neutral as home and host cluster. Cluster 5 is somewhat opposite to cluster 2 and cluster 3. This cluster is compatible with all other clusters as a host but with none of the others as home (two significant and negative coefficients and two insignificant coefficients). It is noteworthy that both significant and negative combinations with cluster 5 as host cluster are related to clusters where "Uncertainty Avoidance" is high. The classifications are summarized in Table 7.

We can also carefully interfere from Fig. 6 about which of Hofstede's cultural dimensions might facilitate or hinder FDI flows. Cluster 2 and cluster 3 are particularly compatible home clusters and incompatible host clusters. Both are characterized by rather high levels of "Individualism" and "Masculinity." High levels of these dimensions seem to promote compatibility with FDI destinations and "Individualism" tends to hinder FDI inflows. High levels of "Power Distance," as observed in clusters 1, 4, and 5, seem to characterize compatible hosts that facilitate FDI inflows.

8. CONCLUSION AND LIMITATIONS

The importance of institutional and cultural distances is well established in the field of IB. But even after decades of research, the exact nature of the

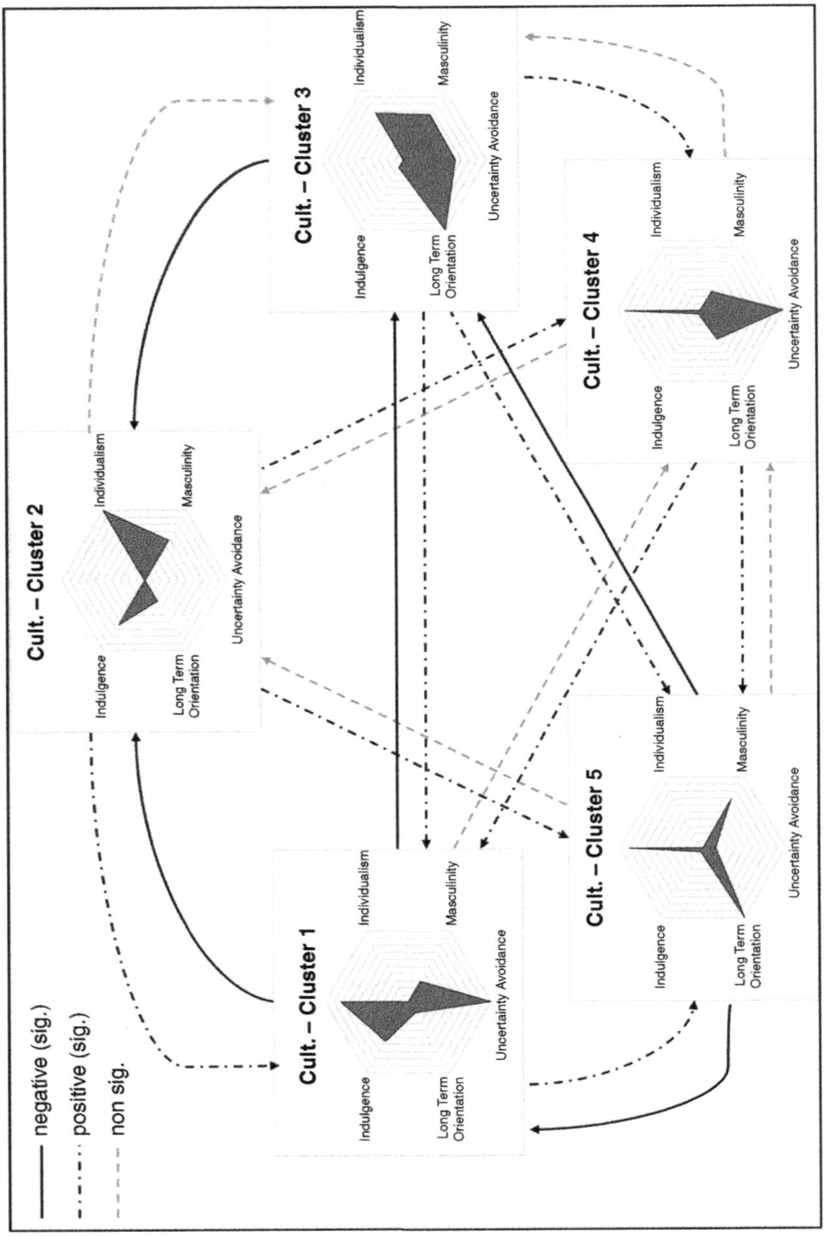

Fig. 6. Compatibility of Cultural Clusters.

influence is still not fully understood. This study aims to extend the understanding of institutional and cultural influences on FDI by proposing the concept of institutional and cultural compatibility. We define compatibility as the synergies created by compatible institutional and cultural patterns of the countries involved in FDI flows (i.e., the home and host country of an investment). Furthermore, we proposed a methodological approach to operationalize institutional and cultural compatibility based on similarities rather than distances. Based on these new measures, we were able to estimate whether institutional and cultural patterns are compatible or not.

In our large-scaled sample of bilateral FDI flows between 127 host and 122 home countries from 2001 to 2012, we found that the majority of institutional and cultural pattern combinations are either compatible or incompatible. That is, some profile combinations facilitate investments while others hinder investments. Our findings thereby demonstrate that the interaction between the institutional environments of countries involved in FDI matters and that the complexity of these interactions exceeds the scope of a mere focus on dissimilarities as measured by distance. Based on our argument we are able to show that certain dissimilarities indeed support investments while others hinder them.

Another interesting finding yields from the differentiation between institutional and cultural compatibility. According to our results, institutional patterns of home and host countries more often tend to be incompatible rather than compatible. Indicating that differences in institutional systems erect barriers that are not easy to overcome even if firms can adjust to institutional environments by additional means of control. For cultural patterns, we find a surprisingly high amount of compatibility between the different clusters. This result supports the notion of Shenkar (2001), who argued that opposing values of, for instance, the masculinity dimension of Hofstede's cultural measurement can support firms doing business together. Finally, our empirical results also demonstrate the importance of directionality. In many of the bilateral cases where we found compatibility from clusters A to B, we found incompatibility from clusters B to A.

From a managerial perspective, our results offer another tool to judge the obstacles involved in a new investment decision as well as to optimize the configuration of the firms' global value chains. The in-/compatibility between two countries or more precisely between the clusters those countries belong to can be used as in indication whether additional means of control or adjustments are necessary. Even though our results only indicate a tendency rather than a concrete measure, this information might proof valuable when location decisions between different potential host countries have to be made. The implications for optimizing the value chain configuration can affect different managerial fields. The human resource management can use information about the compatibility of cultural profiles to optimize global staffing decisions. Moreover, resource allocations can be aligned toward the most promising, that is compatible, location.

As with every empirical work, our study suffers from several limitations. Most important is the limited scope of the measures we employed. Especially Hofstede's cultural measures are criticized in the literature for different reasons. To overcome this limitation, additional robustness checks with different measures (e.g., Globe or the World Value Survey) can be implemented. Based on the variety of measures available, another limitation can be overcome. In the current state, we cannot deduct the reasons why some clusters are compatible or incompatible. With the results from different measures, we might be able to triangulate the findings and clearly identify the causes of compatibility and incompatibility.

REFERENCES

Abdi, M., & Aulakh, P. S. (2012). Do country-level institutional frameworks and interfirm governance arrangements substitute or complement in international business relationships? *Journal of International Business Studies*, *43*(5), 477–497.

Aulakh, P. S., Kotabe, M., & Sahay, A. (1996). Trust and performance in cross-border marketing partnerships: A behavioral approach. *Journal of International Business Studies*, *27*(4), 1005–1032.

Avloniti, A., & Filippaios, F. (2014). Unbundling the differences between psychic and cultural distance: An empirical examination of the existing measures. *International Business Review*, *23*(3), 660–674.

Cantwell, J., Dunning, J. H., & Lundan, S. M. (2010). An evolutionary approach to understanding international business activity: The co-evolution of MNEs and the institutional environment. *Journal of International Business Studies*, *41*(4), 567–586.

Cartwright, S., & Cooper, C. L. (1993). The role of culture compatibility in successful organizational marriage. *Academy of Management Perspectives*, *7*(2), 57–70.

Coeurderoy, R., & Murray, G. (2008). Regulatory environments and the location decision: Evidence from the early foreign market entries of new-technology-based firms. *Journal of International Business Studies*, *39*(4), 670–687.

Cuervo-Cazurra, A. (2016). Corruption in international business. *Journal of World Business*, *51*(1), 35–49.

Cui, A. S., Griffith, D. A., Cavusgil, S. T., & Dabic, M. (2006). The influence of market and cultural environmental factors on technology transfer between foreign MNCs and local subsidiaries: A Croatian illustration. *Journal of World Business*, *41*(2), 100–111.

Cullen, J. B., Johnson, J. L., & Sakano, T. (2000). Sucess through commitment and turst: The soft side of strategic alliance management. *Journal of World Business*, *35*(3), 223–240.

Delios, A., & Henisz, W. J. (2003). Policy uncertainty and the sequence of entry by Japanese firms, 1980–1998. *Journal of International Business Studies*, *34*(3), 227–241.

Dellestrand, H., & Kappen, P. (2012). The effects of spatial and contextual factors on headquarters resource allocation to MNE subsidiaries. *Journal of International Business Studies*, *43*(3), 219–243.

Dikova, D., Sahib, P. R., & van Witteloostuijn, A. (2010). Cross-border acquisition abandonment and completion: The effect of institutional differences and organizational learning in the international business service industry, 1981–2001. *Journal of International Business Studies*, *41*(2), 223–245.

Drogendijk, R., & Slangen, A. (2006). Hofstede, Schwartz, or managerial perceptions? The effects of different cultural distance measures on establishment mode choices by multinational enterprises. *International Business Review*, *15*(4), 361–380.

Dunning, J. H., & Lundan, S. M. (2008). *Multinational enterprises and the global economy. International business* (Vol. 2, 2nd ed.,). Edward Elgar: Cheltenham.

Ghemawat, P. (2001). Distance still matters. *Harvard Business Review*, *79*, 137–147.

Ghoshal, S., & Bartlett, C. A. (1990). The multinational corporation as an interorganizational network. *Academy of Management Review*, *15*(4), 603–626.

Globerman, S., & Shapiro, D. (2002). Global foreign direct investment flows: The role of governance infrastructure. *World Development*, *30*(11), 1899–1919.

Globerman, S., & Shapiro, D. (2003). Governance infrastructure and US foreign direct investment. *Journal of International Business Studies*, *34*(1), 19–39.

Gubbi, S. R., Aulakh, P. S., Ray, S., Sarkar, M. B., & Chittoor, R. (2010). Do international acquisitions by emerging-economy firms create shareholder value? The case of Indian firms. *Journal of International Business Studies*, *41*(3), 397–418.

Habib, M., & Zurawicki, L. (2010). Corruption and foreign direct investment. *Journal of International Business Studies*, *33*(2), 291–307.

Halaszovich, T. F., & Lundan, S. M. (2016). The moderating role of local embeddedness on the performance of foreign and domestic firms in emerging markets. *International Business Review*, *25*(5), 1136–1148.

Heide, J. B., & John, G. (1992). Do norms matter in marketing relationships? *Journal of Marketing*, *56*(2), 32–44.

Henisz, W., & Williamson, O. E. (1999). Comparative economic organization: Within and between countries. *Business and Politics*, *1*(1), 261–278.

Hernández, V., & Nieto, M. J. (2015). The effect of the magnitude and direction of institutional distance on the choice of international entry modes. *Journal of World Business*, *50*(1), 122–132.

Hitt, M. a., Dacin, M. T., Levitas, E., Arregle, J. L., & Borza, A. (2000). Partner selection in a merging and developed market context: Resource-based and organizational learning perspectives. *Academy of Management Journal*, *43*(3), 449–467.

Hutzschenreuter, T., Kleindienst, I., & Lange, S. (2016). The concept of distance in international business research: A review and research agenda. *International Journal of Management Reviews*, 18(2), 160–179.

Hutzschenreuter, T., & Voll, J. C. (2008). Performance effects of "added cultural distance" in the path of international expansion: The case of German multinational enterprises. *Journal of International Business Studies*, *39*, 53–70.

Johanson, J., & Vahlne, J. (1977). The internationalization process of the firm-a model of knowledge development and increasing foreign market commitments. *Journal of International Business Studies*, *8*(1), 23–32.

Khoury, T. A., Cuervo-Cazurra, A., & Dau, L. A. (2014). Institutional outsiders and insiders: The response of foreign and domestic inventors to the quality of intellectual property rights protection. *Global Strategy Journal*, *4*(3), 200–220.

Khoury, T. A., Junkunc, M., & Mingo, S. (2015). Navigating political hazard risks and legal system quality: Venture capital investments in Latin America. *Journal of Management*, *41*(3), 808–840.

Kim, W. C., Hwang, P., & Burgers, W. P. (1993). Multinationals' diversification and the risk-return trade-off. *Strategic Management Journal*, *14*(4), 275–286.

Knack, S., & Keefer, P. (1997). Does social capital have an economic payoff? *Quarterly Journal of Economics*, *112*(4), 1251–1288.

Lambsdorff, J. G. (2003). How corruption affects persistent capital flow. *Economics of Governance*, *4*, 229–243.

Li, Y., Vertinsky, I. B., & Li, J. (2014). National distances, international experience, and venture capital investment performance. *Journal of Business Venturing*, *29*(4), 471–489.

Lu, J., Liu, X., Wright, M., & Filatotchev, I. (2014). International experience and FDI location choices of Chinese firms: The moderating effects of home country government support and host country institutions. *Journal of International Business Studies*, *45*(4), 428–449.

Madhok, A. (1995). Revisiting multinational firms' tolerance for joint ventures: A trust-based approach. *Journal of International Business Studies*, *26*(1), 117–137.

Madhok, A. (1997). Cost, value and foreign market entry mode: The transaction and the firm. *Strategic Management Journal*, *18*(1), 39–61.

Madhok, A., & Tallman, S. B. (1998). Resources, transactions and rents: Managing value through interfirm collaborative relationships. *Organization Science*, *9*(3), 326–339.

Makino, S., & Neupert, K. E. (2000). National culture, transaction costs, and the choice between joint venture and wholly owned subsidiary. *Journal of International Business Studies*, *31*(4), 705–713.

Makino, S., & Tsang, E. W. K. (2011). Historical ties and foreign direct investment: An exploratory study. *Journal of International Business Studies*, *42*(4), 545–557.

Morosini, P., Shane, S., & Singh, H. (1998). National cultural acquisition distance and cross-border performance. *Journal of International Business Studies*, *29*(1), 137–158.

North, D. C. (1990). *Institutions, institutional change and economic performance*. Cambridge: Cambridge University Press.

Oxley, J. E. (1997). Appropriability hazards and governance in strategic alliances : A transaction cost approach. *Journal of Law, Economics, and Organization*, *13*(2), 387–409.

Park, S. H., & Ungson, G. R. (1997). The effect of national culture, organizational complementarity, and economic motivation on joint venture dissolution. *The Academy of Management Journal*, *40*(2), 279–307.

Parkhe, A. (1991). Interfirm diversity, organizational learning, and longevity in global strategic alliances. *Journal of International Business Studies*, *22*(4), 579–601.

Parkhe, A. (1993). Strategic alliance structuring : A game theoretic and transaction cost examination of interfirm cooperation. *Academy of Management Journal*, *36*(4), 794–829.

Putman, R. D., Leonardi, R., & Nanetti, R. Y. (1993). *Making democracy work: Civic traditions in modern Italy*. Princeton, NJ: Princeton University Press.

Reus, T. H., & Lamont, B. T. (2009). The double-edged sword of cultural distance in international acquisitions. *Journal of International Business Studies*, *40*(8), 1298–1316.

Ronen, S., & Shenkar, O. (2013). Mapping world cultures: Cluster formation, sources and implications. *Journal of International Business Studies*, *44*(9), 867–897.

Sarala, R. M., & Vaara, E. (2010). Cultural differences, convergence, and crossvergence as explanations of knowledge transfer in international acquisitions. *Journal of International Business Studies*, *41*(8), 1365–1390.

Sarkar, M., Echambadi, R., Cavusgil, S. T., & Aulakh, P. S. (2001). The influence of complementarity, compatibility, and relationship capital on alliance performance. *Journal of the Academy of Marketing Science*, *29*(4), 358–373.

Saxton, T. (1997). The effects of partner and relationship characteristics on alliance outcomes. *Academy of Management Journal*, *40*(2), 443–461.

Shenkar, O. (2001). Cultural distance revisited: Towards a more rigorous conceptualization and measurement of cultural differences. *Journal of International Business Studies*, *32*(3), 519–535.

Sirmon, D. G., & Lane, P. J. (2004). A model of cultural differences and international alliance performance. *Journal of International Business Studies*, *35*(4), 306–319.

Szulanski, G. (1996). Internal exploring stickiness : Impediments to the transfer of best practice within the firm. *Strategic Management Journal*, *17*, 27–43.

Tan, D., & Mahoney, J. T. (2006). Why a multinational firm chooses expatriates: Integrating resource-based, agency and transaction costs perspectives. *Journal of Management Studies*, *43*(3), 457–484.

van Hoorn, A., & Maseland, R. (2016). How institutions matter for international business: Institutional distance effects vs institutional profile effects. *Journal of International Business Studies*, *47*(3), 374–381.

Woolcock, M. (1998). Social capital and economic development: Toward a theoretical synthesis and policy framework. *Theory and Society*, *27*(2), 151–208.

Zaheer, S., Schomaker, M. S., & Nachum, L. (2012). Distance without direction: Restoring credibility to a much-loved construct. *Journal of International Business Studies*, *43*(1), 18–27.

Zwinkels, R. C. J., & Beugelsdijk, S. (2010). Gravity equations: Workhorse or Trojan horse in explaining trade and FDI patterns across time and space? *International Business Review*, *19*(1), 102–115.

CHAPTER 6

THE DIRECTION OF REGULATORY INSTITUTIONAL DISTANCE AND MNE's SUBSIDIARY OWNERSHIP STRATEGY: RE-EXAMINING THEORY AND EVIDENCE IN THE CASE OF EMERGING MARKETS

Palitha Konara and Vikrant Shirodkar

ABSTRACT

The possibility of institutional distance exerting an asymmetric effect on the entry strategies of multinational enterprises (MNEs) has attracted recent scholarly attention. In this context, we re-examine the relationship described by Hernandez and Nieto (2015) on the effect of the direction of regulatory institutional distance on MNEs' choice of entry mode in host countries. We extend this research by (1) focussing on the context of emerging markets and (2) accounting for a greater variety of MNEs as well as institutions by including both large and small firms, and a larger set of home and host countries. In contrast to Hernandez and Nieto's study, we find that, in the context of emerging markets, institutionally distant MNEs are more likely to choose the full-ownership mode when they originate from

Distance in International Business: Concept, Cost and Value
Progress in International Business Research, Volume 12, 135–154

ISSN: 1745-8862/doi:10.1108/S1745-886220170000012009

an institutionally stronger country in comparison to the host (emerging) country, and they are more likely to choose the joint-ownership mode when they originate from an institutionally weaker country. We discuss our findings with respect to Hernandez and Nieto's study, which explores this relationship more generally (i.e. beyond emerging-market contexts), however in the context of small and medium enterprises.

Keywords: Institutional distance; institutional theory; entry-mode choice; emerging markets

1. INTRODUCTION

The effect of institutional distance on multinational enterprises' (MNEs') entry-mode choice in host countries has been a matter of debate and discussion in several prior studies in international business (Brouthers, 2002; Chao & Kumar, 2010; Eden & Miller, 2004; Gaur & Lu, 2007; Hernández & Nieto, 2015; Hotho, 2009; Ionascu, Meyer, & Estrin, 2004; Phillips, Tracey, & Karra, 2009; Schwens, Eiche, & Kabst, 2011; Van Hoorn & Maseland, 2016; Xu & Shenkar, 2002). The external institutional context of firms comprises regulatory agencies, community groups, socio-cultural norms, supplier and customer characteristics, labour unions, trade associations and competitors, which collectively define the 'rules of the game' and exert pressures on firms to conform to these rules (DiMaggio & Powell, 1983; North, 1990). *Regulatory* institutional distance, in particular, refers to cross-country differences in laws, regulations and political configurations between MNEs' home and host countries (Dikova & Van Witteloostuijn, 2007; Eden & Miller, 2004; Kostova & Roth, 2002; Kostova, Roth, & Dacin, 2008; Shirodkar & Konara, 2016). Such regulative differences present important sources of opportunity as well as risk for MNEs, and therefore form important aspects of their strategic decision-making when entering foreign markets (Berry, Guillen, & Zhou, 2010; Ghemawat, 2001; O'Grady & Lane, 1996).

In this context, recently, research has progressed on the *asymmetry* associated with regulatory institutional distance and its effects on the entry-mode choice in host countries. Hernandez and Nieto (2015) argue that, with increased levels of 'negative regulative distance', defined as when the regulatory development in the host country is lower than that in the MNEs' home country, MNEs would be more likely to choose entry modes characterised by lower levels of resource commitment, for example, by choosing to enter via joint ventures versus wholly owned subsidiaries. In contrast, in the opposite direction, that is, with increased levels of 'positive regulative distance', defined as when the regulatory development in the host country is greater than that in the MNEs' home country, MNEs would be more likely to choose entry modes characterised by higher levels of resource commitment. Hernandez and Nieto (2015) argue that lower levels of regulatory development in host countries increase the perception of risk among MNEs' managers vis-à-vis their needs to exert higher levels of control over host operations, and this results in the likelihood of lower commitment entry modes. On the contrary, when host regulatory institutions are stronger relative to home institutions, the perceived benefits of control exceed transaction cost risks thus enabling MNEs to choose higher commitment modes.

We argue that, *first*, emerging markets provide unique and important contexts to re-examine this relationship. Emerging markets, due to their large resource bases, large populations and high economic growth levels are considered as important destinations of foreign direct investment (FDI) for MNEs from both strongly and weakly institutionalised home countries (UNCTAD, 2015). At the same time, the quality of formal (or regulatory) institutions, as described above, is relatively weaker in emerging markets than in developed countries (Ionascu, et al., 2004; Khanna & Palepu, 2000a; Meyer, Estrin, Bhaumik, & Peng, 2009; Meyer & Nguyen, 2005), leading to perceptions of greater risk and uncertainty among MNEs from developed countries investing in these markets. Yet, over the past decade, several emerging markets (as compared to other developing countries) have made significant progress in regulatory development, such as by improving their regulatory infrastructure, cutting down bureaucratic procedures, improving intellectual property regimes, controlling corruption and improving transparency in business–government interactions (Hoskisson, Wright, Filatotchev, & Peng, 2013). At the same time, MNEs 'from' emerging economies are increasingly investing in both developed and other emerging and developing host countries – with varied institutional contexts (UNCTAD, 2015). Due to these recent developments occurring in emerging markets, we suggest that re-examining the effect of the direction of institutional distance and MNEs' choice of entry mode may provide us with new and valuable insights.

Second, we argue that current research on the link between the direction of institutional distance and MNEs' entry-mode choice is still in its infancy and suffers from methodological limitations. For instance, Hernandez and Nieto's (2015) study on this relationship was limited to the internationalisation of small and medium enterprises (SMEs) among European countries. Since SMEs have fewer resources than large MNEs, their perception of risk arising from weaker host institutions relative to their home would be substantially greater than the risk perceived by large MNEs with greater resources. Therefore, we suggest that extending this research to include both large and small firms would add rigour to current findings. Additionally, Hernandez and Nieto's (2015) study mainly focuses on European Union countries, where the single market agreement potentially reduces the effect of regulative institutional differences between countries. Due to this, and in response to recent calls for including a diverse group of countries in institutional distance research (Van Hoorn & Maseland, 2016), our study aims to re-evaluate the existing findings on the direction of regulative distance–entry mode relationship by including a wider array of home and host countries.

Reflecting the above limitations, our study aims to address the research question – *To what extent does the direction of regulative institutional distance affect entry-mode choice by MNEs in the context of emerging markets?* We believe that by testing our hypotheses on the link between the direction and magnitude of regulatory distance and entry-mode strategy in the context of emerging markets, we make the following contributions. First, we partially replicate Hernandez and Nieto's (2015) model on this link and contribute to a greater generalisation of the link by using observations of subsidiaries of MNEs from 88 home countries operating in 19 emerging market host countries. In this process, we follow the guidelines of a 'good enough' replication (Singh, Ang, & Leong, 2003), that is, we employ constructs that are similar to those employed in Hernandez and Nieto's (2015), although some of our measurements may differ. Second, by focussing on emerging markets, we contribute to existing studies that have previously examined the (symmetric) effect of institutional distance and institutional voids on MNEs' strategic decisions in emerging markets – for example, overall role of psychic distance (Dikova, 2009), business group affiliation (Chacar & Vissa, 2005; Khanna & Rivkin, 2001), managerial ties and connections (Sheng, Zhou, & Li, 2011), embeddedness (Sun, Mellahi, & Thun, 2010), localisation strategies (London & Hart, 2004) and parent–subsidiary integration (Luo, 2003).

In the following sections, we formulate our hypotheses, describe our data and present our findings from the 19 emerging markets. Finally, we discuss our results in relation to Hernandez and Nieto's (2015) findings in addition to other relevant research, and we conclude our chapter by highlighting our contributions and limitations and suggesting important avenues for future research.

2. THEORY AND HYPOTHESES

2.1. Institutions, Institutional Distance and MNEs' Entry-Mode Choice

The choice of entry mode (particularly, full versus partial ownership) in a host country has been regarded as one of the most important decisions surrounding MNEs. Internalisation theory (Williamson, 1985) suggests that the choice of entry mode is based on the relative benefits of exercising greater control over host-country operations versus the risks involved. Greater control modes, achieved through a greater level of equity in a foreign subsidiary, allow the parent to better integrate the subsidiary with the global strategic objectives of the MNE, by transferring people, skills and management practices from headquarters and making subsidiaries comply with headquarters' directives (Kobrin, 1988; Mjoen & Tallman, 1997). Greater control modes can also enable the subsidiary to make strategic decisions more efficiently and avoid potential conflicts with partners, as experienced in lower control and contractual modes (Anderson & Gatignon, 1986). However, on the contrary, lower control modes (such as in the case of international joint ventures) have been argued to be superior if they allow the MNE to benefit from host-location advantages (such as low-cost labour or high growth markets) while taking fewer risks at the same time. In this context, first, the *quality* of host institutions plays an important role (Peng, 2003; Peng, Li, Pinkham, & Chen, 2009). Stronger host institutions, as seen in countries with greater levels of political stability, absence of violence, effective rule of law and control of corruption, reduce contractual costs and risks for foreign MNEs, whereas weaker regulatory institutions increase information asymmetries and external uncertainties – thus increasing overall risk (Meyer, et al., 2009). Second, cross-country *differences* in regulatory institutions also increase 'liabilities of foreignness' to MNEs (Shirodkar & Konara, 2016; Zaheer, 1995). MNEs from institutionally distant home countries (as compared to those from institutionally similar countries) face greater challenges of 'institutional duality' – that is, they experience greater pressures to understand and adapt to the local legitimacy needs of host countries vis-à-vis transferring well-established organisational practices and capabilities developed within their home countries (Kostova & Roth, 2002; Kostova, et al., 2008). Joint ventures, as a mode of entry, provide essential local resources – such as intellectual and managerial knowledge embedded in local firms, and networks and connections that may help counteract the idiosyncrasies of weak and distant host-regulatory contexts (Delios & Beamish, 2001, 2004; Delios & Henisz, 2003). Finally, although acquisitions, as an entry mode, have been argued as effective mechanisms to acquire local intangible resources, while keeping high levels of control at the same time, weak institutions increase information asymmetries and due-diligence costs in finding acquisition targets, making acquisitions riskier (Lin, Peng, Yang, & Sun, 2009). Also, greater institutional differences increase post-merger/acquisition integration costs, thus making acquisitions less cost-effective at greater institutional distances in comparison to joint ventures (Barkema & Vermeulen, 1998).

2.2. The Direction of Institutional Distance, and the Case of Emerging Markets

Scholars have only recently started to examine the issue of asymmetry in the direction of institutional distance and the likely effects that this may have on the strategies of MNEs. The argument on this is that the relative benefits versus risks associated with higher control (or commitment) modes while operating in distant environments may vary depending on the direction of distance. In Hernandez and Nieto's (2015) typology, 'negative regulative distance' is defined as the type of distance that MNEs face when they operate in a host country that has weaker regulatory institutions than its home country. Similarly 'positive regulative distance' is experienced by MNEs that belong to home countries characterised by a weaker regulative environment than the host country. Hernandez and Nieto (2015) argue that with increased negative regulatory distance, the risks of adopting high control modes are greater than the relative benefits, thus causing MNEs to choose low-commitment modes (e.g. JVs). On the contrary, in the opposite direction, when MNEs experience greater positive regulatory distance, they perceive lesser risks relative to benefits of greater control, increasing the likelihood of using high commitment modes (e.g. wholly owned subsidiaries).

We suggest that, subsidiaries located in the context of 'emerging markets' present a special case to re-examine this logic. This is because institutions in emerging markets are characterised by change, reform and transition, and the quality of institutional development (e.g. in terms of political stability, regulatory quality, government effectiveness, rule of law and control of corruption) in emerging economies lies between that observed in institutionally well developed and that in countries with extremely low levels of formal institutional development (Kaufmann, Kraay, & Zoido-Lobatón, 1999). Despite the heterogeneity across various emerging markets, formal institutions in emerging markets remain weak; yet several emerging markets have made significant developments in formal institutions (Hoskisson et al., 2013). Many emerging markets such as China and India have relaxed regulations on full ownership by foreign MNEs, except in a few sectors (Luo, 2007b). At the same time, local resource bases in emerging markets are larger and more context specific (Meyer et al., 2009; Meyer & Nguyen, 2005). Such context-specific resources could be tangible (e.g. land, low-cost labour) or intangible (e.g. managerial knowhow, networks, etc.). Therefore, within emerging markets, lower control modes (e.g. JV) are suggested to be likely choices only when local regulatory institutions are very weak, and there is greater dependence on local resources (both tangible and intangible) at the same time (Meyer et al., 2009). On the contrary, when regulatory institutions within emerging markets are relatively strong, and the local resources needed by the MNE are tangible, there is lesser risk relative to perceived benefits, and greenfield ventures are suggested as likely entry-mode choices. Finally, when emerging market institutions are strong and local resources needed by the MNE are intangible, acquisitions are recommended (Meyer et al., 2009). Although the above logic takes into account the characteristics of weak and strong institutions with regard to the choice of entry modes in emerging markets, it does not fully address the role of distance, and particularly the issue of asymmetry in institutional distance.

2.3. Negative Regulatory Institutional Distance and Entry-Mode Choice in Emerging Markets

In the case of negative regulative distance, MNEs from stronger institutional countries invest in countries with weaker regulative institutions (Hernández & Nieto, 2015). It is widely suggested that MNEs from stronger institutional settings have greater firm-specific advantages (e.g. technological assets and managerial capabilities) relative to local firms in emerging markets. Therefore MNEs' investments in this direction are mainly related to 'exploiting the differences' (Ghemawat, 2001) associated with their sophisticated resources, products or management capabilities developed within their strongly institutionalised home countries and seeking either high-growth markets or low-cost labour in emerging economies (Dunning, 1988; Rugman, 2010). In this context, by using sole-venture modes, that is, by controlling operations tightly, MNEs can exploit these advantages better by reducing spill-overs to local firms. However, firms from institutionally developed contexts depend on reliable information (e.g. regarding market research, coping with emergencies etc.), and such information may not be reliably available in emerging markets due to institutional voids (Chacar & Vissa, 2005; Zhang & Whitley, 2013). Furthermore, particularly in emerging markets, important local resources such as natural resources, markets and licences may be preferentially accessible to state-owned companies or influential business groups due to their greater embeddedness in socio-political networks – and this may put foreign MNEs at a disadvantage (Jakobsen & Torp, 2001; Khanna & Palepu, 2000a, 2000b). Due to these reasons, Hernandez and Nieto (2015) suggest that (albeit, not limited to emerging markets) when MNEs invest in weaker distant institutional countries, they perceive greater risks relative to the potential benefits of exploiting their home advantages derived from stronger institutions. MNEs that are new to weak and distant regulatory environments may fail to understand the adaptation aspects needed to achieve greater legitimacy in such markets. This has been argued to provide support for the notion that the choice of entering via joint venture (vis-à-vis via full ownership) would be more likely.

Alternatively, it has also been argued that although weak regulatory institutions in emerging markets increase risks for MNEs from strongly institutional countries, they do not necessarily justify the choice of lower control modes. Greater external uncertainties experienced due to weak institutions often make the writing and enforcement of contracts (such as in the case of partnership projects) more expensive and inefficient, and under these conditions, sole-venture modes (i.e. greenfield ventures) have been argued to be better than partnership-based modes (Agarwal & Ramaswami, 1992). In line with this, Gaur and Lu (2007) argue that with greater regulative distance in this direction, MNEs face increased 'relational hazards', which include the cost of monitoring, settling disputes and opportunistic behaviour by potential partners to expropriate foreign MNEs' technological assets (Luo, 2006, 2007a). Therefore, with greater distance in this direction, a larger degree of control over subsidiary operations enables MNEs to safeguard against relational hazards and opportunistic behaviour of partners.

Therefore, based on the above alternative arguments, we develop the following opposing hypotheses:

H1a. *Ceteris paribus*, with greater negative regulatory distance, MNEs will be less likely to choose wholly owned subsidiaries in emerging markets.

H1b. *Ceteris paribus*, with greater negative regulatory distance, MNEs will be more likely to choose wholly owned subsidiaries in emerging markets.

2.4. Positive Regulatory Institutional Distance and Entry-Mode Choice in Emerging Markets

In the case of positive regulative distance, MNEs from weaker institutional countries invest in countries with stronger regulatory institutions (Hernández

& Nieto, 2015). Hernandez and Nieto (2015) point out that, in this direction, as firms are entering host environments that are institutionally stronger than their home environments, they perceive lesser risks, and can therefore perceive greater benefits of control by using higher commitment modes (e.g. via full ownership).

We expect that this effect would be different in our context – that is, for the case of subsidiaries of MNEs within emerging markets whose parents are based in countries with further weaker regulatory institutions. MNEs from very weakly institutionalised countries would have very low levels of firm-specific advantages (as derived from their weak home institutions). However, MNEs from such countries are habituated to working in partnership (or cooperation) with the government, other regulatory agencies, business groups or non-governmental organisations that offer greater support in the light of weak formal home institutions. In this process, such MNEs develop natural capabilities in monitoring opportunistic behaviour by partners and dealing with 'relational hazards' while operating in their home countries. Such firms could therefore better exploit their capabilities of working in partnership, while 'escaping' to emerging markets with relatively stronger institutions (Stoian & Mohr, 2016) and catching up with progressive multinationals (Cui, Fan, Liu, & Li, 2016) Therefore, MNEs from distant weaker home institutions are less likely to perceive greater benefits from full ownership (related to the need to control host operations) vis-à-vis the higher costs and risks of full ownership while investing in emerging markets. On the contrary, they could better arbitrage from their natural advantages of operating in partnership while servicing emerging markets. In line with this argument, we suggest that:

> **H2.** *Ceteris paribus*, with greater positive regulatory distance, MNEs will be less likely to choose wholly owned subsidiaries in emerging markets.

3. METHODOLOGY

3.1. Data Collection

We compiled the information of foreign owned firms in year 2011 in 19 emerging markets[1] – Brazil, Chile, China, Columbia, the Czech Republic, Egypt, Hungary, India, Indonesia, Malaysia, Mexico, Morocco, Peru, the Philippines, Poland, Russia, South Africa, Taiwan and Turkey from Bureau van Dijk's ORBIS database. Our final sample consists of 17,457 foreign-owned subsidiaries. Table 1 provides a full list of host and home countries represented by this data set.

Table 1. List of Countries Used in the Study.

Host Countries (19)	Home Countries (88)	
Brazil	Afghanistan	Lebanon
Chile	Algeria	Lithuania
China	Argentina	Luxembourg
Colombia	Australia	Malaysia
Czech Republic	Austria	Malta
Egypt	Bahrain	Mexico
Hungary	Belgium	Nepal
India	Brazil	Netherlands
Indonesia	Bulgaria	New Zealand
Malaysia	Canada	Nigeria
Mexico	Chile	Norway
Morocco	China	Pakistan
Peru	Colombia	Panama
Philippines	Costa Rica	Peru
Poland	Croatia	Philippines
Russian Federation	Czech Republic	Poland
South Africa	Denmark	Portugal
Taiwan	Egypt, Arab Rep.	Qatar
Turkey	El Salvador	Romania
	Estonia	Russian Federation
	Ethiopia	Samoa
	Fiji	Saudi Arabia
	Finland	Serbia
	France	Singapore
	Germany	Slovak Republic
	Greece	Slovenia
	Guatemala	South Africa
	Hong Kong	Spain
	Hungary	Sri Lanka
	Iceland	Sweden
	India	Switzerland
	Indonesia	Syrian Arab Republic
	Iran	Thailand
	Iraq	Turkey
	Ireland	Uganda
	Israel	Ukraine
	Italy	United Arab Emirates
	Japan	United Kingdom
	Jordan	United States
	Kazakhstan	Uruguay
	North Korea	Uzbekistan
	South Korea	Venezuela
	Kuwait	Vietnam
	Latvia	Zimbabwe

3.2. Measures

We measure *subsidiary ownership strategy* (which is our dependent variable) using a dummy variable (WOS) that takes the value of 1 if the subsidiary is wholly owned (i.e. 100% ownership) and 0 if the subsidiary is partially owned with at least a 10% stake.

Our key explanatory variable is the *regulatory institutional distance* between the host country of the subsidiary firm and the home country of the parent firm. We operationalise *regulatory* institutional distance using Kaufmann's Worldwide Governance Indicators, which have been most popularly used in the emerging markets' context (Dikova, 2009; Kolstad & Wiig, 2012). For each country, six dimensions of governance, that is, Voice and Accountability (VA), Political Stability and Absence of Violence (PS), Government Effectiveness (GE), Regulatory Quality (RQ), Rule of Law (RL) and Control of Corruption (CC), are reported in the Worldwide Governance Indicators. Based on these six governance indicators, we constructed a composite variable for each country by carrying out factor analysis. Then we calculated the institutional distance by subtracting the home-country institutional profile score from the host-country institutional profile score; therefore, a negative score represents negative institutional distance and a positive score represents positive institutional distance[2]. We then split the institutional distance (IDIST) measure into the positive ($IDIST_p$) and negative ($IDIST_n$) components as follows:

$$IDIST_p = |IDIST| \text{ if } IDIST > 0$$

$$IDIST_p = 0 \text{ otherwise}$$

$$IDIST_n = |IDIST| \text{ if } IDIST < 0$$

$$IDIST_n = 0 \text{ otherwise}$$

In contrast to Hernandez and Nieto's (2015) approach of interacting the *magnitude of the distance* with the *direction of the distance*, our approach (deconstruction into positive and negative variables) allows us to accurately disentangle the two effects of negative distance ($IDIST < 0$) and positive distance ($IDIST > 0$) compared to the effect of 0 institutional distance ($IDIST = 0$).

Guided by previous literature and empirical evidence, we include several control variables. To control for the effect of informal institutional (cultural) distance between the host and the home country, we include two measures, i.e., the language distance (LDIST) and the religious distance (RDIST) between the host country and the home country. At the subsidiary level, first we include the firm's size and age. We include the number of patents registered under the subsidiary to proxy the technology intensity. We also include a dummy variable to capture whether the subsidiary is a publicly listed firm or not.

In addition to the firm-level determinants, various factors in the host country can influence entry-mode choice. Therefore, we also control for the host country's GDP per capita and the level of human capital. Finally, we control for the geographical distance between the host and the home countries. Table 2 provides a list of all our variables and measures.

4. RESULTS

We use a binary logistic regression model to estimate the odds of choosing the full-ownership mode relative to choosing the joint-ownership mode.

Table 2. Variable Description, Measurement and Sources.

Variable	Description/Measurement	Data Source
WOS	A binary variable which takes the value of 1 if the firm is a wholly owned subsidiary and 0 if the firm is partially owned with at least a 10% stake.	Bureau van Dijk's ORBIS database
$IDIST_n$	Negative institutional distance	Worldwide Governance Indicators
$IDIST_p$	Positive institutional distance	
SIZE	Log (1+ total assets)	Bureau van Dijk's ORBIS database
AGE	Log (1+ Firm age)	
PATENTS	Number of patents	
PUBLIC	A binary variable that takes the value of 1 if the firm is a public firm and 0 otherwise.	
GDPPC	GDP per capita of the host country	World Development Indicators
HC	Human capital of the host country proxied by secondary education enrolment rate	Global Competitiveness Index
LDIST	Five-point scale based on the incidence (p) of the home country's dominant language(s) in the host country. $5 = p < 1\%$; $4 = 1\% \leq p < 5\%$; $3 = 5\% \leq p < 50\%$; $2 = 50\% \leq p < 90\%$; $1 = p \geq 90\%$	Dow and Karunaratna (2004)
RDIST	Five-point scale based on the incidence (p) of the home country's dominant religion(s) in the host country $5 = p < 1\%$; $4 = 1\% \leq p < 5\%$; $3 = 5\% \leq p < 50\%$; $2 = 50\% \leq p < 90\%$; $1 = p > 90\%$	
GDIST	Geographical distance between the home and the host countries	Rose and Spiegel (2011)

Descriptive statistics and correlations are presented in Table 3. Table 4 reports the results of the estimated binary logistic regression model. To help interpret our results better, we report odds ratios instead of the estimated coefficients[3].

In column 1, we report the results when the direction of institutional distance is not taken into account. The odd ratio of IDIST (absolute value of institutional distance) is smaller than 1 (and significant) indicating that with larger institutional distance, MNEs are less likely to opt for full-ownership mode. However, when we include the two directional variables, we can clearly see two distinctive effects from the positive and negative institutional distances. In column 2, both $IDIST_n$ and $IDIST_p$ are significant. The odd ratio of $IDIST_n$ is larger than 1 indicating that institutionally distant MNEs are more likely to choose the full-ownership mode when they originate from an institutionally stronger country in comparison to the host (emerging) country. Therefore, our hypothesis **H1a** is not supported, and hypothesis **H1b** is supported. The odd ratio of $IDIST_p$ is smaller than 1 indicating that institutionally distant MNEs are less likely to choose the full-ownership mode when they originate from an institutionally weaker country in comparison to the host (emerging) country. Therefore, our hypothesis **H2** is supported. Our sample includes all foreign subsidiaries in 2011, irrespective of when they entered these emerging markets. In order to avoid any bias introduced by older subsidiaries, we limited our sample to subsidiaries that were established during the most recent 10 years (i.e. during 2002–2011) and re-estimated the results as a robustness test. All the results remained intact. We further reduced the sample to subsidiaries that were established during the most recent 5 years (i.e. during 2007–2011), and again all our results remained intact.

In terms of control variables, AGE is significant with an odd ratio smaller than 1 indicating that MNEs are more likely to opt for full-ownership mode with newer subsidiaries. This is in line with the studies that have found that MNEs use higher commitment entry modes when they have more experience in markets similar to the host country (Brouthers, 2013; Clarke, Tamaschke, & Liesch, 2013). PUBLIC is significant with an odd ratio smaller than 1 indicating that MNEs are less likely to opt for full-ownership mode when the subsidiary is a publicly listed firm. This is expected given that publicly owned firms are usually owned by more than one shareholder. GDPPC is significant with an odd ratio larger than 1 indicating that MNEs are more likely to opt for full-ownership mode when the GDP per capita in the host country is higher. HC is significant with an odd ratio smaller than 1 indicating that MNEs are less likely to opt for full-ownership mode when the host country has better human capital. GDIST is significant with an odd ratio smaller than 1 indicating that MNEs are less likely to opt for full-ownership mode when

Table 3. Descriptive Statistics and Correlation Matrix.

Variable	Mean	Std. Dev.	Min	Max	Correlation Coefficients										
					1	2	3	4	5	6	7	8	9	10	11
1 WOS	0.66	0.47	0	1											
2 $IDIST_n$	0.4	0.73	0	2.54	0.01										
3 $IDIST_p$	0.99	1.31	0	5.25	−0.05	−0.41									
4 SIZE	1.25	1.57	0	11.03	−0.07	0.27	−0.38								
5 AGE	2	0.8	0	5.31	−0.07	0.05	−0.3	0.36							
6 PATENTS	0.51	26.61	0	2,798	−0.01	0.02	−0.01	0.06	0.03						
7 PUBLIC	0.09	0.28	0	1	−0.11	0.08	−0.15	0.32	0.17	0.02					
8 GDPPC	10,931.53	3,944.17	1,085.73	14,402.01	0.08	−0.71	0.53	−0.46	−0.17	−0.03	−0.24				
9 HC	92.24	7.97	55.85	100.79	0.03	−0.62	0.26	−0.25	−0.01	−0.04	−0.2	0.69			
10 LDIST	4.88	0.45	1	5	0.05	−0.01	0.14	−0.14	−0.12	−0.03	−0.15	0.25	0.08		
11 RDIST	2.73	0.86	1	5	−0.01	−0.13	0.21	0	−0.06	0.02	0	0.11	−0.38	0.19	
12 GDIST	2,042.06	1,944.48	117.31	12,003.92	−0.1	0.4	0.02	0.18	−0.02	0.01	0.16	−0.44	−0.34	−0.02	0.03

Table 4. Estimated Results.

	(1)	(2)
IDIST	0.862***	
	(0.0138)	
$IDIST_n$		1.349***
		(0.0511)
$IDIST_p$		0.809***
		(0.0135)
SIZE	1.021	1.005
	(0.0139)	(0.0138)
AGE	0.842***	0.833***
	(0.0197)	(0.0197)
PATENTS	1.000	1.000
	(0.000583)	(0.000588)
PUBLIC	0.517***	0.581***
	(0.0314)	(0.0359)
GDPPC	1.000***	1.000***
	(8.62e-06)	(9.16e-06)
HC	0.970***	0.989***
	(0.00372)	(0.00402)
LDIST	1.148***	1.008
	(0.0437)	(0.0395)
RDIST	0.866***	0.980
	(0.0218)	(0.0265)
GDIST	1.000***	1.000***
	(1.01e-05)	(1.01e-05)
Constant	26.52***	3.738***
	(10.71)	(1.597)
Observations	17,457	17,457
Pseudo R^2	0.0303	0.0385
chi^2	690.3***	863.6***

Notes: Robust standard errors in parentheses ***$p < 0.01$, **$p < 0.05$, *$p < 0.1$

the geographical distance between the host country and the home country is larger. Other control variables are insignificant. Therefore, control variables have performed modestly well.

5. DISCUSSION AND CONCLUSION

Our study was inspired by the increasing importance of *asymmetry* in regulative institutional distance. Although the role of asymmetry in institutional distance has been gaining momentum, to the best of our knowledge, only one study has previously examined this issue with regard to the entry mode choice (i.e. Hernandez and Nieto, 2015). At the same time, the increasing development of regulatory institutions in emerging markets and continuing investments from both developed and developing countries into these markets demand a more fine-grained analysis of this issue in the context of emerging markets. We therefore make an important contribution by examining how the direction of institutional distance poses distinct opportunities and challenges with regard to the relative risks versus benefits of investing through higher (vs. lower) levels of equity in subsidiaries in emerging markets.

In relation to the effect of increased 'negative institutional distance', that is, when MNEs from stronger institutional countries invest in emerging markets, we presented two alternative arguments (leading to opposite hypotheses) on how this is likely to affect the choice of full versus partial ownership by examining the relative costs versus benefits in each case. Contrary to Hernandez and Nieto (2015), our findings show that, when MNEs investing in emerging markets are from relatively stronger regulatory institutional home countries, greater distance in this direction increases the likelihood of choosing full-ownership modes (in line with our hypotheses **H1b**). This is in line with our argument that, although emerging markets present risks associated with institutional voids to developed-country-based MNEs, MNEs are more likely to deal with these voids via greater ownership of the subsidiary. This is to mainly benefit from the greater need to control their operations and capitalising from arbitrage-related opportunities (such as innovative products, managerial practices, etc.) versus the increasing additional costs and risks associated with 'relational hazards' of monitoring opportunism by local partners in emerging markets (Gaur & Lu, 2007; Luo, 2006, 2007a).

In relation to the effect of increased 'positive institutional distance', we argued that with increased distance in this direction, firms investing in emerging markets are less likely to choose full-ownership modes. Our results support our hypothesis **H2** in this regard. Our argument and findings on this are both contrary to Hernandez and Nieto (2015) who argue that with greater distance in the upward direction, firms would perceive lesser risks and would be more likely to adopt higher commitment modes. We suggest that, with greater positive distance, firms from relatively weaker regulatory environments may not perceive greater benefits of exercising greater control through higher commitment modes and can better arbitrage on their capabilities of operating with partners developed within their home countries.

Our contributions are manifold. First, we contribute to the on-going discussion about the effect of the direction of institutional distance on the entry-mode choice of MNEs by focusing on MNEs subsidiaries within emerging markets – which are important destinations of FDI. Second, we also extend this research by using a more robust methodology – that is in our sample, we use firms of varying sizes and from a greater variety of home and host countries. We thus contribute to the on-going discussion and debate in international business surrounding the link between institutional distance and entry-mode choice (Brouthers, 2002; Hernández & Nieto, 2015; Kogut & Singh, 1988; Schwens, et al., 2011; Tihanyi, Griffith, & Russell, 2005) by not only accounting for the asymmetry in distance but also by providing a robust and fine-grained analysis that undermines some of the findings in prior studies on this important issue.

Our key limitation was our inability to account for complex effects – such as the moderating effects of 'experience' in reducing the effects of the direction of regulatory distance on the choice of entry mode over time. Scholars have also emphasised that experiential learning is an important part of developing unique resources and capabilities while operating in new environments (Delios & Beamish, 2001; Delios & Henisz, 2003). Recent studies show that MNEs that have experience in markets similar to the host country face lesser negative effects or risks of regulatory institutional distance and can therefore use higher commitment entry modes (Brouthers, 2013; Clarke, et al., 2013). However, due to our data limitations, we are unable to examine these effects. Future research could include this moderating effect. Finally, our data are limited to examining the ownership strategy of MNEs at one particular time – that is, in 2011, not at the point of entry into these emerging markets. Therefore, there might have been changes in the ownership levels since their initial entry. Despite these limitations, we believe that we make worthwhile contributions to research in the area of institutional distance and MNEs' entry-mode choice, which remains a topic of much progress, yet on-going discussion and debate within international business.

NOTES

1. These countries were selected based on the classification of emerging markets by four sources – FTSE, Goldman Sachs, Grant Thornton and the International Monetary Fund – and data availability.
2. We stick with Hernandez and Nieto's (2015) terminology of positive and negative distance so that we can easily compare/contrast our findings with the findings of their study.
3. Odds ratio is the probability of choosing the full ownership mode over the probability of choosing the baseline category (joint ownership mode).

REFERENCES

Agarwal, S., & Ramaswami, S. N. (1992). Choice of foreign market entry mode: Impact of ownership, location and internalization factors. *Journal of International business Studies*, *23*(1), 1–27.

Anderson, E., & Gatignon, H. (1986). Modes of foreign entry: A transaction cost analysis and propositions. *Journal of International Business Studies*, *17*(3), 1–26.

Barkema, H. G., & Vermeulen, F. (1998). International expansion through start-up or acquisition: A learning perspective. *Academy of Management Journal*, *41*(1), 7–26.

Berry, H., Guillen, M. F., & Zhou, N. (2010). An institutional approach to cross-national distance. *Journal of International Business Studies*, *41*(9), 1460–1480.

Brouthers, K. D. (2002). Institutional, cultural and transaction cost influences on entry mode choice and performance. *Journal of International Business Studies*, *33*(2), 203–221.

Brouthers, K. D. (2013). A retrospective on: Institutional, cultural and transaction cost influences on entry mode choice and performance. *Journal of International Business Studies*, *44*(1), 14–22.

Chacar, A., & Vissa, B. (2005). Are emerging economies less efficient? Performance persistence and the impact of business group affiliation. *Strategic Management Journal*, *26*(10), 933–946.

Chao, M. C.-H., & Kumar, V. (2010). The impact of institutional distance on the international diversity–performance relationship. *Journal of World Business*, *45*(1), 93–103.

Clarke, J. E., Tamaschke, R., & Liesch, P. W. (2013). International experience in international business research: A conceptualization and exploration of key themes. *International Journal of Management Reviews*, *15*(3), 265–279.

Cui, L., Fan, D., Liu, X., & Li, Y. (2016). Where to seek strategic assets for competitive catch-up? A configurational study of emerging multinational enterprises expanding into foreign strategic factor markets. *Organization Studies*, *38*(8), 1059–1083. 0170840616670441.

Delios, A., & Beamish, P. W. (2001). Survival and profitability: The roles of experience and intangible assets in foreign subsidiary performance. *Academy of Management Journal*, *44*(5), 1028–1038.

Delios, A., & Beamish, P. W. (2004). Joint venture performance revisited: Japanese foreign subsidiaries worldwide. *Management International Review*, *44*(1), 69–91.

Delios, A., & Henisz, W. J. (2003). Political hazards, experience, and sequential entry strategies: The international expansion of Japanese firms, 1980–1998. *Strategic Management Journal*, *24*(11), 1153–1164.

Dikova, D. (2009). Performance of foreign subsidiaries: Does psychic distance matter? *International Business Review*, *18*(1), 38–49.

Dikova, D., & Van Witteloostuijn, A. (2007). Foreign direct investment mode choice: Entry and establishment modes in transition economies. *Journal of International Business Studies*, *38*(6), 1013–1033.

DiMaggio, P. J., & Powell, W. W. (1983). The iron cage revisited: Institutional isomorphism and collective rationality in organizational fields. *American Sociological Review*, *48*(2), 147–160.

Dunning, J. H. (1988). The eclectic paradigm of international production: A restatement and some possible extensions. *Journal of International Business Studies*, *19*(1), 1–31.

Eden, L., & Miller, S. R. (2004). Distance matters: Liability of foreignness, institutional distance and ownership strategy. *Advances in International Management*, *16*, 187–221.

Gaur, A. S., & Lu, J. W. (2007). Ownership strategies and survival of foreign subsidiaries: Impacts of institutional distance and experience. *Journal of Management*, *33*(1), 84–110.

Ghemawat, P. (2001). Distance still matters. *Harvard Business Review*, *79*(8), 137–147.

Hernández, V., & Nieto, M. J. (2015). The effect of the magnitude and direction of institutional distance on the choice of international entry modes. *Journal of World Business*, *50*(1), 122–132.

Hoskisson, R. E., Wright, M., Filatotchev, I., & Peng, M. W. (2013). Emerging multinationals from mid-range economies: The influence of institutions and factor markets. *Journal of Management Studies*, *50*(7), 1295–1321.

Hotho, J. J. (2009). *A measure of comparative institutional distance* (p. 14). Copenhagen: Copenhagen Business School, Center for Strategic Management and Globalization.

Ionascu, D., Meyer, K. E., & Estrin, S. (2004). Institutional distance and international business strategies in emerging economies, William Davidson Institute Working Paper #728.

Jakobsen, G., & Torp, J. E. (2001). *Understanding business systems in developing countries*. London, Sage Publications

Kaufmann, D., Kraay, A., & Zoido-Lobat6n, P. (1999). Governance Matters, World Bank Research Paper No. 2196. The World Bank: Washington, DC

Khanna, T., & Palepu, K. (2000a). The future of business groups in emerging markets: Long-run evidence from Chile. *Academy of Management Journal*, *43*(3), 268–285.

Khanna, T., & Palepu, K. (2000b). Is group affiliation profitable in emerging markets? An analysis of diversified Indian business groups. *The Journal of Finance*, *55*(2), 867–891.

Khanna, T., & Rivkin, J. W. (2001). Estimating the performance effects of business groups in emerging markets. *Strategic Management Journal*, *22*(1), 45–74.

Kobrin, S. J. (1988). Expatriate reduction and strategic control in American multinational corporations. *Human Resource Management*, *27*(1), 63–75.

Kogut, B., & Singh, H. (1988). The effect of national culture on the choice of entry mode. *Journal of International Business Studies*, *19*(3), 411–432

Kolstad, I., & Wiig, A. (2012). What determines Chinese outward FDI? *Journal of World Business*, *47*(1), 26–34.

Kostova, T., & Roth, K. (2002). Adoption of an organizational practice by subsidiaries of multinational corporations: Institutional and relational effects. *Academy of Management Journal*, *45*(1), 215–233

Kostova, T., Roth, K., & Dacin, M. T. (2008). Institutional theory in the study of multinational corporations: A critique and new directions. *Academy of Management Review*, *33*(4), 994–1006.

Lin, Z. J., Peng, M. W., Yang, H., & Sun, S. L. (2009). How do networks and learning drive M&As? An institutional comparison between China and the United States. *Strategic Management Journal*, *30*(10), 1113–1132.

London, T., & Hart, S. L. (2004). Reinventing strategies for emerging markets: Beyond the transnational model. *Journal of International Business Studies*, *35*(5), 350–370.

Luo, Y. (2003). Market-seeking MNEs in an emerging market: How parent–subsidiary links shape overseas success. *Journal of International Business Studies*, *34*(3), 290–309

Luo, Y. (2006). Opportunism in Inter-firm exchanges in emerging markets. *Management and Organization Review*, *2*(1), 121–147.

Luo, Y. (2007a). Are joint venture partners more opportunistic in a more volatile environment? *Strategic Management Journal*, *28*(1), 39–60.

Luo, Y. (2007b). From foreign investors to strategic insiders: Shifting parameters, prescriptions and paradigms for MNCs in China. *Journal of World Business*, *42*(1), 14–34.

Meyer, K. E., Estrin, S., Bhaumik, S. K., & Peng, M. W. (2009). Institutions, resources, and entry strategies in emerging economies. *Strategic Management Journal*, *30*(1), 61–80.

Meyer, K. E., & Nguyen, H. V. (2005). Foreign investment strategies and sub-national institutions in emerging markets: Evidence from Vietnam. *Journal of Management Studies*, *42*(1), 63–93.

Mjoen, H., & Tallman, S. (1997). Control and performance in international joint ventures. *Organization science*, *8*(3), 257–274.

North, D. C. (1990). *Institutions, institutional change and economic performance*. Cambridge: Cambridge University Press.

O'Grady, S., & Lane, H. W. (1996). The psychic distance paradox. *Journal of International Business Studies*, *27*(2), 309–333.

Peng, M. W. (2003). Institutional transitions and strategic choices. *Academy of Management Review*, *28*(2), 275–296.

Peng, M. W., Li, S. S., Pinkham, B., & Chen, H. (2009). The institution-based view as a third leg for a strategy tripod. *Academy of Management Perspectives*, *23*(3), 63–81.

Phillips, N., Tracey, P., & Karra, N. (2009). Rethinking institutional distance: Strengthening the tie between new institutional theory and international management. *Strategic Organization*, *7*(3), 339–348.

Rose, A. K., & Spiegel, M. M. (2011). The olympic effect. *Economic Journal*, *121*(553), 652–677.

Rugman, A. M. (2010). Reconciling internalization theory and the eclectic paradigm. *Multinational Business Review*, *18*(2), 1–12.

Schwens, C., Eiche, J., & Kabst, R. (2011). The moderating impact of informal institutional distance and formal institutional risk on SME entry mode choice. *Journal of Management Studies*, *48*(2), 330–351.

Sheng, S., Zhou, K. Z., & Li, J. J. (2011). The effects of business and political ties on firm performance: Evidence from China. *Journal of Marketing*, *75*(1), 1–15.

Shirodkar, V., & Konara, P. (2016). Institutional distance and foreign subsidiary performance in emerging markets: Moderating effects of ownership strategy and host-country experience. *Management International Review*, *57*(2), 1–29.

Singh, K., Ang, S. H., & Leong, S. M. (2003). Increasing replication for knowledge accumulation in strategy research. *Journal of Management*, *29*(4), 533–549.

Stoian, C., & Mohr, A. (2016). Outward foreign direct investment from emerging economies: Escaping home country regulative voids. *International Business Review*, *25*(5), 1124–1135.

Sun, P., Mellahi, K., & Thun, E. (2010). The dynamic value of MNE political embeddedness: The case of the Chinese automobile industry. *Journal of International Business Studies*, *41*(7), 1161–1182.

Tihanyi, L., Griffith, D. A., & Russell, C. J. (2005). The effect of cultural distance on entry mode choice, international diversification, and MNE performance: A meta-analysis. *Journal of International Business Studies*, *36*(3), 270–283

UNCTAD. (2015). *World Investment Report 2015: Reforming international investment governance*. Geneva: United Nations.

Van Hoorn, A., & Maseland, R. (2016). How institutions matter for international business: Institutional distance effects vs institutional profile effects. *Journal of International Business Studies*, *47*(3), 374–381.

Williamson, O. E. (1985). *The economic institutions of capitalism: Firms, markets, relational contracting*. New York: Free Press/Collier Macmillan.

Xu, D., & Shenkar, O. (2002). Note: Institutional distance and the multinational enterprise. *Academy of Management Review*, *27*(4), 608–618.

Zaheer, S. (1995). Overcoming the liability of foreignness. *Academy of Management Journal*, *38*(2), 341–363.

Zhang, X., & Whitley, R. (2013). Changing macro-structural varieties of East Asian capitalism. *Socio-Economic Review*, *11*(2), 301–336.

PART II
THE COST OF CULTURAL AND PSYCHIC DISTANCE

CHAPTER 7

OWNERSHIP STRATEGY AND SUBSIDIARY SURVIVAL IN FOREIGN ACQUISITIONS: THE MODERATING EFFECTS OF EXPERIENCE, CULTURAL DISTANCE, AND HOST COUNTRY DEVELOPMENT

Yi Wang and Jorma Larimo

ABSTRACT

In this study, we analyze the general effect of acquirers' ownership strategy on the survival in foreign acquisitions. Furthermore, we attempt to address five potential moderating effects: international, regional, target country experience, cultural distance, as well as host country development. The developed hypotheses are tested on a sample of 1,345 acquisitions made by 174 Finnish firms in 59 countries during 1980–2005. The results indicate that in general WOS increases the probability of survival of foreign acquired units. We further find that the impact of WOS on the survival of

Distance in International Business: Concept, Cost and Value
Progress in International Business Research, Volume 12, 157–182

ISSN: 1745-8862/doi:10.1108/S1745-886220170000012008

foreign acquired units is contingent upon cultural distance and host country development but not on the experience of buying firms.

Keywords: Foreign direct investments; foreign acquisitions; subsidiary survival; ownership strategy; Finland

INTRODUCTION

Multinational enterprises (MNEs) are increasingly investing in foreign markets through foreign acquisitions. A foreign acquisition is defined as those involving an acquiring firm and a target company whose headquarters are located in different countries (Shimizu, Hitt, Vaidyanath, & Pisano, 2004; Vermeulen & Barkema, 2001). Foreign acquisition remains one of the most frequent types of foreign direct investment (FDI), since it allows acquirers to establish a quick foreign presence, consolidate market power, acquire knowledge and resources, and gain economies of scale and scope (Chen, 2008; King, Dalton, Daily, & Covin, 2004; Vermeulen & Barkema, 2001). The value of foreign acquisitions increased significantly from US $78 billion in 1987 to US $1045 billion in 2007. While the value of foreign acquisitions plummeted dramatically to US $285 billion during 2008–2009 owing to global financial and economic crisis, it started to grow again since 2010 and reached to US $700 billion in 2015 (UNCTAD, 2015, 2016).

Planning and management of foreign acquisitions is particularly challenging for acquiring firms due to significant differences in national and corporate culture and formal institutional framework (i.e., laws and regulations) as well as problems associated with post-acquisition integration of acquired firms Shimizu, Hitt, Vaidyanath, & Pisano, 2004). Based on results of several studies, the goals set by managers and shareholders for foreign acquisitions have not been reached. Consequently, a significant proportion of foreign acquired units has been divested through closure or sell-off (Zeng, Shenkar, Lee, & Song, 2013). The World Investment Report has indicated that the total value of divested foreign acquisitions reached a record level at US $511 billion in 2014 (UNCTAD, 2015). Further, several studies have reported that the probability of survival for foreign acquisitions is clearly lower than that of greenfield investments (Barkema, Bell, & Pennings, 1996; Benito, 1997; Hennart, Kim, & Zeng, 1998). It is of great importance toward analyzing what factors lead to survival of foreign acquired units.

When MNEs decide to undertake foreign acquisitions, they must determine whether to purchase partial or full equity in an already existing local firm (Chen, 2008; Chen & Hennart, 2004). Equity ownership in FDIs is of great strategic importance since it is associated with the level of organizational control a firm can exercise over its foreign subsidiaries, the amount of resources a company must commit to international markets, and the degree of investment risk a firm must bear in host countries (Chari & Chang, 2009). In foreign acquisition-specific literature, prior studies have addressed the determinants of ownership strategy (Chari & Chang, 2009; Contractor, Lahiri, Elango, & Kundu, 2014; Pinto, Ferreira, Falaster, Fleury, & Fleury, 2016) and its influence on financial (i.e., CARs) and market (i.e., Tobin's Q) performance (Yang, 2015). Our knowledge of survival implications of full versus partial acquisitions is still very limited (Song, 2014a). Moreover, some studies have found a positive relationship between full ownership and subsidiary survival (Chung & Beamish, 2005; Gaur & Lu, 2007; Li, 1995; Song, 2014a); other research has found that there is a nonsignificant (Benito, 1997; Benito & Larimo, 1995) or even a negative relationship (Beamish, 2008; Lu, 2000). Inconclusive findings have prompted IB scholars to look for contingency factors (Gaur & Lu, 2007; Hennart et al., 1998; Peng & Beamish, 2014). Extending this line of research, we argue that ownership–survival relationship in foreign acquisitions is subject to parent firm and host country boundary conditions.

The main goal of this study is to analyze the relationship between acquiring firms' ownership strategy and survival of foreign acquired units. In more detail, this study examines (1) the impact of full versus partial acquisitions at the general level and (2) the moderating effects of parent firm and host country variables that may alleviate or aggravate the general ownership–survival relationship. These moderators include international, regional, target country experience, cultural distance, and host country development. The potential moderating effects of these variables have received still very limited attention in extant subsidiary survival literature (Gaur & Lu, 2007; Peng & Beamish, 2014). These moderators were chosen also because their potential influences on ownership strategy (Zhao, Luo, & Suh, 2004). Drawing on transaction cost economics (TCE), we argue that a proper fit between these moderating variables and ownership strategy influence the survival of foreign acquired units.

Our study contributes to acquisition and survival literature in the field of IB in three important ways. First, extant studies have called for more research on subsidiary survival in general (Berry, 2013; Brauer, 2006; McDermott, 2010), but in particular in the context of foreign acquisitions (Baquero & Longobardi, 2014; Meschi & Metais, 2006, 2015). The present study responds to the calls by analyzing how and why ownership strategy influences survival of foreign acquired units. Second, our chapter addresses a broader range of moderating effects of variables at parent firm and host country level. Third, a significant number of existing studies included Japan (Chung & Beamish, 2005; Gaur & Lu, 2007; Peng & Beamish, 2014) or Korea (Pattnaik & Lee, 2014; Song, 2014a, 2014b, 2014c) as the home country of FDIs. Small and Open Economies (SMOPECs) have insofar received still limited attention (Benito, 1997; Hakason & Kappen, 2016; Scott-Kennel, 2013). Interest to firms based on SMOPECs comes from the importance of them to the overall economy of their home countries (Benito, Larimo, Narula, & Pedersen, 2002; Luostarinen & Gabrielsson, 2006). Our study responds to the calls for more studies focusing on firms based on SMOPECs (Lopez, Kundu, & Ciravegna, 2009) by analyzing survival of foreign acquired units by Finnish MNEs.

To achieve the goals, the structure of this study is as follows. This chapter starts with theoretical discussions leading to study's hypotheses development. Then, this study presents methodology and data collection followed by a discussion of the key research findings. This chapter concludes with discussions concerning study limitations, future research avenues, as well as managerial guidelines.

THEORETICAL BACKGROUND

Ownership Strategy

The choice of wholly-owned subsidiary (WOS) and joint ventures (JVs) is an important strategic consideration since it has significant implications to control, resource commitment, and investment risk (Anderson & Gatignon, 1986; Hill, Hwang, & Kim, 1990). While JVs face limited investment risk owing to lower initial capital investments, the hierarchical control is lower and potential conflict with co-owners is higher. On the other hand, although WOS require a higher level of investments in human, physical, and intangible resources, they provide acquiring firms the greatest level of operational control rights to exploit and integrate the combined resource base (Chen, 2008; Chen & Hennart, 2004). TCE has frequently been applied to explain the ownership strategy in foreign markets (Brouthers & Hennart, 2007). The theoretical argument is that firms tend to opt for a particular governance form which minimizes the total transaction costs (Geyskens, Steenkamp, & Kumar, 2006; Williamson, 1985). Drawing on TCE reasoning, we argue that survival of foreign acquired units requires a proper alignment between ownership strategy and parent firm- and host country-specific variables.

Several studies have addressed the impacts of ownership strategy on subsidiary survival, but their findings have been inconclusive. Some studies have found a positive relationship (Chung & Beamish, 2005; Gaur & Lu, 2007; Li, 1995), whereas others have found an insignificant (Benito, 1997; Benito & Larimo, 1995) or even a negative relationship (Beamish, 2008; Lu, 2000). To resolve inconsistent findings, a limited number of studies have looked for moderating factors on the ownership–survival relationship. The first line of studies has found that the probability of survival across ownership structures is contingent on country-specific variables such as regulative institutional (Gaur & Lu, 2007) and cultural (Barkema et al., 1996; Pattnaik & Lee, 2014) distance, political/social openness (Dhanaraj & Beamish, 2009), and market demand uncertainty (Song, 2014a). The second line of studies has found that firm-specific variables especially host country experience moderate the ownership–survival relationship (Barkema et al., 1996; Gaur & Lu, 2007). The third stream of studies has found that the probability of subsidiaries to survive in full versus partial ownership is attributable to different divestment modes, that is, closure and sell-off (Hennart et al., 1998; Mata & Portugal, 2000).

Extant empirical studies on the ownership–survival relationship have included both greenfield investments and acquisitions into the analysis (Benito, 1997; Gaur & Lu, 2007). Although entry through full (partial) acquisitions shares some advantages and disadvantages with entry through WOS (JV) greenfield investments, there are significant differences between them. First, in the case of a full (partial) acquisition, investing firm buys complete or a part of the equity of an existing company in a foreign country, whereas WOS (JV) greenfield investment entails building an entirely new venture in a target market from scratch. Second, full or partial acquisitions do not add new production capacity and allow a fast entry into foreign markets (Chari & Chang, 2009; Slangen & Hennart, 2007). These differences indicate that acquisitions as a distinct type of FDIs should be investigated in its own right (Chen, 2008). Our study differs from extant survival literature (Barkema et al., 1996; Benito, 1997; Gaur & Lu, 2007) that has grouped full (partial) acquisitions and WOS (JV) greenfield investments into one category by analyzing the survival implications of ownership strategy in foreign acquisitions. The present study also differs from the study by Barkema et al. (1996), Gaur and Lu (2007), and Song (2014a) by analyzing a broader range of parent firm and host country contingency factors on the ownership–survival relationship. In the next, we first develop a hypothesis about the main effect of ownership strategy on survival in foreign acquisitions. We then elaborate how various types of experience, cultural distance, and host country development moderate ownership–survival relationship.

The General Effect of Ownership Strategy on Survival of Foreign Acquired Units

Ownership strategy (i.e., WOS versus JVs) is a critical managerial decision in international expansion (Brouthers & Hennart, 2007; Zhao et al., 2004). The extant literature advocates that WOS would lead to a higher probability of subsidiary survival in the context of foreign acquisitions for two reasons. First, WOS provides parent firms with the greatest level of operational and strategic control over their foreign subsidiaries (Anderson & Gatignon, 1986; Hill et al., 1990). MNEs with complete control can also avoid transaction costs arising from conflicts in sharing proprietary assets (Chen, 2008; Duarte & Garcia-Canal, 2004; Li, 1995; Malhotra & Gaur, 2014). Second, WOS facilitates the transfer of parent firm's specific resources and capabilities to its foreign subsidiaries because there is a less probability of misuse of resources and capabilities by JVs partners. The transfer of firm-specific resources and capabilities should enhance the overall competitiveness of foreign subsidiaries, which in turn increases the probability of subsidiary survival (Gaur & Lu, 2007). In short, TCE-based studies argue that the probability of foreign subsidiaries to survive is higher in WOS relative to JVs. Several IB studies have empirically tested the relationship of WOS and subsidiary survival, but their findings have been mixed. Some studies have found a positive relationship between WOS and subsidiary survival (Chung & Beamish, 2005; Gaur & Lu, 2007; Li, 1995), whereas others have found an insignificant relationship (Benito, 1997; Benito & Larimo, 1995) or even a negative relationship (Beamish, 2008; Lu, 2000). Song (2014a) has found that full ownership is negatively associated with the divestment of foreign acquired units because irreversible and inflexible investments (i.e., full acquisitions) make MNEs harder to exit international markets. Nevertheless, we follow the TCE reasoning and propose that:

H1. There is a positive relationship between WOS and survival of the unit in foreign acquisitions.

The Moderating Effect of International Experience

International experience is an important concept of Uppsala model in explaining firm internationalization. Investing companies increase foreign market commitments and expand into culturally distant markets as they gain experiential knowledge through international experience (Johanson & Vahlne, 1977).

Clarke, Tamaschke, & Liesch (2013) refer to international experience as a "nonlocation-bound" type of experience since firms accrue them from operating in international markets rather than in a particular region or country (Clarke et al., 2013). The TCE-based theoretical argument is that increased international experience is expected to decrease the levels of internal uncertainty (Anderson & Gatignon, 1986; Zhao et al., 2004). In other words, international experience reduces the likelihood of running into problems with various stakeholders (e.g., suppliers, distributors, and customers) in foreign markets (Meyer & Wang, 2015). Further, firms lacking international experience possess limited levels of knowledge in setting up and managing business activities in a foreign market (Barkema & Drogendijk, 2007; Dow & Larimo, 2009). As a result, WOS by inexperienced firms would face increased transaction cost in foreign countries. TCE advocates that inexperienced MNEs should choose JVs as opposed to WOS so that they can lower the transaction costs in dealing with local suppliers, distributors, or customers. This, in turn, will increase the probability of foreign subsidiaries to survive. (Anderson & Gatignon, 1986; Duarte & Garcia-Canal, 2004). Following the theoretical argument, we expect that:

H2. The positive relationship between WOS and survival of foreign acquisitions is stronger if the level of international experience is higher.

The Moderating Effect of Regional Experience

The region, which refers to a group of countries sharing similar cultures, has become an important unit of analysis in existing IB literature (Barkema & Drogendijk, 2007; Barkema et al. 1996). Experience in a specific region is considered as a "location-bound" type of experience since firms accrue such experience by operating in a particular area rather than in global markets (Clarke et al., 2013). Inexperienced MNEs in a particular region possess limited levels of knowledge in planning and management of foreign subsidiaries in target countries located in that region. Such knowledge is usually embedded in incumbent firms who have operated regionally for several years. It can be expected that firms with limited levels of regional experience are more likely to opt for JVs as opposed to WOS to access regional market knowledge possessed by local firms. MNEs with higher levels of regional experience suffer less from "liability of regional foreignness" (LRF), which is defined as the costs of doing business across regions (Qian, Khoury, Peng, & Qian, 2010). We argue that WOS by firms lacking regional experience would face increased costs associated with LRF. It can be expected that experienced MNEs in a particular region are more likely to survive in that area when they opt for WOS relative to JVs. Following the above theoretical argument, we expect that:

H3. The positive relationship between WOS and survival of foreign acquisitions is stronger if the level of regional experience is higher.

The Moderating Effect of Host Country Experience

Apart from international and regional experience, experience from a particular host country is of great importance. Host country experience has been referred as "location-bound" experience since firms accrue them from a particular target country, rather than from international markets (Clarke et al., 2013). Inexperienced MNEs from a particular host country usually possess limited levels of experiential knowledge about local business environment and practices (Hennart, 1991, 2009; Hennart & Park, 1993). Incumbent firms have accumulated host country-specific knowledge through operating in a target market over a long time period. Hence knowledge of a particular target country is embedded in the incumbents and is very costly to duplicate internally or purchase externally (Chen, 2008; Hennart, 2009). TCE posits that inexperienced firms in a particular target country should set up JVs as opposed to WOS to access crucial target market knowledge possessed by local partners. On the other hand, firms with a higher level of host country experience should choose WOS as opposed to JVs so that they can alleviate co-owner-related costs and absorb more rents. Furthermore, Qian, Khoury, Peng, & Qian (2010) argue that inexperienced firms in a particular country suffer from "liability of country foreignness" (LCF), which is referred to the transportation, relational, and institutional costs. The costs associated with LCF are lower in JVs than in WOS since the risk and costs are splitted among JVs partners. Gaur and Lu (2007) have found that the interaction effect of ownership strategy and host country experience on subsidiary survival is significantly positive. In line with both theoretical logic and existing empirical finding, we hypothesize that:

H4. The positive relationship between WOS and survival of foreign acquisitions is stronger if the level of host country experience is higher.

The Moderating Effect of Cultural Distance

The IB literature has defined cultural distance as the differences in national cultural characteristics between home and host country (Hennart & Larimo, 1998; Kogut & Singh, 1988). The internationalization theory argues that MNEs face greater levels of liability of foreignness when conducting business in culturally distant countries (Johanson & Vahlne, 1977). Thus, the probability of survival of foreign subsidiaries is likely to be higher in culturally similar markets. Several studies have supported the notion that subsidiaries are more likely to survive when the cultural distance is shorter (Barkema et al., 1996; Zeng et al., 2013). In this study, we expect that cultural distance moderates the positive relationship between ownership strategy and subsidiary survival. TCE reasoning advocates that cultural distance between home and host country tends to increase the levels of internal uncertainty and transaction costs in dealing with local businesses in a foreign market (Anderson & Gatignon, 1986; Zhao et al., 2004). WOS by MNEs in culturally distant countries would face increased transaction costs in dealing with local suppliers, distributors, and customers. On the other hand, JVs in culturally distant countries would face lower transaction costs since local partners can help the parent firms to deal with the complexity of host country environment (Malhotra & Gaur, 2014; Meyer & Wang, 2015). Following theoretical arguments, we expect that:

H5. The positive relationship between WOS and survival of foreign acquisitions is stronger if the cultural distance to the target country is shorter.

The Moderating Effect of Host Country Development

The level of host country development is an important determinant of foreign subsidiary survival (Garg & Delios, 2007). The relationship of host country development and subsidiary survival has been approached from the perspective of resource exploitation and exploration. MNEs are more likely to survive if they exploit its existing resources in relatively less developed economies and explore new resources in relatively more developed countries (Tsang & Yip, 2007). In this study, we expect that the host country development strengthens the positive relationship between WOS and survival of foreign acquired units. First, Garg and Delios (2007) argue that MNEs prefer to enter economically similar countries since there is a potential for similarities in formal and informal institutional framework. In turn, this reduces the

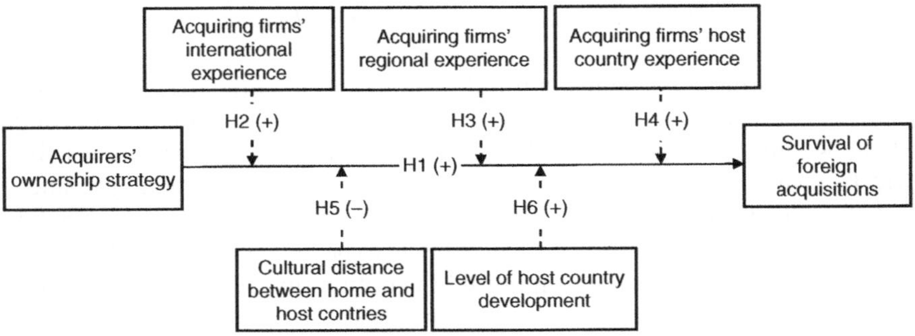

Fig. 1. Research Model (Dotted Lines = Potential Moderating Effects).

liability of doing business in foreign markets. MNEs entering economically similar countries may less dependent on the local partners, making WOS more attractive than JVs. In the context of this study, it can be expected that full acquisitions by Finnish firms more likely to survive in economically advanced countries. Second, the conditions of infrastructure and availability of related and support services in developed areas are more favorable to foreign investors than those in developing areas (Demirbag et al., 2007). Pan (1996) and Demirbag et al. (2007) have noted that the level of investment risk in WOS is much lower for firms located in more developed environments than firms located in less-developed environments. The above theoretical reasoning leads to the following hypothesis:

H6. The positive relationship between WOS and survival of foreign acquisitions is stronger if the level of host country development is higher.

The research model is presented in Fig. 1.

DATA SOURCE, SAMPLE, AND OPERATIONALIZATION OF VARIABLES

Data Source and Sample

The hypotheses will be tested on a sample of foreign acquisitions made by Finnish manufacturing firms around the globe during 1980–2005. Finland as the home country was chosen because it has been considered as an SMOPEC (Laanti, McDougall, & Baume, 2009) and there were significant divestments by Finnish firms during the past years (UNCTAD, 2016). The period of 1980–2005 was chosen because Finnish firms started rapid internationalization in the beginning of 1980s (Benito et al., 2002; Larimo, 2003). The manufacturing sector was selected because it usually represents more strategic decisions than, e.g., sales, marketing, and R&D unit. The main source of the data for the empirical analysis was an internal databank, focusing on FDIs and foreign divestments made by Finnish firms collected over a period of several years. The data were mainly gathered from annual reports and press releases of investing firms but also complemented with the information obtained from Thomson One and Orbis databases, IMD World Competitiveness Yearbook, Euromoney Country Risk (ECR), local business magazines, and based on direct contacts with several of the investing firms. Since we obtained most of our data from multiple secondary sources, Common Method Bias in this study is not likely to be a problem (Chang, Witteloostuijn, & Eden, 2010).

We identified a total of 2,123 FDIs made by Finnish firms during the observation period. Of the total FDIs, 1,345 (63%) were acquisitions, and 778 (37%) were greenfield investments. Hence there was a clear preference for Finnish MNEs to choose acquisitions as opposed to greenfield investments to enter foreign markets. The final sample consists of 1,345 acquisitions made by 174 Finnish firms in 59 countries. In total 1139 (85%) were made in OECD countries and 206 (15%) in non-OECD countries. The three main target countries were Sweden, USA, and Germany. Of the full sample, 673 (50%) units were divested (i.e., closure and sell-off) at the end of the observation period. The mean longevity of foreign acquired units was about 11 years. On average divested units had operated in the target country for 7 years, whereas the average age of survived units was 13 years. Of the total acquisitions, 978 (73%) were WOS, and 367 (27%) were JVs. The average international experience of Finnish acquirers was 27 FDIs at the time of entry. Of the full sample, 106 (8%) acquisitions were the first-time investment in the foreign markets. With regard to host country experience, on average Finnish MNEs had operated 2 years in the home country of acquired firms at the time of entry. The average annual sales of the acquiring companies were approximately Euro 1,500 million before the divestment year or in 2014 if the subsidiaries still existed. Of the total acquisitions, 433 (32%) were in low-tech branches, 285 (21%) in medium-low-tech branches, 507 (38%) in medium-high-tech branches, and 120 (9%) in high-tech branches.

This study applies Cox's proportional hazard model (Cox & Oakes, 1984) to examine the impacts of explanatory variables on the survival of foreign acquisitions. This statistical analysis method was used in most of the earlier survival studies (Demirbag, Apaydin, & Tatoglu, 2011; Dhanaraj & Beamish, 2009; Nadolska & Barkema, 2007; Song, 2015). We choose Cox's proportional hazard analysis because it corrects the problems associated with the censored data and aging effects on subsidiary dissolution and brings the exit rate closer to the failure rate (Gaur & Lu, 2007). The model is expressed as follows:

$$h_i(t) = h_o(t)\exp\ (\beta_1 x_{i1} + \beta_2 x_{i2} + \cdots + \beta_k x_{ik})$$

where $h_i(t)$ is the dependent variable denoting hazard rate of subsidiary i exiting from the host country at time t, $h_o(t)$ is the baseline hazard function, x_{i1} to x_{ik} are independent variables and β_1 to β_k are coefficients which will be estimated. The positive and significant coefficient indicates that a variable is associated with an increased probability of divestment or a decreased probability of survival in foreign acquisitions.

Operationalization of Variables

The dependent variable in the current study is survival of foreign acquisitions, where divested subsidiaries are coded as 1 and survival is coded as 0 (Demirbag et al., 2011; Gaur & Lu, 2007). In this study, foreign acquired units that are either closed down or sold-off are considered as divestments. Analyzing subsidiary survival is of great importance since it is positively correlated with subsequent firm performance (Lee & Madhavan, 2010; Vermeulen & Barkema, 2001). Furthermore, since foreign subsidiaries of MNEs are new entrants in host countries, they are likely to be primarily concerned with long-term survival and viability (Ma & Delios, 2007). The key independent variable is acquiring firms' ownership strategy at the time of divestments or later. It was captured by a dummy variable which receives 1 if the firm owned 95% or more of the subsidiary equity and 0 if it owned at least 10%, but no more than 94% (Benito, 1997; Gaur & Lu, 2007).

This study analyzes moderating effects of international, regional, and target country experience, cultural distance, and host country development. We measured international experience by the ordinal number of foreign manufacturing investments in the globe preceding the observed investment (Clarke et al., 2013). We proxied the regional experience by the ordinal number of foreign manufacturing investments made in the cultural cluster of the host country (Ronen & Shenkar, 2013) before the observed investment. Target country experience was measured by the number of years since the first manufacturing investment of the acquiring firm in the target country (Delios & Beamish, 2001; Gaur & Lu, 2007). We operationalized cultural distance using the methodology developed by Kogut and Singh (1988) based on Hofstede's (1980) four cultural dimensions: power distance, individualism/collectivism, masculinity/femininity, and uncertainty avoidance (Peng & Beamish, 2014; Sousa & Tan, 2015). We measured host country development based on the gross domestic product (GDP) per capita at the time of divestments or later (Garg & Delios, 2007).

Furthermore, we added several control variables that are likely to influence survival of foreign acquisitions (Brauer, 2006). First, we controlled for firm-specific variables. Parent firm size was proxied by worldwide annual sales of acquiring firms (in a million euros) in the year preceding the investments (Hopkins, 1991; Song, 2015). We measured the degree of product diversification by the number of four-digit Standard Industrial Codes (SIC) in which the acquiring company was operating based on the annual reports and websites of the firms (Delios, Xu, & Beamish, 2008; Hopkins, 1991; Nadolska & Barkema, 2007). Second, we controlled for industry-specific variables. The technological intensity of the industry entered was measured by a classification of various four-digit SIC industries into four categories based on their value-added figures (Bandick & Görg, 2010). We controlled for acquisitions made in machinery, paper and pulp, rubber, and chemical industry to control any unobservable effects at the industry level.

Third, we added several control variables at the country level. We measured ease of doing business in the host country using country scores (0–10) based on IMD World Competitiveness Yearbooks. We controlled for change in host country risk at the time of entry and divestment or in 2014 if the acquired units still existed (Benito, 1997; Benito & Larimo, 1995). The host country risk was measured using the country scores taken from Euromoney Country Risk (ECR). We controlled for change in economic growth in the host country, which was measured by difference between GDP growth rate at the time of entry and divestments or in 2014 if the acquired units still existed (Benito, 1997; Benito & Larimo, 1995). In addition, we computed year dummies to control acquisitions made in the period of 1980–1989, 1990–1993, 1994–1999, and 2000–2005. The period of 1980–1989 was treated as the reference group in the analysis. The operationalization of various variables is summarized in Table 1.

Table 1. Operationalization of Variables.

Variables	Operationalization
Dependent variable	
Subsidiary survival	Subsidiary survival is measured by a dummy variable where divested subsidiaries are coded as 1 and survival is coded as 0.
Independent variable	
Ownership strategy at the time of divestments or later	Ownership strategy is captured by a dummy variable which receives one if the firm owned 95% or more of the subsidiary equity and 0 if it owned at least 10%, but no more than 94%.
Moderating variables	
International experience	The ordinal number of foreign manufacturing investments made by the company before the reviewed investment.
Regional experience	The ordinal number of foreign manufacturing investments made in the cultural cluster of host country.
Target country experience	The experience in years from the first manufacturing investment of the firm in the target country.
Cultural distance	Cultural distance is measured by Kogut and Singh's (1988) composite index, which is based on the difference between Finland and host countries along four dimensions of culture identified by Hofstede (1980).
Host country development	GDP per capita at the time of divestments or later
Control variables	
R&D intensity of the industry entered	A classification of various four-digit SIC industries into four categories based on their value-added figures.
Parent firm size	Worldwide annual sales of the company (in a million euros) in the year preceding the investment.
Degree of product diversification	The number of four-digit SIC codes in which the company was operating based on the annual reports and websites of the companies.
Ease of doing business	Country scores (0–10) of the host countries based on IMD World Competitiveness Yearbooks.
Change in host country risk	Differences between host country risk at the time of entry and divestments or in 2014 if the subsidiaries still existed. The source of the data is ECR index.
Change in economic growth	Differences between GDP growth rate at the time of entry and divestments or in 2014 if the subsidiaries still existed. The source of the data is UNCTAD.
Industry dummies	Machinery, paper and pulp, rubber, and chemical industry.
Year dummies	1980–1989, 1990–1993, 1994–1999, and 2000–2005.

RESULTS

Before running Cox's proportional hazard analysis, we conducted a Pearson correlation analysis (Table 2) to diagnose any multicollinearity between various variables. Pallant (2007) has referred that the bivariate correlation of 0.70 indicates a higher probability of multicollinearity. In this study, the correlations between different variables are all below the cut-off point. Following the suggestion by Wetherill (1986), additional multicollinearity diagnostic (variance inflation factor, VIF) was conduced. The VIF values for variables included in the Cox's regression analysis were all below the cut-off point of 2.50. Thus, multicollinearity is not likely to be a major concern in this study. Table 3 presents the results. Model 1 is restricted only to control variables. Model 2 adds ownership strategy (i.e., WOS versus JVs) into the runs. Model 3 adds international, regional, and target country experience, cultural distance, and host country development into the analysis. Models 4a–4e present the results associated with the five interaction terms, respectively. The explanatory powers of all regression models are good, as the chi-square (χ^2) values are good and highly significant at $p < 0.001$ level.

The results show that several control variables exert significant influences on the survival of foreign acquired units. The relationship between parent firm size and survival of foreign acquired units is significant negative ($p < 0.05$). Medium-low technology intensity (as opposed to low technology intensity) is positively associated with survival of foreign acquired units ($p < 0.05$). There is a significant negative relationship between ease of doing business and survival of foreign acquisitions ($p < 0.01$). Change in host country risk is negatively associated with survival of foreign acquisitions ($p < 0.001$). The positive relationship of change in host country economic growth and survival is mildly significant ($p < 0.10$). Acquisitions made in machinery ($p < 0.01$) and paper and pulp industry ($p < 0.10$) increase the probability of survival, whereas rubber industry decreases the survival rate ($p < 0.05$). Acquisitions made in the periods of 1990–1993 ($p < 0.05$), 1994–1999 ($p < 0.001$), and 2000–2005 ($p < 0.001$) are more likely to survive than acquisitions made in the period of 1980–1989.

Our findings depict that full acquisitions increase the probability of survival of foreign acquired units ($p < 0.01$), which is consistent with our expectation. Thus, **H1** is supported. The interaction effect of full acquisitions and international experience on survival is not significant in the pooled sample. A detailed analysis shows that this interaction effect is significantly positive in the USA, Sweden, and Germany. Thus, **H2** is not supported in the pooled sample but supported in the USA, Sweden, and Germany subsample. The

Table 2. Correlation Table.

	Mean	SD	1	2	3	4	5	6	7	8	9	10	11	12	13
1	0.500	0.500	1												
2	0.727	0.446	−0.128**	1											
3	27.130	27.456	−0.175**	0.077**	1										
4	3.050	2.422	0.057*	0.029	0.067*	1									
5	1.890	2.529	0.025	0.082**	0.217**	0.260**	1								
6	1.217	0.758	−0.009	−0.098**	0.143**	−0.018	−0.019	1							
7	18,892.63	8,578.855	−0.215**	0.243**	0.209**	−0.026	0.024	−0.277**	1						
8	2,213.88	3,103.072	−0.058*	0.014	0.563**	0.005	0.169**	0.054*	0.133**	1					
9	2.230	1.000	−0.028	0.073**	0.019	−0.002	0.021	0.085**	0.115**	−0.066*	1				
10	11.600	7.087	0.163**	0.008	0.466**	0.183**	0.252**	−0.015	−0.072**	0.337**	0.051	1			
11	6.416	1.402	0.070*	0.163**	−0.118**	−0.004	0.058*	−0.354**	0.327**	−0.028	0.107**	0.026	1		
12	0.080	3.875	0.064*	−0.152**	−0.096**	−0.023	−0.030	−0.100**	−0.245**	−0.068*	−0.139**	−0.059*	−0.092**	1	
13	−2.620	10.192	0.321**	−0.210**	−0.101**	−0.018	−0.075**	−0.013	−0.392**	−0.071**	−0.171**	−0.007	−0.186**	0.384**	1

Notes: Industry and year dummies included in the correlation analysis, but not reported due to space limit.

Variables: 1 = nonsurvival subsidiaries; 2 = WOS; 3 = international experience; 4 = regional experience; 5 = target country experience; 6 = cultural distance; 7 = host country development; 8 = parent firm size; 9 = technological intensity of industry entered; 10 = the degree of product diversification; 11 = ease of doing business; 12 = change in economic growth of the target country; 13 = change in the country risk of the target country.

*$p < 0.05$, **$p < 0.01$ (two-tailed).

Table 3. Results of Survival of Foreign Acquisitions (Divestments =1).

Variables	Model 1	Model 2	Model 3	Model 4a	Model 4b	Model 4c	Model 4d	Model 4e
Control variables								
Parent firm size[a]	0.089*	0.083*	0.097*	0.096*	0.097*	0.097*	0.083*	0.100*
	(0.040)	(0.040)	(0.042)	(0.021)	(0.042)	(0.042)	(0.042)	(0.042)
Technology intensity of the industry entered								
Low technology (reference group)								
Medium-low technology	−0.334*	−0.333*	−0.319*	−0.322*	−0.319*	−0.320*	−0.331*	−0.293*
	(0.144)	(0.144)	(0.146)	(0.146)	(0.146)	(0.146)	(0.146)	(0.147)
Medium-high technology	−0.149	−0.131	−0.122	−0.129	−0.123	−0.120	−0.115	−0.104
	(0.144)	(0.144)	(0.145)	(0.145)	(0.145)	(0.145)	(0.145)	(0.145)
High technology	0.211	0.200	0.154	0.154	0.154	0.153	0.161	0.176
	(0.153)	(0.152)	(0.154)	(0.154)	(0.154)	(0.154)	(0.154)	(0.155)
Degree of product diversification	0.007	0.008	0.012	0.012	0.012	0.012	0.014	0.012
	(0.008)	(0.008)	(0.009)	(0.009)	(0.009)	(0.009)	(0.009)	(0.009)
Ease of doing business	0.081**	0.090**	0.078**	0.078*	0.077*	0.078*	0.087**	0.088**
	(0.030)	(0.030)	(0.032)	(0.032)	(0.032)	(0.032)	(0.033)	(0.033)
Change in the host country economic growth	−0.026*	−0.029**	−0.019†	−0.019†	−0.019†	−0.019†	−0.020†	−0.018
	(0.011)	(0.011)	(0.011)	(0.011)	(0.011)	(0.011)	(0.011)	(0.011)
Change in the host country risk	0.040***	0.038***	0.042***	0.042***	0.042***	0.042***	0.043***	0.043***
	(0.004)	(0.004)	(0.004)	(0.004)	(0.004)	(0.004)	(0.004)	(0.004)
Machinery industry	−0.420**	−0.422**	−0.395**	−0.392*	−0.395*	−0.397**	−0.406**	−0.394**
	(0.152)	(0.152)	(0.153)	(0.153)	(0.153)	(0.153)	(0.153)	(0.153)

Table 3. (*Continued*)

Paper and paper-related industry	−0.370*	−0.360*	−0.291†	−0.295*	−0.290†	−0.288†	−0.273†	−0.283†
	(0.146)	(0.146)	(0.149)	(0.150)	(0.150)	(0.150)	(0.150)	(0.149)
Rubber industry	0.311†	0.318†	0.331*	0.331*	0.332*	0.329*	0.358*	0.312†
	(0.166)	(0.166)	(0.166)	(0.166)	(0.166)	(0.166)	(0.167)	(0.167)
Chemical industry	−0.059	−0.060	0.003	0.005	0.003	0.000	−0.018	−0.015
	(0.169)	(0.169)	(0.170)	(0.170)	(0.170)	(0.170)	(0.171)	(0.170)
Year of investments								
1980–1989 (reference group)								
1990–1993	−0.249*	−0.255*	−0.284*	−0.288*	−0.284*	−0.282*	−0.295*	−0.268*
	(0.111)	(0.111)	(0.119)	(0.119)	(0.119)	(0.119)	(0.119)	(0.119)
1994–1999	−0.616***	−0.614***	−0.571***	−0.571***	−0.571***	−0.573***	−0.561***	−0.535***
	(0.115)	(0.114)	(0.129)	(0.129)	(0.129)	(0.129)	(0.129)	(0.131)
2000–2005	−0.951***	−0.934***	−0.879***	−0.876***	−0.878***	−0.880***	−0.868***	−0.848***
	(0.148)	(0.148)	(0.177)	(0.177)	(0.177)	(0.177)	(0.177)	(0.178)
Main effects								
WOS ownership strategy		−0.245**	−0.267**	−0.220†	−0.283*	−0.227*	−0.644***	2.642
		(0.088)	(0.090)	(0.124)	(0.142)	(0.110)	(0.156)	(1.650)
International experience			−0.006*	−0.004	−0.006*	−0.006*	−0.006*	−0.005*
			(0.003)	(0.004)	(0.003)	(0.003)	(0.003)	(0.003)
Regional experience			0.009	0.008	0.005	0.009	0.011	0.009
			(0.017)	(0.017)	(0.030)	(0.017)	(0.017)	(0.017)
Target country experience			0.019	0.019	0.019	0.035	0.019	0.018
			(0.017)	(0.017)	(0.017)	(0.030)	(0.017)	(0.017)
Cultural distance			0.143*	0.144*	0.143*	0.145*	−0.002	0.151*
			(0.061)	(0.061)	(0.061)	(0.061)	(0.081)	(0.061)
Host country development[b]			0.305**	0.311**	0.305**	0.303**	0.304**	0.462**
			(0.111)	(0.111)	(0.111)	(0.111)	(0.112)	(0.146)

Interaction effects								
WOS and international experience				−0.002 (0.004)				
WOS and regional experience					0.005 (0.035)			
WOS and target country experience						−0.022 (0.034)		
WOS and cultural distance							0.305** (0.104)	
WOS and host country development								−0.303† (0.172)
−2 Log Likelihood	8,667.370	8,659.924	8,644.709	8,644.411	8,644.685	8,644.311	8,636.113	8,641.616
Model chi-square (c^2)	249.069***	258.188***	278.511***	278.538***	278.515***	279.174***	286.882***	279.535***
Chang in c^2		7.446**	15.216**	0.297	0.023	0.398	8.585**	3.092†
Degree of freedom	15	16	21	22	22	22	22	22
No. of acquisitions (nonsurvival acquisitions)	1,345 (673)	1,345 (673)	1,345 (673)	1,345 (673)	1,345 (673)	1,345 (673)	1,345 (673)	1,345 (673)

Notes: standard errors in parentheses; a, b = logarithm variables.

Level of significance: *$p < 0.05$, **$p < 0.01$, ***$p < 0.001$, † if $p < 0.10$ (all tests two-tailed).

results show that the interaction effect of WOS and regional experience on survival in foreign acquisitions is not significant. **H3** is not supported. The positive interaction effect of full acquisitions and target country experience is not significant. **H4** is not supported. Our results show that the negative interaction effect of WOS and cultural distance on survival is significant ($p < 0.01$). **H5** is supported. Our results indicate that host country development reinforces the positive relationship of full acquisitions and survival of foreign acquired units ($p < 0.10$). Thus, **H6** is supported. In short, our results indicate that the relationship of ownership strategy and subsidiary survival in foreign acquisitions is contingent upon cultural distance and host country development but not on firm experience.

We performed three robustness tests. First, we performed robustness check by using 80% as the cut-off point to distinguish WOS and JVs in foreign acquisitions. Second, a small portion of acquisitions (106 acquisitions) were dropped from the robustness test since they were first-time investments in foreign markets. Third, we run Cox's regression analysis without units that were divested within 1 or 2 years from their establishment year. Most of the results from robustness check were identical to those reported in the study.

DISCUSSION AND CONCLUSION

MNEs face a critical decision concerning the ownership strategy of their subsidiaries when entering foreign markets through acquisitions (Chen, 2008). The ownership strategy of MNEs (i.e. WOS versus JVs) has received considerable scholarly attention in the extant IB literature (Brouthers & Hennart, 2007; Zhao et al., 2004). However, the impact of the ownership strategy on subsidiary survival has received limited attention, and the existing findings have been mixed. In this study, we addressed (1) the impact of the ownership strategy of acquiring firms on the survival of foreign acquisitions at the general level and (2) the moderating effects of selected parent firm and host country variables: acquirers' international, regional, and target country experience, cultural distance, and host country development. The developed hypotheses were tested on a sample of 1,345 acquisitions made by 174 Finnish MNEs in 59 countries during 1980–2005.

In this study, we found that in general WOS increased the probability of foreign acquired units to survive. This finding is inconsistent with studies by Benito (1997) and Benito and Larimo (1995) where the authors found an insignificant relationship between WOS ownership strategy and survival of Norwegian and/or Finnish foreign subsidiaries. The possible explanation is that Benito (1997) and Benito and Larimo (1995) included both greenfield investments and acquisitions into the analysis, whereas this study focused on subsidiary survival in the context of foreign acquisitions. We also found that the general effect of WOS by acquiring firms on subsidiary survival is contextual, depending on (1) cultural distance and (2) host country development. We found that the interaction effect of WOS and cultural distance on subsidiary survival in foreign acquisitions is significantly negative. This finding is in contrast with the study by Pattnaik and Lee (2014) where the authors have found a positive interaction effect. We found that the interaction effect of WOS and host country development (measured as GDP per capita) on the survival of foreign acquired units is significantly positive. The positive interaction effect of WOS and international experience on subsidiary survival was not significant in the pooled sample but significant in the subsample analysis including USA, Sweden, and Germany as the host countries. This finding supports the notion that general international business experience facilitates WOS in more developed nations than in less developed nations (Li & Meyer, 2009). The moderating effects of regional and target country experience were not significant. These results were similar to the study by Barkema et al. (1996) focusing on the longevity of subsidiaries by Dutch firms in multiple host countries.

This study contributes to acquisitions and survival literature in the field of IB in several ways. First, drawing from TCE, this study analyzed how and why ownership strategy of acquiring firms influences survival of foreign acquired units. Past studies focusing on ownership strategy–survival relationship included both greenfield investments and acquisitions into the analysis. Second, this study analyzed the conditions under which WOS most strongly influences survival of foreign acquired units. This study found that the positive effect of WOS on the survival of foreign acquired units is stronger when acquisitions are made in culturally similar or more developed countries. Third, this study contributes to the current literature by analyzing survival of foreign acquisitions by Finnish firms. Extant survival literature has mainly included Japan (Gaur & Lu, 2007; Kim, Delios, & Xu, 2010; Papyrina, 2007) or Korea (Park, Lee, & Hong, 2011; Song 2014a, 2014b, 2014c, 2015) as the home country of FDIs. Analyzing this topic is of great importance because it helps buying firms based on SMOPECs increase the probability of survival in foreign acquisitions. Our findings propose that decision-makers of Finnish acquiring firms should choose WOS over JVs when entering to culturally similar countries or more developed countries.

There are several notable limitations in the study that should be addressed in the future research. First, existing studies have found that the shorter life of JVs relative to WOS is due to a higher probability of sell-off, not to close down (Hennart et al., 1998; Mata & Portugal, 2000). Extending this line of research, we encourage future studies to examine the moderating effect of divestment modes on the relationship between ownership strategy and survival of foreign acquired units. Second, future studies may examine the moderating effect of MNE strategies on the relationship between ownership strategy and survival. MNEs pursuing global strategy may benefit from higher levels of control, while those pursuing multi-domestic strategy may, in contrast, suffer from higher levels of control (Brouthers & Hennart, 2007). WOS by MNEs pursuing global strategy leads to a higher probability of subsidiary survival. Third, this study included a sample of manufacturing firms. Brouthers and Brouthers (2003) have found that FDI behaviors of service firms are significantly different from those of manufacturing firms. It is of great interest toward analyzing survival of foreign acquisitions by service firms (McDermott, 2010). Last but not the least, the empirical part of this study analyzed foreign acquisitions made by Finnish firms. To achieve a higher degree of generalizability, future studies may extend the current study by analyzing firms originating in other SMOPECs especially Nordic countries (Laanti et al., 2009).

REFERENCES

Anderson, E., & Gatignon, H. (1986). Modes of foreign entry: A transaction cost analysis and propositions. *Journal of International Business Studies*, *17*(3), 1–26.

Bandick, R., & Görg, H. (2010). Foreign acquisition, plant survival, and employment growth. *Canadian Journal of Economics*, *43*(2), 547–573.

Baquero, L. M., & Longobardi, T. (2014). Foreign divestment decision process: The pharmaceutical industry experience. *Forum Empresarial*, *19*(2), 1–30.

Barkema, H. G., Bell, J. H., & Pennings, J. M. (1996). Foreign entry, cultural barriers, and learning. *Strategic Management Journal*, *17*(2), 151–166.

Barkema, H. G., & Drogendijk, R. (2007). Internationalising in small, incremental, or larger steps? *Journal of International Business Studies*, *38*(7), 1132–1148.

Beamish, P. W. (2008). *Joint venturing*. Charlotte, NC: Information Age Publishing.

Benito, G. R. G. (1997). Divestment of foreign production operations. *Applied Economics*, *29*(10), 1365–1377.

Benito, G. R. G., & Larimo, J. (1995). Divestment of foreign production operations: The case of foreign direct investment from the Nordic countries. In R. Schiattarella (Ed.), *Proceedings of the 21st annual meeting of the European International Business Academy*, Urbino, Italy.

Benito, G. R. G., Larimo, J., Narula, R., & Pedersen, T. (2002). Multinational enterprises from small economies: Internationalization patterns of large companies from Denmark, Finland, and Norway. *International Studies of Management & Organization*, *32*(1), 57–78.

Berry, H. (2013). When do firms divest foreign operations? *Organization Science*, 24(1), 246–261.

Brauer, M. (2006). What have we acquired and what should we acquire in divestiture research? A review and research agenda. *Journal of Management*, *32*(6), 751–785.

Brouthers, K. D., & Brouthers, L. E. (2003). Why service and manufacturing entry mode choices differ: The influence of transaction cost factors, risk and trust. *Journal of Management Studies*, *40*(5), 1179–1204.

Brouthers, K. D., & Hennart, J. F. (2007). Boundaries of the firm: Insights from international entry mode research. *Journal of Management*, *33*(3), 395–425.

Chang, S. J., Witteloostuijn, A. V., & Eden, L. (2010). From the editors: Common method variance in international business research. *Journal of International Business Studies*, *41*(2), 178–184.

Chari, M. D. R., & Chang, K. (2009). Determinants of the share of equity sought in cross-border acquisitions. *Journal of International Business Studies*, *40*(8), 1277–1297.

Chen, S. F. S. (2008). The motives for international acquisitions: Capability procurements, strategic considerations, and the role of ownership structure. *Journal of International Business Studies*, *39*(3), 454–471.

Chen, S. F. S., & Hennart, J. F. (2004). A hostage theory of joint ventures: Why do Japanese investors choose partial over full acquisitions to enter the United States? *Journal of Business Research*, *57*(10), 1126–1134.

Chung, C. C., & Beamish, P. W. (2005). The impact of institutional reforms on characteristics and survival of foreign subsidiaries in emerging economies. *Journal of International Management*, *42*(1), 35–62.

Clarke, J. E., Tamaschke, R., & Liesch, P. W. (2013). International experience in international business research: A conceptualization and exploration of key themes. *International Journal of Management Review*, *15*(3), 265–279.

Contractor, F. J., Lahiri, S., Elango, B., & Kundu, S. K. (2014). Institutional, cultural and industry related determinants of ownership choices in emerging market FDI acquisitions. *International Business Review*, *23*(5), 931–941.

Cox, D. R., & Oakes, D. (1984). *Analysis of survival data*. London and New York, NY: Chapman and Hall.

Delios, A., & Beamish, P. W. (2001). Survival and profitability: The roles of experience and intangible assets in foreign subsidiary performance. *Academy of Management Journal*, *44*(5), 1028–1036.

Delios, A., Xu, D., & Beamish, P.W. (2008). Within-country product diversification and foreign subsidiary performance. *Journal of International Business Studies*, *39*(4), 706–724.

Demirbag, M., Glaister, K. W., & Tatoglu, E. (2007). Institutional and transaction cost influences on MNE's ownership strategies of their affiliates: Evidence from an emerging market. *Journal of World Business*, 42(4), 418–434.

Demirbag, M., Apaydin, M., & Tatoglu, E. (2011). Survival of Japanese subsidiaries in the Middle East and North Africa. *Journal of World Business*, *46*(4), 411–425.

Dhanaraj, C., & Beamish, P. W. (2009). Institutional environment and subsidiary survival. *Management International Review*, *49*(3), 291–312.

Dow, D., & Larimo, J. (2009). Challenging the conceptualization and measurement of distance and international experience in entry mode choice research. *Journal of International Marketing*, *17*(2), 74–98.

Duarte, C. L., & Garcia-Canal, E. (2004). The choice between joint ventures and acquisitions in foreign direct investments: The role of partial acquisitions and accrued experience. *Thunderbird International Business Review*, *46*(1), 39–58.

Garg, M., & Delios, A. (2007). Survival of the foreign subsidiaries of TMNCs: The influence of business group affiliation. *Journal of International Management*, *13*(3), 278–295.

Gaur, A. S., & Lu, W. (2007). Ownership strategies and survival of foreign subsidiaries: Impacts of institutional distance and experience. *Journal of Management*, *33*(1), 84–110.

Geyskens, I., Steenkamp, J. B. E. M., & Kumar, N. (2006). Make, buy, or ally: A transaction cost theory meta-analysis. *Academy of Management Journal*, *49*(3), 519–543.

Hakason, L., & Kappen, P. (2016). Live and let die: A survival analysis of foreign R&D units in Swedish MNEs. *International Business Review*, *25*(6), 1185–1196.

Hennart, J. F. (1991). The transaction costs theory of joint ventures: An empirical study of Japanese subsidiaries in the United States. *Management Science*, *37*(4), 483–497.

Hennart, J. F. (2009). Down with MNE-centric theories! Market entry and expansion as the bundling of MNE and local asset. *Journal of International Business Studies*, *40*(9), 1432–1454.

Hennart, J. F., Kim, D. J., & Zeng, M. (1998). The impact of joint venture status on the longevity of Japanese stakes in U.S. manufacturing affiliates. *Organization Science*, *9*(3), 382–395.

Hennart, J. F., & Larimo, J. (1998). The impact of culture on the strategy of multinational enterprises. Does national origin affect ownership decisions? *Journal of International Business Studies*, *29*(3), 515–538.

Hennart, J. F., & Park, Y. R. (1993). Greenfield vs. acquisition: The strategy of Japanese investors in the United States. *Management Science*, *39*(9), 1054–1070.

Hill, C. L., Hwang, P., & Kim, W. C. (1990). An eclectic theory of the choice of international entry mode. *Strategic Management Journal*, *11*(2), 117–128.

Hofstede, G. (1980). *Culture's consequences: Internal differences in work-related values*. Newbury Park, CA: Sage.

Hopkins, H. D. (1991). Acquisition and divestiture as a response to competitive position and market structure. *Journal of Management Studies*, *28*(6), 665–677.

Johanson, J., & Vahlne, J. E. (1977). The internationalization process of the firm. A model of knowledge development and increasing foreign market commitment. *Journal of International Business Studies*, *8*(1), 23–32.

Kim, T. Y., Delios, A., & Xu, D. (2010). Organizational geography, experiential learning and subsidiary exit: Japanese foreign expansions in China, 1979–2001. *Journal of Economic Geography*, *10*(4), 579–597.

King, D. R., Dalton, D. R., Daily, C. M., & Covin, J. G. (2004). Meta-analyses of post-acquisition performance: Indications of unidentified moderators. *Strategic Management Journal*, *25*(2), 187–200.

Kogut, B., & Singh, H. (1988). The effect of national culture on the choice of entry mode. *Journal of International Business Studies*, *19*(3), 412–432.

Laanti, R., McDougall, F., & Baume, G. (2009). How well do traditional theories explain the internationalization of service MNEs from small and open economies? Case: National telecommunication companies. *Management International Review*, *49*(1), 121–143.

Larimo, J. (2003). Form of investment by Nordic firms in world markets. *Journal of Business Research*, *56*(10), 791–804.

Lee, D., & Madhavan, R. (2010). Divestiture and firm performance: A meta-analysis. *Journal of Management*, *36*(6), 1345–1371.

Li, J. T. (1995). Foreign entry and survival, the effects of strategic choices on performance in international markets. *Strategic Management Journal*, *16*(5), 333–351.

Li, P. Y., & Meyer, K. E. (2009). Contextualizing experience effects in international business: A study of ownership strategies. *Journal of World Business*, *44*(4), 370–382.

Lopez, L. E., Kundu, S. K., & Ciravegna, L. (2009). Born global or born regional? Evidence from an exploratory study in the Costa Rican Software industry. *Journal of International Business Studies*, *40*(7), 1228–1238.

Lu, J. W. (2000). Characteristics and performance of Japanese FDI in China. *Journal of Asian Business*, *16*(3), 51–71.

Luostarinen, R., & Gabrielsson, M. (2006). Globalization and marketing strategies of born globals in SMOPECs. *Thunderbird International Business Review*, *48*(6), 773–801.

Ma, X., & Delios, A. (2007). A new tale of two cities: Japanese FDIs in Shanghai and Beijing, 1979–2003. *International Business Review*, *16*(2), 207–228.

Malhotra, S. & Gaur, A. S. (2014). Spatial geography and control in foreign acquisitions. *Journal of International Business Studies*, *54*(2), 191–210.

Mata, J., & Portugal, P. (2000). Closure and divestiture by foreign entrants: The impact of entry and post-entry strategies. *Strategic Management Journal*, *21*(5), 549–562.

McDermott, M. C. (2010). Foreign divestment: The neglected area of international business? *International Journal of Management and Organization*, *40*(4), 37–53.

Meschi, P. X., & Metais, E. (2006). International acquisition performance and experience: A resource-based view. Evidence from French acquisitions in the United States. *Journal of International Management*, *12*(4), 430–448.

Meschi, P. X., & Metais, E. (2015). Too big to learn: The effect of major acquisition failures on subsequent acquisition divestment. *British Journal of Management*, *26*(3), 408–423.

Meyer, K. E. & Wang, Y. (2015). Transaction cost perspectives on alliances and joint ventures: Explanatory power and empirical limitations. In J. Larimo, N. Nummela, & T, Mainela (Eds.), *Handbook on international alliances and network research* (pp. 87–136). Cheltenham: Elgar.

Nadolska, A., & Barkema, H. G. (2007). Learning to internationalise: The pace and success of foreign acquisitions. *Journal of International Business*, *38*(7), 1170–1186.

Pallant, J. (2007). *SPSS survival manual: A step by step guide to data analysis using SPSS for Windows*. Buckingham: Open University Press.

Pan, Y. (1996). Influences on foreign equity ownership level in joint ventures in China. *Journal of International Business Studies*, *27*(1), 1–26.

Papyrina, V. (2007). When, how, and with what success? The joint effect of entry timing and entry mode on survival of Japanese subsidiaries in China. *Journal of International Marketing*, *15*(3), 73–95.

Park, Y. R., Lee, J. Y., & Hong, S. (2011). Effects of international entry-order strategies on foreign subsidiary exit: The case of Korean Chaebols. *Management Decision*, *49*(9), 1471–1488.

Pattnaik, C., & Lee, J. Y. (2014). Distance and divestment of Korea MNC affiliates: The moderating role of entry mode and experience. *Asia Pacific Business Review*, *20*(1), 174–196.

Peng, M. W., & Beamish, P. W. (2014). The effect of host country long-term orientation on subsidiary ownership and survival. *Asia Pacific Journal of Management*, *31*(2), 423–453.

Pinto, C. F., Ferreira, M. P., Falaster, C., Fleury, M. T. L., & Fleury, A. (2016). Ownership in cross-border acquisitions and the role of government support. *Journal of World Business*, *52*(4), 533–545.

Qian, G. M., Khoury, T. A., Peng, M. W., & Qian, Z. M. (2010). The performance implications of intra- and inter-regional geographical diversification. *Strategic Management Journal*, *31*(9), 1018–1030.

Ronen, S., & Shenkar, O. (2013). Mapping world cultures: Cluster formation, sources and implications. *Journal of International Business Studies*, *44*(9), 867–897.

Scott-Kennel, J. (2013). Selling to foreign MNEs: End of the road or the beginning of a journey for firms from small advanced economies? *International Studies of Management & Organization*, *43*(1), 52–80.

Shimizu, K., Hitt, M. A., Vaidyanath, D., & Pisano, V. (2004). Theoretical foundations of cross-border mergers and acquisitions: A review of current research and recommendations for the future. *Journal of International Management*, *10*(3), 307–353.

Slangen, A. H. L., & Hennart, J. F. (2007). Greenfield or acquisition entry: A review of the empirical foreign establishment mode literature. *Journal of International Management*, *13*(4), 403–429.

Song, S. (2014a). Entry mode irreversibility, host market uncertainty, and foreign subsidiaries exist. *Asia Pacific Journal of Management*, *31*(2), 455–471.

Song, S. (2014b). Unfavorable market conditions, institutional and financial development, and exit of foreign subsidiaries. *Journal of International Management*, *20*(3), 279–289.

Song, S. (2014c). Subsidiary divestment: The role of multinational flexibility. *Management International Review*, *54*(1), 47–70.

Song, S. (2015). Exchange rate challenges, flexible intra-firm adjustments and subsidiary longevity. *Journal of World Business*, *50*(1), 36–45.

Sousa, C. M. P., & Tan, Q. (2015). Exit from a foreign market: Do poor performance, strategic fit, cultural distance, and international experience matter? *Journal of International Marketing*, *23*(4), 84–104.

Tsang, E. W. K., & Yip, P. S. L. (2007). Economic distance and survival of foreign direct investments. *Academy of Management Journal*, *50*(5), 1156–1168.

UNCTAD [United Nations Conference on Trade and Development] (2015). *World investment report: Reforming international investment governance*. New York, NY and Geneva: UNCTAD.

UNCTAD [United Nations Conference on Trade and Development] (2016). *World investment report: Investor nationality: Policy challenges*. New York, NY and Geneva: UNCTAD.

Vermeulen, F., & Barkema, H. (2001). Learning through acquisitions. *Academy of Management Journal*, *44*(3), 457–476.

Wetherill, G. B. (1986). *Regression analysis with applications*. London: Chapman and Hall.

Williamson, O. E. (1985). *The economic institutions of capitalism: Firms, markets, relational contracting*. New York, NY and London: The Free Press and Collier Macmillan Publishers, cop.

Yang, M. (2015). Ownership participation of cross-border mergers and acquisitions by emerging market firms: antecedents and performance. *Management Decision*, *53*(1), 221–246.

Zeng, Y., Shenkar, O., Lee, S. H., & Song, S. (2013). Cultural differences, MNE learning abilities, and the effect of experience on subsidiary mortality in a dissimilar culture: Evidence from Korean MNEs. *Journal of International Business Studies*, *44*(1), 42–65.

Zhao, H. X., Luo, Y. D., & Suh, T. (2004). Transaction cost determinants and ownership-based entry mode choice: A meta-analytical review. *Journal of International Business Studies*, *35*(6), 524–544.

CHAPTER 8

THE PSYCHIC DISTANCE HAZARDS IN CROSS-BORDER ACQUISITION PERFORMANCE: AN EMPIRICAL STUDY OF CROSS-BORDER ACQUISITIONS FROM 26 COUNTRIES

João Carvalho Santos, Hortênsia Barandas-Karl and Francisco Vitorino Martins

ABSTRACT

In this chapter we test a conceptual model to shed light on the psychic distance (PD) hazards in cross-border acquisitions' (CBAs') performance. Only a few studies have sought to examine the impact of national-level dimensions on CBAs' performance, such as cultural distance or PD, with non-conclusive and contradictory results. Event study methodology is used to scrutinize the impact of the five key dimensions of psychic distance stimuli (PDS) on the stock market performance of the US acquirer firms and 26 countries involved in the CBA. Our results support that PD, as a whole, has a negative impact on CBAs' performance although only in the

Distance in International Business: Concept, Cost and Value
Progress in International Business Research, Volume 12, 183–206

ISSN: 1745-8862/doi:10.1108/S1745-886220170000012010

short term there is a statistically significant negative impact, whereas in the long term no effect is statistically significant. Analyzing the different dimensions of PDS, only differences in language, education, and political systems are significant. This chapter is the first to empirically examine the PD hazards on CBAs by breaking down the PDS and test the effect of each dimension on CBAs' performance. The findings of this study may be useful for managers of firms that wish to undertake CBAs as it denotes important dimensions which hinder post-deal performance.

Keywords: Psychic distance; cross-border acquisitions; performance; internationalization; event study; CAR

INTRODUCTION

Mergers and acquisitions research is important because these transactions have significant implications for firms' performance (Laamanen & Keil, 2008) and account for nearly 70% of worldwide foreign direct investment (Yildiz, 2014). Given its high relevance, numerous studies have addressed M&A's phenomenon both empirically and theoretically (see the overviews by Chi, 2000; Ferreira, Santos, Reis, & Almeida, 2014; Kacpperczyk, 2009). However, even after decades of research on this issue, the research provides no clear consensus on the impact of these transactions on the firms' performance (Haspeslagh & Jemison, 1991; Very, 2004; Very & Gates, 2007). For instance, Chatterjee, Lubatkin, Schweiger, and Weber (1992) and Stahl and Voigt (2008) found a negative impact of cultural differences on cross-border acquisitions' (CBAs') performance, and Morosini, Shane, and Singh (1998) found a positive relationship between cultural differences and CBAs' performance. King, Dalton, Daily, and Covin (2004) perform a meta-analysis of 93 prior empirical studies on M&A's performance and concluded: "our results indicate that post-acquisition performance is moderated by variables unspecified in existing research (…) An implication is that changes to both M&A theory and research methods may be needed" (p. 188).

Cross-border acquisitions are extensively scrutinized due to their long-term effects (Capron & Pistre, 2002). According to Morosini et al. (1998), CBAs have become major strategic tools for corporate growth of multinational corporations. CBAs increase the efficiency and effectiveness of whole industries in addition to affecting individual firms' competitive ability (Hitt, Ireland, & Harrison, 2001). In most cases, CBAs are the only way to acquire resources and knowledge that are not available in the market (Zahra, Ireland, & Hitt, 2000). Firms choose to undertake CBAs for different purposes. CBAs may allow obtaining synergies that would not be acquired otherwise (Bradley, Desai, & Kim, 1988), exploiting economies of scale (Homburg & Bucerius, 2006), overcoming the shortcomings of the financial markets (Brouthers & Brouthers, 2000), or achieving fast access to specialized technological assets (Chen, 2008; Elango, Lahiri, & Kundu, 2013). Managers' self-interest or merely the inadequate evaluation of the potential synergies may also lead to CBAs (Seth, Song, & Pettit, 2000). The outcome of CBAs is contingent on the post- acquisition integration of the acquired firm. For instance, Child and Wong (2002) found that cultural differences are likely to have a negative impact on the firms' post-acquisition performance. The failure of CBA deals is arguably often due to cultural differences (Bauer & Matzler, 2014; Child & Wong, 2002; Haspeslagh & Jemison, 1991; Morosini et al., 1998; Yildiz, 2014).

The present study analyzes the effect of psychic distance (PD) and their dimensions on CBAs' performance. In this study we contribute to the research of the PD hazard on CBAs' performance by studying the performance of 415 CBAs between 2005 and 2012, involving acquirers from the United States and targets from 26 countries. Thus we analyze the PD hazards from one direction (from the United States to other countries) considering the asymmetry of PD (Luo & Shenkar, 2011; Shenkar, Luo, & Yeheskel, 2008). We used an event study methodology to analyze the hazards of the PD on CBAs' performance on the stock market performance of the acquiring firms available in the Security Data Corporation (SDC). We used the formative index based on five key dimensions of psychic distance stimuli (PDS) taken from Dow (2007) and Dow and Karunaratna (2006) to determine "PD" hazard between the US acquirer firms and the target firms from other countries involved in the CBA. Specifically we scrutinize the impact of differences in language, education, religion, industrial development, and political systems on CBA's performance.

This study contributes to international business and strategic management research in different ways. First, this study contributes to the literature on differences between countries by empirically testing the effect of PD on CBAs' performance. Second, it contributes to a better understanding of Dow and Karunaratna (2006) PDS construct by testing the individual effects of the five major variables. We investigate whether certain variables of the stimuli have a more significant impact than others on the CBAs' performance. Overall, this study extends the current understanding of the literature on differences between countries by scrutinizing the relevance of PD on CBAs' operations.

THEORY AND HYPOTHESES

PD and Cross-Border Mergers' and Acquisitions' Performance

According to Johanson and Vahlne (1977, 2009) the internationalization of firms may be examined as an incremental process. As firms internationalize, they accumulate experience and knowledge and are likely to evolve to higher commitment foreign entry modes, namely mergers and acquisitions, and greenfield investments (Johanson & Vahlne, 1977). A crucial element in this evolutionary model is firms' perceived risks that, according to Johanson and Wiedersheim-Paul (1975), lead firms to begin internationalizing to nearby markets – markets in close geographic proximity, with cultural, political, and legal systems that resemble those found in the home country – and only later do they search for more distant markets. The initial expansion to proximate locations seeks to reduce perceived risks by avoiding unfamiliar spaces and by selecting entry modes that entail low commitment of resources. As firms deepen their internationalization they start expanding to more distant countries also assuming greater risks and deploying high involvement entry modes.

Psychic distance, that is, "the sum of factors preventing the flow of information from and to the market. Examples are differences in language, education, business practices, culture, and industrial development" (Johanson & Vahlne, 1977, p. 24), creates a sense of dissimilarity (in factors such as language, culture, and personal relationships between entrepreneurs) that hinders firms' operations. According to the early study of Johanson and Wiedersheim-Paul (1975, p. 307), PD was defined as "factors preventing or disturbing the flow of information between firms and market." Kogut and Singh (1988, p. 413) defined PD as "the degree to which a firm is uncertain of the characteristics of a foreign market," and for Ford (1984, p. 102) PD is the "the extent to which the norms and values of the two companies differ because of their separate national characteristics." Evans, Treadgold, and Mavondo (2000, p. 375) conceptualized PD as "the distance between the home market and a foreign market resulting from the perception and understanding of cultural and business differences." PD is also posited to be asymmetric since the perceptions of differences between two given countries may vary, unlike geographic distance or the traditional measures of cultural distance (Luo & Shenkar, 2011; Shenkar, 2001). The asymmetry of PD is implicit to Uppsala's incremental process of internationalization (Johanson & Vahlne, 1977; Johanson & Wiedersheim-Paul, 1975) although being frequently overlooked (see Håkanson & Ambos [2010] for an overview).

Most of the studies have found an impact of PD on firms' international operations. PD is posited to have an impact on entry-mode decision (Brouthers & Hennart, 2007; Ellis, 2007). According to Dow and Larimo (2007) a high degree of PD between countries is expected to have negative impact on firms' desires for high control of their operations in the foreign market, as in the case of CBA operations. This negative impact has been supported by several empirical studies which have found a significant negative correlation between PD and entry-mode selection (Magnusson, Baack, Zdravkovic, Staub, & Amine, 2008; Zhao, Luo, & Suh, 2004) and also negative influence on trust and satisfaction in international distribution (Obadia, 2013). On the other hand, the impact of PD on firms' international operations may be positive. According to Evans and Mavondo (2002) a greater the PD (and thus a greater uncertainty firms face) will compel firms to "work harder" to reduce this uncertainty instead of overestimating the similarities in close markets (O'Grady & Lane, 1996; Pedersen & Petersen, 2004). Several studies have also shown a positive impact of PD on firms' performance (e.g. Evans & Mavondo, 2002; Morosini et al., 1998; O'Grady & Lane, 1996; Sousa, Ruzo, & Losada, 2010). It appears to be a reasonable explanation that PD positively impacts performance – the PD paradox (O'Grady & Lane, 1996). The PD paradox indicates managers fail to perceive the true PD between countries when they neglect the differences between countries. This may lead managers to "see" a country psychically close when it is not in fact (for a review of this literature see Stahl & Voigt, 2008). Therefore, "learning begins with the ability to see differences" (O'Grady & Lane, 1996, p. 325).

PD has been demonstrated to have an impact on CBAs' performance (Evans & Mavondo, 2002; Evans, Treadgold, & Mavondo, 2000; Morosini et al., 1998). Performance may be conceptualized and measured in several different ways. For example, financial indicators have been used to assess the influence of PD on firms' performance (Evans & Mavondo, 2002). Stahl and Voigt (2008) have also considered organizational performance and synergy realization to assess the hazard of cultural differences in CBAs' performance. International business scholars often adopt the concept of financial performance to measure M&As (Meglio & Risberg, 2011; Venkatraman & Ramanujam, 1986). Financial performance includes market value of the firm and is commonly measured in terms of cumulative abnormal returns (CARs) or cumulative average abnormal returns – event study methodology. According to Meglio and Risberg (2011), the majority of the studies employed the event study method (e.g., Chikh & Filbien, 2011; Shelton, 1988; Wright, Kroll, & Elenkov, 2002).

Grounded in our review into how researchers measure M&As' performance, we employed market-based measure for CBAs' performance. The CARs provide a realistic representation of the wealth effects in M&As (Stahl & Voigt, 2008) and are calculated as the difference between the actual stock return and the return that would be expected given the performance of the market (Datta, Pinches, & Narayanan, 1992).

Conceptual Model

As discussed in the PD literature review, larger country PD is expected for firms to involve in more difficulties. Therefore, firms select markets less psychologically distant, which allow them to gain experience in carrying out international operations generally and operations in a specific market particularly. With the purpose of minimizing risks and learning about customers, suppliers, bureaucratic procedures, exchange rates, taxation, customs barriers, and so forth, firms started to invest in countries with more favorable regulations, incentives, and developed institutions (Dow & Karunaratna, 2006; Johanson & Vahlne, 1977; Martín & Drogendijk, 2014; Xu & Shenkar, 2002).

A larger PD will arguably lead to greater uncertainty in operating in those countries (Dow & Larimo 2009; Håkanson & Ambos, 2010). For instance, when a firm acquires a new firm in a different country the managers need to communicate with suppliers, customers, competitors, and also with the political institutions. Thus, differences between countries, that is, PD, may increase the uncertainty and the cost of interaction and communication between firms and the environment (Hutzschenreuter, Kleindienst, & Lange, 2014). The more differences there are between the home country and host country, the less expected from CBAs' performance. Large PD led to misinterpretation and miscommunication and may result in an inadequate understanding of the foreign market. PD may increase the costs of managing CBAs.

This combined with our early discussions on the definition of PD and CBAs leads us to a first hypothesis:

Baseline Hypothesis 1. PD will be negatively associated with the CBAs' performance.

The next set of hypotheses follow the PDS of Dow and Karunaratna (2006). According to these authors, the PD between two given countries is determined by the differences in language, religion, industrial development, education and political system, colonial ties, and time zone. Following Larimo (2011), we focused on differences in language, religion, industrial development, education and political system; we leave "colonial ties" due to the idiosyncrasies of our sample (all the acquirers are US based and the United States did not have any colonies) and also "time zone" since it was considered to have no significant predictive power under most circumstances (Dow & Karunaratna, 2006; Larimo, 2011). Therefore, using a multi-dimensional approach to PD arguably allows to explain the differences between countries.

Differences in language among countries have been acknowledged as one of the barriers of doing business in the international markets (Dow & Karunaratna, 2006; Evans & Mavondo, 2002; harzing, 2003; Johanson & Wiedersheim-Paul, 1975; Shenkar, 2001; Sousa & Bradley, 2006, 2008). Managers that do not speak the same language will face difficulties in interpreting and understanding the information. The language similarity may explain the trade between countries and increase transaction risks and cost (Dow & Karunaratna, 2006). In CBAs the differences in languages may advance additional problems due to the difficulties in successful integration of the human resources and communication with suppliers and institutions (Bjorkman, Stahl, & Vaara, 2007). Thus, differences in language between countries tend to be negatively associated with the CBAs' performance.

Hypothesis 2. Language differences between countries will be negatively related to CBAs' performance.

Differences in education levels between countries tend to increase the risks and uncertainties of doing business in international markets since these differences may result in uncertainty of understanding and communicating in the international markets (Dow & Karunaratna, 2006). Managers and workers with different education levels may have difficulty working in a team and understanding the new methods of work of the firms resulting from CBAs. The communication itself between the different hierarchical levels and within the same levels can be compromised and negatively influence the CBAs' performance.

Hypothesis 3. Differences in education levels between countries will be negatively associated with the CBAs' performance.

Different levels of industrial development also affect communication and interaction in international markets. According to Dow and Karunaratna (2006) different levels of industrial development may increase costs and uncertainty. For instance, differences in transportation and communication infrastructures that exist between countries with different degrees of industrial development have a negative impact on firms' performance (Evans & Mavondo, 2002; Malhotra, Sivakumar, & Zhu, 2009). According to Ghemawat (2001) the business models may be more easily to be transferred to countries with similar level of industrial development. An M&A between firms from different countries, that is, a CBA, may have a deficient performance by not being able to adapt to these differences. Thus the level of industrial development will be associated with CBAs' performance.

> **Hypothesis 4.** Differences in the degree of industrial development between countries will be negatively associated with CBAs' performance.

Differences in political systems include political stability and democratic character (Dow & Karunaratna, 2006). Firms from relatively stable countries and democratic political system may face political hazard because of the unstable and non-democratic host country government (Hutzschenreuter et al., 2014). According to Johanson and Vahlne (2009), political distance may decrease firm's performance since costs and uncertainty tend to increase in the international markets. Different levels of political stability may yield uncertainty concerning the conditions of doing business and managing the CBAs in different governance system (Zurawicki & Habib, 2010). Thus the differences in political systems will be associated with CBAs' performance.

> **Hypothesis 5.** Differences in political systems between countries will be negatively associated with CBAs' performance.

Differences in religion are related to cultural differences and have a huge influence on culture since religion affects the way people communicate and interact (Blomkvist & Drogendijk, 2013; Ghemawat, 2001; Ronen & Shenkar, 2013). According to Shenkar (2001) and Dow and Karunaratna (2006) religion differences are a factor of conflict between different countries and increase PD hazard. Differences in religion may affect the way the workers, from the firm resulting from the CBA, interact. For instance, the different views of the Christian and the Muslim religion toward the role of men and women in society and business may affect the way of managing the CBAs. The differences in religion may involve differences with regard to communication and interaction norms. Thus the difference in religion will be associated with CBAs' performance.

> **Hypothesis 6.** Differences in religions between countries will be negatively associated with the CBAs' performance.

METHOD

The following section outlines the methodology used to test our hypotheses and understanding the PD hazards on CBAs' performance. We used the standard event study methodology (Campbell, Lo, & MacKinlay, 1997; Fama & MacBeth, 1973) to examine acquirers' returns in US CBAs in the period surrounding the announcement of the deal. Event studies allow scholars to scrutinize whether there are abnormal share price returns associated with an event and capture acquirers' value creation from CBAs consistently (Kohli & Mann, 2012; Zollo & Meier, 2008). This empirical study relies on a sample of CBAs by US multinationals.

Variables

The dependent variable in this study is the CARs obtain through the stock market event study to measure the performance of the acquirers. We used one relatively short event windows (–5, 5) and one relatively long event windows (–20, 20).

Independent Variables

In this study we used the PDS to the USA, which is based on the formative index based on five major dimensions put forward by Dow and Karunaratna (2006) and Dow (2007): differences in language, religion, industrial development, education, and political system. Following Dow and Ferencikova (2010), the PDS index represented the aggregate PDS distance (the five dimensions) of the two acquisition parties. Algebraically:

$$\text{PDS}_j = \sqrt{\sum_{i=1}^{5}(I_{ij} - I_{il})^2}$$

where PDS_j is the psychic distance stimuli difference for the *j*th country to the USA, *i* is fixed and relative to the USA; I_{ij} PDS's score: *i*th PDS dimension for the *j*th country.

The Dow and Karunaratna (2006) scales cover up a huge variety of the factors usually associated with PD (Evans & Mavondo, 2002; Harzing, 2003). According to Dow (2007) and Dow and Karunaratna (2006), the five dimensions of PDS can be defined as: differences in languages – taking into account the two closest major languages for each pair of countries and the ability of the population to speak other major language of another country; differences in religion – the distance between the two closest major religions and population that belong to the same religion in another country; differences in industrial development – taking into account the difference between countries in nine dimensions (the difference in US$ GDP per capita; the difference in energy consumption; the difference in the number of cars; the difference in the % non-agricultural labor; the difference in the % urban population; the difference in the number of daily newspapers; the difference in the number of radios; the difference in the number of telephones; and the difference in the number of televisions); differences in education – taking into account the difference between countries in three dimensions (the difference in the % of literate adults; the difference in the % of population enrolled in second-level education; and the difference in the % of population enrolled in third-level education); Differences in political system – taking into account two distinct dimensions. The degree of democracy that is measured by using three different scales (the difference in the POLCON V scale; the difference in the Modified POLITY IV; and the difference in the Freedom House Political Rights scale) and the differences in political systems that worry the political ideology of the group in power. This is measured by using one scale (the difference in Beck's Political Ideology).

Control Variables

We include a number of firm and industry-level control variables. First, *Firms' size* was measured by the natural logarithm of the firm's total assets (Ahammad & Glaister, 2013). Firms' size is indicative of the firms' ability to obtain economies of scale and scope that may provide the acquirer with higher returns (King et al., 2004; Moeller, Schlingemann, & Stulz, 2004) and better performance (Finkelstein & Haleblian, 2002). Second, *Relatedness* – following the procedures of Morosini et al. (1998), the relatedness of the CBA will be measured based on the industry of the acquirer and the target firms. If a database indicates that the two firms are in the same industry, the CBA receives a score of 1. If a database indicates that the two firms are from different industries, the CBA receives a score of 0. This information is obtained from SDC. Fourth, *Firms' CBA experience* was controlled, because previous experience in conducting CBA may affect the firm's value since prior experience in performing CBA helps firms to better understand all the CBA process and employing them to future deals (Levitt & March, 1988; Nadolska & Barkema, 2007) and eventually avoiding or overcoming problems. This variable is dichotomous, anchored in 1 if the acquirer has performed other CBA deal in the 5 years preceding the focal CBA announcement, and 0 otherwise, with data collected from the SDC. Finally, *Firms' experience in acquisition country* – the previous experience in conducting acquisitions in the target country influences the firm's perceived risk because it may decrease the liability of foreignness and therefore firm value (Eden & Miller, 2004; Zhu, Hitt, Eden, & Tihanyi, 2010). Albeit each CBA may be different, firms with previous experience in the target country will decrease the hazard by increasing the knowledge about a specific market. According to Vermeulen and Barkema (2001), firms will develop target country-specific routines and capabilities that may help the firms manage the M&A process. Takes the value of 1 other CBAs deal in the target country in the 5 years preceding the time of the CBA announcement and 0 otherwise. This information is obtained from the SDC.

Sample

To define the sample we followed eight procedures (Fee & Thomas, 2004). First, we selected only completed transactions. Second, we have excluded public utility firms, public administration, and financial institutions because these industries are profoundly regulated. Third, the acquirer and target are from different countries. Fourth, the acquirer is publicly traded and where both the acquirer's and the target's nation are known. Fifth, the acquirers and target must be in one of 120 countries/areas that are in Douglas Dow's PDS database (Dow, 2007). Sixth, both the acquirer's and the target's *Datastream* code are known to allow for reliable stock return data available for calculations' acquires' abnormal return (AR) and CAR attributable to CBAs announcements. Seventh CBAs announcement dates must be between 2005 and 2012. Finally, we exclude observations of all the offshore countries to avoid including "shell" operations. Our final sample consists of 415 unique acquisitions from US acquirers and 26 different target nations. The majority of the CBAs are in the developed countries (i.e., countries belonging to the OECD): United Kingdom with 124, Canada with 106, and Australia with 32 M&As, represent more than 50% of all acquisitions. Only four acquisitions are targets in Africa and eight acquisitions in South America. The average sum involved in each deal is 256.3 million USD and the last 3 years (2010–2012) represent around 45% of the number of operations.

This sample size satisfies the assumptions of normality (Gubbi, Aulakh, Ray, Sarkar, & Chittoor, 2010), required for an event study (McWilliams & Siegel, 1997). We obtained both the firms' and the CBAs operations' data from Thomson Financials' SDC Platinum database. The SDC Platinum database comprises mergers and acquisitions of international firms and US firms since 1990. We also used *Datastream* database to retrieve the firms' stock prices and the S&P500 index data to compute the returns.

Procedures

We use several models to ascertain the impact of PD on CARs of US firms following CBAs. We test our hypotheses (following Campbell et al., 1997) using weighted least squares estimators (Buckley et al., 2007; Zhu et al., 2010). Since the observations are cross section (different CBAs), we should account for the diversity of firms included in the sample in financial capacity, dimension, number of employees, dividend policy, industry, and so forth. Therefore, according to Gujarati and Porter (2010) and Greene (2011), the observations specificity could be dealt with considering heteroskedasticity, meaning we do not use the classical hypothesis of constant variance. Therefore, we assume heteroskedasticity, where the variance is different in each observation and is dependent of the firms' dimension, that is, $\mathrm{Var}(\in_i) = \sigma^2 Z_i^2$. In this study, the dimension variable (Z_i) is the sales volume of the acquirer. To assess the robustness of our results and analyze eventual differences in the short-term and the long-term effects, we repeated the procedure and used the same independent variables changing the event window of the dependent variable, using an event window (–5, 5). These three models are Models 4–6.

RESULTS

Table 1 reports descriptive statistics (the means and standard deviations (SDs) of the variables, as well as the correlation coefficients) of the dependent, independent, and control variables. A close observation of the correlations between independent variables confirms no multicollinearity issues arise. The strongest correlation is –0.816 between the variables, differences in education level and differences in the degree of industrial development, which is the only coefficient over 0.60 in absolute value. All other correlations present a low coefficient differences indicating no adverse effect in the models.

The sampling probability distributions to test the average CAR and standardized cumulative abnormal return (SCAR) are approximately normal (Campbell et al., 1997). The results on Table 2 show the tests of $CAR_{(-5, 5)}$, $CAR_{(-20, 20)}$, $SCAR_{(-5, 5)}$, $CAR_{(-20, 20)}$, and $SCAR_{(-20, 20)}$. Concerning $CAR_{(-5, 5)}$ and $SCAR_{(-5, 5)}$ tests shows the average accumulated return is statistically significant (significant at 10% level of significance [l.s.] in both cases but also significant at 5% and 1% in SCAR statistics), supporting the most immediate reactions

Table 1. Descriptives and Correlations Matrix.

		Mean	SD	1	2	3	4	5	6	7	8
1	PDS index	5.679	1.551	1.000 –							
2	Differences in languages	2.445	1.668	0.005 0.929	1.000						
3	Differences in education levels	0.359	0.388	−0.039 0.442	−0.575 0.258	1.000 –					
4	Differences in the degree of industrial develop.	1.693	0.483	0.012 0.809	−0.287 0.000***	−0.816 0.000***	1.000 –				
5	Differences in political systems	1.885	0.366	0.067 0.188	−0.269 0.000***	−0.397 0.000***	0.467 0.000***	1.000 –			
6	Differences in religions	0.653	0.683	0.294 0.563	0.106 0.036**	0.528 0.000***	−0.499 0.000***	−0.120 0.000***	1.000 –		
7	CAR $_{(-5, 5)}$	0.023	0.012	0.035 0.494	0.431 0.397	−0.052 0.309	0.031 0.548	0.019 0.715	−0.059 0.245	1.000 –	
8	CAR $_{(-20, 20)}$	−0.027	0.026	0.019 0.707	−0.193 0.000***	0.061 0.233	−0.002 0.976	0.024 0.639	−0.068 0.179	0.208 0.000***	1.000 –

Notes: **Significant at 5% l.s.; **Significant at 1% l.s.

Table 2. Cumulative Abnormal Returns (CARs) and Standardized Cumulative Abnormal Return (SCAR) for CBAs Announcements.

CAR			SCAR		
Event Window	Means	*t*-tests[a]	Event Window	Means	*t*-tests[a]
$CAR_{(-5, 5)}$	0.023	1.879*	$SCAR_{(-5, 5)}$	1.152	3.076***
$CAR_{(-20, 20)}$	−0.027	−1.044	$SCAR_{(-20, 20)}$	−0.124	−2.503**

Notes: [a] *t*-test testing the null hypothesis that the mean of ARs is 0
*Significant at 10% l.s.; **Significant at 5% l.s.; ***Significant at 1% l.s.

of investors close to the operation date. $CAR_{(-20, 20)}$ and $SCAR_{(-20, 20)}$ show only statistically significance for SCAR statistic (significant at 5%), whereas the $CAR_{(-20, 20)}$ statistics are not significantly different from 0.

The interpretation of these results should consider that the statistics are averages and thus hide the diversity of behaviors among the 415 CBAs. Therefore we may conclude the effects on accumulated returns are visible in the short term (the period from five days before until five days after the operation), whereas the longer period (–20, 20) the statistical results do not allow a conclusion.

We ran several models with the dependent variable – CBA Performance. Table 3 presents the results of these analyses. The control variables *Size*, *Related*, and *Experience in acquisition* are significant in the three models, and *Experience in acquisition country* is also significant in model 2.

Model 2 includes as independent variables the five items of the PDS, which allow us to test hypotheses 2–6. We found Differences in languages to be negatively related to acquisition performance with a coefficient of –0.023 (significant at 1%), allowing us to support **Hypothesis 2;** Differences in education levels have been found to be negatively related to acquisition performance with a coefficient of –0.176 (significant at 1%) thus supporting **Hypothesis 3**. Differences in political systems have also been found to have a negative impact with a coefficient of –0.079 (significant at 5%) thus supporting **Hypothesis 5**. As for the impact of Differences in the degree of industrial development and Differences in religion on CBAs' performance, they have not been found significant and thus we may not support **Hypotheses 4** and **6**.

Model 3 allows us to test the PDS index (**Hypotheses 1**) which considers the five items simultaneously. PDS index is found to be negatively – quite strongly – associated with CBAs' performance with a coefficient of –0.445 (significant at 1%). Therefore, as predicted by **Hypothesis 1**, PD is negatively associated with CBAs' performance.

Table 3. Regression Analysis: Determinants of PD on CBA Performance.

Variable	Model 1 Coefficient	Model 2 Coefficient	Model 3 Coefficient	Model 4 Coefficient	Model 5 Coefficient	Model 6 Coefficient
PDS index	–	–	−0.445	–	–	−0.027***
Differences in languages	–	−0.023***	–	–	0.021	–
Differences in education levels	–	−0.176***	–	–	0.013	–
Differences in the degree of industrial develop.	–	0.053	–	–	0.097	–
Differences in political systems	–	−0.079**	–	–	0.006	–
Differences in religions	–	−0.0081	–	–	−0.025	–
Size	0.028***	−0.017***	0.034***	0.030***	0.009	0.034***
Related	0.147***	0.050***	0.057***	0.0580	−0.052	−0.002
Experience in acquisition	0.590***	−0.036***	0.054***	0.009	−0.029	0.005
Experience in acquisition country	0.005	0.051***	0.021	−0.013**	0.006	−0.003
*N*º observations	390	389	388	390	389	388
Adjusted R^2	0.682	0.884	0.745	0.147	0.182	0.167
Log likelihood	−61.489	136.852	−18.637	−294.258	−281.980	−287.967
F-statistic	168.096	295.746	189.232	14.378	9.641	13.972
Prob (*F*-statistic)	0.000	0.000	0.000	0.000	0.000	0.000
Akaike info criterion	0.346	−0.647	0.132	1.540	1.506	1.520
Schwarz criterion	0.407	−0.535	0.204	1.601	1.618	1.592
Hanna-Quinn criterion	0.370	−0.603	0.160	1.564	1.551	1.549

Notes: **Significant at 5% l.s.; ***Significant at 1% l.s.

Models 4–6 analyze the short-term effect of PD. The five items of the PDS are not found to be significant (Model 5) thus not supporting **Hypotheses 2–6** in the short term. However, the PDS index is found to be significant with a coefficient of –0.03 (significant at 1%) (Model 6) thus supporting **Hypothesis 1** also in the short term.

DISCUSSION AND CONCLUSIONS

Firms do business in an increasingly heterogeneous, complex, and uncertain environment (Azar & Drogendijk, 2014; Johanson & Vahlne, 2009). The uncertainty arises from the differences in the international business environment, namely the home–host differences at several levels. The differences between countries may be measured from several perspectives and call for a multidimensional construct which permits gaining a more accurate portrayal of the differences. The PD construct includes factors such as differences in language, religion, education, industrial development, and political systems (Dikova, 2009; Dow & Ferencikova, 2010; Dow & Karunaratna, 2006; Johanson & Wiedersheim-Paul, 1975; Shenkar, 2001) and may be operationalized using the PDS developed by Dow and Karunaratna (2006). The PDS covers an extensive range of factors that may potentially affect the CBAs' performance. In our study we used the PDS to scrutinize the impact of PD hazard on CBAs' performance, using a sample of 415 CBAs operations by US bidder firms that acquired non-US target firms between 2005 and 2012.

The purpose of this study was to break down the PDS developed by Dow and Karunaratna (2006) and test the effect of each dimension on CBAs' performance. Arguably this may produce more specific findings on the importance of the different variables of PD rather than just testing for the PD as a whole. Furthermore, we were interested in testing PDS effects on the CBAs, focusing specifically on their effects on the CBAs' performance. Lastly, as the increasing speed of globalization is supposedly causing cultures to converge, we aimed at testing whether or PD is still an important question in the second decade of the twenty-first century.

Our findings confirm that PD has a negative impact on CBAs' performance (thus broadly supporting **Hypothesis 1**). Both the aggregate index (Model 3) and three individual items (differences in language, education, and political systems) of the five items of the PDS (Model 2) have a significant impact on CBA performance. Our findings confirm that differences in language are still an issue as a potential source of problems when dealing with international acquisitions. According to Dow and Karunaratna (2006) language differences are a central obstacle to conducting business abroad, hindering the development of relationships between the different partners in CBAs and the ability to exploit opportunities. Thus, the managers' ability to speak foreign languages is a central issue and may increase the understanding on the foreign market and decrease the PD hazard on CBA (e.g., Evans & Mavondo, 2002). Our findings are therefore consistent with past research from Evans and Mavondo (2002), Dichtl, Koeglmayr, and Mueller (1990), and Holzmüller and Kasper (1990), who found that the ability to speak other languages decreases the PD hazard.

Our study also supports that differences in education levels hinder the CBAs' performance. The education level has been posited to influence the individual's foreign orientation (Child & Wong, 2002). The managers' foreign orientation arguably influences the desire to operate abroad, either by exporting or by other entry modes (Dichtl et al., 1990), as well as the openness to other cultures (Child & Wong, 2002) and may thus increase the overseas performance. The educational level has also been suggested to impact PD: as the level of education increases the PD decreases (Holzmüller & Kasper, 1990). Thus, differences in education level may affect the relationships between firms from different countries and may cause difficulties in the transfer of information and knowledge. The post-CBA integration may also have additional challenges if firms face an increased difference in educational levels. Our findings are consistent with past research on differences in political systems (e.g., Henisz & Williamson, 1999), which confirm differences in political systems may decrease the CBAs' performance. Firms will face further political hazards caused by different taxation, regulation systems, and property rights legislation (Henisz & Williamson, 1999). Differences in political systems may thus be a source of uncertainty that increase the costs of the operation (Delios & Henisz, 2003). Our results are also consistent with Brewer (2007) and Dow and Karunaratna (2006) that argued that low political difference between the acquirer and the acquired firms' countries is expected to reduce the PD. Greater differences in political systems may obstruct the flow of information and knowledge transfer, thus reducing CBA performance (Brewer, 2007; Dow & Karunaratna, 2006).

In this study, we controlled for size, type of CBAs (related or unrelated), experience in acquisitions, and experience in acquisition in the country. The results indicated the three first control variables have a positive effect on CBAs' performance. Our results are consistent with previous research, which support that CBA performance increases as the size of the firms involved in M&A also increases (Barkema & Vermeulen, 1998; Seth, 1990a): larger firms typically provide brands with high awareness, leaders in their markets, and economies of scale, thus having a higher potential to generate synergies (Barkema & Vermeulen, 1998; Seth, 1990a). Our results on firms' relatedness are also consistent with those of Lubatkin (1983), Datta (1991), and Morosini et al. (1998), which argued that related M&As perform better than unrelated ones. Our results regarding experience in acquisition are also consistent with previous research, which posited that firms with experience in acquisitions are likely to develop routines through experience to support future acquisition processes (Haleblian, Devers, McNamara, Carpenter, & Davison, 2009). Moreover, previous acquisition experience in the focal country is posited to improve the CBAs' performance, since firms gain knowledge on the target country idiosyncrasies (Barkema & Vermeulen, 1998).

Several theoretical contributions stem from the core findings to mergers and acquisitions and distance literature. First, this study uncovers the importance of analyzing the different variables of a PD construct including differences in languages, political systems, education, religion, and industrial development to CBAs' performance. Particularly, highlighting the importance of analyzing each of the different variables individually and not only as a single construct. Second, not all the differences in PDS are significant: only the differences in language, education, and political systems have been found to negatively impact CBAs' performance, whereas differences in religion and differences in industrial development have not been found to be significant. Third, we uncover a different impact of PD on CBA performance in short term and long term: in the short term, there is a statistically significant negative impact, whereas in the long term no effect is statistically significant. Fourth, examining the effects of PD on CBAs' performance provides new insights into hazards' sources influencing CBAs' performance, hence providing contributions to the M&A literature.

Limitations and Future Research

Arguably one of the main limitations of this study is the event study methodology. Although being widely used and able to detect the performance effects, its explanatory power is limited (Zollo & Meier, 2008). The methodological limitations have an impact in our results as the event window $CAR_{(-20, 20)}$ presents non-significant results – a limitation previously acknowledged in the literature (e.g., Madhavan & Prescott, 1995). On the other hand, event study methodology cannot accurately isolate long-term effects on financial performance (Capron & Pistre, 2002) thus may not be employed to analyze the effects of

PD on the long-term CBAs' performance. Future research may overcome this limitation using alternative performance measures, such as financial measures (e.g. return on sales, return on equity, and return on assets). Nevertheless, using financial measures is also problematic, especially in CBAs, since there are different accounting conventions that may bias the results (Hitt et al., 2001).

Another limitation of our study is the analysis perspective we selected. We considered 415 CBA operations in 26 target countries from the same country (USA). Thus we have only examined PD in one direction (from the USA to 26 other countries). Since PD is asymmetric (Håkanson & Ambos, 2010; Luo & Shenkar, 2011; Shenkar et al., 2008) further research may test the model from both directions (i.e. firms acquired in the USA). Therefore, future research may benefit from using a broader approach to confirm and extend our study's findings, namely the asymmetric effect of PD, thus offering a better understanding of the PD's impact on CBA performance.

Finally, we defined the scope of the study. The acquirer firms' country is the USA, a developed country, and a significant number of operations are performed in Anglo-Saxon countries. Nevertheless, other countries' firms are becoming increasingly relevant in cross-border activity and may be worth investigating. For instance, emerging countries are increasingly important in the market for corporate control: for example, the value of Chinese CBAs.

REFERENCES

Ahammad, M., & Glaister, K. (2013). The pre-acquisition evaluation of target firms and cross border acquisition performance. *International Business Review*, *22*(5), 894–904.

Azar, G., & Drogendijk, R. (2014). Psychic distance, innovation, and firm performance. *Management International Review*, *54*(5), 581–613.

Barkema, H., & Vermeulen, G. (1998). International expansion through start-up or through acquisition: An organizational learning perspective. *Academy of Management Journal*, *41*(1), 7–26.

Bauer, F., & Matzler, K. (2014). Antecedents of M&A success: The role of strategic complementarity, cultural fit, and degree and speed of integration. *Strategic Management Journal*, *35*(2), 269–291.

Bjorkman, I., Stahl, G., & Vaara, E. (2007). Cultural differences and capability transfer in cross-border acquisitions: The mediating roles of capability complementarity, absorptive capacity, and social integration. *Journal of International Business Studies*, *38*(4), 658–672.

Blomkvist, K., & Drogendijk, R. (2013). The impact of psychic distance on Chinese outward foreign direct investments. *Management International Review*, *53*(5), 659–686.

Bradley, M., Desai, A., & Kim, E. (1988). Synergistic gains from corporate acquisitions and their division between the stockholders of target and acquiring firms. *Journal of Financial Economics*, *21*(1), 3–40.

Brewer, P. (2007). Operationalizing psychic distance: A revised approach. *Journal of International Marketing*, *15*(1), 44–66.

Brouthers, K., & Brouthers, L. (2000). Acquisition or greenfield start-up? Institutional, cultural and transaction cost influences. *Strategic Management Journal*, *21*(1), 89–97.

Brouthers, K., & Hennart, J.-F. (2007). Boundaries of the firm: Insights from international entry mode research. *Journal of Management*, *33*(3), 395–425.

Buckley, P., Clegg, L., Cross, A., Liu, X., Voss, H., & Zheng, P. (2007). The determinants of Chinese outward foreign direct investment. *Journal of International Business Studies*, *38*(4), 499–518.

Campbell, J., Lo, A., & MacKinlay, C. (1997). *The econometrics of financial markets*. Princeton, NJ: Princeton University press.

Capron, L., & Pistre, N. (2002). When do acquirers earn abnormal returns? *Strategic Management Journal*, *23*(9), 781–794.

Chatterjee, S., Lubatkin, M., Schweiger, D., & Weber, Y. (1992). Cultural differences and shareholder value in related mergers: Linking equity and human capital. *Strategic Management Journal*, *13*(5), 319–334.

Chen, F. (2008). The motives for international acquisitions: Capability procurements, strategic considerations, and the role of ownership structures. *Journal of International Business Studies*, *39*(3), 454–471.

Chi, T. (2000), "Option to acquire or divest a joint venture", *Strategic Management Journal*, Vol. 21, No 6, pp. 665–687.

Chikh, S., & Filbien, J. (2011). Acquisitions and CEO power: Evidence from French networks. *Journal of Corporate Finance*, *17*(5), 1221–1236.

Child, J., & Wong, C. (2002). Psychic distance and internationalization. *International Studies of Management and Organizations*, *32*(1), 36–56.

Datta, K. (1991). Organizational fit and acquisition performance: Effects of post-acquisition integration. *Strategic Management Journal*, *12*(4), 281–297.

Datta, D., Pinches, G., & Narayanan, V. (1992). Factors influencing wealth creation from mergers and acquisitions: A meta-analysis. *Strategic Management Journal*, *13*(1), 67–84.

Delios, A., & Henisz, W. (2003). Political hazards, experience, and sequential entry strategies: The international expansion of Japanese firms, 1980–1998. *Strategic Management Journal*, *24*(11), 1153–1164.

Dichtl, E., Koeglmayr, H., & Mueller, S. (1990). International orientation as a precondition for export Ssccess. *Journal of International Business Studies*, *21*(1), 23–40.

Dikova, D. (2009). Performance of foreign subsidiaries: Does psychic distance matter? *International Business Review*, *18*(1), 38–49.

Dow, D. (2007). *Research web-page for Douglas Dow.* Retrieved from http://www.mbs.edu/home/dow/research/. Accessed on March 20, 2014.

Dow, D., & Ferencikova, S. (2010). More than just cultural distance: Testing new distance scales on FDI in Slovakia. *International Business Review*, *19*(1), 46–58.

Dow, D., & Karunaratna, A. (2006). Developing a multidimensional instrument to measure psychic distance stimuli. *Journal of International Business Studies*, *37*(5), 578–602.

Dow, D., & Larimo, J. (2007). *Entry mode choice: Testing new approaches to measuring psychic distance and international experience*. Catania: European International Business Academy.

Dow, D., & Larimo, J. (2009). Challenging the conceptualization and measurement of distance and international experience in entry mode choice research. *Journal of International Marketing*, *17*(2), 74–98.

Eden, L., & Miller, S (2004). Distance matters: Liability of foreignness, institutional distance and ownership strategy. In T. Devinney, et al. (Eds.), *Philosophy of science and meta-knowledge in international business and management. Advances in International Management* (Vol. 16. pp. 187–221. London: Emerald.

Elango, B., Lahiri, S., & Kundu, K. (2013). How does firm experience and institutional distance impact ownership choice in high-technology acquisitions? *R&D Management*, *43*(5), 505–516.

Ellis, P. (2007). Paths to foreign markets: Does distance to market affect firm internalization? *International Business Review*, *16*(5), 573–593.

Evans, J., & Mavondo, F. (2002). Psychic distance and organizational performance: An empirical examination of international retailing operations. *Journal of International Business Studies*, *33*(3), 515–532.

Evans, J., Treadgold, A., & Mavondo, F. (2000). Psychic distance and the performance of international retailers: A suggested theoretical framework. *International Marketing Review*, *17*(4/5), 373–391.

Fama, E., & MacBeth, J. (1973). Risk, return, and equilibrium: Empirical tests. *The Journal of Political Economy*, *81*(3), 607–636.

Fee, C., & Thomas, S. (2004). Sources of gains in horizontal mergers: Evidence from customer, supplier, and rival firms. *Journal of Financial Economics*, *74*(3), 423–460.

Ferreira, M., Santos, J., Reis, N., & Almeida, M. (2014). Mergers & acquisitions research: A bibliometric study of top strategy and international business journals, 1980–2010. *Journal of Business Research*, *63*(12), 2550–2558.

Finkelstein, S., & Haleblian, J. (2002). Understanding acquisition performance: The role of transfer effects, *Organization Science*, *13*(1), 36–47.

Ford, D. (1984). Buyer/seller relationships in international industrial markets. *Industrial Marketing Management*, *13*(2), 101–13.

Ghemawat, P. (2001). Distance still matters: The hard reality of global expansion. *Harvard Business Review*, *79*(8), 137–147.

Greene, W. (2011). *Econometric analysis* (7th ed.), Upper Saddle River, NJ: Prentice Hall.

Gubbi, S., Aulakh, P., Ray, S., Sarkar, M., & Chittoor, R. (2010). Do international acquisitions by emerging economy firms create shareholder value? The case of Indian firms. *Journal of International Business Studies*, *41*(3), 397–418.

Gujarati, D., & Porter, D. (2010). *Essentials of econometrics* (4th ed.). New York, NY: McGraw Hill.

Håkanson, L., & Ambos, B. (2010). The antecedents of psychic distance. *Journal of International Management*, *16*(3), 195–210.

Haleblian, J., Devers, C., McNamara, G., Carpenter, M., & Davison, R. (2009). Taking stock of what we know about mergers and acquisitions: A review and research agenda. *Journal of Management*, *35*(3), 469–502.

Harzing, A. (2003), The role of culture in entry mode studies: From neglect to myopia. In J. Cheng, M. Hitt (Ed.), *Managing Multinationals in a Knowledge Economy: Economics, Culture* (Advances in International Management, Volume 15) Emerald Group Publishing Limited, pp.75–127.

Haspeslagh, P., & Jemison, D. (1991). *Managing acquisitions: Creating value through corporate renewal*, New York, NY: Free Press.

Henisz, W., & Williamson, O. (1999). Comparative economic organization—within and between countries. *Business and Politics*, *1*(3), 261–278.

Hitt, M., Ireland, D., & Harrison, J. (2001). Mergers and acquisitions: A value creating or value destroying strategy? In M. Hitt, R. Freeman & J. Harrison (Eds.), *Handbook of strategic management* (pp. 384–408). Oxford: Blackwell Business.

Holzmüller, H., & Kasper, H. (1990). The decision-maker and export activity: A cross-national comparison of the foreign orientation of Austrian managers. *Management International Review*, *30*(3), 217–230.

Homburg, C., & Bucerius, M. (2006). Is speed of integration really a success factor of mergers and acquisitions? An analysis of the role of internal and external relatedness. *Strategic Management Journal*, *27*(4), 347–367.

Hutzschenreuter, T., Kleindienst, I., & Lange, S. (2014). Added psychic distance stimuli and MNE performance: Performance effects of added cultural, governance, geographic, and economic distance in MNEs' international expansion. *Journal of International Management*, *20*(1), 38–54.

Johanson, J., & Vahlne, J.-F. (1977). The internationalization process of the firm: A model of knowledge development and increasing foreign market commitment. *Journal of International Business Studies*, *8*(1), 22–32.

Johanson, J., & Vahlne, J.-E. (2009). The Uppsala internationalisation process model revisited: From liability of foreignness to liability of outsidership. *Journal of International Business Studies*, *40*(9), 1411–1431.

Johanson, J., & Wiedersheim-Paul, F. (1975). The internationalization of the firm: Four Swedish cases. *Journal of Management Studies*, *12*(3), 305–322.

Kacperczyk, A. (2009). With greater power comes greater responsibility? Takeover protection and corporate attention to stakeholders. *Strategic Management Journal*, *30*(3), 261–285.

King, D., Dalton, D., Daily, C., & Covin, J. (2004). Meta-analyses of post-acquisition performance: Indications of unidentified moderators. *Strategic Management Journal*, *25*(2), 187–200.

Kogut, B., & Singh, H. (1988). The effect of national culture on the choice of entry mode. *Journal of International Business Studies*, *19*(3), 411–432.

Kohli, R., & Mann, B. (2012). Analyzing determinants of value creation in domestic and cross border acquisitions in India. *International Business Review*, *21*(6), 998–1016.

Laamanen, T., & Keil, T. (2008). Performance of serial acquirers: Toward an acquisition program perspective. *Strategic Management Journal*, *29*(6), 663–672.

Larimo, J. (2011). Disentangling the roles of international experience and distance in establishment mode choice. *Management International Review*, *51*(3), 321–355.

Lubatkin, M. (1983). Merger and the performance of the acquiring firm. *Academy of Management Review*, *8*(2), 218–225.

Luo, Y., & Shenkar, O. (2011). Toward a perspective of cultural friction in international business. *Journal of International Management*, *17*(1), 1–14.

Madhavan, R., & Prescott, J. (1995). Market value impact of joint ventures: The effect of industry information-processing load. *Academy of Management Journal*, *38*(3), 900–915.

Magnusson, P., Baack, D., Zdravkovic, W., Staub, S., & Amine, L. (2008). Meta-analysis of cultural differences: Another slice at the apple. *International Business Review*, *17*(5), 520–532.

Malhotra, S., Sivakumar, K., & Zhu, P. (2009). Distance factors and target market selection: The moderating effect of market potential. *International Marketing Review*, *26*(6), 651–673.

Martín, O., & Drogendijk, R. (2014). Country distance (COD): Development and validation of a new objective measure. *Journal of Small Business Management*, *52*(1), 102–125.

McWilliams, A., & Siegel, D. (1997). Event studies in management research: Theoretical and empirical issues. *Academy of Management Journal*, *40*(3), 626–657.

Meglio, O., & Risberg, A. (2011). The (mis) measurement of M&A performance: A systematic narrative literature review. *Scandinavian Journal of Management*, *27*(4), 418–433.

Moeller, S., Schlingemann, F., & Stulz, R. (2004). Firm size and the gains from acquisitions. *Journal of Financial Economics*, *73*(2), 201–228.

Morosini, P., Shane, S., & Singh, H. (1998). National cultural distance and cross-border acquisition performance. *Journal of International Business Studies*, *29*(1), 137–149.

Nadolska, M., & Barkema, H. (2007). Learning to internationalize: The pace and success of foreign acquisitions. *Journal of International Business Studies*, *38*(7), 1170–1186.

Obadia, C. (2013). Foreignness-induced cognitive disorientation. *Management International Review*, *53*(3), 325–360.

O'Grady, S., & Lane, W. (1996). The psychic distance paradox. *Journal of International Business Studies*, *27*(2), 309–333.

Pedersen, T., & Petersen, B. (2004). Learning about foreign markets: Are entrant firms exposed to a "shock effect"? *Journal of International Marketing*, *12*(1), 103–123.

Ronen, S., & Shenkar, O. (2013). Mapping world cultures: Cluster formation, sources and implications. *Journal of International Business Studies*, *44*(9), 867–897.

Seth, A. (1990a). Value creation in acquisitions: A reexamination of performance issues. *Strategic Management Journal*, *11*(2), 99–115.

Seth, A., Song, K., & Pettit, R. (2000). Synergy, managerialism or hubris? An empirical examination of motives for foreign acquisitions of U.S. firms. *Journal of International Business Studies*, *31*(3), 387–405.

Shelton, M. (1988). Strategic business fits and corporate acquisition: Empirical evidence. *Strategic Management Journal*, *9*(3), 279–288.

Shenkar, O. (2001). Cultural distance revisited: Towards a more rigorous conceptualization and measurement of cultural differences. *Journal of International Business Studies*, *32*(3), 519–535.

Shenkar, O., Luo, Y., & Yeheskel, O. (2008). From "distance" to "friction": Substituting metaphors and redirecting intercultural research. *Academy of Management Review*, *33*(4), 905–923.

Sousa, C., & Bradley, F. (2006). Cultural distance and psychic distance: Two peas in a pod? *Journal of International Marketing*, *14*(1), 49–70.

Sousa, C., & Bradley, F. (2008). Cultural distance and psychic distance: Refinements in conceptualisation and measurement. *Journal of Marketing Management*, *24*(5), 467–488.

Sousa, C., Ruzo, E., & Losada, F. (2010). The key role of managers' values in exporting: Influence on customer responsiveness and export performance. *Journal of International Marketing*, *18*(2), 1–19.

Stahl, G., & Voigt, A. (2008). Do cultural differences matter in mergers and acquisitions? A tentative model and meta-analytic examination. *Organization Science*, *19*(1), 160–176.

Venkatraman, N., & Ramanujam, V. (1986). Measurement of business performance in strategy research: A comparison of approaches. *Academy of Management Review*, *11*(4), 801–814.

Vermeulen, E., & Barkema, H. (2001). Learning through acquisitions. *Academy of Management Journal*, *44*(3), 457–476.

Very, P. (2004), *The management of mergers and acquisition*. Chichester: John Wiley & Sons Ltd.

Very, P., & Gates, S. (2007). Merger and acquisition as project–Controlling the integration Progress with a project monitoring system. Mergers and Acquisitions. London: Blackwell Publishing, pp. 181–203.

Wright, P., Kroll, M., & Elenkov, D. (2002). Acquisition returns, increase in firm size, and chief executive officer compensation: The moderating role of monitoring. *Academy of Management Journal* *45*(3), 599–608.

Xu, D., & Shenkar, O. (2002). Note: Institutional distance and the multinational enterprise. *Academy of Management Review*, *27*(4), 608–618.

Yildiz, E. (2014). Not all differences are the same: Dual roles of status and cultural distance in sociocultural integration in cross-border M&As. *Journal of International Management*, *20*(1), 25–37.

Zahra, S., Ireland, R., & Hitt, M. (2000). International expansion by new venture firms: International diversity, mode of market entry, technological learning, and performance. *Academy of Management Journal*, *43*(5), 925–950.

Zhao, H., Luo, Y., & Suh, T. (2004). Transaction cost determinants and ownership-based entry mode choice: A meta-analytic review. *Journal of International Business Studies*, *35*(6), 524–544.

Zhu, H., Hitt, M., Eden, L., & Tihanyi, L. (2010). *Host country institutions and the performance of cross-border M&As* (p. 113). Working Paper, Chinese University of Hong Kong.

Zollo, M., & Meier, D. (2008). What is M&A performance? *The Academy of Management Perspectives*, *22*(3), 55–77.

Zurawicki, L., & Habib, M. (2010). Corruption and foreign direct investment: What have we learned? *International Business & Economics Research Journal*, *9*(7), 1–10.

CHAPTER 9

WHY DOES PSYCHIC DISTANCE INHIBIT INTERNATIONAL BUYER–SUPPLIER RELATIONSHIPS?

Silviu H. Tierean and Guido A. J. M. Berens

ABSTRACT

In spite of technological advances and the removal or reduction of tariffs and other barriers to trade, international buyer–supplier relationships often struggle. In this conceptual chapter, we examine how purchase intentions are influenced by the effects of the psychic distance between the countries where the buyer and the supplier reside. We look into the causal mechanism through which the psychic distance between the buyer and the supplier influences the extent to which the two will enter a business relationship. Two causal pathways are proposed, a more emotional pathway, through organizational identification, as predicted by the psychological distance theory, and a more rational pathway, through trust and expected relationship quality, as predicted by internationalization theory.

Keywords: Psychic distance; identification; trust; buyer–supplier relationships

Distance in International Business: Concept, Cost and Value
Progress in International Business Research, Volume 12, 207–222

ISSN: 1745-8862/doi:10.1108/S1745-886220170000012018

How the distance between two firms influences international buyer–supplier relationships is an ongoing and relevant topic in international business (Håkanson & Dow, 2012). Recent decades have witnessed a significant progress in communication, such as the world-wide-web revolution, increased speed of transportation, more free-trade agreements, all of these resulting in higher volumes being traded between the different national economies. However, despite increasing globalization, it seems that the effect of distance on international purchasing has actually increased, rather than decreased. Thus, partnerships between foreign business partners continue to struggle or fail (Johnson, Lenartowicz, & Apud, 2006). One of the reasons why international buyer–supplier relationship fails is their inability to appreciate and overcome the differences between them, which stem from the different cultural contexts and development levels of the countries of residence.

The most basic measure of distance is in terms of geographic distance. This approach to measuring distance is the norm when quantifying transportation and other physical costs associated with trading. Examples of such transaction costs that can be largely explained by geographic distance are gathering of information with regard to the quality of products or assessing the reliability of international transaction partners. Furthermore, Portes and Rey (2005) show that the farther away the trading partner is, the higher will be the costs of negotiations, personal interaction, costs which normally should not be associated with geographical distance. Hence, geographical distance diminishes the amount of products transacted by foreign partners. Countries may be distant also because economic, social, cultural, or political differences make it harder for firms to build relationships. Johanson and Vahlne (1977, p. 24) have coined the term "psychic distance" as being the "the sum of factors preventing the flow of information to and from the market," Beckerman (1956) made the first statement with regard to the negative effect of psychic distance by suggesting that countries that have a low psychic distance between each other have higher levels of international trade. The associations held with the country of residence of a supplier may determine how potential buyers interact with the supplier. Differences in language, religious beliefs, social norms, and development are capable of creating distance between two firms, when they are situated in different countries.

Previous research has documented the effects of various dimensions of distance within a broad range of international business issues. Håkansson and Wootz (1975) made the first empirical attempt to link physical distance with purchasing intentions in a business-to-business setting. Their results show that purchasers prefer suppliers who are more proximal. Another study that examines the link between psychic distance and international buyer–supplier relationships (Skarmeas, Katsikeas, Spyropoulou, & Salehi-Sangari, 2008) shows that psychic distance has a negative influence on the quality of importer–exporter relationships in the mature stages of the business relationships. A study by Griffith and Dimitrova (2014) shows that psychic distance is linked to satisfaction with the importer–exporter relationship; however, they take the perspective of the exporting firms in the mature stage of their business relations with importers.

The goal of our chapter is to discuss the effects of the psychic distance dimensions in the context of a firm faced with the situation of choosing an international supplier. Dow and Karunaratna (2006) have shown that large differences between countries predict lower trade-flows, at the country level. In this chapter we aim to provide an explanation of this finding at the micro-level of buyers confronted with the decision whether to choose a particular international supplier or not, depending on the country of residence of the supplier. Furthermore, we aim to explore the causal mechanism through which the distance between the countries of the buyer and the supplier influences the extent to which the two will enter a business relationship.

Subjective and perceptual factors, such as subjective expectations based on own experience, decision makers' personalities, and own assessment of risk, have been shown to have an important role in international marketing and trade decisions (see Evans, Treadgold, & Mavondo, 2000). Managers rely both on objective and subjective information when making decisions related to which foreign markets they should penetrate or which international partners they should trade with. In the particular case of international buyer–supplier relationships, the quantity and quality of objective information is often rather limited due to the distance (Evans et al., 2000). The management is, therefore, faced with having to make decisions based on subjective, emotional cues. In this context it becomes relevant to determine through which causal pathway – more rational or more emotional – distance influences purchasing decisions. We use the concept of "psychological distance," derived from the self-construal theoretical framework, to explore the less rational effects of distance. Therefore, two causal pathways are explored, a more emotional pathway, through organizational identification, as predicted by the psychological distance theory, and a more rational pathway, through trust and expected relationship quality, as predicted by theories from international business.

THE EFFECT OF PSYCHIC DISTANCE DIMENSIONS ON BUYING INTENTIONS

"The farther you are from a country, the harder it will be to conduct business in that country" (Ghemawat, 2001, p. 7). As predicted by the cross-cultural literature, the quality of interaction is influenced by cultural and language barriers. For example, directness in speech perceived as rudeness in Asia whereas in the United States is considered a quality (Hall & Hall, 1990; Pornpitakpan, 2000). Stringfellow, Teagarden, and Nie (2008) coined the term "interaction distance" to incorporate the combined effects of several dimensions of distance between business partners. Therefore, interaction distance denotes the combination of invisible cost that occurs when communicating with foreign partners. According to Stringfellow et al. (2008), there are three conditions which are essential for an effective interaction: a suitable communication channel, a common language, and a common system of interpreting the incoming massages. Although electronic communication is widely available, it cannot be a genuine substitute for face-to-face interaction. Media richness theory (Daft & Lengel, 1986) states that different media of communication vary along a "richness" spectrum, with face-to-face interaction at one end of the spectrum, and e-mail messages at the other end. Communication richness includes all possible interaction types, from spoken words to nonverbal cues, and the richer the communication, the more immediate is the feedback. This richness of communication is even more essential in assessing complex issues that have no a clear solution. To achieve a good level of communication richness, at least one of the international business partners would need to travel to meet the other partner in person. Not making this effort creates an obstacle in the way of rich communication between buyers and suppliers that reside in different countries. Foreign business partners imply cultural and development differences, all of which present challenges to communication, information sharing, problem-solving and, therefore, to operational effectiveness. We discuss the components that contribute to psychic distance as follows.

Cultural Distance

Culture was defined in a various ways (Straub, Loch, Evaristo, Karahanna & Srite, 2002), one often-cited definition being "the collective programming of the mind which distinguishes the members of one group or category of people from another" (Hofstede, 1991, p. 5). Although individuals from different countries have to face similar problems, they might view the solution from different angles. This is because people from different cultures have a different collective programming (Reus & Lamont, 2009). Extensive studies performed on national cultures show that the differences between countries are substantial, and these differences impact the way individuals interact with each other (see Reus & Lamont, 2009). Thus, a high cultural distance has the potential to complicate the communication between the workforces of buyers and suppliers that belong to different cultures.

Compared to language differences, cultural differences are usually more difficult to perceive because they are less apparent and therefore more difficult to notice. Cultural norms which often come in the form of unspoken principles, according to which individuals should behave, are in many instances almost invisible, even to the individuals that follow the principles. Because of this a high level of cultural distance is not easy to overcome and can negatively affect working relationships with foreign partners. For example, Simonin (1999) shows that when cultural distance is high, there is ambiguity between international partners with regard to the knowledge they wish to exchange. Conversely, when cultural distance is low, meaning that the exchange partners share common values and a similar approach to doing business, the transfer of knowledge is facilitated.

The unique characteristics of cultures have been shown to impede building and exploiting resources in distant countries (Luo, 2002). A high cultural distance induces uncertainty, making it more difficult for the firm to predict future events (Magnusson et al., 2008). Magnusson et al. (2008) posit that the effects of cultural distance on importer-exporter relationship quality are becoming increasingly negative and suggest that this may be due to cultural overconfidence. Although in recent years we witnessed a gradual integration of national economies (with the potential exception of the Brexit), it appears that the global economy is still a long way from a "flat world" (Friedman, 2005). Because cultural differences have been linked to and increase in the difficulty of obtaining and interpreting information on foreign market conditions (Boyacigiller, 1990), managers tend to lack objective information and encounter problems in predicting the outcomes of decisions related to foreign markets and exchange partners (Achrol & Stern, 1988). The absence of good quality information about a foreign country can not only lower the firm's ability to respond to changes in the environment in a timely manner, but it can also force managers into making mistakes, which reduces relationship satisfaction and performance (Lee, 1998). Moreover, large differences in culture have been shown to make international marketers less committed to the distant market (Goodnow & Hansz, 1972). For example, Holzmüller and Kasper (1990) show that there is a negative relationship between the perceived differences in culture and the sales to foreign markets.

Language Distance

"All other things being equal, trade between countries that share a language will be three times greater than between countries without a common language" (Ghemawat, 2001, p. 3). Language distance has the potential to become a barrier to communication because the sender and the receiver do not share a common mother tongue. According to the literature on communication theory (i.e., Thomas, 1992), interpersonal communication can by described, on one side, by the core meaning of the message, and, on the other side, by the abstract meaning added by the manner in which the sender delivers the message to the recipient. Both of these characteristics are impacted when attempting to communicate with individuals that speak a different language, and the more dissimilar the language the higher the misunderstanding.

Language distance is another psychic distance dimension that has received empirical confirmation in the research community (Dow & Karunaratna, 2006). Welch, Welch, and Marschan-Piekkari (2001) suggest that organizations tend to expand to countries that speak the same or a similar language, as a measure of reducing risk. Therefore, language distance between national markets tends to inflate the risks of conducting business. As a result, language can be considered as an important factor that influences foreign partner selection. Even if the contact staff members from the supplier and buyer organizations speak the same language, accents can interfere with the process of receiving the message. If the sound of the words is not recognized then the content of the message cannot be processed. Many non-native speakers who carry a heavy accent may be rated as non-intelligible, therefore even in the case of using a common language, the different accents could represent an obstacle in the way of effective communication.

Differences in Religion

Boyacigiller (1990) shows that religions are closely associated with cultures, and imply a set of attitudes and norms. Nevertheless, religion should be treated as a distinct concept relative to culture. At global level, the correlation coefficient between religious distance and cultural distance between any pair of countries in quite low, $r = 0.17$ (Dow & Karunaratna, 2006).

Religions often represent the foundation upon which individuals draw conclusions with regard to the acceptability and desirability of behaviors. Furthermore, the differences in religion are considered to be one of the most important predictors of conflict between groups (Triandis, 2000). In many instances, religious metaphors are a part of the daily language. Consequently, religion may play an important role in how individuals interact with each other. In conclusion, a high level of religious distance may therefore inflate transaction costs and the risk of conflict, and, at the same time, are likely to lower the probability of entering in business relationships.

Differences in Education Levels

The education system is another factor that has the potential to influence how individuals communicate and assess information (see Dow & Karunaratna, 2006). If the differences in education levels between two countries are large, this can have negative consequences on the quality of communication between the foreign business partners, therefore increasing the perceptions of risk of misunderstandings and other types of miscommunication in the market. It is likely that organizational buyers will choose to transact with suppliers from countries that have a similar level of education as their own country of residence.

Differences in Industrial Development

Differences in industrial development were mentioned as a dimension of psychic distance by various researchers in international business (see Dow & Karunaratna, 2006). Similar to how education shapes the way people communicate, how employees perform their duties at work is likely to be shaped by the economic development of their country. The type of jobs that individuals have is likely to have a role in the communication style adopted by those individuals. Furthermore, the standard of business language and interaction are likely to be affected by the industry or economic sector in which the firm operates. "For example, the communication and business norms in a subsistence agrarian economy are likely to be dramatically different from those of a highly industrialized economy with a large service sector" (Dow & Karunaratna, 2006, p. 582). These differences in industrial development imply extra risk and higher transaction costs for organizational purchasing, and thus are likely to influence the country of origin of the business partner.

Differences in Political Systems

Managers can be influenced by the differences in political systems in two distinct ways (Dow & Karunaratna, 2006). First, managing a business relationship with a partner from different country might require interacting with the government of that country. If the difference in political systems is large, then the costs and uncertainties brought by the interaction with the distant government are expected to be higher compared to having to deal with a government that is similar to the one in the country of origin of the buyer firm. Second, governments can interfere with importer–exporter relationships by enforcing contracts and discouraging anti-competitive behavior (Dow & Karunaratna, 2006). Therefore, if the political differences are high, the buyer firm will tend to protect itself from uncertain situations, such as anticipating how the government reacts or the foreign supplier will behave in the case of a potential intervention from their government. Both of the situations described above may drive upward the risks and costs of transacting with a foreign supplier, and hence, have the potential to influence international supplier selection decisions.

In light of these arguments, we expect that a high psychic distance between the countries where the buyer and the supplier reside has negative consequences on the extent to which the buyer will be willing to transact with the supplier.

Proposition 1. Perceived psychic distance to the country where the foreign supplier resides has a negative effect on the intentions to buy from the foreign supplier.

THE "RATIONAL" CAUSAL PATHWAY

Previous research in international trade suggests that a broad set of distance factors have a broad set of consequences. For example, Dow and Ferencikova (2010) show that both the likelihood of foreign direct investment occurring between two countries and the performance of a foreign investment in the host country will be negatively related to the psychic distance dimensions of language distance, differences in religion, differences in industrial development, differences in education, and differences in political systems. Numerous studies support the assumption that firms have better outcomes in foreign countries that are more similar to their home country (see Evans et al., 2000). The most common theoretical claim is that psychic distance negatively influences trade performance because distant countries are more difficult to understand, learn about, and therefore the risk of misunderstandings increases (see Evans et al., 2000). In contrast, when the business partner is located in a more similar country, the level of trust increases, and therefore the chances to enter a business relationship with a proximal supplier also increase.

The development of any relationship is affected by the perception that one business partner has on the other partner. In international business, the concept of psychic distance captures this judgment by proposing that if the characteristics of a firm's national market and those of a foreign business environment differ, it generates uncertainties among business potential business partners which may prevent the formation of business relationships with partners from distant countries. The greater the psychic distance between the foreign country and the domestic environment, the lower is likely to be the quantity and the quality of the available information about the new market. Therefore, it will be more difficult to understand the foreign environment and gather knowledge about it. This idea is supported by Eriksson, Majkgard, and Sharma (2000), who find that large differences between the home country and the foreign country make the process of identifying and analyzing incoming information more demanding, leading to uncertainty regarding the relationship with the distant business partner. Additionally, the more divergent the environments of the two firms are, the more difficult becomes the communication. A low frequency of communication between buyers and suppliers is associated with low trust (Mohr & Nevin, 1990). High levels of psychic distance may make parties hesitant to transact, due to low levels of trust or a general lack of knowledge of the other's home market. Lee (1998) found that exporters' cultural distance positively affects opportunism and this is why cultural distance is negatively related to exporting performance. Conversely, for firms who perceive small differences between the countries in which they reside, in the initial stages of the relationship, perception of risk might be at low levels, similar to those encountered when transacting with domestic business partners, due to the (sometimes wrong) expectation that the foreign business partner is "just like us" (Magnusson & Boyle, 2009). Thus, it has been argued that greater psychic distance can lead to misunderstandings, hence lower trust, and lower business relationship quality (Adler 1997; Lincoln, Hanada, & Olson 1981). Consistent with this reasoning, we argue that psychic distance is negatively related to trust in the supplier, which, in turn, leads to a decreased expected relationship quality.

Proposition 2. Perceived psychic distance to the country where the foreign supplier resides has a negative effect on the trust in the foreign supplier.

Proposition 3. The effect of perceived psychic distance on buying intentions from the foreign supplier is (serially) mediated by trust in the foreign supplier and by the expected quality of the relationship with the foreign supplier.

THE "EMOTIONAL" CAUSAL PATHWAY

Psychological distance

People directly experience themselves and their immediate surroundings at the present moment. Psychologically distant objects are those that are not present in direct experience. Four dimensions of psychological distance can be distinguished: temporal distance, spatial distance, social distance, and hypotheticality – the extent to which an object is real (Trope & Liberman, 2010). The consequence of being removed from the direct exposure of an object is that information about the object becomes less available or less reliable, leading people to rely on schematic, prototypical information (Trope & Liberman, 2003). Construal level theory in consumer psychology conceptualizes spatial distance as one of the key sources of psychological distance (Trope, Liberman, & Wakslak, 2007). In a study by Henderson, Fujita, Trope, and Liberman (2006), in which spatial distance was manipulated, subjects assigned to the spatially distant experimental condition based their estimations on general trends rather than deviations from general trends. In contrast, subjects assigned to the spatially near experimental condition based their estimations equally on general trends and on the deviations from general trends. Thus, individuals tend to construe psychologically distant objects "by their essential, abstract and global features," and psychologically closer objects "by their concrete and local features" (Fujita, Henderson, Eng, Trope, & Liberman, 2006, p. 278). An association is formed between psychological distance and level of construal, and the use of more abstract construals for more distal entities may be generalized beyond the conditions that initially gave rise to the association (Trope & Liberman, 2010). This means that construals of a given entity are more abstract when the entity is psychologically distant compared to when the entity is psychologically near, even when the information known about the entity is identical (Fujita et al., 2006).

The Effect of Distance on Perceptions About the Foreign Supplier and Buyer–Supplier Identification

The construal level theory implies that spatially distant (proximal) objects are represented in more abstract (concrete) manner than corresponding proximal (distant) objects (Trope & Liberman, 2010). The higher level of abstractness would, in turn, lead to a lower level of cognitive fluency (Trope & Liberman, 2010). These findings suggest that buyers would perceive countries located in spatially distant areas more abstractly and thus with less cognitive fluency, while those located in spatially proximal areas more concretely and thus with more cognitive fluency. The positive association between cognitive fluency and consumers' favorable attitudes (Lee & Labroo, 2004) further implies that purchasing managers will have more favorable attitudes toward the proximal objects than distant objects. Moreover, construal-level theory (Trope & Liberman, 2003) proposes that a large spatial distance to an object influences mental representations similar to those having high levels on the other dimensions of psychological distance, including temporal and social distances (Fujita et al., 2006). Trope and Liberman (2010) show that the four types of psychological distance (temporal, spatial, and social distance, and hypotheticality) are cognitively associated with each other, such that imagining an entity as distant on one dimension of psychological distance is linked to thinking about the entity as distant also on the other dimensions and, therefore, the effects of the various dimensions of distances are interchangeable. A consequence of this interchangeability of psychological distance dimensions (i.e., spatial and social distances) is that more spatially distant entities are seen less similar to the self (Trope & Liberman, 2010). In the context of buyer–supplier relationships, the interchangeability of dimensions of psychological distance implies that a high spatial distance to the supplier firms would lead the purchasing officers to perceive a high dissimilarity between them and the suppliers. The fact that construals of a given entity are more abstract when it is psychologically distant versus near, a distant supplier (vs. a nearby supplier) would influence the mental representations of the purchasers, and doing so we distinguish two important consequences. First, the purchasers perceive the information they have on the distant supplier as less reliable, and second, they identify less with the distant suppliers. Organizational identification (which, in our context, refers to the situation where the purchasing officer and the supplier firm share the same goals and values; Efraty & Wolfe, 1988) has been found by several scholars (e.g., Keh & Xie, 2009) to be an important aspect in explaining the performance of business-to-business relationships. Previous research shows that customer–supplier identification fully mediates the effect of perceived company characteristics on both buying behavior (Ahearne, Bhattacharya, & Guen, 2005; Keh & Xie, 2009) and extra-role behaviors (Ahearne et al., 2005). Thus, a buyer's behavior seems to be influenced by the degree to which a seller's values and beliefs are in agreement with his or her value system, with further consequences in buying intentions. In conclusion, by applying the psychological distance approach to a business-to-business context, it seems likely that as distance between the potential exchange partners increases, the organizational identification would decrease, and that organizational identification acts as a mediator of the relation between distance and buying intentions.

> **Proposition 4.** Perceived psychic distance to the country where the foreign supplier resides has a negative effect on the identification with the supplier.

> **Proposition 5.** The effect of perceived psychic distance on buying intentions from the foreign supplier is mediated by the identification with the foreign supplier.

DISCUSSION

The goal of our chapter was to investigate the effects and causal mechanism through which the psychic distance dimensions influence purchase intentions, in the context of a firm faced with the situation of choosing an international supplier. As depicted in Fig. 1, we propose that the distance between the countries where the supplier and the organizational buyer reside has a negative effect on the intentions to buy from the supplier. We also propose two causal pathways – one more rational and one more emotional – through which distance influences purchasing decisions. Using the concept of psychological distance, derived from the self-construal theoretical framework, we propose that, in the case of the more emotional pathway, a large distance negatively influences the identification of the purchasing manager with the supplier, and, in turn, the low degree of identification decreases the purchasing intentions. The other causal pathway that we considered, more rational, uses arguments from international trade theories. We argued that trust and

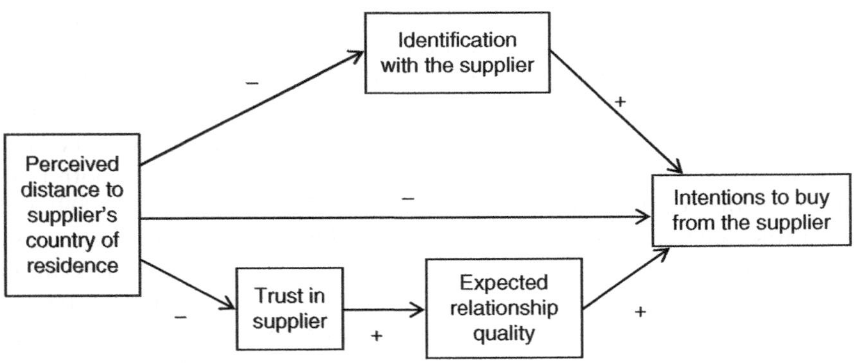

Fig. 1. The Proposed Conceptual Framework.

expected relationship quality serially mediate the effect of distance dimensions on the buyer's intentions to buy from the supplier.

Previous research has documented the effects of various distance-related constructs within a broad range of international business issue, including export market selection, international trade-flows, foreign-direct-investment flows, entry mode choice, establishment mode choice, cross-border acquisitions, adaptation in foreign markets, performance in foreign markets, use of human resource management practices, and the degree of adaptation of the marketing program. The first empirical attempt to link distance (in this case physical) with purchasing intentions in a business-to-business context was made by Håkansson and Wootz (1975). Other studies (Griffith & Dimitrova, 2014; Skarmeas et al., 2008) have also examined the link between psychic distance and international buyer–supplier relationships. However, to the best of our knowledge, no other study has explored the reasons why psychic distance influences the manner in which purchasing managers evaluate foreign suppliers before actually engaging in buying behavior. It is worth mentioning the conceptual work by Magnusson and Boyle (2009) in which they develop a contingency model that suggests that psychic distance might have opposite effects on international channel relationships, depending on the different stages of relationship development.

By highlighting the potential mediating roles of trust, expected relationship quality, and identification with the supplier, our proposed model may provide an explanation for the finding by Dow and Karunaratna (2006) that international trade-flows are dependent on the psychic distance between countries.

Practitioners can benefit from our conceptual study in multiple ways. Our research aims at disentangling the effects of psychic distance, by suggesting an explanation for why psychic distance influences the relationships between buyers and their international suppliers. By considering multiple causal pathways (more rational and more emotional) of the effect of psychic distance on supplier selection, the purchasing managers may become aware of how they make decisions. It could be that sometimes avoiding psychically distant suppliers is a purely emotional decision, which might imply that distance should not become a supplier selection criterion by itself.

On the suppliers' part, the benefits of our study are that they will be aware of which dimensions of psychic distance matter the most and can focus their communication and distribution efforts on those markets on which they can avoid the negative consequences of psychic distance. Furthermore, knowing through which mechanisms distance affects buying decisions might give suppliers guidance on how to approach "distant" buyers. For example, if identification would indeed play an important role in why distance has an effect, suppliers could try to foster identification with distant buyers in other ways (e.g., by demonstrating their values through initiatives aimed at societal issues).

REFERENCES

Achrol, R. S., & Stern, L. W. (1988). Environmental determinants of decision-making uncertainty in marketing channels. *Journal of Marketing Research, 25*(1), 36–50.

Adler, E. (1997). Seizing the middle ground: Constructivism in world politics. *European Journal of International Relations, 3*(3), 319–363.

Ahearne, M., Bhattacharya, C. B., & Gruen, T. (2005). Antecedents and consequences of customer-company identification: Expanding the role of relationship marketing. *Journal of Applied Psychology, 90*(3), 574.

Beckerman, W. (1956). Distance and the pattern of intra-European trade. *The Review of Economics and Statistics, 38*(1), 31–40.

Boyacigiller, N. (1990). The role of expatriates in the management of interdependence complexity and risk in multinational corporations. *Journal of International Business Studies, 21*(3), 357–381.

Daft, R. L., & Lengel, R. H. (1986). Organizational information requirements, media richness and structural design. *Management Science, 32*(5), 554–571.

Dow, D., & Ferencikova, S. (2010). More than just national cultural distance: Testing new distance scales on FDI in Slovakia. *International Business Review, 19*(1), 46–58.

Dow, D., & Karunaratna, A. (2006). Developing a multidimensional instrument to measure psychic distance stimuli. *Journal of International Business Studies, 37*(5), 578–602.

Efraty, D., & Wolfe, D. M. (1988). The effect of organizational identification on employee affective and performance responses. *Journal of Business and Psychology, 3*(1), 105–112.

Eriksson, K., Majkgård, A., & Sharma, D. D. (2000). Path dependence and knowledge development in the internationalization process. *Management International Review, 40*(4), 307–328.

Evans, J., Treadgold, A., & Mavondo, F. T. (2000). Psychic distance and the performance of international retailers – A suggested theoretical framework. *International Marketing Review, 17*(4/5), 373–391.

Friedman, T. L. (2005). *The world is flat: A brief history of the twenty-first century*. New York: Farrar, Straus and Giroux.

Fujita, K., Henderson, M. D., Eng, J., Trope, Y., & Liberman, N. (2006). Spatial distance and mental construal of social events. *Psychological Science, 17*(4), 278–282.

Ghemawat, P. (2001). Distance still matters. *Harvard Business Review, 79*(8), 137–147.

Goodnow, J. D., & Hansz, J. E. (1972). Environmental determinants of overseas market entry strategies. *Journal of International Business Studies, 3*(1), 33–50.

Griffith, D. A., & Dimitrova, B. V. (2014). Business and cultural aspects of psychic distance and complementarity of capabilities in export relationships. *Journal of International Marketing, 22*(3), 50–67.

Håkanson, L., & Dow, D. (2012). Markets and networks in international trade: On the role of distances in globalization. *Management International Review, 52*(6), 761–789.

Håkansson, H., & Wootz, B. (1975). Supplier selection in an international environment: An experimental study. *Journal of Marketing Research*, 46–51.

Hall, E. T., & Hall, M. R. (1990). *Understanding cultural differences* (Vol. 12). Yarmouth, ME: Intercultural Press.

Henderson, M. D., Fujita, K., Trope, Y., & Liberman, N. (2006). Transcending the "here": The effect of spatial distance on social judgment. *Journal of Personality and Social Psychology*, *91*(5), 845.

Hofstede, G. (1991). *Cultures and organizations. Intercultural cooperation and its importance for survival. Software of the mind*. London: McGraw-Hill.

Holzmüller, H. H., & Kasper, H. (1990). The decision-maker and export activity: A cross-national comparison of the foreign orientation of Austrian managers. *MIR: Management International Review*, *30*(3), 217–230.

Johanson, J., & Vahlne, J. E. (1977). The internationalization process of the firm – A model of knowledge development and increasing foreign market commitments. *Journal of International Business Studies*, *8*(1), 23–32.

Johnson, J. P., Lenartowicz, T., & Apud, S. (2006). Cross-cultural competence in international business: Toward a definition and a model. *Journal of International Business Studies*, *37*(4), 525–543.

Keh, H. T., & Xie, Y. (2009). Corporate reputation and customer behavioral intentions: The roles of trust, identification and commitment. *Industrial Marketing Management*, *38*(7), 732–742.

Lee, D. J. (1998). Developing international strategic alliances between exporters and importers: The case of Australian exporters. *International Journal of Research in Marketing*, *15*(4), 335–348.

Lee, A. Y., & Labroo, A. A. (2004). The effect of conceptual and perceptual fluency on brand evaluation. *Journal of Marketing Research*, *41*(2), 151–165.

Luo, Y. (2002). Capability exploitation and building in a foreign market: Implications for multinational enterprises. *Organization Science*, *13*(1), 48–63.

Lincoln, J. R., Hanada, M., & Olson, J. (1981). Cultural orientations and individual reactions to organizations: A study of employees of Japanese-owned firms. *Administrative Science Quarterly*, *26*(1), 93–115.

Magnusson, P., & Boyle, B. A. (2009). A contingency perspective on psychic distance in international channel relationships. *Journal of Marketing Channels*, *16*(1), 77–99.

Magnusson, P., Baack, D. W., Zdravkovic, S., Staub, K. M., & Amine, L. S. (2008). Meta-analysis of cultural differences: Another slice at the apple. *International Business Review*, *17*(5), 520-532.

Pornpitakpan, C. (2000). Trade in Thailand: A three-way cultural comparison. *Business Horizons*, *43*(2), 61–70.

Portes, R., & Rey, H. (2005). The determinants of cross-border equity flows. *Journal of International Economics*, *65*(2), 269–296.

Simonin, B. L. (1999). Ambiguity and the process of knowledge transfer in strategic alliances. *Strategic Management Journal*, *20*(7), 595–623.

Skarmeas, D., Katsikeas, C. S., Spyropoulou, S., & Salehi-Sangari, E. (2008). Market and supplier characteristics driving distributor relationship quality in international marketing channels of industrial products. *Industrial Marketing Management*, *37*(1), 23–36.

Straub, D., Loch, K., Evaristo, R., Karahanna, E., & Srite, M. (2002). Toward a theory-based measurement of culture. *Human Factors in Information Systems*, *10*(1), 61–65.

Stringfellow, A., Teagarden, M. B., & Nie, W. (2008). Invisible costs in offshoring services work. *Journal of Operations Management*, *26*(2), 164–179.

Thomas, K. W. (1992). Conflict and conflict management: Reflections and update. *Journal of Organizational Behavior*, *13*(3), 265–274.

Triandis, H. C. (2000). Culture and conflict. *International Journal of Psychology*, *35*(2), 145–152.

Trope, Y., & Liberman, N. (2003). Temporal construal. *Psychological Review*, *110*(3), 403.

Trope, Y., & Liberman, N. (2010). Construal-level theory of psychological distance. *Psychological Review*, *117*(2), 440.

Trope, Y., Liberman, N., & Wakslak, C. (2007). Construal levels and psychological distance: Effects on representation, prediction, evaluation, and behavior. *Journal of Consumer Psychology*, *17*(2), 83.

Welch, D. E., Welch, L. S., & Marschan-Piekkari, R. (2001). The persistent impact of language on global operations. *Prometheus*, *19*(3), 193–209.

PART III
THE COST OF INSTITUTIONAL DISTANCE

CHAPTER 10

INSTITUTIONAL DISTANCE AND LOCATION CHOICE: NEW EMPIRICAL EVIDENCE FROM EMERGING-MARKET MNEs

Diego Quer, Enrique Claver and Laura Rienda

ABSTRACT

Outward foreign direct investment (FDI) from emerging economies, in particular from China and India, is on the rise. As a result, the international expansion of emerging-market multinational enterprises (MNEs) is attracting growing attention among scholars. However, existing research comparing the location patterns of Chinese and Indian MNEs is still scant. In order to fill this gap, we aim to analyze the impact of political risk and cultural distance on the location choice of Chinese and Indian MNEs. Drawing on an institutional approach, we propose several hypotheses regarding the influence of political risk and cultural distance on location decisions. We test our hypotheses using a sample of FDIs carried out by Chinese and Indian MNEs. Our findings suggest that the behavior of Chinese MNEs is less conventional than that of their Indian counterparts when facing institutional obstacles in host countries. Previous papers dealing with location decisions of China's and India's outward FDI did not specifically address

Distance in International Business: Concept, Cost and Value
Progress in International Business Research, Volume 12, 225–237

ISSN: 1745-8862/doi:10.1108/S1745-886220170000012003

the impact of political risk and cultural distance. This comparative study provides new empirical evidence on the influence of these traditional host country institutional factors.

Keywords: Emerging-market MNEs; location choice; political risk; cultural distance

INTRODUCTION

Outward foreign direct investment (FDI) from emerging economies is one of the most important trends in international business over the past few years. In particular, emerging-market multinational enterprises (MNEs) from China and India are increasingly becoming leading players in many industries from energy and metals to automotive, engineering, information technology, or tourism. Large corporations such as China National Petroleum Corporation (CNPC), Sinopec, Huawei, Lenovo or Wanda Group, in the case of China, and Tata Group, Infosys, Reliance Industries or Indian Oil, in the case of India, are some outstanding examples.

Several recent literature reviews report that empirical research comparing the international behavior of Chinese and Indian MNEs is still scarce (Quer, Claver, & Rienda, 2015; Rienda, Claver, & Quer, 2011). Although prior studies analyzed several issues, only a few of them focused on the locational determinants of China's and India's outward FDI decisions (Brienen, Burger, & van Oort, 2010; De Beule & Duanmu, 2012; De Beule & Van Den Bulcke, 2012; Duanmu & Guney, 2009; Pradhan, 2011).

However, these past studies did not specifically address the simultaneous influence of political risk and cultural distance, two traditional host country institutional factors that affect location strategies of MNEs. We aim to fill this research gap by investigating the impact of the abovementioned factors on the location decisions of Chinese and Indian MNEs. More precisely, we seek to analyze the potential differences between the behavioral pattern of these emerging-market MNEs and that shown by developed-country MNEs in the past.

THEORETICAL FRAMEWORK

Among host country institutional factors, political risk is one of the most researched topics. Prior studies reported a negative influence of political risk on outward FDI. A less repressive institutional environment in the host country tends to be preferred by foreign MNEs (Kang & Jiang, 2012). Furthermore, factors such as uncertainty and the hazard of an eventual expropriation usually deter foreign companies (Brouthers, 2002; Pak & Park, 2004).

However, this traditional view is challenged by emerging-market MNEs. Since they use to compete in a weak underdeveloped institutional environment in their home country, they may enjoy an advantage over developed-country MNEs when operating in a similar underdeveloped host country institutional environment (Cuervo-Cazurra & Genc, 2008).

In spite of this, we argue that this effect may depend on the unique characteristics of the respective China's and India's home country institutional environments. The government in China has played a more active role in China's economic development in comparison with India (Das, 2010). As a consequence, whereas the largest Chinese MNEs are state-owned enterprises (SOEs), the vast majority of Indian MNEs are private firms (Devonshire-Ellis, 2010; Pradhan, 2011). Because of the support of the home government, Chinese SOEs may be not deterred by host country political risk (Duanmu, 2012, 2014; Ramasamy, Yeung, & Laforet, 2012). For instance, they may not pursue only profit maximization (Buckley et al., 2007). Moreover, bilateral diplomatic relations between China and several host countries may represent a risk-reduction device (Zhang, Jiang, & Zhou, 2014). Therefore, we propose our first hypothesis as follows:

H1. Host country political risk has a negative impact on India's outward FDI but a non-significant impact on China's outward FDI.

Cultural distance is the other host country institutional factor that has been extensively analyzed in the literature on location decisions of MNEs. The conventional wisdom suggests that cultural distance deters foreign MNEs, since it creates several obstacles when doing business abroad (Blomkvist & Drogendijk, 2013; Cui & Jiang, 2010; Kang & Jiang, 2012; Malhotra, Zhu, & Locander, 2010). There is abundant empirical evidence supporting this negative relationship between cultural distance and location decisions (Bhardwaj, Dietz, & Beamish, 2007).

Despite this general understanding, there are several arguments suggesting differences between Chinese and Indian MNEs when dealing with cultural distance. Since 1991, India's outward FDI has concentrated in developed countries, in particular, the United Kingdom and the United States, two countries with which India shares cultural ties and a common language (Pradhan, 2008a, 2008b). Actually, prior studies report that the presence of overseas Indian in English-speaking countries is a factor that may attract Indian investments (Anwar & Mughal, 2013; Brienen et al., 2010; Nunnenkamp, Sosa, Vadlamannati, & Waldkirch, 2012; Pradhan & Singh, 2011).

As for Chinese MNEs, the unique characteristics of their internationalization path suggest a less conventional behavior. First, it is worth mentioning the influence of prior inward internationalization, that is, the strategic alliances established in China with foreign MNEs since the late 1970s. These provided Chinese companies with a useful international experience for their subsequent outward internationalization (Luo & Wang, 2012; Luo, Zhao, Wang, & Xi, 2011; Ning & Sutherland, 2012; Xia, Ma, Lu, & Yiu, 2014). Huawei is a good example of how joint ventures at home strengthened international competitive capabilities of a Chinese firm (Child & Rodrigues, 2005). Therefore, inward FDI is a factor that may reduce the potential negative influence of cultural distance on Chinese MNEs' international decisions (Luo & Tung, 2007).

Second, over recent years, strategic asset-seeking is becoming an important driver of China's outward FDI (Buckley et al., 2007; Huang & Renyong, 2014; Rui & Yip, 2008; Yang, Yang, Chen, & Allen, 2014). Many Chinese companies used these investments to access technological, managerial, or commercial resources in order to improve their international competiveness. The main destinations of this type of outward FDI are developed countries with a higher cultural distance from China.

Based on the foregoing discussion, we argue that the conventional negative influence of cultural distance is more evident in the case of Indian MNEs' location decisions than in the case of their Chinese counterparts. Therefore, we propose:

H2. Cultural distance has a negative impact on India's outward FDI but a non-significant impact on China's outward FDI.

METHODOLOGY AND RESEARCH DESIGN

Our sample consists of 832 outward FDIs carried out by Chinese and Indian MNEs between 2005 and 2014. We collected data from several secondary sources. In the case of China, we used the China Global Investment Tracker (a large database on China's outward FDI published by the American Enterprise Institute and The Heritage Foundation). We also checked news reported by several media such as *China Daily* or *Global Times*. In the case of India, we used information from the Centre for Monitoring Indian Economy

(India's largest database on individual companies) and from several Indian media, including *The Economic Times*, *The Hindu Business Line*, and *Business Standard*.

Next we present descriptive statistics for our sample. First, it should be pointed out that 599 outward FDIs were carried out by Chinese MNEs, accounting for 72 percent of the total, whereas the remaining 233 (28 percent) were carried out by Indian MNEs. Table 1 shows the top destinations of both China's and India's investments, while Table 2 reports the top Chinese and Indian investing companies included in our sample.

As to destination countries, it emerges that the United States and Australia are the top host countries of both China's and India's investments abroad, although in the case of China, the United States clearly leads the ranking, accounting for a 14.9 percent of the total China's investments covered by our sample. Furthermore, it should be highlighted that China is the third

Table 1. Top Destinations of China's and India's Outward FDI (2005–2014).

China's Outward FDI			
Rank	Country	FDI number	Percent
1	US	89	14.9
2	Australia	63	10.5
3	Canada	32	5.3
4	UK	30	5
5	Brazil	28	4.7
6	Russia	24	4
7	Indonesia	22	3.7
8	Germany	15	2.5
9	Singapore	13	2.2
10	Malaysia	12	2
India's Outward FDI			
1	Australia	19	8.2
2	US	18	7.7
3	China	14	6
4	UK	13	5.6
5	Mozambique	9	3.9
	Singapore	9	3.9
6	Brazil	8	3.4
	Hong Kong, China	8	3.4
7	Canada	7	3
	Italy	7	3
	South Africa	7	3

Table 2. Top Chinese and Indian Investing Companies (2005–2014).

Rank	Company	Industry	FDI number	Percent
	China's Outward FDI			
1	CNPC	Oil and gas	35	5.8
2	Sinopec	Oil and gas	31	5.2
3	CNOOC	Oil and gas	16	2.7
4	ICBC	Banking	9	1.5
	Greenland Group	Real estate	9	1.5
	Sinochem	Chemicals (conglomerate)	9	1.5
5	Chinalco	Metals	8	1.3
6	Fosun	Conglomerate	7	1.2
	China Minmetals	Metals	7	1.2
	Sinosteel	Mining, equipment, engineering	7	1.2
	State Grid	Electric utility	7	1.2
	India's Outward FDI			
1	Tata Steel	Steel	19	8.2
2	Infosys	Information Technology	16	6.9
	Tata Consultancy Services	Information Technology	16	6.9
3	HCL Technologies	Information Technology	15	6.4
4	Mahindra & Mahindra	Automotive	13	5.6
5	Hindalco Industries	Metals	11	4.7
6	Bank of Baroda	Banking	9	3.9
	Tata Motors	Automotive	9	3.9
7	ICICI Bank	Banking	8	3.4
	Jindal Steel & Power	Steel, energy	8	3.4
	NMDC	Mining	8	3.4
	Sun Pharmaceutical	Pharmaceuticals	8	3.4

destination of India's outward FDIs, but India is not among the top 10 destinations of China's investments.

With regard to the main investors, oil and gas companies such as CNPC, Sinopec, and CNOOC are the top Chinese investors, accounting for 13.7 percent of total China's investments. In the case of India, although Tata Steel leads the ranking of top investors, it is worth mentioning that three information and technology companies – Infosys, Tata Consultancy Services, and HCL Technologies – are the next main investors, accounting for 20.2 percent of India's investments.

Table 3 summarizes the variables we used for hypothesis testing as well as the measurement for each variable and what prior studies on Chinese and Indian MNEs used similar variables and measures. Apart from the dependent and explanatory variables related to our two hypotheses (outward FDI,

Table 3. Variables and Measures.

	Variable	Measure	Past Studies Using This Measure
Dependent variable	Number of outward FDIs	Total number of investments carried out by Chinese and Indian MNEs in each country	Brienen et al. (2010), Deng and Yang (2015), Malhotra et al. (2010), Pradhan and Singh (2011), Ramasamy et al. (2012)
Explanatory variables	Political risk	Political risk rating (International Country Risk Guide, Political Risk Services Group)	Buckley et al. (2007), Duanmu (2012), Duanmu and Guney (2009), Han, Chu, and Li (2014), Quer et al. (2012), Rienda, Claver, and Quer (2013)
	Cultural distance	Kogut and Singh (1988) index	Blomkvist and Drogendijk (2013), Kang and Jiang (2012), Li, Li, and Shapiro (2012), Malhotra et al. (2010), Quer et al. (2012)
Control variables	Natural resource-seeking motivation	Host country natural resource endowment (ore and metal exports to total exports, annual %)	Buckley et al. (2007), De Beule and Duanmu (2012), De Beule and Van Den Bulcke (2012), Duanmu and Guney (2009)
	Market-seeking motivation	Host market size (log host country GDP)	Buckley et al. (2007), De Beule and Duanmu (2012), De Beule and Van Den Bulcke (2012), Duanmu and Guney (2009), Malhotra et al. (2010), Nunnenkamp et al. (2012)
		Host market growth (host country GDP growth, annual %)	Buckley et al. (2007), Duanmu and Guney (2009), Kang and Jiang (2012), Nunnenkamp et al. (2012), Ramasamy et al. (2012)
	Strategic asset-seeking motivation	Host country patent registrations (log number of patent registration)	Buckley et al. (2007), De Beule and Duanmu (2012), De Beule and Van Den Bulcke (2012)
	Geographical distance	Log distance (kilometers) between each host country, capital city and Beijing, China, and New Delhi, India	Anwar, Hasse, and Rabbi (2008), Anwar and Mughal (2013), Buckley et al. (2007), Duanmu and Guney (2009), Malhotra et al. (2010)

political risk and cultural distance), we also included several control variables which previous researchers identified as potential determinants of location decisions of MNEs. Thus, we controlled for FDI motivation, namely, natural resource-, market- or strategic asset-seeking, as well as for the geographical distance between home and host countries.

RESULTS

Since our dependent variable is a count variable (number of investments in each country), it is more appropriate to use a negative binomial regression for hypothesis testing instead of an ordinary least square regression (Greene, 2003; Long, 1997). Actually, prior studies using a similar discrete dependent variable also employed a negative binomial regression (Brienen et al., 2010; Buckley, Munjal, Enderwick, & Forsans, 2016; Deng & Yang, 2015).

Table 4 presents the results of our analysis. Model 1 reports the findings for the subsample of Chinese MNEs (599 observations) and Model 2 shows those of Indian MNEs (233 observations).

As reported in Table 4, whereas the coefficient of political risk is not statistically significant as predictor of China's number of investments in each

Table 4. Negative Binomial Regression Analysis.

	Model 1 (China)	Model 2 (India)
Explanatory variables		
Political risk	0.002	−0.017*
Cultural distance	−0.088	−0.572***
Control variables		
Natural resource-seeking	0.013*	0.014
Market-seeking (host market size)	0.293	0.330
Market-seeking (host market growth)	0.050	0.057
Strategic asset-seeking	0.704***	0.321*
Geographical distance	0.908*	0.872*
Log likelihood	−180.929	−115.978
LR Chi-square	54.193***	18.877**
N	599	233

Notes: Dependent variable: no. of outward FDIs.
$*p < 0.05$; $**p < 0.01$; $***p < 0.001$.

country, it turns out to be negative and significant in the case of India's investments ($\beta = -0.017$, $p < 0.05$). Therefore, Hypothesis 1 is supported.

Likewise, the coefficient of cultural distance is not significant in the subsample of China's outward FDI, but it has a highly significant negative influence on the number of India's investments in each host country ($\beta = -0.572$, $p < 0.001$). This provides strong support for Hypothesis 2.

Regarding control variables, Table 4 shows that natural resource endowment ($\beta = 0.013$, $p < 0.05$) and the number of patent registrations in the host country ($\beta = 0.704$, $p < 0.001$) are positively associated with the number of China's investments in that host country. As for India's investments, only patent registration shows a positive impact ($\beta = 0.321$, $p < 0.05$). This suggests that whereas China's outward FDI is driven by both natural resource- and strategic asset-seeking, Indian investments abroad are mainly driven by a strategic asset-seeking motivation. In addition, geographical distance has a positive influence on both the number of China's and India's investments ($\beta = 0.908$, $p < 0.05$ and $\beta = 0.872$, $p < 0.05$, respectively). The specific motivation for each FDI decision and the type of FDI may explain this finding. For instance, a greater geographical distance could lead Chinese and Indian MNEs seeking market access to carry out manufacturing investments in distant host countries in order to save transportation costs derived from exporting.

DISCUSSION AND CONCLUSION

Our study was motivated by the desire to compare the influence of two of the most researched host country institutional factors on the location choice of emerging-market MNEs from China and India. The findings of our comparative analysis suggest that, when dealing with higher levels of political risk and cultural distance in a host country, the behavior of Indian MNEs is more conventional, that is, more similar to that reported by prior studies focusing on developed-country MNEs. In other words, our results indicate that political risk and cultural distance negatively influence India's outward FDI location choice. Conversely, both host country institutional factors do not affect Chinese MNEs location decisions. These findings show the importance of considering home country institutions when analyzing the role of host country institutions for FDI location choice (Nielsen, Asmussen, & Weatherall, 2017).

Regarding political risk, our finding supports past empirical evidence on the location decisions of China's and India's outward FDI. Several prior studies report that host country political risk does not deter Chinese MNEs (Buckley et al., 2007; Duanmu, 2012, 2014; Han et al., 2014; Kang & Jiang, 2012; Kolstad & Wiig, 2012; Malhotra et al., 2010; Quer et al., 2012; Ramasamy et al., 2012). On the contrary, past empirical evidence suggests a more conventional negative influence of host country risk on the location decisions of Indian MNEs (De Beule & Duanmu, 2012; De Beule & Van Den Bulcke, 2012; Nunnenkamp et al., 2012).

As for cultural distance, it is worth mentioning that prior comparative studies on the location choice of Chinese and Indian MNEs did not address the influence of cultural distance. However, its impact was indeed analyzed by several prior studies focusing independently on China's and India's outward FDI. Thus, our finding is similar to that of several researchers analyzing location decisions of Indian MNEs, who also reported a negative impact of cultural distance (Anwar & Mughal, 2013; Brienen et al., 2010; Nunnenkamp et al., 2012; Pradhan & Singh, 2011). As for Chinese MNEs, our finding on the non-significant effect of cultural distance is in line with the lack of conclusive support obtained in prior research (Kang & Jiang, 2012; Li et al., 2012; Quer et al., 2012; Ramasamy et al., 2012).

In our view, this study contributes to the epistemological debate on the validity of extant theories originated from developed-country MNEs for explaining the behavioral pattern of emerging-market MNEs as newcomers (Buckley et al., 2016; Cuervo-Cazurra, 2012). Moreover, we also contribute to the empirical research on Chinese and Indian MNEs, since comparative studies addressing their international behavior are still scarce.

Notwithstanding these contributions, this study is not free from limitations. First, because we used secondary data, the measurement of several variables is limited. Second, since we used an index for measuring political risk, we focused on the so called macro political risk, that is, on the environmental factors that affect all foreign firms doing business in a specific host country. Third, given that we focused on Chinese and Indian MNEs, our findings may not apply to other emerging-market MNEs. Future research could overcome these limitations by considering managerial perceptions on host country institutional factors, by analyzing the impact of political risk depending on the unique features of the foreign MNE, and by replicating our study in other emerging markets.

REFERENCES

Anwar, A. I., Hasse, R., & Rabbi, F. (2008). *Location determinants of Indian outward foreign direct investment: How multinationals choose their investment destinations?* Munich Personal RePEc Archive (MPRA) Paper, No. 47397.

Anwar, A., & Mughal, M. (2013). The role of diaspora in attracting Indian outward FDI. *International Journal of Social Economics*, *40*(11), 944–955.

Bhardwaj, A., Dietz, J., & Beamish, P. W. (2007). Host country cultural influences on foreign direct investment. *Management International Review*, *47*(1), 29–50.

Blomkvist, K., & Drogendijk, R. (2013). The impact of psychic distance on Chinese outward foreign direct investments. *Management International Review*, *53*(5), 659–686.

Brienen, M. J., Burger, M. J., & van Oort, F. G. (2010). The geography of Chinese and Indian greenfield investments in Europe. *Eurasian Geography and Economics*, *51*(2), 254–273.

Brouthers, K. D. (2002). Institutional, cultural and transaction cost influences on entry mode choice and performance. *Journal of International Business Studies*, *33*(2), 203–221.

Buckley, P. J., Clegg, L. J., Cross, A. R., Liu, X., Voss, H., & Zheng, P. (2007). The determinants of Chinese foreign direct investment. *Journal of International Business Studies*, *38*(4), 499–518.

Buckley, P. J., Munjal, S., Enderwick, P, & Forsans, N. (2016). Cross-border acquisitions by Indian multinationals: Asset exploitation or asset augmentation? *International Business Review*, *25*(4), 986–996.

Child, J., & Rodrigues, S. B. (2005). The internationalization of Chinese firms: A case for theoretical extension? *Management and Organization Review*, *1*(3), 381–410.

Cuervo-Cazurra, A. (2012). Extending theory by analyzing developing country multinational companies: Solving the Goldilocks debate. *Global Strategy Journal*, *2*(3), 153–167.

Cuervo-Cazurra, A., & Genc, M. (2008). Transforming disadvantages into advantages: Developing-country MNEs in the least developed countries. *Journal of International Business Studies*, *39*(6), 957–979.

Cui, L., & Jiang, F. (2010). Behind ownership decision of Chinese outward FDI: Resources and institutions. *Asia Pacific Journal of Management*, *27*(4), 751–774.

Das, D. K. (2010). *China and India: Differentiating economic growth paradigms* (pp. 1–33). China Papers-New Zealand Contemporary China Research Centre-Victoria University of Wellington, No. 27.

De Beule, F., & Duanmu, D. (2012). Locational determinants of internationalization: A firm-level analysis of Chinese and Indian acquisitions. *European Management Journal*, *30*(3), 264–277.

De Beule, F., & Van Den Bulcke, D. (2012). Locational determinants of outward foreign direct investment: An analysis of Chinese and Indian greenfield investments. *Transnational Corporations*, *21*(1), 1–34.

Deng, P., & Yang, M. (2015). Cross-border mergers and acquisitions by emerging market firms: A comparative investigation. *International Business Review*, *24*(1), 157–172.

Devonshire-Ellis, C. (2010). *China-India comparison: An examination of 2011 direction and developments.* New Delhi: Dezan Shira & Associates.

Duanmu, J. L. (2012). Firm heterogeneity and location choice of Chinese multinational enterprises (MNEs). *Journal of World Business*, *47*(1), 64–72.

Duanmu, J. L. (2014). State-owned MNCs and host country expropriation risk: The role of home state soft power and economic gunboat diplomacy. *Journal of International Business Studies*, *45*(8), 1044–1060.

Duanmu, J. L., & Guney, Y. (2009). A panel data analysis of locational determinants of Chinese and Indian outward foreign direct investment. *Journal of Asia Business Studies*, *3*(2), 1–15.

Greene, W. (2003). *Econometric analysis* (5th ed.) Upper Saddle River, NJ: Prentice Hall.

Han, J., Chu, X. Y., & Li, K. (2014). China's ODI motivations, political risk, institutional distance and location choice. *Theoretical Economics Letters*, *4*, 540–547.

Huang, X., & Renyong, C. (2014). Chinese private firms' outward foreign direct investment: Does firm ownership and size matter? *Thunderbird International Business Review*, *56*(5), 393–406.

Kang, Y., & Jiang, F. (2012). FDI location choice of Chinese multinationals in East and Southeast Asia: Traditional economic factors and institutional perspective. *Journal of World Business*, *47*(1), 45–53.

Kogut, B., & Singh, H. (1988). The effect of national culture on the choice of entry mode. *Journal of International Business Studies*, *19*(3), 411–432.

Kolstad, I., & Wiig, A. (2012). What determines Chinese outward FDI? *Journal of World Business*, *47*(1), 26–34.

Li, J., Li, Y., & Shapiro, D. (2012). Knowledge seeking and outward FDI of emerging market firms: The moderating effect of inward FDI. *Global Strategy Journal*, *2*(4), 277–295.

Long, J. S. (1997). *Regression models for categorical and limited dependent variables*. Thousand Oaks, CA: Sage.

Luo, Y., & Tung, R. L. (2007). International expansion of emerging market enterprises: A springboard perspective. *Journal of International Business Studies*, *38*(4), 481–498.

Luo, Y., & Wang, S. L. (2012). Foreign direct investment strategies by developing country multinationals: A diagnostic model for home country effects. *Global Strategy Journal*, *2*(3), 244–261.

Luo, Y., Zhao, H., Wang, Y., & Xi, Y. (2011). Venturing abroad by emerging market enterprises. A test of dual strategic intents. *Management International Review*, *51*(4), 433–459.

Malhotra, S., Zhu, P., & Locander, W. (2010). Impact of host-country corruption on U.S. and Chinese cross-border acquisitions. *Thunderbird International Business Review*, *52*(6), 491–507.

Nielsen, B. B., Asmussen, C. G., & Weatherall, C. D. (2017). The location choice of foreign direct investments: Empirical evidence and methodological challenges. *Journal of World Business*, *52*(1), 62–82.

Ning, L., & Sutherland, D. (2012). Internationalization of China's private-sector MNEs: An analysis of the motivations for foreign affiliate formation. *Thunderbird International Business Review*, *54*(2), 169–182.

Nunnenkamp, P., Sosa, M., Vadlamannati, K. C., & Waldkirch, A. (2012). *What drives India's outward FDI?* Kiel Working Paper, No. 1800.

Pak, Y. S., & Park, Y. R. (2004). Global ownership strategy of Japanese multinational enterprises: A test of internalization theory. *Management International Review*, *44*(1), 3–21.

Pradhan, J. P. (2008a). Rise of Indian outward FDI: What implications does it hold for host developing countries? *Revista Economía: Teoría y Práctica*, *29*, 9–49.

Pradhan, J. P. (2008b). The evolution of Indian outward foreign direct investment: Changing trends and patterns. *International Journal of Technology and Globalisation*, *4*(1), 70–86.

Pradhan, J. P. (2011). Emerging multinationals: A comparison of Chinese and Indian outward foreign direct investment. *International Journal of Institutions and Economies*, *3*(1), 113–148.

Pradhan, J. P., & Singh, N. (2011). Business group affiliation and location of Indian firms' foreign acquisitions. *Journal of International Commerce, Economics and Policy*, *2*(1), 19–41.

Quer, D., Claver, E., & Rienda, L. (2012). Political risk, cultural distance, and outward foreign direct investment: Empirical evidence from large Chinese firms. *Asia Pacific Journal of Management*, *29*(4), 1089–1104.

Quer, D., Claver, E., & Rienda, L. (2015). Chinese outward foreign direct investment: A review of empirical research. *Frontiers of Business Research in China*, *9*(3), 326–370.

Ramasamy, B., Yeung, M., & Laforet, S. (2012). China's outward foreign direct investment: Location choice and firm ownership. *Journal of World Business*, *47*(1), 17–25.

Rienda, L., Claver, E., & Quer, D. (2011). Doing business in India: A review of research in leading international journals. *Journal of Indian Business Research*, *3*(3), 192–216.

Rienda, L., Claver, E., & Quer, D. (2013). The internationalisation of Indian multinationals: Determinants of expansion through acquisitions. *Journal of the Asia Pacific Economy*, *18*(1), 115–132.

Rui, H., & Yip, G. S. (2008). Foreign acquisitions by Chinese firms: A strategic intent perspective. *Journal of World Business*, *43*(2), 213–226.

Xia, J., Ma, X., Lu, J. W., & Yiu, D. W. (2014). Outward foreign direct investment by emerging market firms: A resource dependence logic. *Strategic Management Journal*, *35*(9), 1343–1363.

Yang, Y., Yang, X., Chen, R., & Allen, J. P. (2014). What drives emerging-economy outbound FDI decisions to obtain strategic assets? *Asian Business & Management*, *13*(5), 379–410.

Zhang, J., Jiang, J., & Zhou, C. (2014). Diplomacy and investment – the case of China. *International Journal of Emerging Markets*, *9*(2), 216–235.

CHAPTER 11

FIRM RESOURCES, INSTITUTIONAL DISTANCE, AND THE CHOICE OF ENTRY MODE

Jonas F. Puck, Markus Hödl, Igor Filatotchev and Thomas Lindner

ABSTRACT

We build on the resource-based view and extend entry mode research by focusing on firms' intention to transfer different resources from the parent firm to its overseas subsidiary. In line with our hypotheses, we find that parent firms that plan to transfer high levels of intangible resources to their foreign subsidiaries tend to choose wholly owned subsidiaries, while firms that intend to transfer high levels of tangible resources tend to choose international joint ventures. Moreover, we find that these relationships are moderated by institutional distance. We test our hypotheses using unique primary data from a sample of 128 foreign subsidiaries in the People's Republic of China. Our results have important theoretical implications for international business strategy research as they develop further existing entry-mode theories.

Keywords: Entry mode; institutional distance; intangible resources; tangible resources

Distance in International Business: Concept, Cost and Value
Progress in International Business Research, Volume 12, 239–270

ISSN: 1745-8862/doi:10.1108/S1745-886220170000012019

INTRODUCTION

A significant amount of international business (IB) research has dealt with the choice of entry mode, predominantly addressing the question of whether firms should retain full control over their foreign resources (wholly owned subsidiaries, or WoS) or share control with other firms (international joint ventures, or IJVs) (Brouthers & Hennart, 2007; Morschett, Schramm-Klein, & Swoboda, 2010). These scholars have argued that the choice of entry mode is one of the most important decisions firms have to make in the course of internationalization since modes entail different levels of control, risk, and resource commitment (Morschett, Swoboda, & Schramm-Klein, 2008; Zhao, Luo, & Suh, 2004). Prior research primarily drew on transaction cost economics (TCE) to investigate predictors of entry levels in subsidiaries and their performance implications (Brouthers & Hennart, 2007; Canabal & White, 2008; Werner, 2002). TCE assumes that firms are concerned with achieving transaction-specific efficiency, preferring hierarchical governance structures over cooperative modes with increasing governance costs (Brouthers, 2002; Brouthers, Brouthers, & Werner, 2003; Williamson, 1985). However, such approaches fall short of explaining how firms expect to create and maintain value through the intended deployment of different resource types in alternative governance structures (Chen & Chen, 2003), and this is the main focus of our study.

Previous studies that have aimed to develop a better understanding of entry-mode choices available to the firm suffer from a number of theoretical shortfalls. First, their heavy focus on efficiency criteria and cost minimization has often neglected the potential for value creation (Tsang, 2000). While efficiency criteria are undoubtedly crucial for mode choices, it is also important to understand how intended resource endowments affect the structuring of foreign operations. With the majority of these studies being based on TCE, prior research has focused on the contractual relationship between the parent firm and the foreign subsidiary, explaining entry modes as a result of failures of external markets (Zhao et al., 2004). Consequently, these studies have insufficiently taken into account firm resources that are intended to be transferred to the host market and their influence on the choice of entry mode (Peng, 2001).

Second, previous entry-mode research drawing on the resource-based view (RBV) looked at different resource endowments of a parent, primarily experience-based resources, to explain entry-mode choice (Brouthers & Hennart, 2007). However, these studies did not analyse different types of resources that are intended to be transferred from the multinational corporation (MNC) to the subsidiary. Specifically, characteristics underlying the effect of intended intangible and tangible resource transfers on entry-mode choices have not been systematically differentiated. The majority of previous studies used RBV explanations to analyse under which conditions parent firms opt for hierarchical governance structures to maintain the valuable resources they endow the subsidiary with (Chiao, Lo, & Yu, 2010; Claver & Quer, 2005; Ekeledo & Sivakumar, 2004). However, little is known about how the intended transfer of different types of resources influences the parent firm's choice between IJVs and WoS in the process of internationalization.

Finally, prior RBV-grounded entry-mode research has insufficiently examined how intended resource transfers affect mode choices and how institutional contexts and distance interact with these dependences (for notable exception, see Brouthers, Brouthers, & Werner, 2008) even though institutional differences may require parent firms to structure their foreign operations differently to create value from the resources that they intend to transfer (Sirmon, Hitt, & Ireland, 2007). Overall, we find that there is a dearth of empirical studies that looks at how the intended transfer of different resources affects the choice of entry mode and how these dependencies are influenced by institutional differences. For instance, Brouthers and Hennart (2007, p. 407) argue in their review of the field that studies drawing on resource-based explanations for mode choices are still limited. These authors conclude that more studies investigating the 'interactive effects of institutional factors' on mode choices are warranted. Moreover, Peng (2001) argues that combining RBV with institutional theory provides a promising direction for future research, especially in emerging markets. Finally, Schwens, Eiche, and Kabst (2011) recently report that there is still a scarcity of studies that analyse how institutional environments interact with firm capabilities.

In our study, we explore how the firm's intended transfer of resources influences its choice of entry mode. By grounding our study within the RBV, we take an intended transfer of firm resources as our starting point, suggesting that the nature of MNC resources to be transferred to the foreign market determines the choice of entry mode. Further, we distinguish between intended intangible and tangible resource transfers between the parent and the subsidiary and highlight their opposite effect on the entry mode choice. Specifically, we argue that parent firms that intend to transfer high levels of intangible resources tend to choose WoS, while firms that intend to transfer high levels of tangible resources tend to choose IJVs. As our RBV-based reasoning is thus focusing on the efficient deployment of transferred resources and not on the costs of controlling them we test for the comparative contribution of our RBV-based explanatory factors. Of course, we control for TCE constructs in our empirical observation to test the additional explanatory effect of our RBV model.

In addition, we examine whether the relationship between intended resource transfers and the mode choice is affected by institutional differences. By integrating resource-based explanations with insights from institutional theory, we suggest that the effect of firms' intended resource transfers on the choice of entry mode depends on the institutional distance between the firm's home and the host markets (Brouthers et al., 2008; Sirmon et al., 2007). We argue that institutional distance should have a significant impact on the liability of foreignness and uncertainty associated with the deployment of resources in host markets, and this interactive effect should have a profound impact on the mode choice. Specifically, we suggest that parent firms that intend to transfer high intangible or tangible resources are expected to show a greater propensity of selecting IJVs as institutional distance increases.

We test our hypotheses using a sample of foreign subsidiaries in the People's Republic of China (PRC). With more than US \$105 billion in inward FDI flows in 2010 (UNCTAD, 2011) the country is one of the largest recipients of FDI globally. Moreover, IJVs and WoS are the dominant FDI modes in the PRC (Puck, Holtbrügge, & Mohr, 2009). In 2010, out of 27,420 new FDI projects 18 per cent were organized as equity joint ventures, whereas 80 per cent were organized as wholly foreign-owned enterprises (MOFCOM, 2012). Therefore, we focus on IJVs and WoS in our analysis. Finally, due to the large number of subsidiaries set up by investors from an institutionally diverse range of countries, we believe that China provides a valuable research context for analysing the moderating effect of institutional distance.

We make a number of contributions to the global strategy research in general and entry-mode research in particular. In contrast to the majority of previous studies that primarily looked at firm experience as a resource-based variable (Cho & Padmanabhan, 2001; Delios & Henisz, 2000; Erramilli, 1991) or analysed under which conditions parent firms strive to embed their valuable resource endowments in hierarchical governance structures (Chiao et al., 2010; Claver & Quer, 2005; Ekeledo & Sivakumar, 2004), we focus on the intended transfer and deployment of different types of resources. We thus contribute to the RBV by highlighting the value creation aspect associated with entry mode choices, given a certain intention to commit resources to a foreign operation. Specifically, we analyse how the nature of the intended transfer of firm resources influences the choice of entry mode. We distinguish between intended intangible and tangible resource deployment and examine how different characteristics underlying the intended transfers of these affect entry modes (Molloy, Chadwick, Ployhart, & Golden, 2011).

Further, we contribute by integrating insights from institutional theory into the RBV framework. In particular, we analyse how differences in institutional environments require parent firms to adapt their structuring of foreign operations (Brouthers et al., 2008; Sirmon et al., 2007). We argue that institutional distance between the parent firm and the foreign subsidiary enhances the liability of foreignness and uncertainty associated with the firm's intended resource transfers, thus increasing the propensity of parent firms that intend to deploy high levels of intangible and tangible resources to select IJVs. Overall, by combining resource-based explanations with insights from institutional theory, we develop novel insights to advance our understanding of internationalization strategy.

The remainder of this study is organized as follows. In the next section, we present our theoretical framework and develop our hypotheses. The ensuing section presents our data collection and measures followed by a discussion of our empirical results and implications. The final sections outline directions for future research and provide a conclusion.

THEORETICAL FRAMEWORK AND HYPOTHESES

Resources and the Choice of Entry Mode

In line with the majority of previous studies, we conceptualize entry-mode choice as the firm's choice between WoS and IJV – that is, whether the firm should retain full control over its resources (WoS) or share control with other firms when investing in foreign markets (IJV; Brouthers & Hennart, 2007). To investigate this choice prior entry-mode research mostly relied upon TCE as a leading theoretical framework, arguing that firms strive to minimize transaction costs when venturing abroad (Brouthers & Hennart, 2007; Canabal & White, 2008). Consequently, entry-mode research has primarily focused on operationalizing TCE's core attributes such as asset specificity and uncertainty (both external and internal to the firm) to explain the boundaries of firms (Anderson & Gatignon, 1986; Brouthers et al., 2003). From the TCE perspective, parent firms are advised to internalize foreign operations with increasing transaction costs stemming from market imperfections. While TCE expects firms to choose the most transaction cost-efficient mode, critics, however, maintain that TCE's applicability is limited in the sense that it solely focuses on efficiency and cost minimization (Tsang, 2000).

The RBV, on the other hand, is often considered complementary to TCE since it helps to overcome some of these limitations (Mahoney, 2001; Peng, 2001). Specifically, instead of transaction costs minimization, RBV is more concerned with how value is created and maintained in international expansion by looking at resources and capabilities the firm possesses (Aulakh & Kotabe, 1997). RBV suggests that firms need to develop valuable, rare, and hard to imitate resources and capabilities to sustain competitive advantage in the long term (Barney, 1991). However, the sole development and possession of these intangible and tangible resources is not sufficient, they also need to be deployed through appropriate governance structures (Barney, Wright, & Ketchen, 2001; Brouthers et al., 2008). Firms thus have to design their governance structures in a way that maximum value is obtained from their resource endowments (Tsang, 2000). To achieve this, companies may venture into new markets in order to exploit existing resources through internal structures or acquire new, complementary resources from local partners in cooperatives modes. Building on RBV arguments, we thus suggest that the nature of resources intended to be transferred to foreign markets determines the mode choice as modes serve as governance structures for deploying these resources abroad (Sharma & Erramilli, 2004, p. 9). Chandler (1992, p. 86) highlights this effect by arguing that 'the specific nature of the firm's facilities and skills become the most significant factor in determining what will be done by the firm and what in the market'.

However, only few scholars have applied this theoretical perspective to entry-mode studies (Brouthers & Hennart, 2007). Ekeledo and Sivakumar (2004, p. 69) suggest that entry-mode research drawing on RBV explanations has predominantly been conceptual, thus 'systematic empirical research on entry mode choice, using the resource-based perspective, is lacking'. Indeed, the empirical studies in the field have mostly investigated the effects of experience-based resources on mode choices. Aulakh and Kotabe (1997) found, for instance, partial support for a positive relationship between international experience and hierarchical governance structures. Erramilli (1991), on the other hand, detected a U-shaped relationship between length and scope of international experience and mode choice for his sample of service firms. Comparable results were obtained by Cho and Padmanabhan (2001).

Ekeledo and Sivakumar (2004), Chen and Hennart (2002), Chiao et al. (2010), Claver and Quer (2005) and Mutinelli and Piscitello (1998) develop a more comprehensive approach by including in their analysis non-experience-based resources of the parent firm such as proprietary technology, reputation, R&D, customer following, firm size, among others (for a review, see Brouthers & Hennart, 2007). However, these studies primarily use RBV to explain under which conditions parent firms aim to protect their valuable resource endowments and thus seek control by opting for WoS. However, studies that untangle conditions under which firms choose IJVs or WoS still remain rare (for notable exception, see Mutinelli & Piscitello, 1998). Therefore, following Brouthers and Hennart (2007), we suggest that our understanding of mode decisions can be improved by looking at other classifications of resources and, more importantly, by untangling how the intended deployment of these resources influence the choice between IJVs and WoS.

We distinguish in our study between intended transfers of intangible and tangible resources (Wernerfelt, 1984). Specifically, and in contrast to most studies mentioned above looking at parent firm resources, we conceptualize them as a collection of resources that parent firms and foreign subsidiaries exchange in order to create value in the host market (Barney et al., 2001). Intangible resources have three characteristics that distinguish them from tangible resources such as they do not deplete with use and entail benefits for an undefined time frame; they can be used simultaneously in multiple ways, making them a non-rivalrous good; and they are immaterial and thus not separable from the owner (Molloy et al., 2011). Due to the very different nature underlying intangible and tangible resources, we argue that their intended deployment has different effects on the choice of entry mode.

It is important to highlight specific differences between intangible and tangible resources on the one hand, and assets of high specificity on the other hand. While assets of high specificity lose their value outside of the transaction at hand (Williamson, 1979), this is not the case for firm resources. A strong brand, for example, is a highly valuable intangible resource, but its value is not constrained to a specific transaction. Rather the opposite, strong brands are often those that apply to a broad scope of activities. With regard to tangible resources, a fully automated production facility may be a valuable resource but it is not necessarily specific to a transaction. In conclusion, while there are cases where firm-specific advantages directly translate into transaction-specific advantages, the two concepts are substantially different.

For our hypotheses development we rely on two mechanisms that are key for the efficient deployment of contributed resources: First, we discuss the potential creation of competitive advantage by the respective kinds of resources that are intended to be transferred, or the lack thereof, and their consequences for mode choice. Then, we discuss organizational factors like the embeddedness of resources in the organization structure as well as the ease of bundling them. Taken together, our reasoning concludes that from an RBV, the recommendations that emerge in terms of ownership structure are different for the intended transfer of tangible and intangible resources.

For intangible resources we suggest that firms that intend to contribute high levels of intangible resources tend to choose WoS as the value of these resources can best be exploited through hierarchical governance structures. First and from a competitive advantage creating perspective, intangible resources are often the direct source of competitive advantage and enable firms to differentiate their products or services, and ultimately generate higher profits (Zhao et al., 2004). Thus, firms with high levels of intangibles are in a powerful strategic position and have only limited incentives to cooperate with local partners (Eisenhardt & Schoonhoven, 1996). Li and Qian (2008) found in their study, for instance, that innovation advantage (operationalized as R&D intensity) was positively related to the choice of WoS. They maintain that firms that are in possession of these resources do not need to rely on the contribution of local complementary resources as they can efficiently deploy their own advantages to compete in overseas markets. Moreover, Meyer, Wright, and Pruthi (2009) propose in their conceptual analysis of RBV and entry mode strategies that firms with high R&D capabilities tend to choose hierarchical governance structures to exploit their firm-specific advantages. Furthermore, Chen and Hennart (2002) found that firms with high levels of advertising resources in the host market tended to choose WoS over IJVs in a sample of Japanese MNCs in the US. Finally, Chen and Hu (2002) found empirical evidence that high control entry modes provide parent firms with advantages when deploying marketing skills, brands, and highly advertised products. Overall, from a competitive advantage creating perspective, firms would thus prefer to use wholly owned entry modes when intending to transfer major intangible resources.

Second, from an organizational perspective, intangible resources are usually of tacit nature, often embedded in social interactions and routines within organizations (Madhok, 1997). Scholars have argued that these types of intangibles cannot be systematically coded and are thus difficult to deploy outside of firm boundaries (Ekeledo & Sivakumar, 2004; Kogut & Zander, 2003; Sharma & Erramilli, 2004). For example, Claver and Quer (2005) point to the difficulty of transferring intangibles to other firms as proper implementation by local firms is difficult to achieve, and Madhok (1997) suggests that the transfer of embedded resources across firm boundaries may erode competitive advantage. RBV thus suggests that control over resources is required to assure that the resources and capabilities transferred abroad yield their highest productive value (Brouthers et al., 2008; Sirmon et al., 2007). Brouthers et al. (2008, p. 191) argue, for instance, that 'international expansion through wholly owned structures enables firms to create and maintain resource-based value through developed routines'. Consequently, prior research suggests that, in order to exploit these advantages, firms should establish WoS as the extant internal routines prevalent in these modes ensure that their value is secured (Kogut & Zander, 2003). Overall, building on these arguments we suggest:

> **Hypothesis 1a (H1a).** The higher the level of intangible resources a parent firm intends to transfer to its foreign subsidiary, the more likely it will select a WoS as entry mode.

In contrast to intangible resources, parent firms that intend to contribute high levels of tangible resources should tend to choose IJVs, as the cooperation with local firms may increase the value of their investments for several reasons. First, from a competitive advantage perspective, parent firms that intend to transfer high levels of tangible resources are often confronted with high liability of foreignness and uncertainty (Haiyang Chen & Hu, 2002) as these types of resources seldom form the basis of competitive advantage that differentiates firms from competitors. In contrast to intangibles, tangible resources can more easily be replicated by local firms. Prior research thus argues that IJVs are an attractive vehicle for parent firms to share not only equity, but also mitigate liability of foreignness and uncertainty (Chan & Makino, 2007; Gatignon & Anderson, 1988; Kim & Hwang, 1992). Pan (1996) found, for instance, that parent firms that undertake large investments preferred to reduce their ownership stakes in foreign subsidiaries in order to mitigate their risk exposure. Similar empirical results were obtained by the studies of Chen and Hu (2002) and Shan (1991). Also, concerns about knowledge dissemination related to tangible resources are negligible since these resources are highly visible and can thus be more easily safeguarded in IJVs than intangibles. Specifically, tangibles are clearly attributable to an owner (Molloy et al., 2011); therefore, local partners have limited possibility to act opportunistically and misappropriate these resources which leads to lower risk of additional transaction cost stemming from partner supervision.

Second, from an organizational perspective, IJVs permit parent firms to exploit economies of scale and scope in the host market. From the RBV perspective, bundling tangible resources with local firms in cooperative modes allows parent firms to augment their resource base and realize synergy effects. Compared to intangibles, tangible resources can be more easily bundled with local complementary resources in IJVs. RBV scholars maintain that resources which are not of tacit nature and embedded in organizational routines can be more effectively transferred across firm boundaries as these types of resources can be easily absorbed and put to use by outside firms (Claver & Quer, 2005; Madhok, 1997). Consequently, we extend the RBV argument concerning establishment mode (green- vs. brownfield) to the entry mode discussion.

We argue that local partner's absorptive capacity is higher for tangible resources than for intangibles.

Further, increasing time-to-market pressure and high competition in many markets for manufactured products require firms to quickly get their business operations in place which requires substantial investment of tangible resources. In these markets, parent firms lack the time to build their operations from scratch on their own. Instead, firms are pressured to quickly launch their operations in order to deploy their invested resources as fast as possible. Consequently, collaboration with local partners becomes a viable option to quickly establish large-scale business operations. Tsang (2000, p. 231) argues, for instance, that 'collaboration is a popular means of gaining fast market access'. Similarly, Combs and Ketchen (1999) maintain that cooperative modes allow parent firms to quickly establish a foothold in the market (compared to WoS). Moreover, Hennart and Park (1993) found that large amounts of investments abroad impose managerial constraints on parent firms and thus induce firms to look out for local partners. Consequently, the potential benefit from partnering with local companies is higher for parents that intend to transfer tangible resources to their foreign-market subsidiary. Overall, building on these arguments we suggest:

Hypothesis 1b (H1b). The higher the level of tangible resources a parent firm intends to transfer to its foreign subsidiary, the more likely it will select an IJV as entry mode.

The Moderating Effects of Institutional Distance

Prior institutional theory research has highlighted the importance of institutional differences for MNC behaviour (Kostova, Roth, & Dacin, 2008; Peng, Wang, & Jiang, 2008; Xu & Shenkar, 2002) and entry-mode choices (Brouthers et al., 2008; Chan & Makino, 2007; Yiu & Makino, 2002). In general, institutional differences concern the differences in the firm's external environment and have been argued to be an important source of uncertainty, creating a liability of foreignness that firms are confronted with abroad (Zaheer, 1995). Firms are thus expected to incur additional costs when doing business in distant host markets. Specifically, with increasing institutional differences between the home and the host market, parent firms are pressured to adapt their governance structures to the 'rules of the game' (North, 1990, p. 3) in the host environment to gain legitimacy from both the internal organization and the external environment (Yiu & Makino, 2002).

The institutional pressures and parent firm's quest for legitimacy thus influence the governance structures through which firms exploit their resource endowments and maintain their value.

Existing research argues that the interaction of firm resources and institutional characteristics influences the choice of entry mode in foreign markets (Chiao et al., 2010; Meyer et al., 2009). For instance, Brouthers, Brouthers and Werner (2008, p. 192) argue that 'institutional idiosyncrasies create market imperfections that may influence the value of resource-based advantages' which may in turn bear on how parent firms structure their foreign operations. Following North (1990) and Scott (1995) scholars have usually divided a host country's institutional environment into formal (political, legal, and economic factors) and informal dimensions (normative and social factors) in order to systematically analyse differences between countries and their impact on mode choices. In line with prior research (Gaur & Lu, 2007; Salomon & Wu, 2012), we conceptualize institutional differences as the distance between the home country of the parent firm and host market since the higher the distance, the greater is the 'degree of foreignness (…) and the less understandable [are] the messages issued by the environment' (Garnier, 1982, p. 894).

We argue that parent firms that intend to transfer high levels of intangible or tangible resources to their subsidiaries increase their preference for IJVs as institutional distance increases, for several reasons. First, with increasing institutional difference the resources that parent firms intend to transfer are associated with higher liability of foreignness and uncertainty in the host market. Increased liability of foreignness erodes competitive advantage derived from resource transfers. Prior entry-mode research maintains that firms may mitigate uncertainty and liability of foreignness by sharing equity with local firms. Lu and Hébert (2005, p. 738) argue, for instance, that 'forming an IJV permits foreign investors to access complementary assets and to reduce the uncertainty they are confronting'. From an institutional perspective, parent firms that cooperate with local IJV partners increase the legitimacy of their business operations and thus the value of their intended resource deployment in institutionally distant markets. Specifically, local firms may assist foreign firms in adapting their strategies to the 'rules of the game' (North, 1990, p. 3) in the host environment (Canabal & White, 2008). Yiu and Makino (2002, p. 668) state, for instance, that 'pressure from host-country institutions may induce firms to trade their ownership for legitimacy in the local environment' and thus opt for IJVs. Hence, the local IJV partner can assist the parent firm in dealing with institutional idiosyncrasies by contributing 'social knowledge' (Sohn,

1994), alleviating information requirements and facilitating the deployment of firm resources. Empirical evidence for this line of reasoning comes from Ando (2011), Demirbag, Glaister, and Tatoglu (2007), Dikova (2012) and Kaynak, Demirbag, and Tatoglu (2007), among others, who found that high institutional distance induce parent firms to reduce their equity stakes in foreign subsidiaries.

Second, in institutionally distant environments, parent firms are assumed to be unable to rely on their own capacity to deploy intangible or tangible resources. Madhok (1997) argues, for instance, that large differences between home and host market reduce the appropriateness as well as applicability of organizational routines since these differences increase costs of implementation and adaption. Madhok (1997, p. 47) thus suggests that 'in such cases, a firm may well prefer collaborative modes'. Moreover, using established organizational routines and practices in the process of resources transfers only provide the firm with limited legitimacy in the host market and may subsequently be sanctioned by customers' actions. This is all the more true in situations of high institutional distance between the firm's home and host countries as differences are expected to mitigate the value that intended resource transfers may generate abroad. Finally, parent firms that intend to transfer high levels of resources attract attention from host country governments that may react with discriminatory policies in order to protect domestic competitors. Cooperating with local firms permits parent firms to benefit from spill over effects and 'free ride on the reputational capital' of the IJV partner (Yiu & Makino, 2002, p. 671), thus alleviating risks associated with political hazards and discriminatory actions. Therefore, with increasing institutional distance, we argue that parent firms are more dependent on the contributions of local partners in order to mitigate disadvantages associated with liability of foreignness and to conform to new institutional conditions. The effect of institutional distance thus leads to an increase in the likelihood of IJVs for both kinds of firms.

Of course, setting up IJVs in institutionally distant markets also carries risks. Difficulties to understand local regulations and practices may increase the likelihood of partner firms to misappropriate transferred resources. The potential damage is higher for firms intending to transfer substantial intangible assets because of the abovementioned reasons related to competitive advantage. Consequently, companies that intend to transfer substantial intangible resources will still have a stronger preference for WoS but this effect will be stronger in less distant investment locations. As argued above, this effect is negligible for firms intending to transfer high amounts of tangible resources as they already have a preference for IJV modes.

Overall, building on the arguments above, we suggest:

Hypothesis 2a (H2a). Institutional distance reinforces the negative relation between the intended transfer of tangible resources and firms' choice of WoS.

Hypothesis 2b (H2b). Institutional distance weakens the positive relation between intended transfer of intangible resources and firms' choice of WoS.

RESEARCH DESIGN AND METHODOLOGY

Data Collection

To test our hypotheses, we collected primary data from foreign companies located in the PRC using a questionnaire survey over a two month period in 2012. In order to compile a comprehensive database of contact addresses we contacted national chambers of foreign trade of Japan, the United States, the United Kingdom, Germany and the European Union. Furthermore, we analysed company home pages and articles in newspapers such as China Business Review. In total, we identified contact details of 1,979 IJVs and WoS of foreign companies in the PRC.

The original German language questionnaire was translated into English, Japanese, French, and Spanish by professional translators. We used translate/back-translate method to ensure the equivalency of the questionnaires (Brislin, 1970). The questionnaire was distributed via e-mail accompanied by an executive summary explaining the objectives of the study. Those companies that had not replied by the original deadline subsequently received a reminder two weeks later. After a second deadline, we collected 195 questionnaires from 156 companies (response rate of 9.90 per cent). The collected sample covers 29 industries (based on two-digit SIC) with the largest contributors being industrial machinery and equipment (SIC: 35) with 19 per cent of responses and transportation equipment (SIC: 37) with 15 per cent of respondents. Due to missing information in secondary data or the fact that companies were active in industries with major ownership restrictions data analysis was based on a subsample of 128 cases. The relatively low response rate may in part be explained by the questionnaire fatigue reported by many managers of subsidiaries of foreign firms in the PRC (one respondent who declined to participate in the study explained that he would receive more than seven questionnaires per week). Scholars from several fields report low response rates because of high research-intensity particularly in East-coast China. Yang (2012), for example, reports that effective response rates around 7 per cent have become common in recent mail surveys.

In our sample, subsidiaries were established by companies headquartered in 13 countries, with the United States, Germany, Japan and the United Kingdom accounting for the majority of investments. Mean age of subsidiaries was about 5 years (SD: 3.4 years). The majority of the respondents (82 per cent) were general managers of the respective subsidiary, 7 per cent were subsidiary Chief Financial Officers (CFOs) and 6 per cent marketing managers. We acknowledge that there is a chance that subsidiary managers' perception of intended resource transfers does not mirror those of parent company decision-makers. Yet, we maintain that subsidiary managers have the best understanding of the importance of the respective transferred resources for the subsidiary, which is the logic of resource transfer intentions that underlies our theoretical reasoning.

We assessed non-response bias by using the approach developed by Armstrong and Overton (1977). A comparison of early- and late-arriving responses by means of logistic regression indicated that the likelihood of a non-response bias for our study variables was low and insignificant. Consequently, non-response bias was not considered to be a problem. As data in the responses were self-reported and collected using a single questionnaire, we took precautions to avoid a self-reporting bias by following the methodological approach suggested by Podsakoff, MacKenzie, Jeong-Yeon, and Podsakoff (2003). In particular, we separated items measuring the same construct in the questionnaire, protected and assured respondent anonymity, and reduced the danger of self-reporting biases by explaining in the executive summary that there were neither 'right' nor 'wrong' answers.

In addition, we tested for the presence of a common method bias. We used Harman's (1967) one factor test and supplementary confirmatory factor analysis. All variables were entered into an exploratory factor analysis using unrotated principal component, principal component with varimax rotation and principal axis analysis with varimax rotation to determine the number of factors necessary to account for the variance in the variables. In the case of a substantial common method effect, either one single factor will emerge or the majority of covariance among variables will be explained by a single variable (Krishnan, Martin, & Noorderhaven, 2006; Podsakoff & Organ, 1986; Podsakoff et al., 2003). All analyses revealed the presence of six single factors with eigenvalues greater than 1, explaining approximately 71 per cent of the variance. As the largest factor did not account for the majority of the variance (16–19 per cent, depending on method of extraction), no general factor seems to be present. Further, confirmatory factor analysis revealed that a single-factor model did not fit our data well, with all fit indices showing unsatisfactory results. While our analyses cannot preclude the existence of common method variance in our data, findings do suggest that common method bias is of no great concern and unlikely to confound the interpretation of results.

Operationalization of Variables

Dependent variable. Entry mode of the subsidiary was measured using a dichotomous variable, assigned 0 if the subsidiary operated as an IJV and 1 if the subsidiary was a WoS (Brouthers et al., 2003; Jean-François Hennart & Larimo, 1998; Padmanabhan & Cho, 1996). We classified a subsidiary as an IJV if the parent firm held between 30 and 70 per cent of the subsidiary. Ownership above 70 per cent was classified as WoS. In our sample, we only included Sino–foreign ventures, but no foreign–foreign or Sino–Sino ventures. Fifty-six per cent of observations decided to form WoS and 44 per cent opted for an IJV.

Independent variables. Given the cross-sectional nature of our data we cannot capture managerial intentions for resource contributions. We, thus, use realized resource contributions for both intangibles and tangibles and argue that inferring from realized resource contributions on intended contributions is the best solution to measure our phenomenon for three reasons. First, subsidiaries in our sample are relatively young (mean age: 5 years, SD: 3.4 years), thus intended action and action will probably be strongly correlated as only limited time-effects occur. Second, asking about intended transfers after the realization of transfer may be confronted with at least two relevant biases: a memory bias as managers may not remember or may not have been in place when decided; and a social desirability bias as managers prefer to report successful operations. Third, we statistically control for endogeneity using a two-step procedure and are thus able to solve the empirical challenge associated with simultaneous measures.

The intended level of intangible resource contributions was measured following the suggestions of Davis, Desai and Francis (2000) and operationalized by a three-item measure. We asked managers to evaluate resource sharing between the parent firm and the subsidiary in the following activities of the value chain: research and development, advertising and promotional efforts, and common sales force. Answers to these questions were measured on seven-point Likert-type scales ranging from 1 (very low) to 7 (very high). To examine whether these items represented a single construct we ran a factor analysis that confirmed a single factor solution for our data. We thus used the average score of these items in our analyses. Calculating factor scores using regression analyses may be used as an alternative. Yet, Grice (2001) notes that averages can be considered as a specific type of factor score (using unit weights instead of a weight matrix derived mathematically) and they typically yield highly similar and robust results.

The level of intended tangible resource contributions was measured with a one-item measure obtained by asking managers about the amount of financial investment in their subsidiary made by a parent in million US dollars. We used the amount of financial investment as intended tangible resource transfer can be of different types and the measure includes all physical investments. We took a logarithm of this variable in order to account for diminishing returns (Contractor & Kundu, 1998). We include firm size as a control variable. Consequently, the tangible and intangible asset transfers are tested in relation to overall company size. As a robustness check, we also ran our model with a multi-item measure of perceived investment of tangible assets which we obtained from our survey and observed similar effects. Since financial investment is defined more clearly and hence easier to interpret for managers, we believe that it is a more rigorous measure of tangible asset transfer than a multi-item construct that depends on managers' perception of what distinguishes tangible and intangible resources.

Moderator variable. Berry, Guillén and Nan (2010) point out that there is a variety of definitions of institutional environment. Johanson and Vahlne (1977, p. 24) were among the first who pointed to the multidimensionality of environments, arguing that differences between countries are manifested in 'differences in language, education, business practices, culture, and industrial development'. Institutional theorists have divided the institutional environment into formal and informal dimensions (North, 1990; Scott, 1995), which prompted IB scholars to include both types of measures in empirical studies (Gaur & Lu, 2007; He, Brouthers, & Filatotchev, 2013; Slangen, 2011; Xu, Pan, & Beamish, 2004). Following the conceptualization and suggestions of prior research, we thus included both formal and informal measures of distance. We used differences in industrial development, levels of education, and political systems (both differences in degree of democracy and political ideology) to reflect the formal dimension of the institutional environment and differences in language and religion to reflect the informal dimension. We used the multi-item factor scores developed by Dow and Karunaratna (2006). Factor scores of these six dimensions were averaged to form a composite measure of institutional distance (Tanure, Barcellos, & Fleury, 2009). Our sample includes companies from 13 countries that are on the one hand quite uniform since their home country institutions can all be argued to be more developed than those in China. On the other hand, their within-group variation is significant. The institutional background particular with regard to institutional development over the past years is considerably different between, for example, Slovenia and

Japan or the United States and the Czech Republic which are all featured in our final sample.

Control variables. Four control variables were included in the analysis. The selection of control variables was based on previous entry-mode studies with the majority of them being the TCE determinants of the entry-mode choice in order to demonstrate the additional explanatory power of our analysis compared to the TCE-dominated entry-mode literature. We used a questionnaire-item quantifying asset specificity and, in addition, we included the level of technology intensity of the industry as a proxy for industry-specific asset specificity (Zhao et al., 2004). Prior entry-mode research maintained that high technology intensity prompts parent firms to choose WoS instead of IJVs to avoid know-how diffusion and appropriation risks (Gatignon & Anderson, 1988; Kogut & Singh, 1988). We used the SIC 10 category division coding system as our broad sample yielded a host of sparsely populated two-digit major industry codes. We classified these SIC-coded industries into five categories based on their R&D intensities following a definition by Hatzichronoglou (1997) and the OECD (2003). The categories included service, low-technology, medium-low technology, medium-high technology, and high-technology industry (Larimo, 2003). For the industries in our sample, five dummy variables were created and entered into the analysis. Service was used as reference category. With this two-pronged approach we covered perceptional and objective characteristics of asset specificity.

To measure the level of external uncertainty perceived by firms, we followed the recommendations of Agarwal and Ramaswami (1992), Brouthers (2002) and Brouthers and Brouthers (2003) and asked about the development of the political, economic and social stability in the PRC on seven-point Likert-type scales ranging from 1 (very low) to 7 (very high). Following the suggestions of Aulakh and Kotabe (1997), we also included a question about the legal stability. The majority of entry-mode scholars argue that high perceived external uncertainty prompt parent firms to opt for lower levels of integration, that is, by establishing IJVs instead of WoS. These scholars suggest that IJVs tie up fewer resources and offer MNCs greater flexibility in case the external environment in the host country deteriorates, thus reducing the firm's exposure to uncertain conditions (Erramilli & Rao, 1993; Gatignon & Anderson, 1988; Kim & Hwang, 1992). We used the average score of these items in our analyses ($\alpha = 0.85$).

With regard to internal uncertainty, we included grouped variables identifying the number of subsidiaries the companies in question have in all foreign countries and in the PRC. Also, the time that has passed since the first subsidiary in the PRC was founded was considered. Finally, we included size of the parent firm as a control variable since prior research suggested an influence of size on entry mode (Combs & Ketchen, 1999; Contractor & Kundu, 1998; Jean-François -Hennart & Larimo, 1998). Further, we believe it is specifically relevant to control for firm size as firms' intended tangible and intangible resource contributions should be evaluated in relation to firm size. In line with many existing studies we used number of worldwide employees as a measure of a parent firm's size (Brouthers et al., 2008; Chan & Makino, 2007).

Instrumental Variables

The research design unfortunately only allows asking subsidiary managers about the company's motivation for WoS or IJV formation after the fact. As a result, regression-based testing of our hypotheses may severely suffer from endogeneity. In order to counter endogeneity, we introduced instrumental variables that are not subject so simultaneity of measurement of dependent and independent variables. For the intended transfer of tangible resources we employed the time passed since the parent company founded its first subsidiary abroad. The exogeneity of this instrument is straightforward and the F-value from the first-stage regression confirms the instrument's strength ($F = 4.89$). For intended intangible resource transfer isomorphic pressure was chosen as an instrument. It was argued that sustainable change of isomorphic policies occurs quite slowly (Slack & Hinings, 1994). Consequently, we assume that isomorphic pressures are constant between the time of subsidiary formation and time of research. Regarding strength of the instrument, the F-value of the first-stage regression again indicates a robust instrument ($F = 7.46$). For the interaction terms, interaction instruments were estimated with the exogenous institutional distance estimator interacted with the respective intended tangible or intangible resource transfer instrument ($F = 10.45$ and $F = 8.37$). It can be assumed that the reduction of bias by introducing instruments outweighs the IV bias since for all first-stage regression the statistic nR^2 (Murray, 2006) greatly exceeds the number of instruments used ($nR^2 = \{33.42; 56.38; 81.39; 68.90\}$).

RESULTS

Table 1 shows the means, standard deviations and bivariate Pearson correlations. In our sample, 55 per cent of the subsidiaries are WoS, while 45 per cent

Table 1. Bivariate Pearson Correlations.

	Mean	Standard Deviation	*techigh*	*tecmedhigh*	*tecmedlow*	*teclow*	*econstab*	*exunc*	*assetspec*	*wwempl*	*prcsubs*	*instdist*	*intan-gible*	*tangible*
ownfound	0.4419	0.4985												
isompress	4.2973	0.9131												
firstsub	3.3516	0.9547												
techigh	0.0409	0.1987	1											
tecmedhigh	0.6082	0.4896	−0.2887***	1										
tecmedlow	0.0936	0.2921	−0.0690	−0.4183***	1									
teclow	0.0526	0.2240	−0.0476	−0.2887***	−0.0690	1								
econstab	4.7784	1.5884	0.0831	−0.0173	0.0534	−0.0789	1							
exunc	4.7258	1.1479	0.0962	0.0330	0.0186	−0.1143	0.8029***	1						
assetspec	3.9371	1.6208	0.1344	0.1001	−0.2619**	0.1344	−0.2133**	−0.3133***	1					
wwempl	63,566	125,729	0.0468	0.1981*	−0.1426	−0.0987	0.1746*	0.1919*	0.0468	1				
prcsubs	6.9583	10.6211	0.0833	0.2095*	−0.1170	−0.0789	0.1467	0.1960*	0.0154	0.7869***	1			
instdist	1.2230	0.1040	0.0465	0.0735	−0.0599	0.0247	−0.0316	0.0082	−0.0349	0.0833	0.0646	1		
intangible	4.3511	1.4826	0.0063	−0.0237	0.0519	−0.0990	0.0801	0.1062	−0.2175*	−0.0027	−0.0329	−0.0524	1	
tangible	1.4490	2.4425	0.0018	0.3481	−0.0375	−0.0117	0.1675	0.2353**	0.0677	0.3841***	0.2815**	0.1331	0.0457	1

Notes: 71 observed WoS and 57 IJVs. *ownfound* is the dummy depicting WoS or IJV choice (0 = IJV, 1 = WoS), *isompress* is isomorphic pressures (instrument 1) and *firstsub* is the year when the first foreign subsidiary was founded (instrument 2). *techigh* is a dummy indicating high technology intensity; *tecmedhigh* indicates medium to high technology intensity; *tecmedlow* indicates medium to low; *teclow* low technology intensity; *econstab* is economic stability; *exunc* external uncertainty; *assetspec* is asset specificity; *prcsubs* is the number of subsidiaries in the PRC preceding the respective investment; *wwempl* is total worldwide employees of the mother company; *instdist* is the compound measure of institutional distance as explained above; *intangible* and *tangible* are the originally obtained resource transfer intention variables (before IV estimation).

Significance value indicates at *0.05, **0.01 and ***0.001 levels.

are IJV. Despite a number of statistically significant correlations concerns about multicollinearity are not warranted (Hair, Black, Babin, Anderson, & Tatham, 2006). To address multicollinearity concerns variance inflation factors (VIFs) were calculated. The average of VIFs is 3.66, significantly below the threshold of 10 where literature proposes additional measures against multicollinearity (Neter, Kutner, Nachtsheim, & Wasserman, 1996). The highest VIF is recorded for the medium-high dummy in technology intensity (6.52). However, to further mitigate multicollinearity concerns and to ease the interpretation of the interaction effect, the predictor and moderator variables were standardized prior to the analyses. Some scholars recommend centring variables and aligning their mean to 0 in order to reduce collinear effects (Aiken & West, 1991). While having the same effect in terms of multicollinearity as centring, standardized variables offer some other advantages: With a standard deviation equal to 1 and a mean equal to 0, the interpretation of the interactions are easier (Frazier, Tix, & Barron, 2004). Also, standardization helps to draw comparisons between different models, as non-standardized variables are dependent on their unique unit of measurement.

We employed logistic regressions to test our hypotheses as applied in previous entry-mode studies (Brouthers, 2002; Brouthers & Nakos, 2004; Erramilli, 1991). The results of the logistic regression analyses are shown in Table 2. Since distribution of our sample was asymmetric, we used the proportional chance criterion to examine the predictive power of our regression results. Tatoglu, Glaister and Erdal (2003) argue that the power of a regression is acceptable if it explains 25 per cent more than the proportional chance criterion. The predictive power of our regression (67.97 per cent) exceeds this reference value (62.55 per cent) and is thus acceptable. Of course, the instrumental estimation under-estimates the explanatory power of our model due to the reduction in variance in the instrumental variables as opposed to the original descriptive variables. The R^2 values reported in Table 2 are also significantly lowered because of the two-stage regression.

We calculate five models to test our hypotheses. In Model 1, only control variables are entered. Out of the control variables, parent firm size has a significant effect on the choice of entry mode. Moreover, technology intensity of industry shows significances for medium-high technology and medium-low technology dummies. Also, the model shows a significant constant in favour of WoS, which is an indication of it being not correctly specified since in the underlying sample the shares of WoS and IJV are almost equal. In Model 2, direct effects are added. The intended transfer of intangible resources is significantly related to the choice of entry mode, with higher intended levels of intangible resources increasing the propensity of parent

Table 2. Logit Regression Results for IV Estimation of Entry Mode.

DV: ownfound	Model 1	Model 2	Model 3	Model 4	Model 5
const	1.1783**	0.0424	−0.1041	0.2685	0.1157
	(2.74)	(0.05)	(−0.12)	(0.27)	(0.10)
techigh	−1.1079	−0.0252	0.0647	−0.2309	−0.1343
	(−1.78)	(−0.03)	(0.08)	(−0.26)	(−0.14)
tecmedhigh	−1.3282***	−0.1132	0.0501	−0.2173	−0.0220
	(−3.21)	(−0.13)	(0.05)	(−0.20)	(−0.02)
tecmedlow	−1.8154***	−0.4296	−0.2396	−0.7977	−0.6022
	(−3.25)	(−0.43)	(−0.23)	(−0.60)	(−0.43)
teclow	−0.9739	0.1921	0.3550	0.0439	0.2341
	(−1.41)	(0.16)	(0.31)	(0.03)	(0.16)
econstab	−0.0384	0.0020	0.0951	0.1189	0.2531
	(−0.13)	(0.01)	(0.37)	(0.48)	(0.97)
exunc	−0.1467	−0.0786	−0.1958	−0.1123	−0.2769
	(−0.45)	(−0.24)	(−0.57)	(−0.30)	(−0.69)
assetspec	−0.2858	−1.0190	−0.1322	0.0465	0.0175
	(−1.45)	(−0.46)	(−0.59)	(0.20)	(0.07)
prcsubs	−0.0397	−0.1653	−0.1205	−0.1445	−0.0858
	(−0.31)	(−1.08)	(−0.66)	(−0.77)	(−0.39)
wwempl	−0.3328***	0.1827	0.1597	0.2115	0.1856
	(−3.77)	(0.72)	(0.61)	(0.76)	(0.57)
instdist		0.3037	0.8262	−0.5761	−0.0396
		(1.14)	(1.04)	(−1.41)	(−0.08)
intangible		0.5122***	0.7139*	0.5339***	0.7991***
		(4.19)	(2.27)	(4.00)	(4.42)
tangible		−0.9603	−1.1184	−1.1439	−1.3783*
		(−1.38)	(−1.60)	(−1.85)	(−2.19)
*intangible * instdist*			−0.9117		−1.2364*
			(−0.93)		(−2.03)
*tangible * instdist*				−0.8209**	−0.9155**
				(−2.87)	(−2.74)
N	128	128	128	128	128
$\overline{R}^2$	0.090	0.077	0.084	0.1014	0.1138
LLH	−98.9612	−81.1790	−80.5706	−79.0362	−77.9458

Notes: 0 indicates IJV, 1 indicates WoS. *ownfound* is the dummy depicting WoS or IJV choice, *techigh* is a dummy indicating high technology intensity, *tecmedhigh* indicates medium to high technology intensity, *tecmedlow* indicates medium to low and *teclow* low technology intensity. *econstab* is economic stability, *exunc* external uncertainty, *assetspec* is asset specificity, *prcsubs* is the number of subsidiaries in the PRC preceding the respective investment and *wwempl* is total worldwide employees of the mother company. *instdist* is the compound measure of institutional distance as explained above. *tangible* and *intangible* stand for the IV-simulated results of intended tangible and intangible resource transfers. *N* is the number of observations, $\overline{R}^2$ is adjusted pseudo R^2 for the logit regression (underestimating the real R^2 because of IV estimation) and LLH is the pseudo limited likelihood of the logit regression (for model comparison). Significance value indicates at *0.05, **0.01 and ***0.001 levels for two-sided tests.

firms choosing WoS. In Models 3 and 4, we enter the interaction terms of intangible resources and institutional distance and tangible resources and institutional distance individually. Our theory and hypotheses are, however, symmetrical. Consequently, the relevant test of our hypotheses occurs in Model 5. There, we find that higher intended transfer of intangible resources indicates propensity to opt for WoS (**H1a**), while the intended transfer of tangible resources makes opting for IJVs more likely (**H1b**). The coefficients of the interaction terms for intended intangible resource transfers and institutional distance are significant as well, confirming that institutional distance tilts the impact of intended tangible and intangible resource transfers towards shared entry modes. Therefore, **H2a** and **H2b** are supported.

In terms of controls, technology intensity of the industry as a proxy for asset specificity is partially significant, with medium levels of intensity (i.e. medium-high technology and medium-low technology dummies) resulting in a higher propensity of choosing IJVs. This finding is in line with traditional TCE reasoning, suggesting that WoS represent the cost-efficient governance structure for high degrees of asset specificity, while IJVs are the cost-efficient governance structure for medium degrees of specificity (Anderson & Gatignon, 1986).

The majority of entry mode scholars argue that high external uncertainty prompt parent firms to opt for IJVs instead of WoS (Erramilli & Rao, 1993; Gatignon & Anderson, 1988; Kim & Hwang, 1992). However, we do not find a significant effect for external uncertainty. An explanation for this result could be that the entry-mode literature can, from a theoretical point of view, equally accommodate the opposite line of reasoning. Specifically, some scholars noted that highly uncertain conditions make it difficult for MNCs to rely on contributions of external firms in the host market, thus increasing the likelihood of choosing WoS instead of IJVs (Anderson & Gatignon, 1986; Padmanabhan & Cho, 1996). Consequently, the effect of external uncertainty on the choice of entry mode does not appear to be clear-cut, which may explain our insignificant results.

Finally, parent firm size in our sample does not increase the propensity of firms choosing IJVs. It is argued that because of their size, international experience, and bargaining power larger firms are less affected by internal uncertainty within IJV operations, which may increase their willingness to engage in cooperative modes. Larimo (1993), Mutinelli and Piscitello (1998) and Sanna-Randaccio (1990), among others, find that very large firms were more likely to set up IJVs. With the inclusion of resource transfer intentions, however, it seems that size effects in the parent companies are accounted for.

We conducted robustness checks of our model with regard to the clustering of error terms. In a fixed-effects hierarchical linear model (HLM) that accounts for the different levels of classification of errors related to country differences and errors related to company difference we did not find significant differences to the presented results. We report the logit model since it is proposed that for country-level groups of below 30 observations the coefficients are more efficient in a moderated regression model than in a HLM (Meuleman & Billiet, 2009; Peterson, Arregle, & Martin, 2012). Also, when the logit approach was exchanged for a probit approach, the coefficients in the regression did not change significantly.

DISCUSSION

Our study has a number of important implications for entry-mode studies in IB. By grounding our study within the RBV, we contribute to the literature by highlighting the value creation aspect of entry-mode choices. We demonstrate that parent firms select their governance structures based on the nature of intended resource transfers abroad to maintain value that may be obtained from their intended resource endowments. Moreover, we differentiate between the intended transfer of intangible and tangible resources and show their opposite effects on the choice of entry mode. In particular, our analysis shows that from an RBV perspective, WoSs serve as appropriate governance structures for facilitating the transfer of intangible resources, while IJVs appear to be the appropriate structures for facilitating the transfer of tangible resources. We thus suggest that the choice of entry mode is not purely driven by failure on external markets, but also by failures of hierarchical governance structures as not all modes appear to be equally effective in preserving the expected value derived from intended resource transfers (Madhok, 1997). Furthermore, our findings support the notion that while parent firms tend to leverage intangibles in WoS, they tend to bundle deployed tangibles with local IJV partners (Sirmon et al., 2007). The RBV argument that mainly concerned the establishment mode choice hence is extended to ownership-based entry mode. Our reasoning shows that TCE and RBV are compatible. We argue that their explicit inclusion in one empirical framework makes it possible to observe resource-based effects while controlling for the transaction-related impact of TCE argumentation. In empirical terms, our analysis shows that the RBV determinants have a significant impact when TCE constructs are controlled for. Altogether, our findings indicate that the firm's resource transfer intentions have a profound impact on the choice of entry mode.

Furthermore, we contribute by integrating insights from institutional theory into the RBV framework. We suggest that the expected value derived from intended resource transfers is far from being universal, but contingent on differences in the institutional environment between home and host country. We thus address the criticism of scholars who maintained that prior research has failed to control for the institutional environment of firms (He et al., 2013; Sirmon et al., 2007). Our analysis clearly indicates that the level of institutional distance affects the governance structures through which parent firms intend to deploy their resources. We show that with increasing institutional distance parent firms that intend to transfer high levels of intangible or tangible resources may increase the legitimacy of their business operations and thus the value of their resource endowments by cooperating with local IJV partners. In particular, our results demonstrate that parent firms that intend to transfer high levels of intangible resources are more dependent on the contributions of local partners in situations of high institutional differences. Due to their often tacit nature and organizational embeddedness intangible resources thus appear to be highly location sensitive, which complicates the deployment through hierarchical governance structures with increasing institutional distance. Our analysis thus provides important evidence that insights from institutional theory can be meaningfully combined with RBV explanations to enhance the explanatory power of entry mode decisions.

Furthermore, we contribute to theories that go beyond the scope of this study. In particular, we also contribute to entry mode studies grounded within the TCE framework. Previous TCE-related entry-mode studies heavily relied on the concept of asset specificity to capture the nature of assets that parent firms transact with foreign subsidiaries, suggesting that high asset specificity induce parent firms to opt for hierarchical governance structures such as WoS (Cleeve, 1997; Gatignon & Anderson, 1988). Apart from their focus on the contractual relationship and not the transfer of resources, the majority of these studies did not differentiate between intangible and tangible resources (Brouthers & Brouthers, 2003; Brouthers et al., 2003; Puck et al., 2009). While the focus of our study is not on measuring specificity inherent in the transferred resources, we suggest that the intangible component of the to-be-deployed resources appears to exert a stronger influence on the choice of hierarchical governance structures than the tangible component. Specifically, our study shows that parent firms that transfer high levels of tangibles are not solely concerned with minimizing transaction costs and thus opt for hierarchical governance structures in order to achieve cost reduction effects, but also with value creation by bundling resources jointly with local IJV partners. Chen and Chen (2003) highlight that, in contrast to RBV, TCE falls short of explaining the benefits of resource sharing in strategic alliances. Our study shows that the benefits derived from sharing tangibles with local IJV partners appear to drive cooperative mode choices – a factor that is often overlooked by traditional TCE studies. Overall, with respect to further development of TCE, we suggest that the insufficient differentiation between effects of intangible and tangible resource contributions may partially explain mixed empirical evidence regarding the effect of asset specificity on entry mode choice besides the conceptual and methodological concerns about the asset specificity construct stated in the literature (Brouthers & Hennart, 2007). In line with our findings, we thus recommend future studies to more clearly untangle the effect of intangible and tangible resource transfer intentions in order to enhance our understanding of mode choices.

LIMITATIONS AND FUTURE RESEARCH

This study is not without limitations. First, we focused on foreign subsidiaries in one country, the PRC. This approach helps to keep one part of the institutional distance equation constant and thus may lead to a range restriction in our institutional distance variable. Therefore, as range restriction decreases statistical power, our results may generate a conservative estimate of the effects of institutional distance on the choice of entry mode. Future research should include a broader geographic sample to address this potential shortcoming.

Second, the size of both parent firms and subsidiaries in our sample was relatively large. Larger firms have more experience and resources to deal with liability of foreignness and uncertainty stemming from institutional hazards which may influence their governance choices (Salomon & Wu, 2012; Schwens et al., 2011). In order to enhance our understanding future studies should verify whether the nature of firm resource transfer intentions and institutional distance influences SME's entry-mode choice in a similar way.

Third, from the results of our study we are unable to draw any performance implications. Nevertheless, it would be interesting to analyse how strategic matches/mismatches from the perspective of RBV and institutional theory influence performance outcomes. Brouthers (2002), Brouthers et al. (2003), and Brouthers and Nakos (2004), for instance, have conducted research analysing possible performance outcomes of similar strategic matches/mismatches with regard to entry-mode choices. Future studies could thus use an RBV approach and analyse how firms make decisions about entry-mode choices and how these choices affect performance.

Finally, a further limitation concerns the measurement of constructs, their subjective evaluation by a single firm representative and the possibility of common method bias on the level of control variables. In addition, even though we relied on scales that have been used in other research, few of these scales have been designed for a cross-cultural research framework.

CONCLUSION

Building on the RBV and insights from institutional theory, we extend the extant TCE-grounded entry-mode literature. We show that intra-firm resource transfer intentions have a significant effect on the choice of entry mode (IJVs/WoS). Our results indicate that the entry-mode choice does not solely depend on efficiency and cost minimization aspects, but also on the intentions concerning firm resources to be transferred to foreign markets, as these resources may be differently exploited in IJVs and WoS. More importantly, the value that firms expect to generate with the resources they plan to transfer abroad is far from being universal, but is influenced by institutional differences between the firm's home and the host country. Overall, our focus on intended firm resource transfers and institutional distance provides important guidance for future entry mode research.

REFERENCES

Agarwal, S., & Ramaswami, S. N. (1992). Choice of foreign market entry mode: Impact of ownership, location and internalization factors. *Journal of International Business Studies*, *23*(1), 1–27.

Aiken, L. S., & West, S. G. (1991). *Multiple regression: Testing and interpreting interactions*. Newbury Park, CA, London: Sage.

Anderson, E., & Gatignon, H. (1986). Modes of foreign entry: A transaction cost analysis and propositions. *Journal of International Business Studies*, *17*(3), 1–26.

Ando, N. (2011). The ownership structure of foreign subsidiaries and the effect of institutional distance: A case study of Japanese firms. *Asia Pacific Business Review*, *18*(2), 259–274. doi:10.1080/13602381.2010.502315

Armstrong, J. S., & Overton, T. S. (1977). Estimating nonresponse bias in mail surveys. *Journal of Marketing Research*, *14*(3), 396–402.

Aulakh, P. S., & Kotabe, M. (1997). Antecedents and performance implications of channel integration in foreign markets. *Journal of International Business Studies*, *28*(1), 145–175.

Barney, J. (1991). Firm resources and sustained competitive advantage. *Journal of Management*, *17*(1), 99–120.

Barney, J., Wright, M., & Ketchen, D. J. (2001). The resource-based view of the firm: Ten years after 1991. *Journal of Management*, *27*(6), 625–641. doi:10.1177/014920630102700601

Berry, H., Guillén, M. F., & Nan, Z. (2010). An institutional approach to cross-national distance. *Journal of International Business Studies*, *41*(9), 1460–1480. doi:10.1057/jibs.2010.28

Brislin, R. W. (1970). Back-translation for cross-cultural research. *Journal of Cross-Cultural Psychology*, *1*(3), 185–216.

Brouthers, K. D. (2002). Institutional, cultural and transaction cost influences on entry mode choice and performance. *Journal of International Business Studies*, *33*(2), 203–221.

Brouthers, K. D., & Brouthers, L. E. (2003). Why service and manufacturing entry mode choices differ: The influence of transaction cost factors, risk and trust. *Journal of Management Studies*, *40*(5), 1179–1204. doi:10.1111/1467-6486.00376

Brouthers, K. D., Brouthers, L. E., & Werner, S. (2003). Transaction cost-enhanced entry mode choices and firm performance. *Strategic Management Journal*, *24*(12), 1239–1248. doi:10.1002/smj.362

Brouthers, K. D., Brouthers, L. E., & Werner, S. (2008). Resource-based advantages in an international context. *Journal of Management*, *34*(2), 189–217. doi:10.1177/0149206307312508

Brouthers, K. D., & Hennart, J.-F. (2007). Boundaries of the firm: Insights from international entry mode research. *Journal of Management*, *33*(3), 395–425.

Brouthers, K. D., & Nakos, G. (2004). SME entry mode choice and performance: A transaction cost perspective. *Entrepreneurship: Theory & Practice*, *28*(3), 229–247. doi:10.1111/j.1540-6520.2004.00041.x

Canabal, A., & White, G. O. (2008). Entry mode research: Past and future. *International Business Review*, *17*(3), 267–284. doi:10.1016/j.ibusrev.2008.01.003

Chan, C. M., & Makino, S. (2007). Legitimacy and multi-level institutional environments: Implications for foreign subsidiary ownership structure. *Journal of International Business Studies*, *38*(4), 621–638. doi:10.1057/palgrave.jibs.8400283

Chandler, A. D. (1992). Organizational capabilities and the economic history of the industrial enterprise. *Journal of Economic Perspectives*, *6*(3), 79–100.

Chen, H., & Chen, T.-J. (2003). Governance structures in strategic alliances: Transaction cost versus resource-based perspective. *Journal of World Business*, *38*(1), 1–14. doi:10.1016/s1090-9516(02)00105-0

Chen, H., & Hu, M. Y. (2002). An analysis of determinants of entry mode and its impact on performance. *International Business Review*, *11*(2), 193–210. doi:10.1016/s0969-5931(01)00055-5

Chen, S.-F. S., & Hennart, J.-F. (2002). Japanese investors' choice of joint ventures versus wholly-owned subsidiaries in the US: The role of market barriers and firm capabilities. *Journal of International Business Studies*, *33*(1), 1–18.

Chiao, Y.-C., Lo, F.-Y., & Yu, C.-M. (2010). Choosing between wholly-owned subsidiaries and joint ventures of MNCs from an emerging market. *International Marketing Review*, *27*(3), 338–365. doi:10.1108/02651331011047998

Cho, K. R., & Padmanabhan, P. (2001). The relative importance of old and new decision specific experience in foreign ownership strategies: An exploratory study. *International Business Review*, *10*(6), 645–659. doi:10.1016/s0969-5931(01)00036-1

Claver, E., & Quer, D. (2005). Choice of market entry mode in China: The influence of firm-specific factors. *Journal of General Management*, *30*(3), 51–70.

Cleeve, E. (1997). The motives for joint ventures: A transaction costs analysis of Japanese MNEs in the UK. *Scottish Journal of Political Economy*, *44*(1), 31–43.

Combs, J. G., & Ketchen, D. J., Jr. (1999). Explaining interfirm cooperation and performance: Toward a reconciliation of predictions from the resource-based view and organizational economics. *Strategic Management Journal*, *20*(9), 867–888.

Contractor, F. J., & Kundu, S. K. (1998). Modal choice in a world of alliances: Analyzing organizational forms in the international hotel sector. *Journal of International Business Studies*, *29*(2), 325–357.

Davis, P. S., Desai, A. B., & Francis, J. D. (2000). Mode of international entry: An isomorphism perspective. *Journal of International Business Studies*, *31*(2), 239–258.

Delios, A., & Henisz, W. J. (2000). Japanese firms' investment strategies in emerging economies. *The Academy of Management Journal*, *43*(3), 305–323.

Demirbag, M., Glaister, K. W., & Tatoglu, E. (2007). Institutional and transaction cost influences on MNEs' ownership strategies of their affiliates: Evidence from an emerging market. *Journal of World Business*, *42*(4), 418–434. doi:10.1016/j.jwb.2007.06.004

Dikova, D. (2012). Entry mode choices in transition economies: The moderating effect of institutional distance on managers' personal experiences. *Journal of East-West Business*, *18*(1), 1–27. doi:10.1080/10669868.2012.675807

Dow, D., & Karunaratna, A. (2006). Developing a multidimensional instrument to measure psychic distance stimuli. *Journal of International Business Studies*, *37*(5), 578–602.

Eisenhardt, K. M., & Schoonhoven, C. B. (1996). Resource-based view of strategic alliance formation: Strategic and social effects in entrepreneurial firms. *Organization Science*, *7*(2), 136–150.

Ekeledo, I., & Sivakumar, K. (2004). International market entry mode strategies of manufacturing firms and service firms: A resource-based perspective. *International Marketing Review*, *21*(1), 68–101.

Erramilli, M. K. (1991). The experience factor in foreign market entry behavior of service firms. *Journal of International Business Studies*, *22*(3), 479–501.

Erramilli, M. K., & Rao, C. P. (1993). Service firms' international entry-mode choice: A modified transaction-cost analysis approach. *Journal of Marketing*, *57*(3), 19–38.

Frazier, P. A., Tix, A. P., & Barron, K. E. (2004). Testing moderator and mediator effects in counselling psychology research. *Journal of Counselling Psychology*, *51*(1), 115–134.

Garnier, G. H. (1982). Context and decision making autonomy in the foreign affiliates of U.S. multinational corporations. *Academy of Management Journal*, *25*(4), 893–908.

Gatignon, H., & Anderson, E. (1988). The multinational corporation's degree of control over foreign subsidiaries: An empirical test of a transaction cost explanation. *Journal of Law, Economics & Organization*, *4*(2), 305–336.

Gaur, A. S., & Lu, J. W. (2007). Ownership strategies and survival of foreign subsidiaries: Impacts of institutional distance and experience. *Journal of Management*, *33*(1), 84–110.

Grice, J. W. (2001). Computing and evaluating factor scores. *Psychological Methods*, *6*(4), 430–450. doi:10.1037/1082-989x.6.4.430

Hair, J. F., Black, B., Babin, B., Anderson, R. E., & Tatham, R. L. (2006). *Multivariate data analysis* (6th ed.). Upper Saddle River, NJ: Pearson Education.

Harman, H. H. (1967). *Modern factor analysis*. Chicago, IL: University of Chicago Press.

Hatzichronoglou, T. (1997). *Revision of the high-technology sector and product classification*. OECD Science, Technology and Industry Working Papers, No. 1997/02, OECD Publishing, Paris. doi:10.1787/134337307632

He, X., Brouthers, K. D., & Filatotchev, I. (2013). Resource-based and institutional perspectives on export channel selection and export performance. *Journal of Management*, *39*(1), 27–47.

Hennart, J.-F., & Larimo, J. (1998). The impact of culture on the strategy of multinational enterprises: Does national origin affect ownership decisions? *Journal of International Business Studies*, *29*(3), 515–538.

Hennart, J.-F., & Park, Y.-R. (1993). Greenfield vs. acquisition: The strategy of Japanese investors in the United States. *Management Science*, *39*(9), 1054–1070.

Johanson, J., & Vahlne, J.-E. (1977). The internationalization process of the firm – A model of knowledge development and increasing foreign market commitments. *Journal of International Business Studies*, *8*(1), 25–34.

Kaynak, E., Demirbag, M., & Tatoglu, E. (2007). Determinants of ownership-based entry mode choice of MNEs: Evidence from Mongolia. *Management International Review*, *47*(4), 505–530. doi:10.1007/s11575-007-0028-y

Kim, C. W., & Hwang, P. (1992). Global strategy and multinationals' entry mode choice. *Journal of International Business Studies*, *23*(1), 29–53.

Kogut, B., & Singh, H. (1988). The effect of national culture on the choice of entry mode. *Journal of International Business Studies*, *19*(3), 411–432.

Kogut, B., & Zander, U. (2003). Knowledge of the firm and the evolutionary theory of the multinational corporation: 2003 decade award winning article. *Journal of International Business Studies*, *34*(6), 516–529.

Kostova, T., Roth, K., & Dacin, M. T. (2008). Institutional theory in the study of multinational corporations: A critique and new directions. *Academy of Management Review*, *33*(4), 994–1006.

Krishnan, R., Martin, X., & Noorderhaven, N. G. (2006). When does trust matter to alliance performance? *Academy of Management Journal*, *49*(5), 894–917.

Larimo, J. (1993). *Foreign direct investment behaviour. An analysis of Finnish direct manufacturing investments in OECD countries.* University of Vaasa, Vaasa.

Larimo, J. (2003). Form of investment by nordic firms in world markets. *Journal of Business Research*, *56*(10), 791–803. doi:10.1016/s0148-2963(02)00467-8

Li, L., & Qian, G. (2008). Partnership or self-reliance entry modes: Large and small technology-based enterprises' strategies in overseas markets. *Journal of International Entrepreneurship*, *6*(4), 188–208.

Lu, J. W., & Hébert, L. (2005). Equity control and the survival of international joint ventures: A contingency approach. *Journal of Business Research*, *58*(6), 736–745. doi:10.1016/j.jbusres.2003.08.012

Madhok, A. (1997). Cost, value and foreign market entry mode: The transaction and the firm. *Strategic Management Journal*, *18*(1), 39–61.

Mahoney, J. T. (2001). A resource-based theory of sustainable rents. *Journal of Management*, *27*(6), 651–660. doi:10.1016/s0149-2063(01)00116-7

Meuleman, B., & Billiet, J. (2009). *A Monte Carlo sample size study: How many countries are needed for accurate multilevel SEM?* Paper presented at the Survey Research Methods.

Meyer, K. E., Wright, M., & Pruthi, S. (2009). Managing knowledge in foreign entry strategies: A resource-based analysis. *Strategic Management Journal, 30*(5), 557–574. doi:10.1002/smj.756

MOFCOM. (2012). *Foreign investment Department of the Chinese Ministry of Commerce: Statistics of FDI by form in 2010*. Retrieved from http://www.fdi.gov.cn/pub/FDI_EN/Statistics/AnnualStatisticsData/AnnualFDIData/FDIStatistics,2010/t20120207_140889.htm. Accessed on 22 February 2012.

Molloy, J. C., Chadwick, C., Ployhart, R. E., & Golden, S. J. (2011). Making intangibles "Tangible" in tests of resource-based theory. *Journal of Management, 37*(5), 1496–1518. doi:10.1177/0149206310394185

Morschett, D., Schramm-Klein, H., & Swoboda, B. (2010). Decades of research on market entry modes: What do we really know about external antecedents of entry mode choice? *Journal of International Management, 16*(1), 60–77. doi:10.1016/j.intman.2009.09.002

Morschett, D., Swoboda, B., & Schramm-Klein, H. (2008). Einflussfaktoren auf die Wahl einer Markteintrittsstrategie: Eine meta-analytische Untersuchung der Entscheidung zwischen Tochtergesellschaft und Kooperation. *Zeitschrift für Betriebswirtschaft, 78*(5), 509–552. doi:10.1007/s11573-008-0031-1

Murray, M. P. (2006). Avoiding invalid instruments and coping with weak instruments. *The Journal of Economic Perspectives, 20*(4), 111–132.

Mutinelli, M., & Piscitello, L. (1998). The entry mode choice of MNEs: An evolutionary approach. *Research Policy, 27*(5), 491–506. doi:10.1016/s0048-7333(98)00063-8

Neter, J., Kutner, M. H., Nachtsheim, C. J., & Wasserman, W. (1996). *Applied linear statistical models* (Vol. 4). Chicago, IL: Irwin.

North, D. C. (1990). *Institutions, institutional change, and economic performance*. Cambridge: Cambridge University Press.

OECD. (2003). *OECD science, technology and industry scoreboard 2003*. doi:10.1787/sti_scoreboard-2003-en

Padmanabhan, P., & Cho, K. R. (1996). Ownership strategy for a foreign affiliate: An empirical investigation of Japanese Firms. *Management International Review, 36*(1), 45–65.

Pan, Y. (1996). Influences on foreign equity ownership level in joint ventures in China. *Journal of International Business Studies, 27*(1), 1–26.

Peng, M. W. (2001). The resource-based view and international business. *Journal of Management, 27*(6), 803–829. doi:10.1177/014920630102700611

Peng, M. W., Wang, D. Y. L., & Jiang, Y. (2008). An institution-based view of international business strategy: A focus on emerging economies. *Journal of International Business Studies, 39*(5), 920–936. doi:10.1057/palgrave.jibs.8400377

Peterson, M. F., Arregle, J.-L., & Martin, X. (2012). Multilevel models in international business research. *Journal of International Business Studies, 43*(5), 451–457.

Podsakoff, P. M., MacKenzie, S. B., Jeong-Yeon, L., & Podsakoff, N. P. (2003). Common method biases in behavioral research: A critical review of the literature and recommended remedies. *Journal of Applied Psychology, 88*(5), 879–903.

Podsakoff, P. M., & Organ, D. W. (1986). Self-reports in organizational research: Problems and prospects. *Journal of Management, 12*(4), 531–544.

Puck, J. F., Holtbrügge, D., & Mohr, A. T. (2009). Beyond entry mode choice: Explaining the conversion of joint ventures into wholly owned subsidiaries in the People's Republic of China. *Journal of International Business Studies, 40*(3), 388–404. doi:10.1057/jibs.2008.56

Salomon, R., & Wu, Z. (2012). Institutional distance and local isomorphism strategy. *Journal of International Business Studies*, *43*(4), 343–367.

Sanna-Randaccio, F. (1990). *The ownership structure of foreign subsidiaries: Evidence from the Italian multinationals*. Paper presented at the Annual Meeting of the European International Business Association, Madrid.

Schwens, C., Eiche, J., & Kabst, R. (2011). The moderating impact of informal institutional distance and formal institutional risk on SME entry mode choice. *Journal of Management Studies*, *48*(2), 330–351. doi:10.1111/j.1467-6486.2010.00970.x

Scott, W. R. (1995). *Institutions and organizations/W. Richard Scott*. Thousand Oaks, CA: Sage.

Shan, W. (1991). Environmental risks and joint venture sharing arrangements. *Journal of International Business Studies*, *22*(4), 555–578.

Sharma, V. M., & Erramilli, M. K. (2004). Resource-based explanation of entry mode choice. *Journal of Marketing Theory and Practice*, *12*(1), 1–18.

Sirmon, D. G., Hitt, M. A., & Ireland, R. D. (2007). Managing firm resources in dynamic environments to create value: Looking inside the black box. *Academy of Management Review*, *32*(1), 273–292. doi:10.5465/amr.2007.23466005

Slack, T., & Hinings, B. (1994). Institutional pressures and isomorphic change: An empirical test. *Organization Studies*, *15*(6), 803–827.

Slangen, A. H. L. (2011). A communication-based theory of the choice between greenfield and acquisition entry. *Journal of Management Studies*, *48*(8), 1699–1726. doi:10.1111/j.1467-6486.2011.01013.x

Sohn, J. H. D. (1994). Social knowledge as a control system: A proposition and evidence from the Japanese FDI behavior. *Journal of International Business Studies*, *25*(2), 295–324.

Tanure, B., Barcellos, E. P., & Fleury, M. T. L. (2009). Psychic distance and the challenges of expatriation from Brazil. *International Journal of Human Resource Management*, *20*(5), 1039–1055. doi:10.1080/09585190902850257

Tatoglu, E., Glaister, K. W., & Erdal, F. (2003). Determinants of foreign ownership in Turkish manufacturing. *Eastern European Economics*, *41*(2), 5–41.

Tsang, E. W. K. (2000). Transaction cost and resource-based explanations of joint ventures: A comparison and synthesis. *Organization Studies*, *21*(1), 215–242.

UNCTAD. (2011). *Inward and outward foreign direct investment flows, annual, 1970-2010*. Retrieved from United Nations http://unctadstat.unctad.org. Accessed on 22 February 2012.

Werner, S. (2002). Recent developments in international management research: A review of 20 top management journals. *Journal of Management*, *28*(3), 277–305.

Wernerfelt, B. (1984). A resource-based view of the firm. *Strategic Management Journal*, *5*(2), 171–180.

Williamson, O. (1979). Transaction-cost economics: The governance of contractual relations. *Journal of Law and Economics*, *22*(2), 233–261.

Williamson, O. E. (1985). *The economic institutions of capitalism: Firms, markets, relational contracting*. New York, NY: Free Press.

Xu, D., Pan, Y., & Beamish, P. W. (2004). The effect of regulative and normative distances on MNE ownership and expatriate strategies. *Management International Review*, *44* (3), 285–307.

Xu, D., & Shenkar, O. (2002). Institutional distance and the multinational enterprise. *Academy of Management Review*, *27*(4), 608–618.

Yang, C. (2012). Restructuring the export-oriented industrialization in the Pearl river delta, China: Institutional evolution and emerging tension. *Applied Geography*, *32*(1), 143–157.

Yiu, D., & Makino, S. (2002). The choice between joint venture and wholly owned subsidiary: An institutional perspective. *Organization Science*, *13*(6), 667–683.

Zaheer, S. (1995). Overcoming the liability of foreignness. *Academy of Management Journal*, *38*(2), 341–363.

Zhao, H., Luo, Y., & Suh, T. (2004). Transaction cost determinants and ownership-based entry mode choice: A meta-analytical review. *Journal of International Business Studies*, *35*(6), 524–544.

CHAPTER 12

HOW THE DIRECTION OF INSTITUTIONAL DISTANCE INFLUENCES FOREIGN ENTRY MODE CHOICES: AN INFORMATION ECONOMICS PERSPECTIVE

Michael J. Mueller, Guus Hendriks and Arjen H.L. Slangen

ABSTRACT

In this chapter, we aim to shed more light on the role of formal institutional distance in firms' foreign entry mode choices by accounting for the direction of that distance. Specifically, we distinguish between foreign entries where the host country is institutionally less developed than the investing firm's home country (negative institutional distance) and those where the host country's institutions are comparatively more developed (positive institutional distance), and explore whether these different types of entries are implemented through different equity-based modes. We take an information economics perspective to develop hypotheses on the effects of positive and negative

Distance in International Business: Concept, Cost and Value
Progress in International Business Research, Volume 12, 271–296

ISSN: 1745-8862/doi:10.1108/S1745-886220170000012020

formal institutional distance on firms' choices between greenfields and acquisitions, and between full and partial ownership of greenfield and acquired subsidiaries. We test our hypotheses on a sample of 1,070 foreign entries made by 796 emerging market multinationals originating from 14 countries. Controlling for the host country's formal institutional quality and other factors, we find that negative institutional distance increases the likelihood that a foreign entry takes the form of a greenfield investment rather than an acquisition and that positive institutional distance decreases that likelihood. We also find that negative institutional distance increases the chances that firms choose greenfield joint ventures over wholly owned greenfields and full over partial acquisitions. Finally, we find that positive institutional distance does not affect firms' ownership stake choices, neither for greenfields nor for acquisitions. Overall, these findings argue for a nuanced, contingency view of the role of formal institutional distance in foreign entry mode choices. To the best of our knowledge, this study is the first to use information economics to construct a holistic picture of firms' equity-based entry mode choices, taking into account both establishment and ownership modes.

Keywords: Information economics; institutional distance; entry mode choice; emerging market multinationals

INTRODUCTION

When a firm decides to engage in foreign direct investment, it faces two strategic decisions (Brouthers & Hennart, 2007). First, it has to decide whether to acquire an existing firm or to start up a greenfield subsidiary (i.e., the establishment mode choice). Second, it needs to decide whether it will hold full ownership in the foreign subsidiary or share ownership with a local partner (i.e., the ownership mode choice). Extant studies have shown that these decisions depend in part on the quality of the formal institutions in the selected host country, finding that this quality has a positive effect on the chance that firms enter through acquisitions rather than through greenfields and on the chance that they opt for full rather than shared ownership of the foreign subsidiary (Dikova & van Witteloostuijn, 2007; Meyer, Estrin, Bhaumik, & Peng, 2009; Slangen & van Tulder, 2009). Yet besides depending on a host country's institutional quality per se, foreign entry mode choices may also depend on whether that quality compares favorably or unfavorably to the institutional quality in the entrant's home country. This institutional position of a host country vis-à-vis an entrant's home country is not captured by the popular concept of institutional distance, which only takes into account the magnitude of the difference in institutional quality between home and host countries, thus disregarding the direction of that difference (e.g., Kostova, 1999; Kostova & Zaheer, 1999; Liou, Chao, & Yang, 2016). Recent theoretical advances therefore refined the concept of institutional distance by distinguishing between negative and positive institutional distance (Hernández & Nieto, 2015; Miletkov, Poulsen, & Wintoki, 2016; Trąpczyński & Banalieva, 2016). Negative institutional distance indicates that a host country's institutions are less developed than in the entrant's home country, while positive institutional distance implies that they are comparatively more developed.

In this study we aim to shed more light on the role of the direction of institutional distance in firms' foreign entry mode choices. To do so, we take an information economics perspective, given that the quality of a country's formal institutions determines the amount of information that buyers have at their disposal about the assets that they purchase. Well-functioning formal institutions reduce information asymmetries between exchange partners in various markets, such as the market for corporate control and the markets for intermediary inputs (Meyer et al., 2009; Yao, 1988). If institutions do not effectively reduce information asymmetries, buyers face the risks of overpayment and adverse selection and the respective market may break down (Akerlof, 1970; McCann, Reuer, & Lahiri, 2016; Stiglitz, 2002).

We argue that foreign entrants' perceptions of how well host country institutions reduce information asymmetries not only depend on the quality of a host country's institutions per se, but also on how that quality compares to the quality of home-country institutions, that is, on the direction of the institutional distance. The greater the negative institutional distance, we argue, the higher the information asymmetries that the entrant will likely perceive and, hence, the higher its inclination to select entry modes that reduce the risks associated with information asymmetries. More specifically, we hypothesize that negative institutional distance encourages firms to enter through greenfields rather than through acquisitions, since acquisitions often come with at least some undesired assets, which foreign entrants will consider harder to sell in host countries characterized by greater negative institutional distance. We further hypothesize that such distance will increase the chance that acquisition entries take the form of partial rather than full acquisitions because remaining prior owners signal information accuracy. Moreover, we hypothesize that among the subset of greenfield entries, negative institutional distance increases the chance that such entries take the form of greenfield joint ventures (JVs) rather than wholly owned greenfields. The reason is that a local JV partner may function as a mediator in market transactions, therewith lowering the information asymmetries that the foreign entrant perceives in the market for intermediary inputs.

For the reverse case of positive institutional distance, we argue that such distance reduces the degree of information asymmetries perceived by foreign entrants since they have access to more complete information than they are used to in their home environment and, hence, their perception of information asymmetry-related risks such as the risk of overpayment. Accordingly, we hypothesize that positive institutional distance increases the chance that foreign firms enter through acquisitions rather than greenfields and that they opt for full rather than partial ownership of acquired and greenfield subsidiaries.

We test our hypotheses on a sample of 1,070 entries into 50 foreign countries made by 796 emerging market multinationals (EMNEs) from 14 home countries. Controlling for host country institutional quality and other factors, we find that negative institutional distance increases the likelihood that foreign entrants set up greenfields rather than acquire an already established firm and that positive institutional distance decreases that likelihood. We further find that negative institutional distance increases the chance that firms choose greenfield JVs over wholly owned greenfields and, unexpectedly, that it causes firms to choose full acquisitions over partial ones. We find no significant effect of positive institutional distance on ownership mode decisions, neither for greenfields nor for acquisitions.

Our study makes two noteworthy contributions to the foreign entry mode literature. First, to the best of our knowledge, we are the first to explore how the direction of institutional distance influences establishment choices, and whether this direction has explanatory power above and beyond the host country's institutional quality. In addition, we extend Hernández and Nieto's (2015) work on how the direction of institutional distance influences ownership mode choices by distinguishing between and performing separate analyses for greenfield and acquired subsidiaries. Second, ours is the first entry mode study to adopt an information economics perspective to explain the effects of institutional differences across countries. By bridging insights from information economics and the institution-based view, we shed more light on the effects of formal institutions on foreign entry mode choices. More specifically, we show that a foreign firm's perception of local institutions' capacity to reduce information asymmetries is contingent on the firm's home institutional environment and that this perception affects its entry mode choices in several ways.

THEORETICAL BACKGROUND AND HYPOTHESES

Information Economics and Institutions

The information economics perspective goes back to the works of Akerlof (e.g., 1970), Spence (e.g., 1974), and Stiglitz (see for a review Stiglitz, 2002) who jointly received the Nobel Prize in economics in 2001 for demonstrating how information asymmetries among market players affect the efficiency of markets (Reuer & Ragozzino, 2012). This theoretical view deals with the hazards that exchange partners experience in market transactions and emphasizes that the market for an asset may break down if potential buyers cannot determine the asset's quality, since in that case they are exposed to the risk of adverse selection and overpayment (McCann et al., 2016). While insights from information economics were subsequently used widely in research on public policy, as well as in a number of functional areas in management (for a review, see Reuer & Ragozzino, 2012), its applications to domestic governance choices (e.g., Balakrishnan & Koza, 1993; McCann et al., 2016) and especially foreign entry mode decisions are scarce. Notable exceptions are the studies by Malhotra and Gaur (2013) and Dow, Cuypers, and Ertug (2016), who argue that geographic distance and within-country diversity, respectively, elevate information asymmetries in cross-border acquisitions and that acquirers mitigate the risks of such asymmetries via lower ownership stakes in target firms.

These exceptions, however, did not consider the role of institutions, even though their nature and quality may have a substantial impact on the extent of information asymmetry that foreign entrants face. This void is surprising since "institutions have an essential role in a market economy to support the effective functioning of the market mechanism, such that firms and individuals can engage in market transactions without incurring undue costs or risks" (Meyer et al., 2009, p. 63). Weaker institutions generally reduce the amount and reliability of information about exchange partners' characteristics and likely future behavior (Arrow, 1971; Casson, 1997; Meyer et al., 2009). The reason is that the lower a market's institutional development, the lower the efficiency and number of intermediaries such as market and financial analysts as well as accounting firms (Li & Atuahene-Gima, 2002; Marquis & Raynard, 2015; Peng & Heath, 1996). In addition, lower institutional development comes with less codified and less reliable information, which in turn requires higher degrees of interpretation (Child & Rodrigues, 2011). Thus, while information asymmetries between sellers and buyers always exist to some extent, they are larger when market supporting institutions are less developed. Such circumstances may contribute to the presence of 'lemons' (Akerlof, 1970) in markets for assets, including the market for corporate control and the market for intermediary inputs such as land, labor, and equipment, posing substantial risks to foreign entrants. In line with existing research on institutional development, we therefore expect foreign entrants to be more likely to choose risk-mitigating entry modes when the quality of the formal institutions in a host country is low (cf. Meyer et al., 2009; Slangen & van Tulder, 2009).

Yet, foreign firms' responses to local institutions may not only be determined by the quality of host country institutions, given that firms' experiences in their home contexts shape their routines and "DNA" (cf. Landau, Karna, Richter, & Uhlenbruck, 2016; Luiz, Stringfellow, & Jefthas, 2017; Madhok & Keyhani, 2012; Martin, 2014). We therefore propose that firms' perceptions of and responses to given levels of information asymmetry in the host country vary, based on the differences between home and host country institutions. Building on the body of work on institutional distance (e.g., Kostova, 1999; Kostova & Zaheer, 1999; Liou et al., 2016), recent theoretical advances further take into account the direction of institutional differences, introducing the concepts of negative and positive institutional distance (cf. Hernández & Nieto, 2015; Miletkov et al., 2016; Trąpczyński & Banalieva, 2016). We draw on these recent developments to explain entry-modes as a function of perceived information asymmetries arising from the magnitude and direction of institutional distance, above and beyond the information asymmetries that originate from the sheer quality of host country institutions.

We broadly follow Meyer et al. (2009) and consider institutions to be "stronger" (i.e., positive institutional distance) if they better support effective market mechanisms based on voluntary exchange than home-country institutions and "weaker" (i.e., negative institutional distance) if they support effective market mechanisms to a lower extent than in a firm's home country. Like several prior studies (Coeurderoy & Murray, 2008; Dikova & van Witteloostuijn, 2007; Hernández & Nieto, 2015; Meyer et al., 2009), we focus on formal institutions given their likely role in determining the efficiency of the markets for corporate control and intermediary inputs (Meyer et al., 2009; Peng & Heath, 1996) and the fact that they are frequently targeted toward firms and their activities (Dikova & van Witteloostuijn, 2007).[1]

How Negative Institutional Distance Influences Entry Mode Choices

We argue that the greater the extent to which home-country institutions are superior to the host country's, the higher are the perceived information asymmetries by the foreign firm entering a given host country as the availability and reliability of information about local assets is lower, less codified and more ambiguous compared to what the firm is typically exposed to. We therefore propose that negative institutional distance increases the degree of information asymmetry perceived by foreign firms. If firms perceive higher information asymmetries, they perceive a higher risk of overpayment and adverse selection. We further suggest that foreign firms mitigate this risk by choosing entry modes that entail foreign firms to greater information asymmetry disadvantages than others.

One way through which foreign firms mitigate such risks, we argue, is to set up a greenfield subsidiary instead of acquiring an existing firm. The reason is that acquisitions are more vulnerable to information asymmetries because targets' desired assets are frequently complemented by undesired assets (e.g., redundant functions such as distribution centers that exist in both target and acquirer or unrelated business units) which the buyer will eventually sell off (Capron, Mitchell, & Swaminathan, 2001; Hennart & Reddy, 1997). Given that information asymmetries negatively affect market efficiency, that is the matching of supply and demand (Reuer & Ragozzino, 2012), we expect entrants to anticipate potential buyers of these assets to equally suffer from information asymmetries, thus expecting the latter to limit their bids or to stay away from the deal altogether. We therefore suggest that, everything else equal, acquisitions have an information asymmetry disadvantage over greenfields as the latter come with undesired assets, which a foreign entrant will perceive harder to sell off at a reasonable price in host countries where it perceives information asymmetries to be greater (i.e., in host countries characterized by greater negative institutional distance). Hence:

Hypothesis 1a. The higher the negative institutional distance to a host country, the higher the likelihood that a foreign firm will enter that country through a greenfield investment rather than through an acquisition.

Both greenfield and acquired subsidiaries can be either fully or partly owned by a foreign entrant (Brouthers & Hennart, 2007). Extant studies have shown that ownership modes provide firms with an option to mitigate exogenous risks (e.g., Dow et al., 2016; Henisz, 2000; Hill, Hwang, & Kim, 1990). In line with the existing literature, we propose that foreign firms are more likely to opt for shared ownership in both acquired and greenfield subsidiaries when risks due to higher perceived information asymmetries are higher. Yet, the theoretical underpinnings we propose for each establishment mode differ.

Extant work on ownership preferences in acquisitions argues that full ownership in the acquired firm is favorable when it comes to the integration of the target into the acquiring firm as higher levels of control ease the achievement of target top management's and employees' full commitment and cooperation during the integration process (Cain, Denis, & Denis, 2011; Capron & Shen, 2007; Kostova, 1999; Malhotra & Gaur, 2013). Yet, we argue that with greater perceived information asymmetries (i.e. higher negative institutional distance), firms may be more likely to trade these control advantages for risk reduction. According to Chen and Hennart (2002, p. 1128), shared ownership can mitigate adverse selection and overpayment risks as it incentivizes the target to reveal accurate information, functioning as an alternative ex-ante selection mechanism to more efficient markets. The reason is that owners of 'lemons' can be expected to apply a "hit-and-run strategy" while only sellers that are confident about the value of their firms agree to maintain partial ownership in the acquired entity. Through this hostage effect, 'lemons' may be separated from targets that believe in their future prospects (Akerlof, 1970; Malhotra & Gaur, 2013). A large negative institutional distance implies a high perceived information asymmetry on the part of a foreign acquirer and, thus, a higher need for such ex-ante quality signals in order for the market for corporate control to function effectively (cf. Chari & Chang, 2009). Hence, the higher the negative institutional distance, the higher the chance that acquirers and targets will agree on shared ownership. That is:

Hypothesis 1b. The higher the negative institutional distance to a host country, the higher the likelihood that a foreign firm will enter that country through a partial acquisition rather than through a full acquisition.

Similar to their counterparts which make foreign acquisitions, firms which set up foreign greenfields can also reduce information asymmetry-related risks through their choice of ownership mode. We propose that foreign entrants will be inclined to partner with a local firm when they perceive such risks since the latter can function as a mediator in subsequent market transactions – that are required given that greenfields are built from scratch. The reason for this proposition is that information asymmetries not only exist in the market for corporate control, but also in the market for intermediary inputs, inputs that play a crucial role in the construction of a greenfield subsidiary (Hennart, 2009). For reasons discussed earlier, greenfield investors entering countries characterized by a greater negative institutional distance will likely perceive greater information asymmetries in the market for intermediary inputs. The risks associated with such asymmetries can be reduced by performing the purchase of local intermediary inputs such as land and equipment together with a local partner, since such a partner is likely to be more familiar with local institutions and better able to distinguish high-quality local inputs from lemons. The reason is that local partners are more likely to have social ties with sellers of intermediary inputs and location-bound knowledge of how to interpret claims by these sellers about the alleged quality of a local input (Child & Rodrigues, 2011; Peng, 2003; Shi, Sun, Yan, & Zhu, 2017). To incentivize the local partner to assess the quality of local inputs fairly, it needs to be given an equity stake in the greenfield venture (Hennart, 1988). We therefore hypothesize:

> **Hypothesis 1c.** The higher the negative institutional distance to a host country, the higher the likelihood that a foreign firm will enter that country through a greenfield JV rather than through a wholly owned greenfield.

How Positive Institutional Distance Influences Entry Mode Choices

We now turn our discussion to firms' foreign entries that are characterized by positive institutional distance. We propose that firms from institutionally less developed countries perceive host country institutions in a different light than firms which internationalize from more developed institutional environments. In line with our arguments for **Hypotheses 1a–1c**, we argue that the degree to which home-country institutions are inferior to those in the host country matters on top of the sheer quality of host country institutions. Specifically, we argue that whereas host country institutional quality captures actual information asymmetries, positive institutional distance captures foreign entrant's inclination to assume the absence of information asymmetries. The greater that distance, the more developed the host country's institutions are compared to those in a foreign entrant's home country and, hence, the more information about local assets the entrant will have at its disposal than it is used to in its home country. The greater the comparative information availability, the greater the entrant's inclination to conclude that it has all the necessary information about a local asset and, hence, that it faces no information asymmetry vis-à-vis the seller whatsoever. This argument is in line with literature on overconfidence that suggests that entrepreneurs tend to overestimate themselves compared to others when facing more trivial tasks (Cain, Moore, & Haran, 2015; Moore & Cain, 2007). Similarly, Trąpczyński and Banalieva (2016) found the performance of Polish MNEs to decrease when these firms enter countries characterized by positive institutional distance. Hence, the greater the positive institutional distance, the lower a foreign entrant's inclination to select an entry mode that mitigates information asymmetry-related risks.

We argued that acquisitions have an information asymmetry disadvantage over greenfields. The reason is that acquisitions usually involve at least some undesired assets (Capron et al., 2001; Hennart & Reddy, 1997). That is, the higher the perceived information asymmetries, the higher the perceived risk related to selling off these assets efficiently after the acquisition. Yet, we argue that foreign firms perceive information asymmetries to be lower when institutional distance is positive and even more so when it is high. This suggests that the information asymmetry disadvantages of acquisitions are less decisive in this case, since foreign firms perceive lower risks in relation to information asymmetries. We therefore suggest that the likelihood of entrants to acquire an existing firm increases with larger degrees of positive institutional distance as they anticipate selling off undesired assets to be less cumbersome. Hence:

> **Hypothesis 2a.** The higher the positive institutional distance to a host country, the higher the likelihood that a foreign firm will enter that country through an acquisition rather than through a greenfield investment.

We further argued that firms that make acquisitions under high levels of perceived information asymmetries will be more likely to trade control advantages that come with full ownership for additional ex-ante quality signals of prior owners maintaining a partial ownership stake post acquisition (cf. Chari & Chang, 2009; Chen & Hennart, 2002; Malhotra & Gaur, 2013). Yet, we argue that the marginal value of additional information decreases when information asymmetries are perceived to be lower or virtually absent. We therefore suggest that foreign firms will be less likely to give up full control over the target when positive institutional distance is higher.

> **Hypothesis 2b.** The higher the positive institutional distance to a host country, the higher the likelihood that a foreign firm will enter that country through a full acquisition rather than through a partial acquisition.

Last, we argued that firms that experience higher information asymmetries mitigate the risks of overpayment in the markets for intermediary goods by setting up a greenfield JV instead of a wholly owned greenfield. When foreign firms experience lower information asymmetries, they are likely to value the benefits of operating through a local intermediary to a lesser extent as they experience lower risks related to overpayment and adverse selection in the markets for intermediary assets (cf. Akerlof, 1970). Entrants will therefore feel more confident in operating on their own when they perceive lower information asymmetries. Hence:

Hypothesis 2c. The higher the positive institutional distance to a host country, the higher the likelihood that a foreign firm will enter that country through a wholly owned greenfield rather than through a greenfield JV.

METHODS

Data Collection and Sample

To perform a strong and reliable test of our hypotheses, we require a sample of entries characterized by varying degrees of institutional distance, both positively and negatively. We therefore compiled a sample of foreign entries by EMNEs as many of these firms have entered both institutionally more developed countries (characterized by positive institutional distance) and institutionally less developed ones (characterized by negative institutional distance) (cf. Banalieva & Santoro, 2009; Cuervo-Cazurra & Genc, 2008; Luo & Tung, 2007). Moreover, recent research has called for more multiple reference point studies in order to be able to distinguish institutional profile effects from institutional distance effects (Van Hoorn & Maseland, 2016). We therefore collected information on cross-border acquisitions and greenfield investments on a variety of home–host country pairings using the Emerging Market Global Player Reports provided by the Columbia Center on Sustainable Investment. These reports contain lists of the biggest (mainly full) acquisitions and wholly owned greenfield investments made by MNEs from 14 emerging economies. We complemented these lists with data on (i) other acquisitions made by EMNEs originating from the countries covered in the Emerging Market Global Player Reports, including partial acquisitions, and (ii) any greenfield JVs established by these firms. These additional data were obtained from SDC Platinum. We only included subsidiaries in which the EMNEs had an equity stake of at least 10%. We then collected firm-level data on the EMNEs from the Orbis database. Country-level data on home and host countries' institutional quality were obtained from the World Bank.

After discarding observations with missing data, our final sample consists of 1,070 entries made into 50 countries by 796 EMNEs from 14 emerging economies over the period 2005–2015. The main characteristics of the sample are summarized in Table 1.

Dependent Variables

The first dependent variable in this study is the *establishment mode choice* between greenfield investments and acquisitions. To measure this construct,

Table 1. Sample Statistics.

Sample characteristic	Description
Ownership mode	487 full investments (46%), 583 partial investments (54%)
Establishment mode	862 acquisitions (81%), 208 greenfields (19%)
Type of FDI	420 full acquisitions (39%), 442 partial acquisitions (41%), 67 wholly owned greenfield investments (6%), 141 greenfield JVs (13%)
Number of transactions per year	2005: 29, 2006: 47, 2007: 121, 2008: 123, 2009: 106, 2010: 108, 2011: 125, 2012: 122, 2013: 97, 2014: 100, 2015: 92
Number of transactions per home country	Argentina: 9, Brazil: 52, Chile: 33, China: 340, Hungary: 4, India: 141, Israel: 71, Mexico: 93, Poland: 26, Russia: 66, South Korea: 123, Taiwan: 46, Turkey: 15, United Arab Emirates: 51
Number of host countries	50

we use a binary dummy variable that is coded 1 for acquisitions and 0 for greenfields. The second dependent variable, the *ownership mode* firms apply is captured with a dummy variable that takes the value 1 for full ownership and 0 for partial ownership. Following previous studies, we set the cutoff point between partial and full ownership at 95% of equity ownership (e.g., Arslan & Dikova, 2015; Chen & Hennart, 2004). We consider this cutoff point to be well suited for this study since it indicates whether a local partner has significant influence in the business or not.

Explanatory Variables

The explanatory variables in this study are *negative institutional distance* and *positive institutional distance.* We measure these distances using the World Bank's rule of law indicator (Liu, Feils, & Scholnick, 2011), since the availability and reliability of information about local assets is likely to be strongly related to the strength of the rule of law in a country (Meyer et al., 2009; Peng & Heath, 1996; Reuer, Shenkar, & Ragozzino, 2004).

We calculate institutional distance by subtracting the home-country Rule of Law indicator from the host country score. We then created *positive institutional distance (negative institutional distance)* by adapting the approach of and set all values that coincide with a positive (negative) value to 0 (cf. Kim, Finkelstein, & Haleblian, 2015). Subsequently, we transform all institutional distance scores into absolute values. Accordingly, higher values in either direction represent greater distance.

Control Variables

To control for other factors that may affect firms' entry mode choices, we enter several variables at the firm, industry, and country levels.

At the firm level, we control for whether the firm is stock listed. We enter a dummy variable that takes the value of 1 if the firm is listed at a stock exchange and the value 0 if it is not. In addition, we control for firm size using the logarithm of the firm's assets 1 year prior to the focal entry as the literature suggests that both stock listed and larger firms tend to have more resources at their disposal, which potentially results in in cross-border investments that involve higher commitment (Agarwal & Ramaswami, 1992; Chang & Rosenzweig, 2001; Schwens, Eiche, & Kabst, 2011). Further, we control for the investment size relative to firm size using the logarithm of that fraction.

At the industry level we control for the focal firm's industry. Prior research suggests that firms' governance choices may not be independent from their industrial sector (Kogut & Singh, 1988; Slangen, 2013). Following Contractor, Lahiri, Elango, & Kundu (2014), all focal firms with primary SIC codes ranging from 20 to 39 are considered as active in the manufacturing sector (coded as 0) while we consider firms with a primary SIC code of 40 and higher to be part of the service sector (coded as 1). Second, we measure the relatedness of the industry into which a firm expands. This is also measured through a binary dummy variable, which takes the value of 1 if the partner or target firm has the same two-digit SIC code and the value of 0 if the two-digit SIC codes do not match (Ang, Benischke, & Doh, 2015).

At the country level we consider different dimensions of national distance that can influence entry mode choices (Berry, Guillén, & Zhou, 2010; Dow & Larimo, 2009; Hernández & Nieto, 2015). We control for cultural distance between country pairings using Hofstede's (2001) four original items applying Kogut and Singh's (1988) formula (Liu et al., 2011; Perkins, 2014). We further include geographic distance measured via the logarithm of the great circle distance in kilometers between the capitals of the home and the host country (Coeurderoy & Murray, 2008; Slangen & Beugelsdijk, 2010). To measure economic distance we apply the logarithm of the absolute distance between the home and the host countries' GDP per capita (Hernández & Nieto, 2015; Tsang & Yip, 2007). In addition to these distances, we control for the market size of the host economy using the logarithm of its GDP (Liou et al., 2016;

Slangen, 2013), as a higher market size may lead firms to prefer entry modes that involve a higher resource commitment (Agarwal & Ramaswami, 1992; Kwon & Konopa, 1993). In addition, even though most countries substantially reduced restrictions on foreign acquisitions, some are still in place and may potentially influence cross-border mode choices (Barkema & Vermeulen, 1998; Cho & Padmanabhan, 1995; Slangen & Hennart, 2008). We therefore control for foreign acquisition restrictions using the IMD's World Competitiveness Yearbook item "Foreign investors are free to acquire control in domestic companies." Following Slangen and Hennart (2008) we reverse coded the reported scores. Accordingly, higher values connote more restrictive host countries. We include this item to rule out that regulations which prevent acquisitions in general may drive firms' mode choices instead of their reactions on an environment that is less conducive to acquisition activity (Henisz, 2000). Last, we control for the quality of the host country's formal institutions using the Rule of Law score based on the same WGI index we have used to measure our explanatory variable. We do so to ensure that the variation in our dependent construct is driven by the magnitude and direction of the institutional distance between the home and the host country and not by the institutional quality in the host country on its own.

Statistical Model

Due to the dichotomous nature of our dependent variables we apply binary logistic regression models to analyze determinants of establishment and ownership modes. Binary logistic regression has frequently been used in the past and has proven to produce reliable statistical analyses regarding several aspects of entry mode choices (Arslan & Dikova, 2015; Dikova & van Witteloostuijn, 2007; Hennart & Larimo, 1998). The dependent variable takes the value 1 in case of an acquisition (full ownership) and the value 0 in case of a greenfield (shared ownership). Hence, a positive regression coefficient indicates that a certain explanatory variable increases the probability of an acquisition (full ownership). We use Stata/MP 14.1 to estimate our regression models.

RESULTS

Table 2 presents descriptive statistics and correlations for the data set we use in our analysis. The table shows no evidence for high correlations among the first-order variables since their correlation coefficients are below 0.70, the

Table 2. Descriptive Statistics and Correlations[a].

Variables	Mean	SD	(1)	(2)	(3)	(4)	(5)	(6)	(7)	(8)	(9)	(10)	(11)	(12)	(13)	(14)
(1) Establishment mode[b]	0.81	0.40	1.00													
(2) Ownership mode[c]	0.46	0.50	0.13	1.00												
(3) Positive institutional distance	1.23	0.87	0.42	0.06	1.00											
(4) Negative institutional distance	0.19	0.46	−0.44	−0.10	−0.57	1.00										
(5) Firm size	5.77	3.03	−0.44	−0.03	−0.14	0.16	1.00									
(6) Investment size	−1.32	2.61	0.50	0.21	0.20	−0.21	−0.68	1.00								
(7) Stock listed[d]	0.62	0.49	−0.19	0.12	−0.17	0.13	0.20	−0.18	1.00							
(8) Industry[e]	0.47	0.50	0.12	−0.07	0.04	−0.02	−0.13	0.08	−0.28	1.00						
(9) Industry relatedness[f]	0.55	0.50	−0.08	0.17	−0.11	0.09	0.18	−0.04	0.23	−0.26	1.00					
(10) Cultural distance	2.29	1.49	0.16	0.11	0.37	−0.21	−0.05	0.15	−0.09	−0.09	0.01	1.00				
(11) Economic distance	9.85	1.13	0.24	−0.03	0.60	−0.21	−0.17	0.11	−0.02	−0.05	−0.11	0.28	1.00			
(12) Geographic distance	8.48	0.78	0.11	0.20	0.22	−0.34	−0.02	0.14	−0.03	−0.15	0.07	0.29	0.14	1.00		
(13) Market size	14.26	1.46	0.00	0.19	0.06	−0.04	−0.00	−0.03	0.10	−0.12	0.07	0.40	0.26	0.20	1.00	
(14) Acquisition restrictions	2.74	1.33	−0.45	−0.14	−0.58	0.52	0.23	−0.28	0.10	−0.17	0.10	−0.13	−0.30	−0.15	0.12	1.00
(15) Host country institutional quality	1.10	0.89	0.51	0.11	0.79	−0.70	−0.26	0.28	−0.13	0.07	−0.13	0.40	0.60	0.25	0.18	−0.68

Notes: [a]N = 1,070; [b]Acquisition = 1; [c]Full ownership = 1; [d]Listed firm = 1; [e]Non-manufacturing = 1; [f]Same industry = 1.

commonly applied threshold, with exception of the host country's rule of law score that correlates highly with our explanatory variables. This correlation is comprehensible since our aim is to tease out the additional effects that positive and negative institutional distances have above and beyond a host country's institutional development. To further test for multicollinearity, we ran collinearity diagnostics. The variance inflation factors we obtained were all below 10, the generally accepted multicollinearity level (Cohen, Cohen, West, & Aiken, 2003; Neter, Kutner, Nachtsheim, & Wasserman, 1996), with the maximum value being 6.10 for the host country's institutional quality. Our positive and negative institutional distance variables had values of 3.29 and 2.62, respectively. Based on these results, we conclude that our analysis is not biased by effects of multicollinearity.

The results of our regression models are presented in Table 3. Models 1, 3, and 5 contain only control variables and their effects on the establishment mode choice, the ownership mode choice in acquisitions and the ownership mode choice in greenfields, respectively. Our explanatory variables are then added in Models 2, 4, and 6. The addition of these variables significantly improves the explanatory power of Models 1 and 5, yet not of Model 3. We will limit our discussion of control variables to the ones that show significant effects on the respective dependent construct. In correspondence with the order of our hypotheses, we first discuss the results for the establishment mode choice. We find relative investment size to be positively associated with the ocurrence of acquisitions compared to greenfields. This is in line with prior research as acquisitions are typically more expensive than greenfield investments due to the purchase price premiums and undesired assets they typically contain (Kusewitt, 1985). This result may also partly be explained by our finding that firm size is negatively associated with the choice of an acquisition. A fairly surprising result because one could assume that larger firms have more financial resources at their disposal, which generally tends to increase the likelihood that a firm can pay price premiums that typically come with acquisitions. Model 1 further suggests that our sampled firms are more likely to acquire within their main industry than across industries. This is in line with our assumptions that firms' decisions to acquire may be dependent on the information asymmetries between the acquirer and a potential target (cf. Malhotra & Gaur, 2013). Furthermore, in line with our expectations we find acquisition restrictions to be negatively associated with the choice of an acquisition. Last, the host country's institutional quality is positively associated with the choice of an acquisition over a greenfield investment. This finding supports our baseline assumption that higher institutional quality reduces information asymmetries facilitating acquisitions. In Model 2 the explanatory variables negative and positive institutional distance are added to

Table 3. Logit Models.

Variables	Establishment Mode[a]		Ownership Mode in Acquisitions[b]		Ownership Mode in Greenfields[b]	
	Model 1	Model 2	Model 3	Model 4	Model 5	Model 6
Firm level						
Firm size	−0.277***	−0.302***	0.050	0.053	1.059***	1.068***
	(0.060)	(0.062)	(0.036)	(0.037)	(0.231)	(0.235)
Investment size	0.342***	0.351***	0.148**	0.139**	1.038***	1.030***
	(0.060)	(0.061)	(0.050)	(0.051)	(0.214)	(0.221)
Stock listed[c]	−0.255	−0.126	0.619***	0.609***	0.805	1.649+
	(0.291)	(0.296)	(0.166)	(0.167)	(0.778)	(0.904)
Industry level						
Industry[d]	0.233	0.354	−0.296+	−0.318+	1.849**	2.542**
	(0.248)	(0.255)	(0.169)	(0.170)	(0.660)	(0.803)
Same industry[e]	0.482+	0.486+	0.295+	0.292+	1.782**	2.365**
	(0.257)	(0.261)	(0.166)	(0.166)	(0.627)	(0.770)
Country level						
Cultural distance	−0.074	−0.107	−0.037	−0.039	−0.083	0.050
	(0.111)	(0.113)	(0.062)	(0.064)	(0.265)	(0.297)
Economic distance	−0.162	−0.094	−0.256**	−0.276**	−0.673*	−0.317
	(0.131)	(0.144)	(0.094)	(0.106)	(0.287)	(0.327)
Geographic distance	−0.172	−0.251	0.447***	0.491***	−0.629+	−0.994*
	(0.162)	(0.170)	(0.113)	(0.116)	(0.371)	(0.444)
Market size	−0.016	0.007	0.456***	0.449***	−0.301	−0.270
	(0.094)	(0.094)	(0.064)	(0.065)	(0.235)	(0.260)
Acquisition restrictions	−0.351**	−0.303*	−0.276**	−0.288**	−0.224	−0.565
	(0.121)	(0.124)	(0.088)	(0.090)	(0.307)	(0.366)
Host country institutional quality	1.248***	0.541+	0.154	0.372+	0.805	−0.809
	(0.214)	(0.289)	(0.172)	(0.216)	(0.563)	(1.016)
Negative institutional distance (H1a, b, c)		**−0.580+**		**0.539+**		**−2.432****
		(0.305)		**(0.317)**		**(0.866)**
Positive institutional distance (H2a, b, c)		**0.676****		**−0.073**		**−0.244**
		(0.241)		**(0.159)**		**(0.736)**
Constant	8.122***	7.880***	−7.809***	−8.068***	−10.127	−10.999
	(2.291)	(2.264)	(1.360)	(1.384)	(1,469.211)	(1,876.037)
Observations	1,070	1,070	862	862	208	208

Table 3. (*Continued*)

Variables	Establishment Mode[a]		Ownership Mode in Acquisitions[b]		Ownership Mode in Greenfields[b]	
	Model 1	Model 2	Model 3	Model 4	Model 5	Model 6
Model chi-squared symbol χ^2	512.8	525.9	192.6	195.7	154.7	165.1
Log likelihood	−270.6	−264.1	−500.9	−499.3	−53.38	−48.18
Likelihood ratio test of focal model vs. prior model		13.08**		3.19		10.40**
Pseudo R^2	0.486	0.499	0.161	0.164	0.592	0.631

Notes: Standard errors in parentheses. Year dummies are included in the regression models but not shown.
[a] Acquisition = 1; [b] full ownership = 1; [c] listed firm = 1; [d] non-manufacturing = 1; [e] same industry = 1.
***$p < 0.001$, **$p < 0.01$, *$p < 0.05$, and $^{+}p < 0.10$ (two-tailed).

the base model. The results show a marginally significant negative association between negative institutional distance and the choice of an acquisition over a greenfield ($p < 0.1$) and a positive association in the case of positive institutional distance ($p < 0.01$). Hypotheses 1a and 2a are thus supported.

Next, we proceed with the discussion of the results of the ownership mode choice in acquisitions (Models 3 and 4). As could be expected, relative investment size, whether a firm is stock listed, industry relatedness, whether a firm is active in the manufacturing industry, and the size of the host market are all positively associated with the choice of full ownership and thus in line with prior research (e.g., Ang et al., 2015; Malhotra & Gaur, 2013). Interestingly, our results further suggest that EMNEs prefer full over partial acquisitions when geographic distance increases, whereas earlier studies relying on a global sample have found a negative effect (e.g., Malhotra & Gaur, 2013). We further find economic distance and acquisition restrictions to be negatively related with full ownership. The host country's institutional quality is positive but insignificant in Model 3 and becomes moderately significant when our explanatory variables are added in Model 4. Based on our analysis we do not find positive institutional distance to significantly affect ownership mode preferences in acquisitions. In addition, not in line with our hypothesis, we find a moderately significant positive association between negative institutional distance and the choice of a full acquisition. Therefore, we do not find support for Hypotheses 1b and 2b.

Last, we discuss our results regarding ownership mode preferences in greenfield investments (Models 5 and 6). As expected and in line with prior findings, firm size and relative investment size are positively associated with firms' preference for wholly owned greenfields over JVs. Furthermore, service firms and firms investing in their core industry are more likely to opt for full ownership. Hence, in line with existing research on acquisitions, firms which set up greenfields seem to experience higher information asymmetries when entering new industries than when operating in their main industry, thus limiting their resource commitment (cf. Montgomery & Hariharan, 1991). In line with this, we also find economic and geographic distance to be negatively associated with full ownership. Unexpectedly, the host country's institutional quality is not significantly associated with any ownership mode preferences in greenfields. The variables positive and negative institutional distances are subsequently added to the model. We find negative institutional distance to be associated with the preference of a greenfield JV ($p < 0.01$). Yet, we find no support for a preference of wholly owned greenfields over greenfield JVs when positive institutional distance is higher. Thus, Hypothesis 1c is supported while Hypothesis 2c is not supported by our analysis.

DISCUSSION AND CONCLUSION

In this chapter, we aimed to provide answers to the questions how the direction and magnitude of formal institutional distance affect the decisions on (i) whether firms are more likely to acquire or set up a greenfield, and whether they opt for a full or a partial ownership stake in (ii) acquired and (iii) greenfield subsidiaries. To answer these questions, we took an information economics perspective and hypothesized that negative institutional distance increases the likelihood that firms will enter via modes that mitigate information asymmetry-related risks, that is, set up greenfields and hold partial ownership in both acquired and greenfield subsidiaries. On the contrary, we hypothesized that positive institutional distance decreases that likelihood, that is, firms will rather enter via acquisitions and hold full ownership in acquired and greenfield subsidiaries. We tested these hypotheses on a sample of 1,070 MNEs from 14 emerging economies and found support for some, but not all of our hypotheses while controlling for host country institutional quality and other factors.

More specifically, the finding that negative institutional distance first increases the likelihood that firms choose a greenfield over an acquisition and subsequently partial ownership in these greenfields indicates that it is not only the sheer quality of host country institutions that impacts entry mode choices, but also the extent to which host country institutions are inferior to the ones in the firm's home country. That is, this difference will shape the information asymmetry-related risks that managers perceive in both the market for corporate control and the markets for intermediary inputs (Child & Rodrigues, 2011; Hennart, 2009). Firms therefore reduce these risks by avoiding the first and engage in transactions in the latter via a local mediator (i.e., a JV partner). These results indicate that our information economics-based arguments may also improve our understanding of ownership choices in greenfields – a setting that has been regarded to a lesser extent through an information economics lens. We further hypothesized that negative institutional distance increases the likelihood that firms which do choose an acquisition opt for partial stakes rather than full ownership. That is, the fact that a former owner agrees to retain partial ownership can be interpreted as a quality signal and therewith make up for higher institution-based information asymmetries (Chen & Hennart, 2002; Malhotra & Gaur, 2013). Unexpectedly, we find moderate support for an opposite effect. Yet, it needs to be acknowledged that firms do not always do what they should do (Hennart & Slangen, 2015), either because they do not have sufficient knowledge and cognitive capacity or because certain factors prevent the firm from doing so. Extant research has found that firms in lesser developed markets frequently are reluctant to share control with other parties (Bruton, Ahlstrom, & Wan, 2003; Peng, Wang, & Jiang, 2008). Our unexpected result may thus relate to the limited options that a firm has – either acquiring an entire firm or walking away from the deal – even though they would generally tend to prefer acquiring a partial ownership stake in a target that operates in an environment characterized by inferior institutions.

Our finding that positive institutional distance increases the likelihood with which a firm will acquire instead of setting up a greenfield supports our argument which states that positive institutional distance inclines firms to assume information asymmetries to be largely absent, thus being overconfident when making acquisition decisions. Nonetheless, we do not find statistical significant effects for ownership mode preferences in any of the two establishment modes. Prior research found that some EMNEs internationalize to acquire strategic assets and to catch up quickly with established players (Luo & Tung, 2007). These EMNEs may prefer a local partner that gives them immediate access to its resources (Meyer et al., 2009). These motives may thus counterbalance the abovementioned theoretical explanation, thereby showing an effect that is overall non-significant.

One of the limitations of our study, therefore, is that we did not measure whether the firms in our sample have a strategic-asset-seeking motive.

This opens up potential future research opportunities. Future studies could more rigorously investigate under which conditions firms follow such motives and how they affect governance choices. A further limitation is that, despite controlling for cultural distance that is typically used to proxy informal institutional distance (cf. Shao, Kwok, & Zhang, 2013), we focused our reasoning exclusively on formal institutions and thereby neglected the role informal institutions have in reducing information asymmetries (Dikova & van Witteloostuijn, 2007; Hernández & Nieto, 2015). Yet, informal norms and constraints complement formal institutions in a nation's institutional framework (Dikova, Sahib, & van Witteloostuijn, 2010; North, 1990). Future research may thus complement our work by investigating the effects that this institutional dimension could have on the flows of information and asymmetries between firms and whether it changes our identified determinants of firms' strategic responses. Last, another limitation of this chapter is that we (and the vast majority of other scholars) consider all firms from a given context to be equipped with the same capabilities. We therefore take the stand that more studies are required which will investigate firm-specific capabilities in dealing with institutions and thus we call for more research on institutional competitive advantages (cf. Landau et al., 2016).

NOTE

1. In this chapter we follow authors such as Peng, Sun, Pinkham, & Chen (2009) and bridge the broadly complementary sociological (e.g., Scott, 1995) and economic (e.g., North, 1990) traditions of institutional theory by pooling the best available insights on institutional mechanisms. In this vein, we loosely map North's (1990) dimension of formal institutions with Scott's (1995) regulatory pillar and use the determinations of both traditions interchangeably.

REFERENCES

Agarwal, S., & Ramaswami, S. N. (1992). Choice of foreign market entry mode: Impact of ownership, location and internationalization factors. *Journal of International Business Studies*, *23*(1), 1–27.

Akerlof, G. A. (1970). The market for 'Lemons': Quality uncertainty and the market mechanism. *The Quarterly Journal of Economics*, *84*(3), 488.

Ang, S. H., Benischke, M. H., & Doh, J. P. (2015). The interactions of institutions on foreign market entry mode. *Strategic Management Journal*, *36*(10), 1536–1553.

Arrow, K. (1971). *Essays in the theory of risk-bearing*. Chicago, IL: Markham Publishing Co.

Arslan, A., & Dikova, D. (2015). Influences of institutional distance and MNEs' host country experience on the ownership strategy in cross-border M&As in emerging economies. *Journal of Transnational Management*, *20*(4), 231–256.

Balakrishnan, S., & Koza, M. P. (1993). Information asymmetry, adverse selection and joint-ventures. *Journal of Economic Behavior & Organization*, *20*(1), 99–117.

Banalieva, E. R., & Santoro, M. D. (2009). Local, regional, or global? Geographic orientation and relative financial performance of emerging market multinational enterprises. *European Management Journal*, *27*(5), 344–355.

Barkema, H. G., & Vermeulen, F. (1998). International expansion through start up or acquisition: A learning perspective. *The Academy of Management Journal*, *41*(1), 7–26.

Berry, H., Guillén, M. F., & Zhou, N. (2010). An institutional approach to cross-national distance. *Journal of International Business Studies*, *41*(9), 1460–1480.

Brouthers, K. D., & Hennart, J.-F. (2007). Boundaries of the firm: Insights from international entry mode research. *Journal of Management*, *33*(3), 395–425.

Bruton, G. D., Ahlstrom, D., & Wan, J. C. C. (2003). Turnaround in East Asian firms: Evidence from ethnic overseas Chinese communities. *Strategic Management Journal*, *24*(6), 519–540.

Cain, M. D., Denis, D. J., & Denis, D. K. (2011). Earnouts: A study of financial contracting in acquisition agreements. *Journal of Accounting and Economics*, *51*(1), 151–170.

Cain, D. M., Moore, D. A., & Haran, U. (2015). Making sense of overconfidence in market entry. *Strategic Management Journal*, *36*(1), 1–18.

Capron, L., Mitchell, W., & Swaminathan, A. (2001). Asset divestiture following horizontal acquisitions: A dynamic view. *Strategic Management Journal*, *22*(9), 817–844.

Capron, L., & Shen, J.-C. (2007). Acquisitions of private vs. public firms: Private information, target selection, and acquirer returns. *Strategic Management Journal*, *28*(9), 891–911.

Casson, M. C. (1997). *Information and organization: A new perspective on the theory of the firm*. Oxford: Clarendon.

Chang, S. J., & Rosenzweig, P. M. (2001). The choice of entry mode in sequential foreign direct investment. *Strategic Management Journal*, *22*(8), 747–776.

Chari, M. D., & Chang, K. (2009). Determinants of the share of equity sought in cross-border acquisitions. *Journal of International Business Studies*, *40*(8), 1277–1297.

Chen, S.-F., & Hennart, J.-F. (2002). Japanese investors' choice of joint ventures vs. wholly-owned subsidiaries in the US: The role of market barriers and firm capabilities. *Journal of International Business Studies*, *33*(1), 1–18.

Chen, S.-F. S., & Hennart, J.-F. (2004). A hostage theory of joint ventures: Why do Japanese investors choose partial over full acquisitions to enter the United States? *Journal of Business Research*, *57*(10), 1126–1134.

Child, J., & Rodrigues, S. B. (2011). How organizations engage with external complexity: A political action perspective. *Organization Studies*, *32*(6), 803–824.

Cho, K. R., & Padmanabhan, P. (1995). Acquisition versus new venture: The choice of foreign establishment mode by Japanese firms. *Journal of International Management*, *1*(3), 255–285.

Coeurderoy, R., & Murray, G. (2008). Regulatory environments and the location decision: Evidence from the early foreign market entries of new-technology-based firms. *Journal of International Business Studies*, *39*(4), 670–687.

Cohen, J., Cohen, P., West, S. G., & Aiken, L. (2003). *Applied multiple regression/correlation analysis for the behavioral sciences* (3rd ed.). Hillsdale, NJ: Lawrence Erlbaum Associates.

Contractor, F. J., Lahiri, S., Elango, B., & Kundu, S. K. (2014). Institutional, cultural and industry related determinants of ownership choices in emerging market FDI acquisitions. *International Business Review, 23*(5), 931–941.

Cuervo-Cazurra, A., & Genc, M. (2008). Transforming disadvantages into advantages: Developing-country MNEs in the least developed countries. *Journal of International Business Studies, 39*(6), 957–979.

Dikova, D., Sahib, P. R., & van Witteloostuijn, A. (2010). Cross-border acquisition abandonment and completion: The effect of institutional differences and organizational learning in the international business service industry, 1981–2001. *Journal of International Business Studies, 41*(2), 223–245.

Dikova, D., & van Witteloostuijn, A. (2007). Foreign direct investment mode choice: Entry and establishment modes in transition economies. *Journal of International Business Studies, 38*(6), 1013–1033.

Dow, D., Cuypers, I. R. P., & Ertug, G. (2016). The effects of within-country linguistic and religious diversity on foreign acquisitions. *Journal of International Business Studies, 47*(3), 319–346.

Dow, D., & Larimo, J. (2009). Challenging the conceptualization and measurement of distance and international experience in entry mode choice research. *Journal of International Marketing, 17*(2), 74–98.

Henisz, W. (2000). The institutional environment for multinational investment. *Journal of Law, Economics, and Organization, 16*(2), 334–364.

Hennart, J.-F. (1988). A transaction costs theory of equity joint ventures. *Strategic Management Journal, 9*(4), 361–374.

Hennart, J.-F. (2009). Down with MNE-centric theories! Market entry and expansion as the bundling of MNE and local assets. *Journal of International Business Studies, 40*(9), 1591–1591.

Hennart, J.-F., & Larimo, J. (1998). The impact of culture on the strategy of multinational enterprises: Does national origin affect ownership decisions? *Journal of International Business Studies, 29*(3), 515–538.

Hennart, J. F., & Reddy, S. (1997). The choice between mergers/acquisitions and joint ventures: The case of Japanese investors in the United States. *Strategic Management Journal, 18*(1), 1–12.

Hennart, J.-F., & Slangen, A. H. L. (2015). Yes, we really do need more entry mode studies! A commentary on shaver. *Journal of International Business Studies, 46*(1), 114–122.

Hernández, V., & Nieto, M. J. (2015). The effect of the magnitude and direction of institutional distance on the choice of international entry modes. *Journal of World Business, 50*(1), 122–132.

Hill, C. W. L., Hwang, P., & Kim, W. C. (1990). An eclectic theory of the choice of international entry mode. *Strategic Management Journal, 11*(2), 117–128.

Hofstede, G. H. (2001). *Culture's consequences: Comparing values, behaviors, institutions, and organizations across nations*. Thousand Oaks, CA: Sage Publications.

Kim, J. Y., Finkelstein, S., & Haleblian, J. (2015). All aspirations are not created equal: The differential effects of historical and social aspirations on acquisition behavior. *Academy of Management Journal, 58*(5), 1361–1388.

Kogut, B., & Singh, H. (1988). The effectof national culture on the choice of entry mode. *Journal of International Business Studies*, *19*(3), 411–432.

Kostova, T. (1999). Transnational transfer of strategic organizational practices: A contextual perspective. *Academy of Management Review*, *24*(2), 308–324.

Kostova, T., & Zaheer, S. (1999). Organizational legitimacy under conditions of complexity: The case of the multinational enterprise. *Academy of Management Review*, *24*(1), 64–81.

Kusewitt, J. B. (1985). An exploratory study of strategic acquisition factors relating to performance. *Strategic Management Journal*, *6*(2), 151–169.

Kwon, Y.-C., & Konopa, L. J. (1993). Impact of host country market characteristics on the choice of foreign market entry mode. *International Marketing Review*, *10*(2), 60–75.

Landau, C., Karna, A., Richter, A., & Uhlenbruck, K. (2016). Institutional leverage capability: Creating and using institutional advantages for internationalization. *Global Strategy Journal*, *6*(1), 50–68.

Li, H., & Atuahene-Gima, K. (2002). The adoption of agency business activity, product innovation, and performance in Chinese technology ventures. *Strategic Management Journal*, *23*(6), 469–490.

Liou, R. S., Chao, M. C. H., & Yang, M. (2016). Emerging economies and institutional quality: Assessing the differential effects of institutional distances on ownership strategy. *Journal of World Business*, *51*(4), 600–611.

Liu, R., Feils, D. J., & Scholnick, B. (2011). Why are different services outsourced to different countries? *Journal of International Business Studies*, 42, 558–571.

Luiz, J., Stringfellow, D., & Jefthas, A. (2017). Institutional complementarity and substitution as an internationalization strategy: The emergence of an African multinational giant. *Global Strategy Journal*, *7*(1), 83–103.

Luo, Y., & Tung, R. L. (2007). International expansion of emerging market enterprises: A springboard perspective. *Journal of International Business Studies*, *38*(4), 481–498.

Madhok, A., & Keyhani, M. (2012). Acquisitions as entrepreneurship: Asymmetries, opportunities, and the internationalization of multinationals from emerging economies. *Global Strategy Journal*, *2*(1), 26–40.

Malhotra, S., & Gaur, A. S. (2013). Spatial geography and control in foreign acquisitions. *Journal of International Business Studies*, *45*(2), 191–210.

Marquis, C., & Raynard, M. (2015). Institutional strategies in emerging markets. *The Academy of Management Annals*, 9.

Martin, X. (2014). Institutional advantage. *Global Strategy Journal*, *4*(1), 55–69.

McCann, B. T., Reuer, J. J., & Lahiri, N. (2016). Agglomeration and the choice between acquisitions and alliances: An information economics perspective. *Strategic Management Journal*, *37*(6), 1085–1106.

Meyer, K. E., Estrin, S., Bhaumik, S. K., & Peng, M. W. (2009). Institutions, resources, and entry strategies in emerging economies. *Strategic Management Journal*, *30*(1), 61–80.

Miletkov, M., Poulsen, A., & Wintoki, M. B. (2016). Foreign independent directors and the quality of legal institutions. *Journal of International Business Studies*.

Montgomery, C. A., & Hariharan, S. (1991). Diversified expansion by large established firms. *Journal of Economic Behavior & Organization*, *15*(1), 71–89.

Moore, D. A., & Cain, D. M. (2007). Overconfidence and underconfidence: When and why people underestimate (and overestimate) the competition. *Organizational Behavior and Human Decision Processes*, *103*(2), 197–213.

Neter, J., Kutner, M. H., Nachtsheim, C. J., & Wasserman, W. (1996). *Applied linear statistical models* (Vol. 4). McGraw-Hill/Irwin.

North, D. 1990. *Institutions, institutional change and economic performance*. Cambridge: Cambridge University Press.

Peng, M. W. (2003). Institutional transitions and strategic choices. *Academy of Management Review*, *28*(2), 275–296.

Peng, M. W., & Heath, P. S. (1996). The growth of the firm in planned economies in transition: Institutions, organizations, and strategic choice. *Academy of Management Review*, *21*(2), 492–528.

Peng, M. W., Sun, S. L., Pinkham, B., & Chen, H. (2009). The institution-based view as a third leg for a strategy tripod. *Academy of Management Perspectives*, *23*(3), 63–81.

Peng, M. W., Wang, D. Y. L., & Jiang, Y. (2008). An institution-based view of international business strategy: A focus on emerging economies. *Journal of International Business Studies*, *39*(5), 920–936.

Perkins, S. E. (2014). When does prior experience pay? Institutional experience and the multinational corporation. *Administrative Science Quarterly*, *59*(1), 145–181.

Reuer, J. J., & Ragozzino, R. (2012). The choice between joint ventures and acquisitions: Insights from signaling theory. *Organization Science*, *23*(4), 1175–1190.

Reuer, J. J., Shenkar, O., & Ragozzino, R. (2004). Mitigating risk in international mergers and acquisitions: The role of contingent payouts. *Journal of International Business Studies*, *35*(1), 19–32.

Schwens, C., Eiche, J., & Kabst, R. (2011). The moderating impact of informal institutional distance and formal institutional risk on SME entry mode choice. *Journal of Management Studies*, *48*(2), 330–351.

Scott, W. R. (1995). *Institutions and organizations*. Thousand Oaks, CA: Sage.

Shao, L., Kwok, C. C. Y., & Zhang, R. (2013). National culture and corporate investment. *Journal of International Business Studies*, *44*(7), 745–763.

Shi, W., Sun, S. L., Yan, D., & Zhu, Z. (2017). Institutional fragility and outward foreign direct investment from China. *Journal of International Business Studies*.

Slangen, A. H. L. (2013). Greenfield or acquisition entry? The roles of policy uncertainty and MNE legitimacy in host countries. *Global Strategy Journal*, *3*(3), 262–280.

Slangen, A. H. L., & Beugelsdijk, S. (2010). The impact of institutional hazards on foreign multinational activity: A contingency perspective. *Journal of International Business Studies*, *41*(6), 980–995.

Slangen, A. H. L., & Hennart, J. F. (2008). Do multinationals really prefer to enter culturally distant countries through greenfields rather than through acquisitions? The role of parent experience and subsidiary autonomy. *Journal of International Business Studies*, *39*(3), 472–490.

Slangen, A. H. L., & van Tulder, R. J. M. (2009). Cultural distance, political risk, or governance quality? Towards a more accurate conceptualization and measurement of external uncertainty in foreign entry mode research. *International Business Review*, *18*(3), 276–291.

Spence, A. M. (1974). Market signaling : Information transfer in hiring and related screening processes. Cambridge, MA: Harvard University Press.

Stiglitz, J. E. (2002). Information and the change in the paradigm in economics information and the change in the paradigm in economicist. *The American Economic Review*, *92*(3), 460–501.

Trąpczyński, P., & Banalieva, E. R. (2016). Institutional difference, organizational experience, and foreign affiliate performance: Evidence from Polish firms. *Journal of World Business*, *51*, 826–842.

Tsang, E. W. K., & Yip, P. S. L. (2007). Economic distance and the survival of foreign direct investments. *Academy of Management Journal*, *50*(5), 1156–1168.

Van Hoorn, A., & Maseland, R. (2016). How institutions matter for international business: Institutional distance effects vs institutional profile effects. *Journal of International Business Studies*, *47*(3), 374–381.

Yao, D. A. (1988). Beyond the reach of the invisible hand: Impediments to economic activity, market failures, and profitability. *Strategic Management Journal*, *9*(1S), 59–70.

CHAPTER 13

EQUITY COMMITMENT IN CROSS-BORDER ACQUISITIONS: THE INFLUENCE OF DISTANCE AND ORGANIZATIONAL RESOURCES

Desislava Dikova, Ahmad Arslan and Jorma Larimo

ABSTRACT

We investigate the effect of distance – political, economic, cultural and spatial, on developed-economy multinational enterprises' (MNEs') ownership decisions in cross-border (CB) acquisitions. We start with the premise that distance discourages full and majority ownership in CB acquisitions, and further investigate the moderating role of distance-reducing factors. We examine how the relationship between distance and acquisition ownership decision is moderated by firm-specific characteristics, such as firm size, general international experience, and specific host country experience. Our data sample consists of 1,041 CB acquisitions under taken by Finnish MNEs in 58 countries during the time period 1990–2010. We find substantial support for all our hypotheses and conclude that the negative

Distance in International Business: Concept, Cost and Value
Progress in International Business Research, Volume 12, 297–337

ISSN: 1745-8862/doi:10.1108/S1745-886220170000012021

effects of distance on CB acquisition equity stake are positively moderated by the three firm-specific resources but their individual importance is conditional on the host country type (developed or emerging).

Keywords: Cross-border acquisitions; equity commitment; distance; organizational resources

1. INTRODUCTION

The concept of distance has assumed a critical role in international business (IB) research over last few decades (Stahl, Tung, Kostova, & Zellmer-Bruhn, 2016; Williams & Gregoire, 2015). Perhaps the centrality of this topic is best explained by the notion that "international management *is* management of distance" (Zaheer, Schomaker, & Nachum, 2012, p. 19; emphasis in original). Past studies have addressed distance from a range of perspectives including administrative, cultural, economic, geographic, institutional, linguistic, and psychic distances but also reported inconsistent and often controversial results (e.g., Arslan, Tarba, & Larimo, 2015; Choi, Lee, & Shoham, 2016; Demirbag, Tatoglu, & Glaister, 2009; Dow & Larimo, 2011; Drogendijk & Martin, 2015; Ghemawat, 2007; Kuo & Fang., 2009; Stahl et al., 2016; Tang, 2012). A recent paper by Williams and Gregoire (2015) points to some critical aspects of research on distance. For example, there is the "distance paradox" where apparent closeness between the home and host country may lead managers to overlook critical differences. There is also the call for more nuanced understanding of distance (Stahl et al., 2016) that goes beyond the typical problem-focused approach. This positivist approach draws attention to the potential benefits of foreignness and cultural diversity in creating value, rather than problems, for global organizations. Despite all advances in the field, there is furthermore the opinion that the lack of or the presence of distance on a particular dimension does not necessarily mean that the two countries in question are close or not (Zaheer et al., 2012, p. 20). Instead it means that distance depends on (a) the type of international activity examined (e.g., decisions related to investment location, timing, or mode) and (b) on specific effects that increase distance or reduce it by allowing firms to bridge that distance (Williams & Gregoire, 2015). In this chapter we further advance research on distance by focusing on a popular international activity and specific distance-reducing factors.

We study cross-border (CB) acquisitions which have become a popular entry-mode strategy for both developed- and emerging-market firms

(Contractor, Lahiri, Elango, & Kundu, 2014). There is an increase in value of CB acquisition deals reaching US $721 billion in 2015, representing ca. 41% of global foreign direct investment (FDI) flows (UNCTAD, 2016, p. 2). The popularity of CB acquisitions can be explained with the associated strategic possibilities for investing multinational enterprises (MNEs) such as speedy entry into new markets and industries, consolidation of power, taking advantage of new opportunity, or reducing competitive threats in future (Arslan & Dikova, 2015; Collins, Holcomb, Certo, Hitt, & Lester, 2009). Moreover, CB acquisitions have been found to offer MNEs a possibility to access key assets like technologies, reputable brands, and local talents (experienced human resources; Chen & Zeng, 2004; Newmeyer, Swaminathan, & Hulland, 2016). Valuation, wealth creation, post-acquisition integration, and performance have received by far the greatest research interest while equity commitment in CB acquisitions remains relatively under-researched (e.g., Chang & Tsai, 2013; Chari & Chang, 2009; Dikova & Sahib, 2013; Du & Boateng, 2015; Malhotra & Gaur, 2014; Stahl et al., 2012).

We consider foreign investor's equity commitment an important aspect of CB acquisitions prospective research for numerous reasons, for example, it is a likely condition for the efficient access to and transfer of valuable assets from the target firm, it determines the MNE's influence over target firm's strategic direction, often determines the success of integration, and has serious financial implications for the foreign investor. Despite MNEs' general preference for full ownership and control of foreign acquisitions, partial CB acquisitions have been found useful in mitigating asymmetric information-exchange problems, controlling foreign expansion risk and facilitating the fast penetration into foreign markets (e.g. Zhu & Dutta, 2011). Distance seems to play a critical role in equity-related decisions in CB acquisition deals. On the one hand it can exacerbate the asymmetric exchange problems between acquirer and target firm, cause uncertainty, increase the level of investment risk, and create obstacles for the access to and the transfer of valuable assets thus negatively influencing equity choice in CB acquisitions. On the other hand, it can be a source of synergy, innovation, and leaning (Stahl et al., 2016) thus positively influencing equity choice in CB acquisitions.

We hereby link the literature on distance to the literature on ownership decisions in CB acquisition and ask how does distance affects the ownership choice in CB acquisitions? In line with recent conceptualization of types of distance, we consider the four main categories of country-specific determinants of CB acquisitions proposed by Xie, Reddy, and Liang (2017) and thus examine economic, political (institutional, regulatory), social (cultural), and spatial (geographic) distance. We further investigate the moderating role of two distinct categories of distance-reducing factors. We analyze whether the relationship between distance and acquisition ownership decision is moderated by firm-specific characteristics, such as firm size, general international experience, and specific host country experience.

The empirical setting of our research is based on CB acquisitions undertaken by Finnish MNEs in both developed and emerging economies. The sample heterogeneity offers several benefits. The first benefit is related to the relationship between distance and the choice between full or partial CB acquisitions. Our sample allows us to perform several different types of analysis of ownership preferences in CB acquisitions: a general analysis distinguishing between full and partial ownership and also sub-sample analysis based on the equity commitment choice in partial CB acquisitions (i.e., majority versus minority acquisition). Second, by keeping the home country constant, we can investigate whether the ownership choices in CB acquisitions of the same developed-market originating MNEs are substantially different in developed or emerging-market context.

2. LITERATURE REVIEW AND HYPOTHESES

Our review summarized in Table 1 allows us to make several interesting observations. First, the majority of studies examining the relationship between distance and equity (ownership) stake in CB acquisitions use institutional theory and to a lesser extent Transaction cost economics TCE (or any other IB theory) as the basic reference point of discussion. This is not surprising considering that on the one hand the concept of distance resonates best with the theoretical postulates of institutional theory, and on the other hand the effect of distance on ownership decisions in acquisitions is primarily related to transaction cost (and uncertainty/risk) issues. Only one study uses resource-based view (RBV) in tandem with institutional theory to investigate possible effects of distance-reducing factors such as acquisition experience and technological intensity of the industry.

We advance this approach by further investigating firm-level (e.g., resource-based determined) distance-reducing factors. Second, the majority of studies use selected measures of distance with cultural distance being the most popular of them, followed by various measures of formal institutional distance. Perhaps the variations in the choice of distance measures explain the diverse findings about the impact of distance on the choice of equity stake in CB acquisitions ranging from linear to curvilinear effects. Perhaps the divergent findings can also be explained by the focus on either emerging economy or developed economy firms. We contribute to this literature by firstly,

Table 1. Literature on the Link between Distance and Ownership in CB Acquisitions.

Author	Theory	Dep. Variable	Key Predictor	Key Findings
Chari and Chang (2009)	TCE	Equity control in acquisitions (full or partial)	Cultural distance	Firms tend to acquire partially in culturally distant countries. Host country's risk and greater GAAP differences result in partial equity control
Chikhouni et al. (2016)	TCE, institutional theory	Equity control in acquisitions (5%–100%)	Psychic distance	Firms tend to acquire smaller stakes when psychic distance is large. This is moderated by directionality: EM firms acquire higher stakes in high psychic distance countries while DM firms prefer smaller stakes
Contractor et al. (2014)	Institutional theory	Equity control in acquisitions (minority, 50% and majority)	Institutional distance, uncertainty avoidance distance	At higher uncertainty avoidance distance firms tend to choose minority over majority ownership but institutional distance has insignificant effect. The joint effect of institutional distance and industry relatedness leads to minority equity control
Di Guardo et al. (2016)	Institutional theory	Equity control in acquisitions (full or partial)	Corruption	Firms tend to acquire full control at low and highly corrupt countries and partial control at moderate levels of corruption. Industry relatedness and economic connectivity moderate this relationship
Elango et al. (2013)	RBV, institutional theory	Equity control in acquisitions (full or partial)	Institutional distance	At greater institutional distance firms tend to choose partial equity but acquisition experience moderates this relationship. Acquisitions in high-tech industries are of full ownership in institutionally distant countries
Ferreira et al. (2016)	Institutional theory	Equity control in acquisitions (full or partial)	Economic, financial, political, administrative, cultural, demographic, knowledge, geo distance	At higher financial and cultural distance between home country and Brazil, firms tend to choose full ownership and at higher geographic distanced firms choose partial over full ownership in acquisitions

Table 1. (*Continued*)

Author	Theory	Dep. Variable	Key Predictor	Key Findings
Gaffney et al. (2016)	Institutional theory	Equity control in acquisitions (0.1%–100%)	Economic distance	UK firms are less likely to acquire larger equity stakes in economically distant countries, but EM firms tend to acquire larger equity stakes in distant countries with higher levels of economic development
Kedia and Bilgili (2015)	Institutional theory	Equity control in acquisitions (10–49, 50, 51–99, 100%)	Institutional distance	Firms tend to acquire smaller stakes when institutional distance is large. Historical ties and open markets moderate this relationship
Lahiri et al. (2014)	Institutional theory	Equity control in acquisitions (full or partial)	Institutional distance	At greater institutional distance EM firms tend to acquire full equity in both soft-service and hard-service industries
Liou et al. (2016)	Institutional theory	Equity control in acquisitions (0.1%–100%)	Formal and informal institutional distance	Firms tend to acquire partial equity control when informal institutional distance is large but formal institutional distance has no effect on equity ownership. Human capital mitigates the link between distance and equity control
Malhotra (2012)	Institutional theory	Equity control in acquisitions (full or partial)	Cultural and geographic distance	Firms tend to choose partial/full equity control in geographically distant/close targets. At moderate and high cultural distance firms tend to choose full control acquisitions in geographically distant countries
Malhotra and Gaur (2014)	Institutional economics	Equity control in acquisitions (0.1%–100%)	Geographic distance	Firms tend to acquire small equity stakes at low and moderate geographic distance, and large stakes at high cultural distance. This is moderated by pubic status and industry relatedness: public status firms and firms launching related acquisitions take larger states in geographically distant countries
Malhotra et al. (2016)	TCE	Equity control in acquisitions (full or partial)	Institutional, geographic and cultural distance	There is negative relationship between distance and full equity control but the relationship is weaker for Latin American firms than US firms (L.A. firms tend to acquire higher equity in more distant countries.)

Malhotra et al. (2011)	Institutional theory	Equity control in acquisitions (0.1%–100%)	Cultural distance	Firms tend to acquire large equity stakes at low and high cultural distance, and small stakes at moderate cultural distance. Industry relatedness moderates this relationship by increasing the magnitude of the effect at any given distance level
Moschieri et al. (2014)	Institutional theory	Equity control in acquisitions (5%–100%)	Uncertainty avoidance and risk (distance)	Firms tend to acquire full over partial equity control in EU at higher uncertainty avoidance and higher risk especially prior to 2001
Piaskowska and Trojanowski (2014)	Upper echelons theory, Institutional theory	Equity control in acquisitions (full or partial)	Cultural distance, country risk	Firms tend to acquire partially when cultural distance and country risk are large. This is moderated by TMT characteristics: international experience and career, and executives' foreign nationality positively moderate the negative link between distance and full ownership stake
Pinto et al. (2016)	Institutional theory	Equity control in acquisitions (full or partial)	Institutional distance	Brazilian firms tend to acquire full over partial equity control when institutional distance is large; government ownership through financial support strengthens the link but not political ties (the effect is insignificant). Firms with government ownership tend to make partial deals in institutionally distance countries
Yang (2015)	TCE, institutional theory, agency theory	Equity control in acquisitions (0.1%–100%)	Institutional and cultural distance	Firms tend to acquire full over partial equity control when institutional distance is small, when acquisitions are related and when acquirer board members own a large percentage of company shares

examining the case of Finnish firms CB acquisitions and thus keeping the investor's country fixed and secondly, by employing a more comprehensive approach to distance. We adopt the political economy view of determinants of CB acquisitions proposed by Xie et al. (2017) and investigate the direct and moderated effect of four groups of distance measures, namely, economic distance, political (formal institutional) distance, social (cultural) distance, and spatial (geographic) distance.

2.1. Distance and Equity Commitments in CB Acquisitions

Contemporary research shows that MNEs take internationalization-related decisions in light of two types of uncertainties, specifically external and internal uncertainty. According to Chikhouni et al. (2017) external uncertainty is caused by challenges faced by the MNE in the host country (e.g., specific business conditions, insufficient level of institutional development, frequency of macro-economic changes, etc.) and internal uncertainties are related to the distance between the MNE's home and host country. According to our reasoning, internal uncertainties by default are idiosyncratic and related to the distance-bridging factors introduced earlier, rather than solely capturing distance effects. We treat internal uncertainties as the direct result of the interaction between external uncertainties caused by various forms of distance (differences) between home and host country and firm-specific, distance-bridging factors such as knowledge-based resources (general and specific experience), and resource slack (firm size).

Distance has been traditionally conceptualized in a variety of ways. The concept of psychic distance was introduced by Beckerman (1956) to explain how differences between home and host countries affect the internationalization of Swedish firms. The cultural distance index was introduced by Kogut and Singh (1988) as a construct based on Hofstede's (1984) dimensions of culture and further applied to other cultural measures such as those created by Schwartz (1992) and the GLOBE study (House, Hanges, Javidan, Dorfman, & Gupta, 2004). Kostova (1999) introduced the notion of institutional distance as a means to capture differences in regulatory, normative, and social institutional differences while Ghemawat (2001) extended the concept of distance to include cultural, administrative, geographic, and economic distances. Finally, Berry, Guillén, and Zhou (2010) broadened the concept even further by adding knowledge and global connectedness distance thus proposing the most detailed account of distance (nine measures in total). The relevance of this extended range of distance dimensions for MNEs' international ownership decisions has not yet been investigated (Lee, Hemmert, & Kim, 2014).

Clearly, operationalization of the distance concept has presented numerous challenges to researchers and we recognize the importance of capturing the multidimensionality of the concept. This study considers four sources of uncertainty – cultural distance, geographic distance, (formal) institutional distance, and economic distance. We postulate that uncertainty caused by distance influences MNEs' decision to opt for shared equity ownership in CB acquisitions. Our basic premise is that the presence of uncertainty (measured by the four distinct distances between the home and host countries) will increase information-processing and transaction costs. As a result, acquirers will forego the option of obtaining full ownership by counterbalancing their need for control with the necessity to contain the costs associated with the acquisition and full integration of an ongoing operation (organization) in a substantially different context. Furthermore, the strength of this relationship will vary depending on the acquirers' resources that can be utilized as distance-bridging factors. Below we provide more detailed account of the specific effects of each type of distance on equity commitment in CB acquisitions and the proposed moderating effects.

Cultural distance has been traditionally considered a major source of uncertainty (Caves, 1982; Kim & Hwang, 1992; Malhotra, Sivakumar, & Zhu, 2009, 2011). The most popular reasons given for the negative effect of cultural distance on ownership levels and the subsequent preference of MNEs for shared risk through joint ownership include high information costs, organizational and administrative costs (Kogut & Singh, 1988), expropriation risks (Gatignon & Anderson, 1988) or the difficulties associated with the transfer of home grown management systems and technologies to culturally distant subsidiaries (Richman & Copen, 1972).

Past research has also examined the impact of institutional distance, captured by the degree of dissimilarity between home and host country institutions (Kostova, 1999). According to Kostova and Zaheer (1999), on the one hand MNEs face more difficulty in establishing legitimacy in host countries that are institutionally distant and on the other hand they are challenged in transferring strategic routines to these institutionally distant foreign subsidiaries. An equity involvement by a local partner may assist in establishing local legitimacy hence high institutional distance encourages MNEs to seek lower equity share in CB acquisitions. In addition, locally embedded competitive advantages of the target firm are viewed as a substitute for the difficult to transfer MNE practices

(Xu & Shenkar, 2002). Research has also pointed to problems in performing due diligence in institutionally distant locations due to different accounting standards, stakeholder interests, and restructuring restrictions (e.g.,Boussard, 2016; Dikova, Sahib, & Witteloostuijn, 2010). In emerging economies, researchers report challenges associated with target-firms financial evaluation and estimating potential post CB acquisition benefits (Arslan & Dikova, 2015; Lebedev et al., 2015). In such cases MNEs may prefer to reduce their financial exposure (Dikova et al., 2010) by avoiding fully owned CB acquisitions.

External uncertainty can also be related to geographical distance. The development of information technology and transportation systems has made it easier for MNEs to manage and control subsidiaries in geographically distant locations (Grosse & Trevino, 1996). However, recent studies have confirmed the relevance of geographical distance for MNEs' international ownership decisions (Chakrabarti & Mitchell, 2013; Ragozzino, 2009). Geographical distance increases the costs of transportation and communication (Anderson, 1979). In the context of CB acquisitions it intensifies the problem of information asymmetry (Grote, 2007) thus exacerbating the risk of adverse selection for spatially remote acquirers (Ragozzino & Reuer, 2011). Malhotra (2012) finds that for US firms the greater the geographic distance the more likely the US firms will choose shared ownership over full control in CB acquisitions. Others have also confirmed that MNEs likely choose to acquire a smaller equity stake in a target-firm based in geographically more remote location and a larger stake in a neighboring market (Ragozzino, 2009).

Economic distance is typically defined as the level of economic development of the host country relative to that of the home country (Ghemawat, 2001). Some researchers have argued that substantial economic distance provides MNEs with the benefits of exploiting or exploring competitive advantages (Tsang & Yip, 2007; Xu & Meyer, 2013). Early research suggests that firms invest in economically distant (different) locations either as a result of accumulating foreign market knowledge from similar locations (Johanson & Vahlne, 1977) or as a result of adjustments to product life cycles (Vernon, 1966). Tsang and Yip (2007) suggest that firms invest in economically distant countries to access valuable complementary resources but they prefer to invest in economically close locations when they pursue vertical or horizontal expansion that strengthens their home market base. Fully owned CB acquisitions imply integration as a result of a vertical or horizontal expansion. Here we suggest that such deals create risks for MNEs due to heightened uncertainty and increasing liabilities of foreignness in economically less-developed locations.

In sum, there is a negative relationship between cross-national uncertainty and firms' propensity to use full ownership in CB acquisitions, where uncertainty is a result of cultural distance, institutional distance, geographic distance, and economic distance. We propose:

Hypothesis 1. Distance (economic, political, cultural, and spatial) is negatively associated with equity commitment in CB acquisitions.

2.2. Distance, Firm Resources, and Equity Commitment in CB Acquisitions

The control dynamics vary significantly in CB acquisitions depending upon the ownership (minority or majority) stake (e.g., Malhotra & Gaur, 2014). The size of the investing MNE captured either by annual sales, geographic diversification or number of employees has been chosen as a good proxy of the available tangible and intangible resources that can be employed for strategic purposes (Cozza, Rabellotti, & Sanfilippo, 2015; Li & Li, 2014). Earlier studies have found it to be significantly related to the equity commitment at time of market entry (e.g., Wooster, Blanco, & Sawyer, 2016). MNE size has been associated with availability of financial resources required to undertake an FDI, which in many cases is an expensive venture (e.g., Anil, Tatoglu, & Ozkasap, 2014; Drogendijk & Slangen, 2006; Li & Li, 2014). MNE size has also been associated with the risk propensity of MNEs, where large size allows them to engage in risky ventures because they possess enough resources to cover the associated costs (e.g., Fillat, Garetto, & Oldenski, 2015). In similar vein we argue that since CB acquisitions are expensive ventures (Wooster et al., 2016), we expect that MNE size will influence the relationship between distance and equity commitment.

Previous research has shown that large MNEs prefer higher control in their subsidiaries, as it eases the integration in global strategy as well transfer of required practices (e.g., Fang, Wade, Delios, & Beamish, 2013; Kawai and Strange, 2014). In CB acquisitions, the only possibility to have a high control is via obtaining high stake in the acquired firm (Malhotra & Gaur, 2014). Moreover, larger firms are found more capable of making an acquisition in the first place (Larimo, 2003). We expect that large size will also mitigate the negative influences of distance on equity stake in CB acquisitions in such a way that larger MNEs may opt for higher equity commitment in distant locations, due to availability of resources required to better manage distant subsidiaries. Therefore, we hypothesize that:

Hypothesis 2. MNE's size moderates the influences of distance on equity commitment in CB Acquisitions in such a way that large MNEs will prefer high equity commitment in CB acquisitions undertaken in such locations.

From RBV perspective, experience of investing firms has been referred as a key resource for them especially during internationalization to the new markets (Rammal et al., 2014). Researchers have referred that as firms accumulate international experience, their organizational capabilities to deal with unfamiliar contexts increase (e.g., Das & Teng, 2000; Dow & Larimo, 2011; Meschi, 2005). Therefore, earlier research has argued that firms lacking international experience tend to prefer collaborative modes like joint ventures or partial acquisitions (Clarke, Tamaschke, & Liesch, 2013). In specific context of CB acquisitions, international experience of managers has been found to result in higher equity stakes choice (e.g., Piasskowska & Trojanowski, 2014). Piakowska and Trojanowski (2014) also revealed that international experience of top managers tend to moderate influences of cultural differences and risk on choice of ownership stake in CB acquisitions. Slangen and Hennart (2008) examined at the interaction between cultural distance and international experience. They found that internationally experienced MNEs are more likely to make acquisitions in culturally distant locations than their inexperienced counterparts. We extend this argument to suggest that internationally experience is likely to moderate the negative relationship between distance and equity stake in CB acquisitions. So we have:

Hypothesis 3. MNE international experience moderates the influences of distance on equity commitment in CB acquisitions in such a way that experienced MNEs will prefer high equity commitment in CB acquisitions undertaken in such locations.

Studies have focused on the importance of host country experience, as it equips investing MNEs with important knowledge about local market dynamics (Arslan & Dikova, 2015; Li & Meyer, 2009) and key players in industrial sectors those MNEs operate (Lindsay, Rod, & Ashill, 2015). Host country experience has been found to moderate some influences of uncertainty coming from institutional differences in emerging economies, as well as offer useful information on useful local firms as a target for acquisition (Arslan & Dikova, 2015). The lack of host country experience has been found to determine the likelihood of MNEs potentially overpaying for a CB acquisition deal (e.g., Chakrabarti & Mitchell, 2013; Cuypers, Cuypers, & Martin, 2016). As a result, MNEs without host country experience are more likely to seek the cooperation of the target-firm owners to reduce their motivation to inflate the value of the assets (Chen & Hennart 2004; Reuer, Tong, Tyler, &

Ariño, 2013) and also to avoid prolonging the deal negotiations or incurring additional unforeseen costs. Earlier literature has also suggested that MNEs engaging in CB acquisitions typically have to collect, analyze, distribute, and utilize information about the target firm, often under severe time constraints (Dikova et al., 2010). Host country experience equips MNEs with knowledge about country specific disclosure requirements and dynamics of the negotiation process (Ahammad, Tarba, Liu, Glaister, & Cooper, 2016; Ahmadjian, 2016; Zaheer et al., 2012). Therefore, it is reasonable to expect that host country experience of MNEs moderates the influence of distance on equity commitment in CB acquisitions. We hypothesize that:

Hypothesis 4. MNE host country experience moderates the influences of distance on equity commitment in CB acquisitions in such a way that experienced MNEs will prefer high equity commitment in CB acquisitions undertaken in such locations.

3. EMPIRICAL RESEARCH DESIGN AND METHODOLOGY

3.1. Data Sources

The study data have been collected and constantly updated over a period of 30 years. The database contains FDI and CB acquisition activities of Finnish MNEs in the manufacturing sector and has been compiled with information from annual reports of investing firms, corporate website and stock release information, articles, and information in leading Finnish business magazines (Kauppalehti and Talouselämä). The data has further been supplemented with data from Thompson One database, as well as archival FINNFUND reports. The CB acquisition information consists of basic investing firm and deal-related information like year of investment, field of industry, location, ownership (full vs. partial acquisition and minority vs. majority acquisition) at the time of entry and subsequent changes, such as the potential divestment of the acquired unit. The data set is relatively unique and representative of the CB acquisitions undertaken by the Finnish MNEs in the manufacturing sector. The dependent variables of the study and many of the control variables like investment relatedness, R&D intensity, and product diversity are derived from this data set. Other control variables and the country-level independent variables are based on reliable and established external data sources, as explained in the forthcoming section.

3.2. Operationalization of Study Variables

3.2.1. Dependent Variable

There are two dependent variables in this study. The first one is CB acquisition equity which is coded 1 for full CB acquisition (95% or more equity ownership at time of investment), while 0 for partial CB acquisition (94% or less equity ownership at time of investment). In order to better understand equity commitment in CB acquisitions by Finnish MNEs, we further divide sample and analyze partial acquisitions in greater depth. The second dependent variable is partial CB acquisition coded as 1 for majority acquisition (equity ownership between 51% and 94% by acquiring MNEs at time of entry), and 0 for minority acquisition (equity ownership of 50% or less at time of market entry). Therefore, for the sake of simplicity and clarity, we consider the few cases of equal (50–50) ownership as minority equity.

3.2.2. Independent Variables

Political Distance: Political institutions of a country form an important part of formal institutional environment of a country (North, 1990). They tend to ensure "freedoms of transacting, security of property rights, and transparency of government and legal process" (Globerman & Shapiro, 2003, p. 19). To operationalize the political distance, we use the country scores in the pillar of *legal structure and security of property rights* from economic freedom of the world annual reports (Gwartney, Lawson, & Hall, 2016). This pillar includes the aspects of judicial independence, impartial courts, protection of property rights, integrity of legal system, and legal enforcement of contracts. Therefore, we argue that this pillar captures the essence of formal institutions as conceptualized by North (1990). We use the difference in country scores in year of CB acquisition or nearest available year, calculated using Kogut and Singh (1988) formula, which considers variance as well.

Cultural Distance: The current book chapter uses the Kogut and Singh (1988) cultural distance index, in this case using the differences between the scores of the host foreign country and Finland on Hofstede's (1980) dimensions of national culture for the four original dimensions of culture.

Spatial Distance: In line with prior studies (Malhotra, Sivakumar, & Zhu, 2009; Slangen & Beugelsdijk, 2010), we measured spatial (geographic) distance as the actual distance in kilometers between the capital cities of the acquiring and the target countries. To correct for any skewness in the data, we use natural logarithm of these distance values, as done in earlier studies.

Economic Distance: We measure the economic distance using the difference in real GDP per capita in US Dollars between Finland and host country. GDP per capita is a variable commonly used by researchers and organizations, such as the United Nations, to measure the level of economic development of a country. Following the suggestions of earlier studies, we use natural logarithmic value of difference instead of simple difference (e.g., Tsang & Yip, 2007).

MNE Size: We measured MNE size by using the natural log of global sales (in Euros) of the investing firms in the year preceding to the investment (e.g., Dow & Larimo, 2011; Hennart & Park, 1993; Taylor, Zou, & Osland, 2000). The data for this variable is compiled from annual reports of the investing firms.

MNE International Experience: We measured international experience of investing MNEs by the number of earlier market entries undertaken by investing firms in different international markets, as done in several earlier studies (e.g., Kaynak, Demirbag, & Tatoglu, 2007; Shaver, Mitchell, & Yeung, 1997, 2000). The data for this variable are based on internal database of Finnish FDIs.

MNE Host Country Experience: We measured host country experience of investing MNEs by using the number years of presence in host country calculated from the time of the first manufacturing investment in that particular market (Arslan & Dikova, 2015; Hennart & Park, 1993; Larimo, 2003). The data for this variable are based on internal database of Finnish FDIs.

3.2.3. Control Variables

In line with past literature, we use a number of control variables at the country, industry, and firm levels, in order to enhance the validity of the study findings. We explain the operationalization of these control variables as follows.

Investment unrelatedness: We use a dummy variable where 0 means that the CB acquisition is undertaken in a related industry (the four-digit SIC code of the investment is the same as the industry where the firm already operates) and 1 which means that the CB acquisition was undertaken in an industry that is new for the firm (unrelated investment). Similarly, operationalization has been reported by earlier IB studies (e.g., Barkema & Vermeulen, 1998; Chen & Hennart, 2004; Contractor et al., 2014).

MNE Product Diversity: We use the number of four-digit SIC codes of the products in which investing firm has been operating based on the annual reports and websites of the acquiring firms (Chung, Lee, Beamish, Southam, & Nam, 2013; Hennart & Larimo, 1998).

R&D Intensity: We use a classification of various four-digit SIC industries into four categories (Low-Tech, Low-MediumTech, Medieum-Tech, and

High-Tech) based on value-added figures of investing firms (Arslan & Dikova, 2015; Dow & Larimo, 2011). The data for this variable are based on internal database of Finnish FDIs as well as annual reports and websites of investing firms.

Host Country Economic Growth: We use % of GDP growth in host country of in the preceding the investment based on UCTAD data (e.g., Brouthers & Brouthers, 2000; Hennart, 1991; Larimo & Arslan, 2013).

Host Country Risk: We use Euromoney country risk ratings for this variable. It is operationalized by subtracting country score from 100, in the year of investment or nearest available year (e.g., Arslan et al., 2015; Click, 2005; Demirbag et al., 2009; Larimo, 2003).

3.3 Sample Description

The study sample consists of 1,041 CB acquisitions under taken by Finnish MNEs in 58 countries representing both developed and emerging economies during the time period 1990–2010. Out of 1,041 CB acquisitions, 761 (73.1%) were undertaken in developed economies, while 280 (26.9%) were undertaken in emerging economies. Major destinations for CB acquisitions for Finnish firms are the USA (156 CB acquisitions), Sweden (140 CB acquisitions), and Germany (115 CB acquisitions). Moreover, there are 692 (66.5%) full CB acquisitions, while 349 (33.5%) are partial CB acquisitions. We can further observe in sub-sample focusing on partial acquisitions that 157 (45%) out of 349 are majority CB acquisitions, while rest are minority CB acquisitions. Moreover, the sample distribution on basis of R&D intensity shows that Finnish MNEs undertook 189 (17.2%) CB acquisitions in low-tech industries, 175 in low-medium tech industries (16.8%), 400 (38.4%) in medium-tech industries, and 287 (27.6%) in high-tech industries. It is also important to mention that our study sample includes CB acquisitions undertaken by experienced and relatively large-sized Finnish MNEs like Ahlstrom, Fazer, Hartwall, Fiskars, Fortum, Kemira, Kone, Metso, Neste, Nokia, Raisio, Rautaruukki, and UPM, as well as a number of newly internationalizing, relatively small-sized, and inexperienced MNEs.

3.4. Statistical Method

The dependent variables of the current study are dichotomous (i.e., full vs. partial acquisition and majority vs. minority acquisitions). Therefore, we use binomial logistic regression analysis to analyze the impact of the control and independent variables on CB acquisitions undertaken by Finnish MNEs. Binary logistic regression has been used often as a reliable statistical analysis technique in past IB studies addressing different aspects of foreign market entry strategies of MNEs (e.g., Demirbag et al., 2009; Dikova & van Witteloostuijn 2007; Larimo 2003) as well as acquisition strategy of MNEs specifically (e.g., Arslan & Dikova, 2015). The binomial logistic regression model is formally expressed as

$$P(yi = 1) = 1 / 1 + \exp(-a - XiB)$$

where yi is the dependent variable, Xi is the vector of independent variables for the ith observation, a is the intercept parameter, and B is the vector of regression coefficients (Amemiya, 1981). A recent version of SPSS, that is, PASW 23, is used for the binomial regression analysis in this study. Since the dependent variables have been coded with value 1 for full acquisition in full sample, and for majority acquisition (in sub-sample), a positive regression coefficient indicates that a particular control and independent variable increases the probability of preference of full CB acquisition/majority CB acquisition by acquiring MNEs.

4. RESULTS

The correlation matrix showing pairwise correlations among all the variables of the study is presented in Table 2. The pairwise correlations do not appear to present any potential multicollinearity problems for the multivariate analysis, as none of the variables have correlation coefficients above 0.60 (Hair, Anderson, Tatham, & Black, 2013, p. 230). However, following the recommendations by Pallant (2007), we conduct additional multicollinearity diagnostic (tolerance and variance inflation factor (VIF)). According to Wetherill (1986), the VIF value should not exceed 10. In the current study, the VIF values of the all the variables are lower than 5 (highest being 4.3) and consequently, the potential collinearity among variables is not expected to influence the results of binomial logistic regression analysis.

Tables 3 and 4 display the results of our binomial regression analyses. The explanatory power of all the statistical models of the study is good, as their chi-square (χ^2) values are significant at $p \leq 0.01$. Moreover, Nagelkerke R^2 values further show relatively satisfactory predictive capability of all models. Model 1 in all tables shows the influences of control and independent

Table 2. Descriptive Statistics and Pearson Correlations.

	Mean	SD	1.	2.	3.	4.	5.	6.	7.	8.	9.	10.	11.	12.	13.
1. CB acquisition	0.66	0.472	1												
2. Unrelatedness	0.03	0.180	0.120	1											
3.R&D Intensity	2.76	1.038	−0.209*	−0.120	1										
4. Product Diversity	10.25	7.077	−0.010	0.052	0.133*	1									
5. Economic Growth	2.782	3.785	0.085	−0.038	−0.072	−0.008	1								
6. Country Risk	18.214	19.506	−0.339*	−0.076	−0.266*	−0.086	−0.130*								
7. MNE Size	6.86	2.554	0.033	−0.054	−0.002	0.533	0.080	−0.061	1						
8. MNE Int. Experience	34.42	31.915	0.147*	−0.064	−0.069	0.340*	−0.130*	−0.053	0.553*	1					
9. MNE Host Country Experience	7.23	0.289	0.147*	0.008	−0.082	0.277*	0.024	−0.288*	0.400*	0.330*	1				
10. Political Distance	1.3445	0.995	−0.266*	−0.083	−0.162*	−0.021	0.073	0.413*	0.052	0.062	−0.236*	1			
11. Cultural Distance	1.480	0.852	−0.069	−0.045	0.142*	0.043	0.174*	0.148*	0.097	0.127*	−0.014	0.434*	1		
12. Spatial Distance	7.603	1.218	−0.143*	0.028	0.326*	0.115	−0.212*	0.263*	0.177*	0.159*	0.124	−0.008	0.456*	1	
13. Economic Distance	1.777	1.076	−0.127*	−0.082	−0.072	−0.011	0.432*	0.486*	0.086	0.107	−0.143*	0.530*	0.408*	0.109	1

Note: * Correlation is significant at the $p \leq 0.01$ level (two-tailed).

Table 3. Full Sample Binomial Logistic Regression Estimates (Full Acquisition = 1).

Variable	Model 1: Total	Model 2: Moderating Political Distance	Model 3: Moderating Cultural Distance	Model 4: Moderating Spatial Distance	Model 5: Moderating Economic Distance
Unrelatedness	−0.467*	−0.431*	−0.431*	−0.529*	−0.444*
R&D Intensity	0.334***	0.315***	0.315***	0.345***	0.324***
Product Diversity	−0.043***	−0.044***	−0.044***	−0.042***	−0.043***
Economic Growth	0.043*	0.041*	0.043*	0.041*	−0.045*
Country Risk	−0.034***	−0.034***	−0.033***	−0.035***	−0.033***
MNE Size	0.028*				
MNE Int. Experience	0.006*				
MNE Host Country Experience	0.015**				
Political Distance	−0.120**		−0.088*	−0.136	−0.121*
Cultural Distance	−0.271**	−0.284**		−0.246**	−0.255**
Spatial Distance	−0.097*	−0.105*	−0.74*		−0.096
Economic Distance	−0.03*	−0.022*	−0.013*	−0.021	
Political Distance × MNE Size		0.071			
Political Distance × MNE Int Experience		0.468			
Political Distance × MNE Host country Experience		0.037**			
Cultural Distance × MNE Size			0.025		
Cultural Distance × MNE Int Experience			0.006		

Table 3. (*Continued*)

Variable	Model 1: Total	Model 2: Moderating Political Distance	Model 3: Moderating Cultural Distance	Model 4: Moderating Spatial Distance	Model 5: Moderating Economic Distance
Cultural Distance × MNE Host Country Experience			0.019*		
Spatial Distance × MNE Size				0.023**	
Spatial Distance × MNE Int Experience				0.001	
Spatial Distance × MNE Host Country Experience				0.016*	
Economic Distance × MNE Size					0.031*
Economic Distance × MNE Int Experience					0.185**
Economic Distance × MNE Host Country Experience					0.026*
N (Full Acquisition)	1,041(692)	1,041(692)	1,041(692)	1,041(692)	1,041(692)
Model x^2	157.990***	162.012***	163.225***	151.458**	162.929***
−2 Log Likelihood	1,169.988	1,164.753	1,164.757	1,166.410	1,165.049
Nagelkerke R^2	0.195	0.202	0.209	0.199	0.201
Correctly Classified (%)	71.7%	72.1%	75.5	71.8%	71.9%

Notes: Levels of significance: $^{*}p \leq 0.1$, $^{**}p \leq 0.05$, $^{***}p \leq 0.01$.

variables, while Models 2–5 show the moderating influences on political, cultural, spatial and economic distances.

The results in Model 1 of Table 3 show that Finnish MNEs preferred partial CB acquisitions in unrelated industries. Moreover, highly diversified

Table 4. Full Sample Binomial Logistic Regression Estimates (Majority Acquisition = 1).

Variable	Model 1: Total	Model 2: Moderating Political Distance	Model 3: Moderating Cultural Distance	Model 4: Moderating Spatial Distance	Model 5: Moderating Economic Distance
Unrelatedness	0.442	0.468	0.453	−0.529*	0.346
R&D Intensity	−0.010	−0.034	0.012	0.345***	0.034
Product Diversity	−0.039*	−0.040**	−0.046*	−0.042***	−0.038*
Economic Growth	0.079*	0.078*	0.079*	0.041*	0.072
Country Risk	−0.021*	−0.016*	−0.021**	−0.035***	−0.034**
MNE Size	0.087*				
MNE Int. Experience	0.007				
MNE Host Country Experience	0.022**				
Political Distance	−0.431*		−0.201*	−0.136*	−0.454**
Cultural Distance	−0.204*	−0 204*		−0.246**	−0.198**
Spatial Distance	−0.014*	−0 025	−0.74*		−0.003
Economic Distance	0.016	0 016	0.015	0.02	
Political Distance × MNE Size		0.059*			
Political Distance × MNE Int Experience		0.005			
Political Distance × MNE Host Country Experience		0.019*			
Cultural Distance × MNE Size			0.010*		
Cultural Distance × MNE Int Experience			0.003		

Table 4. (*Continued*)

Variable	Model 1: Total	Model 2: Moderating Political Distance	Model 3: Moderating Cultural Distance	Model 4: Moderating Spatial Distance	Model 5: Moderating Economic Distance
Cultural Distance × MNE Host Country Experience			0.015		
Spatial Distance × MNE Size				0.011*	
Spatial Distance × MNE Int Experience				0.005	
Spatial Distance × MNE Host Country Experience				0.023**	
Economic Distance × MNE Size					0.001
Economic Distance × MNE Int Experience					0.002
Economic Distance × MNE Host Country Experience					0.014
N (Majority Acquisition)	349(157)	349(157)	349(157)	349(157)	349(157)
Model x^2	124.589***	125.782***	126.576***	126.281***	122.503***
−2 Log Likelihood	455.712	454.519	454.725	454.020	447.798
Nagelkerke R^2	0.219	0.225	0.221	0.220	0.228
Correctly Classified (%)	72.8%	72.9%	71.9%	71.9%	73.5%

Notes: Levels of significance: $^{*}p \leq 0.1$, $^{**}p \leq 0.05$, $^{***}p \leq 0.01$.

MNEs also preferred partial CB acquisitions. These findings are in line with earlier studies that referred to the lack of product-specific knowledge to properly evaluate an acquisition deal in an unrelated industry, as well as the need for collaboration with the acquired firm owners to gain that knowledge (e.g., Contractor et al., 2014; Hennart, Sheng, & Pimenta, 2015; Mazon, Silva, Ferreira, & Serra, 2017). We can further observe that Finnish MNEs operating in industries with high R&D intensity preferred full CB acquisitions. This finding is in line with earlier studies that referred to the importance of intellectual property in high-tech sectors and the reluctance of MNEs to share it with other firms leading to a preference of fully owned establishments (e.g., Hennart et al., 2015). The results further show that Finnish MNEs preferred full CB acquisitions in host country representing high economic growth, while they preferred partial CB acquisitions in high risk host countries. These findings are similar to earlier studies focusing on the influences of economic growth (e.g., Lu, Karpova, & Fiore, 2011) and country risk (e.g., Chari & Chang, 2009). The results further show that key factors causing external uncertainty (i.e., political, cultural, spatial, and economic distances) are negatively associated with preference of full CB acquisition by Finnish MNEs. Therefore, we get support for Hypothesis 1 of the study. Finally, Table 1 also shows that large-sized MNEs, as well as the ones with high international and host country experience tend to prefer full CB acquisitions over partial CB acquisitions.

Models 2–5 show interesting results concerning potential moderating influences of MNE size, international experience, and host country experience on all four measures of distance. We can see from Model 2 that political distance is only moderated by MNE host country experience, as shown by positive and significant regression coefficient. We further observe in Table 3 of Model 2 that cultural distance is moderated by MNE host country experience; interaction term mildly significant at $p \leq 0.1$. Therefore, it can be concluded that Finnish MNEs with high host country experiences tended to prefer full CB acquisitions despite high political and cultural differences. Moreover, Model 4 shows that spatial distance is moderated by investing MNE size along with host country experience. Finally, we see that economic distance is moderated by investing MNE size and international experience. Based on these study findings, we can say that we receive partial support for Hypotheses 2, 3, and 4 of our study suggesting that different distance measures are positively moderated by MNE's resources.

In order to better understand the equity commitment by Finnish MNEs in CB acquisitions, we performed binomial logistic regression analysis of our sample of partial CB acquisitions (majority vs. minority CB acquisitions). The results are shown in Table 4.

Model 1 in Table 4 shows the influences of control and independent variables on preference of minority of majority partial CB acquisitions by Finnish MNEs. The results show that highly diversified MNEs tended to prefer minority CB acquisitions at time of entry. High economic growth led to a preference for majority CB acquisitions, while minority CB acquisitions have been preferred by Finnish MNEs in high risk countries. Some interesting findings can be observed concerning the influences of our independent variables, where both MNE international experience and economic distance are non-significant. The insignificance of international experience can be explained by referring to specificities of managing collaborative ventures in new markets, where generic international experience may not offer specific insights to managers (e.g., Barkema, Shenkar, Vermeulen, & Bell, 1997); however, no references in past literature can assist us in explaining why economic distance has no impact on equity commitment dynamics within a partially acquired subsidiary. We can further see that political, cultural, and spatial distances are negatively associated with high equity commitment (i.e., majority CB acquisition in this case), while large MNE size and host country experience are positively associated with high equity commitment. Therefore, we receive partial support for Hypothesis 1.

The results further show that MNE size moderates political, cultural, and spatial distances. This means that large-sized Finnish MNEs preferred high equity commitment (majority CB acquisitions in this case) despite high political and cultural distances. We can further see that MNE host country experience moderates political and spatial distances, that is, host country experienced Finnish MNEs preferred majority CB acquisitions despite high political and spatial distances. Based on these findings, we can say that we receive partial support for Hypotheses 2–4 from this sub-sample analysis.

To further understand the dynamics of equity commitment in CB acquisitions, we sub-divide sample on the bases of level of economic development of host economies, that is, developed vs. emerging economies. Table 5 shows the results of developed economies sample for choice between full vs. partial acquisition by Finnish MNEs.

The results are rather similar to the full sample results as shown in Table 2, which is quite logical as developed economies comprise majority of study sample (ca. 73.1%). However, there are few interesting findings that need to be highlighted. Firstly, investing MNE size is non-significant for choice between full and a partial acquisition. This aspect can be partially explained by the attractiveness of developed economies due to economic opportunities, liberal M&A policies and the potential for stable return on investments that both large- and relatively smaller-sized MNEs undertook high equity commitment deals (i.e., full CB acquisition). We can also see that spatial distance is positively associated with high equity commitment. This means that Finnish MNEs preferred full CB acquisitions despite high distance between home and

Table 5. Developed Economies Binomial Logistic Regression Estimates (Full Acquisition = 1).

Variable	Model 1: Total	Model 2: Moderating Political Distance	Model 3: Moderating Cultural Distance	Model 4: Moderating Spatial Distance	Model 5: Moderating Economic Distance
Unrelatedness	−0.487*	−0.542	−0.562*	−0.483	−0.594*
R&D Intensity	0.229**	0.226**	0.210**	0.282**	0.225**
Product Diversity	−0.038**	−0.026**	−0.020*	−0.044**	−0.019
Economic Growth	−0.027	−0.021	0.023	0.021	0.010
Country Risk	−0.051**	−0.057**	−0.057**	−0.054**	−0.056**
MNE Size	0.074				
MNE Int. Experience	0.011**				
MNE Host Country Experience	0.062*				
Political Distance	−0.227**		−0.213*	−0.034*	−0.084*
Cultural Distance	−0.534*	−0.534**		−0.405**	−0.505**
Spatial Distance	0.285**	0.298**	0.278**		0.321**
Economic Distance	0.150	−0.015	0.256		
Political Distance × MNE Size		−0.072			
Political Distance × MNE Int Experience		0.087**			
Political Distance × MNE Host Country Experience		0.032*			
Cultural Distance × MNE Size			0.094***		
Cultural Distance × MNE Int Experience			0.035**		

Table 5. (*Continued*)

Variable	Model 1: Total	Model 2: Moderating Political Distance	Model 3: Moderating Cultural Distance	Model 4: Moderating Spatial Distance	Model 5: Moderating Economic Distance
Cultural Distance × MNE Host Country Experience			0.005		
Spatial Distance × MNE Size				0.001	
Spatial Distance × MNE Int Experience				0.001	
Spatial Distance × MNE Host Country Experience				0.006	
Economic Distance × MNE Size					0.012
Economic Distance × MNE Int Experience					0.031
Economic Distance × MNE Host Country Experience					−0.004
N (Full Acquisition)	761(569)	761(569)	761(569)	761(569)	761(569)
Model x^2	50.723***	56.296***	55.618***	55.545**	52.927***
−2 Log Likelihood	808.896	803.402	804.080	804.152	806.771
Nagelkerke R^2	0.175	0.187	0.186	0.187	0.181
Correctly Classified (%)	75%%	75.8%	75.6%	75.1%	75.3%

Notes: Levels of significance: $^{*}p \leq 0.1$, $^{**}p \leq 0.05$, $^{***}p \leq 0.01$.

host countries. This finding can be partially explained by referring to full CB acquisitions undertaken by Finnish MNEs in distant developed economies like Australia, Canada, and USA. Another interesting finding relates to the significance of the interaction effect of MNE international experience which reduces the negative effects of political and cultural distance on equity commitment in developed economies. MNEs size positively moderates the effect of cultural distance on full acquisition ownership in developed economies.

Table 6 shows equity commitment by Finnish MNEs in case of partial CB acquisitions (majority vs. minority CB acquisitions) undertaken in the developed economies.

The results are similar to full sample results presented in Table 4 with couple of interesting exceptions. Firstly, spatial distance is positively associated with high equity commitment (i.e., majority owned CB acquisitions). This finding can also be partially explained by referring to sample characteristics and equity commitment in distant developed economies. Moreover, MNE international experience moderates influences of political and cultural distances while political distance is moderated by MNE host country experience. It is interesting to note that in the subsample of developed host economies, both types of experiences (general and host-country-specific international experiences) have significant direct effects on both full acquisition and majority acquisition ownership but general international experience is more frequently a significant moderator of the negative distance effects than host country-specific experience in developed economies sample.

Table 7 shows the equity commitment by Finnish MNEs in the emerging economies sample. The results offer some interesting differences compared to the full sample results presented in Table 3. Firstly, MNE international experience is a non-significant determinant for equity commitment. This finding echoes earlier studies noting that generic international experience is less useful for acquiring MNEs in emerging economies (e.g., Arslan & Dikova, 2015; Li & Meyer, 2009). As emerging economies represent high information asymmetry and uncertainty, host country experience has been considered more useful to evaluate a potential target firm and manage post-CB acquisition process effectively (Arslan & Dikova, 2015; Aybar & Ficici, 2009). This experience can also further reduce uncertainties associated with the external environment, as MNE is equipped with practical tools to deal with market specificities, as well as possesses knowledge of good potential target firms (Ahmadjian, 2016; Arslan & Dikova, 2015). This claim is further supported by the moderating effects of MNE host country experience on distance, as it appears to reduce the negative influences of political, cultural, and spatial distances.

Table 8 shows the regression results for equity commitment (i.e. majority vs. minority CB acquisition) by Finnish MNE in the case of partial CB acquisitions in emerging host economies. The results show that general international experience does not have an impact on equity commitment

Table 6. Developed Economies Binomial Logistic Regression Estimates (Majority Acquisition = 1).

Variable	Model 1: Total	Model 2: Moderating Political Distance	Model 3: Moderating Cultural Distance	Model 4: Moderating Spatial Distance	Model 5: Moderating Economic Distance
Unrelatedness	0.474	0.467	0.426	0.479	0.535
R&D Intensity	−0.74	−0.063	−0.043	−0.048	−0.061
Product Diversity	−0.051*	−0.061**	−0.058**	−0.054*	−0.062**
Economic Growth	0.018**	0.012**	0.024*	0.023**	0.105**
Country Risk	−0.024	−0.030	−0.027	−0.022	−0.027
MNE Size	0.140				
MNE Int. Experience	0.006*				
MNE Host Country Experience	0.17*				
Political Distance	−0.395**		−0.404**	−0.364**	−0.113*
Cultural Distance	−0.142*	−0.118*		−0.197*	−0.151*
Spatial Distance	0.047**	0.053**	0.052**		0.061**
Economic Distance	0.235	0.314	0.298	0.223	
Political Distance × MNE Size		−0.019			
Political Distance × MNE Int Experience		0.100**			
Political Distance × MNE Host Country Experience		0.046*			
Cultural Distance × MNE Size			0.021		
Cultural Distance × MNE Int Experience			0.015*		

Table 6. *(Continued)*

Variable	Model 1: Total	Model 2: Moderating Political Distance	Model 3: Moderating Cultural Distance	Model 4: Moderating Spatial Distance	Model 5: Moderating Economic Distance
Cultural Distance × MNE Host Country Experience			0.043		
Spatial Distance × MNE Size				−0.010	
Spatial Distance × MNE Int Experience				0.21**	
Spatial Distance × MNE Host Country Experience				0.032*	
Economic Distance × MNE Size					0.001
Economic Distance × MNE Int Experience					−0.002
Economic Distance × MNE Host Country Experience					−0.036
N (Majority Acquisition)	192(74)	192(74)	192(74)	192(74)	192(74)
Model x^2	112.263***	112.833***	113.971***	113.646***	113.100***
−2 Log Likelihood	243.732	243.112	242.024	242.349	242.895
Nagelkerke R^2	0.184	0.188	0.187	0.188	0.186
Correctly Classified (%)	72.1%	73.5%	72.5%	72.5%	75.6%

Notes: Levels of significance: $^{*}p \leq 0.1$, $^{**}p \leq 0.05$, $^{***}p \leq 0.01$.

in partial CB acquisitions by Finnish MNEs. Moreover, cultural distance is positively associated with high equity commitment (i.e., choice of majority CB acquisition). This finding is opposite to our expectation but can be explained by referring to earlier studies where high ownership stake in

Table 7. Emerging Economies Binomial Logistic Regression Estimates (Full Acquisition = 1).

Variable	Model 1: Total	Model 2: Moderating Political Distance	Model 3: Moderating Cultural Distance	Model 4: Moderating Spatial Distance	Model 5: Moderating Economic Distance
Unrelatedness	−0.771	−0.431*	0.716	0.596	0.232
R&D Intensity	0.545***	0.315***	0.518***	0.516***	0.546***
Product Diversity	−.020	−0.044***	0.02	−0.019	−0.001
Economic Growth	0.012*	0.041*	0.011*	0.016*	0.129**
Country Risk	−0.039***	−0.034***	−0.041**	−0.038**	−0.040**
MNE Size	0.076*				
MNE Int. Experience	−0.004				
MNE Host Country Experience	0.025**				
Political Distance	−0.099*			−0.093*	−0.483*
Cultural Distance	−0.138**	−0.284**	−0.100*	−0.182*	−0.066**
Spatial Distance	−0.062*	−0.106*	−0.089*		−0.088*
Economic Distance	−0.228**	−0.022*	−0.269*	−0.254*	
Political Distance × MNE Size		0.071			
Political Distance × MNE Int Experience		0.468			
Political Distance × MNE Host Country Experience		0.037**			
Cultural Distance × MNE Size			−0.003		
Cultural Distance × MNE Int Experience			0.001		

Table 7. *(Continued)*

Variable	Model 1: Total	Model 2: Moderating Political Distance	Model 3: Moderating Cultural Distance	Model 4: Moderating Spatial Distance	Model 5: Moderating Economic Distance
Cultural Distance × MNE Host Country Experience			0.043**		
Spatial Distance × MNE Size				0.002	
Spatial Distance × MNE Int Experience				0.071	
Spatial Distance × MNE Host Country Experience				0.41*	
Economic Distance × MNE Size					0.001
Economic Distance × MNE Int Experience					0.032
Economic Distance × MNE Host Country Experience					0.021
N (Full Acquisition)	280(123)	280(123)	280(123)	280(123)	280(123)
Model x^2	43.584***	43.313***	44.024***	44.919**	48.543***
−2 Log Likelihood	340.169	1,164.753	339.901	337.105	335.480
Nagelkerke R^2	0.194	0.202	0.195	0.195	0.213
Correctly Classified (%)	69.3%	72.1%	69.8%	69.6%	69.6%

Notes: Levels of significance: $^{*}p \leq 0.1$, $^{**}p \leq 0.05$, $^{***}p \leq 0.01$.

culturally distant economies (e.g., López-Duarte & Vidal-Suárez, 2013) has been linked to better subsidiary management. It appears that in emerging economies, high ownership can reduce potential problems in managing a collaborative venture (a partially acquired firm) for MNE, as it can transfer

Table 8. Emerging Economies Binomial Logistic Regression Estimates (Majority Acquisition = 1).

Variable	Model 1: Total	Model 2: Moderating Political Distance	Model 3: Moderating Cultural Distance	Model 4: Moderating Spatial Distance	Model 5: Moderating Economic Distance
Unrelatedness	2.464	2.350	2.076	2.135	1.909
R&D Intensity	0.118	0.096	0.130	0.134	−0.011
Product Diversity	−0.036*	−0.030*	−0.033*	−0.026***	−0.019*
Economic Growth	0.012	0.012*	0.017	0.010*	0.099
Country Risk	−0.019*	−0.018	−0.018*	−0.019**	−0.018*
MNE Size	0.036*				
MNE Int. Experience	0.009				
MNE Host Country Experience	0.015				
Political Distance	−0.181**		−0.124*	−0.112**	−0.210*
Cultural Distance	0.376*	0.406*		0.320*	0.302*
Spatial Distance	−0.067*	−0.084*	−0.023*		−0.024*
Economic Distance	−0.781**	−0.813**	−0.614**	−0.780**	
Political Distance × MNE Size		0.006			
Political Distance × MNE Int Experience		0.003			
Political Distance × MNE Host Country Experience		0.113*			
Cultural Distance × MNE Size			0.026**		
Cultural Distance × MNE Int Experience			0.005		

Table 8. (*Continued*)

Variable	Model 1: Total	Model 2: Moderating Political Distance	Model 3: Moderating Cultural Distance	Model 4: Moderating Spatial Distance	Model 5: Moderating Economic Distance
Cultural Distance × MNE Host Country Experience			0.051*		
Spatial Distance × MNE Size				0.092	
Spatial Distance × MNE Int Experience				0.001	
Spatial Distance × MNE Host Country Experience				0.002	
Economic Distance × MNE Size					0.023**
Economic Distance × MNE Int Experience					0.002
Economic Distance × MNE Host Country Experience					0.016**
N (Majority Acquisition)	157(83)	157(83)	157(83)	157(83)	157(83)
Model x^2	35.482***	36.129***	36.678***	35.939***	36.503***
−2 Log Likelihood	211.290	211.003	210.364	210.193	204.762
Nagelkerke R^2	0.149	0.151	0.156	0.150	0.151
Correctly Classified (%)	67.3%	67.3%	67.6%	68.6%	68.0%

Notes: Levels of significance: $^{*}p \leq 0.1$, $^{**}p \leq 0.05$, $^{***}p \leq 0.01$.

practices and perform some required restructuring as well. We can further see that MNE host country experience moderates the negative influence of political and economic distances while MNE size moderates the negative effect of economic distance.

5. IMPLICATIONS, LIMITATIONS, AND FUTURE RESEARCH DIRECTIONS

Our study offers several implications for both academic and managerial audiences. The first implication is linked to our findings that regardless of the type of distance, the effect is mostly negative on equity commitment in CB acquisition. However, not all four types of distance (economic, political, spatial, and cultural) show consistently significant effects for the different measures of equity commitment in CB acquisitions, hence their separate examination should be considered. In line with previous research, we associated distance with external uncertainty; however, our results show that different types of distances tend to have different influences depending upon what kind of equity commitment is analyzed (e.g., full vs. partial or majority vs. minority CB acquisition). We highlight that in case of partial CB acquisition, the choice between majority and minority CB acquisitions deserves attention as the empirical results showed differences compared to the dynamics concerning full vs. partial CB acquisitions. In addition, the effects of various types of distance become more divergent when we consider the type of host country, whether it is a developed or emerging economy. Assuming that distance is always negative in the context of both developed and emerging economies would be inaccurate. Moreover, the interaction between MNE resources (size, international experience, and host country experience) with the four types of distance produced different results especially in case of developed vs. emerging host economies. Therefore, we argue that it is very difficult to give a generic statement about the influence of distance on CB acquisitions, as in certain cases, it can have positive influence.

Our study shows that despite the predominant negative connotation associated with distance, it can have positive effects in CB acquisitions at the presence of certain types of firms-specific resources. For example, the importance of host country experience is best illustrated in case of partial CB acquisitions in emerging economies where MNEs' generic international experience is less relevant. Particularly the effect of spatial distance should be considered in the specific context of host economies, for example, their level of economic development and stability. Introducing context explains the preference for high equity commitment in CB acquisitions by Finnish (European) MNEs in the geographically distant developed economies of Australia, Canada, and USA. High equity CB acquisitions in the emerging economies of Asia, Central and Eastern Europe, and Latin America were only registered in more recent times (from year 2000 onward), since they offered high growth opportunities and restrictions were relatively eased. Clearly distance is as a source of uncertainty, but it also presents a range of opportunities that can be utilized by implementing specific resources (financial as well as experiential). Therefore, we should not hastily conclude that entering distant markets happens primarily through low equity acquisitions, as distance is positively moderated by key resources applicable in international context. Finally, we should be cautious in generalizing the applicability of international experience as general international experience may be less useful in the context of partial CB acquisitions, as well as CB acquisitions undertaken in emerging economies.

Like all studies, our study has certain limitations. Firstly, this study only addresses CB acquisitions undertaken by Finnish MNEs. However, according to earlier research (e.g., Gabrielsson, Seppälä, & Gabrielsson, 2016; Nummela, Saarenketo, Jokela, & Loane, 2014), internationalization behavior of Finnish MNEs have been found to be representative of MNEs from small, open and highly internationalized economies (SMOPEC). Therefore, we believe in the generalizability of our findings. Secondly, we only considered three MNE resources (size, international experience, and host country experience) as potential moderators for equity commitment. Other MNE resources such as level of diversification, technological capabilities, and human capital can also potentially moderate certain influences of distance. We urge more research in the future that examines a broader set of conditions that would determine under what circumstances various types of distance would be beneficial or detrimental for CB acquisitions. Our study analyzed CB acquisitions in large and small host economies together. However, there can be potential differences in equity commitment by MNEs in CB acquisitions undertaken in large developed economies like USA, United Kingdom, France, Italy, Japan, and Germany or large emerging countries like the BRICS. Therefore, future studies should analyze differences in equity commitment in large and small host economies by bringing the discussion on the combined effects of distance and MNE resources in such context analysis. Finally, future studies can try to link equity commitment to subsequent performance of acquired subsidiaries by analyzing the performance differences in minority, majority, and full CB acquisitions in more or less distant locations.

REFERENCES

Ahammad, M. F., Tarba, S. Y., Liu, Y., Glaister, K. W., & Cooper, C. L. (2016). Exploring the factors influencing the negotiation process in cross-border M&A. *International Business Review*, *25*(2), 445–457.

Ahmadjian, C. L. (2016). Comparative institutional analysis and institutional complexity. *Journal of Management Studies*, *53*(1), 12–27.

Amemiya, T. (1981). Qualitative response models, a survey. *Journal of Economic Literature*, *4*(4), 1483–1536.

Anderson, J. (1979). A theoretical foundation for the gravity equation. *American Economic Review*, *69*(1), 106–116.

Anil, I., Tatoglu, E., & Ozkasap, G. (2014). Ownership and market entry mode choices of emerging country multinationals in a transition country, evidence from Turkish multinationals in Romania. *Journal for East European Management Studies*, *19* (4), 413–452.

Arslan, A., & Dikova, D. (2015). Influences of institutional distance and MNEs' host country experience on the ownership strategy in cross-border M&As in emerging economies. *Journal of Transnational Management*, *20*(4), 231–256.

Arslan, A., Tarba, S. Y., & Larimo, J. (2015). FDI entry strategies and the impacts of economic freedom distance, evidence from nordic FDIs in transitional periphery of CIS and SEE. *International Business Review*, *24*(6), 997–1008.

Aybar, B., & Ficici, A. (2009). Cross-border acquisitions and firm value, an analysis of emerging-market multinationals. *Journal of International Business Studies*, *40*(8), 1317–1338.

Barkema, H. G., Shenkar, O., Vermeulen, F., & Bell, J. H. (1997). Working abroad, working with others, how firms learn to operate international joint ventures. *Academy of Management Journal*, *40*(2), 426–442.

Beckerman, W. (1956). Distance and the pattern of intra-European trade. *The Review of Economics and Statistics*, *38*(1), 31–40.

Berry, H., Guillén, M. F., & Zhou, N. (2010). An institutional approach to cross-national distance. *Journal of International Business Studies*, *41*(9), 1460–1480.

Boussard, V. (2016). *Who creates value creation? Systems for measuring the value and growth of the mergers and acquisitions (M&A) market in France since the 1990s*. Retrieved from https,//hal.archives-ouvertes.fr/hal–01326238

Brouthers, K. D., & Brouthers, L. E. (2000). Acquisition or greenfield start-up? Institutional, cultural and transaction cost influences. *Strategic Management Journal*, *21*(1), 89–97.

Brummer, C. (2015). *Soft law and the global financial system, rule-making in the 21st century*. Cambridge: Cambridge University Press.

Buckley, P. J., Yu, P., Liu, Q., Munjal, S., & Tao, P. (2016). The institutional influence on the location strategies of multinational enterprises from emerging economies, evidence from China's cross-border mergers and acquisitions. *Management and Organization Review*, *12*(3), 425–445.

Caves, R. E. (1982). *Multinational enterprise and economic analysis*. Cambridge, MA: Cambridge University Press.

Chakrabarti, A., & Mitchell, W. (2013). The persistent effect of geographic distance in acquisition target selection. *Organization Science*, *24*(6), 1805–1826.

Chang, S. J., Chung, J., & Moon, J. J. (2013). When do wholly owned subsidiaries perform better than joint ventures? *Strategic Management Journal*, *34*(3), 317–337.

Chang, S. C., & Tsai, M. T. (2013). The effect of prior alliance experience on acquisition performance. *Applied Economics*, *45*(6), 765–773.

Chari, M. D. R., & Chang, K. (2009). Determinants of the share of equity sought in cross-border acquisitions. *Journal of International Business Studies*, *40* (8), 1277–1297.

Chen, S. F., & Hennart, J.-F. (2004). A hostage theory of joint ventures, why do Japanese investors choose partial over full acquisitions to enter the United States? *Journal of Business Research*, *57*(10), 1126–1134.

Chen, S. F., & Zeng, M. (2004). Japanese investors' choice of acquisitions vs. startups in the US, the role of reputation barriers and advertising outlays. *International Journal of Research in Marketing*, *21*(2), 123–136.

Chikhouni, A., Edwards, G., & Farashahi, M. (2017). Psychic distance and ownership in acquisition, direction matters. *Journal of International Management*, *23*, 32–42.

Choi, J. J., Lee, S. M., & Shoham, A. (2016). The effects of institutional distance on FDI inflow, general environmental institutions (GEI) versus minority investor protection institutions (MIP). *International Business Review*, *25*(1), 114–123.

Chung, C. C., Lee, S. H., Beamish, P. W. Southam, C., & Nam, D. D. (2013). Pitting real options theory against risk diversification theory, international diversification and joint ownership control in economic crisis. *Journal of World Business*, *48*(1), 122–136.

Clarke, J. E., Tamaschke, R., & Liesch, P. W. (2013). International experience in international business research, a conceptualization and exploration of key themes. *International Journal of Management Reviews*, *15*(3), 265–279.

Click, R. W. (2005). Financial and political risks in US direct foreign investment. *Journal of International Business Studies*, *36*(5), 559–575.

Collins, J. D., Holcomb, T. R., Certo, S. T., Hitt, M. A., & Lester, R. H. (2009). Learning by doing, cross-border mergers and acquisitions. *Journal of Business Research*, *62*(12), 1329–1334.

Contractor, F. J., Lahiri, S., Elango, B., & Kundu, S. K. (2014). Institutional, cultural and industry related determinants of ownership choices in emerging market FDI acquisitions. *International Business Review*, *23*(5), 931–941.

Cozza, C., Rabellotti, R., & Sanfilippo, M. (2015). The impact of outward FDI on the performance of Chinese firms. *China Economic Review*, *36*(1), 42–57.

Cuypers, I. R., Cuypers, Y., & Martin, X. (2016). When the target may know better, effects of experience and information asymmetries on value from mergers and acquisitions. *Strategic Management Journal*. Retrieved from http://onlinelibrary.wiley.com/doi/10.1002/smj.2502

Das, T. K., & Teng, B.-S. (2000). A resource-based theory of strategic alliances. *Journal of Management*, *26*(1), 31–61.

Demirbag, M., Tatoglu, E., & Glaister, K. W. (2009). Equity-based entry modes of emerging country multinationals, lessons from Turkey. *Journal of World Business*, *44*(4), 445–462.

Dikova, D., & Sahib, P. R. (2013). Is cultural distance a bane or a boon for cross-border acquisition performance? *Journal of World Business*, *48*(1), 77–86.

Dikova, D., Sahib, P. R., & Witteloostuijn, A. (2010). Cross-border acquisition abandonment and completion, the effect of institutional differences and organizational learning in the international business service industry, 1981–2001. *Journal of International Business Studies*, *41*(2), 223–245

Dow, D., & Larimo, J. (2011). Disentangling the roles of international experience and distance in establishment mode choice. *Management International Review*, *51*(3), 321–355.

Drogendijk, R., & Martín, O. M. (2015). Relevant dimensions and contextual weights of distance in international business decisions, evidence from Spanish and Chinese outward FDI. *International Business Review*, *24*(1), 133–147.

Drogendijk, R., & Slangen, A. (2006). Hofstede, Schwartz, or managerial perceptions? The effects of different cultural distance measures on establishment mode choices by multinational enterprises. *International Business Review*, *15*(4), 361–380.

Du, M., & Boateng, A. (2015). State ownership, institutional effects and value creation in cross-border mergers & acquisitions by Chinese firms. *International Business Review*, *24*(3), 430–442.

Fang, Y., Wade, M., Delios, A., & Beamish, P. W. (2013). An exploration of multinational enterprise knowledge resources and foreign subsidiary performance. *Journal of World Business*, *48*(1), 30–38.

Fillat, J. L., Garetto, S., & Oldenski, L. (2015). Diversification, cost structure, and the risk premium of multinational corporations. *Journal of International Economics*, *96*(1), 37–54.

Gabrielsson, M., Seppälä, T., & Gabrielsson, P. (2016). Realizing a hybrid competitive strategy and achieving superior financial performance while internationalizing in the high-technology market. *Industrial Marketing Management*, *54*(1), 141–153.

Gatignon, H., & Anderson, E. (1988). The multinational corporation's degree of control over foreign subsidiaries. An empirical test of a transaction cost explanation. *Journal of Law, Economics and Organization*, *4*(2), 305.

Gaur, A. S., Kumar, V., & Singh, D. (2014). Institutions, resources, and internationalization of emerging economy firms. *Journal of World Business*, *49*(1), 12–20.

Ghemawat, P. (2001). Distance still matters, the hard reality of global expansion. *Harvard Business Review*, *79*(8), 137–147.

Ghemawat, P. (2007). Why the world isn't flat. *Foreign Policy*, *159*, 54–60.

Globerman, S., & Shapiro, D. (2003). Governance infrastructure and US foreign direct investment. *Journal of International Business Studies*, *34*(1), 19–39.

Grosse, R., & Trevino, L. J. (1996). Foreign direct investment in the United States, an analysis by country of origin. *Journal of International Business Studies*, *27*(1), 139–155.

Gwartney, J. D. R., Lawson, S., & Hall, J. (2016). *Economic freedom of the world, 2016 Annual report*. Vancouver, BC: The Fraser Institute.

Hair, J. F. Jr., Anderson, R. E., Tatham, R. L., & Black, W. C. (2013). *Multivariate data analysis* (7th ed.). Upper Saddle River, NJ: Prentice Hall.

Hennart, J. F. (1991). A transaction costs theory of equity joint ventures, an empirical study of Japanese subsidiaries in the United States. *Strategic Management Journal*, *9*(4), 361–374.

Hennart, J. F., & Larimo, J. (1998). The impact of culture on the strategy of multinational enterprises, does national origin affect ownership decisions? *Journal of International Business Studies*, *29*(3), 515–538.

Hennart, J. F., & Park, Y. R. (1993). Greenfield vs. acquisition, the strategy of Japanese investors in the United States. *Management Science*, *39*(9), 1054–1070.

Hennart, J. F., Sheng, H. H., & Pimenta, G. (2015). Local complementary inputs as drivers of entry mode choices, the case of US investments in Brazil. *International Business Review*, *24*(3), 466–475.

Hofstede, G. (1984). *Culture's consequences, international differences in work-related values* (Vol. 5). Thousand Oaks, CA: Sage.

House, R. J., Hanges, P. J., Javidan, M., Dorfman, P. W., & Gupta, V. (2004). *Culture, leadership and organizations, the GLOBE study of 62 societies*. Thousand Oaks, CA: Sage Publications.

Johanson, J., & Vahlne, J. E. (1977). The internationalization process of the firm – A model of knowledge development and increasing foreign market commitments. *Journal of International Business Studies*, *8*(1), 23–32.

Kawai, N., & Strange, R. (2014). Subsidiary autonomy and performance in Japanese multinationals in Europe. *International Business Review*, *23*(3), 504–515.

Kaynak, E., Demirbag, M., & Tatoglu, E. (2007). Determinants of ownership-based entry mode choice of MNEs, evidence from Mongolia. *Management International Review*, *47*(4), 505–530.

Kim, W. C., & Hwang, P. (1992). Global strategy and multinational's entry mode choice. *Journal of International Business Studies*, *23*(1), 29–53.

Kogut, B., & Singh, H. (1988). The effect of national culture on the choice of entry mode. *Journal of International Business Studies*, *19*(3), 411–432.

Kostova, T. (1999). Transnational transfer of strategic organizational practices, a contextual perspective. *Academy of Management Review*, *24*(3), 308–324.

Kostova, T., & Zaheer, S. (1999). Organizational legitimacy under conditions of complexity, the case of the multinational enterprise. *Academy of Management Review*, *24*(1), 64–81.

Kuo, C. L., & Fang, W. C. (2009). Psychic distance and FDI location choice, empirical examination of Taiwanese firms in China. *Asia Pacific Management Review*, *14*(1), 85–106.

Larimo, J. (2003). Form of investment by nordic firms in world markets. *Journal of Business Research*, *56*(10), 791–803.

Larimo, J., & Arslan, A. (2013). Determinants of foreign direct investment ownership mode choice, evidence from nordic investments in central and eastern Europe. *Journal for East European Management Studies*, *18*(2), 232–263.

Lee, Y., Hemmert, M., & Kim, J. (2014). What drives the international ownership strategies of Chinese firms? The role of distance and home country institutional factors in outward acquisition. *Asian Business and Management*, *13*(3), 197–2125.

Li, Y., & Li, H. (2014). FDI spillovers over time in an emerging market, the roles of entry tenure and barriers to imitation. *Academy of Management Journal*, *57*(3), 698–722.

Li, P. Y., & Meyer, K. E. (2009). Contextualizing experience effects in international business, a study of ownership strategies. *Journal of World Business*, *44*(4), 370–382.

Lindsay, V. J., Rod, M., & Ashill, N. (2015). SME entry into an emerging market, a resource-based and institutional approach. Retrieved from http://www.ro.uow.edu.au/cgi/viewcontent.cgi?article=1698&context=dubaipapers.

López-Duarte, C., & Vidal-Suárez, M. M. (2013). Cultural distance and the choice between wholly owned subsidiaries and joint ventures. *Journal of Business Research*, *66*(11), 2252–2261.

Lu, Y., Karpova, E. E., & Fiore, A. M. (2011). Factors influencing international fashion retailers' entry mode choice. *Journal of Fashion Marketing and Management*, *15*(1), 58–75.

Malhotra, S. (2012). Geographic distance as a moderator of curvilinear relationship between cultural distance and shared ownership. *Canadian Journal of Administrative Sciences*, *29*(3), 218–230.

Malhotra, S., & Gaur, A. S. (2014). Spatial geography and control in foreign acquisitions. *Journal of International Business Studies*, *45*(2), 191–210.

Malhotra, S., Sivakumar, K., & Zhu, P. (2009). Distance factors and target market selection, the moderating effects of market potential. *International Market Review*, *26*(6), 651–673.

Malhotra, S., Sivakumar, K., & Zhu, P. (2011). A comparative analysis of the role of national culture on foreign market acquisitions by US firms and firms from emerging countries. *Journal of Business Research*, *64*(7), 714–722.

Mazon, G., Silva, F. M., Ferreira, M. P., & Serra, F. R. (2017). Knowledge motives in the cross-border acquisitions, a case research of three Brazilian multinationals. *Management Research, Journal of the Iberoamerican Academy of Management*, *15*(1), 15–37.

Meschi P.-X. (2005). Environmental uncertainty and survival of international joint ventures, the case of political and economic risk in emerging countries. *European Management Review*, *2*(2), 143–152.

Newmeyer, C. E., Swaminathan, V., & Hulland, J. (2016). When products and brands trade hands, a framework for acquisition success. *Journal of Marketing Theory and Practice*, *24*(2), 129–146.

North, D. C. (1981). *Structure and change in economic history*. Norton.

North, D. C. (1990). *Institutions, institutional change and economic performance*. Cambridge, MT: Cambridge University Press.

Nummela, N., Saarenketo, S., Jokela, P., & Loane, S. (2014). Strategic decision-making of a born global, a comparative study from three small open economies. *Management International Review*, *54*(4), 527–550.

Pallant, J. (2007). *SPSS survival manual, a step by step guide to data analysis using SPSS for windows*. Buckingham, Open University Press.

Piaskowska, D., & Trojanowski, G. (2014). Twice as smart? The importance of managers' formative-years' international experience for their international orientation and foreign acquisition decisions. *British Journal of Management*, *25*(1), 40–57.

Ragozzino, A. P. R. (2009). The effects of geographic distance on the foreign acquisition activity of US firms. *Management International Review*, *49*(4), 509–535.

Ragozzino, R., & Reuer, J. J. (2011). Geographic distance and corporate acquisitions, signals from IPO firms. *Strategic Management Journal*, *32*(8), 876–894.

Reuer, J. J., Tong, T. W., Tyler, B. B., & Ariño, A. (2013). Executive preferences for governance modes and exchange partners, an information economics perspective. *Strategic Management Journal*, *34*(9), 1104–1122.

Richman, B. M., & Copen, M. R. (1972). International management and economic development. *Thunderbird International Business Review*, *14*(4), 2–3.

Schwartz, S. H. (1992). Universals in the content and structure of values, theoretical advances and empirical tests in 20 cultures. In M. P. Zanna (Ed.), *Advances in experimental social psychology* (Vol. 25, pp. 1–65). San Diego, CA: Academic Press.

Shaver, J., & Flyer, F. (2000). Agglomeration economies, firm heterogeneity, and foreign direct investment in the United States. *Strategic Management Journal*, *21*(12), 1175–1193.

Shaver, J., Mitchell, W., & Yeung, B. (1997). The effect of own-firm and other-firm experience on foreign direct investment survival in the United States, 1987–92. *Strategic Management Journal*, *18*(10), 811–824

Slangen, A. H. L., & Hennart, J.-F. (2008) Do multinationals really prefer to enter culturally distant countries through greenfields rather than through acquisitions? The role of parent experience and subsidiary autonomy. *Journal of International Business Studies*, *39*(3), 472–490.

Stahl, G., Björkman, I., Farndale, E., Orris, S., Paauwe, J., Stiles, P., & Wright, P. M. (2012). Leveraging your talent, six principles of effective global talent management. *Sloan Management Review*, *53*(2), 25–42.

Stahl, G. K., Tung, R. L., Kostova, T., & Zellmer-Bruhn, M. (2016). Widening the lens, rethinking distance, diversity, and foreignness in international business research through positive organizational scholarship. *Journal of International Business Studies*, *47*(6), 621–630.

Tang, L. (2012). The direction of cultural distance on FDI, attractiveness or incongruity? *Cross Cultural Management, An International Journal*, *19*(2), 233–256.

Taylor, C. R., Zou, S., & Osland, G. E. (2000). Foreign market entry strategies of Japanese MNCs. *International Marketing Review*, *17*(2), 146–163.

Tsang, E. W. K., & Yip, P. S. L. (2007). Economic distance and survival of foreign direct investments. *Academy of Management Journal*, *50*(5), 1156–1168.

UNCTAD (2016). *World investment report 2016 (investor nationality and policy challenges)*. Geneva: United Nations Publications.

Vernon, R. (1966). International investment and international trade in the product cycle. *The Quarterly Journal of Economics*, *80*(2), 190–207.

Williams, D. W., & Gregoire, D. A. (2015). Seeking commonalities or avoiding differences? Re-conceptualizing distance and its effects on internationalization decisions. *Journal of International Business Studies*, *46*(3), 253–284.

Wetherill, G. B. (1986). *Regression analysis with applications*. London: Chapman and Hall.

Wooster, R. B., Blanco, L., & Sawyer, W. C. (2016). Equity commitment under uncertainty, A hierarchical model of real option entry mode choices. *International Business Review*, *25*(1), 382–394.

Xie, E., Reddy, K. S. & Liang, J. (2017). Country-specific determinants of cross-border mergers and acquisitions, A comprehensive review and future research directions. *Journal of World Business*, *52*(2), 127–183.

Xu, D., & Meyer, K. E. (2013). Linking theory and context, "Strategy research in emerging economies" after Wright et al. (2005). *Journal of Management Studies*, *50*(7), 1322–1346.

Xu, D., & Shenkar, O. (2002). Institutional distance and the multinational enterprise. *Academy of Management Review*, *27*(4), 608–618.

Yan, A., & Luo, Y. (2016). *International joint ventures, theory and practice*. London: Routledge.

Zaheer, S., Schomaker, M. S., & Nachum, L. (2012). Distance without direction, Restoring credibility to a much-loved construct. *Journal of International Business Studies*, *43*(1), 18–27.

Zhu, P., & Dutta, S. (2011). Partial acquisition, motivation and consequences on firm performance. In H. K. Baker, & H. Kiymaz (Eds.), *The art of capital restructuring, Creating shareholder value through mergers and acquisitions*. Hoboken, NJ: John Wiley & Sons, Inc.

PART IV
THE VALUE OF DISTANCE

CHAPTER 14

THE GEOGRAPHY OF INTERNATIONAL KNOWLEDGE SOURCING: LOOKING BACK AND MOVING FORWARD

Alessandra Perri and Grazia D. Santangelo

ABSTRACT

Multinational corporations (MNCs) have increasingly sourced knowledge across borders, and foreign subsidiaries operations have played a critical role in MNC international knowledge sourcing strategies. The growing responsibility of foreign subsidiaries has paralleled an interest on the geography of this phenomenon by international business and international management scholars. In this chapter, we review this research. In addition, based on recent research in economics and management drawing on economic geography and innovation studies, we highlight possible avenues of research to enrich our understanding of the geographical aspects of international knowledge sourcing. In particular, we suggest three lines of research opportunities. A first opportunity relates to the explicit consideration of distance and border effects. A further research opportunity arises from investigating the geographical distance of heterogeneous host country knowledge sources from the foreign subsidiary. A final research opportunity we discuss

Distance in International Business: Concept, Cost and Value
Progress in International Business Research, Volume 12, 341–361

ISSN: 1745-8862/doi:10.1108/S1745-886220170000012015

is about the contribution of heterogeneous host country knowledge sources to the variety of knowledge developed by the foreign subsidiary.

Keywords: International knowledge sourcing; foreign subsidiary; geography

1. INTRODUCTION

Sourcing knowledge across borders is a major strategy of multinational corporations (MNCs), which geographically disperse their research and development (R&D) activities to tap into novel ideas and capabilities where these are created and available (Cantwell & Santangelo, 1999; Singh, 2008). Initially questioned (Patel & Pavitt, 1991), the magnitude of this phenomenon has been amplified by the diffusion of Information and Communications Technology (ICT) technologies and the opportunities of knowledge sourcing offered by the availability of talents in emerging markets (Lewin, Massini, & Peeters, 2009; Santangelo, 2001).

Within the MNC, knowledge-sourcing efforts are usually demanded to foreign subsidiary operations (Bartlett & Ghoshal, 1986; Frost, Birkinshaw, & Ensign, 2002; Gupta & Govindarajan, 1994). These operations are increasingly designed to enhance linkages with external knowledge sources and access new knowledge in the respective host countries in order to contribute to MNC innovation performance (Almeida, 1996; Singh, 2007). To this end, foreign subsidiaries are eager to maximize incoming knowledge spillovers and minimizing outgoing knowledge spillovers when relating to local knowledge sources and partners (Alcacer, 2006; Perri & Andersson, 2014; Santangelo, 2012). Such a tension reflects on MNC location strategies because the ability to source knowledge critically depends on the geographical distance from the host country knowledge sources (Almeida, 1996; Criscuolo, Narula, & Verspagen, 2005; Frost, 2001). Proximity eases access and monitoring of local knowledge development and, at the same time, may favor unintended knowledge spillovers to nearby firms (Cantwell & Santangelo, 2002; Narula & Santangelo, 2009; Santangelo, 2012; Perri, Andersson, Nell, & Santangelo, 2013), adversely affecting the innovation performance of co-located firms (Lahiri, 2010). If the role of geography may be moderated by the quality of local institutions offering safeguards against local knowledge leakages (Santangelo, Meyer, & Jindra, 2016), still geography and geographical distance bear strategic relevance for the success of international knowledge sourcing.

Traditionally, international business and international management scholars have investigated external knowledge sourcing by foreign subsidiaries mainly in terms of comparison between home and host country knowledge sourcing (Almeida, 1996; Criscuolo et al., 2005; Frost, 2001) or have focused on specific features of the host country as a whole (Almeida & Phene, 2004). More recently geography has been in the spotlight in research on international knowledge sourcing in connection to opportunities and challenges associated to R&D offshoring in emerging markets (D'Agostino, Laursen, & Santangelo, 2013; D'Agostino & Santangelo, 2012; Piscitello & Santangelo, 2009). In less and more recent studies, geographical distance between the subsidiary and the external sources has been accounted for in terms of co-location of source and recipient (Almeida, Dokko, & Rosenkopf, 2003; Frost, 2001) or has been associated with challenges/opportunities for complementarity/substitution between host and home country knowledge creation.

We believe that there is scope to further extend our understanding and conceptualization of geography and geographical distance in connection with international knowledge sourcing to better grasp the implications for subsidiary and MNC innovation performance. In particular, we suggest that fresh insights can be offered by recent research in economics and management drawing on economic geography and innovation studies. To this end, we offer a critical review of these streams of research to ultimately identify elements that may help refine the conceptualization of geography and geographical distance in international business and international management. Based on this review, we then identify research questions that can advance our understanding of the role of geography and geographical distance in international knowledge sourcing.

The chapter is organized into five sections. In the next section, we offer a critical overview of the knowledge sourcing literature in international business and international management. In Section 3, we focus on the specific role of geography and geographical distance in international knowledge sourcing to pinpoint how international business and international management scholars have accounted for geography and geographical distance. In Section 4, we take the discussion further by looking at research in other research fields to grasp the conceptualization of the two constructs in connection with cross-border knowledge sourcing. Section 5 concludes our discussion by highlighting future avenues of investigation that may help advance international knowledge sourcing research in business and international management.

2. SOURCING KNOWLEDGE ACROSS BORDERS

Originally regarded as "an important case of non-globalization" (Patel & Pavitt, 1991, p. 1), the production of technology by MNCs has over time become more internationally dispersed. A significant number of foreign R&D subsidiaries are increasingly established to target very specific locales, to which they are attracted by the availability of distinct technological profiles and where they engage in a broad spectrum of activities (Dunning & Lundan, 2008; Florida, 1997). This trend reflects in the qualitative evolution of subsidiary operations, and in the heterogeneity of foreign subsidiaries in sourcing knowledge.

2.1 The Evolution of Foreign Subsidiary Operations

In the past, the establishment of foreign subsidiaries with R&D responsibilities was mainly motivated by the willingness to exploit a firm's domestic advantages abroad (Cantwell, 1995). This type of technological activity performed by these units was adaptive and its locational patterns followed primarily the MNC foreign market priorities. Over time, the motivation behind the MNC choice to internationalize its R&D activities has changed. MNCs have identified opportunities for enriching, rather than just exploiting, their technological base abroad, in accordance with the comparative advantages available in different potential host countries (Cantwell, 1989, 1995; Cantwell & Janne, 1999; Pearce, 1999; Pearce & Papanastassiou, 1997). As a consequence, nowadays foreign R&D subsidiaries are increasingly responsible for tapping into the knowledge endowment of their host locations in order to ensure that new sources of technological advantage, in addition to those that can be found in the home country, can nourish the MNC technological position (Cantwell, 1995; Florida, 1997).

The evolution from a merely adaptive, demand-driven R&D responsibility toward more creative and supply-driven technological activities in foreign subsidiaries has been widely documented in international business literature. Since the early 1990s, an array of classifications has been proposed to highlight the existence of different types of foreign subsidiaries. Hakånson and Nobel (1993) distinguish the *research unit* type from the traditional *market-oriented* and *production support units* as a subsidiary located in a foreign site with the distinctive strategic objective of acquiring local knowledge irrespective of the presence of any other manufacturing or commercial operations of the MNC. A multitude of studies have then further qualified R&D units as units committed to scan and monitor the local knowledge environment (i.e., *listening post*) *versus* those committed to the generation of new knowledge through the leverage of local technological resources (i.e., *generation station*) (Graham, 1992). This distinction echoes the separation between *research-oriented* and *local-support-oriented* (Iwasa & Odagiri, 2004), *home base exploiting* and *home base augmenting* (Kuemmerle, 1997), and more recently between *competence-creating* and *competence-exploiting* (Cantwell & Mudambi, 2005) subsidiaries.

More articulated taxonomies have disentangled the *international creator*, which performs an active role in both upstream and downstream innovation activities and maintains direct relationships with the central R&D offices, and those units defined as *local* or *international adaptors*, whose R&D activities are mainly driven by the needs to adapt to the specificities of the foreign demand (Birkinshaw & Hood, 1998). An equally elaborated taxonomy concerns the distinction between *research*, *development* of new products and processes, and *adaptation* to customers' needs (Dunning & Narula, 1995; Le Bas & Sierra, 2002; Pearce, 1999; Pearce & Papanastassiou, 1999).

2.2 Heterogeneity of Foreign Subsidiaries

The increasing responsibilities of foreign subsidiaries toward knowledge sourcing have spurred interest in the heterogeneity of foreign subsidiaries along at least three dimensions.

A first dimension concerns the subsidiary's capabilities to identify and absorb relevant knowledge from both internal and external repositories and to combine it creatively with its own technology base (Phene & Almeida, 2008). These capabilities, defined as *sourcing* and *combinative* capabilities, are a driver of greater subsidiary heterogeneity within industries and host countries. Subsidiary technological capabilities have also been related to the intensity of knowledge sourcing from the host location. In particular, Song, Asakawa, and Chu (2011) suggest that the relationship between them is inverted U-shaped because an appropriate level of technological capabilities is essential to effectively assimilate host country knowledge, but highly capable subsidiaries tend to source knowledge also beyond the boundaries of the host location in order to evolve from local into global innovators. The critical role of capabilities also reflects in the analysis of Collinson and Wang (2012), who suggest that the existence of subsidiary-specific skills in the design of the subsidiary linkages portfolio affects the extent to which foreign units are able to take advantage of the expertise residing in the host location and in their firm-internal network. Focusing on a sample of foreign MNC subsidiaries based in Taiwan, the authors show that, even when sharing the same industry background and host country, different foreign units evolve along different paths of specialization, partly due to a heterogeneous leverage of internal and external linkages and sources.

A further dimension that contributes to the differential ability to source knowledge by foreign subsidiaries connects to the subsidiary's local embeddedness, intended as the involvement in a network of linkages with the local technical and scientific community (Song et al., 2011). Subsidiary embeddedness is a key enabler of knowledge sourcing because the different types of relationships subsidiaries maintain with local partners act as rich communication channels, through which knowledge can flow from the external environment into the subsidiary to nurture its technological competences (Cantwell & Mudambi, 2011; Gnyawali & Hatfield, 2007; Song et al., 2011). Greater integration in the local network increases significantly over time the reliance of subsidiaries on the local knowledge contexts (Phene & Almeida, 2003). In a similar vein, Li, Poppo, and Zhou (2010) show that both relational and contractual mechanisms that govern a subsidiary's linkages with its local partners play a significant role in the subsidiary's ability to acquire codified and tacit knowledge from the host country.

Ultimately, governance and organizational attributes at the subsidiary and MNC level have been associated with the subsidiary ability to relate to the local context and effectively source knowledge. The presence of a heterogeneous subsidiary top management team enables to activate more diverse local relationships and, hence, enhances the subsidiary ability to tap into localized pockets of knowledge and expertise. Also, an entrepreneurial corporate culture tends to trigger a favorable environment for stimulating learning practices (Gnyawali & Hatfield, 2007).

3. THE GEOGRAPHY OF INTERNATIONAL KNOWLEDGE SOURCING

The role of geography in international knowledge sourcing by foreign subsidiaries has been investigated in connection with the dichotomy home–host country (Cantwell & Santangelo, 1999; Criscuolo et al., 2005; Frost, 2001; Phene & Almeida, 2008) or in the context of the host country/region to observe the patterns of local knowledge flows (Almeida, 1996; Almeida & Phene, 2004; Perri & Andersson, 2014; Phene & Almeida, 2003; Singh, 2007).

Also, the geographical dimension has been more explicitly investigated in connection with the opportunities and challenges associated with localized knowledge spillovers.

A common feature of these studies is that the geographical distance between the subsidiary and its knowledge sources has been conceptualized primarily in terms of co-location *versus* non-co-location of source and recipient (Almeida, 1996; Almeida & Phene, 2004; Criscuolo et al., 2005; Frost; 2001; Phene & Almeida, 2008; Singh, 2007).

In what follows we review these streams of research.

3.1 Home–Host Country Dichotomy

Subsidiary knowledge sources have been traditionally identified based on the distinctiveness of MNC subsidiary organizational context that offers the opportunity to span both organizational and geographical boundaries (Almeida & Phene, 2004; Perri, 2015). Every foreign subsidiary is simultaneously part of an internal and an external network (Almeida & Phene, 2004; Frost, 2001; Zanfei, 2000). The internal network relates to the MNC organizational network, which consists of the headquarters (HQ) located in the home country and the sister units potentially located in the home and in a variety of host countries. The external network relates to the local knowledge network, which consists of external firms and other actors in the host country (e.g., competitors, suppliers, distributors, universities and research centers, and any other member of the local technological community). This double organizational embeddedness reflects on the privileged access of foreign subsidiaries to both *MNC-external, locally embedded* knowledge sources and *MNC-internal, globally dispersed* knowledge sources (Phene and Almeida, 2008).

Based on this distinction, research has investigated the extent to which foreign subsidiaries rely on one over the other type of source.

Foreign subsidiaries seem to draw more on host country knowledge sources when the MNC relies on foreign units to overcome domestic technological weaknesses by tapping into globally distributed areas of technological excellence (Cantwell, 1989; Dunning & Narula, 1995; Kuemmerle, 1997). Drawing on a sample of US-based greenfield subsidiaries, Frost (2001) suggests that foreign subsidiaries are more likely to source local knowledge when they innovate in technical domains in which the host country and the home country exhibit, respectively, an advantage and a disadvantage. More creative subsidiaries then rely more on host country knowledge sources. Also, a subsidiary's innovation in technical fields in which it enjoys a leadership position within the MNC is associated with a more extensive leverage of the host country knowledge. In a similar vein, Cantwell and Santangelo (1999) point out that MNCs use their foreign subsidiaries to source even highly tacit technologies, such as those encompassing a heavy reliance on science, particularly when the foreign location provides access to a locally embedded sectoral specialization.

Yet, Criscuolo et al. (2005) argue that the extent to which foreign subsidiaries source knowledge from the host *versus* the home country may depend on the marginal costs of maintaining integration in the home country against the marginal costs of integrating into a new location. In their analysis of foreign R&D subsidiaries of European and US firms operating, respectively, in the United States and Europe, they found that subsidiaries rely more on the home country knowledge base, although they also source knowledge from the host country. This conclusion is qualified by Awate, Larsen, and Mudambi (2015) who contrast the R&D internationalization of advanced country and emerging country MNCs in relation to the knowledge sourcing behavior of their foreign R&D subsidiaries. They suggest that the extent to which foreign subsidiaries rely more on home *versus* host country knowledge critically depends on the relative sophistication of technological resources and knowledge they can access in each of the two locations. Hence, sourcing home country knowledge from the HQ is more valuable to foreign R&D subsidiaries of advanced country MNCs investing in emerging countries, particularly in the first stages of their life cycle when they often serve as competence exploiting units, and less to foreign R&D subsidiaries of emerging country MNCs investing in advanced countries, which usually possess a more advanced technology than the HQ. Phene and Almeida (2008) explore the home–host country dichotomy in relation with the subsidiary innovation performance and find that, while sourcing knowledge from the host country and from home-based external organizations positively contributes to the scale and quality of their innovation, sourcing knowledge from the HQ has no effect on the subsidiary innovative performance. Phene and Almeida (2003) analyze this phenomenon dynamically and find that, as subsidiaries mature, they rely increasingly more both on the home country knowledge from the HQ and on host country technology sources.

In addition to assessig the extent of home and host country knowledge sources, scholars have zoomed in knowledge sourcing in the host country to evaluate the net knowledge sourcing benefit foreign subsidiaries enjoy when relating with local actors. Observing a set of foreign subsidiaries operating in the United States, Almeida (1996) shows that foreign subsidiaries both give and get more knowledge to and from the host location than it could be predicted based on the geographic distribution of innovative activities in the industry. Instead, using a larger sample of knowledge flows between foreign MNC subsidiaries and domestic companies in 30 countries, Singh (2007) demonstrates not only that MNC subsidiaries draw extensively on the knowledge embedded in the host country but also that the flow of knowledge from host country organizations to foreign subsidiaries is substantially greater than the knowledge flowing in the opposite direction.

3.2 The Role of Localized Knowledge Spillovers

A major premise of international knowledge sourcing research is that knowledge stays to some extent confined within geographic boundaries (Almeida, 1996; Singh, 2008). The location-bound nature of knowledge and knowledge-related assets motivates the establishment of foreign subsidiaries where relevant knowledge is created in the attempt to benefit from localized knowledge spillovers (Almeida & Kogut, 1999; Audretsch & Feldman, 1996; Feldman, 1994; Jaffe, Trajtenberg, & Henderson, 1993). Geographical proximity is generally associated with the sharing of a common social context (Gertler, 2003), which facilitates the establishment and the coordination of linkages through personal interactions and face-to-face contacts (Storper & Venables, 2004; Zucker, Darby, & Armstrong, 1998). These linkages favor knowledge sourcing because they improve a firm's ability to recognize and assess the characteristics of knowledge (Tallman & Phene, 2007) and to effectively assimilate it, especially when it is highly tacit (Gertler, 2003; Howells, 2006; Morgan, 2004; Storper, 1997).

Geographical distance offers opportunities to source diverse knowledge to the extent that countries develop idiosyncratic patterns of technological specialization, which remain relatively stable over time and become increasingly distinctive (Cantwell, 1989; Lundvall, 1992; Nelson, 1993; Patel & Pavitt, 1994). This cross-country variation in technological specialization creates incentives for MNCs to gain access to technological inputs that are different from those available in the home country (Almeida, 1996; Almeida & Phene, 2004; Bartholomew, 1997; Frost, 2001; Phene & Almeida, 2008; Singh, 2008). Cantwell and Janne (1999) show that, driven by the willingness to access to the host country technological expertise, leading MNCs carry out innovative activities abroad in areas that are substantially different from their domestic technological strengths. Hence, they point to the existence of a hierarchy of national locations that contributes to explain the patterns of technological specialization of foreign subsidiaries. Almeida and Phene (2004) add to this stream of literature by demonstrating that not only the establishment of local knowledge linkages, but also the host country's technological richness and diversity matter for subsidiary knowledge sourcing and, in turn, for its innovative performance. More recently, the idea that geography reflects differences in technological specialization across location has been revamped by research on the opportunities and challenges of R&D offshoring in emerging markets (D'Agostino & Santangelo, 2012; D'Agostino et al., 2013; Piscitello & Santangelo 2009). Adopting the region as a level of analysis that more effectively than the country captures the systemic dynamics underlying the innovation process (Braczyk, Cooke, & Heidenreich, 1998), D'Agostino and Santangelo (2012) and D'Agostino et al. (2013) show that international knowledge sourcing from advanced country regions in emerging countries are beneficial to the extent that the geographical distance between source and destination region reflects differences in technological and R&D activity specialization. In other words, the authors point to the existence of a complementarity relationship between R&D offshoring in specific technologies and activities, and home R&D.

Yet, reaching out geographically distant locations with the strategic intent to source complementary knowledge exposes foreign subsidiaries to the risks of knowledge leakages, which geographical proximity amplifies. Local knowledge spillovers are bi-directional (Alcacer & Chung, 2007; Shaver & Flyer, 2000). They generate opportunities for effective knowledge sourcing and, at the same time, activate channels for unintended knowledge spillovers to nearby agents (Cantwell & Santangelo, 2002; Narula & Santangelo, 2009; Perri & Andersson, 2014; Perri et al., 2013). Foreign subsidiaries then confront with a tension of maximizing incoming knowledge spillovers from the local environment, while minimizing outgoing spillovers that erode the subsidiary technology-based competitive advantages (Alcacer & Chung, 2007; Santangelo, 2012). In this perspective, the role of geography has been investigated in connection with the competitive dynamics animating a subsidiary's host location.

Research emphasizing the concerns of knowledge protection by MNCs clustering into foreign locations (also referred to as the "strategic deterrence" thesis) has argued that tension between a MNC's willingness to tap into local sources of knowledge and the need to protect its own technology from unwanted dissemination is first governed at the HQ level through location choices (Alcacer & Chung, 2007). Not surprisingly, technologically advanced MNCs avoid establishing their subsidiaries in areas of intense industrial activity to minimize close contacts with competitors. Also, they cherry-pick a number of selected locations featuring high levels of academic innovative activities, where outgoing knowledge spillovers would not represent a serious competitive risk (Alcacer & Chung, 2007). While location choices are a one-shot tool for strategically managing the balance between sourcing and protecting knowledge, the relationship between a foreign subsidiary and its location is not immutable, with brand-new opportunities and threats possibly emerging after the subsidiary has been established in a given location. Consistent with this idea, a number of studies have highlighted that, once the location decision is made at the corporate level, also subsidiaries take an active role in this realm, and try to govern the trade-off between sourcing and protecting knowledge (Perri & Andersson, 2014; Perri et al., 2013; Santangelo, 2012), for instance through a careful design of their relationships with local partners (Narula & Santangelo, 2009).

Challenging the conclusions of the strategic deterrence thesis, the "physical attraction" perspective suggests that, far from being deterred from entry into locations featuring high industrial activity, dominant foreign MNCs enjoy a privileged local position because their technological capabilities generate relational advantages that positively affect their ability to absorb relevant knowledge from local sources (Cantwell & Mudambi, 2011). Yet, a high *concentration* of industrial activity where the dominant position is held by a local firm results in a local innovation network closed to outsiders, and in a lower range of opportunities for linkages and spillovers to foreign subsidiaries (Cantwell & Mudambi, 2011).

Table 1 summarizes the lines of research reviewed in this section by highlighting the nature of the empirical methodology (qualitative vs. quantitative), the type of data used, the level of analysis, the focus of the study, the geographical unit, and the conceptualization of geography adopted in the study, and time dimension of the empirical setting.

4. INSIGHTS ON THE ROLE OF GEOGRAPHY FROM OTHER RESEARCH FIELDS

The role of geography in connection with international knowledge sourcing hinges upon the importance of localized knowledge spillovers, which has found support in a broad range of disciplines including economic geography and innovation studies, to name a few. The widespread interest for this concept lies in that spillovers are key to new knowledge generation and innovation and, in turn, to economic growth (Belenzon & Schankerman, 2013; Singh & Marx, 2013).

Table 1. Literature on the Geography of Knowledge Sourcing by Foreign Subsidiaries.

	Authors and Year	Methodology	Data	Level of Analysis[a]	Focus	Geographical Unit[a]	Period
Home-host country dichotomy	Almeida, 1996	Quantitative	Patent data	Citation	Local learning and contributing patterns by foreign subsidiaries	Country and region	1980–1990
	Frost, 2001	Quantitative	Patent data	Citation	Geography of subsidiary knowledge sourcing	Country	1980–1990
	Cantwell & Santangelo, 1999	Quantitative	Patent data	Region	Subsidiary sourcing of highly tacit knowledge in the host location	Country	1969–1995
	Phene & Almeida, 2003	Quantitative	Patent data	Subsidiary	Subsidiary evolution and host country knowledge sourcing	Country	1981–1992
	Criscuolo et al., 2005	Quantitative	Patent data	Subsidiary	Subsidiary reliance on host vs. home country knowledge sources	Macro-region	1995–1997
	Singh, 2007	Quantitative	Patent data	Citation	Knowledge spillovers between MNCs and host country firms	Country	1986–1995
	Phene & Almeida, 2008	Quantitative	Patent data	Subsidiary	Subsidiary knowledge assimilation, capabilities and innovation performance	Country	1981–1992
	Awate et al., 2015	Qualitative	Case study and patent data	Firm	Home/host country knowledge sourcing by advanced and emerging MNCs	Country	1970s–2011

Role of localized knowledge spillovers	Cantwell & Janne, 1999	Quantitative	Patent data	National group of firms	Geographical and sectoral dispersion of MNCs' technological activity	Country	1969–1995
	Cantwell & Santangelo, 2002	Quantitative	Patent data	Region	Co-location and co-specialization of corporate R&D	Region	1969–1995
	Almeida & Phene, 2004	Quantitative	Patent data	Subsidiary	Features of host country and subsidiary knowledge creation	Country	1981–1992
	Alcacer & Chung, 2007	Quantitative	Patent and FDI data	Firm	Bi-directionality of knowledge spillovers and location choices	Region	1985–1994
	Narula & Santangelo, 2009	Quantitative	Alliances and patent data	Alliance	Co-location and the propensity to engage in R&D alliances	Country and region	1978–1995
	Cantwell & Mudambi, 2011	Quantitative	Survey data and patent data	Subsidiary	Technological heterogeneity and subsidiary knowledge sourcing	Country and region	1995
	D'Agostino & Santangelo, 2012	Quantitative	Patent and FDI project data	Region	Complementarity between home and host R&D investment (activity and sector)	Region	2003–2007
	Santangelo, 2012	Quantitative & Qualitative	Survey data and case study	Subsidiary	Local competition and subsidiary embeddedness	Region	2004–2005
	D'Agostino et al., 2013	Quantitative	Patent and FDI project data	Region	Complementarity between home and host R&D investment (sector)	Region	2003–2007
	Perri et al., 2013	Quantitative	Survey data	Subsidiary	Bi-directionality of knowledge spillovers and subsidiary local linkages	Country	1990–2005
	Perri & Andersson, 2014	Quantitative	Patent data	Subsidiary	Local knowledge sourcing and spillovers by foreign subsidiaries	Region	1990–2005

Note: [a]"Region" refers to subnational spatial units (i.e., metropolitan statistical area, state, etc.).

Recently, research in economics and management drawing on economic geography and innovation studies has provided a significant contribution to our understanding of the geography of knowledge spillovers. In these fields two important geographic dimensions that shape knowledge spillovers have been refined: (1) the multi-level character of the border effects that contribute to define the geographic scope of knowledge spillovers (Belenzon & Schankerman, 2013; Singh & Marx, 2013; Toedtling, Grillitsch, & Hoeglinger, 2012) and (2) the continuous nature of spatial distance as a determinant of the spillover decay effect (Belenzon & Schankerman, 2013; Singh & Marx, 2013).

The first dimension deals with the realm of the different geopolitical borders that are likely to constrain the spatial diffusion of knowledge. Traditionally the focus has been on national boundaries, and knowledge spillovers have been considered as a country-level phenomenon (Branstetter, 2001; Jaffe & Trajtenberg, 2002; Keller, 2002; Singh, 2007). The reason behind the popularity of national borders in empirical research on spillovers lies in that national borders usually differentiate territories in terms of languages, culture, economic, and political institutions (Belenzon & Schankerman, 2013; Singh & Marx, 2013), which are widely recognized as critical aspects that influence the degree to which actors can interact and communicate effectively to facilitate the dissemination of knowledge.

A second group of studies have considered more fine-grained spatial units, such as the state (Audretsch & Feldman, 1996; Jaffe, 1989; Rosenthal & Strange, 2001) or the metropolitan area (Almeida & Kogut, 1999; Tallman & Phene, 2007), in accordance with the regional system of innovation approach (Asheim & Gertler, 2005; Braczyk et al., 1998; Morgan, 2004). These studies have suggested that it is in these less aggregated areas that social and organizational relationships that are more conducive to knowledge diffusion take place.

The arguments supporting the relevance of national and regional borders are both plausible. Yet, the prevailing approach in the empirical literature has long been the use of a single geographic unit of analysis. Even in studies that employ different spatial scales, geopolitical borders are in reality considered disjointedly (Almeida, 1996; Jaffe et al., 1993) rather than simultaneously (Singh & Marx, 2013).

A number of studies have recently underlined the methodological weakness of this approach based on empirical evidence (Belenzon & Schankerman, 2013; Singh & Marx, 2013). Rather uncontroversial findings show that country borders significantly limit the diffusion of knowledge. These findings could be driven in reality by the combination of state and metropolitan effects (Singh & Marx, 2013). As a solution, these scholars recommend to simultaneously account for different levels of geopolitical borders as a way to more precisely assess the geography of knowledge spillovers (Belenzon & Schankerman, 2013; Singh & Marx, 2013; Toedtling et al., 2012). While the disjoint use of different political borders results in an overestimation of their respective strength, national, state, and metropolitan boundaries all seem to maintain a significant role in the localization of knowledge spillovers after controlling for each other (Singh & Marx, 2013), although country-level mechanisms are the most significant.

Besides acknowledging the simultaneous effect of multiple geopolitical borders on the geography of knowledge spillovers, scholars have also stressed the importance of accounting for the continuous nature of spatial distance as a driver of the spillover decay effect (Belenzon & Schankerman, 2013; Singh & Marx, 2013). Irrespective of the spatial level of analysis, spatial proximity has been widely captured as a dichotomous phenomenon through the use of co-location measures. While this choice has partly been driven by the complexity of developing accurate measures of geographical distance between knowledge sources and receivers (Singh & Marx, 2013), its implications are not trivial as it is assumed that co-location with a given knowledge source produces the same knowledge access benefits for different recipients, regardless of the geographical distance that separates them from the source.

Yet, operating in the same region might create a common social, institutional, and cultural background that certainly favor the occurrence of spillovers that may be subject to a distance decay effect, which, by definition, cannot be captured by a discrete variable such as co-location. In other words, this methodological approach prevents to account for both borders and distance effects (Belenzon & Schankerman, 2013; Singh & Marx, 2013), thereby limiting our understanding of the extent to which the localization of knowledge spillovers should be ascribed to political and administrative boundaries rather than to proximity effects.

Studies that have emphasized the flaws plaguing existing research have endorsed the need to use appropriate continuous measures to capture spatial proximity and have empirically demonstrated that border and distance effects exert an independent, significant influence on the diffusion of knowledge across space (Belenzon & Schankerman, 2013; Singh & Marx, 2013), thus confirming the idea that geopolitical borders and spatial proximity are distinct phenomena, potentially operating through different channels and thus requiring separate research attention.

As we shall explain in the next paragraph, we believe that the findings of these studies open up new and valuable research avenues that may help international business research to more effectively grasp knowledge sourcing by foreign subsidiaries.

5. MOVING FORWARD: THE TAKE AWAY FOR INTERNATIONAL BUSINESS SCHOLARS

The geography of knowledge sourcing by foreign subsidiaries has attracted great attention in international business and international management mainly in terms of co-location of source and recipient, and different specialization of distant sources and recipients. Discrete border and continuous distance effects have been instead collapsed in a single construct. Yet, the distinctiveness of these constructs has been recently recognized in connection with the more general MNC operations (Beugelsdijk & Mudambi, 2013). MNCs face more or less abrupt changes in a variety of institutional conditions when crossing country borders and the magnitude of these changes increase with the firm's liability of foreignness (Zaheer, 1995). At the same time, subnational spatial heterogeneity drives the establishment of foreign subsidiaries *"in particular agglomerations and not at random locations within a country"* (Beugelsdijk & Mudambi, 2013: 413) due to the spillover's decay effect.

The implications of these continuous and discontinuous spatial variations have been overlooked in the analysis of subsidiaries knowledge sourcing. We believe that recent research in economics and management drawing on innovation studies and economic geography (Belenzon & Schankerman, 2013; Singh & Marx, 2013; Toedtling et al., 2012) may help advance our knowledge in this direction. In particular, we see at least three avenues that intentional business scholars can fruitfully explore.

First of all, accounting for the role of the continuous nature of geographical distance in combination with multiple intra-host country border effects in the study of subsidiary knowledge sourcing is likely to offer significant opportunities to gain a more nuanced understanding of how subsidiaries deal with the geography of host country knowledge sources. Previous empirical studies have compressed the full range of information regarding these potential effects into binary measures of co-location between source and recipient. Yet, the theoretical relevance of distance and border effects points to a distinctive contribution of each of these effects to subsidiary host country knowledge sourcing. An analysis explicitly accounting for these effects will then enable to ascertain how subsidiaries vary in their ability to source knowledge depending (1) on the geographical distance that separates them from knowledge sources that are heterogeneously located within the host country territorial boundaries and (2) on the different types of intra-host country borders that stand between them.

The refined approach to the role of the geographical distance between subsidiaries and knowledge sources opens up research opportunities also in relation with other aspects of knowledge sourcing by foreign subsidiaries. More accurate definitions of geographical distance could be leveraged in combinations with the heterogeneity of the knowledge sources subsidiaries may access to. The diversity of the knowledge sources potentially accessible to foreign subsidiaries has received very limited attention by international business scholars. Yet, when MNCs establish their R&D subsidiaries abroad, they aim to tap into the knowledge embedded in the host country business network as well as into the local scientific system of knowledge production, as composed by local universities and other research institutions (Chung & Alcacer, 2002, Santangelo, 2005). To the best of our knowledge, the only attempt to address this heterogeneity in knowledge sources in the context of foreign subsidiaries is the study by Yamin and Otto (2004). The authors investigate the contribution of host country scientific and industrial sources as well as of different intra-MNC knowledge sources, but account for the geography of the different sources only in relation to the internal MNC dimension. Thus, it remains an open question whether the finding that only scientific sources of local knowledge contribute to the subsidiary knowledge creation, as opposed to industrial sources is robust to the geographical origin of each of these host country knowledge sources. Innovation studies and economic geography would suggest that geographical proximity/distance between source and recipient does play a role. The relationship between geographical distance and the heterogeneity of host country knowledge sources remains then a missing link, which is worth exploring to enrich our understanding of knowledge sourcing by foreign subsidiaries.

A third promising avenue of research concerns a further question that remains open in relation with the geography of different host country knowledge sources and relates to subsidiary innovation performance. More or less geographically distant heterogeneous sources can reasonably influence, in addition to the ability of the subsidiary to access local knowledge, different types of subsidiary innovation performances. Different locations evolve in diverse systems of knowledge, even within the same technological domain (Phene, Fladmoe-Lindquist, & Marsh, 2006). Knowledge sourcing from geographically distant/proximate diverse host country sources located in different sub-national regions arguably contributes to the novelty of the knowledge accumulated by the subsidiary. At the same time, the geography and type of knowledge diversity would arguably contribute to variety in subsidiary innovation performance.

There are certainly several empirical challenges that come along with the opportunities associated with each of the avenues of research we have highlighted. Such challenges are also part of the explanation why previous studies have chosen to rely on discrete measures of co-location to indirectly capture the role of geographical distance (Singh & Marx, 2013). Yet, we believe it is time for international business scholars to take on these challenges in order to advance the knowledge of the field in connection to the themes discussed in this chapter.

REFERENCES

Alcacer, J. (2006). Location choices across the value chain: How activity and capability influence collocation. *Management Science*, *52*(10), 1457–1471.

Alcacer, J., & Chung, W. (2007). Location strategies and knowledge spillovers. i, *53*(5), 760–776.

Almeida, P. (1996). Knowledge sourcing by foreign multinationals: Patent citation analysis in the US semiconductor industry. *Strategic Management Journal*, *17*(S2), 155–165.

Almeida, P., Dokko, G., & Rosenkopf, L. (2003). Startup size and the mechanisms of external learning: increasing opportunity and decreasing ability? *Research Policy*, *32*(2), 301–315.

Almeida, P., & Kogut, B. (1999). Localization of knowledge and the mobility of engineers in regional networks. *Management Science*, *45*(7), 905–917.

Almeida, P., & Phene, A. (2004). Subsidiaries and knowledge creation: The influence of the MNC and host country on innovation. *Strategic Management Journal*, *25*(8–9), 847–864.

Asheim, B., & Gertler, M. (2005). *The geography of innovation: Regional innovation systems*. Oxford Handbooks Online. Retrieved from http://www.oxfordhandbooks.com/view/10.1093/oxfordhb/9780199286805.001.0001/oxfordhb-9780199286805-e-11. Accessed on February 13, 2017.

Audretsch, D. B., & Feldman, M. P. (1996). R&D spillovers and the geography of innovation and production. *The American Economic Review*, *86*(3), 630–640.

Awate, S., Larsen, M. M., & Mudambi, R. (2015). Accessing vs sourcing knowledge: A comparative study of R&D internationalization between emerging and advanced economy firms. *Journal of International Business Studies*, *46*(1), 63–86.

Bartholomew, S. (1997). National systems of biotechnology innovation: Complex interdependence in the global system. *Journal of International Business Studies*, *28*(2), 241–266.

Bartlett, C. A., & Ghoshal, S. (1986). Tap your subsidiaries for global reach. *Harvard Business Review*, *64* (4), 87–94.

Belenzon, S., & Schankerman, M. (2013). Spreading the word: Geography, policy, and knowledge spillovers. *Review of Economics and Statistics*, *95*(3), 884–903.

Beugelsdijk, S., & Mudambi, R. (2013). MNEs as border-crossing multi-location enterprises: The role of discontinuities in geographic space. *Journal of International Business Studies*, *44*(5), 413–426.

Birkinshaw, J., & Hood, N. (1998). Multinational subsidiary evolution: Capability and charter change in foreign-owned subsidiary companies. *Academy of Management Review*, *23*(4), 773–795.

Braczyk, H. J., Cooke, P. N., & Heidenreich, M. (1998). *Regional innovation systems: The role of governances in a globalized world*. University College London Press, London.

Branstetter, L. G. (2001). Are knowledge spillovers international or intranational in scope? Microeconometric evidence from the US and Japan. *Journal of International Economics*, *53*(1), 53–79.

Cantwell, J. (1989). *Technological innovation and multinational corporations*. Oxford: Basil Blackwell.

Cantwell, J. (1995). The globalisation of technology: What remains of the product cycle model? *Cambridge Journal of Economics*, *19*, 155–155.

Cantwell, J., & Janne, O. (1999). Technological globalisation and innovative centres: The role of corporate technological leadership and locational hierarchy. *Research Policy*, *28*(2), 119–144.

Cantwell, J., & Mudambi, R. (2005). MNE competence-creating subsidiary mandates. *Strategic Management Journal*, *26*(12), 1109–1128.

Cantwell, J., & Mudambi, R. (2011). Physical attraction and the geography of knowledge sourcing in multinational enterprises. *Global Strategy Journal, 1*(3–4), 206–232.

Cantwell, J., & Santangelo, G. D. (1999). The frontier of international technology networks: Sourcing abroad the most highly tacit capabilities. *Information Economics and Policy, 11*(1), 101–123.

Cantwell, J., & Santangelo, G. D. (2002). The new geography of corporate research in information and communications technology (ICT). *Journal of Evolutionary Economics, 12*(1–2), 163–197.

Chung, W., & Alcacer, J. (2002). Knowledge seeking and location choice of foreign direct investment in the United States. *Management Science, 48*(12), 1534–1554.

Collinson, S. C., & Wang, R. (2012). The evolution of innovation capability in multinational enterprise subsidiaries: Dual network embeddedness and the divergence of subsidiary specialisation in Taiwan. *Research Policy, 41*(9), 1501–1518.

Criscuolo, P., Narula, R., & Verspagen, B. (2005). Role of home and host country innovation systems in R&D internationalisation: A patent citation analysis. *Economics of Innovation and New Technology, 14*(5), 417–433.

D'Agostino, L. M., Laursen, K., & Santangelo, G. D. (2013). The impact of R&D offshoring on the home knowledge production of OECD investing regions. *Journal of Economic Geography, 13*(1), 145–175.

D'Agostino, L. M., & Santangelo, G. D. (2012). Do overseas R&D laboratories in emerging markets contribute to home knowledge creation? *Management International Review, 52*(2), 251–273.

Dunning, J. H., & Lundan, S. M. (2008). *Multinational enterprises and the global economy*. Cheltenham, Edward Elgar Publishing.

Dunning, J. H., & Narula, R. (1995). The R&D activities of foreign firms in the United States. *International Studies of Management & Organization, 25*(1–2), 39–74.

Feldman, M. P. (1994). *The geography of innovation*. Boston, MA: Kluwer Academic Publishers.

Florida, R. (1997). The globalization of R&D: Results of a survey of foreign-affiliated R&D laboratories in the USA. *Research Policy, 26*(1), 85–103.

Frost, T. S. (2001). The geographic sources of foreign subsidiaries' innovations. *Strategic Management Journal, 22*(2), 101–124.

Frost, T. S., Birkinshaw, J. M., & Ensign, P. C. (2002). Centers of excellence in multinational corporations. *Strategic Management Journal, 23*(11), 997–1018.

Gertler, M. S. (2003). Tacit knowledge and the economic geography of context, or the undefinable tacitness of being (there). *Journal of Economic Geography, 3*(1), 75–99.

Gnyawali, D. R., & Hatfield, D. E. (2007). Foreign subsidiaries' learning from local environments: An empirical test. *Management International Review, 47*(1), 79–102.

Graham, E. (1992). Japanese control of R&D activities in the United States: Is there cause for concern. In T. Arrison, & C. F. Bergsten (Eds.), *Japan's growing technological capability: Implications for the U.S. economy* (pp. 191–206). Washington, DC: National Academy Press.

Gupta, A. K., & Govindarajan, V. (1994). Organizing for knowledge flows within MNCs. *International Business Review, 3*(4), 443–457.

Håkanson, L., & Nobel, R. (1993). Foreign research and development in Swedish multinationals. *Research Policy, 22*(5), 373–396.

Howells, J. (2006). Intermediation and the role of intermediaries in innovation. *Research Policy, 35*(5), 715–728.

Iwasa, T., & Odagiri, H. (2004). Overseas R&D, knowledge sourcing, and patenting: An empirical study of Japanese R&D investment in the US. *Research Policy, 33*(5), 807–828.

Jaffe, A. B. (1989). Real effects of academic research. *The American Economic Review*, *79*(5), 957–970.

Jaffe, A. B., & Trajtenberg, M. (2002). *Patents, citations, and innovations: A window on the knowledge economy*. Cambridge, MA, MIT press.

Jaffe, A. B., Trajtenberg, M., & Henderson, R. (1993). Geographic localization of knowledge spillovers as evidenced by patent citations. *The Quarterly Journal of Economics*, *108*(3), 577–598.

Keller, W. (2002). Geographic localization of international technology diffusion. *The American Economic Review*, *92*(1), 120–142.

Kuemmerle, W. (1997). Building effective R&D capabilities abroad. *Harvard Business Review*, *75*, 61–72.

Lahiri, N. (2010). Geographic distribution of R&D activity: How does it affect innovation quality? *Academy of Management Journal*, *53*(5), 1194–1209.

Le Bas, C., & Sierra, C. (2002). Location versus home country advantages' in R&D activities: Some further results on multinationals' locational strategies. *Research Policy*, *31*(4), 589–609.

Lewin, A. Y., Massini, S., & Peeters, C. (2009). Why are companies offshoring innovation? The emerging global race for talent. *Journal of International Business Studies*, *40*(6), 901–925.

Li, J. J., Poppo, L., & Zhou, K. Z. (2010). Relational mechanisms, formal contracts, and local knowledge acquisition by international subsidiaries. *Strategic Management Journal*, *31*(4), 349–370.

Lundvall, B. A. (1992). *National innovation system: Towards a theory of innovation and interactive learning*. London: Pinter.

Morgan, K. (2004). The exaggerated death of geography: Learning, proximity and territorial innovation systems. *Journal of Economic Geography*, *4*(1), 3–21.

Narula, R., & Santangelo, G. D. (2009). Location, collocation and R&D alliances in the European ICT industry. *Research Policy*, *38*(2), 393–403.

Nelson, R. R. (Ed.). (1993). *National innovation systems: A comparative analysis*. Oxford: Oxford University Press.

Patel, P., & Pavitt, K. (1991). Large firms in the production of the world's technology: An important case of "non-globalisation." *Journal of International Business Studies*, *22*(1), 1–21.

Patel, P., & Pavitt, K. (1994). National innovation systems: Why they are important, and how they might be measured and compared. *Economics of Innovation and New Technology*, *3*(1), 77–95.

Pearce, R. (1999). Decentralised R&D and strategic competitiveness: Globalised approaches to generation and use of technology in multinational enterprises (MNEs). *Research Policy*, *28*(2), 157–178.

Pearce, R., & Papanastassiou, M. (1997). European markets and the strategic roles of multinational enterprise subsidiaries in the UK. *JCMS: Journal of Common Market Studies*, *35*(2), 243–266.

Pearce, R., & Papanastassiou, M. (1999). Overseas R&D and the strategic evolution of MNEs: Evidence from laboratories in the UK. *Research Policy*, *28*(1), 23–41.

Perri, A. (2015). *Innovation and the multinational firm: Perspectives on foreign subsidiaries and host locations*. Palgrave Macmillan, UK.

Perri, A., & Andersson, U. (2014). Knowledge outflows from foreign subsidiaries and the tension between knowledge creation and knowledge protection: Evidence from the semiconductor industry. *International Business Review*, *23*(1), 63–75.

Perri, A., Andersson, U., Nell, P. C., & Santangelo, G. D. (2013). Balancing the trade-off between learning prospects and spillover risks: MNC subsidiaries' vertical linkage patterns in developed countries. *Journal of World Business*, *48*(4), 503–514.

Phene, A., & Almeida, P. (2003). How do firms evolve? The patterns of technological evolution of semiconductor subsidiaries. *International Business Review*, *12*(3), 349–367.

Phene, A., & Almeida, P. (2008). Innovation in multinational subsidiaries: The role of knowledge assimilation and subsidiary capabilities. *Journal of International Business Studies*, *39*(5), 901–919.

Phene, A., Fladmoe-Lindquist, K., & Marsh, L. (2006). Breakthrough innovations in the US biotechnology industry: The effects of technological space and geographic origin. *Strategic Management Journal*, *27*(4), 369–388.

Piscitello, L., & Santangelo, G. D. (2009). Does R&D offshoring displace or strengthen knowledge production at home? Evidence from OECD countries. Contractor, F. J., Kumar, V., Kundu, S. K., & Pedersen, T. (Eds.), (2010). *Global outsourcing and offshoring: an integrated approach to theory and corporate strategy*. Cambridge, Cambridge University Press.

Rosenthal, S. S., & Strange, W. C. (2001). The determinants of agglomeration. *Journal of Urban Economics*, *50*(2), 191–229.

Santangelo, G. D. (Ed.). (2005). *Technological change and economic catch-up: the role of science and multinationals*. Cheltenham, Edward Elgar Publishing.

Santangelo, G. D. (2001). The impact of the information and communications technology revolution on the internationalisation of corporate technology. *International Business Review*, 10(6), 701–726.

Santangelo, G. D. (2012). The tension of information sharing: Effects on subsidiary embeddedness. *International Business Review*, *21*(2), 180–195.

Santangelo, G. D., Meyer, K. E., & Jindra, B. (2016). MNE subsidiaries' outsourcing and in sourcing of R&D: The role of local institutions. *Global Strategy Journal*, *6*(4), 247–268.

Shaver, J. M., & Flyer, F. (2000). Agglomeration economies, firm heterogeneity, and foreign direct investment in the United States. *Strategic Management Journal*, *21*(12), 1175–1193.

Singh, J. (2007). Asymmetry of knowledge spillovers between MNCs and host country firms. *Journal of International Business Studies*, *38*(5), 764–786.

Singh, J. (2008). Distributed R&D, cross-regional knowledge integration and quality of innovative output. *Research Policy*, *37*(1), 77–96.

Singh, J., & Marx, M. (2013). Geographic constraints on knowledge spillovers: Political borders vs. spatial proximity. *Management Science*, *59*(9), 2056–2078.

Song, J., Asakawa, K., & Chu, Y. (2011). What determines knowledge sourcing from host locations of overseas R&D operations? A study of global R&D activities of Japanese multinationals. *Research Policy*, *40*(3), 380–390.

Storper, M. (1997). *The regional world: Territorial development in a global economy*. New York, NY: Guilford Press.

Storper, M., & Venables, A. J. (2004). Buzz: Face-to-face contact and the urban economy. *Journal of Economic Geography*, *4*(4), 351–370.

Tallman, S., & Phene, A. (2007). Leveraging knowledge across geographic boundaries. *Organization Science*, *18*(2), 252–260.

Toedtling, F., Grillitsch, M., & Hoeglinger, C. (2012). Knowledge sourcing and innovation in Austrian ICT companies—how does geography matter? *Industry and Innovation*, *19*(4), 327–348.

Yamin, M., & Otto, J. (2004). Patterns of knowledge flows and MNE innovative performance. *Journal of International Management*, *10*(2), 239–258.

Zaheer, S. (1995), Overcoming the liability of foreignness. *Academy of Management Journal*, *38*(2), 341–363.

Zanfei, A. (2000). Transnational firms and the changing organisation of innovative activities. *Cambridge Journal of Economics*, *24*(5), 515–542.

Zucker, L. G., Darby, M. R., & Armstrong, J. (1998). Geographically localized knowledge: Spillovers or markets? *Economic Inquiry*, *36*(1), 65–86.

CHAPTER 15

CSR IMPLEMENTATION IN MNEs: THE ROLE OF DISTANCE AND PRIORITIZATION OF DEMANDS

Anne Jacqueminet

ABSTRACT

How does distance influence the type of corporate social responsibility (CSR) implementation strategy the subsidiaries of a multinational enterprise (MNE) adopt? In this chapter, I argue that the relationship between distance and CSR relies on the subsidiaries' relative need for internal versus external legitimacy. I propose that, on average, subsidiaries that are more distant from the MNE's home country pay more attention to the demands of their local stakeholders compared to those of their headquarters because they want to acquire local legitimacy. I propose that this local prioritization will broaden the set of practices that distant subsidiaries implement on a certain CSR issue as they try to satisfy a larger set of stakeholders but reduce the extent to which they implement each of them. Furthermore, I expect that dependence on the parent MNE should limit the effect of distance on local prioritization, and therefore reduce the overall negative relationship between distance and CSR implementation level and

Distance in International Business: Concept, Cost and Value
Progress in International Business Research, Volume 12, 363–378

ISSN: 1745-8862/doi:10.1108/S1745-886220170000012002

focus. And finally, in case of high local stakeholders' consensus, the overall negative relationship between distance and CSR implementation level and focus should again be assuaged. Thus, by looking at the subsidiaries' simultaneous need for internal and external legitimacy and introducing the moderating effects of dependence on the parent and consensus among local stakeholders, this chapter nurtures the current discussions on the impact of distance on CSR implementation in MNEs.

Keywords: Corporate social responsibility (CSR); distance; practice implementation; institutional duality; attention

INTRODUCTION

> *If multinationals would commit to promoting sustainability and responsible business conduct throughout their supply chains this would have a decisive impact on the success of the [Sustainable Development Goals].*
>
> UNEP, September 2015.

As suggested by the above citation, multinational enterprises (MNEs) are considered as instrumental to tackle today's global sustainability challenges. As a result, MNEs are increasingly pressed to conform to international standards regarding their corporate social responsibility (CSR) performance throughout their operations and make commitments at a global level (Christmann, 2004; Devinney, Mcgahan, & Zollo, 2013). Thus, today, more than 90 percent of the world's 250 largest companies report on their global CSR performance (KPMG, 2015). But the organizational complexity of MNEs makes the achievement of CSR compliance and the satisfaction of a large set of stakeholders difficult. In particular, while the headquarters may define the global CSR strategy, the implementation of the practices and the satisfaction of the demands of local stakeholders largely depend on the subsidiaries (Crilly, Zollo, & Hansen, 2012; Kostova & Roth, 2002). The risk of such a separation is that, by attending to local expectations, subsidiaries might lose attention to the demands of the headquarters (Durand & Jacqueminet, 2015) and prioritize practices that are not fully consistent with the corporate mandate or the global sustainability demands. In extreme cases, there is a risk of irresponsible behavior or misconduct in one of the MNE's subsidiaries, which would reflect badly on the whole organization because of legitimacy spillovers (Kostova & Zaheer, 1999). Regulators are also more and more concerned about MNE's

CSR in their foreign affiliates. For instance, on February 21, 2017, the French Parliament adopted a "duty of vigilance" obligation for companies headquartered in France and employing at least 5,000 people, making France the first country to require MNEs to perform human right due diligence within all their worldwide subsidiaries. Given those coordination challenges and legal and reputational risks, it is crucial for MNEs to understand what drives the subsidiaries' choices when it comes to implementing CSR practices.

In particular, the role of distance in CSR implementation in MNEs has gained scholarly interest. Campbell, Eden, & Miller (2012) have unveiled two mechanisms that could drive the relationship between distance and CSR implementation in opposite directions. On the one hand, distance could increase the level of CSR implementation because subsidiaries suffer from a liability of foreignness (Rathert, 2016; Zaheer, 1995) and need to gain local legitimacy (Campbell et al., 2012; Salomon & Wu, 2012; Yang & Rivers, 2009). But on the other hand, subsidiaries that are further away from the headquarters might have a reduced ability to implement CSR. Campbell et al. (2012) suggest that this second mechanism dominates, which is supported by their empirical analysis. However, in this chapter, I argue that we need a more fine-grained understanding of the legitimacy-related mechanisms at play in the complex context of MNEs. In particular, we need to consider not only the need for local legitimacy, but the trade-off that exists at the subsidiary level between internal and external legitimacies (Drori & Honig, 2013; Yang & Rivers, 2009), given the subsidiary's situation of institutional duality (Hillman & Wan, 2005; Kostova & Roth, 2002). Indeed, prior work showed that the conformity pressures from both the headquarters and local stakeholders should enhance CSR implementation in the subsidiaries (Durand & Jacqueminet, 2015). But given the attention capacity of the subsidiaries is limited (Ocasio, 1997), the allocation of attention to external versus internal demands should be studied in conjunction. Therefore, to better conceptualize the relationship between distance and CSR implementation, we need to understand how distance can influence the prioritization by the subsidiary of an MNE of the demands of its local stakeholders versus the internal demands of the parent regarding its CSR.

In addition, attention to local versus internal demands can shape the subsidiaries' practice implementation choices beyond the mere implementation level. For instance, previous work has proposed that the power of local stakeholders could increase the extent to which a subsidiary *adapts* its CSR practices to the local norms (Yang & Rivers, 2009). But little attention has been paid to the potential fragmentation of local stakeholders and inconsistencies in their demands. In particular, a high attention to local demands relative to the demands of the headquarters might not only influence the degree of adaptation of existing practices, but also the portfolio of practices that subsidiaries choose to implement to satisfy all their local stakeholders.

In this chapter, I aim to address these two gaps by (1) articulating the relationship between distance and the amount of attention the subsidiary pays to the demands of its local stakeholders relative to the demands of the headquarters as far as CSR is concerned – that is, the extent to which it prioritizes local demands over internal ones and (2) exploring the consequences of such prioritization for the subsidiaries' level and scope of CSR implementation. Thus, while previous work has looked at the role of dual institutional pressures and distance as separate explanations for heterogeneous CSR implementation within MNEs, in this chapter, I focus on the relationship between the two and its consequences for CSR implementation. Drawing on arguments related to a mechanism of search for internal and external legitimacy at the subsidiary level, I make a set of testable propositions.

This chapter is intended to nurture discussions on the influence of distance on the implementation of CSR in MNEs (e.g., Campbell et al., 2012; Gardberg & Fombrun, 2006; Yang & Rivers, 2009) by superimposing a consideration for the institutional duality in which subsidiaries of MNEs find themselves and the conditions under which the search for internal rather than local legitimacy is the prevalent mechanism linking distance to CSR. I conclude the chapter with a discussion of the potential avenues for future research.

THEORETICAL BACKGROUND

Corporate Social Responsibility in Multinational Enterprises

CSR practices are implemented by companies to maximize their net positive environmental and social impact (Aguilera, Rupp, Williams, & Ganapathi, 2007; Bansal, 2005), above and beyond legal compliance (McWilliams & Siegel, 2001; Rodriguez, Siegel, Hillman, & Eden, 2006). These practices include the consideration of environmental and social impacts and benefits throughout the activities of the company – operations, research and development, procurement, marketing and sales, human resources – as well as partnerships and donations in money, time, or kind. Thus, CSR is not limited to stakeholder engagement but means actual changes in the way organizations operate (Zollo et al., 2009). MNEs seek to achieve a certain level of standardization in their CSR practices so as to respond to global demands in a consistent manner (Christmann, 2004), and limit decoupling, which can represent a reputational threat (Kostova & Zaheer, 1999; MacLean & Behnam, 2010; Marquis & Qian, 2013). Therefore, CSR is clearly a crucial strategic issue for complex organizations such as MNEs and one that represents important conformity challenges. As illustrated by previous work (Crilly, 2011; Crilly et al., 2012; Durand & Jacqueminet, 2015), the context of CSR is particularly well suited to look at subsidiary strategies and the consequences of subsidiary's attention to local stakeholders. Indeed, CSR issues are at the heart of the subsidiary's local stakeholders' demands and needs. CSR implementation also displays a lot of heterogeneity within an MNE, as various subsidiaries may understand and interpret CSR objectives differently (Crilly et al., 2012; Gardberg & Fombrun, 2006) and also vary in how they translate them into practice (Crilly et al., 2012). And at the same time, the implementation of CSR is an efficient way for the subsidiaries to gain local legitimacy in foreign markets (e.g., Fiaschi, Giuliani, & Nieri, 2016; Marano & Kostova, 2016; Marano, Tashman, & Kostova, 2016; Rathert, 2016).

Institutional Duality and CSR Implementation

The subsidiaries of an MNE are in a situation of "institutional duality": they need to simultaneously follow guidelines defined by the parent MNE and address the demands of their local stakeholders (Hillman & Wan, 2005; Kostova & Roth, 2002). Therefore, they face a constant tension between corporate integration and local responsiveness.

The means to balance "standardization versus local tailoring" (Westney, 1993, p. 58) and the respective pressures toward one or the other have long been studied by international management scholars, following contingency arguments (Doz & Prahalad, 1991; Prahalad & Doz, 1987) and institutional ones (Kostova & Zaheer, 1999; Rosenzweig & Singh, 1991; Salomon & Wu, 2012; Westney, 1993). Rosenzweig and Singh (1991) focused more specifically on the subsidiaries and on the dual conformity pressures they undergo: "a pressure for conformity to conditions in the local environment and an imperative for consistency within the multinational enterprise" (Rosenzweig & Singh, 1991, p. 344). Most of these earlier works on the integration/responsiveness challenge aimed at explaining under what conditions and circumstances, internal or local pressures prevailed.

Somewhat more recently, international management scholars have looked at the consequences of this "institutional duality" (Hillman & Wan, 2005;

Kostova & Roth, 2002) and showed that both internal and external pressures for conformity could foster practice adoption (Durand & Jacqueminet, 2015), drawing on isomorphic arguments introduced by neo-institutional scholars (DiMaggio & Powell, 1983). In parallel to this line of work, some international business scholars have more specifically studied the performance implications of local embeddedness (Andersson, Forsgren, & Holm, 2001; Figueiredo, 2011) and subsidiary initiative-taking (Birkinshaw, 1997; Birkinshaw, Hood, & Jonsson, 1998). Contrasting with the works on institutional duality, this stream of research is more concerned with subsidiary-level strategies, beyond isomorphism.

While some of the work cited above suggests that both internal and local demands for CSR implementation can increase subsidiaries' implementation of CSR (Durand & Jacqueminet, 2015, Figueiredo, 2011), we lack an understanding of the way in which subsidiaries prioritize these various demands and how putting more weight on either internal or local demands might affect their implementation of CSR. Consistent with the attention based view of the firm (Ocasio, 1997, 2011), I consider attention as limited and focused, so that we need to consider the relative attention the subsidiary pays to the demands of local stakeholders versus the demands of the parent MNE. In this chapter, I am interested in the extent to which, depending on its economic, cultural, and institutional distance from the headquarters of the MNE, a subsidiary prioritizes either local or internal CSR demands, that is, the amount of attention its key decision-makers pay to the demands of local stakeholders compared to the demands of the headquarters as far as CSR in concerned.

Distance and CSR Implementation

Over the past decade, scholars have started to theorize the relationship between a subsidiary's distance from the MNE's headquarters and its implementation of CSR with the assumption that CSR could compensate for the subsidiary's liability of foreignness (Zaheer, 1995). For instance, building on the conceptualization of citizenship programs as intangible assets, Gardberg and Fombrun (2006, p. 341) proposed that "[the] greater the institutional distance between a company's home and host institutional environments, the less likely its citizenship profile is to fall within the range of acceptability and the greater the degree to which the company has to customize its citizenship profile to the local institutional environment." Similarly, Yang and Rivers (2009) argued that greater institutional distance from the MNE's home country increases a subsidiary's tendency to adapt to local practices. In one of the first attempts to test empirically the role of distance in the extent of CSR implementation, Campbell et al. (2012) concede that distant subsidiaries might suffer from greater liability of foreignness and might therefore need to implement CSR practices to enhance their local legitimacy and acceptability. However, the authors argue and observe empirically that this legitimating mechanism is counterbalanced by another, stronger, mechanism through which distance actually reduces CSR implementation. According to them, this effect is attributable to the subsidiaries' willingness and ability to implement CSR. More specifically, they suggest that more distant subsidiaries are less willing – because they identify less with local stakeholders and therefore care less about satisfying their demands – and less able – because they receive fewer resources from the MNE and the adaptation to local norms is too expensive – to implement CSR (Campbell et al., 2012).

What is however missing in these works is the simultaneous understanding of the role of the headquarters, that is, the consideration for the institutional duality situation depicted above, which might make the legitimation mechanism more complex. Indeed, more distant subsidiaries might also have more difficulties being legitimate within the MNE, so that we need to consider how distance affects the trade-off between the search for internal and local legitimacy, which in turn influences CSR implementation.

PROPOSITIONS DEVELOPMENT

In order to unveil and disentangle the internal and local legitimation mechanisms at play in the relationship between distance and CSR implementation, I describe thereafter the model step by step, first focusing on the role of distance in prioritizing demands, and then on the influence of local demands' prioritization on CSR implementation strategies.

Distance and CSR Demands Prioritization

Drawing on previous work, we can suggest that more distant subsidiaries should be more eager to gain local legitimacy, that is, "comply with the rules and belief systems of the local stakeholder environment in which they operate" (Rathert, 2016; Reimann, Ehrgott, Kaufmann, & Carter, 2012) because, in such cases, the liability of foreignness is greater (Zaheer, 1995). Liability of foreignness is defined as "all of the additional costs that a firm operating in a market overseas incurs compare to a local firm" (Zaheer, 1995, p. 343). As distance increases, so do those costs, so that subsidiaries need to increase their level of local responsiveness in order to keep them minimal. In particular, previous work suggests that local isomorphism increases with distance (Salomon & Wu, 2012), although it might not be the optimal strategy at the MNE level as replicating local practices may prove challenging (Campbell et al., 2012; Zaheer, 1995). In any case, as distance increases, standards for legitimacy differ more and more, so that it becomes more difficult for subsidiaries to establish local legitimacy. Thus, "the greater the institutional distance, the higher the need will be to adapt organizational practices to meet host country legitimacy requirements" (Kostova & Zaheer, 1999, p. 68). In particular, Gardberg and Fombrun (2006) suggest that MNEs' subsidiaries engage in corporate citizenship programs to reduce their liability of foreignness and enhance their local legitimacy. Campbell et al. (2012) point out that motivations to reduce liability of foreignness through CSR should be greater in more distant subsidiaries. And Yang and Rivers (2009, p. 158) propose that "When MNCs' subsidiaries operate in countries with very different institutional environments, they have a greater propensity to adapt to local CSR practices to deal with the greater legitimacy challenges as a result of institutional distance."

As a result, I expect that, on average, distance will increase the tendency of subsidiaries to pay greater attention to local demands versus the demands of the headquarters in order to adopt/adapt in priority practices that are locally legitimate. In other words, because they have a greater need for local legitimacy, more distant subsidiaries will prioritize the demands of their local stakeholders vis-à-vis the demands of their parent firm. As distance is a multifaceted construct (Berry, Guillén, & Zhou, 2010; Salomon & Wu, 2012), recent studies focusing on distance have typically distinguished between economic, cultural, and institutional distance (e.g., Salomon & Wu, 2012). Therefore, I propose:

Proposition 1. The greater the economic, cultural, and institutional distances between the MNE home country and the subsidiary's host country, the higher the subsidiary's prioritization of the CSR demands of its local stakeholders (versus the parent).

The relationship between a subsidiary and the MNE headquarters however does not depend solely on distance. In particular, the level of autonomy of the subsidiary, as it shapes its level of dependence on the parent firm for resources such as knowledge, human capital, technology, or financial resources (Pfeffer & Salancik, 1978), is bound to influence the need for internal versus local legitimacy (Rosenzweig & Singh, 1991; Yang & Rivers, 2009).

Therefore, I expect that dependence on the parent firm will influence the relationship between distance and prioritization of demands. I argued above that distance increased the need for local legitimacy. But for entities that depend more on the parent firm, gaining or maintaining internal legitimacy might be the priority, and distance might make it harder to obtain. Therefore, instead of prioritizing local demands, these subsidiaries might focus their attention on the demands of the headquarters to gain internal legitimacy in spite of their distance – or at least rebalance their attention to some extent toward addressing the demands of their parent more.

Proposition 2. The positive relationship between economic, cultural, and institutional distances and the subsidiary's prioritization of the CSR demands of its local stakeholders (versus the parent) is negatively moderated by the subsidiary's dependence on the parent firm.

CSR Demands Prioritization and CSR Implementation

When it comes to the diffusion of CSR practices among their subsidiaries, MNEs face a dilemma as a high level of attention to local demands gives the subsidiaries greater access to local specific resources and knowledge but shifts their attention away from the headquarters' demands (Andersson, Forsgren, & Holm, 2007; Durand & Jacqueminet, 2015). Prior work has shown that attention to both headquarters' and local stakeholders' demands can enhance practice implementation (Durand & Jacqueminet, 2015). But given stakeholders' interests might point toward different priorities than those of the MNE and given subsidiaries have limited attention capacity (Ocasio, 1997), the subsidiaries' CSR implementation strategies will depend on the relative weight they place on each of the two types of demands.

In particular, depending on the extent to which it prioritizes one or the other types of demands, an MNE subsidiary will need to attend to a more concentrated and consistent set of demands – from the headquarters – or wider and more heterogeneous set of demands –from its local stakeholders. Given they face demands from a larger number of stakeholders that might require different responses, we can reasonably expect that subsidiaries that prioritize local demands need to implement a large set of practices to satisfy them. This is consistent with the idea that subsidiaries that face high local demands need to adopt locally legitimate practices (Yang & Rivers, 2009). The implementation of CSR in particular has been shown to be a way for firms to improve their local legitimacy (Rathert, 2016). But diverse CSR practices can be locally legitimate as local stakeholders may have different (sometimes inconsistent) expectations. As a result, subsidiaries are bound to implement a wide set of practices to meet those expectations and ensure local legitimacy.

By contrast, subsidiaries that place more importance on the demands of their headquarters compared to the demands of their local stakeholders might choose to focus on implementing a few visible CSR practices that are valued internally to signal conformity to the corporate mandate.

> **Proposition 3.** The higher the subsidiary's prioritization of the CSR demands of its local stakeholders (versus the parent), the lower its degree of focus in the implementation of CSR practices.

In addition, since subsidiaries that give priority to local demands relative to the demands of the parent firm are faced with more numerous and potentially inconsistent demands, it might be hard for them to prioritize certain practices to be implemented fully. They might also have a harder time identifying the best ways to implement them if they receive inconsistent requests. And understanding, processing, prioritizing demands can drive time and cognitive resources away from the actual implementation. This means not only that they will implement practices in a more balanced way as suggested above but also to a lesser extent overall. As Pache and Santos (2010, p. 463) propose, one way to respond to plural demands is to "achieve partial conformity in order to accommodate at least partly all institutional demands." They further argue that such compromise is most likely when the demands are inconsistent at the level of the means – in other words of the concrete implementation of practices.[1]

On the contrary, for the subsidiaries that pay more attention to the demands of the headquarters, implementing changes in their processes should be easier. Indeed, they get clear and precise guidelines and implementation recommendations, specific and coherent demands that are tailored to the organization and easier to combine with their everyday business. In addition, it might be more difficult to get away with a partial implementation of the corporate CSR policy. As a result:

> **Proposition 4.** The higher the subsidiary's prioritization of the CSR demands of its local stakeholders (versus the parent), the lower its average level of implementation of CSR practices.

The main assumption behind **Propositions 3** and **4** is that local stakeholders are fragmented and have diverse expectations in terms of what types of CSR practices MNE subsidiaries should implement. While I believe this is a reasonable assumption, it points to the central role of the degree of agreement among stakeholders. The mechanisms described above should be more salient if the demands of local stakeholders are really conflicting. On the one hand, when a subsidiary prioritizes the demands of its local stakeholders, if these stakeholders do not agree about which practices should be implemented in priority, the need for the subsidiary to accommodate this large set of demands (Crilly et al., 2012) by simultaneously adopting a large set of practices is greater. In addition, in such a context, the lack of time and resources to implement all practices fully and the absence of clear signals are also heightened. In other words, if the subsidiaries prioritize the local CSR demands, more conflicting demands might lead to greater inertia in the response (Pache & Santos, 2010). On the other hand, the more consensus there will be among local stakeholders about what practices the subsidiary should implement, the more the prioritization of local demands should result in a focused and deep implementation of CSR. Therefore, I further propose:

Proposition 5.: The negative relationship between the subsidiary's prioritization of CSR demands of its local stakeholders (versus the parent) and its degree of focus in the implementation of CSR practices is positively moderated by the level of conflict among local stakeholders

Proposition 6.: The negative relationship between the subsidiary's prioritization of CSR demands of its local stakeholders (versus the parent) and its average level of implementation of CSR practices is positively moderated by the level of conflict among local demands.

Fig. 1 summarizes the six propositions developed in this chapter.

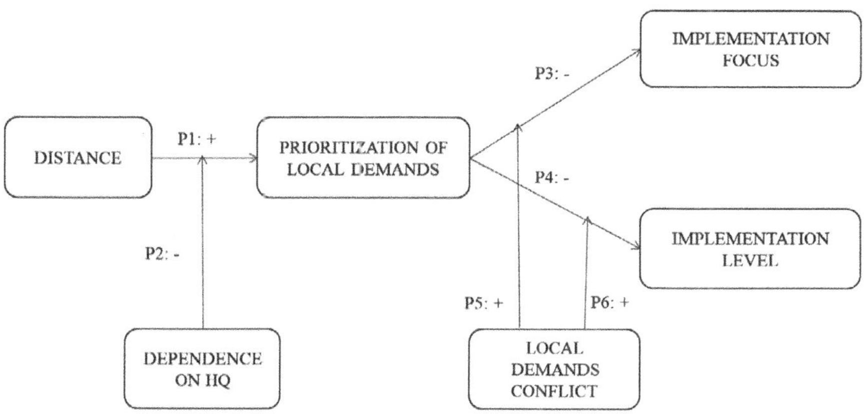

Fig. 1. Summary of the Propositions.

CONCLUSIONS AND AVENUES FOR FUTURE RESEARCH

In this chapter, I propose that the relationship between distance and CSR implementation is mediated by the prioritization of local versus internal demands and moderated by the subsidiary's dependence on its parent firm and on the level of conflict among its local stakeholders' demands. On average, I expect that more distant subsidiaries will prioritize local demands at the expense of the corporate mandate, and therefore implement more practices but less extensively. But for subsidiaries that depend more heavily on their parent MNE, as internal legitimacy is key, distance might in fact increase the attention to the headquarters and therefore have a smaller effect on local prioritization. As a result, dependence on the parent firm will reduce the overall negative relationship between distance and CSR implementation level and focus. And the effect of the prioritization of local demands on CSR implementation will be more prevalent if local demands are conflicting. Thus, in case of high local stakeholder consensus, the overall negative relationship between distance and CSR implementation level and focus will again be assuaged.

I believe this chapter has the potential to contribute to the international management literature in several ways.

First, this chapter intends to join the recent discussion on the role of distance in the implementation of CSR in MNEs. I start with the premise that distance increases the need for local legitimacy, but, by introducing the idea of demand prioritization, I propose that it can paradoxically reduce the level of CSR implementation. This more nuanced understanding of the legitimacy trade-off at play at the subsidiary level could help explain why prior work found a negative relationship between distance and CSR implementation (Campbell et al., 2012). In addition, I propose some moderating factors which, if tested, could both further strengthen the main mechanism and represent boundary conditions.

Second, by studying the context of CSR, this chapter contributes to discussions on the strategic implications of subsidiaries' institutional duality. I propose that the prioritization of local demands influences subsidiaries' implementation strategies by favoring the implementation of a larger set of practices but limiting their overall implementation level. This means that an important antecedent of subsidiaries' initiatives is the extent to which they prioritize local demands. As they attend to local demands, subsidiaries might implement practices that are not central to the corporate policy and even reduce their overall average implementation of practices but introduce additional innovative and complementary practices to the ones suggested by the headquarters.

And finally, this chapter speaks to research on CSR implementation in MNEs. Previous works either focused on the role of external constituents in shaping CSR strategies (e.g. Crilly, Hansen, & Zollo, 2016; Marquis & Qian, 2013) or opposed the headquarters and local stakeholders' interests suggesting that "parent corporations' demands for earnings [could] prompt efficiency concerns that crowd out the voices of local stakeholders, and produce a focus on shareholder returns" (Crilly, 2011, p. 695). However, increasingly, the headquarters are also concerned with CSR, so that both types of pressures point toward enhanced CSR (Durand & Jacqueminet, 2015). In this chapter, I wished to address the need to consider the subsidiary's attention to the demands of its parent and the demands of its local stakeholders in relative terms, given attention capacity is limited (Ocasio, 1997). Thus, I proposed that more attention to local constituents as opposed to the MNE headquarters highly influences the subsidiary's implementation of practices, in that it will foster the implementation of a larger set of practices, but to a lesser extent on average.

Avenues for Future Research

I believe this chapter can initiate discussions and open avenues for future research. First, future research could prolong and test my propositions empirically. Given the intra-organizational focus of this theoretical model and the role of attention allocation, an efficient way to measure the proposed relationships would be to design ad-hoc surveys and administrate them in the subsidiaries of one or several MNEs. Another option would be to conduct field or lab experiments.

Second, my model was designed to address heterogeneity in implementation within one MNE. However, additional insight could be gained from thinking about the role of MNE-level characteristics, such as the level of centralization, that might shape the relative need for internal and external legitimacy, or the location of the headquarters, that could influence the way the parent firm deals with CSR in the first place.

And third, future work could study more specifically what type of practices subsidiaries decide to implement, depending on their level of prioritization of local versus internal demands. For instance, it would be interesting to understand how such prioritization might affect the extent to which a subsidiary implements rather substantive or symbolic practices, or focuses on the implementation of highly visible practices that may act as stronger conformity signals.

NOTE

1. Pache and Santos (2010) propose that compromise is a prevalent response strategy when the demands are conflicting over means – that is, the implementation requests the subsidiaries need to manage are inconsistent in this case – and there is either no or a balanced internal representation of the demands. The only situation in which it is not the most likely strategy is when one type of demand is strongly represented internally.

REFERENCES

Aguilera, R. V., Rupp, D. E., Williams, C. A., & Ganapathi, J. (2007). Putting the S back in corporate social responsibility: A multilevel theory of social change in organizations. *Academy of Management Review*, *32*(3), 836–863.

Andersson, U., Forsgren, M., & Holm, U. (2001). Subsidiary embeddedness and competence development in MNCs a multi-level analysis. *Organization Studies*, *22*(6), 1013–1034.

Andersson, U., Forsgren, M., & Holm, U. (2007). Balancing subsidiary influence in the federative MNC: A business network view. *Journal of International Business Studies*, *38*(5), 802–818.

Bansal, P. (2005). Evolving sustainably: A longitudinal study of corporate sustainable development. *Strategic Management Journal*, *26*(3), 197–218.

Berry, H., Guillén, M. F., & Zhou, N. (2010). An institutional approach to cross-national distance. *Journal of International Business Studies*, *41*(9), 1460–1480.

Birkinshaw, J. (1997). Entrepreneurship in multinational corporations: The characteristics of subsidiary initiatives. *Strategic Management Journal*, *18*(3), 207–229.

Birkinshaw, J., Hood, N., & Jonsson, S. (1998). Building firm-specific advantages in multinational corporations: The role of subsidiary initiative. *Strategic Management Journal*, *19*(3), 221–242.

Campbell, J. T., Eden, L., & Miller, S. (2012). Multinationals and corporate social responsibility in host countries: Does distance matter? *Journal of International Business Studies*, *43*(1), 84–106.

Christmann, P. (2004). Multinational companies and the natural environment: Determinants of global environmental policy. *Academy of Management Journal*, *47*(5), 747–760.

Crilly, D. (2011). Predicting stakeholder orientation in the multinational enterprise: A mid-range theory. *Journal of International Business Studies*, *42*(5), 694–717.

Crilly, D., Hansen, M. T., & Zollo, M. (2016). The grammar of decoupling: A cognitive-linguistic perspective on firms' sustainability claims and stakeholders' interpretation. *Academy of Management Journal*, *59*(2), 705–729.

Crilly, D., Zollo, M., & Hansen, M. T. (2012). Faking it or muddling through? Understanding decoupling in response to stakeholder pressures. *Academy of Management Journal*, *55*(6), 1429–1448.

Devinney, T. M., Mcgahan, A. M., & Zollo, M. (2013). A research agenda for global stakeholder strategy. *Global Strategy Journal*, *3*(4), 325–337.

DiMaggio, P., & Powell, W. (1983). The iron cage revisited: Institutional isomorphism and collective rationality in organizational fields. *American Sociological Review*, *48*(2), 147–160.

Doz, Y. L., & Prahalad, C. K. (1991). Managing DMNCs: A search for a new Paradigm. *Strategic Management Journal*, *12*(S1), 145–164.

Drori, I., & Honig, B. (2013). A process model of internal and external legitimacy. *Organization Studies*, *34*(3), 345–376.

Durand, R., & Jacqueminet, A. (2015). Peer conformity, attention, and heterogeneous implementation of practices in MNEs. *Journal of International Business Studies*, *46*(8), 917–937.

Fiaschi, D., Giuliani, E., & Nieri, F. (2017). Overcoming the liability of origin by doing no harm: Emerging country firms' social irresponsibility as they go global. *Journal of World Business*, *52*(4), 546–563.

Figueiredo, P. N. (2011). The role of dual embeddedness in the innovative performance of MNE subsidiaries: Evidence from Brazil. *Journal of Management Studies*, *48*(2), 417–440.

Gardberg, N. A., & Fombrun, C. J. (2006). Corporate citizenship: Creating intangible assets across institutional environments. *Academy of Management Review*, *31*(2), 329–346.

Hillman, A., & Wan, W. P. (2005). The determinants of MNE subsidiaries' political strategies: Evidence of institutional duality. *Journal of International Business Studies*, *36*(3), 322–340.

Hofstede, G. H. (2001). *Culture's consequences: Comparing values, behaviors, institutions and organizations across nations*. Thousand Oaks, CA: Sage.

Kogut, B., & Singh, H. (1988). The effect of national culture on the choice of entry mode. *Journal of international business studies*, 411–432.

Kostova, T., & Roth, K. (2002). Adoption of an organizational practice by subsidiaries of multinational corporations: Institutional and relational effects. *Academy of Management Journal*, *45*(1), 215–233.

Kostova, T., & Zaheer, S. (1999). Organizational legitimacy under conditions of complexity: The case of the multinational enterprise. *Academy of Management Review*, *24*(1), 64–81.

KPMG. (2015). *KPMG international survey of corporate responsibility reporting 2015*. Amstelveen, The Netherlands: KPMG International.

MacLean, T. L., & Behnam, M. (2010). The dangers of decoupling: The relationship between compliance programs, legitimacy perceptions, and institutionalized misconduct. *Academy of Management Journal*, *53*(6), 1499–1520.

Marano, V., & Kostova, T. (2016). Unpacking the institutional complexity in adoption of CSR practices in multinational enterprises. *Journal of Management Studies*, *53*(1), 28–54.

Marano, V., Tashman, P., & Kostova, T. (2017). Escaping the iron cage: Liabilities of origin and CSR reporting of emerging market multinational enterprises. *Journal of International Business Studies*, *48*(3), 386-408.

Marquis, C., & Qian, C. (2013). Corporate social responsibility reporting in China: Symbol or substance? *Organization Science*. *25*(1), 127–148.

McWilliams, A., & Siegel, D. (2001). Corporate social responsibility: A theory of the firm perspective. *Academy of Management Review*, *26*, 117–127.

Ocasio, W. (1997). Towards an attention-based view of the firm. *Strategic Management Journal*, *18*(S1), 187–206.

Ocasio, W. (2011). Attention to attention. *Organization Science*, *22*(5), 1286–1296.

Pache, A. C., & Santos, F. (2010). When worlds collide: The internal dynamics of organizational responses to conflicting institutional demands. *Academy of Management Review*, *35*(3), 455–476.

Pfeffer, J., & Salancik, G. R. (1978). *The external control of organizations: A resource dependence approach*. New York, NY: Harper and Row Publishers.

Prahalad, C. K., & Doz, Y. L. (1987). *The multinational mission: Balancing global integration with local responsiveness*. New York, NY: Free Press.

Rathert, N. (2016). Strategies of legitimation: MNEs and the adoption of CSR in response to host-country institutions. *Journal of International Business Studies, 47*(7), 858–879.

Reimann, F., Ehrgott, M., Kaufmann, L., & Carter, C. R. (2012). Local stakeholders and local legitimacy: MNEs' social strategies in emerging economies. *Journal of International Management, 18*(1), 1–17.

Rodriguez, P., Siegel, D. S., Hillman, A., & Eden, L. (2006). Three lenses on the multinational enterprise: Politics, corruption, and corporate social responsibility. *Journal of International Business Studies*, *37*(6), 733–746.

Rosenzweig, P. M., & Singh, J. V. (1991). Organizational environments and the multinational enterprise. *Academy of Management Review*, *16*(2), 340–361.

Salomon, R., & Wu, Z. (2012). Institutional distance and local isomorphism strategy. *Journal of International Business Studies*, *43*(4), 343–367.

Westney, D.E.(1993). Institutionalization theory and the multinational corporation. In S. Ghoshal & D. E. Westney (Eds.), *Organization theory and the multinational corporation*: 53–76. New York: St. Martin's Press.

Yang, X., & Rivers, C. (2009). Antecedents of CSR practices in MNCs' subsidiaries: A stakeholder and institutional perspective. *Journal of Business Ethics*, *86*(2), 155–169.

Zaheer, S. (1995). Overcoming the liability of foreignness. *Academy of Management Journal*, *38*(2), 341–363.

Zollo, M., Minoja, M., Casanova, L., Hockerts, K., Neergaard, P., Schneider, S., & Tencati, A. (2009). Towards an internal change management perspective of CSR: Evidence from project RESPONSE on the sources of cognitive alignment between managers and their stakeholders, and their implications for social performance. Corporate Governance. *The International Journal of Business in Society, 9*(4), 355–372.

CHAPTER 16

BREAKING BAD? THE EFFECT OF FAULTLINE STRENGTH AND DISTANCE ON RELATIONSHIP CONFLICT, AND PERFORMANCE IN TEAMS. A CONDITIONAL PROCESS MODEL.

Ursula Pregernig

ABSTRACT

Demographic faultlines (i.e., potential subgroup splits based on demographic attributes) have been argued to have effects over and above those of diversity. Yet, faultlines, much like diversity, do not seem to have positive or negative effects on performance per se, but to be affected by contextual variables as well as intermediate outcomes, such as relationship conflict. Relationship conflicts, a major threat to teamwork, are particularly likely to arise between subgroups. Thus, with the objective to shed some light on why and how exactly faultlines impact group outcome, we investigate the effect of faultline strength and distance on performance through relationship conflict as well as the effect of faultline strength on performance via relationship conflict, contingent on the level of faultline distance. To

Distance in International Business: Concept, Cost and Value
Progress in International Business Research, Volume 12, 379–402

ISSN: 1745-8862/doi:10.1108/S1745-886220170000012022

test our hypotheses we used data gathered in a laboratory setting with 267 graduate students. Results provide strong support for the extension of the faultline model.

Keywords: Teams; faultlines; faultline strength; faultline distance; relationship conflict

INTRODUCTION

Due to organizational (Gibson, Zellmer-Bruhn, & Schwab, 2003; Jackson, Joshi, & Erhardt, 2003; Jehn, Northcraft, & Neale, 1999) as well as demographic changes (Jehn & Bezrukova, 2004; Mohammed & Angell, 2004; Pelled, Eisenhardt, & Xin, 1999; Puck, Neyer, & Dennerlein, 2010; Van Knippenberg & Schippers, 2007), diverse teams have become a key feature of today's business environment. Diverse teams promise to provide a broader set of knowledge, expertise, and viewpoints, and thus, appear to be the solution to successfully adjust to new market conditions and stay competitive (Mannix & Neale, 2005). Yet, differences on demographic attributes can also cause disruptions and conflict among team members which can harm team effectiveness (Jehn et al., 1999). In particular, conflicts on a personal level are likely to be triggered by demographic differences and, thus, have been argued to be a major threat to teamwork (e.g., De Dreu & Weingart, 2003; Jehn & Bendersky, 2003). Such "interpersonal incompatibilities" (Jehn & Mannix, 2001, p. 238) are referred to as relationship or relational conflict and are characterized by frictions and tensions among team members, not related to the task itself (Jehn et al., 1999). Given that a majority of studies found relationship conflict to be detrimental (De Dreu & Weingart, 2003; De Wit, Greer, & Jehn, 2012), it is essential to understand circumstances that stimulate this type of conflict.

Diversity is often measured based on single features at a time. A recent and "more comprehensive approach" (Bezrukova, Jehn, Zanutto, & Thatcher, 2009, p. 35) to study the effects of demographic diversity is the faultline framework (Lau & Murnighan, 1998, 2005). Faultlines have been defined as "hypothetical dividing lines that split a group into relatively homogeneous subgroups based on the group members' demographic alignment along multiple attributes" (Bezrukova et al., 2009, p. 35). Building on underlying theoretical principles of faultline theory, subgroups based on combinations of attributes like cultural background, gender, and age may emerge, which provide a base for in- and out-group behaviors, such as personal disagreements

(Lau & Murnighan, 2005; Turner, Hogg, Oakes, Reicher, & Wetherell, 1987). Further, subgroup formation will increase team-level relational conflict, since team members are likely to exaggerate differences they feel toward the other subgroup (Brewer, 1991). In turn, relationship conflict is likely to negatively affect team performance, due to cognitive overload and emotional strain involved with it (Carnevale & Probst, 1998; Swann, Polzer, Seyle, & Ko, 2004). Thus, the effect of faultlines on performance seems to run via relationship conflict. However, while many researchers have argued that faultlines affect performance via relationship conflict, few have explicitly tested for its effect (for an exception see Thatcher & Patel, 2011).

Investigating the effect of faultlines, researchers have mainly focused on the "extent of demographic alignment across members within a group" (Zanutto, Bezrukova, & Jehn, 2011, p. 702), which is referred to as faultline strength. However, faultline strength does not capture the difference between subgroups emerging from such an alignment (Bezrukova et al., 2009). Based on theories of distance (for a review see Thatcher & Patel, 2012) a larger distance between subgroups is likely to intensify processes and behavior evoked by the formation of subgroups (i.e., faultline strength). Thus, if team members of the respective subgroups are "farther apart," interaction can become even more inimical (Jetten, Spears, & Manstead, 1998) and team members are more likely to psychologically remain within their subgroup (Bezrukova et al., 2009; Nesdale & Mak, 2003). Therefore, faultline distance can increase the negative effects of faultline strength on group outcomes. Beyond its moderating effect, larger distance might also directly affect team outcomes positively since team members expect others, who are demographically more different from them to act respectively different, and, thus, strengthening the capacity to deal with differences. This reasoning is derived drawing from foundations of expectations state theory (Bettencourt, Dill, Greathouse, Charlton, & Mulholland, 1997), according to which team members associate certain characteristics with demographic attributes such as gender. In sum, scholars have recently refined measures of group faultlines, taking into account not only faultline strength (Shaw, 2004; Thatcher, Jehn, & Zanutto, 2003) but also faultline distance (Zanutto et al., 2011). In line with this, Zanutto et al. (2011) argue that both concepts provide unique information but can also be considered simultaneously as interaction. However, so far, there are few studies incorporating both concepts.

Thus, the objective of this study is to integrate relationship conflict as a relevant process between faultlines and team performance. In specific, we investigate the effect of faultline strength and faultline distance on performance via relationship conflict. Furthermore, we investigate whether the indirect effect of faultline strength on performance is contingent on the level of faultline distance.

We contribute to theory in the following ways. First, we contribute by proposing and analyzing an extended faultline model. We move beyond existing research and account for different dimensions of faultlines by also including distance between subgroups, as well as dynamics and outcomes triggered by both. Thereby, we aim to uncover deeper mechanisms of how and why faultlines affect team outcomes. This is crucial for our understanding of faultlines in teams as the two dimensions of faultlines (i.e., faultline strength and faultline distance) provide different information and can, thus, differently affect team outcomes. Second, we expand existing theory by conceptualizing and testing the specific role of interpersonal conflicts in this relation. By doing so we provide a more complete picture of the much discussed causal chain between team composition, team processes, and team outcomes. This is an important addition to existing knowledge as the effect of different dimensions of faultlines on team outcome seems be better understood through the mediating role of relationship conflict.

In order to reach the objective of this study we proceed in the following way. First, we will provide an overview of existing literature on demographic diversity, focusing on faultline theory and intra-team conflict. Based on this theoretical background we will develop hypotheses of the effect of faultline strength and distance on performance via relationship conflict, and whether the mediating chain of faultline strength on performance via relationship conflict is moderated by faultline distance. This will be followed by a description of our sample and data analysis. Next, we will discuss the results as well as limitations and derive implications for future research and practice.

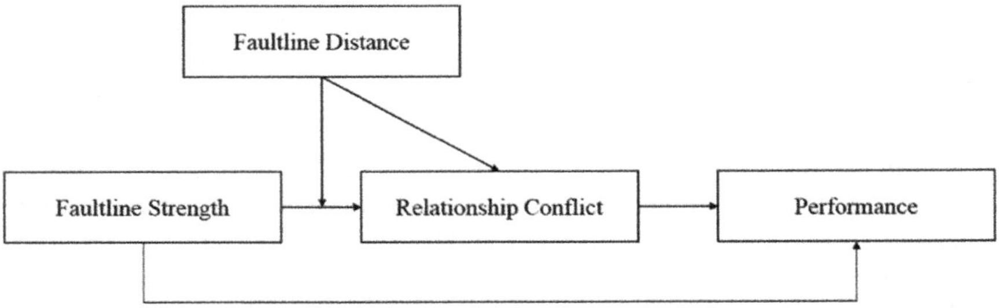

Fig. 1. Moderated Mediation Model. The Conditional Indirect Effect of Faultline Strength on Perceived Performance through Relationship Conflict, Moderated by Faultline Distance.

THEORETICAL BACKGROUND AND HYPOTHESES

In order to increase understanding of diversity in teams, researchers (e.g., Van Knippenberg & Schippers, 2007) have highlighted the importance of more fine-grained conceptualizations of diversity as well as the inclusion of contextual and intervening variables into research models (Bezrukova et al., 2009; Horwitz & Horwitz, 2007; Stahl, Maznevski, Voigt, & Jonsen, 2010). Addressing the former, that is, the issue of conceptualizing and measuring diversity, the concept of faultlines (Lau & Murnighan, 2005) has been receiving ever growing attention. The concept focuses on the alignment of different attributes of diversity, such as gender, culture, and age, which can trigger the formation of subgroups and, thus, create potential dividing lines, that is, faultlines. Therefore, the alignment of several diversity attributes potentially serves as a base for the formation of subgroups within a team, again evoking particular intra-team dynamics. Hence, demographic faultlines have been argued to have effects "over and above" those of demographic diversity by itself (Thatcher & Patel, 2011, p. 1120).

The theoretical base for the formation of demographic faultlines (Lau & Murnighan, 1998) is derived from self-categorization and social identity theories (Tajfel, 1981; Turner et al., 1987) as well as the similarity attraction paradigm (Byrne, 1971). According to self-categorization and social identity theory, individuals categorize themselves and others into different groups, based on demographic attributes, leading to the formation of in- and out-groups within a team. Further, social identity theory serves as a base to form in- and out-groups as people seem to be more attracted to those who have similar demographic attributes and also to get along better. Thus, these theories suggest that driven by the alignment of demographic attributes, subgroups and faultlines emerge (Lau & Murnighan, 1998) which can increase relationship conflict and, in turn, decrease performance (for reviews see Thatcher & Patel, 2011, 2012). Moreover, explanations for the consequences and mechanisms of faultlines can be derived from optimal distinctiveness theory (Brewer, 1991), the categorization-elaboration model (van Knippenberg, De Dreu, & Homan, 2004), and distance theories (Bezrukova et al., 2009; Jetten et al., 1998). Optimal distinctiveness theory and the categorization-elaboration model explain intra- and inter-group dynamics, thus, support the effect of faultline strength (i.e., likeliness of subgroups to emerge) on outcomes and processes. Distance theories, again, help to explain why and how the level of difference between possible subgroups, that is, faultline distance, influences the effect of faultline strength on group outcomes (Bezrukova et al., 2009). Apart from its moderating effect, faultline distance can also affect team outcomes directly and evoke separate and different dynamics and outcomes (Zanutto et al., 2011). Yet, previous studies have mostly focused only on faultline strength (see Thatcher & Patel, 2011, for a review), but neglected the concept of faultline distance, which is why we incorporate faultline distance as independent variable and moderator into our research model. In specific we argue that the indirect effect of faultline strength on performance, via relationship conflict, is contingent on the level faultline distance, but faultline distance also indirectly affects performance through relationship conflict.

Faultline Strength

Faultline strength has been used to conceptualize potential subgroup splits and describes the degree to which subgroups can emerge within a team, based on the alignment of similar attributes (Lau & Murnighan, 2005; Thatcher et al., 2003). Zanutto et al. (2011, p. 702) define faultine strength "as the extent of demographic alignment across members within a group." The strength of a faultline increases, the more attributes there are along which two subgroups can potentially align. Thus, for example, a team of two middle-aged women with Asian background and two young men with North-American background represents a strong faultline, as this team could easily break into two similar subgroups. However, a team of a young woman with North-American background, a young man with European background, a middle-aged man with African background, and a middle-aged women with European background represents a weak faultline, as demographic attributes do not clearly align. Weak faultlines are compositions where either all members of a team are homogeneous or very heterogeneous, as in the example above (Lau & Murnighan, 1998).

Among the most commonly researched consequences of faultline strength is intra-team conflict (for a review see Thatcher & Patel, 2012). As, most of the time, relationship conflict seems to have a detrimental effect on group outcomes (De Dreu & Weingart, 2003; De Wit et al., 2012), this type of conflict requires particular attention with regard to its antecedents as well as effects. Relational conflicts can be described as frictions and tensions on a personal level (Jehn, 1997; Pelled, 1996). Previous studies of the effect of faultlines have found them to both increase (Li & Hambrick, 2005; Pearsall, Ellis, & Evans, 2008) and decrease (Lau & Murnighan, 2005) relationship conflict, but a recent meta-analysis (S. Thatcher & Patel, 2011) provides further support for the assumption that faultlines increase relationship conflict. This assumption is mainly based on social categorization, self-identity (Tajfel, 1981; Turner et al., 1987), and similarity attraction (Byrne, 1971) perspectives. Cultural background, gender, and age represent "relationship-oriented" (Bezrukova, Thatcher, Jehn, & Spell, 2012, p. 78) attributes that can be associated with social identities and encourage social categorization (Carton & Cummings, 2012) leading to the emergence of subgroups. Members of a subgroup tend to develop in-group favoritism, that is, they regard their in-group as superior to the out-group which can evoke tensions, frictions, and hostility. Thus, teams with strong faultlines are likely to experience more relationship conflict than teams with weak faultlines, in which subgroup identities are not as salient (Bezrukova et al., 2009; Chung et al., 2015). Further support for this line of argumentation can be derived from optimal distinctiveness theory (Brewer, 1991) according to which team members seek an equilibrium between assimilation (i.e., being part of the in-group) and differentiation (i.e., being dissimilar from the out-group). Moreover, the comparative fit element of the categorization-elaboration model (van Knippenberg et al., 2004) describes that team members experience strong similarity among their sub-group members, but differences toward out-group members. Hence, team members are likely to form bonds with members of their own subgroup but distance themselves from out-group members, providing breeding ground for relationship conflict between subgroups (Pearsall et al., 2008; Thatcher & Patel, 2011). Therefore, we derived the following hypothesis:

H1. The higher faultline strength, the higher the level of relationship conflict.

Faultline Distance

Faultline distance can be defined as "the extent to which subgroups formed by faultlines diverge as a result of accumulated differences" (Zanutto et al., 2011, p. 702). Zanutto et al. (2011) presented the concept of faultline distance in response to criticism regarding the conceptualization of faultlines. While faultline strength reflects the likelihood of teams to break into subgroups based on similarity of team members' characteristics, faultline distance addresses the difference between these subgroups and is thus a metric to capture how conceptually different subgroups can be. Faultline distance captures the possibility that groups which might have similar faultline strength differ with regard to how far apart subgroups within a team are, which can affect behavior and outcomes directly, as well as the relation between faultline strength and group outcomes (Zanutto et al., 2011).

Based on their findings, Bezrukova et al. (2009, p. 45) argue that "faultline distance may trigger additional negative categorization effects, potentially resulting in stereotyping and bias in groups." Thus, faultline distance is likely to aggravate the effects of faultline strength on relationship conflict, as adverse subgroup interaction can increase at a large distance (Jetten et al., 1998). Researchers who investigated a moderating effect of faultline distance in relation with other group outcomes also found it to intensify the negative effect of faultline strength on group outcomes (for a review see Thatcher & Patel, 2012). The theoretical rational underlying the moderating effect of faultline distance on the relation between faultline strength and relationship conflict can be derived from cultural-, psychological-, and social distance theories (Bezrukova et al., 2009; Blau, 1977; Hraba, Hagendoorn, & Hagendoorn, 1989; Leong & Ward, 2000; Thatcher & Patel, 2012). These theories support the notion that intra-team differences affect the relation between faultlines and group outcomes and amplify distinctions between groups. Particularly demographic differences (such as culture, gender, or age) seem to be a driver for distinctions which further increase social barriers and possible misunderstandings. Again, such perceived gaps and misunderstandings will intensify the negative effect of faultline strength on relationship conflict, particularly if distance (i.e., the gap) is large. Therefore, we argue that while faultline strength reflects "awareness of membership into separate and distinct subgroups" (Bezrukova et al., 2009, p. 39), a large faultline distance will further increase the effect of faultline strength on relationship conflict. Thus, we derive the following hypothesis:

H2. Faultline distance will moderate the relationship of faultline strength and relationship conflict such that the relationship between faultline strength and relationship conflict will be stronger for groups with high faultline distance.

Beyond the moderating effect described above, faultline distance can also be considered as an additional dimension of faultlines, providing separate information. While the information provided is related to that of faultline strength, this dimension can evoke own particular mechanisms (Zanutto et al., 2011). Building on the reasoning of expectation state theory which suggest that team members associate certain expectations with characteristics of other team members (Bettencourt et al., 1997), we believe that team members might attribute certain behavior or comments to greater demographic differences and, thus, do not feel personally attacked by or associate negative emotions with respective behavior of members of a subgroup very different to them. In light of this argumentation, personal conflicts seem to be less likely to occur. Therefore, we developed the following hypothesis:

H3. The higher faultline distance, the lower the level of relationship conflict.

Faultline Strength, Distance, Relationship Conflict, and Performance

Performance has been investigated as one of the major direct outcomes of faultline strength (Thatcher & Patel, 2012), and while effects for both an increase and decrease thereof have been found, Thatcher and Patel (2011) provided support for an overall negative effect on performance in their meta-analysis. Also in their literature review, Thatcher and Patel (2012) come to the conclusion that high faultline strength leads to lower levels of performance as various scholars found strong faultlines to have a detrimental effect on performance (Homan et al., 2008; Jehn & Bezrukova, 2010; Li & Hambrick, 2005; Thatcher et al., 2003; Zanutto et al., 2011) as well as to decrease perceived performance (Kunze & Bruch, 2010) and negatively impact behavior related to performance (Choi & Rainey, 2010; Lau & Murnighan, 2005; Molleman, 2005). However, since scholars also found support for positive effects of faultlines (Gibson & Vermeulen, 2003; Lau & Murnighan, 2005), there is reason to assume that the effect can be further explained by additional variables, such as processes as well as contingencies.

When explaining the effects of faultlines on performance, scholars often base their argumentation for a negative effect on performance on the fact that faultline strength affects performance via intra-team conflict. Thus, a similar theoretical rational (i.e., social categorization, self-identity, similarity attraction) for why faultline strength affects relationship conflict has been applied. To give an example, Bezrukova et al. (2009) argued that tensions which are evoked by categorization processes are likely to decrease group performance. Lau and Murnighan (2005) hypothesized that strong faultlines lead to more conflict and poorer performance based on identity literature. In specific, subgroup members are more likely to take comments of a member of another subgroup as criticism (even if it is not meant as such), thus decreasing performance. In line with the initial proposition of Lau and Murninghan (1998), Thatcher et al. (2003) argued that due to conflict, faultlines will negatively affect outcomes. Thus, faultlines will increase the level of conflict which will, again, decrease performance. However, the mediating effect of conflict has, so far, only been tested in Thatcher and Patel's (2011) meta-analysis as well as by Jehn and Bezrukova (2010) who investigated the mediating role of conflicts between activated faultlines and group outcomes. Both studies found support for the (at least partial) mediating role of conflict.

Relationship conflict, in turn, is likely to have a negative impact on performance for the following reasons. It is argued that, in the case of relational conflict, team members' attention shifts to a personal, emotional level impeding them in achieving their objectives and constraining their decision-making ability (Jehn, 1995; Jehn et al., 1999). In specific, the ability to process information is supposed to be limited, since team members do not focus on the task, but themselves (De Dreu & Weingart, 2003), which can have a negative effect on team performance. This reasoning is supported by an information-processing perspective, according to which any kind of conflict is leading to a decline in the quality of decision-making as, due to a cognitive overload, the processing of information and the ability to make effective decisions are constrained (Carnevale & Probst, 1998; Jehn, Greer, Levine, & Szulanski, 2008). For the particular case of relationship conflict, processing of information or cognitive ability can be limited since people associate threat to damage working relationships with personal disagreements (Jehn & Bendersky, 2003; Roseman, Wiest, & Swartz, 1994; Staw, Sandelands, & Dutton, 1981). Apart from the limited processing ability, Pelled (1996) stated two further reasons for a negative influence of relational conflicts. First, members who experience personal incompatibilities are likely to reject each other's ideas, suggestions, and opinions. Second, time is spent on dealing with existing relational conflicts instead of pursuing the objective. A theoretical base indorsing these negative effects is self-verification theory (Swann et al., 2004), which suggests that team members cannot separate their viewpoints and opinions being challenged from "a negative assessment of their own abilities and competences" (De Wit et al., 2012, p. 362). Furthermore, a negative view of relationship conflict is confirmed by several studies, such as the meta-analysis by De Dreu and Weingart (2003) in which the authors also explain the negative effect of relationship conflict on performance by information-processing theory.

Summarized, we argue that the negative effect of faultline strength on performance can at least be partially explained through relationship conflict. Further, as predicted in **H2** the effect of faultline strength on relationship conflict depends on faultline distance. Thus, faultline distance possibly moderates the strength of the mediated relationship between faultline strength and performance via relationship conflict, such that the mediated relationship will be stronger if faultline distance is large. Furthermore, the effect of faultline distance on performance is also likely to run via relationship conflict. Building on the argumentation of **H3**, and the reasoning above, faultline distance can directly affect relationship conflict, which, in turn, will decrease performance, and, thus, partially explain the effects of faultline distance. Hence, we develop the following hypotheses:

H4. Faultline distance will moderate the partially mediated effect of faultline strength on perceived performance via relationship conflict such that the mediated effect will be stronger for groups with high levels of faultline distance.

H5. Relationship conflict will partially mediate the effect of faultline distance on performance, such that faultline distance decreases relationship conflict, which again, increases performance.

METHOD

Sample and Procedure

In order to test the abovementioned relations, primary data was gathered using a quasi-experimental laboratory setting, given its benefits of control, such as through similarity of the task, duration, and comparability of outcome measures (Jehn, 1994) as well as the possibility to determine cause–effect relationships. Thus, the design facilitated a systematic investigation of intra-team behavior and outcomes. Research participants were 268 graduate students from the business school of a large university who participated in exchange for course credit. While the results of student samples have been found to be comparable to those of work teams (De Dreu & Van Vianen, 2001), a particular advantage over the latter is that student teams usually share limited history of prior interaction which could affect the relations to be investigated (i.e., pre-existing conflict dynamics). The sample included 169 (63%) females and 99 males (37%). Mean age of all participants was 24, and the number of different national cultures within the teams varied between 1 and 5.

A CV had to be handed in by all participants 2 weeks before the study. Information from the CV was used in order to divide the students into heterogeneous teams. The information collected helped to split the students into teams with varying heterogeneity and size. Nationality and gender within the teams as well as team size were unevenly distributed by the researchers in order to enhance the standard deviation and therefore improve the possibilities of statistical analysis.

The introduction was followed by an assignation of each team to a conference table. After all teams had settled, each team received its first task from the observer assigned to the team. Each team member received a printed copy of the task. After its distribution all students had three minutes to read the task and to address any open question. Afterward, teams worked on the respective task for 20 minutes. All teams, irrespectively of their heterogeneity or size, were treated equally during this time period and were neither coached nor in any other way supported by the observer or other members of the research team. After 20 minutes, the observer collected the presentations of the teams and provided each participant with a questionnaire to assess the intra-team conflict level. After a 10-minute break that followed the collection of the questionnaires in which the students had to remain seated at their tables, the procedure above was repeated with the second task. Again the same questionnaires were distributed after the task was completed.

MEASURES

Faultline Strength

We measured faultline strength along gender, cultural background, and age and applied the algorithm developed by Thatcher et al. (2003). This algorithm computes "the percent of total variation in overall group characteristics accounted for by the strongest group split by calculating the ratio of the between-group sum of square to the total sum of squares" (Bezrukova et al., 2009, p. 41). Values for faultline strength can possibly range from 0 to 1 whereas larger values indicate a greater strength. Values for faultline strength ranged from 0.36 to 1.

$$Fau_g = \left(\frac{\sum_{j=1}^{p} \sum_{k=1}^{2} n_k^g \left(\bar{x}_{\cdot jk} - \bar{x}_{\cdot j} \right)^2}{\sum_{j=1}^{p} \sum_{k=1}^{2} \sum_{i=1}^{n_k^g} \left(x_{ijk} - \bar{x}_{\cdot j} \right)^2} \right)$$

Faultline Distance

The faultline distance measure is based on Bezrukova et al. (2009) reflecting the distance between subgroups, after the strongest split has been detected. Faultline distance values ranged from 0.98 to 3.96.

$$D_e(X,Y) = \sqrt{\sum_i (x_i - y_i)^2}$$

Thus, faultline strength indicates options in which a group possibly subdivides, whereas faultline distance shows the distance between these possible subgroups. While a group could potentially split into several subgroups, we followed the argumentation of Zanutto et al. (2011) that given the small to moderate size of teams, a break into two subgroups is the most common type and thus focused on measurement of two subgroups. We applied the macro provided by Meyer and Glenz (2013) to calculate both faultine strength and faultline distance.

Relationship conflict was operationalized with items provided by Jehn (1995) and measured on 7-point Likert-scales. The specific items we used were

"How much friction is there among members in your team?," "Are personality conflicts evident in your group?," and "How much tension is there among members of the team?" Similar to Jehn's study, participants evaluated the individual perceptions of existing conflicts within the team from 1 = "none" to 7 = "a lot." Cronbach's alpha was computed with 0.69. The result for relational conflict is slightly below those of previous studies, nevertheless it is considered satisfactory (Nunnally, 1970).

Perceived Performance

We measured perceived performance, using 7-point Likert scales. Self-assessments of performance have been found to reliably predict performance in previous studies (Bandura, 1997) as groups seem to accurately evaluate themselves (Costa, Roe, & Taillieu, 2001) as well as the level of satisfaction with their performance (Rispens, Greer, & Jehn, 2007). Based on Stewart and Barrick (2000, p. 140) we applied items relating to the "quality of work, initiative, planning and allocation [...] and overall performance." In specific we used the following items: "I feel good about my team's achievements," "I think, most of our team members are very satisfied with our achievement," "I believe, most of the team members enjoyed the work," "In my opinion, we did a good job," "In my eyes, we have thought about all relevant items of the task," "There was enough time to solve the task," "I believe the team members put considerable effort into their tasks," "Team members are concerned about the quality of their work," and "Team members did their part to ensure that the task is answered in time." A factor analysis revealed that all items were loaded high (from 0.81 to 0.92) on one factor and we achieved a Cronbach's alphas of 0.88.

Controls

Based on their consistency with our faultline variables and in line with previous studies we controlled for diversity effects by applying Blau's (1977) formula for gender and culture as well as the coefficient of variation for age and averaged all three to receive our measure for social category diversity (Bezrukova et al., 2009; Jehn et al., 1999). Further, we integrated team size and task type as controls since both have been argued to be influential variables in the context of faultlines and facilitators for subgroup interaction (Thatcher & Patel, 2011).

Table 1. Means, Standard Deviations, and Correlations among Variables.

	Mean	SD	1	2	3	4	5	6
1. Perceived performance	5.60	0.96						
2. Relationship conflict	2.33	1.33	−0.342**					
3. Faultline strength	0.64	0.14	0.127**	−0.098*				
4. Faultline distance	1.84	0.78	0.250**	−0.121**	0.428**			
5. Diversity	0.50	0.09	0.008	0.060	−0.318**	−0.103*		
6. Team size	6.00	1.05	0.115**	−0.073	−0.022	0.315**	0.060	
7. Task type	0.50	0.50	−0.04	0.01	0.00	0.00	0.00	0.00

Notes: $^{*}p < 0.05$; $^{**}p < 0.01$. $N = 487$

RESULTS

In a first step, we applied Harman's single factor test to check for common method variance (CMV) and found that CMV does seem to be a problem in this study (Chang, van Witteloostuijn, & Eden, 2010). Next, we conducted a correlation analysis. The results as well as means and standard deviations of all variables are shown in Table 1.

In a next step, we ran several multi-level linear regression models in STATA 14, addressing the multi-level nature of our data set. First, we tested the main effect of faultline strength on relationship conflict and the moderating effect of faultline distance. Table 2 shows the results of this first model.

Faultline strength has a highly significant positive effect on relationship conflict ($\beta = 0.236$, $p < 0.05$), thus supporting **H1** predicting that faultline strength will increase the level of relationship conflict. Further, we found support for a highly significant positive moderating effect of faultline distance on the relationship between faultline strength and relationship conflict ($\beta = 0.199$, $p < 0.05$). Thus, in line with **H2** we found that faultline distance further increased the positive effect of faultline strength on relationship conflict. We conducted additional analysis of the significance of the moderating effect, by applying the Johnson Neyman technique (Johnson & Fay, 1950) which revealed that the moderating effect becomes significant at medium levels of faultline distance, and, as faultline distance increases is becoming stronger. However, the moderating effect is insignificant at low levels of faultline distance.

Table 2. Results of Multilevel Linear Regression on Relationship Conflict.

	Model 1 DV: Relationship Conflict
Faultline strength	0.236*
	(2.15)
Faultline distance	−0.401**
	(−3.50)
Faultline Strength	0.199*
*Faultline distance controls:	(2.41)
Diversity	0.140
	(2.02)
Team size	0.008
	(0.12)
Task type	0.021
	(0.35)
Observations	487
teams	84
Observations/group	Min = 3
	Avg = 5.8
	Max = 10
Model Deviance[a]	1,337.662

Notes: [a]Deviance is a measure of model fit; it equals −2 × log-likelihood of the maximum likelihood estimate. A smaller model deviance means a better fit.
*, ** indicate significance on 0.05 and 0.01 levels, respectively. *Z*-statistics are reported in brackets.

Thus, we found partial support for **H2**. To increase understanding we plotted the effect of faultline strength on relationship conflict at low, medium, and high levels of faultline distance (see Fig. 2), that is, one standard deviation below the mean ($\beta = 0.50$, $p < 0.492$), at the mean ($\beta = 2.01, p < 0.01$) and one standard deviation above the mean ($\beta = 3.51$, $p < 0.01$; Aiken, West, & Reno, 1991). The plots show that with increasing faultline strength, the level of relationship conflict also increased. Also, teams experienced more relationship conflict at medium levels of distance than at high levels of distance.

Further, we found support for **H3**, that is, faultline distance highly significantly decreased relationship conflict ($\beta = -0.401, p < 0.01$).

Next, addressing the nested nature of our data (i.e., individuals, level 1, nested within teams, level 2) we used multi-level linear regressions to test for the mediating role of relationship conflict between faultline strength and perceived performance as well as between faultline distance and perceived performance following the procedure by Baron and Kenny (1986). Thus, faultline

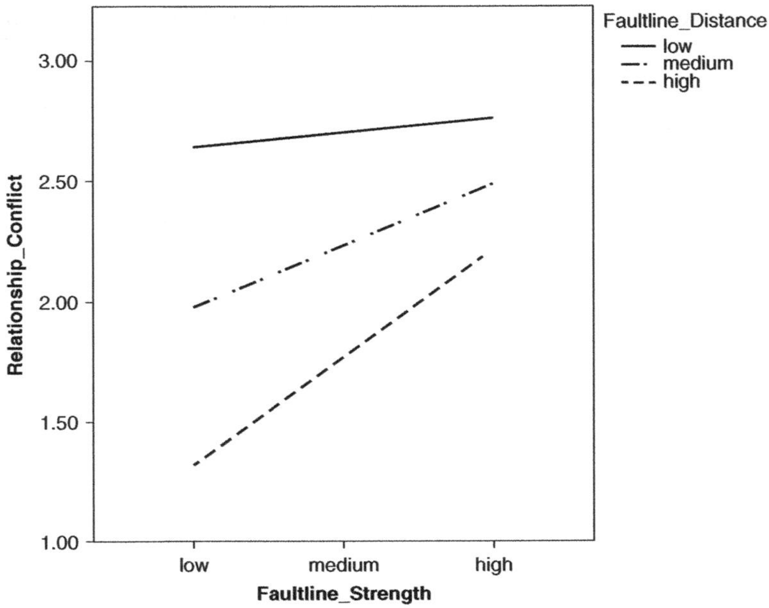

Fig. 2. Interactions: Moderated Effect of Faultline Distance.
Note: Low, medium, and high values represent 1 standard deviation below the mean, and 1 standard deviation above the mean. The analysis is based on centered values
Source: Aiken et al., 1992

strength and distance need to significantly predict relationship conflict (which has been tested in Model 1) and performance (see Model 2). Furthermore, the effects of faultline strength and distance on performance have to become less when controlled for relationship conflict (see Model 3). Table 3 shows the results of Models 2 and 3.

The negative direct effect of faultline strength on perceived performance is significant by tendency ($\beta = -0.200$, $p < 0.1$). When relationship conflict is entered into the model, this effect becomes insignificant. Hence, we found support for **H4**. Additionally, we tested for moderated mediation following the procedure suggested by Hayes (2013) using bias-corrected bootstrapped moderated mediation analysis. The total model (including covariates and moderator) made up for about 17% ($R^2 = 17.27$, $p < 0.01$) of the variance of perceived performance. Results show that at medium and high levels of faultline distance, the 95% bias-corrected bootstrapped confidence intervals

Table 3. Results of Multilevel Linear Regression on Perceived Performance.

	Model 2 DV: Perceived Performance	Model 3 DV: Perceived Performance
Faultline strength	$-0.200^{\dagger}$	-0.141
	(-1.88)	(-1.44)
Faultline distance	0.438**	0.338**
	(3.95)	(3.31)
Relationship conflict controls:		-0.248**
		(-5.72)
Diversity	-0.089	-0.055
	(-1.33)	(-0.89)
Team size	-0.010	-0.008
	(-0.16)	(-0.14)
Task type	-0.042	-0.037
	(-0.74)	(-0.71)
Observations	487	487
teams	84	84
Observations/group	Min = 3	Min = 3
	Avg = 5.8	Avg = 5.8
	Max = 10	Max = 10
Model Deviance[a]	1,315.776	1,283.348

Notes: [a]Deviance is a measure of model fit; it equals $-2 \times$ log-likelihood of the maximum likelihood estimate. A smaller model deviance means a better fit.
†, *, ** indicate significance on 0.1, 0.05, and 0.01 levels, respectively. *Z*-statistics are reported in brackets.

for the indirect effect of faultline strength on perceived performance (through relationship conflict) was significantly different from zero (medium: CI: –0.93 to –0.17 and high: CI –1.51 to –0.38), but nonsignificant at low levels of faultline distance (CI: –0.50 to 0.21). The effect sizes of the negative indirect effect of faultline strength on perceived performance via relationship conflict increased from medium ($f^2 = -0.48$) to high levels ($f^2 = -0.85$) of faultline distance, thus further supporting **H4**. As proposed in **H5**, faultline distance had a highly significant positive and direct effect on performance ($\beta = 0.438$, $p < 0.01$) in Model 2 which decreased in Model 3 when relationship conflict was entered ($\beta = 0.338$, $p < 0.01$). Further, a 95 % bootstrap confidence interval for the indirect effect of faultline distance on performance via relationship conflict was entirely different from 0 (0.038, 0.161), thus, significant and supporting **H5**.

DISCUSSION

While recognition of the importance of faultlines over and above those of diversity in teams is increasing, knowledge on how and when exactly faultlines might affect team outcomes is still limited. In this study we contribute to research on faultlines and intra-team conflict by investigating a conditional process model which has not been tested so far. In particular, we examined whether the effect of faultline strength on performance runs via relationship conflict and is contingent on the level of faultline distance. Further we incorporated faultline distance as an independent variable, testing whether its effect on performance also runs via relationship conflict. Our findings show that indeed, if the level of faultline distance was medium to large, the effect of faultline strength on performance through relationship conflict was stronger. Thus, we found support for a moderating effect of faultine distance, and a partially mediating effect of relationship conflict. Further, we found support for a partially mediating effect of relationship conflict between faultline distance and performance.

Specifically, we found that faultline strength had a direct negative impact on both performance and relationship conflict. Thus, the stronger the faultline, the worse the team members perceived their performance and the higher the level of relationship conflict. This finding is in line with the initial assumptions of the faultline model (Lau & Murnighan, 1998) and can be derived from theories and perspectives of social category, similarity attraction, self-identity, optimal distinctiveness, and categorization elaboration (Byrne, 1971; Tajfel, 1981; Turner et al., 1987; van Knippenberg et al., 2004) arguing that subgroups and, thus, divides occur, based on the alignment of different demographic attributes. Demographic attributes like cultural background, age, and gender are particularly salient and, therefore, are likely to lead to subgroup formation and different behavior toward people who are perceived as more or less alike oneself. Team members tend to be more sympathetic to those who are more alike them and less toward those who are not. Furthermore, they seem to take comments more personal if they come from members who are not in their in-group which, again, is increasing the level of relationship conflict. In turn, relationship conflict will decrease the level of perceived performance as team members seem to rate their performance worse if they experience relationship conflict. Moreover, we found that the effect of faultline strength on relationship conflict was intensified if faultline distance was medium to large. This finding is in line with various distance theories, such as social, psychological, and cultural distance (Blau, 1977; Hraba et al., 1989; Leong & Ward, 2000). If distance between subgroups increases, the "gap" between subgroups becomes stronger; thus, all the above mentioned behavioral processes become more pronounced. Such behavior can be rooted in demographic differences and become more severe if these differences are large. When entered as predictor, we found faultline distance to have a significant negative effect on relationship conflict and a significant positive direct effect on perceived performance. This finding is in line with the principles of expectations state theory (Bettencourt et al., 1997) and can be explained by the fact that if the gap between two subgroups is very large, subgroup members might expect other team members to behave in a certain way and, in line with the "value in diversity" argument (Jehn et al., 1999), might even view such difference as an advantage which could positively affect overall performance.

Limitations

There are several limitations which require consideration when interpreting these results. First, we tested your hypothesis using a student sample. While Lau and Murninhan (2005) also tested their hypotheses based on a sample of students and found strong support for the faultline model, we believe that our hypothesized relations should additionally be tested in a work setting to increase the external validity of our results. Second, teams only had to work together for a very limited period of time which might have affected our findings. Hollenbeck et al. (2012) pointed out the theoretical perception that newly formed teams are substantially different from more mature teams. Third, sample size was rather small. Fourth, we investigated the effect of so-called dormant faultlines, that is, these are faultlines that could potentially occur, but are not necessarily perceived as such by team members as is the case with active faultlines. However, "faultline researchers find that the presence of dormant faultlines has consequences even when faultlines are not activated (Chrobot-Mason et al., 2009), and there is evidence from one study (Zanutto et al., 2010) that there is a high correlation between dormant and active faultlines" (Thatcher & Patel, 2012). Thus, there is sufficient reason to believe that potential faultlines have strong effects on intra-team behavior, processes, and outcomes. Fifth, we only investigated the effect of demographic faultlines, while more recent research highlighted the importance of investigating different types faultlines (Chung et al., 2015), as some types of faultlines, such as information-based faultlines, can have positive outcomes (Bezrukova, 2009). Sixth, we measured performance based on the subjective rating of team members themselves. Therefore, results could differ if performance is evaluated differently. This is supported by the results of De Wit et al. (2012) who found that the effect of conflict depended on how performance is measured. Subjective variables, such as perceived performance, could be negatively biased because of the negative effect which is provoked by relationship conflict. Also, we only included relationship conflict into our model but did not test for the mediating role of other types of conflict, such as task- or process conflict which could potentially positively affect team outcomes (Jehn et al., 1999).

Implications

The following implications can be derived from this study. First, we found support for a conditional process model, which highlights the importance of, both, contingencies and processes when trying to explain the effects of subgroup formation based on demographic attributes. Hence, faultline research might need to follow the trail of diversity research, acknowledging that effects might not be clear cut, but depend on context or can be explained through additional variables, and might thus not necessarily have detrimental effects. Therefore, we call for further investigation of moderating as well mediating variables to shed light on both possible negative and positive effects of demographic faultline splits. It would be particularly interesting to further investigate under which circumstances faultlines could have positive effects on team outcome since there seems to be a prevalence of studies investigating negative effects (Meyer, Glenz, Antino, Rico, & González-Romá, 2014; Thatcher & Patel, 2012). Since we found support for particular effects of different dimensions of faultlines (i.e., faultline strength and faultline distance) we call for further research regarding the specific effects involved with different aspects of faultlines to uncover circumstances under which positive effects prevail. In order to identify such circumstances we suggest to borrow from literatures of diversity and conflict, for example, to include variables that might positively affect performance, such as emergent states (e.g., trust and respect; Jehn et al., 2008) or processes like cooperation (De Cremer, 2002). Apart from this, another possible alley of future research could be potential additional dimensions of faultlines, such as faultline depth (Thatcher & Patel, 2012).

Nonetheless, our results support a negative effect of faultline strength, that is, the possibility of subgroups was linked to an increase of relationship conflict, which was intensified in case of medium to large faultline distance and, in turn, decreased perceived performance. Thus, management should apply measures to avoid or mitigate such potential negative effects, such as by adapting demographic composition of teams or increasing team identity

(Jehn & Bezrukova, 2010; Thatcher & Patel, 2011), particularly in case of medium distance between subgroups. On the other hand, large distance between subgroups could prove beneficial for a team's success.

CONCLUSION

Faultlines, and their different dimensions, are a phenomenon which is of high relevance in teams. In this study, we investigated the links between faultline strength, relationship conflict, performance, and faultline distance. We found that faultline strength has a negative effect on perceived performance, partially via relationship conflict, which is contingent on the level of faultline distance. Further, we found that faultline distance increased performance, and this relation was, again, partially mediated via relationship conflict. Thus, our findings support the underlying reasoning of the faultline model (Lau & Murnighan, 1998), that is, faultlines affect performance via conflict, as well as the extended faultline framework (i.e., unique effects of faultline strength and faultine distance), and highlight the importance of including process and contingency variables into research models, as well as to introduce practical measures to mitigate potentially negative effects of subgroup formation.

REFERENCES

Aiken, L. S., West, S. G., & Reno, R. R. (1991). *Multiple regression: Testing and interpreting interactions*. New York, NY: Sage.

Bandura, A. (1997). *Self-efficacy: The exercise of control*. New York, NY: W. H. Freeman.

Baron, R. M., & Kenny, D. A. (1986). The moderator-mediator variable distinction in social psychological research: Conceptual, strategic, and statistical considerations. *Journal of Personality and Social Psychology*, *51*(6), 1173–1182.

Bettencourt, B. A., Dill, K. E., Greathouse, S. A., Charlton, K., & Mulholland, A. (1997). Evaluations of ingroup and outgroup members: The role of category-based expectancy violation. *Journal of Experimental Social Psychology*, *33*(3), 244–275.

Bezrukova, K., Jehn, K. A., Zanutto, E. L., & Thatcher, S. M. (2009). Do workgroup faultlines help or hurt? A moderated model of faultlines, team identification, and group performance. *Organization Science*, *20*(1), 35–50.

Bezrukova, K., Thatcher, S., Jehn, K. A., & Spell, C. S. (2012). The effects of alignments: Examining group faultlines, organizational cultures, and performance. *Journal of Applied Psychology*, *97*(1), 77.

Blau, P. M. (1977). *Inequality and heterogeneity: A primitive theory of social structure*: New York, NY: Free Press.

Brewer, M. B. (1991). The social self: On being the same and different at the same time. *Personality and Social Psychology Bulletin*, *17*(5), 475–482.

Byrne, D. (1971). *The attraction paradigm*. San Diego, CA: Academic Press.

Carnevale, P. J., & Probst, T. M. (1998). Social values and social conflict in creative problem solving and categorization. *Journal of Personality and Social Psychology*, *74*(5), 1300–1309.

Carton, A. M., & Cummings, J. N. (2012). A theory of subgroups in work teams. *Academy of Management Review*, *37*(3), 441–470.

Choi, S., & Rainey, H. G. (2010). Managing diversity in US federal agencies: Effects of diversity and diversity management on employee perceptions of organizational performance. *Public Administration Review*, *70*(1), 109–121.

Chung, Y., Liao, H., Jackson, S. E., Subramony, M., Colakoglu, S., & Jiang, Y. (2015). Cracking but not breaking: Joint effects of faultline strength and diversity climate on loyal behavior. *Academy of Management Journal*, *58*(5), 1495–1515.

Costa, A. C., Roe, R. A., & Taillieu, T. (2001). Trust within teams: The relation with performance effectiveness. *European Journal of Work and Organizational Psychology*, *10*(3), 225–244. doi:10.1080/13594320143000654

Chang, S. J., Van Witteloostuijn, A., & Eden, L. (2010). From the editors: Common method variance in international business research. *Journal of International Business Studies*, *41*(2), 178–184.

Chrobot-Mason, D., Ruderman, M. N., Weber, T. J., & Ernst, C. (2009). The challenge of leading on unstable ground: Triggers that activate social identity faultlines. *Human Relations*, *62*(11), 1763–1794.

De Cremer, D. (2002). Respect and cooperation in social dilemmas: The importance of feeling included. *Personality and Social Psychology Bulletin*, *28*(10), 1335–1341.

De Dreu, C. K., & Van Vianen, A. E. (2001). Managing relationship conflict and the effectiveness of organizational teams. *Journal of Organizational Behavior*, *22*(3), 309–328.

De Dreu, C. K., & Weingart, L. R. (2003). Task versus relationship conflict, team performance, and team member satisfaction: A meta-analysis. *Journal of Applied Psychology*, *88*(4), 741–749.

De Wit, F. R. C., Greer, L. L., & Jehn, K. A. (2012). The paradox of intragroup conflict: A meta-analysis. *Journal of Applied Psychology*, *97*(2), 360–390. doi:10.1037/a0024844

Gibson, C., & Vermeulen, F. (2003). A healthy divide: Subgroups as a stimulus for team learning behavior. *Administrative Science Quarterly*, *48*(2), 202–239.

Gibson, C. B., Zellmer-Bruhn, M. E., & Schwab, D. P. (2003). Team effectiveness in multinational organizations: Evaluation across contexts. *Group & Organization Management*, *28*(4), 444–474. doi:10.1177/1059601103251685

Hayes, A. F. (2013). *Introduction to mediation, moderation, and conditional process analysis: A regression-based approach*. New York, NY: Guilford Press.

Hollenbeck, J. R., Beersma, B., & Schouten, M. E. (2012). Beyond team types and taxonomies: A dimensional scaling conceptualization for team description. *Academy of Management Review*, *37*(1), 82–106. doi:10.5465/armr.2010.0181

Homan, A. C., Hollenbeck, J. R., Humphrey, S. E., Van Knippenberg, D., Ilgen, D. R., & Van Kleef, G. A. (2008). Facing differences with an open mind: Openness to experience, salience of intragroup differences, and performance of diverse work groups. *Academy of Management Journal*, *51*(6), 1204–1222.

Horwitz, S. K., & Horwitz, I. B. (2007). The effects of team diversity on team outcomes: A meta-analytic review of team demography. *Journal of Management*, *33*(6), 987–1015.

Hraba, J., Hagendoorn, L., & Hagendoorn, R. (1989). The ethnic hierarchy in the Netherlands: Social distance and social representation. *British Journal of Social Psychology*, *28*(1), 57–69.

Jackson, S. E., Joshi, A., & Erhardt, N. L. (2003). Recent research on team and organizational diversity: SWOT analysis and implications. *Journal of Management*, *29*(6), 801. doi:10.1016/s0149-2063(03)00080-1

Jehn, K. A. (1994). Enhancing effectiveness: An investigation of the advantages and disadvantages of value-based intragroup conflict. *International Journal of Conflict Management*, *5*(3), 223–238.

Jehn, K. A. (1995). A multimethod examination of the benefits and detriments of intragroup conflict. *Administrative Science Quarterly*, *40*(2), 256–256.

Jehn, K. A. (1997). A qualitative analysis of conflict types and dimensions in organizational groups. *Administrative Science Quarterly*, *42*(3), 530–557.

Jehn, K. A., & Bendersky, C. (2003). Intragroup conflict in organizations: A contingency perspective on the conflict-outcome relationship. *Research in Organizational Behavior*, *25*, 187–243.

Jehn, K. A., & Bezrukova, K. (2004). A field study of group diversity, workgroup context, and performance. *Journal of Organizational Behavior*, *25*(6), 703–729. doi:10.1002/job.266

Jehn, K. A., & Bezrukova, K. (2010). The faultline activation process and the effects of activated faultlines on coalition formation, conflict, and group outcomes. *Organizational Behavior and Human Decision Processes*, *112*(1), 24–42.

Jehn, K. A., Greer, L., Levine, S., & Szulanski, G. (2008). The effects of conflict types, dimensions, and emergent states on group outcomes. *Group Decision and Negotiation*, *17*(6), 465–495.

Jehn, K. A., & Mannix, E. A. (2001). The dynamic nature of conflict: A longitudinal study of intragroup conflict and group performance. *Academy of Management Journal*, *44*(2), 238–251.

Jehn, K. A., Northcraft, G. B., & Neale, M. A. (1999). Why Differences make a difference: A field study of diversity, conflict, and performance in workgroups. *Administrative Science Quarterly*, *44*(4), 741–763.

Jetten, J., Spears, R., & Manstead, A. S. (1998). Defining dimensions of distinctiveness: Group variability makes a difference to differentiation. *Journal of Personality and Social Psychology*, *74*(6), 1481.

Johnson, P. O., & Fay, L. C. (1950). The Johnson-Neyman technique, its theory and application. *Psychometrika*, *15*(4), 349–367.

Kunze, F., & Bruch, H. (2010). Age-based faultlines and perceived productive energy: The moderation of transformational leadership. *Small Group Research*, *41*(5), 593–620.

Lau, D. C., & Murnighan, J. K. (1998). Demographic diversity and faultlines: The compositional dynamics of organizational groups. *Academy of Management Review*, *23*(2), 325–340.

Lau, D. C., & Murnighan, J. K. (2005). Interactions within groups and subgroups: The effects of demographic faultlines. *Academy of Management Journal*, *48*(4), 645–659.

Leong, C.-H., & Ward, C. (2000). Identity conflict in sojourners. *International Journal of Intercultural Relations*, *24*(6), 763–776.

Li, J., & Hambrick, D. C. (2005). Factional groups: A new vantage on demographic faultlines, conflict, and disintegration in work teams. *Academy of Management Journal*, *48*(5), 794–813.

Mannix, E., & Neale, M. A. (2005). What differences make a difference? The promise and reality of diverse teams in organizations. *Psychological Science in the Public Interest*, *6*(2), 31–55.

Meyer, B., & Glenz, A. (2013). Team faultline measures a computational comparison and a new approach to multiple subgroups. *Organizational Research Methods*, *16*(3), 393–424.

Meyer, B., Glenz, A., Antino, M., Rico, R., & González-Romá, V. (2014). Faultlines and subgroups a meta-review and measurement guide. *Small Group Research*, *45*(6), 633–670.

Mohammed, S., & Angell, L. C. (2004). Surface- and deep-level diversity in workgroups: Examining the moderating effects of team orientation and team process on relationship conflict. *Journal of Organizational Behavior*, *25*(8), 1015–1039.

Molleman, E. (2005). Diversity in demographic characteristics, abilities and personality traits: Do faultlines affect team functioning? *Group Decision and Negotiation*, *14*(3), 173–193.

Nesdale, D., & Mak, A. S. (2003). Ethnic identification, self-esteem and immigrant psychological health. *International Journal of Intercultural Relations*, *27*(1), 23–40.

Pearsall, M. J., Ellis, A. P., & Evans, J. M. (2008). Unlocking the effects of gender faultlines on team creativity: Is activation the key? *Journal of Applied Psychology*, *93*(1), 225.

Pelled, L. H. (1996). Demographic diversity, conflict, and work group outcomes: An intervening process theory. *Organization Science*, *7*(6), 615–631.

Pelled, L. H., Eisenhardt, K. M., & Xin, K. R. (1999). Exploring the black box: An analysis of work group diversity, conflict, and performance. *Administrative Science Quarterly*, *44*(1), 1–28.

Puck, J. F., Neyer, A.-K., & Dennerlein, T. (2010). Diversity and conflict in teams: A contingency perspective. *European Journal of International Management*, *4*(4), 417–439. doi:10.1504/ejim.2010.03361

Rispens, S., Greer, L. L., & Jehn, K. A. (2007). It could be worse: A study on the alleviating roles of trust and connectedness in intragroup conflicts. *International Journal of Conflict Management*, *18*(4), 325–344.

Roseman, I. J., Wiest, C., & Swartz, T. S. (1994). Phenomenology, behaviors, and goals differentiate discrete emotions. *Journal of Personality and Social Psychology*, *67*(2), 206–221. doi:10.1037/0022-3514.67.2.206

Shaw, J. B. (2004). The development and analysis of a measure of group faultlines. *Organizational Research Methods*, *7*(1), 66–100.

Stahl, G. K., Maznevski, M. L., Voigt, A., & Jonsen, K. (2010). Unraveling the effects of cultural diversity in teams: A meta-analysis of research on multicultural work groups. *Journal of International Business Studies*, *41*(4), 690–709.

Staw, B. M., Sandelands, L. E., & Dutton, J. E. (1981). Threat rigidity effects in organizational behavior: A multilevel analysis. *Administrative Science Quarterly*, 501–524.

Stewart, G., & Barrick, M. (2000). Team structure and performance: Assessing the mediating role of intrateam process and the moderating role of task type. *Academy of Management Journal*, *43*(2), 135–148. doi:10.2307/1556372

Swann, W. B., Polzer, J. T., Seyle, D. C., & Ko, S. J. (2004). Finding value in diversity: Verification of personal and social self-views in diverse groups. *Academy of Management Review*, *29*(1), 9–27. doi:10.5465/amr.2004.11851702

Tajfel, H. (1981). *Human groups and social categories: Studies in social psychology*. Cambridge: Cambridge University Press.

Thatcher, S., & Patel, P. C. (2011). Demographic faultlines: A meta-analysis of the literature. *Journal of Applied Psychology*, *96*(6), 1119.

Thatcher, S. M., Jehn, K. A., & Zanutto, E. (2003). Cracks in diversity research: The effects of diversity faultlines on conflict and performance. *Group Decision and Negotiation*, *12*(3), 217–241.

Thatcher, S. M., & Patel, P. C. (2012). Group faultlines a review, integration, and guide to future research. *Journal of Management*, *38*(4), 969–1009.

Turner, J. C., Hogg, M. A., Oakes, P. J., Reicher, S. D., & Wetherell, M. S. (1987). Rediscovering the social group: A self-categorization theory. *Contemporary Sociology*.

Van Knippenberg, D., De Dreu, C. K. W., & Homan, A. C. (2004). Work group diversity and group performance: An integrative model and research agenda. *Journal of Applied Psychology*, *89*(6), 1008–1022. doi:10.1037/0021-9010.89.6.1008

Van Knippenberg, D., & Schippers, M. C. (2007). Work group diversity. *Annual Review of Psychology*, *58*, 515–541.

Zanutto, E. L., Bezrukova, K., & Jehn, K. A. (2011). Revisiting faultline conceptualization: Measuring faultline strength and distance. *Quality & Quantity*, *45*(3), 701–714.

CHAPTER 17

WHEN DISTANCE IS GOOD: AN UPPER-ECHELONS PERSPECTIVE ON THE ROLE OF DISTANCE IN INTERNATIONALIZATION

Dorota Piaskowska

ABSTRACT

Prior research has tended to view cross-country distance as an obstacle. Yet, differences across countries are a key reason for firms to internationalize. To address this discrepancy, this paper puts forward a unifying framework which (1) synthesizes and delineates the different types of cross-country distance, (2) provides a logic for analyzing cross-level influences of distance on internationalization decisions, and (3) highlights the opportunities brought about by distance. The paper argues that firms are more likely to be able to realize these opportunities when they have internationally experienced managers and diverse, well-functioning top management teams at the helm. The paper also highlights the complex influences of distance, calling for the use of cognitive and behavioral research methodologies to further our understanding of the role of distance in internationalization. An illustrative example of Vodafone Group PLC is included.

Distance in International Business: Concept, Cost and Value
Progress in International Business Research, Volume 12, 403–423

ISSN: 1745-8862/doi:10.1108/S1745-886220170000012011

Keywords: Cross-country distance; internationalization; cross-level influences

1. INTRODUCTION

Distance is a central concept in international business research. Its use can be traced back to the influential works of Uppsala scholars on the internationalization of Swedish multinationals (e.g., Johanson & Vahlne, 1977; Johanson & Wiedersheim-Paul, 1975). Hundreds of studies have since employed the concept of distance as an intuitive metaphor for various differences across countries (Ghemawat, 2001; Hutzschenreuter, Kleindienst, & Lange, 2016; Shenkar, 2012; Zaheer, Schomaker, & Nachum, 2012) to explain why, when, where, and how firms internationalize, as well as how well they manage in their foreign markets (e.g., Barkema, Bell, & Pennings, 1996; Johanson & Vahlne, 1977; Malhotra, Sivakumar, & Zhu, 2009; Vermeulen & Barkema, 2002).

The existence of differences across countries is one of the key, long-established reasons for firms to internationalize. Cross-country differences enable firms to benefit from arbitrage opportunities, access to new markets and resources, and improved efficiency (Ambos & Håkanson, 2014; Dunning & Lundan, 2008; Zaheer et al., 2012). In spite of these benefits, research into the role of cross-country differences in internationalization has tended to take a negative view on them (Berry, Guillen, & Zhou, 2010; Stahl, Tung, Kostova, & Zellmer-Bruhn, 2016). In this literature, firms are typically seen as suffering from liabilities of foreignness and perceived "psychic" distance due to their lack of understanding of foreign markets and lack of local networks (Johanson & Vahlne, 1977, 2009; Zaheer, 1995). These challenges arise due to the cultural, administrative, political, economic, and geographic differences between countries (Delios & Henisz, 2003; Ghemawat, 2001; Kogut & Singh, 1988) and are seen as a source of risk, uncertainty, friction, and complexity (e.g., Cuypers & Martin, 2010; Shenkar, Luo, & Yeheskel, 2008; Vermeulen & Barkema, 2002).

Hence, an important question in prior research has been how to mitigate the challenges associated with cross-country distance in internationalization. A common advice has been for firms to expand incrementally without adding excessive complexity, identify knowledgeable partners with whom to share risks, and learn from experience in the process (e.g., Barkema et al.,

1996; Johanson & Vahlne, 1977; Vermeulen & Barkema, 2002). At the core of these arguments has been the idea that a firm's experiential knowledge about foreign countries, the process of internationalization, and expansion modes (Dow & Larimo, 2009) is the antidote to the challenges of cross-country distance.

While the step-wise and risk-sharing approaches to internationalization have clear advantages, they are time-consuming and may lead firms to forego attractive investment opportunities. At the same time, firms which possess the necessary internationalization knowledge and abilities may become trapped in their competencies (cf. Levitt & March, 1988; Zeng, Shenkar, Lee, & Song, 2013), underestimate the challenges of distant markets (Ghemawat, 2001), and be outpaced by other players in their markets. This leads to a key question: what sets apart the companies which can capitalize on opportunities in variously distant locations from those which cannot?

To address this question, this chapter zooms in on the locus of internationalization decisions in firms: the top management. Top-management research has long argued that executives are the key decision-makers as well as the key learners in strategic decisions (Hambrick & Mason, 1984; Nadolska & Barkema, 2007; Nielsen & Nielsen, 2011; Piaskowska & Trojanowski, 2014). Hence, top managers can be seen as the locus of knowledge and abilities required when taking and executing internationalization decisions, including in otherwise inexperienced multinationals (Maitland & Sammartino, 2015a). Furthermore, top managers' cognitions and backgrounds play a role in their decision-making, including in how managers perceive and handle cross-country differences (Dow & Karunaratna, 2006; Nebus & Chai, 2014; Piaskowska & Trojanowski, 2014). In spite of this, top managers are rarely considered in distance-related research in international business.

This chapter aims to fill this gap by combining insights from literature on the role of distance in international business and the upper-echelons literature. The key insight is that managerial cognitions and values are central to how institutional distance stimuli are received and interpreted to form managerial perceptions, that is, psychic distance. Hence, having the right individuals at their helms enables firms to realize the investment and learning opportunities associated with distance.

These insights are illustrated with the example of UK's Vodafone Group Plc.. Under the leadership of Arun Sarin between 2003 and 2008, Vodafone embarked on a major expansion drive in emerging markets, which were distant from the firm's portfolio and experience at the time. The success of these expansions has been possible in part due to Mr. Sarin's background and experience in emerging markets combined with his understanding of the developed markets.

The chapter offers two contributions to prior research. One, it proposes a framework to analyze the multifaceted and cross-level influences of distance on internationalization, thereby helping to address some of the issues highlighted in prior distance research (Zaheer et al., 2012). Two, by synthesizing and systematizing prior distance-related research, the chapter aims to start refocusing it on firms' abilities to realize the benefits of distance. Suggestions for future research are also discussed.

BACKGROUND LITERATURE

Distance-related research in the field of international business has produced hundreds of studies over the past four decades (Hutzschenreuter et al., 2016). While a range of conceptual and empirical inconsistencies and disagreements persist (Ambos & Håkanson, 2014; Zaheer et al., 2012), the literature is in broad agreement on three points. One, cross-country distance encompasses differences along multiple, often related dimensions (Berry et al., 2010; Dow & Karunaratna, 2006). Two, the literature is nearly uniform in its negative view of the different dimensions of cross-country distance as sources of challenges for companies, affecting their internationalization trajectories and outcomes (Ambos & Håkanson, 2014; Hutzschenreuter et al., 2016). Three, there is a broad acceptance in the literature of the idea that, at least to an extent, distance is endogenous to the perceiver (Dow & Karunaratna, 2006; Zaheer et al., 2012). The following sections expand on these points.

Dimensions of Cross-Country Distance

Past research has identified a multitude of dimensions of cross-country distance (e.g., Berry et al., 2010; Brewer, 2007; Dow & Karunaratna, 2006; Ghemawat, 2001; Hutzschenreuter et al., 2016). These dimensions can be grouped into five categories: cultural, administrative, political, economic, and geographic distances.

The first and most frequently studied category is *cultural distance*, encompassing differences in attitudes to authority, work, groups, time orientation, and associated business practices, among others (Drogendijk & Slangen,

2006; Hutzschenreuter et al., 2016; Tihanyi, Griffith, & Russell, 2005; Tung & Verbeke, 2010). Despite much criticism (Shenkar, 2001), cultural distance is typically conceptualized using four of Hofstede's (2001) cultural dimensions (power distance, individualism vs. collectivism, masculinity vs. femininity, and uncertainty avoidance) and measured using Kogut and Singh's (1988) index.

The second category is *administrative distance*. It encompasses colonial ties and legal system differences (Berry et al., 2010; Ghemawat, 2001) and relates closely to the third category, namely *political distance*. Political distance encompasses differences in the political systems and the systems' stability (Berry et al., 2010). The stability of political systems can be quantified with the use of Henisz's (2000) political hazards index.

Next is *economic distance*, which includes cross-country differences in economic and financial development, macroeconomic characteristics, and commercial ties among countries (Anderson & Gatignon, 1986; Berry et al., 2010; Brewer, 2007; Ghemawat, 2001). Administrative, political, and economic distances are typically operationalized using publicly available data from sources such as the World Bank and World Trade Organization.

The fifth and final category is *geographic distance*, which refers to physical separation between countries. It is perhaps the most straightforward type of distance to measure, for example, as the great circle distance between geographic centers of countries (Berry et al., 2010). Geographic distance may also include climate differences and the existence of a common border (Ghemawat, 2001).[1]

The above five categories of distance are not mutually exclusive, and different scholars have used different groupings of dimensions for conceptual and measurement purposes. For example, Berry et al. (2010) have used linguistic and religious commonalities as part of their administrative distance measure, whereas Ghemawat (2001) has viewed linguistic and religious differences as elements of cultural distance instead. At the same time, Ghemawat has included aspects of political systems, specifically political hostility and government policies, in his administrative distance concept. For Berry and colleagues, political distance has been a separate category.

Overarching Concepts of Distance

Beyond the above five distance categories, there are two overarching concepts commonly used in the distance-related literature to encapsulate multiple types of distance under a single umbrella. These terms are institutional distance

(Berry et al., 2010; Kostova, 1999; Xu & Shenkar, 2002) and psychic distance (Dow & Karunaratna, 2006; Johanson & Vahlne, 1977; O'Grady & Lane, 1996).

The notion of *institutional distance* is grounded in institutional theory and based on the formal (regulative) and informal (normative and cognitive) pillars of the institutional environment (Gaur & Lu, 2007; Kostova, 1999). As such, institutional distance encompasses a wide range of factors. Berry et al. (2010) have proposed one of the most comprehensive approaches to institutional distance. Their measures covered the five categories of distance listed above and included several less commonly studied dimensions, such as differences in scientific and touristic activities across countries. Other studies have tended to account for a smaller range of factors. In particular, cultural distance is often excluded from studies of institutional distance, or it is treated as a separate concept (e.g., Ang, Benischke, & Doh, 2015; Gaur & Lu, 2007), although there are also studies which equate cultural distance with the informal aspects of institutional distance (e.g., Dikova, 2009; Müller, Hendriks, & Slangen, 2016).

The second of the overarching concepts is *psychic distance*. Its roots trace back to Beckerman (1956), who noted the importance of an individual's knowledge and relationships in effectuating international trade transactions. The concept of psychic distance has been revived by scholars within the Uppsala school, who defined it as the collective of factors hindering information flows between the firm and its markets (Johanson & Vahlne, 1977; Johanson & Wiedersheim-Paul, 1975). Subsequent research has included a plethora of such factors under the psychic distance umbrella, from cultural differences to political, linguistic, religious as well as economic ones. In terms of measurement, similar and oftentimes the same measures have been used to operationalize psychic distance as for institutional distance (e.g., Brewer, 2007; Dikova, 2009; Dow & Karunaratna, 2006).

One reason for this apparent empirical and conceptual overlap between psychic distance and institutional distance is the convergence in the level of analysis and the reference points at which the two concepts operate. Institutional distance focuses on differences between country pairs. It operates at the country-dyad level, in practice referring to a firm's home country's distance to its host country. Unlike institutional distance, psychic distance has been conceived originally as an individual-level concept and elevated through anthropomorphism to the firm level by the early Uppsala works. In practice, this has led to psychic distance being operationalized at the home–host country-dyad level, too. It is only more recently that scholars have started putting the "psychic" aspect back in its place (Nebus & Chai, 2014; Zaheer et al., 2012). Still, empirical work remains scant and the country-dyad measures remain in use as the so-called psychic distance stimuli received by managers (e.g., Dikova, 2009; Dow & Karunaratna, 2006). Thus, at least empirically, the two overarching concepts of institutional distance and psychic distance continue to overlap. This lack of conceptual and empirical clarity coincides with divergent empirical findings in distance-related literature, as discussed next.

Is Distance Good or Bad for Internationalizing Firms?

Prior research has tended to take a negative view on the role of cross-country distance in firm internationalization. Distance has been seen as a liability to overcome, a barrier to be surmounted, uncertainty to be resolved, or risk to be mitigated (Ambos & Håkanson, 2014; Johanson & Vahlne, 1977; Makino & Tsang, 2011; Zaheer, 1995). Looking at cultural distance alone, Stahl et al. (2016) have found a 17:1 ratio of studies that made negative rather than positive assumptions about it. Distance has been argued to increase the transactional and managerial costs of doing business, complicate learning and knowledge transfer, and increase organizational complexity following international expansion (e.g., Barkema et al., 1996; Demirbag, Glaister, & Tatoglu, 2007; Simonin, 1999; Vermeulen & Barkema, 2002).

However, empirical findings are not unequivocal. Many studies have found positive, insignificant, or nonlinear effects of various dimensions of distance on the choice of international markets, entry-mode selection, as well as firm and subsidiary performance (see appendices to Hutzschenreuter et al., 2016 for a recent collection). This is not surprising if one considers that, fundamentally, firms internationalize in order to exploit the cross-country differences for commercial reasons. Yet, only very recently have scholars begun to argue for a more positive view of distance (e.g., Ambos & Håkanson, 2014; Klitmøller & Lauring, 2016; Stahl et al., 2016). In this respect, prior research suggests two types of benefits of distance for internationalizing firms; learning benefits and differentiation benefits.

Regarding the *learning benefits*, O'Grady and Lane (1996) have been among the first to identify what they termed the "psychic distance paradox," a situation when perceived or assumed similarities between the home and host countries can leave decision-makers complacent, unlikely to seek insight, and unable to learn about the new countries. Hence, larger distance should lead to more learning and better internationalization outcomes.

In a similar vein, Evans and Mavondo (2002) have observed that in order to reduce uncertainty, firms are more likely to undertake extensive research, learning, and planning when expanding into distant markets as compared to more proximate or similar ones. Thanks to the more extensive preparation, the resulting internationalization decisions are likely to be more comprehensive and ultimately lead to better performance when distance is higher.

Another learning benefit from distance is associated with the breadth of knowledge. Distance can enhance learning and performance of internationalizing firms by broadening a firm's knowledge base through access to new routines and repertoires embedded in other cultures and organizations (Morosini, Shane, & Singh, 1998). Larger distance may also increase knowledge transfer potential, for example, in international acquisitions (Sarala & Vaara, 2010). Furthermore, a more diverse knowledge base is likely to increase a firm's awareness of potential differences across countries, making firm less likely to misapply prior experience, and better able to recombine prior knowledge to generate new solutions to problems encountered in new markets (Piaskowska, 2005). Diverse knowledge base can also help firms develop new capabilities and overcome inertial forces (Vermeulen & Barkema, 2001). Thus, exposure to higher distances is associated with learning benefits, leading to better decisions, improved problem solving, greater adaptability, and ultimately higher performance (Piaskowska, 2005; Reus & Lamont, 2009; Stahl et al., 2016).

Apart from the learning benefits, prior research has also pointed to *differentiation benefits* associated with higher cross-country distances, over and beyond the long-recognized benefits of international expansion associated with access to new markets, resources, and improved efficiency (Dunning & Lundan, 2008). Being different in a distant market opens new opportunities for a firm and may shield it from local competition (Evans & Mavondo, 2002), in particular when coupled with a positive perception of the firm and its products or services due to country-of-origin effects (Insch & Miller, 2005). Similarly, for some firms, being foreign in a distant market may bring reputational and signaling benefits, for example, when the foreign firms adopt high sustainability and corporate social responsibility standards beyond regulatory requirements in their host markets (Doh, Littell, & Quigley, 2015).

Summary

Cross-country distance comprises cultural, administrative, political, economic, and geographic differences. Two overarching concepts encompassing some and all of these categories are institutional distance and psychic distance. While institutional distance is normally seen as a set of environmental factors, psychic distance is more appropriately conceptualized as perceptions of the environmental stimuli. Despite this conceptual distinction, both institutional distance and psychic distance have been measured at the country-dyad level,[2] often with the use of the same or similar empirical indicators.

Irrespectively of the type of distance, its predominant effect on firm internationalization is seen as negative. Yet, empirical findings do not support this view uniformly, and two types of benefits of distance can be seen in prior literature: differentiation benefits and learning benefits. Differentiation benefits are associated with firm origin and country-of-origin effects. Learning benefits are endogenous and depend on the firm's and its decision-makers' perceptions and assumptions about its environments.

In what follows, we employ the upper-echelons perspective (Carpenter, Geletkanycz, & Sanders, 2004; Hambrick & Mason, 1984; Piaskowska & Trojanowski, 2014) as a unifying framework to analyze the multifaceted influences of distance on internationalization and to provide a logic for when cross-country distance is beneficial to internationalizing firms.

UPPER-ECHELONS PERSPECTIVE ON CROSS-COUNTRY DISTANCE

Upper-echelons theory has been proposed first by Hambrick and Mason (1984). It stipulates that top managers have a profound impact on strategic decisions of firms, including decisions concerning internationalization (Carpenter et al., 2004; Hambrick, 2007; Hambrick & Mason, 1984; Maitland & Sammartino, 2015b). This is because managers rely on their own values, personalities, biases, cognitions, and experiences when faced with ambiguity and uncertainty normally associated with strategic decisions. Managerial cognitions and values influence which contextual stimuli are seen and received, and how they are interpreted. The resulting managerial perceptions become reflected in strategic decisions and outcomes (Carpenter, Pollock, & Leary, 2003; Hambrick, 2007; Li & Tang, 2010; Nadkarni & Herrmann, 2010).

Of particular relevance to internationalization decisions are managerial perceptions of distance and attitudes to risk. Prior research has shown that perceptions and attitudes to distance and risk depend on the managers' family and cultural backgrounds and experiences (e.g., Dohmen et al., 2011; Piaskowska & Trojanowski, 2014; Tse, Lee, Vertinsky, & Wehrung, 1988) and affect their expectations regarding the likelihood of success or failure (Carpenter et al., 2003). These influences are particularly pronounced in situations which allow managers' significant discretion, for example, due to a country's governance regulations (Crossland & Hambrick, 2007, 2011; Finkelstein & Hambrick, 1990).

Considering the importance of top managers in internationalization decisions, prior research has adopted upper-echelons theory to study foreign entry-mode choices (e.g., Herrmann & Datta, 2006; Nielsen & Nielsen, 2011), expansions into new geographic areas (e.g., Barkema & Shvyrkov, 2007), the extent of firm internationalization (e.g., Tihanyi, Ellstrand, Daily, & Dalton, 2000), and firm performance (e.g., Hutzschenreuter & Horstkotte, 2013; Nielsen & Nielsen, 2013). For the most part, this research has linked demographic characteristics of CEOs or top-management teams directly to internationalization decisions and outcomes. Less research has considered how decision-makers may perceive distance-related stimuli, and how their perceptions may influence firm internationalization (cf. Maitland & Sammartino, 2015b; Piaskowska & Trojanowski, 2014; Williams & Grégoire, 2015).

Based on the distance-related research reviewed earlier, we argue that the exogenous, contextual stimuli received and interpreted when making internationalization decisions pertain to institutional distance (Fig. 1). Institutional distance stimuli arise from political, economic, administrative, cultural, as well as geographic differences between the host country and the firm. Such differences can be seen and interpreted from different reference points, including in comparison to the firm's home country or other countries in the firm's portfolios, and in comparison to countries with which top management are familiar.

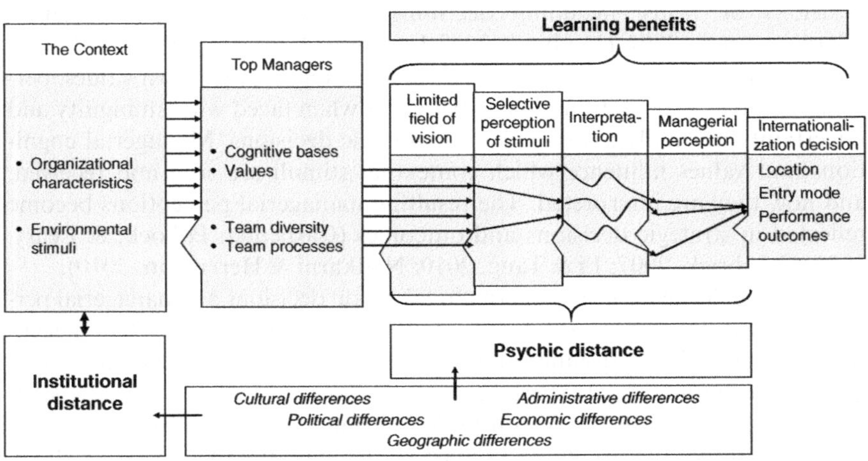

Fig. 1. Upper-Echelons Framework for the Influence of Cross-Country Distance on Internationalization Decisions. *Source*: Adapted based on Hambrick and Mason (1984, p. 195) and Carpenter et al. (2004, p. 760).

Thus, distance-related stimuli may operate at several levels and from different reference points (cf. Hutzschenreuter et al., 2016). Once interpreted, with some simplification and potential errors, the stimuli become the subjective perceptions. In this way institutional distance translates into psychic distance. Because these processes take place across different levels, team diversity and team processes also matter for how distance stimuli are received and interpreted (Carpenter et al., 2004; Nielsen & Nielsen, 2013; Piaskowska & Trojanowski, 2014).

The above logic allows us to delineate the institutional and psychic distance concepts and suggests that psychic distance is a complex, cross-level phenomenon dependent on individual managerial cognitions, the top team characteristics and processes, and the organizational contexts, with multiple reference points possible simultaneously (cf. Maitland & Sammartino, 2015a, 2015b; Stahl, Miska, Lee, & De Luque, 2017). Thus, there can be no simple answer to the question of whether cross-country distance is generally good or bad for internationalizing firms.

When Distance is Good

Beyond the earlier-discussed benefits of distance, the framework proposed in this chapter suggests that distance is good when managers have a wide "field of vision" and are able to receive and accurately interpret multiple stimuli from the environment. Wider fields of vision and more accurate interpretations of distance stimuli are more likely when managers have international experience (Herrmann & Datta, 2006; Levy, Beechler, Taylor, & Boyacigiller, 2007; Sambharya, 1996; Tihanyi et al., 2000). Both deep and broad experience of different institutional contexts is needed, as it helps managers avoid undue confidence and interpret the institutional stimuli more accurately (Piaskowska, 2005). The breadth of experience can be achieved by including managers with diverse backgrounds in the top team. Nationally diverse top management teams tend to consider a larger variety of perspectives (Nielsen & Nielsen, 2011) and are likely to receive and process more distance stimuli as compared to single-nationality teams, ultimately leading to higher performance (Nielsen & Nielsen, 2013). Furthermore, bicultural top managers, or managers who are able to bridge across various cultural schema, may be particularly well positioned to help their (diverse) teams process distance stimuli (Brannen & Doz, 2010; Piaskowska & Trojanowski, 2014), ultimately helping their firms to benefit from distance.

Thus, distance is good for companies whose executives possess relevant (international) knowledge, abilities, and attitudes, and whose top teams have a level of diversity they can capitalize on (cf. Stahl, Mäkelä, Zander, & Maznevski, 2010), even when their companies lack relevant organizational experience (Maitland & Sammartino, 2015a). This insight adds to prior research which has long recognized organizational experience as an antidote to the challenges of distance in internationalization (Barkema et al., 1996; Johanson & Vahlne, 1977).

The Case of Vodafone Group PLC

Vodafone is an illustrative example of a company which was successful expanding into institutionally distant markets while having only a limited experience in such markets at the organizational level. The company is one of the largest mobile phone and fixed network operators in the world. Headquartered in the UK, Vodafone owns or part-owns operations in 26 other countries on 5 continents, including such institutionally distant locations as Turkey, India, Ghana, and Lesotho, and has partnership agreements in further 49 countries (www.vodafone.com, Annual Reports). Despite these achievements, Vodafone's road to global presence has been bumpy.

The company emerged as an independent business in 1991, when it separated from Racal Electronics and became listed on London and New York stock exchanges (www.vodafone.com). Its initial strategy was that of organic growth. This has changed under the leadership of Christopher Gent, who took over as the CEO in 1997 and embarked on what business press described as aggressive empire building (*The Economist*, 2008). Sir Gent, a British-born and raised businessman with a career in British multinationals (www.bloomberg.com), had focused Vodafone's expansions on the developed markets. By the time he was replaced by Arun Sarin in 2003, Vodafone had ownership interests and partnerships in 28 countries, of which the most significant were in Europe (www.vodafone.com). Outside of Europe, Vodafone was struggling with its American and Japanese operations, and needed to integrate the global collection of mobile-phone operators assembled by Sir Gent.

Mr. Sarin has been described as "the archetypal international executive" (*The Economist*, 2003) who "is equally at home with both cricket and baseball analogies, as you might expect from someone born and brought up in India, and now an American citizen," married to a fellow Indian he met while studying at University of California at Berkley (*The Economist*, 2004). It is no wonder then that Mr. Sarin's international experience – both the formative, childhood influences, and his later life, career experiences – has been seen as an asset for Vodafone at the time when it needed to integrate the various units acquired under the leadership of his predecessor. As *The Economist* (2003) remarked, "to put another Brit into the top job might have bred resentment."

Despite the initial positive reception of Mr. Sarin's leadership, soon "it became clear that quietly fitting the pieces together would not be enough" (*The Economist*, 2008). Thus, in mid-2005, Mr. Sarin begun shifting Vodafone's strategy toward emerging markets. Step by step, Vodafone moved to take control of operators in Central Europe and then outbid a number of rivals to acquire Turkey's Telsim for $4.5 billion in December 2005 (*The Economic Times*, 2007). This strategic shift toward emerging markets was crowned by the $11.1 billion acquisition of Hutchison Essar, an Indian operator, in February 2007 (*The Economist*, 2007).

In retrospect, *The Economist* (2008) remarked that "Mr. Sarin's Indian roots were an asset during the fight for Hutchison Essar" and "having an Indian-American running Vodafone was exactly the right choice for a company that is now trying to bridge mature and developing markets." In 2008, the group reported strong financial results and revealed that it had more customers outside of Western Europe than within it.

Vodafone's example illustrates that expanding and integrating operations across multiple institutionally distant markets has been a major opportunity the company was able to notice and capitalize on at the right time, despite relatively limited organizational-level experience. Strikingly, the success has come under the leadership of an internationally experienced CEO who had an in-depth understanding of both the developed and the emerging markets thanks to his personal experience. He also surrounded himself by other internationally experienced directors. By 2004, his six-person executive director team counted three non-British members, with further internationally minded senior managers included in the company's Executive Committee (www.vodafone.com). For Vodafone, distance has been an opportunity, and the top management has been central to turning expansions into distant markets into a success.

DISCUSSION

In their recent study into the role of managerial cognitions in internationalization, Maitland and Sammartino (2015b, p. 753) observed that international business researchers have "a tendency to fall back on easy-to-access data and variables." Our review of distance-related studies has shown a similar tendency; the same or similar measures have been repeatedly used to operationalize conceptually distinct types of distance, in particular the two overarching concepts of institutional and psychic distance, with limited regard to the mechanisms, levels of analysis, and reference points (Hutzschenreuter et al., 2016; Zaheer et al., 2012). We have also observed that scholars have typically viewed distance as a negative factor in firm internationalization, despite distance being the very reason for firms to try to gain an arbitrage of doing business in foreign markets (Ambos & Håkanson, 2014). It is no wonder then that empirical results regarding the effect of cross-country distance on internationalization have been far from uniform (Hutzschenreuter et al., 2016).

This chapter sought to provide a unifying framework which would (1) synthesize and delineate the different types of cross-country distance conceptually, (2) provide a logic for analyzing cross-level influences of distance in internationalization, and (3) address the inconsistency between the predominantly negative view of distance in prior research and distance being the very reason for firms to internationalize. We proposed that combining insights from prior distance-related research with upper-echelons theory provides such a framework.

The combined framework indicates that distance influences internationalization at multiple levels and across levels, of which the organizational, managerial, and top management team levels are the most apparent. Most prior research has focused on the organizational level. At this level, distance is associated with differences between a host country and a firm's home country or portfolio of countries (e.g., Hutzschenreuter et al., 2011). However, this level of analysis is not consistent with conceptualization of distance as a perception. By focusing on the decision-makers, upper-echelons theory provides a framework for putting the "psychic" back into the concept of distance (Dikova, 2009; Nebus & Chai, 2014) and can help resolve some of the inconsistencies in distance research (Zaheer et al., 2012).

This chapter focused on one such inconsistency to clarify when distance is a negative factor in internationalization, and when firms can capitalize on the opportunities distance brings. While prior research has long argued that organizational experience helps firms mitigate the negative influence of distance (e.g., Barkema et al., 1996; Johanson & Vahlne, 1977), the framework and example shown in this chapter indicate that managerial cognitions, experiences, and values can enable firms to benefit from distance even in the absence of firm-level experience (cf. Maitland & Sammartino, 2015a). Indeed, distance itself opens opportunities for new learning, further contributing to a firm's ability to internationalize successfully.

FUTURE RESEARCH AVENUES

The relationships between exogenous and perceived distances and their influence on internationalization are complex and multiple mechanisms can be at play simultaneously. For example, in the case of Vodafone, Arun Sarin's plan to integrate the units acquired under the leadership of his predecessor involved some sell-offs. His efforts in this respect were slowed down by counteracting forces due to prior decisions taken by Vodafone. Thus, it is possible that managerial experience may not turn distance into an opportunity and the learning benefits associated with distance may not realize if organizational context is unfavorable. It is also possible that managers may become overconfident, especially those with some but limited experience (cf. Menkhoff, Schmeling, & Schmidt, 2013), and overestimate their ability to capitalize on opportunities in distant markets, leading to increased risk-taking (Li & Tang, 2010). While the framework proposed in this chapter offers a logic for analyzing such multifaceted influences, future theorizing would benefit from in-depth studies aiming to disentangle these influences. Specifically, cognitive mapping approaches (e.g., Calori, Johnson, & Sarnin, 1994; Maitland & Sammartino, 2015b) and experimental designs (e.g., Kraus, Ambos, Eggers, & Cesinger, 2015; Menkhoff et al., 2013) may be particularly useful. At a minimum, future research would benefit from recognizing the cross-level and (partly) endogenous nature of distance through the use of appropriate methodologies to better capture the complex relationships and to advance our theorizing.

The concept of distance has been widely used within various theoretical perspectives to explain firm internationalization, from transaction cost economics (Anderson & Gatignon, 1986), to the Uppsala internationalization process model (Barkema et al., 1996) and institutional theory (Gaur & Lu, 2007), to name a few. There is a potential in these theories to account for the managerial role in internationalization by integrating insights from upper-echelons literature and the broader cognitive and behavioral research. Such extensions may help advance our understanding of the microfoundations of internationalization (Foss & Pedersen, 2016; Gavetti, 2012), and allow for a more precise modeling of the heterogeneity in internationalization approaches and outcomes among firm.

There is also an opportunity for future research to study distance-related phenomena in contexts other than traditional multinationals. For example, the past few years have witnessed the emergence of new breeds of globally present companies such as i-businesses (Brouthers, Geisser, & Rothlauf, 2016). Such companies often internationalize fast and early, despite their inexperience, newness, and sometimes even smallness. It is not clear to what extent distance may matter, either positively or negatively, for such firms, nor is it clear what matters in their internationalization more broadly (Brouthers et al., 2016).

Finally, future research may develop new, practical insights regarding top-management team composition and talent development for firms to benefit from distance. Opportunities to do so would exist by bridging into the areas of global talent management research (Cerdin & Brewster, 2014; Puck, Kittler, & Wright, 2008), cultural intelligence (Earley & Ang, 2003), biculturals (Brannen & Doz, 2010), and diversity (Stahl et al., 2010), to name a few.

CONCLUSION

Cross-country distance can be good for internationalizing firms. It presents opportunities in terms of access to markets, resources, improved efficiency, differentiation, and learning. For these opportunities to materialize, firms need the right individuals at their helms, as managerial cognitions and values influence how distance stimuli are received and interpreted when internationalization decisions are being made and implemented. Internationally experienced managers and diverse, well-functioning top-management teams are a step in the right direction. By considering *who* perceives and interprets institutional distance stimuli, the framework proposed in this chapter offers a logic for analyzing the multifaceted and cross-level influences of distance on internationalization, highlighting the possibility for future research to refocus on how firms can benefit from opportunities brought about by cross-country distance.

NOTES

1. Another interesting though less-studied aspect of geographic distance is the "hassle factor," that is, how troublesome it is for managers from one country to travel to or live in another country (Schotter & Beamish, 2013).

2. There are a few notable exceptions to this. They include recent studies into the so-called added or marginal distance, which considered firm country portfolios instead of firms' home countries as the relevant reference points (e.g., Hutzschenreuter & Voll, 2008; Hutzschenreuter, Voll, & Verbeke, 2011; Popli & Kumar, 2016).

REFERENCES

Ambos, B., & Håkanson, L. (2014). The concept of distance in international management research. *Journal of International Management, 20*(1), 1–7.

Anderson, E., & Gatignon, H. (1986). Modes of foregin entry: A transaction cost analysis and propositions. *Journal of International Business Studies, 17*(3), 1–26.

Ang, S. H., Benischke, M. H., & Doh, J. P. (2015). The interactions of institutions on foreign market entry mode. *Strategic Management Journal, 36*(10), 1536–1553.

Barkema, H. G., Bell, J. H. J., & Pennings, J. M. (1996). Foreign entry, cultural barriers, and learning. *Strategic Management Journal, 17*(2), 151–166.

Barkema, H. G., & Shvyrkov, O. (2007). Does top management team diversity promote or hamper foreign expansion? *Strategic Management Journal, 28*(7), 663–680.

Beckerman, W. (1956). Distance and the pattern of intra-European trade. *The Review of Economics and Statistics, 38*(1), 31–40.

Berry, H., Guillen, M. F., & Zhou, N. (2010). An institutional approach to cross-national distance. *Journal of International Business Studies, 41*(9), 1460–1480.

Brannen, M. Y., & Doz, Y. L. (2010). From a distance and detached to up close and personal: Bridging strategic and cross-cultural perspectives in international management research and practice. *Scandinavian Journal of Management, 26*(3), 236–247.

Brewer, P. A. (2007). Operationalizing psychic distance: A revised approach. *Journal of International Marketing, 15*(1), 44–66.

Brouthers, K. D., Geisser, K. D., & Rothlauf, F. (2016). Explaining the internationalization of ibusiness firms. *Journal of International Business Studies, 47*(5), 513–534.

Calori, R., Johnson, G., & Sarnin, P. (1994). CEOs' cognitive maps and the scope of the organization. *Strategic Management Journal, 15*(6), 437–457.

Carpenter, M. A., Geletkanycz, M. A., & Sanders, W. G. (2004). Upper echelons research revisited: Antecedents, elements, and consequences of top management team composition. *Journal of Management, 30*(6), 749–778.

Carpenter, M. A., Pollock, T. G., & Leary, M. M. (2003). Testing a model of reasoned risk-taking: Governance, the experience of principals and agents, and global strategy in high-technology IPO firms. *Strategic Management Journal, 24*(9), 803–820.

Cerdin, J.-L., & Brewster, C. (2014). Talent management and expatriation: Bridging two streams of research and practice. *Journal of World Business, 49*(2), 245–252.

Crossland, C., & Hambrick, D. C. (2007). How national systems differ in their constraints on corporate executives: A study of CEO effects in three countries. *Strategic Management Journal, 28*(8), 767–789.

Crossland, C., & Hambrick, D. C. (2011). Differences in managerial discretion across countries: How nation-level institutions affect the degree to which CEOs matter. *Strategic Management Journal, 32*(8), 797–819.

Cuypers, I. R. P., & Martin, X. (2010). What makes and what does not make a real option? A study of equity shares in international joint ventures. *Journal of International Business Studies, 41*(1), 47–69.

Delios, A., & Henisz, W. J. (2003). Political hazards, experience, and sequential entry strategies: The international expansion of Japanese firms, 1980–1998. *Strategic Management Journal, 24*(11), 1153–1164.

Demirbag, M., Glaister, K. W., & Tatoglu, E. (2007). Institutional and transaction cost influences on MNEs' ownership strategies of their affiliates: Evidence from an emerging market. *Journal of World Business, 42*(4), 418–434.

Dikova, D. (2009). Performance of foreign subsidiaries: Does psychic distance matter? *International Business Review*, *18*(1), 38–49.

Doh, J. P., Littell, B., & Quigley, N. R. (2015). CSR and sustainability in emerging markets: Societal, institutional, and organizational influences. *Organizational Dynamics*, *44*(2), 112–120.

Dohmen, T., Huffman, D., Schupp, J., Falk, A., Sunde, U., & Wagner, G. G. (2011). Individual risk attitudes: Measurement, determinants, and behavioral consequences. *Journal of the European Economic Association*, *9*(3), 522–550.

Dow, D., & Karunaratna, A. (2006). Developing a multidimensional instrument to measure psychic distance stimuli. *Journal of International Business Studies*, *37*(5), 578–602.

Dow, D., & Larimo, J. (2009). Challenging the conceptualization and measurement of distance and international experience in entry mode choice research. *Journal of International Marketing*, *17*(2), 74–98.

Drogendijk, R., & Slangen, A. (2006). Hofstede, Schwartz, or managerial perceptions? The effects of different cultural distance measures on establishment mode choices by multinational enterprises. *International Business Review*, *15*(4), 361–380.

Dunning, J. H., & Lundan, S. M. (2008). *Multinational enterprises and the global economy* (2nd ed.). Cheltenham: Edward Elgar.

Earley, P. C., & Ang, S. (2003). *Cultural intelligence: Individual interactions across cultures*. Stanford, CA: Stanford University Press.

Evans, J., & Mavondo, F. T. (2002). Psychic distance and organizational performance: An empirical examination of international retailing operations. *Journal of International Business Studies*, *33*(3), 515–532.

Finkelstein, S., & Hambrick, D. C. (1990). Top management team tenure and organizational outcomes: The moderating role of managerial discretion. *Administrative Science Quarterly*, *35*(3), 484–503.

Foss, N. J., & Pedersen, T. (2016). Microfoundations in strategy research. *Strategic Management Journal*, *37*(13), E22–E34.

Gaur, A. S., & Lu, J. W. (2007). Ownership strategies and survival of foreign subsidiaries: Impacts of institutional distance and experience. *Journal of Management*, *33*(1), 84–110.

Gavetti, G. (2012). Toward a behavioral theory of strategy. *Organization Science*, *23*(1), 267.

Ghemawat, P. (2001). Distance still matters: The hard reality of global expansion. *Harvard Business Review*, *79*(8), 137–147.

Hambrick, D. C. (2007). Upper echelons theory: An update. *Academy of Management Review*, *32*(2), 334–343.

Hambrick, D. C., & Mason, P. A. (1984). Upper echelons: The organization as a reflection of its top managers. *Academy of Management Review*, *9*(2), 193–206.

Henisz, W. J. (2000). The institutional environment for economic growth. *Economics & Politics*, *12*(1), 1–31.

Herrmann, P., & Datta, D. K. (2006). CEO experiences: Effects on the choice of FDI entry mode. *Journal of Management Studies*, *43*(4), 755–778.

Hofstede, G. (2001). *Culture's consequences: Comparing values, behaviors, institutions, and organizations across nations* (2nd ed.). Beverly Hills, CA: Sage.

Hutzschenreuter, T., & Horstkotte, J. (2013). Performance effects of international expansion processes: The moderating role of top management team experiences. *International Business Review*, *22*(1), 259–277.

Hutzschenreuter, T., Kleindienst, I., & Lange, S. (2016). The concept of distance in international business research: A review and research agenda. *International Journal of Management Reviews*, *18*(2), 160–179.

Hutzschenreuter, T., & Voll, J. C. (2008). Performance effects of "added cultural distance" in the path of international expansion: The case of German multinational enterprises. *Journal of International Business Studies*, *39*(1), 53.

Hutzschenreuter, T., Voll, J. C., & Verbeke, A. (2011). The impact of added cultural distance and cultural diversity on international expansion patterns: A Penrosean perspective. *Journal of Management Studies*, *48*(2), 305–329.

Insch, G. S., & Miller, S. R. (2005). Perception of foreignness: Benefit or liability? *Journal of Managerial Issues*, *17*(4), 423–438.

Johanson, J., & Vahlne, J.-E. (1977). The internationalization process of the firm: A model of knowledge development and increasing foreign market commitments. *Journal of International Business Studies*, *8*, 23–32.

Johanson, J., & Vahlne, J. E. (2009). The Uppsala internationalization process model revisited: From liability of foreignness to liability of outsidership. *Journal of International Business Studies*, *40*(9), 1411–1431.

Johanson, J., & Wiedersheim-Paul, F. (1975). The internationalizaiton of the firm: Four Swedish cases. *Journal of Management Studies*, *12*(3), 305–323.

Klitmøller, A., & Lauring, J. (2016). When distance is good: A construal level perspective on perceptions of inclusive international language use. *International Business Review*, *25*(1), 276–285.

Kogut, B., & Singh, H. (1988). The effect of national culture on the choice of entry mode. *Journal of International Business Studies*, *19*(3), 411–432.

Kostova, T. (1999). Transnational transfer of strategic organizational practices: A contextual perspective. *Academy of Management Review*, *24*(2), 308–324.

Kraus, S., Ambos, T., Eggers, F., & Cesinger, B. (2015). Distance and perceptions of risk in internationalization decisions. *Journal of Business Research*, *68*(7), 1501–1505.

Levitt, B., & March, J. G. (1988). Organizational learning. *Annual Review of Sociology*, *14*(1), 319–340.

Levy, O., Beechler, S., Taylor, S., & Boyacigiller, N. A. (2007). What we talk about when we talk about "global mindset": Managerial cognition in multinational corporations. *Journal of International Business Studies*, *38*(2), 231–258.

Li, J. T., & Tang, Y. (2010). CEO hubris and firm risk taking in China: The moderating role of managerial discretion. *Academy of Management Journal*, *53*(1), 45–68.

Maitland, E., & Sammartino, A. (2015a). Decision making and uncertainty: The role of heuristics and experience in assessing a politically hazardous environment. *Strategic Management Journal*, *36*(10), 1554–1578.

Maitland, E., & Sammartino, A. (2015b). Managerial cognition and internationalization. *Journal of International Business Studies*, *46*(7), 733–760.

Makino, S., & Tsang, E. W. K. (2011). Historical ties and foreign direct investment: An exploratory study. *Journal of International Business Studies*, *42*(4), 545–557.

Malhotra, S., Sivakumar, K., & Zhu, P. (2009). Distance factors and target market selection: The moderating effect of market potential. *International Marketing Review*, *26*(6), 651–673.

Menkhoff, L., Schmeling, M., & Schmidt, U. (2013). Overconfidence, experience, and professionalism: An experimental study. *Journal of Economic Behavior & Organization*, *86*, 92–101.

Morosini, P., Shane, S., & Singh, H. (1998). National cultural distance and cross-border acquisition performance. *Journal of International Business Studies*, *29*(1), 137–158.

Müller, M., Hendriks, G., & Slangen, A. (2016). *Institutional distance and emerging market multinationals' establishment mode choices: The importance of context, direction, and interaction*. Paper presented at the European International Business Academy, Vienna, Austria.

Nadkarni, S., & Herrmann, P. (2010). CEO personality, strategic flexibility, and firm performance: The case of the Indian business process outsourcing industry. *Academy of Management Journal*, *53*(5), 1050–1073.

Nadolska, A., & Barkema, H. G. (2007). Learning to internationalize: The pace and success of foreign acquisitions. *Journal of International Business Studies*, *38*(7), 1170–1186.

Nebus, J., & Chai, K. H. (2014). Putting the "psychic" back in psychic distance: Awareness, perceptions, and understanding as dimensions of psychic distance. *Journal of International Management*, *20*(1), 8–24.

Nielsen, B. B., & Nielsen, S. (2011). The role of top management team international orientation in international strategic decision-making: The choice of foreign entry mode. *Journal of World Business*, *46*(2), 185–193.

Nielsen, B. B., & Nielsen, S. (2013). Top management team nationality diversity and firm performance: A multilevel study. *Strategic Management Journal*, *34*(3), 373–382.

O'Grady, S., & Lane, H. W. (1996). The psychic distance paradox. *Journal of International Business Studies*, *27*(2), 309–333.

Piaskowska, D. (2005). *Essays on firm growth and value creation*. Tilburg: Tilburg University.

Piaskowska, D., & Trojanowski, G. (2014). Twice as smart? The importance of managers' formative-years' international experience for their international orientation and foreign acquisition decisions. *British Journal of Management*, *25*(1), 40–57.

Popli, M., & Kumar, V. (2016). Jumping from springboard? The role of marginal cultural distance in cross-border M&A deal completion. *Thunderbird International Business Review*, *58*(6), 527–536.

Puck, J. F., Kittler, M. G., & Wright, C. (2008). Does it really work? Re-assessing the impact of pre-departure cross-cultural training on expatriate adjustment. *International Journal of Human Resource Management*, *19*(12), 2182–2197.

Reus, T. H., & Lamont, B. T. (2009). The double-edged sword of cultural distance in international acquisitions. *Journal of International Business Studies*, *40*(8), 1298–1316.

Sambharya, R. B. (1996). Foreign experience of top management teams and international diversification strategies of U.S. multinational corporations. *Strategic Management Journal*, *17*(9), 739–746.

Sarala, R. M., & Vaara, E. (2010). Cultural differences, convergence, and crossvergence as explanations of knowledge transfer in international acquisitions. *Journal of International Business Studies*, *41*(8), 1365–1390.

Schotter, A., & Beamish, P. W. (2013). The hassle factor: An explanation for managerial location shunning. *Journal of International Business Studies*, *44*(5), 521–544.

Shenkar, O. (2001). Cultural distance revisited: Towards a more rigorous conceptualization and measurement of cultural differences. *Journal of International Business Studies*, *32*(3), 519–535.

Shenkar, O. (2012). Beyond cultural distance: Switching to a friction lens in the study of cultural differences. *Journal of International Business Studies*, *43*(1), 12–17.

Shenkar, O., Luo, Y., & Yeheskel, O. (2008). From "distance" to "friction": Substituting metaphors and redirecting intercultural research. *Academy of Management Review*, *33*(4), 905–923.

Simonin, B. L. (1999). Ambiguity and the process of knowledge transfer in strategic alliances. *Strategic Management Journal*, *20*(7), 595–623.

Stahl, G. K., Mäkelä, K., Zander, L., & Maznevski, M. L. (2010). A look at the bright side of multicultural team diversity. *Scandinavian Journal of Management*, *26*(4), 439–447.

Stahl, G. K., Miska, C., Lee, H.-J., & De Luque, M. S. (2017). The upside of cultural differences: Towards a more balanced treatment of culture in cross-cultural management research. *Cross Cultural & Strategic Management*, *24*(1), 2–12.

Stahl, G. K., Tung, R. L., Kostova, T., & Zellmer-Bruhn, M. (2016). Widening the lens: Rethinking distance, diversity, and foreignness in international business research through positive organizational scholarship. *Journal of International Business Studies*, *47*(6), 621–630.

The Economic Times. (2007). *Vodafone digests its prey in three stages globally*. Retrieved from http://www.economictimes.indiatimes.com

The Economist. (2003). *A new voice at Vodafone*. Retrieved from http://www.economist.com/node/1956966

The Economist. (2004). *Foundation and empire*. Retrieved from http://www.economist.com/node/3423126

The Economist. (2007). *Business this week*. Retrieved from http://www.economist.com/node/8717698

The Economist. (2008). *Ringing off*. Retrieved from http://www.economist.com/node/11452433

Tihanyi, L., Ellstrand, A. E., Daily, C. M., & Dalton, D. R. (2000). Composition of the top management team and firm international diversification. *Journal of Management*, *26*(6), 1157–1177.

Tihanyi, L., Griffith, D. A., & Russell, C. J. (2005). The effect of cultural distance on entry mode choice, international diversification, and MNE performance: A meta-analysis. *Journal of International Business Studies*, *36*(3), 270–283.

Tse, D. K., Lee, K.-h., Vertinsky, I., & Wehrung, D. A. (1988). Does culture matter? A cross-cultural study of executives' choice, decisiveness, and risk adjustment in international marketing. *Journal of Marketing*, *52*(4), 81–95.

Tung, R. L., & Verbeke, A. (2010). Beyond Hofstede and GLOBE: Improving the quality of cross-cultural research. *Journal of International Business Studies*, *41*(8), 1259–1274.

Vermeulen, F., & Barkema, H. G. (2001). Learning through acquisitions. *Academy of Management Journal*, *44*(3), 457–476.

Vermeulen, F., & Barkema, H. G. (2002) Pace, rhythm, and scope: Process dependence in building a profitable multinational corporation. *Strategic Management Journal*, *23*(7), 637–654.

Williams, D. W., & Grégoire, D. A. (2015). Seeking commonalities or avoiding differences? Re-conceptualizing distance and its effects on internationalization decisions. *Journal of International Business Studies*, *46*(3), 253–284.

Xu, D., & Shenkar, O. (2002). Institutional distance and the multinational enterprise. *Academy of Management Review*, *27*(4), 608–618.

Zaheer, S. (1995). Overcoming the liability of foreignness *Academy of Management Journal*, *38*(2), 341–363.

Zaheer, S., Schomaker, M. S., & Nachum, L. (2012). Distance without direction: Restoring credibility to a much-loved construct. *Journal of International Business Studies*, *43*(1), 18–27.

Zeng, Y., Shenkar, O., Lee, S.-h., & Song, S. (2013). Cultural differences, MNE learning abilities, and the effect of experience on subsidiary mortality in a dissimilar culture: Evidence from Korean MNEs. *Journal of International Business Studies*, *44*(1), 42–65.

CHAPTER 18

HOW TO INTERNATIONALIZE A TRADITIONAL PORTUGUESE-STYLE FOOD – LIABILITY OR ASSET OF PORTUGUESENESS?

Susana Costa e Silva and Maria Elo

ABSTRACT

In an increasingly competitive global market, firms try to conquer a special place in customers' minds and – when possible – in their hearts and spirits in order to succeed. Hence, through a competitive strategy based on differentiation, companies tend to focus their efforts in creating the right value proposition for consumers. They also establish upstream and/or downstream partnerships based on win–win relationships for the parties that constitute their value chain. The particular characteristics of ethnic products influence these strategies and the brand crossover. How can the ethnic-national identity of a product be employed successfully – regarding its liabilities and assets – in international sales? This case study[1] *focuses on Nata Pura, a rather young Portuguese firm that has built its internationalization strategy based on exporting a traditional product pastel de nata using innovative solutions, which include the development of partnerships*

Distance in International Business: Concept, Cost and Value
Progress in International Business Research, Volume 12, 425–442

ISSN: 1745-8862/doi:10.1108/S1745-886220170000012007

to produce and promote this as an organic pastry made with high-quality-adapted ingredients. Earlier, the traditional product was mainly sold and distributed within Portuguese Diaspora. Nata Pura company markets and distributes the re-invented product, originally a traditional Portuguese food product, and bridges cultural and administrative distances by combining the traditional with global tendencies and tastes.

Keywords: Case study; differentiation; internationalization; international market selection; adaptation; marketing mix; Portugal; pastel de nata; Nata Pura

INTRODUCTION

In January 2012, during a press conference regarding the internationalization of the Portuguese economy, the minister of economy and employment Álvaro Santos Pereira stressed the fact that despite its success, heretofore there hadn't been any entrepreneur – Portuguese or foreigner – willing to promote and commercialize one of the most famous products in Portugal: the pastel de nata (TSF, 2012). At the time, this statement hit the headlines of newspapers, but many tended to welcome it with disregard, because there were already several companies exporting this product to different host markets around the globe. Nevertheless, none of them was promoting pastel de nata as a Portuguese delicacy, but rather as a non-branded staple.

Although not in line with the incentive of the minister, more than one year later, in May 2013, Mabílio de Albuquerque and his partner Gonçalo Albuquerque decided to join efforts and search for traditional Portuguese agri-business products that could be accepted by consumers worldwide and be exported, respectively. Originally, they considered three distinct products: olive oil, wine, and pastel de nata. However, the first two items were already well established in the market and dominated by major players, which created strong barriers of entry to newcomers and increased the chances of failure. Hence, the two entrepreneurs opted to spread their chances of entering foreign markets with a product that they thought to be less difficult to introduce, due to its uniqueness as a Portuguese delicacy, good quality, and tradition. They also stressed that regarding pastel de nata it could also be fully controlled in terms of production quality. However, is an ethnic product strategy viable for internationalization, isn't it facing particular liabilities of foreignness? How could the firm employ the ethnic-national identity of the product reducing its liabilities as a foreign product and increasing its assets as a recognized delicacy in international sales? Bridging the distance in taste and demand in distant markets positively requires a strategic fit and cultural asset employment following the idea of semantic fit in strategy in the case of Walt Disney Company's internationalization (Brannen, 2004).

In this case, the delicacy offered them the opportunity to tell a story, which combined with a strong tradition in the country of origin – Portugal – could allow the two partners to differentiate Nata Pura from their competitors, following a business strategy based on differentiation, rather than on costs Palavras, H. de. (2014, July). Nata Pura com personalidade. Pontos de Vista, 57. In fact, according to Nata Pura's CMO, Nuno Costa, it seems that "clients, especially end consumers, like to know that there is a story behind the product." The CEO of Nata Pura, Mabílio de Albuquerque, considered that differentiation (from other suppliers) was an extremely relevant part of the internationalization process, because it added credibility and sustainability not only to the product but also to the business, especially when competing in foreign markets. Furthermore, the firm regarded branding and promotion as being very important to achieve the right kind of differentiation and the correct positioning that was still missing concerning the other pastel de nata in international markets. While the origin of the food product (country of origin) can represent a liability of foreignness for consumers, it may particularly be so in the minds of the gatekeepers to new foreign markets and increase entry difficulties (Knight, Holdsworth, & Mather, 2007). With this Portuguese custard tart, the firm Nata Pura attempts to develop a contemporary and dynamic wise-activated brand, turning it into a global concept of delight with Portuguese origin that may crossover to mainstream markets abroad. Simultaneously, the brand was designed to be adopted and recognized in any part of the world, permitting it to be used in distinct situations, not only in terms of marketing but also considering its concept as a global product-ethnic delicacy (Palavras, 2014).

THEORETICAL VIEWS ON DISTANCE AND FOREIGNNESS

Distance and otherness remain central problems in internationalization. There are several concepts of distance between foreign and indigenous firms from linking information asymmetry to aspects of foreignness as a taste. "The psychic distance is defined as the sum of factors preventing the flow of information from and to the market" (Johanson & Vahlne, 1977, p. 24). It is constituted by aspects like language, education, business practices, culture, and industrial development. The concept of liability of foreignness can be credited to Hymer (1976) who claimed that there are unavoidable costs faced by foreign firms when operating in a different environment than their home market. International market selection is frequently linked with the liability of foreignness due to the costs associated with the acquisition of market knowledge and the respective hazards.

Later, the concept of liability of foreignness was complemented with a new view on deficiency: the liability of outsidership. This extended concept on entry problems as well as the liability of outsidership illustrate the significance of the establishment of a network that involves different actors like suppliers, customers, and stakeholders, which places foreign entrant firms in a competitive disadvantage relative to incumbent firms enjoying stronger ties with relevant players in the host market (Gallego & Casillas, 2014; Johanson & Vahlne, 2003, 2006, 2009; Muzychenko & Liesch, 2015; Zaheer, 2002). The Uppsala model (e.g., Johanson & Vahlne, 1977) for market entry proposed an entry order starting with exports via an agent, followed by established sales subsidiary and later in some cases by beginning production, as exporters attempt to reduce psychic distance between home and host countries. Accordingly, we can claim that the existence of stronger and larger business networks may contribute to firms' establishment of important relationships in foreign markets, which apparently can help the companies to diminish the costs of doing business abroad (i.e., liability of foreignness), as well as those associated with being considered outsiders (i.e., liability of outsidership; Johanson & Vahlne, 2009; Muzychenko & Liesch, 2015).

In addition, other scholars have pointed out that the distance or liability of foreignness may influence the business positively and constitute an asset (cf. Brannen, 2004; Nachum, 2010). Brannen (2004) illustrates how foreignness can facilitate the international marketing process of a product or concept in a foreign market entry. Market-based resources are central in generating assets, such as classic firm-specific advantages, and may enable overcoming liability of foreignness (LOF) (Barnard, 2010). Thus, there are two dynamics to consider in ethnic-national product entry: (1) how the liability of foreignness is diminished to enable local acceptance and (2) how the assets of foreignness are created for a product's differentiation strategy that may leverage the foreignness positively.

In marketing and advertising literature, the promotion of branded products toward ethnically diverse target groups is referred to as "brand crossover" (Puzakova, Kwak, & Bell, 2015), which implies that a certain degree of ethnic-national character is employed in international marketing across distant markets. In brand crossover, the role of the product itself may play an instrumental role in satisfying customers and creating value for them (e.g., Fang, Palmatier, & Evans, 2008), potentially due to its ethnic features (Chaudhry & Crick, 2004) or those of the customers (Dimofte, Johansson, & Bagozzi, 2010).

As the research literature on international distribution underlines, there is a network of actors involved in international marketing and international diffusion of a product but also shaping its value proposal (cf. Grier et al., 2006). The integration of this actor network into the strategic planning may reduce the business distance in multiple ways; it may reduce the meaning of geographical distance by developing manufacturing and logistics solutions together to serve the distant markets better; it may decrease the uncertainty and perceived liabilities of foreignness by building strong working relations with channel partners; and finally, the market-specific knowledge of this network may be crucial in generating the right product adaptation mix that makes the foreignness into an asset. The constellation of the international strategy and the product's value proposal may obtain advantages from cooperation with experts, for example, for the acceptance of a correct dosage needed for local consumption. Such adaptation in terms of the international marketing-mix program (Walters, 1986) does not have to relate to the ethnic value of the product. Still, it can balance the differences between the traditional national style and needs of the target markets. Thus, incremental innovation on various aspects of the marketing-mix aligned with international market preferences may contribute to higher acceptance while protecting the authenticity of the product, such as recipe in this case. A modular type of product strategy that allows the core to remain authentic but anticipates local purchasing preferences in other product characteristics may enable the assets of foreignness to be employed while reducing the respective liabilities.

METHODOLOGICAL APPROACH

Case Study

This is a qualitative single case study. It employs ethnographic and qualitative methods on a complex real-life phenomenon with ethnic-cultural dimensions (Alasuutari, 1995; Ghauri & Grønhaug, 2005; Stake, 1995). Because ethnic liabilities and assets related to a product and its diffusion and distribution are less known, a case study approach can be particularly useful (cf. Dana & Dana, 2005; Eisenhardt, 1989). The study follows an explorative and descriptive strategy. Its purpose is to further develop international marketing and product theory on ethnic products in an interchanging data- and theory-driven reflection without rigid hypotheses, instead by interpreting the findings in our theorizing and discussion using a more progressive focus (cf. Piekkari et al., 2010; Sinkovics & Alfoldi, 2012). The case selection has been purposeful focusing on a traditional flagship-ethnic product representing a critical case for Portugal.

The data collection builds strongly on primary sources, such as in-depth interviews, observations, and company documents. In addition, other data such as photographic materials, reports, newspaper articles, and marketing material are collected and analyzed. The data are compared and content analyzed in reflection to the ethnic nature of the product's Portugueseness and its implications and meanings in the international marketing context.

Mr. Mabílio Albuquerque and Mr. Nuno Costa, respectively, the CEO and the CMO of Nata Pura, are primary information sources. This primary data, the secondary data obtained in public presentations made by the company, as well as their public reports are used. A representative of Portugal Foods, a private organization that assists firms willing to further develop their international operations in the agri-business sector, Ms. Ondina Afonso, was also interviewed for the catalyst role played by this actor in the internationalization process of the firm. Interviews took place between December 2015 and March 2016. The data collection is summarized in Table 1.

THE CASE OF NATA PURA

Pastel de Nata: The Story Behind the Product

Pastel de nata is a Portuguese traditional pastry that can assume different names around the world, such as egg tarts, custard tarts, cream custards, or even Portuguese-style cakes – the latter is the name adopted by McDonald's (Pinto, 2015). According to *The Guardian* (Fox, 2009), pastel de nata was considered one of the best foods in the world (ranked at number 15, among 50); it suggests that these "creamy, flaky custard tarts – served with cinnamon – are one of Portugal's great culinary gifts to the world" (Fox, 2009).

The historical origin of this pastry cannot be traced with accuracy; it is assumed that pastel de nata was originally produced in the 18th century by Jerónimos' monks, who lived in a monastery located in Belém – currently

Table 1. Data Collected in the Interviews.

Primary	Secondary		
In-depth, recorded and transcribed interviews with Mr. Albuquerque and Mr. Costa, in Porto/Portugal, and with Ms. Ondina Afonso in Maia/Portugal in 2016, non-recorded interviews with consumers of "pastel de nata" and mainstream customers in various contexts, photos, observations	http://www.natapura.biz/ http://www.natapura.com/ https://twitter.com/nata_pura https://www.facebook.com/natapura/ http://www.logisticaetransporteshoje.com/sobre/nata-pura/ http://www.natapura.biz/blog-detail9.html All retrieved on March 22, 2016.	http://www.theguardian.com/lifeandstyle/2009/sep/13/best-foods-in-the-world, accessed on March 17, 2016 http://www.agroportal.pt/x/agronoticias/2005/11/23.htm and http://www.dinheirovivo.pt/buzz/ementa-do-mccafe-completamente-renovada/, accessed on March 17, 2016 http://www.portugaldailyview.com/whats-new/pasteis-de-nata-portuguese-pastry-around-the-world, accessed on March 22, 2016 http://www.portugaldailyview.com/whats-new/pasteis-de-nata-portuguese-pastry-around-the-world, accessed on March 22, 2016 http://www.natapura.biz/blog-detail12.html, accessed on May 5, 2016 https://wilkes888.wordpress.com/2013/04/25/london-coffee-festival-2013-50-pics/london-coffee-festival-2013-tasty-nata-from-nata-pura/, accessed on May 5, 2016 http://www.mytaste.co.uk/s/bbc-good-food-custard-slice-recipe.html, accessed on May 5, 2016	http://www.portugalfoods.org/catalogo/files/assets/common/downloads/page0130.pdf, accessed on March 23, 2016 http://www.portugalfoods.org/catalogo/files/assets/common/downloads/page0131.pdf, accessed on March 23, 2016 http://www.portugalventures.pt/pt-pt/article/portugal-ventures-anuncia-investimento-na-nata-pura-no-%C3%A2mbito-do-programa-inova%C3%A7%C3%A3o-ind%C3%BAstria, accessed on April 14, 2016

part of Lisbon, but at the time considered an independent village. Over the years, many people have tasted this cake not only in Portugal but also in other countries where the Portuguese diaspora has taken it, most of the times, combined with an espresso, which is the traditional way of consuming this product in Portugal. In Portugal, the espresso, a small shot of caffeine that most of the Portuguese consume several times a day – 80% of the Portuguese population drinks coffee on an everyday basis (RTP, 2015) – is bundled with a pastel de nata. Interestingly, this tradition has already been imitated and incorporated by McDonald's, which has created a specific menu for Portugal that includes a coffee mingled with the pastel de nata (Brito, 2011). This shows how McDonald's has adapted its product range to meet the needs of the Portuguese market. In Portugal, it tends to be mandatory to always have these sweet custard tarts available in any bakery, pastry, or coffee shop. This stresses the idea that more than popular, pastel de nata is considered an ethnic cultural tradition of consumers in its country of origin.

One of the most well-known pastries selling pastel de nata is located in Lisbon and has branded this cake as Pastel de Belém. This shop is considered by many as the birthplace of this custard tart, and it also contains the story that its founder bought the original secret recipe from the Jerónimos' monks in 1837. Currently, the shop is owned by the descendants of the person who has purchased the formula in the 19th century. It is the only one that, until 2013, had branded this product, trying to convince consumers that other coffee shops, bakeries, and pastries simply sell copies of the original cake, no-name products of little authenticity. The positioning of that brand in Portugal allowed the firm to benefit from an excellent reputation that permits it to charge a premium price for the product and at the same time have customers queuing for hours just to buy the traditional cakes. Consequently, Pastel de Belém attracts people from different parts of the world – tourists visiting Lisbon – as well as locals.

Regarding the international markets (Garcia, 2012) from London to Los Angeles, through Paris and Berlin, there are many places where one can find pastel de nata; since, for decades, Portuguese have been selling this product abroad, especially in shops located in the vicinity of the Portuguese Diaspora. In light of the aforementioned facts, it was indeed pertinent to think that pastel de nata could go further than just playing a small role in small businesses as an exquisite tart. It was a challenge to establish a branded product with ethnic-national heritage. Other firms selling it were not employing branding strategies or developing the marketing mix. In 2013, Nata Pura decided to pursuit novel branding and embrace more innovative international marketing.

Additionally, the company was able to verify that this delight was becoming popular not only among Diasporas suggesting potential for an ethnic cross-over. When looking at the percentage of Portuguese buying pastel de nata at Kensal Town, London, the proportion of Portuguese buyers has been decreasing over time and substituted by foreigners (70% of the buyers are not Portuguese). Similarly, the increasing number of recommendations posted on TripAdvisor, it becomes visible that pastel de nata is no longer just a delicacy that Portuguese living abroad like to purchase in order to experience something from their home country. In fact, it seems that pastel de nata is definitely conquering the delicacy market in foreign markets. This is illustrated by the current consumption trends in cities like New York, Paris, and São Paulo (in the latter it is also possible to find shops fully devoted to this pastry).

Nata Pura: Paving the Road to International Expansion

Nata Pura is a rather young company founded in 2013, which has currently five people working in international sales management, design, marketing, and communication. Since day one, the firm wanted to have a project based on exports that was also driven by the desire of having a product that could be an international sales champion, built on a clean label. Hence, Nata Pura started developing a business on the basis of an organic product, made with high-quality ingredients, combining a three-centuries-old traditional product in its home country, with an innovation in marketing abroad. The firm currently sells the pastel de nata made with high-quality ingredients in a business model characterized by upstream and downstream partnerships, as the authors will describe next.

According to Nata Pura's CEO, Mabílio de Albuquerque, the entry barriers to this market can be considered low, especially after getting experience in this business, which was not, however, this case. Having obtained the experience in the production of pastel de nata, Nata Pura realized that with little incremental costs, it was possible to serve different markets using distinct channels: indie coffee shops, coffee chains, catering services, department stores (gourmet), restaurants, hotels, and supermarkets (Nata Pura, 2016), regardless of their location, independently from the geographical distance to Portugal.

In the road to the achievement of testing the concept, the product, and the brand in foreign markets, Nata Pura decided to attend events in several places, starting by the Waldorf Hilton Hotel in London, the Portuguese consulate in Seville, as well as other Portuguese consulates in the Middle Eastern markets, such as the United Arabs Emirates. The result of these events was extremely positive for the firm which was able to get constructive and encouraging feedbacks that helped to define Nata Pura's strategy, placing the project in a more focused and effective path. In one of these events, Nata Pura was also able to meet and establish a fruitful relationship with AICEP Portugal Global (a Trade and Investment governmental agency, created in 2007, focused in encouraging the best foreign companies to invest in Portugal and contribute to the success of Portuguese companies abroad in their internationalization processes or export activities.),[2] which offered the company full support, provided by a team of experts in the international business and marketing arenas (Palavras, 2014).

Nata Pura considers itself as a marketing firm that sells a product using a differentiation approach, focused on quality, texture, color, and lightness, which are the result of producing pastel de nata only with fresh and high-quality organic ingredients. Therefore, to reach distant host markets, Nata Pura's internationalization process is based on finding the right partners with whom it can develop a win–win relationship, where the firm provides not only the product and the brand but also all the marketing tools necessary to penetrate the market and engage consumers into a long-lasting relationship. This way the firm believes to be able to address administrative distance and the foreignness of the product positively. At the same time, the firm increases its sales and helps its partners to achieve customer loyalty through customized communication that can go from ads to social media, through an appealing packaging, as well as the promotion of events (Nata Pura, 2016).

At the moment, the firm has already conquered markets across the European Union and beyond, in Saudi Arabia, and the United Arab Emirates – in the latter it opened a kiosk at the Barsha Mall, Dubai. Using the same strategy employing the Portuguese tradition and the high organic quality, the firm is currently serving also very distant markets, such as South Korea. Thus, it has been able to overcome distance and related liabilities and to benefit from the distinct ethnic speciality character of the product.

Australia and New Zealand are targeted during 2016, along with other European markets, for example, the Nordic countries. Regarding the European market, Nata Pura established a partnership with a reference partner in the United Kingdom. These local partnerships allow the firm to access foreign markets, retrieve information about them, and obtain local acceptance (Nata Pura, 2016, cf. Rana & Elo, 2016). This has been, in fact, the *modus operandi* that the firm found to be effective in the international market selection process: Nata Pura establishes partnerships with local actors met in trade fairs that guide the firm to its next markets. By doing so, the firm mainly follows a relational approach on international market selection and an opportunistic approach exploring opportunities to which the firm is exposed that lead the process instead of having a systematic way of pre-defined strategies. This network-based, rather organic way of approaching the foreign markets assists the firm to build on the value creation of its products that is emerging from a more emic perspective.

Adaptation Versus Standardization: The Path that Nata Pura Follows

Product Policy

The company intentionally chose differentiation over price strategy. Following the guidelines that resulted from Nata Pura's research and development activities, the product is produced only with high-quality ingredients, such as real eggs, fresh milk, and sugar cane – avoiding the use of high-fructose corn syrup (HFCS) which is considered to be related to health problems like diabetes. Nata Pura is concerned about food safety and the key role played by certifications, which in the food industry can be considered by end consumers as more relevant than the brand *per se*. Thus, the company needed to search for a manufacturer that would be able to comply with certifications like the standardization of quality, safety, operational criteria, and legal obligations (i.e., BRC Global Standards is a leading brand and consumer protection organisation, used by over 25,000 certificated suppliers over 130 countries, with certification issued through a global network of accredited certification bodies. (in https://www.brcglobalstandards.com/) – Grade A), International Featured Standards (IFS) and Halal – an extremely important certificate for Muslim communities. Moreover, due to the relevance of the Jewish community in some of the countries where Nata Pura is present, the company is now aiming to get the Kosher certification. Genuine and certified quality is essential in order to reach certain markets and partners like Harrods. Also some events require that to be eligible to participate. Nata Pura is aware of the relevance and need of having internationally recognized certifications. At the same time, the certifications seem to help the company to differentiate its products from others in the market while establishing its own standards for the quality of its pastel de nata. The externalized production of Nata Pura guarantees manufactured according to the firm's instructions, under strict rules in terms of ingredients and specific certification standards. The firm was awarded with two of the three stars granted by the Great Taste Awards in 2015.

As part of the differentiation strategy, Nata Pura tries to adapt the product to the tastes of consumers in diverse distant markets. After attending some trade shows and processing all the information retrieved from the interaction with potential partners, clients, and other stakeholders, the firm realized that in order for its pastel de nata to thrive in the international market, Nata Pura would have to show the superior quality of the product. This could be done by the use of high-quality ingredients, such as margarine (or butter, as the team subsequently learned to be almost mandatory when producing for the French market), leaving behind the use of powder eggs, powder milk, trans fats, and HFCS. Thus, the incremental innovations used in the production of pastel de nata enabled Nata Pura to excel and to define its differentiation strategy in marketing communication addressing local preferences. It also called the attention of trade visitors who tasted the product during international food events and exhibitions.

This openness to innovation is relevant for the product per se, but also for the markets where the company is present and for the target markets. The firms follow the rule: "be where the market requests us to be," as said by Nuno Costa, Nata Pura's CMO. This mindset enabled in 2013 that in the world's most important food exhibition, ANUGA Food-Fair in Cologne Germany, the firm got acquainted with a Japanese chef who was delighted with the brand and product of pastel de nata. The chef was so enthusiastic about this delicacy that he requested some product adaptation to Japan in order for the tart to be included in Japanese restaurant Yosushi menus. This was the seed for the development and production of pastel de nata with green tea flavor (being added to the inner part of the pastry), which resulted in a new creation that was successfully introduced in other south eastern markets, like South Korea, where the brand can currently be found in 79 shops. In this specific case, the firm not only adapted the product to the market, as it also changed its entry-mode choice, which resulted in a full conjoint partnership with the local associate. Furthermore, in this entry process it was not the firm that selected the market but it was the partner who developed the entry in the host country with Nata Pura's new products. The firm employed a relational approach to its international market selection.

In terms of product adaptation, it is also important to stress the fact that instead of the determined attitude revealed by some players about not changing the traditional recipe of pastel de nata, the company decided to introduce some changes and capitalize on a modification that seems to be effective and fruitful for all parties involved in particular new markets. In fact, the CEO of the firm stated that: "we know about the product, but they know about the market. Thus we have to rely on their knowledge of the local preferences and if the market requests a green tea and a passion fruit pastel de nata, that is what we are going to develop." According to Nuno Costa, CMO, adaptation pays off when it is technically viable. Hence, after considering the knowledge of the market of the selected partners, it can be transformed in a win–win situation with appealing outcomes for both parties. Thus, as the CEO Mabílio Albuquerque commented, apart from having the original formula, Nata Pura also produces other flavors, such as chocolate, passion fruit, green tea, and wild berries, and although the latter may "definitively not be successful in Portugal," the CEO argues that this is not one of the target markets, mainly due to the fact that only 0.5 million people will be willing to purchase these products. Consequently, Nata Pura focuses its attention and efforts on more attractive markets like the United Kingdom, where it is possible to find 15 million people keen to buy premium pastel de nata with different flavors, as well as the French market with its 10 million potential consumers for this kind of product. Moreover, Nata Pura's CEO suggests that "Europe is our home market, not Portugal." To sum up, country of origin effect and the original recipe do not seem to be the key drivers of the success achieved by Nata Pura in its distant host markets, where South Korea and Saudi Arabia tend to play a key role. Instead, the branded high-quality Portuguese tradition of real ingredients, intrinsic for the product range, and the value created through adaptation tends to be the real motivator for partners to start a business relationship and for customers to buy this delicacy and develop customer loyalty. Regarding the firm's perspective, one of the key elements for the success of its strategy is the partner selection and integration in the overall internationalization process and in international product development. This strategy has enabled overcoming of the liabilities and selecting the best of "Portugueseness" for the target markets.

Surprisingly, in most of the international markets the product seems to be sometimes considered as overcooked, due to its brownish crispy surface, which has a rather different perception in Portugal, where consumers tend to see this as the normal color of this kind of products. Bearing in mind the reaction of potential and actual clients in the host markets, Nata Pura decided to decrease the tanned surface in the overall area of the top, leaving the pastel de nata with a more yellowish tone. This assisted in diminishing the perception that some new consumers of nata may have that the product did not have an "optimal outline."

Promotion Policy

As far as B2B communication is concerned, Nata Pura chose to use international trade shows as the main communication vehicle, mostly driven by pastry tasting, which tends to help the brand to establish contacts with several agents, distributors, retail chains, restaurants, hotels, coffee chains, indie coffee shops, as well as catering service providers. These are usually contacted after the end of the event. So far, this approach has granted the firm a number of partnerships that have been subsequently developed into businesses and seem to set the path in terms of market selection. In fact, as the CEO of the firm said: "in our presence in these fairs, we were not constrained by any previous decision in the markets to enter. We may have been thinking about entering the French market, but we have always remained open to other possibilities that might appear."

As part of Nata Pura's communication strategy, the firm relies on being innovative and traditional in both approaches: above and below the line. It mainly communicates in the B2B market, but the company also wants to assist its partners by developing B2C communication campaigns, which tend to increase top-of-the-mind awareness for these delicacies. B2C marketing communication is not standardized but developed in these partnerships to enable right kind of acceptance and perception. The image and the brand activation are developed centrally, as well as the creation and making off of the videos that try to inform about the product and, at the same time, tease consumers by positioning the product as the second best delight in the world, since there is no consensus about the first one, as the firm's slogan mentions. Concerning brand activation, Nata Pura prefers to partner with its local intermediaries and in most of the cases the brand employs degustation which is inexpensive and also a good way of associating the product with the senses and the experience of seeing, touching, smelling, and tasting it. The firm has also elected some events to sponsor, such as the London Coffee Fest, BBC Good Food, and the RHS Flower Show, which in its opinion highlights the right associations to the brand, as the CMO recognized. In the absence of another place to insert the brand, the company chose to imprint it on the paper cup in which the pastel de nata is served that is simultaneously essential to absorb any fat left by the pastry.

Regarding Nata Pura's presence online, the firm has created two domains: a ".biz"' for distributors and a ".com" for end consumers. Moreover, the brand has a Facebook page as well as a YouTube channel that have been activated by the generation of new contents, where the core message is focused on the presentation of a new product, with an innovative approach to the requisites of the market, taking into account the local preferences of consumers. At the same time, the note also carries a traditional value proposition, since it refers to a product that transmits hundreds of years of history.

Distribution Policy

As for distribution and strategic product placement, the company relies on a structure that includes the partner's retail chain, hotels, restaurants, and coffee shops, as well as food retail stores. Thus, Nata Pura provides some solutions for partners in the retail business, distributing and marketing the product. However, the firm does not tend to do the same thing when dealing with the latter (i.e., hotels, restaurants, and coffee shops, as well as food retail stores) that are normally more independent in these decisions.

As for the transport of the products, in order to maintain the original quality of the pastries, they need to be sealed in refrigerated containers that are needed to move the frozen pastel de nata. Then, the product flies into the destination markets and remains appropriate for consumption for a long period as it has, at least, a 12-month shelf life. Furthermore, Nata Pura's products can go straight from the freeze to the oven, reducing wastes and shortening the need for space – especially in small coffee shops – since these pastries can be baked as they go. Nata Pura's clients welcome these features as they generate value and flexibility.

Pricing Policy

Retail prices vary across contexts. Regarding retail price, even though in Portugal a typical coffee shop can sell pastel de nata at a price that ranges from 0.75 euro to 1 euro, in the United Kingdom, for instance, it is marketed at 2 pounds and can easily reach 2.5 pounds in some stores. This provides distributors a good margin, which also contributes to the success of the product abroad.

CONCLUSION AND DISCUSSION

The strategy pursued by the firm is granting it the success that Álvaro Santos Pereira longed for in 2012. Nata Pura has been able to merge tradition with innovation in a combination where the accomplishment of its partners' suggestions plays a central role in overcoming barriers to entry and foreignness of the product. Their brand crossover strategy (cf. Fang et al., 2008; Puzakova et al., 2015) in international expansion has been successful and has bridged the distance of Portugueseness and the foreign markets.

It is important to observe that in Nata Pura's strategy, international markets are not regarded as extensions of the domestic one. In fact, the firm did not build on any previous domestic business experience before going abroad. It started as a born international. The same way it did not insist – as many did before – in using and copying the "Portuguese" traditional formula of pastel de nata to be sold abroad (cf. Brannen, 2004). The firm reveals to be open-minded enough to accommodate changes suggested by its international partners while building on the strong reputation and organic ingredients, as tastes are vital for foreign consumer acceptance. Systematically,

Nata Pura recognized and integrated the market knowledge of its partners into its international marketing policies, contrary to other Portuguese firms in this sector.

Nata Pura can be considered a success on the basis of its product co-development with partners and incremental innovation on its product character as Portuguese delicacy. This strategy has been integrative and a flexible way to internationalize. One can say that being open to adaptation made this traditional product competitive and generated a positive ethnic character, that is foreignness, which was easier to welcome in target markets. The openness to innovation is not common when it comes to the traditional or ethnic delight market. Thus, even though Nata Pura may have played down the "Portugueseness" of pastel de nata as its central feature, it has shown to be able to promote the high-quality perception of the country (ethnic-national character) in the innovation carried, in what is considered the second best delight of the world. Thus, its hybrid brand cross-over strategy following a global logic has combined the best features for each market and leveraged on these assets of foreignness when crossing borders and consumer tastes. As a result, Nata Pura has become a global product.

NOTES

1. Which has a teaching note, as well as some visual representations that can be provided upon request.
2. See more at http://www.portugalglobal.pt/EN/about-us/Pages/about-us.aspx

REFERENCES

Alasuutari, P. (1995) *Researching culture: Qualitative method and cultural studies*. London: Sage.

Barnard, H. (2010) Overcoming the liability of foreignness without strong firm capabilities – The value of market-based resources. *Journal of International Management*, *16*(2010), 165–176.

Brannen, M. Y. (2004). When Mickey loses face: Recontextualization, semantic fit, and the semiotics of foreignness. *Academy of Management Review*, *29*(4), 593–616.

Brito, P. (2011). Ementa do McCafé completamente renovada. Retrieved from http://www.dinheirovivo.pt/buzz/ementa-do-mccafe-completamente-renovada/. Accessed on March 17, 2016.

Chaudhry, S., & Crick, D. (2004). Understanding practices at the "ethnic" marketing/entrepreneurship interface: A case study of Kirit Pathak. *Qualitative Market Research: An International Journal*, *7*(3), 183–193.

Dana, L. P., & Dana, T. E. (2005). Expanding the scope of methodologies used in entrepreneurship research. *International Journal of Entrepreneurship and Small Business*, *2*(1), 79–88.

Dimofte, C. V., Johansson, J. K., & Bagozzi, R. P. (2010). Global brands in the United States: How consumer ethnicity mediates the global brand effect. *Journal of International Marketing*, *18*(3), 81–106.

Eisenhardt, K. M. (1989). Building theories from case study research. *Academy of Management Review*, *14*(4), 532–550.

Fang, E., Palmatier, R. W., & Evans, K. R. (2008). Influence of customer participation on creating and sharing of new product value. *Journal of the Academy of Marketing Science*, *36*(3), 322–336.

Fox, K. (2009). The 50 best things to eat in the world, and where to eat them. Retrieved from http://www.theguardian.com/lifeandstyle/2009/sep/13/best-foods-in-the-world. Accessed on March 17, 2016.

Gallego, Á., & Casillas, J. C. (2014). Choice of markets for initial export activities: Differences between early and late exporters. *International Business Review*, *23*(5), 1021–1033. Retrieved from http://doi.org/10.1016/j.ibusrev.2014.03.004

Garcia, P. C. (2012). Pastel de Nata: Where to savour Portugal's iconic pastry around the world. Retrieved from http://www.portugaldailyview.com/whats-new/pasteis-de-nata-portuguese-pastry-around-the-world. Accessed on March 22, 2016.

Ghauri, P. N., & Grønhaug, K. (2005). *Research methods in business studies: A practical guide*. FT Prentice Hall, Pearson Education, Harlow, UK

Grier, S. A., Brumbaugh, A. M., & Thornton, C. G. (2006). Crossover dreams: Consumer responses to ethnic-oriented products. *Journal of Marketing*, *70*(2), 35–51.

Hymer, S. H. (1976). The international operations of national firms: A study of direct investment. Cambridge, MA: MIT Press.

Johanson, J., & Vahlne, J. E. (1977). The internationalization process of the firm – A model of knowledge development and increasing foreign market commitments. *Journal of International Business Studies*, *8*(1), 23–32.

Johanson, J., & Vahlne, J.-E. (2003). Business relationship learning and commitment in the internationalization process. *Journal of International Entrepreneurship*, *1*(1), 83–101. Retrieved from http://doi.org/10.1023/A:1023219207042

Johanson, J., & Vahlne, J. (2006). Commitment and opportunity development in the internationalization process: A note on the Uppsala internationalization. *Management International Review*, *46*(2), 165–178.

Johanson, J., & Vahlne, J.-E. (2009). The Uppsala internationalization process model revisited: From liability of foreignness to liability of outsidership. *Journal of International Business Studies*, *40*(9), 1411–1431. Retrieved from http://doi.org/10.1057/jibs.2009.24

Knight, J. G., Holdsworth, D. K., & Mather, D. W. (2007). Country-of-origin and choice of food imports: An in-depth study of European distribution channel gatekeepers. *Journal of International Business Studies*, *38*(1), 107–125.

Muzychenko, O., & Liesch, P. W. (2015). International opportunity identification in the internationalisation of the firm. *Journal of World Business*, *50*(4), 704–717. Retrieved from http://doi.org/10.1016/j.jwb.2014.12.001

Nachum, L. (2010). When is foreignness an asset or a liability? Explaining the performance differential between foreign and local firms. *Journal of Management*, *36*(3), 714–739.

Nata Pura. (2016). Retrieved from http://www.natapura.com. Accessed on April 7, 2016.

Palavras, H. de. (2014, July). Nata Pura com personalidade. *Pontos de Vista*, 57.

Piekkari, R., Plakoyiannaki, E., & Welch, C. (2010). 'Good'case research in industrial marketing: Insights from research practice. *Industrial Marketing Management*, *39*(1), 109–117.

Pinto, S. P. (2015, June 8). O mundo já é de nata. *Jornal I* (8), 1–9.

Puzakova, M., Kwak, H., & Bell, M. (2015). Beyond seeing Mcdonald's fiesta menu: The role of accent in brand sincerity of ethnic products and brands. *Journal of Advertising*, *44*(3), 219–231.

Rana, M. B., & Elo, M. (2017). Transnational Diaspora and Civil Society Actors Driving MNE Internationalisation: The Case of Grameenphone in Bangladesh. *Journal of International Management*, *23*(1), 87–106.

RTP. (2015). *Cerca de 80 por cento dos portugueses consome café*. Retrieved from http://www.rtp.pt/noticias/pais/cerca-de-80-por-cento-dos-portugueses-consome-cafe_v820186. Accessed on March 17, 2016.

Sinkovics, R. R., & Alfoldi, E. A. (2012). Progressive focusing and trustworthiness in qualitative research. *Management International Review*, *52*(6), 817–845.

Stake, R.E. (1995) *The art of case study research*. London: Sage.

TSF. (2012). Ministro não percebe porque não há «franchising» do pastel de nata. The link for the information retrived is http://www.tsf.pt/economia/interior/ministro-nao-percebe-porque-nao-ha-franchising-do-pastel-de-nata-2236280.html (retrieved in 13 Sept 2017)

Walters, P. (1986), International marketing policy: A discussion of the standardization construct and its relevance for corporate policy. *Journal of International Business Studies*, *17*(2), 55–69. doi:10.1057/palgrave.jibs.8490424

Zaheer, S. (2002). The liability of foreignness, redux: A commentary. *Journal of International Management*, *8*(3), 351–358. Retrieved from http://doi.org/10.1016/S1075-4253(02)00070-4

PART V
ALTERNATIVE LENSES FOR IB RESEARCH

CHAPTER 19

LIABILITIES OF DISTANCE: GOVERNANCE COST DYNAMICS IN MNE HEADQUARTERS–SUBSIDIARY RELATIONSHIPS

Sverre Tomassen

ABSTRACT

Cultural and geographical distances create friction in multinational enterprises (MNEs), friction that indigenous firms do not experience in the same manner. This friction or liabilities of distance is conceptualized as governance costs in this chapter. Unfortunately, governance costs seem to be a rather equivocal concept, although it is one of the building blocks of internalization theory, and the raison d'être of the idea that certain kind of transactions have to be internalized to overcome the most prohibitive consequences of business activities across cultural and geographical distances. By going back to an award-winning paper, published in IBR in 2009, we put forward some nuances and reflections upon theory and findings presented in that paper, as well as upon implications and behavior of governance costs. The reason for this endeavor is grounded in the idea that theories must be challenged, empirical finding, just as well. Building upon survey data from 159 Norwegian MNEs, we explore and test six hypotheses by structural equation modeling (SEM).

Distance in International Business: Concept, Cost and Value
Progress in International Business Research, Volume 12, 445–470

ISSN: 1745-8862/doi:10.1108/S1745-886220170000012023

The results indicate that information fallacies seem to be the main driver of monitoring – and bargaining costs in the relationship between MNE HQs and their foreign subsidiaries, and thereby also the indirect driver of the observed negative effects of monitoring and bargaining on subsidiary performance. On the other hand, trust shaped by bonding activities seems to be an important factor in reducing bargaining costs and improving subsidiary performance.

Keywords: Headquarter–subsidiary relations; distance; governance costs dynamics; TCE; structural equation modeling

INTRODUCTION

The use of foreign direct investments (FDIs) as a governance mechanism in the globalization of businesses has been a noticeable move in the last decades, and the importance of the multinational enterprise (MNE) in the world economy has thereby increased dramatically. The ratio of multinational sales to world GDP increased from 23 percent in 1990 to 47 percent in 2014,[1] and the value of FDI inflow and outflow increased from 449 billion dollars to 2,528 trillion dollars during the same period (UNCTAD, 2015). Despite this trend, and despite those positive effects of trade and cross-border investments that we have seen the last decades, both at the macro, as well as at the firm level (see, e.g., Contractor, 2007; Dellestrand & Kappen, 2012; Li, Strange, Ning, & Sutherland, 2016; Liang, 2017; OECD, 2002, 2008), one cannot underestimate the extra burdens of managing subsidiaries located across geographical and cultural borders that create both fictional and factual distances.

In several host countries, "spatially related transaction costs" (Dunning, 1998, p. 50) might increase substantially for the MNE due to higher level of political risk, weak legal systems, limited access to skilled workers, and elevated trade barriers. In addition, together with expenditures related to employment, equipment, land and buildings, etc. (which indeed, can be substantially lower than corresponding expenses at home), governance costs that are more elusive in its character are generated in the daily management of the foreign subsidiary. Before entering a foreign market, these subtle costs are in many cases underestimated and indistinct for the companies. However, when the structure is set and the habitual business progresses, the liability of managing dispersed entities across geographical and cultural distances becomes more apparent and acknowledged throughout the MNE. Hence, although distance might be beneficial, it creates disadvantages and extra costs for the MNE (Ghemawat, 2001; Zaheer, 1995).

These acknowledgements are surely not ground breaking among international business (IB) scholars and have been at the center of the debate about; why firms go international, where to locate, and what organizational structure to set up, for example, Buckley and Casson (1976), Caves (1971), Dunning (1988), Hennart (1982), Hymer (1960), Kindleberger (1969), Kogut and Zander (1993), Rugman and Verbeke (2001), and several others. More recent studies show that larger distance between HQ and subsidiary, be it geographical and cultural, decreases the ability to share knowledge efficiently (Ambos & Ambos, 2009; Gupta & Govindarajan, 2000; Verbeke & Yuan, 2016), increases the costs of coordinating activities (Bouquet & Birkinshaw, 2008; Ceci & Prencipe, 2013; Richter, 2014; Tan & Mahoney, 2006), and augments information costs (Casson, 1999). Further, majority-owned affiliates in host countries might experience higher costs than local firms due to closer monitoring from HQ and thereby also lower degree of flexibility compared to what local firms experience (Nachum, 2010).[2]

In this chapter, we focus on the relationship between MNE headquarters (HQ) and their foreign subsidiaries and examine matters of governance and performance consequences in such relationships. Different theoretical perspectives have been used to explore the MNE, and without disregarding any other views, internalization theory/transaction cost economics (TCE; Buckley & Casson, 1976; Hennart, 1982; Rugman, 1981; Williamson, 1975) has been one of the most prominent perspective in that respect.[3] However, TCE is primarily concerned with the consequences of aligning different kinds of transactions to discrete governance structures; hence, little attention is devoted to, for example, firm performance and what is going on inside the boundaries of the MNE (Casson, 1999). Still, it would be wrong to claim that the performance issue is totally neglected, since the core puzzle to solve is about contrasting and choosing the governance structure that is most efficient in the long run. Hence, efficiency refers to the minimization of both production costs and organization costs, with the latter often labeled as transaction costs when resources are organized across markets, and management costs, when the transactions are internalized (Demsetz, 1993).[4]

Yet, there is no reason to believe that management costs generated in hierarchical solutions like foreign subsidiaries are conceptually different from those costs generated in market transactions – "they only manifest themselves somewhat differently in different contexts," according to Milgrom and Roberts (1992, p. 20). Therefore, this chapter follows Demsetz's recommendation and denotes both transaction costs and management costs as "governance costs" (Demsetz, 1993, pp. 161–162).

Neither, is it likely that an internalized solution even out the extra burden of cultural and geographical distances that often create additional friction in MNEs (Shenkar, 2012; Shenkar, Luo, & Yeheskel, 2008). This friction or liabilities of distance is in the present chapter conceptualized as governance costs. Hence, to be able to cope with governance challenges created by, among other things, cultural and geographical distance, at least four aspects with respect to governance costs have to be in place: The fundamental comprehension of governance costs, the factors that drive these costs, the possible performance effects of the costs, and governance cost dynamics.

Even though these aspects seem straightforward to solve at the outset, the exercises are certainly not that easy to execute. Governance costs occur both *ex ante* and *ex post* of the exchanged transactions (Williamson, 1985). They do not diminish by integrating the transactions (Casson, 1999; Eisenhardt, 1989; Jensen & Meckling, 1976), and some of them are hard to observe and measure (Masten, Meehan, & Snyder, 1991). Consequently, although we have recognized an increasing number of studies within the field of IB that address several of the critical aspects above,[5] there is still a way to go before the conceptualization, the measurements, and the dynamics of these costs are fully comprehended.

The present paper's principal concern is to explore the dynamic issues of governance costs in the relationship between MNE HQs and respective foreign subsidiaries, although both measurement issues and subsidiary performance will be addressed both theoretically and empirically.[6] Building upon survey data from 159 Norwegian MNEs, with subsidiaries across the globe, this exploratory study indicates that governance costs might interact and affect subsidiary performance in ways that have not been explored in former studies, for example, Tomassen and Benito (2009).

THEORY AND HYPOTHESES

Distance, in all its nuances, creates an extra burden for the MNE. It increases transportation and communication costs, as well as coordination, and monitoring costs (Hutzschenreuter & Voll, 2008; Hutzschenreuter, Kleindienst, & Lange, 2016; Tan & Mahoney, 2006). To reduce information asymmetries and uncertainty caused by distance, surplus resources will be required to learn and to refine the basis for decision-making in the MNE (Evans & Mavondo, 2002; Makino & Tsang, 2011; Morosini, Shane, & Singh, 1998). Likewise, the costs of essential initiatives such as job rotation, project organizations across units, specific management training, and socialization activities to bind the different parts of the organization closer together, will probably be higher

(Nohria & Ghoshal, 1994; Rabbiosi, 2011). It is therefore likely to anticipate a higher level of governance costs in internalized solutions when geographical and cultural distance is high, compare to what normally would be expected in purely domestic firms. Hence, in many cases – gains earned by lowering production costs, are gains lost by elevated governance costs in MNEs, which points toward the close link between governance costs and firm performance.

According to TCE, the make or buy decision is a trade-off between the costs of market transactions against the costs of internalization, and the most efficient governance structure is the one that minimizes production and governance costs in the long run (Hennart, 1982; Williamson, 1985). However, if this logic should have strong validity, the governance costs have to be conceptualized and measured in a clear fashion, scrutinized, and tested – that is, we have to investigate and test conceivable relationships between governance costs and various dimensions of firm performance.

Therefore, and before we go deeper into the conceptions of governance costs, a few words about firm performance would be pertinent. There seems to be numerous approaches to study and measure firm performance. Both objective and subjective evaluation criteria have been used in former studies. However, focusing on subsidiary performance, as in this study, faces the researcher with extra difficulties – objective data are hard to find and they are often biased by different accounting practices, transfer price issues, and dissimilar tax regimes across geographical borders (Dess & Robinson, 1984). As an alternative, different kinds of subjective performance data have been used in former studies, for example, Ariño (2003) and Brouthers (2002).

Consequently, and aware of the problems with such data, the present study relies on a set of satisfaction measures that altogether try to grasp the effectiveness of the subsidiaries (see Appendix for details). Hence, we believe that governance costs in some ways are related to subsidiaries' performance (Tomassen & Benito, 2009).

Governance Costs and Performance

Different literature has been occupied with the interpretation of governance costs, and according to Allen (2000, pp. 893–894), there are two distinct traditions: the "property right tradition" and the "neoclassical" tradition. The former is occupied with the role that governance costs play in the distribution of property rights – here defined as laws, rules, social customs, and organizations that are able to generate incentives for behavior. The latter is much more narrow in its approach, and according to Allen (2000), define governance costs analytically identical to transportation costs and taxes. Several will also claim that the latter type of costs arises only in market exchanges, and not within firms (Langlois, 2006).[7] Hence, due to our intra-MNE focus, the "property right" tradition will be the theoretical basis for a conceptual understanding of governance costs.

According to Williamson (1985, p. 19), governance costs are: "[…] the economic equivalent of friction in physical systems – it is the 'costs of running the economic system' (Arrow, 1969, p. 48), and must be distinguished from production costs." Hence, it is about the costs of governing the transactions – be it across markets or within organizational boundaries (Langlois, 2006). Being more specific, "friction" – or governance costs in general, are by Williamson (1985) classified into *ex ante* and *ex post* costs. The former are the costs of drafting, negotiating, and safeguarding agreements. The latter are the costs of (a) inadequate adaptation due to imperfections in the communication between parties, (b) the costs of bargaining with the intentions of correcting misalignments, (c) bonding activities with the purpose of aligning actors involved in the transactions, and (d) preparing and running the contract.

Transacting in a market when asset specificity and/or uncertainty are high, MNEs will probably be faced with elevated governance costs since such conditions trigger potential opportunistic behavior from other transacting parties.[8] This, according to TCE, is curbed most efficiently by hierarchical governance structures – that is, greenfield, acquisition, and joint venture (Hennart, 2009; Williamson, 1985). However, it would be credulous to assume zero governance costs in such solutions. In an intra-MNE setting, adaptation and coordination problems, communication failure due to cultural and geographical distances, are all common traits (Casson, 1999; Ceci & Prencipe, 2013; Ghemawat, 2001; Lu & Beamish, 2004). Likewise, extensive resources spent on supervision and control are likely to be frequent (Baliga & Jaeger, 1984; Chang & Taylor, 1999; Hennart, 1991). Hence, distances create *ex post* governance costs for the MNE, which at the outset should indicate negative associations towards firm performance.

Williamson's description of governance costs is rather general, but unfortunately, there has been rather limited emphasis on specifying and measuring such costs within the field of IB as well as in strategy and economics (Allen, 2006; Masten et al., 1991). The reason for this might have something to do with the general belief that such costs are difficult to observe and measure (Masten et al., 1991). Likewise, the idea that the problem of quantifying governance costs is somewhat mitigated due to the fact that they "always are assessed in a comparative institutional way […] by employing rather primitive apparatus" (Williamson, 1985, p. 22), certainly fortifies the absence of measurement of governance costs in empirical research. However, this stand is a major obstacle when testing the normative guidelines in the theory. It is actually imperative to understand and measure these costs (Allen, 2006; Milgrom & Roberts, 1992). The comparison of attributes will be rather superficial if the understanding and the measurement of the governance costs are ambiguous. Likewise, governance costs effects on performance will be difficult to comprehend.

Hence, a few, but growing number of attempts can be recognized (Buvik & Andersen, 2002; Buvik & John, 2000; Dahlstrom & Nygaard, 1999; Masten et al., 1991; Richter, 2014; Tomassen & Benito, 2009; Tomassen et al., 2012).[9] In the further description, we will follow Tomassen and Benito (2009) in their description of four different facets of *ex post* governance costs, as this study utilizes the same variables and data set in its analysis.

Bargaining costs are costs related to time spent on bargaining, resources used during bargaining, and losses that occur because of failure in reaching efficient agreements (Milgrom & Roberts, 1992, p. 301; Walker & Poppo, 1991). In an MNE context, this might be of an extra burden due to cultural complexity and geographical separation of the entities. Negotiations and renegotiation of unclear agreements between HQ and its subsidiaries are common attributes of the relationship (Andersson, Forsgren, & Holm, 2007). Tensions and disagreements between HQ and subsidiary regarding transfer prices and knowledge sharing in the MNE are also well-known sources for disagreements and bargaining (Mahnke, Pedersen, & Venzin, 2009). All these create extra costs that would hurt performance (at least in the short run).

Monitoring costs occur when resources and expenses are used to reduce shirking and other types of opportunistic behavior that violate the agreement between parties (Hennart, 1991; Jensen & Meckling, 1976). Since MNEs per definition are present in different countries and thereby exposed to a wide range of differences in legal and economic systems, as well as language, culture, and business behavior, *ex post* information asymmetries and risk of "moral hazards" (Knight, 1921, p. 249), are probably prevalent in some subsidiaries, probably also at a higher level than in purely domestic firms. Controlling delivered services, both to and from the local unit, create extra time and resources. Likewise, resources spent on accounting issues will probably be higher, and finally yet importantly; travel expenses to control working effort, so on, will be a significant extra burden for the MNE (Tomassen & Benito, 2009).

Information costs, in general, rise from communication and coordination failures between corporate HQs and subsidiaries. Due to larger geographical distances, and higher cultural differences in MNEs, one would expect that the information fallacies are substantial in such companies (Casson, 1999; Fisch &

Zschoche, 2011; Richter, 2014). Information received from the foreign unit might be incomplete, or too voluminous, or too poorly formulated to provide a proper basis for decision-making regarding adequate courses of action. Information costs are simply the opportunity costs of ineffective and inappropriate responses, which make the MNE unable to react rapidly to changing conditions.

In theory, with full information and complete agreements, the above three categories of governance costs should be negligible. However, the real world of MNEs is far from the ideal world of zero friction, and normally we will expect, *ceteris paribus*, that any extra costs incurred will have negative associations with firm performance, which also is confirmed by Tomassen and Benito (2009).

Bonding costs, on the other hand, seems to behave somewhat different. They occur when there is a need to integrate different entities, not by formal systems, but by building a more common corporate culture through social coordination mechanisms, which are essential building blocks in establishing and developing distant entities. Activities of this kind could be resources used in establishing personal ties between HQ and subsidiaries – for example, through social events, building common incentive systems, cooperation with subsidiaries to solve conflicts with third parties, close communication with foreign units, and time used to develop a common company culture (Rabbiosi, 2011; Tomassen et al., 2012). Although bonding brings about costs, Tomassen and Benito (2009, p. 294) contend that: "… in a real world, positive bonding would most often be better than no bonding because the costs derived from these activities may lead to improved firm value in the long-run. As such, bonding may be seen as an investment rather than costs."

Hence, we propose the following four base line hypotheses (all, in accordance with the results of Tomassen and Benito (2009), and all with direct effects toward subsidiary performance):

Hypothesis 1. The higher the bargaining costs, the lower the subsidiary performance.

Hypothesis 2. The higher the information costs, the lower the subsidiary performance.

Hypothesis 3. The higher the monitoring costs, the lower the subsidiary performance.

Hypothesis 4. The higher the bonding costs, the higher the subsidiary performance.

Governance Costs Dynamics

In their IBR article from 2009, Tomassen and Benito (2009) treated governance costs as four independent and unique latent variables, that each had a single and direct effect on subsidiary performance (i.e., HQ's satisfaction with the specific subsidiary along different dimensions). However, this could be challenged for several reasons, and Benito and Tomassen (2010, pp. 152–153) present a line of thinking that certain types of costs are more endogenous than others. Hence, one might observe systematic associations between particular types of governance costs, which expose MNEs to trade-offs. The arguments are as follows:

Firstly, information costs occur due to communication problems between MNE HQ and the local unit. Hence, higher level of communication problems due to cultural and geographical distance might intensify both bargaining and monitoring activities, which at the outset should have a negative effect on subsidiary performance since incomplete and/or poorly formulated information from the local unit may lead to wrong decisions and inefficient solutions (Dahlstrom & Nygaard, 1999; Tomassen & Benito, 2009).

Secondly, adaptation is perhaps the key economic problem of organizations. Hence, when foreign markets are volatile, difficult to predict, and quite different from the home market, information from subsidiaries will soon be inferior and incomplete, which probably augment both monitoring and bargaining activities (Nachum, 2010; Tomassen et al., 2012). Additional monitoring activities are implemented to hinder further negative developments, and bargaining becomes essential in correcting misalignments between MNE HQ and the subsidiaries (Andersson et al., 2007). The direct costs of both bargaining and monitoring activities are probably quite easy to identify; managers observe time spent in meetings, travel expenses are explicit costs, formal auditing as well. However, it is trickier to do the same with information costs. MNE managers may see information costs as drivers of other – more observable – costs that are the results of necessary actions, but they may find it difficult to link information costs directly to the performance of the subsidiary.

Thirdly, intensifying bonding, which in many senses can be seen as efforts in trust building activities with the purpose to reduce the needs for formal control, should decrease bargaining costs as well as monitoring costs. According to Chiles and McMackin (1996, p. 88): "Trust decreases monitoring costs as a result of each party's confidence in the other's performance, even though short term incentives may favor opportunism. [Further,] trust decreases negotiating costs by fostering a game-type approach to negotiations in which actors are cooperative and quick to come to a resolution rather than a tactical-type approach in which actors are cautious and slow to come to a resolution." Still, some bonding activities such as education programs (e.g., aimed at building a common company culture), and conflict solving with third parties, may lead to more control due to the necessity of evaluating the effect of putting additional resources into bonding activities. Hence, the following two hypotheses are proposed:

Hypotheses 5. Information costs affect both bargaining costs and monitoring costs positively, thus having a negative effect on subsidiary performance.

Hypothesis 6. Bonding costs affect both bargaining costs and monitoring cost negatively, thus having a positive effect on subsidiary performance.

METHODS

This chapter is using the same data set, with the same key variables as Tomassen and Benito (2009). Hence, we have no intention to deviate from what already has been done with respect to data collection, sampling frame, as well as validation of measurements. The initial part of this section will therefore be rather superficial.

Data Collection and Sampling Frame

The data were collected through a mail survey among Norwegian MNEs and their foreign subsidiaries, which at the outset were picked from the Dun & Bradstreet database of Norwegian firms. By checking all companies in the database, the original number of firms of approximately 1,300 MNEs with more than 3,000 foreign subsidiaries was reduced to an appropriate sampling frame of 346 MNEs that fitted the criteria and were willing to participate.[10]

Only one subsidiary for each MNE was chosen, and the study relied on a single key informant approach (Campbell, 1955; Seidler, 1974). The informants were all well informed about the relationship between HQ and the subsidiary, and the subsidiaries were between 3 and 11 years old at the time of the study. The total number of usable respondents was 159, which gives us a response rate of 46 percent.

Non-response bias was checked; according to Armstrong and Overton's (1977) procedures (i.e., late respondents were compared with early respondents by a *t*-test), no such problems were detected.

Since the data come from a questionnaire, different precautions, *ex ante*, were taken to reduce eventually *common method biases (CMV)*. (1) Some scales were reversed, (2) questions of interest for the present study were mixed with questions not so relevant, and (3) items belonging to different theoretical and latent construct were mixed. *Ex post*, two remedies were conducted:

(1) A Harman's single factor test was conducted without detecting any serious problem. (2) In the present study, we have specified a research model with complex relationships (yet, out of theoretical reasons), that probably not are part of the cognitive maps of the respondents (Chang, van Witteloostuijn, & Eden, 2010; Podsakoff, MacKenzie, Lee, & Podsakoff, 2003).

Measurements and Validation

Following Bollen and Lennox (1991), multi-item reflective scales were developed for all the different categories of governance costs and subsidiary performance. To validate the measures, both unrotated and rotated (oblique) principal component analysis were conducted in the initial phases of the validation. A final validation of the measurement model was done through a confirmatory factor analysis executed in LISREL 8.8. The final measurement model with three measures on information costs, four measures on bonding costs, two measures on bargaining costs, three measures on monitoring costs, and four measures on subsidiary performance shows excellent fit on all relevant fit statistics:[11] $\chi^2 = 97.00$ ($p > 0.395$; RMSEA = 0.014; AGFI = 0.90; CFI = 0.99 (Bollen, 1989; Jöreskog & Sörbom, 1981; Tanaka & Huba, 1985). Reliability was assessed by three measures: Cronbach's α (Nunnally & Bernstein, 1994), individual item reliability, and average variance extracted (AVE; Bagozzi & Yi, 1988; Gerbing & Anderson, 1988). The Cronbach's α values (ranging from 0.71 to 0.84) indicate that the scales are reasonably reliable. All factor loadings are significant. AVE values are, on the other hand, somewhat low on monitoring and bonding costs, but acceptable.[12] Discriminant validity seems also to be good, although there are some noticeable correlation coefficients among some of the governance cost constructs. See Appendix for an overview of items included in the measurement model. These items will also be included in the following section where several structural models are explored and tested.

ESTIMATION AND RESULTS

Since there are few studies of the relationship between governance costs and subsidiary performance, the main intention by presenting and testing this alternative model is to open up for reflections and deliberations upon a subject that may play an important role in firms' international activities. Since the focus in this study is on the relationship between perceived governance costs and subsidiary performance and not to explain subsidiary performance per se, control variables are omitted.[13]

Tomassen and Benito (2009) tested the hypotheses by using OLS and 2SLS. However, both theoretically and empirically (i.e., high correlation among some of the governance costs constructs), there are indications of interdependences among the governance costs variables.[14] Therefore, a structural equation modeling (SEM) approach with LISREL 8.8 (see Fig. 1) will serve as a basis for further explorations and analyses (Goldberger, 1973; Jöreskog & Sörbom, 1982).

The structural model in Fig. 1 contains three latent endogenous variables – "bargaining costs," "monitoring costs," and "subsidiary performance," and two latent exogenous variables – "information costs" and "bonding costs," all according to the six hypotheses that we proposed. In addition to testing the proposed effects, the LISREL approach also analyzes the whole model. As in an analysis of a measurement model, fit indices will also be produced for the structural model, and to assess the overall fit, the same fit statistics will be reported for the structural analysis.

The most common modeling strategy involves a comparison of competing models. Model difference can then be tested for statistical significance by following the recommendation from Anderson and Gerbing (1988, p. 419): "Significance between models can be tested by a χ^2 difference test with degrees

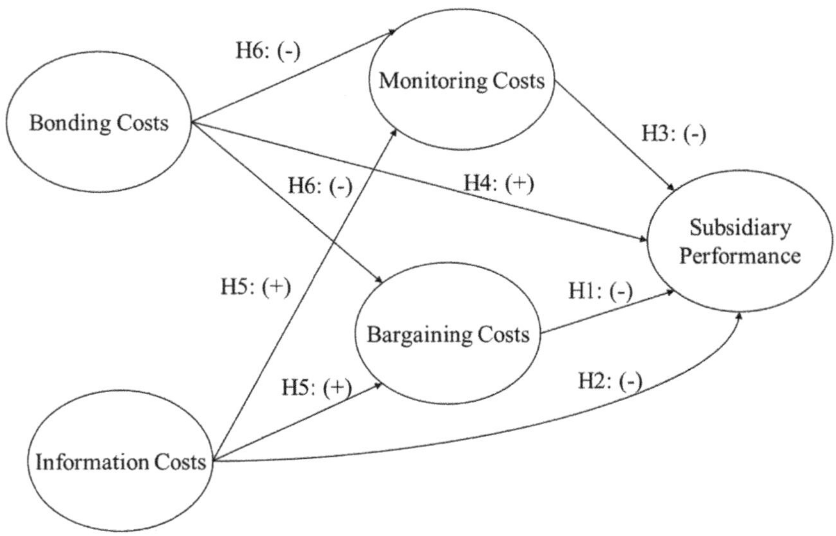

Fig. 1. Structural Model with Hypotheses.

of freedom equal to the differences in degree of freedom for the two models." The only requirement if this procedure is to be followed is that the number of constructs and indicators are the same for the different models (i.e., that we have a set of nested models). If the models are non-nested, we have to rely on a comparison of the parsimonious fit measures (AGFI, and the normed χ^2) since the χ^2 difference test is inappropriate in this case (Hair, Black, Babin, & Anderson, 2009). Only nested models are compared; hence, possible significant differences among models are tested by χ^2 difference tests (Anderson & Gerbing, 1988; Rust, Lee, & Valente, 1995).

RESULTS

Three different nested models were compared (Model S1, Model S2, and Model S3). *Model S3*, which represents our hypotheses **H1** through **H6**, is the proposed model described in Fig. 1. *Model S1* has no bonding cost effects towards "bargaining costs" and "monitoring costs" but is otherwise equal to *Model S3*. *Model S2* is also a reduced version of *Model S3* with no direct information cost effect on "subsidiary performance," otherwise equal to *Model S3*. Hence, *Model S1* < *Model S2* < *Model S3*. All models have the same number of observed indicators and latent constructs as for the measurement model estimated and reported earlier. Fit indices and χ^2 differences for the three competing models are presented in Table 1.

All three models show relatively excellent fit by most of the fit statistics. However, *Model S1* has a somewhat low CN value (CN = 179) and an AGFI below the recommended threshold value of 0.90 (AGFI = 0.89). When testing for significantly differences, it is observed that *Model S2* and *Model S3* are significantly better fitted than *Model S1*. χ^2 for *Model S1* is 110.49 with 97 degrees of freedom. For *Model S2*, the respective values are 100.17 and 96, and for *Model S3*: 97.83 and 95, which gives a $\Delta\chi^2$ of 12.66 with 2 degrees of freedom and a significance of $p < 0.01$ (critical value = 9.210) for the difference between *Model S1* and *Model S3*. Respective numbers for *Model S1* and *Model S2* are: $\Delta\chi^2 = 10.32$ with 1 degree of freedom, $p < 0.01$ (critical value = 6.64). However, there is no significant difference between *Model S2* and *Model S3* with respect to fit. $\Delta\chi^2 = 2.34$ with 1 degree of freedom (critical value for $p < 0.10 = 2.71$).

In addition to comparing the fit between structural models, Anderson and Gerbing (1988) also recommend a final comparison of fit differences between the structural model and the measurement model. If a significant difference is observed, there are reasons to believe that it is possible to improve

Table 1. Fit Indices and χ^2 Differences for Three Competing Structural Models.

Fit Statistics	*Model S1*	*Model S2*	*Model S3*
χ^2	110.49	100.17	97.83
(df)	(97)	(96)	(95)
p-Value	0.1650	0.3653	0.4006
RMSEA	0.030	0.017	0.014
p-Value close fit	0.92	0.97	0.98
NCP	13.49	4.17	2.83
GFI	0.92	0.93	0.93
AGFI	0.89	0.90	0.90
RMR	0.076	0.067	0.065
NFI	0.93	0.94	0.94
NNFI	0.98	0.99	0.99
CFI	0.99	0.99	0.99
IFI	0.99	0.99	0.99
CN	179 (179.46)	196 (196.89)	199 (199.80)
$\Delta\chi^2$:			
Model S1 – Model S2 (1 df)		10.32***	
Model S1 – Model S3 (2 df)		12.66***	
Model S2 – Model S3 (1 df)		2.34	

Notes: *Model S1:* Minus H6 (two *Bonding costs* relationships); *Model S2:* Minus H2 (the *Information costs–Subsidiary performance* relationship)
***$p < 0.01$.

the structural model by respecifying it. The formal χ^2 difference tests are reported in Table 2, together with some of the recommended fit indices used when comparing structural models with a baseline model (RMSEA, NNFI, CFI, and IFI).

Table 2. Comparing the Structural Models with the Measurement Model.

Fit Indices	Measurement Model	Structural Model (*Model S1*)	Structural Model (*Model S2*)	Structural Model (*Model S3*)
χ^2 (df)	97.00 (94)	110.49 (97)	100.17 (96)	97.83 (95)
$\Delta\chi^2$ (df)	—	17.49***	3.17	0.83
RMSEA	0.014	0.030	0.017	0.014
NFI	0.94	0.93	0.94	0.94
NNFI	0.99	0.98	0.99	0.99
CFI	0.99	0.99	0.99	0.99
IFI	0.99	0.99	0.99	0.99

Note: ***$p < 0.01$.

The results from the χ^2 difference test indicate that *Model S1* needs some improvements since the χ^2 difference is highly significant ($p < 0.01$ (3 df)). On the other hand, there are no significant differences between the measurement model (the baseline model) and the two structural models: *Model S2* and *Model S3*. Hence, both structural models seem to be well specified. Therefore, in accordance with the logic presented by Anderson and Gerbing (1988, pp. 419–420), one should accept the theoretical model of interest if not a constrained or unconstrained model is significantly better fitted. Therefore, the conclusion regarding the best overall model of *Model S2* and *Model S3* must be based on theoretical bases rather than on statistical justifications.[15] Still,

Table 3. Parameter Estimates for Three Competing Structural Models.

Model		Information Cost	Bonding Cost	Bargaining Cost	Monitoring Cost	R^2
Model S3	Bargaining cost	$\gamma = 0.68$ $p < 0.001$ (6.63)	$\gamma = -.23$ (−2.68) $p < 0.01$	—	—	0.53
	Monitoring cost	$\gamma = 0.62$ (6.13) $p < 0.001$	$\gamma = 0.22$ (2.37) $p < 0.05$	—	—	0.41
	Performance	$\gamma = -0.26$ (−1.57) NS	$\gamma = 0.23$ (2.44) $p < 0.05$	$\beta = -0.22$ (−1.48) NS	$\beta = -0.15$ (−1.20) NS	0.37
Model S2	Bargaining cost	$\gamma = 0.69$ (6.84) $p < 0.001$	$\gamma = -0.22$ (−2.64) $p < 0.01$	—	—	0.55
	Monitoring cost	$\gamma = 0.63$ (6.22) $p < 0.001$	$\gamma = 0.22$ (2.45) $p < 0.05$	—	—	0.42
	Performance	—	$\gamma = 0.23$ (2.31) $p < 0.05$	$\beta = -0.38$ (−3.38) $p < 0.001$	$\beta = -0.26$ (−2.35) $p < 0.05$	0.36
Model S1	Bargaining cost	$\gamma = 0.70$ (6.75) $p < 0.001$	—	—	—	0.49
	Monitoring cost	$\gamma = 0.59$ (5.94) $p < 0.001$	—	—	—	0.35
	Performance	$\gamma = -0.26$ (−1.63) NS	$\gamma = 0.23$ (2.77) $p < 0.01$	$\beta = -0.24$ (−1.74) $p < .10$	$\beta = -0.13$ (−1.12) NS	0.36

Notes: γ and β are standardized coefficients; *t*-values in parentheses; NS, not significant; $N = 159$.

some indications of what is the most proper model can be given by the parameter estimates for the three competing structural models presented in Table 3.

In all three models, governance costs explain approximately 36 percent of the variance in subsidiary performance, which is approximately at the same level as in the 2SLS regressions presented by Tomassen and Benito (2009, p. 299). In spite of this, both *Model S3* and *Model S1* have some insignificant relationships. In *Model S3*, it is observed that *Information costs* and *Monitoring costs,* both have insignificant effects towards *Subsidiary performance*, and the rather strong effect of *Bargaining costs* that is observed in *Model S2* ($\beta = -0.38$, $t = -3.38$, $p < 0.001$) becomes insignificant when the direct effect of *Information costs* is included as in *Model S3* ($\beta = -0.22$, $t = -1.48$).

Furthermore, there are strong indications of a relationship between *Information costs* on the one hand and *Bargaining Cost* and *Monitoring Cost* on the other hand, as proposed in hypothesis **H5**. In *Model S3* (as well as in the other two models), *Information cost* has a strong and significant positive effect on *Bargaining cost* and *Monitoring cost* ($\gamma_{InfBarg} = 0.68$, $t = 6.63$, $p < 0.001$; $\gamma_{\text{InfMon}} = 0.62$, $t = 6.13$, $p < 0.001$). These effects are only slightly lower than the effects estimated in *Model S2*, where the direct effect between *Information cost* and *Subsidiary performance* is included. However, this direct effect is insignificant $\gamma_{InfPerf} = -0.26$ ($t = -1.57$, $p > 0.10$) in Model S3, and excluding this effect (Model S2) had only modest effects on the explained variance in subsidiary performance ($\Delta R^2 = 0.01$ – going from 0.36 to 0.37). When excluding the relationships between *Information cost* and *Bargaining cost* and between *Information cost* and *Monitoring cost*, and keeping everything else equal, a rather poor fit was obtained (RMSEA = 0.086; NFI = 0.88; AGFI = 0.80), and the explained variance in *Subsidiary performance* dropped to 28 percent.

Hence, it seems reasonable to conclude that information costs affect subsidiary performance through bargaining costs and monitoring costs, rather than through a direct effect when only governance costs are included as explanatory variables of subsidiary performance. Therefore, it may be so that *Model S2* is more in line with reality than the two other models. If so, then we have to reject **H2** – that there should be a direct negative information costs effect toward subsidiary performance.

It is also worth emphasizing that bonding costs have a strong and significant positive effect on performance whatever model is proposed. In *Model S2*, the effect is significant at $p < 0.05$ ($\gamma_{\text{BonPerf}} = 0.23$, $t = 2.31$). The same effect size is observed in *Model S3* and *Model S1* although the significance level is somewhat higher in *Model S1*. In addition, we also observe, strong effects towards monitoring and bargaining, but somewhat surprising; there is a significant strong and positive effect between bonding and monitoring, which is the opposite of what we hypothesized in **H6**. Hence, we must *reject* **H6** – *but only partially*.

DISCUSSION AND IMPLICATIONS

Even though we have recognized several and important positive effects of the growth in foreign trade and exchange, we cannot deny that establishing subsidiaries across cultural and geographical distances might also create an extra burden for the MNEs. We have to admit that even though firms choose internalized solutions for their international expansions, these hierarchical governance forms are staffed with actors that have diverse and complex backgrounds, they suffer from misconceptions and subjective interpretations about almost every issue we can think of. Sometimes they also behave in ways that are harmful to the company. Hence, and in short – governance costs do not disappear by internalizing the transactions, and they might be very much present and affect the MNEs in ways that we need to know more about.

Therefore, we have tried in this paper to shed light on this debate by going back to an award-winning paper, published in IBR by Tomassen and Benito (2009), and put forward some nuances and reflections upon their findings.

The reason for this endeavor is grounded in the idea that theories have to be challenged, empirical finding, just as well. Therefore, bringing nuances into a theory (TCE) with such paramount influence on the thinking of economic organization will always be important. We have among other things, focused on the rather limited number of studies of governance costs per se. Governance costs play a crucial role in the economics of organization, and they also might serve as a signal on the extra burden of organizing the firm across distances – cultural as well as geographical. Hence, if the theoretical notion and the measurement of such costs are ambiguous, it is imperative to accentuate this limitation. Tomassen and Benito (2009) made a candid attempt on this, but their modeling approach and results open up for some critical questions and comments. Hence, three circumstances pointed toward an alternative modeling strategy.

First, relatively high correlation coefficients were observed among some of the governance cost constructs. Second, it is theoretically possible with both interconnections and some kind of trade-offs between these costs (Chiles & McMackin, 1996). Third, the relationships between the different costs will most certainly change over time in a rather dynamic fashion. For example, a feeling of shared purpose makes organizations able to create an atmosphere that shapes the values and goals of their members. Hence, bonding activities incurred yesterday may lead to the development of trust and commitment, which is of major importance in reducing the negative effects of geographical and cultural distance and thereby also governance costs tomorrow (Moran & Ghoshal, 1996).

Instead of modeling the relationships as direct effects toward subsidiary performance, the alternative research model (see Fig. 1), presumed in addition, interdependencies between the governance costs, and an SEM approach was therefore conducted to further investigate these possible relations. However, it is worth mentioning that a cross-sectional snapshot, still gives limited understanding of such dynamism as described in the line of reasoning above. The following discussion will by and large be concentrated around two major findings: first, and most importantly, the role of information costs, and second, the effect of bonding costs.

As we already have pointed toward, geographical and cultural distances are major sources for information fallacies in MNEs. They distort the communication and information flows and enforce the MNEs to actuate additional governance initiatives, such as bargaining and monitoring, but also long-term investments in bonding activities.

According to the results presented in Table 3, information costs and bonding costs are the two exogenous "drivers" in the model. Bargaining costs and monitoring costs, on the other hand, are intervening variables, which are highly dependent on especially the information costs. In addition, according to further analysis, 36 percent of the total 42 percent variation in monitoring costs explained by the model can be attributed to information costs. The respective figures for bargaining costs are even higher with 51 percent and 55 percent. Since adaptation (internal as well as external) is one of the most central economic problems of organization, information costs are also assessed as the most important of the governance costs (Williamson, 1988, p. 572). Therefore, given that the logic in the alternative research model is correct, these results seem quite logical. Information fallacies caused by for example geographical and cultural distance, are those opportunity costs that most certainly are seen as sources for increased *ex post* governance costs. When it is difficult for the subsidiary to anticipate changes in consumer preferences, distribution arrangements, competition in the foreign market, and/or is faced with opportunism, there is a great chance of misalignments. The most likely action then, is to increase both monitoring and bargaining activities. The first is done to control for further detrimental developments, the latter is a necessity if misaligned agreements are to be corrected. Direct costs of these activities are therefore easy to spot and to attribute. It is much more difficult to do the same with the information costs. Most likely, the management in MNEs will have problems attributing these costs directly to the performance of the subsidiary but may see them as sources for other observable costs that are the results of necessary actions.

The results in fact indicate such an assumption. Information cost effects on subsidiary performance is mostly of an indirect nature, and work through monitoring costs and bargaining costs. Explained variance in subsidiary performance dropped only from 37 percent to 36 percent when the direct effect from information costs on subsidiary performance was skipped (see Table 3). In addition, a rather poor fit was obtained when the information costs effect was modeled only as a direct effect on subsidiary performance.

Bonding costs have both direct and indirect effects according to the findings. Bonding expenses can certainly be attributed to subsidiary performance (with the same proviso as taken above), but it is also possible that bonding costs influence the level of bargaining costs and monitoring costs. The first relationship is probably the easiest to explain. Costs used on bonding activities, in many cases bring the foreign subsidiary more in line with the MNE HQ, which then probably leads to reduced disputes about settled agreements (Anderson, 1988). Bargaining costs that occur between HQ and subsidiary will thereby go down (Dahlstrom & Nygaard, 1999).

The positive relationship on monitoring costs is more difficult to understand. Intuitively, frequent meetings, building personal relationships, and support from HQ in conflicts with third parties should develop a more trustful relationship, which thereby reduces the needs for monitoring (Chiles & McMackin, 1996). In addition, there may also be a built-in control effect in increased communication and time together with the subsidiary (with the intention to bind the entities more closely together), which also should have reduced the need for control precautions. One reason for a positive relationship could be rooted in the need of evaluating activities that are introduced actively and consciously from the management in the MNE (i.e., bonding activities). However, saying that, it is of course also possible that the positive relationship is purely accidental. Therefore, a further discussion of this relationship will only be based on highly speculative arguments, so that an answer on the observed positive relationship between bonding costs and monitoring costs must instead be left to future studies.

CONCLUDING REMARKS

We subscribe to several of Tomassen and Benito's conclusions in their paper. Governance costs are important when we discuss performance effects in MNEs. They affect the performance of the subsidiaries, although in a more complex fashion than what was modeled in their paper. Hence, the burden of distance in MNEs may be a lesser burden if we fully understand the dynamics of governance costs. The results point to the important fact that reducing information fallacies in MNEs must be imperative and that trust building through bonding activities have a direct positive effect on subsidiary performance, while it also reduce the needs for bargaining and renegotiations, which is costly for the MNE.

Modeling governance costs as interdependent variables has been a travel in a somewhat unknown terrain, and part of this exploration has perhaps been more empirically driven, than theoretically. However, since the relationship between governance costs and performance seldom is investigated, pushing the forefront of the accumulated knowledge about governance costs and their behavior and effects may stimulate others to dig more deeply into the area.

Summarized, five key issues could be extracted from this exploratory modeling effort: (1) It is probably wrong, modeling all the four categories of governance costs as independent variables, and they cannot be treated as such in future research either. (2) Most certainly, there are trade-offs between such costs, which must be tested with longitudinal designs. (3) Distance creates information fallacies, which seems to be an important driver of the extra needs for monitoring and bargaining in MNEs, and as such, this seems to be one of the most important variables to be aware of. (4) Bargaining costs, monitoring costs, and bonding costs represent direct effects of governance costs on subsidiary performance, and a large proportion of these costs are observable direct expenses, which should be rather easy to observe and measure. (5) Information fallacies, which affect subsidiary performance negatively, most certainly work through bargaining costs and monitoring costs, and not as a direct effect on subsidiary performance.

APPENDIX

Items Used in the Structural Model (as in the Measurement Model).

Scales	Items
Bargaining costs	1. Our meetings with employees from our foreign company are very effective and systematic (reversed). 2. Both parties are always well prepared in the meetings so that decisions can be made (reversed).
Monitoring costs	1. We use a lot of time to control the delivered services from the foreign subsidiary. 2. We spend a lot of time on accounting issues related to the foreign subsidiary. 3. We spend a lot of time to control deliveries of important input resources to the foreign subsidiary.

(Continued)

Scales	Items
Bonding costs	1. We spend a lot of time in communicating with our foreign company. 2. We spend a lot of time in developing personal ties between headquarter and subsidiary. 3. We spend a lot of time in developing a common company culture. 4. We spend a lot of time together with our subsidiary in order to solve conflicts with third parties.
Information costs	1. Information from the foreign subsidiary is often incomplete and therefore difficult to understand. 2. Information from the foreign subsidiary is often too voluminous and therefore difficult to understand. 3. Important information from the foreign subsidiary seldom comes at the right time.
Subsidiary performance	1. How satisfied are you with your market share in the specific market? 2. How satisfied are you with your profitability in the specific market? 3. How satisfied are you with your current distribution arrangement in the specific market? 4. How satisfied are you with your access to the specific market?

NOTES

1. Author's calculation based on numbers reported in Table 1.5, UNCTAD (2015).
2. It is worth mentioning that Nachum (2010) did not find any evidence that differences associated with nationality, per se, create higher costs for foreign firms compared to local firms. However, as she reflects upon, the type of industry (financial services) and the location (London) that was chosen for the study can explain the reason for this.
3. Further, in this paper, "TCE" will be used as the all-embracing abbreviation for the internalization perspectives, in full knowledge that the Williamsonian version of TCE and the classic internalization approach (Buckley & Casson, 1976), differ to some extent from the international business version of internalization theory (Hennart, 1982; Rugman & Verbeke, 2003).
4. See also Baldwin's (2008, p. 164) definition of "mundane transaction costs."
5. See for example, Richter (2014) for a review.
6. We will not go specifically into the issue of sources of governance costs in the present paper. See for example Tomassen et al. (2012), for a more in-depth presentation and analysis of that issue.
7. Which is why Demsetz (1993) prefers governance costs as a common term for transaction costs when resources are transferred across markets as well as within firms.

8. The concept of asset specificity is probably most useful when explaining vertical integrated value chains, and less useful to explain internalization of knowledge and goodwill, which, according to Hennart (2010), can be traced down to a problem of information asymmetry.

9. According to Allen (2006), the first formal attempt to measure transaction costs was Wallis and North (1986). However, that study used a macro perspective and divided the economy into two sectors – production and transaction. Then the total value of resources used in the transaction sector were measured and labeled, transaction costs. Hence, it gives no sense labeling such costs as "governance costs" (Benito & Tomassen, 2010).

10. The D&B database were quite unreliable concerning the filed firms. Many of the listed firms were in reality sleeping construction without any activities. Likewise, accounting data and other information, such as key personnel, were in many cases outdated. Much time and effort have been dedicated in cleaning the database.

11. See Table 1, Model 3, p. 296, in Tomassen and Benito (2009).

12. Ref. Table 2, p. 297, *Ibid.*

13. This can also be justified by the fact that no spurious and intervening effects were present in the original study by Tomassen and Benito (2009, Table 4, p. 299).

14. Ref. Table 3, Panel A, p. 298, *Ibid.*

15. Probably many other parametric structures summarize the data equally well if the relationships are based on empirical grounds rather than on theoretical fundaments (Bagozzi & Baumgartner, 1994).

REFERENCES

Allen, D. W. (2000). Transaction costs. In B. Bouckaert & G. De Gest (Eds.), *The encyclopedia of law and economics* (Vol. 1, pp. 893–926). Cheltenham: Edward Elgar.

Allen, D. W. (2006). Theoretical difficulties with transaction cost measurement. *Division of Labour & Transaction Costs*, *2*(1), 1–14.

Ambos, T. C., & Ambos, B. (2009). The impact of distance on knowledge transfer effectiveness in multinational corporations. *Journal of International Management*, *15*(1), 1–14.

Anderson, E. (1988). Transaction costs as determinants of opportunism in integrated and independent sales forces. *Journal of Economic Behavior & Organization*, *9*(3), 247–264.

Andersson, U., Forsgren, M., & Holm, U. (2007). Balancing subsidiary influence in the federative MNC: A business network view. *Journal of International Business Studies*, *38*(5), 802–818.

Anderson, J. C., & Gerbing, D. W. (1988). Structural equation modeling in practice: A review and recommended two-step approach. *Psychological Bulletin*, *103*(3), 411–423.

Ariño, A. (2003). Measures of strategic alliance performance: An analysis of construct validity. *Journal of International Business Studies*, *34*(1), 66–79.

Armstrong, J. S., & Overton, T. S. (1977). Estimating nonresponse bias in mail surveys. *Journal of Marketing Research*, *14*(3), 396–402.

Arrow, K. J. (1969). The organization of economic activity: Issues pertinent to the choice of market versus nonmarket allocation. In U.S. Joint Economic Committee 91st Congress 1st Session (Ed.), *The analysis and evaluation of public expenditure: The PPB system* (Vol. 1, pp. 47–64). Washington, DC: U.S. Government Printing Office.

Bagozzi, R. P., & Baumgartner, H. (1994). The evaluation of structural equation models. In R. P. Bagozzi (Ed.), *Principles of marketing research* (pp. 386–422). Cambridge, MA: Blackwell Publishers.

Bagozzi, R. P., & Yi, Y. (1988). On the evaluation of structural equation models. *Journal of the Academy of Marketing Science*, *16*(1), 74–94.

Baldwin, C. Y. (2008). Where do transactions come from? Modularity, transactions, and the boundaries of firms. *Industrial and Corporate Change*, *17*(1), 155–195.

Baliga, B. R., & Jaeger, A. M. (1984). Multinational corporations: Control systems and delegation issues. *Journal of International Business Studies*, *15*(2), 25–40.

Benito, G. R. G., & Tomassen, S. (2010). Governance costs in headquarters-subsidiary relationships. In U. Andersson & U. Holm (Eds.), *Managing the contemporary multinational: The role of headquarters* (pp. 138–160). Cheltenham: Edward Elgar.

Bollen, K. A. (1989). *Structural equations with latent variables*. New York, NY: John Wiley & Sons.

Bollen, K. A., & Lennox, R. (1991). Conventional wisdom on measurement: A structural equation perspective. *Psychological Bulletin*, *110*(2), 305–314.

Bouquet, C., & Birkinshaw, J. (2008). Weight versus voice: How foreign subsidiaries gain attention from corporate headquarters. *Academy of Management Journal*, *51*(3), 577–601.

Brouthers, K. D. (2002). Institutional, cultural and transaction cost influences on entry mode choice and performance. *Journal of International Business Studies*, *33*(2), 203–221.

Buckley, P. J., & Casson, M. C. (1976). *The future of the multinational enterprise*. London: Macmillan.

Buvik, A., & Andersen, O. (2002). The impact of vertical coordination on ex post transaction costs in domestic and international buyer-seller relationship. *Journal of International Marketing*, *10*(1), 1–24.

Buvik, A., & John, G. (2000). When does vertical coordination improve industrial purchasing relationships? *Journal of Marketing*, *64*(4), 52–64.

Campbell, D. T. (1955). The informant in quantitative research. *American Journal of Sociology*, *60*(4), 339–342.

Casson, M. (1999). The organisation and evolution of the multinational enterprise: An information cost approach. *Management International Review (MIR)*, *39*(1), 77–121.

Caves, R. E. (1971). International corporations: The industrial economics of direct foreign investments. *Economica*, *38*(149), 1–27.

Ceci, F., & Prencipe, A. (2013). Does distance hinder coordination? Identifying and bridging boundaries of offshored work. *Journal of International Management*, *19*(4), 324–332.

Chang, E., & Taylor, M. S. (1999). Control in multinational corporations (MNCs): The case of Korean manufacturing subsidiaries. *Journal of Management*, *25*(4), 541–565.

Chang, S.-J., van Witteloostuijn, A., & Eden, L. (2010). Common method variance in international business research. *Journal of International Business Studies*, *41*(2), 178–184.

Chiles, T. H., & McMackin, J. F. (1996). Integrating variable risk preferences, trust, and transaction cost economics. *Academy of Management Review*, *21*(1), 73–99.

Contractor, F. J. (2007). Is international business good for companies? The evolutionary or multi-stage theory of internationalization vs. the transaction cost perspective. *Management International Review (MIR)*, *47*(3), 453–475.

Dahlstrom, R., & Nygaard, A. (1999). An empirical investigation of ex post transaction costs in franchized distribution channels. *Journal of Marketing Research*, *36*(2), 160–170.

Dellestrand, H., & Kappen, P. (2012). The effects of spatial and contextual factors on headquarters resource allocation to MNE subsidiaries. *Journal of International Business Studies*, *43*(3), 219–243.

Demsetz, H. (1993). The theory of the firm revisited. In O. E. Williamson & S. G. Winter (Eds.), *The nature of the firm: Origins, evolution and development* (pp. 159–178). New York, NY: Oxford University Press.

Dess, G. G., & Robinson, R. B., Jr. (1984). Measuring organizational performance in the absence of objective measures: The case of the privately-held firm and conglomerate business unit. *Strategic Management Journal*, *5*(3), 265–273.

Dunning, J. H. (1988). *Explaining international production*. London: Unwin Hyman.

Dunning, J. H. (1998). Location and the multinational enterprise: A neglected factor? *Journal of International Business Studies*, *29*(1), 45–66.

Eisenhardt, K. M. (1989). Agency theory: An assessment and review. *Academy of Management Review*, *14*(1), 57–74.

Evans, J., & Mavondo, F. T. (2002). Psychic distance and organizational performance: An empirical examination of international retailing operations. *Journal of International Business Studies*, *33*(3), 515–532.

Fisch, J. H., & Zschoche, M. (2011). The effects of liabilities of foreignness, economies of scale, and multinationality on firm performance: An information cost view. *Schmalenbach Business Review*, *63*(3), 51–68.

Gerbing, D. W., & Anderson, J. C. (1988). An updated paradigm for scale development incorporating unidimensionality and its assessment. *Journal of Marketing Research*, *25*(2), 186–192.

Ghemawat, P. (2001). Distance still matters. The hard reality of global expansion. *Harvard Business Review*, *79*(8), 137–147.

Goldberger, A. S. (1973). Structural equation models: An overview. In O. D. Duncan & A. S. Goldberger (Eds.), *Structural equation models in the social sciences* (pp. 1–18). New York, NY: Seminar Press.

Gupta, A. K., & Govindarajan, V. (2000). Knowledge flows within multinational corporations. *Strategic Management Journal*, *21*(4), 473–496.

Hair, J. F., Jr., Black, W. C., Babin, B. J., & Anderson, R. E. (2009). *Multivariate data analysis* (7th ed.). Upper Saddle River, NJ: Prentice Hall.

Hennart, J.-F. (1982). *A theory of multinational enterprise*. Ann Arbor, MI: University of Michigan Press.

Hennart, J.-F. (1991). Control in multinational firms: The role of price and hierarchy. *Management International Review*, *31*(Special Issue), 71–96.

Hennart, J.-F. (2009). Theories of the multinational enterprise. In A. M. Rugman (Ed.), *The Oxford handbook of International business* (2nd ed.). (pp. 125–145) Oxford: Oxford University Press.

Hennart, J.-F. (2010). Transaction cost theory and international business. *Journal of Retailing*, *86*(3), 257–269.

Hutzschenreuter, T., Kleindienst, I., & Lange, S. (2016). The concept of distance in international business research: A review and research agenda. *International Journal of Management Reviews*, *18*(2), 160–179.

Hutzschenreuter, T., & Voll, J. C. (2008). Performance effects of "added cultural distance" in the path of international expansion: The case of German multinational enterprises. *Journal of International Business Studies*, *39*(1), 53–70.

Hymer, S. H. (1960). *The international operations of national firms: A study of direct foreign investment*. Cambridge, MA: MIT Press (Published in 1976).

Jensen, M. C., & Meckling, W. H. (1976). Theory of the firm: Managerial behavior, agency costs, and capital structure. *Journal of Financial Economics*, *3*(4), 305–360.

Jöreskog, K. G., & Sörbom, D. (1981). *Lisrel V: Analysis of linear structural relationships by maximum likelihood and least squares methods*. Mooresville, IL: Scientific Software International.

Jöreskog, K. G., & Sörbom D. (1982). Recent developments in structural equation modeling. *Journal of Marketing Research*, *19*(4), 404–416.

Kindleberger, C. P. (1969). *American business abroad: Six lectures on direct investment*. New Haven, CT: Yale University Press.

Knight, F. H. (1921). *Risk, uncertainty and profit*. Boston, MA: Houghton Mifflin Co.

Kogut, B., & Zander, U. (1993). Knowledge of the firm and the evolutionary theory of the multinational corporation. *Journal of International Business Studies*, *24*(4), 625–645.

Langlois, R. N. (2006). The secret life of mundane transaction costs. *Organization Studies*, *27*(9), 1389–1410.

Li, J., Strange, R., Ning, L., & Sutherland, D. (2016). Outward foreign direct investment and domestic innovation performance: Evidence from China. *International Business Review*, *25*(5), 1010–1019.

Liang, F. H. (2017). Does foreign direct investment improve the productivity of domestic firms? Technology spillovers, industry linkages, and firm capabilities. *Research Policy*, *46*(1), 138–159.

Lu, J. W., & Beamish, P. W. (2004). International diversification and firm performance: The s-curve hypothesis. *Academy of Management Journal*, *47*(4), 598–609.

Mahnke, V., Pedersen, T., & Venzin, M. (2009). Does knowledge sharing pay? An MNC subsidiary perspective on knowledge outflows. *Advances in International Management*, *22*, 123–139.

Makino, S., & Tsang, E. W. K. (2011). Historical ties and foreign direct investment: An exploratory study. *Journal of International Business Studies*, *42*(4), 545–557.

Masten, S. E., Meehan, J. W., Jr., & Snyder, E. A. (1991). The costs of organization. *Journal of Law, Economics, and Organization*, *7*(1), 1–25.

Milgrom, P., & Roberts, J. (1992). *Economics, organization and management*. Englewood Cliffs, NJ: Prentice-Hall International.

Moran, P., & Ghoshal, S. (1996). Theories of economic organization: The case for realism and balance. *Academy of Management Review*, *21*(1), 58–72.

Morosini, P., Shane, S., & Singh, H. (1998). National cultural distance and cross-border acquisition performance. *Journal of International Business Studies*, *29*(1), 137–158.

Nachum, L. (2010). When is foreignness an asset or a liability? Explaining the performance differential between foreign and local firms. *Journal of Management*, *36*(3), 714–739.

Nohria, N., & Ghoshal, S. (1994). Differentiated fit and shared values: Alternatives for managing headquarters-subsidiary relations. *Strategic Management Journal*, *15*(6), 491–502.

Nunnally, J. C., & Bernstein, I. H. (1994). *Psychometric theory* (3rd ed.). New York, NY: McGraw-Hill.

OECD. (2002). *Foreign direct investment for development*. OECD, Paris: OECD.

OECD. (2008). *The impact of foreign direct investment on wages and working conditions*. OECD, Paris: OECD.

Podsakoff, P. M., MacKenzie, S. B., Lee, J.-Y., & Podsakoff, N. P. (2003). Common method biases in behavioral research: A critical review of the literature and recommended remedies. *Journal of Applied Psychology*, *88*(5), 879–903.

Rabbiosi, L. (2011). Subsidiary roles and reverse knowledge transfer: An investigation of the effects of coordination mechanisms. *Journal of International Management*, *17*(2), 97–113.

Richter, N. F. (2014). Information costs in international business: Analyzing the effects of economies of scale, cultural diversity and decentralization. *Management International Review (MIR)*, *54*(2), 171–193.

Rugman, A. M. (1981). *Inside the multinationals: The economics of internal markets*. London: Croom Helm.

Rugman, A. M., & Verbeke, A. (2001). Subsidiary-specific advantages in multinational enterprises. *Strategic Management Journal*, *22*(3), 237–250.

Rugman, A. M., & Verbeke, A. (2003). Extending the theory of the multinational enterprise: Internalization and strategic management perspectives. *Journal of International Business Studies*, *34*(2), 125–137.

Rust, R. T., Lee, C., & Valente, E., Jr. (1995). Comparing covariance structure models: A general methodology. *International Journal of Research in Marketing*, *12*(4), 279–291.

Seidler, J. (1974). On using informants: A technique for collecting quantitative data and controlling measurement error in organization analysis. *American Sociological Review*, *39*(6), 816–831.

Shenkar, O. (2012). Beyond cultural distance: Switching to a friction lens in the study of cultural differences. *Journal of International Business Studies*, *43*(1), 12–17.

Shenkar, O., Luo, Y., & Yeheskel, O. (2008). From "distance" to "friction": Substituting metaphors and redirecting intercultural research. *Academy of Management Review*, *33*(4), 905–923.

Tan, D., & Mahoney, J. T. (2006). Why a multinational firm chooses expatriates: Integrating resource-based, agency and transaction costs perspectives. *Journal of Management Studies*, *43*(3), 457–484.

Tanaka, J. S., & Huba, G. J. (1985). A fit index for covariance structure models under arbitrary GLS estimation. *British Journal of Mathematical and Statistical Psychology*, *38*(2), 197–201.

Tomassen, S., & Benito, G. R. G. (2009). The costs of governance in international companies. *International Business Review*, *18*(3), 292–304.

Tomassen, S., Benito, G. R. G., & Lunnan, R. (2012). Governance costs in foreign direct investments: A MNC headquarters challenge. *Journal of International Management*, *18*(3), 233–246.

UNCTAD. (2015). *World investment report 2015: Reforming international investment governance*. Geneva: United Nations.

Verbeke, A., & Yuan, W. (2016). The impact of "distance" on multinational enterprise subsidiary capabilities. *Multinational Business Review*, *24*(2), 168–190.

Walker, G., & Poppo, L. (1991). Profit centers, single-source suppliers, and transaction costs. *Administrative Science Quarterly*, *36*(1), 66–87.

Wallis, J. J., & North, D. C. (1986). Measuring the transaction sector in the American economy, 1870–1970. In S. L. Engerman & R. E. Gallman (Eds.), *Long-term factors in American economic growth*. (pp. 95–161) Chicago, IL: Chicago University Press.

Williamson, O. E. (1975). *Markets and hierarchies: Analysis and antitrust implications – A study in the economics of internal organization*. New York, NY: Free Press.

Williamson, O. E. (1985). *The economic institutions of capitalism: Firms, markets, relational contracting*. New York, NY: Free Press.

Williamson, O. E. (1988). Corporate finance and corporate governance. *Journal of Finance 43*(3): 567–591.

Zaheer, S. (1995). Overcoming the liability of foreignness. *Academy of Management Journal*, *38*(2), 341–363.

CHAPTER 20

REDUCING PSYCHIC DISTANCE THROUGH SPRINGBOARD SUBSIDIARIES: AN EXPLORATORY CASE STUDY

Nina Magomedova, Fariza Achcaoucaou and Paloma Miravitlles

ABSTRACT

The aim of this study is to explore how springboard subsidiaries affect the psychic distance between the headquarters (HQ) of multinational companies (MNCs) and a distant target region. The study applies a single case study methodology to analyse a springboard subsidiary located in Spain that helps its German HQ to pursue opportunities in a psychically distant Latin American region. The findings suggest that springboard subsidiaries help MNCs to reduce the perceived psychic distance between their HQ and a target region due to (1) their intermediate psychic proximity in both directions (i.e. to the HQ and the target region) and (2) their location outside the target region, which makes them somewhat 'impartial' and not involved in intra-regional conflicts; the study also shows that the sum of psychic distance stimuli between HQ's home country –springboard subsidiary's country and springboard subsidiary's – Latin American countries is

Distance in International Business: Concept, Cost and Value
Progress in International Business Research, Volume 12, 471–493

ISSN: 1745-8862/doi:10.1108/S1745-886220170000012024

actually smaller than the direct psychic distance between HQ's home country and Latin American countries. No previous studies have explored the effect of springboard subsidiaries on psychic distance.

Keywords: Springboard subsidiary; psychic distance; single case study

INTRODUCTION

During the past 30 years international business (IB) has witnessed a drastic increase in foreign direct investments (FDIs) in most geographically, economically, and culturally dispersed directions (UNCTAD, 2016). Driven by an attempt to benefit from the progressively globalized market place, multinational companies (MNCs) move increasingly away from their home countries to pursue business opportunities in distant new markets. However, the successful exploitation of these geographically dispersed opportunities is hindered by what IB researchers refer to as psychic distance (Dow, 2000; Dow & Karunaratna, 2006; Drogendijk & Zander, 2010; Hakanson, 2014; Hakanson & Ambos, 2010; Hakanson, Ambos, Schuster, & Leicht-Deobald, 2016; Hutzschenreuter, Kleindienst, & Lange, 2014; Johanson & Vahlne, 1977, 1990, 2009).

The concept of psychic distance was first used by Beckerman (1956) and is understood as the 'factors that prevent or disturb the flow of information between firms and markets' (Johanson & Wiedersheim-Paul, 1975, p. 308). Since Beckerman's (1956) seminar work, prolific research has evidenced the significant effects of psychic distance on many outcomes of MNC internationalization process, including entry-mode choice, trade flows, sequence of internationalization, and even organizational performance (see, e.g., Brewer, 2007; Evans & Mavondo, 2002; Kogut & Singh, 1988; Morosini, Shane, & Singh, 1998; Nebus & Chai, 2014; Nordstrom & Vahlne, 1994; Reuss & Lamont, 2009). Notably, recent studies suggest that despite the advances in transportation and communication technologies, as well as an increase of volumes of international trade, the concern about psychic distance is still relevant (Berry & Brock, 2004; Brock, Johnson, & Zhou, 2011; Dow & Karunaratna, 2006).

Given the significant impact of psychic distance on international operations, MNCs are prone to use mechanisms that allow them to overcome barriers and obtain better results in psychically distant markets. One of such mechanisms is the creation of an integrated matrix of local subsidiaries in a distant region administered through intermediate organizational units called springboard subsidiaries (Caicedo Marulanda, Mora Rodriguez, Pla Barber, & Leon

Darder, 2015; Pla Barber & Camps, 2012; Pla Barber, Villar, & Silva Domingo, 2015).

Despite the advancements in springboard subsidiary literature (Caicedo Marulanda et al., 2015; Pla Barber & Camps, 2012; Pla Barber et al., 2015), there is still a lack of empirical studies on their role as intermediate organizational units. Therefore, the objective of our study is to explore how springboard subsidiaries affect the psychic distance between a HQ and a target market. Specifically, we use a single case study methodology to analyse a springboard subsidiary located in Spain that helps its German HQ to pursue opportunities in psychically distant Latin American market. Hence, based on our exploratory analysis, this chapter contributes to a deeper understanding of the role played by a springboard subsidiary in reducing psychic distance between its HQ and a distant target market.

The chapter proceeds with the theoretical framework on psychic distance in IB literature and springboard subsidiaries as intermediate level units. Afterwards, the paper methodology is presented. Furthermore, we demonstrate the results of the case study analysis, exploring the influence of a springboard subsidiary on the perceived psychic distance. And finally, we present the conclusions, managerial implications, and proposals for future research.

THEORETICAL BACKGROUND

Psychic Distance in IB Literature

The concept of psychic distance has become a 'cornerstone of IB research' over the past three decades because of its powerful impact on international trade and business (Hutzschenreuter et al., 2014, p. 38). Since the first appearance of this concept in the study by Beckerman (1956), numerous researches have contributed to further clarification (Dow & Karunaratna, 2006; Dikova, 2009; Evans, Treadgold, & Mavondo, 2000; Hutzschenreuter et al., 2014; Johanson & Vahlne, 1977; Kogut & Singh, 1988). Moreover, recent studies underline the importance of differentiation of country-level factors preventing or disturbing the flows of information between different markets, that is, psychic distance stimuli, and the decision-maker's perception of psychic distance (Dow & Karunaratna, 2006). In our study, we follow the logic proposed by these scholars and compare country-level psychic distance stimuli and the MNC management's perception of psychic distance.

Among the factors that constitute psychic distance, language, culture, institutional and country development, and industrial development seem to be of a significant concern among IB scholars. First, language dissimilarities are evident stimuli of psychic distance, because international trade and FDI flows are fundamentally based on verbal and written communication, that is, spoken, printed, and digitalized language (Selmier II & Oh, 2012). Language dissimilarities often hinder communication between business partners, decrease efficiency of negotiations and increase transaction costs (Klitmoller & Lauring, 2013). Therefore, the effects of differences in language are included in numerous studies on psychic distance (Dow & Karunaratna, 2006; Hakanson & Ambos, 2010; López-Duarte & Vidal-Suárez, 2013). Additionally, using English as a *lingua franca* of IB can alleviate language dissimilarities (Nickerson, 2005). Therefore some studies suggest to measure not only the country's national language but also consider the command of English (Kedia & Reddy, 2016; Reiche, Harzing, & Pudelko, 2015), proposing the TOEFL (Test of English as a Foreign Language) as an indicator of the level of English in a country (Nickerson, 2005; Reiche et al., 2015).

Second, cultural differences may lead to misinterpretation and miscommunication between the negotiating parties and result in the increased costs of doing business abroad (Zaheer, 1995). Indeed, some scholars recognize that culture plays a key role in psychic distance, and consider it a central factor for measuring psychic distance (Morosini et al., 1998; Shenkar, Luo, & Yeheskel, 2008; Tihanyi, Griffith, & Russell, 2005). Cultural distance is often calculated as a difference among a combination of Hofstede's four original dimensions: power distance, individualism, uncertainty avoidance, and masculinity (Hofstede, 1980). However, since 1980 the study of Geert Hofstede was extended and the four-dimensional framework was amplified by two more dimensions: long-term orientation and indulgence (Minkov & Hofstede, 2011). In this chapter we consider both four-dimensional and six-dimensional frameworks.[1]

Third, psychic distance is also affected by the political and institutional conditions in countries (Kostova, 1997; Kostova & Zaheer, 1999). Recent analyses of divergences in institutional development of countries have revealed that countries with poorly developed regulatory institutions appear to be perceived as less transparent and more difficult to understand by managers from countries with stronger institutional structures (Hakanson & Ambos, 2010). Moreover, distance in country economic development has been acknowledged as an important factor in influencing demand structure, consumption patterns, and even communication and interaction norms (Dow & Karunaratna, 2006; Hutzschenreuter et al., 2014; Malhotra, Sivakumar, & Zhu, 2009). In IB research, country development is often measured by Gross Domestic Product (GDP) in current prices and GDP per capita, which have proven to be effective indicators of differences in country industrial development

(Chan, Isobe, & Makino, 2008; Dow & Karunaratna, 2006; Hakanson & Ambos, 2010; Malhotra et al., 2009).

Additionally, recent studies suggest that the psychic distance can be affected by migration flows. For instance, Hakanson et al. (2016) propose that people who have emigrated to a particular foreign country are likely to have conveyed the information about this country to their friends and relatives at home, which raises familiarity to this country and makes it seem less distant. Thus, this factor is also an important contributor to the perception of psychic distance between countries. Specifically, if some country receives many immigrants from a particular geographical region, it will be perceived as less distant by this same region, even despite language, cultural, institutional and industrial differences that exist between them.

All in all, the IB literature shows that psychic distance cannot be considered as a single factor but rather a set of diverse antecedents. Hence, the multidimensional character of psychic distance and its inhibiting effects on internationalization processes are one of the major drawbacks to overcome by MNCs.

Springboard Subsidiary as an Intermediate Organizational Unit

Among possible alternatives to address the problem of psychic distance between a home country and its target regions, the use of a springboard subsidiary appears to be a relevant solution. The intermediate position of these organizational units may help to reduce the perceived psychic distance and, consequently, propose MNCs an alternative approach to administering psychically distant target regions.

The conceptualization of a springboard subsidiary was first proposed in the study of Pla Barber and Camps (2012) on the example of Spain as a 'springboard country' to coordinate MNC's activities in the Latin American region. These scholars call such subsidiaries as springboards and define them as organizational units that are 'located in the intermediate position in terms of institutional distance and business knowledge between the MNC home country and a target region and that have successfully incorporated the specific advantages of their location' (Pla Barber & Camps, 2012, p. 533).

In particular, they find that the lack of institutional and business knowledge about a psychically distant target market forces MNCs to use an indirect way of acquiring this knowledge through the experience of their subsidiaries located in a country with strong business ties and experiential knowledge about this target region (Pla Barber & Camps, 2012). In that sense, the ease of knowledge flows between a HQ and a host region is one of the most influential factors that help to exploit efficiently target market opportunities (Johanson & Vahlne, 1977; Reiche et al., 2015), and springboard subsidiaries seem to be an effective mechanism to this end. Consequently, MNCs are prone to give these subsidiaries the role of an administrative centre for the whole target in order to exploit synergies and implement key strategic decisions, such as decisions on investment, internationalization, and even introduction of new product lines (Pla Barber & Camps, 2012; Pla Barber et al., 2015). Accordingly, these intermediate units are endowed with a high level of autonomy from HQ, which 'is not limited to activities within the local market but extends to activities on a regional scale, i.e., the countries for which it serves as a springboard' (Pla Barber & Camps, 2012, p. 531).

To sum up, in the case of psychic distant regions, it is difficult for the HQ to exploit local opportunities directly because of information deficiencies. Hence, channelling knowledge flow through an autonomous springboard subsidiary, which shares to a greater degree of HQ's organizational goals, ambitions and understanding, results in a significant reduction of psychic distance.

Moreover, springboard subsidiaries are characterized by their 'extra-regional location', that is, location outside the target region (Pla Barber & Camps, 2012). More specifically, they are likely to be located in a place that is not necessarily within the target region (like regional HQ), but is rather in the midway between a target region and a HQ in terms of psychic distance (Bergström, Johansson, & Brundin, 2006). Such intermediate location of springboard subsidiaries places them simultaneously close towards both a HQ and a target region. Additionally, the 'extra-regional' location puts these organizational units in a somewhat 'impartial', or unbiased, position, towards the target region. In other words, these springboard subsidiaries are not perceived by the target region as business or political rivals on the one hand and have important cultural or historical ties with this market on the other hand. Consequently, we posit that the extra-regional midway location of springboard subsidiaries, along with a high level of autonomy given to these intermediate level units will help MNCs to reduce psychic distance between a HQ and a target region.

METHODOLOGY

To explore how springboard subsidiaries shorten psychic distance between HQ and a target region we use a single case study methodology (Yin, 1989). This methodology is an appropriate means when the case is extremely revelatory and exemplar (Eisenhardt & Graebner, 2007; Yin, 2009). In fact, methodologies based on single cases allow to fit theory exactly to the many details of a particular case (Eisenhardt & Graebner, 2007), contributing to a deeper and broader understanding of specifics of a phenomenon, and providing further theoretical meanings to an already crystallized understanding of reality (Mariotto, Zanni, & Moraes, 2014; Tsoukas, 2009).

To identify and select an information-rich case, we used purposeful sampling technique (Patton, 2002). In particular, we applied critical case technique that involves identifying and selecting individuals that are especially knowledgeable about or experienced with the phenomenon of interest (Creswell & Plano Clark, 2011). To do so, we scrutinized Factiva database, looking for the information of MNCs that used springboard subsidiaries to expand in psychically distant regions. Given the novelty of the phenomenon of a springboard subsidiary, only a handful of cases were identified. Some of the MNCs were contacted via emails and telephone calls, and based on the collected preliminary information and telephone talks, we chose only one case as the most information-rich and exemplar.

As a result, we selected a German MNC that coordinates its activities in Latin America through its Spanish springboard subsidiary. The MNC is one of the world biggest corporations in the publishing and communication industry. It is headquartered in Munich, Germany, and all the Latin American activities related to publishing business are controlled through its subsidiary located in Barcelona. The MNC presence in Latin America includes Argentina, Chile, Colombia, Mexico, Peru, and Uruguay. The overview of publishing industries of the corresponding countries is presented in Table 1.

Given the fact that psychic distance can be analysed through MNC's perceived psychic distance and country-level psychic distance stimuli (Dow & Karunaratna, 2006) we conducted analysis on both levels. First, the data on MNC's perceived psychic distance between the HQ and the target region were collected through in-depth, personal semi-structured interview. Specifically, the interview was held with the Spanish subsidiary top manager that had worked in the MNC since late 1990s and has witnessed all the organizational transformation processes and structural changes of the MNC over time. Thus, the interviewee has extensive knowledge and experience in the springboard subsidiary and has worked in a direct contact with the HQ management. The interview was conducted in May 2016. The duration of the interview was about 3 hours and was recorded and transcribed within subsequent 24 hours. The data collected through the interview was triangulated using secondary data (media interviews, press releases, newspaper and academic articles, annual reports, etc.).

Second, country-level stimuli of the corresponding countries – Germany as the HQ home country, Spain as a springboard subsidiary's country, and Latin American region countries Argentina, Chile, Colombia, Mexico, Peru, and

Table 1. Publishing Industry Overview for 2014.

Country	GDP ($ millions)	GDP per Capita ($)	Population (millions)	IPA[a] ranking	Market Value ($ millions sales)	Number of titles (thousands)
Germany	3,868,291	47,966	81.5	3	9,896	93,600
Spain	1,381,342	29,861	47	9	2,331	90,802
Mexico	1,294,695	10,326	127	17	461.5	29,895
Argentina	543,490	12,645	42	25	620	30,850
Colombia	377,740	7,904	49.8	29	37.9	16,030
Uruguay	57,471	16,807	3.3	n/a	n/a	1,896
Chile	258,062	14,528	17.8	n/a	n/a	5,702
Peru	201,809	6,516	31.6	n/a	1.07	6,152

Note: The ranking estimates the publishing industry development of countries and is primarily based on a country's market value in terms of sales.
Source: [a]International Publishers Association (IPA, 2014). *Source*: Proper elaboration.

Uruguay where the MNC has direct presence – were analysed and compared. The stimuli that were used for the case study are presented in Table 2. All the stimuli, except *Country's language* distance, were calculated using Kogut & Singh index[2] (1988). To measure *Country's language* distance we followed Dow and Karunaratna (2006) that quantifies the difference between the major languages of 120 countries on a 5-point scale, based on Gordon's (2005) hierarchical classification on languages. Thus, distance between Spain and Latin American countries was equal to 1 (same language), and between Germany and Latin American countries was equal to 4 (same language family).

We also analysed *Migration* between Latin American countries, Spain and Germany, as it contributes to the asymmetry of psychic distance (Hakanson et al., 2016). Migration is given in absolute numbers and taken from UN Statistical Yearbook (2014).

RESULTS

Psychic Distance Between MNC'S HQ and the Target Region

The MNC first entered Latin American market in the 1960s, and during several decades key decisions were taken directly from the German HQ. By the beginning of the XXI century the company's presence in this region was weakening due to, as the interviewee posits, 'overall economic instability in Latin American countries on the one hand, and the erroneous investment decisions

Table 2. Psychic Distance Stimuli.

Psychic Distance Stimulus	Composites	Reference	Data Source
Language	Country's language	Dow & Karunaratna (2006); López-Duarte & Vidal-Suárez (2013)	Dow & Karunaratna (2006); Gordon (2005)
	TOEFL	Nickerson (2005); Reiche et al. (2015)	TOEFL (2015)
Culture	Hofstede's four dimensions[a]	Fletcher & Bohn (1998); Evans & Mavondo (2002)	Hofstede (1980)
	Hofstede's six dimensions[b]	Minkov & Hofstede (2011); Choi, Im, & Hofstede (2016)	The Hofstede Centre (2017)
Institutional distance	Worldwide governance indicators[c]	Dikova (2009); Globerman & Shapiro (2003); Hakanson & Ambos (2010); Kaufmann, Kraay, & Mastruzzi (2009);	World Bank (2014)
Country development	GDP in current prices (in $ millions)	Dow & Karunaratna (2006); Hutzschenreuter et al. (2014);	UN Statistical Yearbook (2014)
	GDP per capita (in $)	Chan et al. (2008); Dow & Karunaratna (2006); van Veen, Sahib, & Aangeenbrug (2014)	UN Statistical Yearbook (2014)
Publishing industry development	Marker value per population: Sales (in $ millions) divided by population (in millions)	IPA (2014)	Agencia ISBN (2016); Boersenverein des Deutschen Buchhandels (2016); Camara Colombiana del Libro (2016); Camara del Libro de Chile (2016); CANIEM (2016); INFOARTES (2016); IPA (2014)

Notes: [a]Hofstede's four dimensions include: power distance, individualism versus collectivism, masculinity versus femininity, uncertainty avoidance (Hofstede, 1980).
[b]Hofstede's six dimensions include: power distance, individualism versus collectivism, masculinity versus femininity, uncertainty avoidance, long-term orientation, indulgence (Minkov & Hofstede, 2011).
[c]Worldwide Governance indicators include: voice and accountability, political stability and absence of violence, government effectiveness, regulatory quality, rule of law, control of corruption (World Bank, 2014).
Source: Proper elaboration.

on the other hand'. This situation was even more complicated because of the significant psychic distance between the HQ and the target region, in terms of language, cultural, institutional, and industrial dissimilarities.

If we compare psychic distance stimuli between MNC's home country and each Latin American country where the company operates, we see dissimilarities in diverse aspects of psychic distance (see Table 3). To begin with, there is a significant language distance, as Spanish and German belong to different language groups, which results in the score of 4 according to Dow and Karunaratna (2006). In addition, the comparison of TOEFL scores shows that Latin American countries, with the only exception of Argentina and Uruguay, have a significantly lower English proficiency level in comparison with Germany, with the average value of TOEFL index difference of 4.26. Moreover, if we look at cultural distance indicators we observe that, with the exception of Argentina, the difference is significant as well, especially when all six dimensions are taken into account (see Hofstede's 6 dimensions, on Table 3). In terms of institutional distance, Argentina and Mexico are the farthest countries from Germany, whereas the distance in country development – measured as GDP and GDP per capita – is high in all cases.

Similarly, the MNC's perception of these psychic distance stimuli was also high. In particular, according to the interviewee, at that time the HQ had little understanding of the host market, which was caused by a significant distance between the German HQ and Latin America, in terms of language, culture, business practices and industry trends. To begin with, language distance slowed down business processes. In order to cope with this problem, the HQ put a German person who speaks Spanish in charge of Latin American market. However, even after that, the communication was inhibited because of

Table 3. Psychic Distance Between Germany and Latin American Countries.

	Language distance	TOEFL index difference	Hofstede's 4 dimensions	Hofstede's 6 dimensions	Institutional distance	GDP in current prices	GDP per capita	Market value per population
Argentina	4	1.30	1.93	2.81	6.29	6.95	6.36	4.99
Chile	4	7.07	5.29	4.75	0.36	8.20	5.70	n/a
Colombia	4	8.12	4.16	5.17	4.76	7.66	8.18	6.38
Mexico	4	4.37	4.72	5.65	5.17	4.17	7.22	6.08
Peru	4	4.37	5.02	4.49	4.98	8.45	8.76	6.46
Uruguay	4	0.32	5.71	4.96	0.73	9.13	4.95	n/a
Average	4	4.26	4.47	4.64	3.71	7.43	6.86	5.98

Note: All indicators, except Language distance, are calculated using Kogut & Singh (1988) index.
Source: Proper elaboration.

the cultural aspect that influences *the way of doing things* in general: 'Cultural differences influence the way of thinking, behaving, and even working, and a simple knowledge of language is not enough to eliminate these differences'. Additionally, because of a great distance in industry development, there was a problem of understanding local customers' needs. The interviewee posits: 'These markets [German and Latin American] have different maturation rhythm, and the industry trends of more advanced countries will probably enter Latin American market in 5 years. Because of such a great gap, it's very difficult for the HQ to foresee what will be popular in Latin America'.

Another peculiarity of Latin American market is its internal heterogeneity, and the existence of intra-regional psychic distance, that is, dissimilarities among Latin American countries. As Table 4 demonstrates, while country and industry development of Latin American countries in terms of GDP (with the average value 0.25), GDP per capita (with the average value 0.16) and market value per population (average value 0.04) are quite similar, they differ to a large extent culturally and institutionally. In particular, Hofstede's four dimensions and the institutional distance indicators show that, in some cases, the distance between two Latin American countries is greater than between HQ home country and the target region; for instance, the cultural distance between Chile and Mexico (2.36) or Mexico and Uruguay (2.43), is higher than between Germany and Argentina (1.93), whereas the institutional distance between Argentina and Chile (4.43) is almost reaching the one between Germany and Colombia (4.76).

Likewise, this intra-regional heterogeneity of Latin American countries was especially strongly perceived by the MNC. Because of the strong psychic distance between the country's HQ and Latin America, the HQ failed to understand the intra-regional psychic distance. As the interviewee posits, the difference of doing business in local subsidiaries from different Latin American countries is quite significant, which is often 'overlooked by the HQ, as they try to work with Latin America as a homogeneous region'. As a result, the German MNC could not fully exploit the growing potential of the distinct Latin American countries on the one hand, and did not benefit from the existing activities on the other hand. Additionally, the company was gradually losing control over its operations in this area as a consequence of mutual misunderstandings and miscommunication.

Springboard Subsidiary as an Intermediate Level Unit

Meanwhile, in 2001, Spanish subsidiary started making its first steps as an intermediate level unit taking advantage of important structural changes

Table 4. Psychic Distance among Countries of Latin America.

	Hofstede's 4 dimensions	Hofstede's 6 dimensions	Institutional distance	GDP in current prices	GDP per capita	Market value per population
Argentina-Chile	1.51	1.06	4.43	0.05	0.02	n/a
Argentina-Colombia	1.41	1.13	1.42	0.02	0.11	0.0859
Argentina-Mexico	1.83	1.72	1.32	0.35	0.03	0.0543
Argentina-Peru	1.18	0.90	1.04	0.07	0.19	0.0951
Argentina-Uruguay	1.10	0.78	3.36	0.15	0.09	n/a
Chile-Colombia	1.61	1.27	2.68	0.01	0.22	n/a
Chile-Mexico	2.36	1.94	3.11	0.68	0.09	n/a
Chile-Peru	0.25	0.38	3.01	0.00	0.33	n/a
Chile-Uruguay	0.71	0.57	0.44	0.03	0.03	n/a
Colombia-Mexico	0.52	0.47	0.21	0.53	0.03	0.0036
Colombia-Peru	0.68	1.07	0.25	0.02	0.01	0.0002
Colombia-Uruguay	2.18	1.88	3.02	0.06	0.40	n/a
Mexico-Peru	1.41	2.00	0.31	0.75	0.07	0.0057
Mexico-Uruguay	2.43	2.42	3.47	0.96	0.21	n/a
Peru-Uruguay	0.72	0.50	2.93	0.01	0.54	n/a
Average	1.33	1.21	2.07	0.25	0.16	0.04

Note: All indicators are calculated using Kogut & Singh (1988) index.

Source: Proper elaboration.

within the corporation. The MNC created a joint venture with another editorial company that had vast activities in Latin American region. The first task that the German MNC faced was to merge its existing activities in the region with the ones of their partner. That was the time when the Spanish subsidiary began to actively take over all the merger operations in the region. Such proactive behaviour resulted in a gradual build-up of a strategic importance of the subsidiary unit within the MNC. Hence, when the HQ needed to select an intermediate unit that would consolidate control over Latin American operations, it did not hesitate to choose the Spanish subsidiary. In particular, the Spanish subsidiary demonstrated robust capabilities to take control of the complex, but promising, market, had a rich experiential knowledge of managing important more-than-a-unit tasks and, finally, was psychically close to the target region, while at the same time having psychic similarity towards the HQ. As a result, in 2012 the Spanish subsidiary was officially appointed a mandate of a springboard subsidiary for expansion into Latin America.

As a result, nowadays the Spanish subsidiary has all the basic features of an intermediate level unit. For instance, when asked which Latin American operations the Spanish springboard controls the interviewee responds: 'All the Latin American subsidiaries report to us, each general director reports to the general director here, and each financial director reports here. On the editorial level everything is coordinated from here. On the level of human resources everything is coordinated from Spain. It's Spain who directs strategies of Latin American subsidiaries'.

Another intermediate unit feature of the Spanish subsidiary is its high level of autonomy. Springboard subsidiary's autonomy is somewhat curious. It finds itself in a complex paradigm relationships that extend into two different directions: (1) its relationship with the HQ and (2) its relationship with the target region. First, according to the interviewee, the HQ gives the Spanish intermediate unit an 'unconditional support' from its HQ not only in terms of financial investment, but also strategically, believing in their actions and supporting their initiatives. Second, when the Spanish subsidiary coordinates the firm's activities in the target region it copies to some extent, this decentralized approach of the HQ and delegates solid autonomy to its units in the target region: ' [Local subsidiaries] have quite a solid autonomy. In fact they are quite independent in their daily operations, and can publish whatever books they want on the local level'. Such approach is crucial when a company deals with a heterogeneous market that requires the use of multi-domestic strategy.

This double autonomy might seem concerning, because, as some IB scholars recognize, giving too much autonomy to a psychically distant subsidiary may result in the loss of control of overseas operations, restricted knowledge flow and eventually can inhibit international expansion in the target region (Forsgren et al., 2000; Gammelgaard et al., 2004; Noorderhaven and Harzing, 2009). In the case of springboard subsidiary, it may seem that these negative effects must double, because first, HQ gives autonomy to the Spanish subsidiary, and second, the Spanish subsidiary gives autonomy to the target region. Nevertheless, using a springboard subsidiary as an intermediate level unit for expansion into a target region paradoxically leads to the opposite results; it improves control, facilitates knowledge flow and eases international expansion by reducing the perception of psychic distance between the HQ and the target region.

The Impact of Springboard Subsidiaries on HQ – Target Market Relationships

The comparison of psychic distance stimuli between Latin American and Germany and those between Latin American and Spain helps to clarify why the Spanish subsidiary has the effect of reducing psychic distance between the HQ and the target region. In particular, Table 5 demonstrates that the average values of psychic distance of Spain respect the target region are relatively much smaller (from 1.01 to 1.78) than those of Germany (from 3.75 to 7.43). Moreover,

Spain finds itself psychically more proximate towards both Germany and Latin American countries: for example, Hofstede's six dimensions indicator for *Spain – Germany* is 2.22, and that for *Spain–Mexico* 2.65. This double proximity of Spain both to the MNC's home country and the target region puts this country in a somewhat midway between the HQ's home country and the target market.

Moreover, if we sum the psychic distance *Germany – Spain* and *Spain – Latin American country*, we see that in the majority of the cases, it will still be lower than the distances *Germany – Latin American country*. This is represented in Formula (1) as:

$$AB + BC < AC, \tag{1}$$

where AB is the distance between Germany and Spain, BC is the distance between Spain and Latin American country, and AC is distance between Germany and Latin American country. For example, the sum of institutional distances between Germany – Spain (0.56) and Spain – Mexico (2.44) will still be lower than the institutional distance between Germany – Mexico (5.17).

Table 6 represents the calculations to Formula (1) and indicates in black the results in which using Spain as springboard country lower the psychic distance between de HQ home country and the target region, and in grey otherwise.

Finally, if we compare the migration flows from and to each of the eight countries, we will see that Spain is the favourite destination for migrants from Germany, Argentina, Peru, Colombia, and Mexico, and the second favourite for migrants from Chile and Uruguay, with a total number of immigrants of 1.2 million people in 2013 (see Table 7). Such a big number of migrants creates stronger ties between countries, especially in the direction from country A to country B (Hakanson et al., 2016), and, consequently, reduces the perceived distance in this direction.

Considering Spain as the intermediate point between Germany and Latin-American countries, the perception of psychic distance between the MNC's HQ and the target region decreases after introducing the Spanish springboard subsidiary between them. As the interviewee posits, Spain serves as an 'important filter' between the German HQ and Latin America, because '[Latin American people] are very informal, and the Germans are very strict and the Spanish are somewhere in between'. He adds: 'I always defend that everything that goes from Germany to Latin America needs to pass through Spain first, because we contribute to a better understanding between the HQ and the target region, and if we don't do it, [the communication] is very difficult'. The interviewee concludes that Spain is closer to Latin America not only in the

Table 5. Psychic Distance Between Spain and Countries of Latin America, and the HQ's Home Country.

	Language distance		TOEFL index difference		Hofstede's 4 dimensions		Hofstede's 6 dimensions		Institutional distance		GDP in current prices		GDP per capita		Market value per population	
	Spain	Germany	Spain	Germany	Spain	Germany	Spain	Germany	Spain	Germany	Spain	Germany	Spain	Germany	Spain	Germany
Germany	4	-	2.31	-	2.71	-	2.22	-	0.56	-	3.89	-	1.67	-	2.26	-
Spain	-	4	-	2,31	-	2.71	-	2,22	-	0,56	-	3.89	-	1.67	-	2.26
Argentina	1	4	0.14	1.30	0.32	1.93	0.61	2.81	3.30	6.29	0.44	6.95	1.51	6.36	0.53	4.99
Chile	1	4	1.30	7.07	0.83	5.29	0.89	4.75	0.17	0.36	0.79	8.20	1.20	5.70	n/a	n/a
Colombia	1	4	1.77	8.12	1.81	4.16	2.24	5.17	2.27	4.76	0.63	7.66	2.46	8.18	1.05	6.38
Mexico	1	4	0.32	4.37	1.95	4.72	2.65	5.65	2.44	5.17	0.01	4.17	1.95	7.22	0.93	6.08
Peru	1	4	0.32	4.37	0.96	5.02	0.82	4.49	2.44	4.98	0.87	8.45	2.78	8.76	1.08	6.46
Uruguay	1	4	0.90	0.32	0.67	5.71	0.64	4.96	0.39	0.73	1.10	9.13	0.87	4.95	n/a	n/a
Average	1	4	1.01	4.26	1.32	4.47	1.44	4.64	1.65	3.71	1.11	7.43	1.78	6.86	1.17	5.98

Notes: All indicators, except Language distance, are calculated using Kogut and Singh (1988) index.

Source: Proper elaboration.

Table 6. Sum of Psychic Distance Stimuli.

AB + BC	TOEFL index difference	Hofstede's 4 dimensions	Hofstede's 6 dimensions	Institutional distance	GDP in current prices	GDP per capita	Market value per population
Germany – Spain – Argentina	2.45	3.03	2.83	3.87	4.33	3.18	2.79
Germany – Spain – Chile	3.61	3.54	3.11	0.74	4.68	2.87	n/a
Germany – Spain – Colombia	4.08	4.53	4.47	2.83	4.52	4.13	3.31
Germany – Spain – Mexico	2.63	4.67	4.87	3.00	3.89	3.62	3.19
Germany – Spain – Peru	2.63	3.67	3.04	3.01	4.76	4.45	3.34
Germany – Spain – Uruguay	3.21	3.39	2.87	0.96	4.99	2.54	n/a

Note: All indicators are calculated using Kogut & Singh (1988) index.
Source: Proper elaboration.

language but also in the way of conducting business. Moreover, even in terms of the industry-level development and trends, Spain, according to the interviewee, finds itself somewhere in the midway between more advanced countries and Latin America: 'Those tendencies [from advanced markets] enter Spain with the delay of 2–3 years, and will enter in Latin America in 2–3 years more. This intermediate position helps us to forecast more correctly, which products will be successful in Latin America, and which not'. When the industrial differences are too big, this forecast is less reliable, which explains why the US and German HQ had troubles to foresee the trends of Latin American market.

Furthermore, unlike psychically distant HQ that overlooks this intra-regional heterogeneity, Spanish subsidiary understands the differences between Latin American countries: 'Each country there is a unique culture, unique traditions, and we [Spanish subsidiary] treat subsidiaries from different countries in Latin America differently'. Thus, Spanish psychic proximity to the target region helps to detect important intra-regional dissimilarities and improves the communication between them.

All in all, the interviewee confirms that the coordination of Latin American activities through the Spanish springboard subsidiary has resulted

Table 7. Migration Flows for 2013.

Migration	From Mexico	From Colombia	From Peru	From Chile	From Argentina	From Uruguay	From Spain	From Germany	TOTAL
To Mexico	0	16,005	6,767	6,056	15,746	2,726	**21,700**	7,145	76,145
To Colombia	2,779	0	4,911	1,970	3,115	424	**6,455**	2,299	21,953
To Peru	1,735	6,902	0	8,350	13,199	713	**5,900**	3,403	40,202
To Chile	2,153	15,525	149,335	0	66,701	2,834	**10,950**	7,238	254,736
To Argentina	1,931	2,301	171,964	193,007	0	119,533	**90,494**	8,405	587,635
To Uruguay	483	n/a	1,368	1,393	22,425	0	**14,453**	877	40,999
To Spain	**47,441**	**359,178**	**190,004**	**62,031**	**268,129**	**79,899**	**0**	**240,003**	**1,246,685**
To Germany	7,219	12,375	12,375	5,156	7,219	658	**88,688**	0	133,690
Total	63,741	412,286	536,724	277,963	396,534	206,787	238,640	269,370	

Source: Proper elaboration.

in remarkably positive results, and summarizes: 'in our case it worked, and we can't imagine to work it out in any other way'. Thus, we can assume that the MNC's use of Spanish springboard subsidiary helped the company to achieve its objectives to gain control over Latin American market and take full advantage of the market opportunities there.

CONCLUSIONS

This chapter is an attempt to understand the effect of springboard subsidiaries as intermediate level units on MNC's international expansion into psychically distant markets. Although, recently there have been done substantial advancements on the topic of a springboard subsidiary (Caicedo Marulanda et al., 2015; Pla Barber & Camps, 2012; Pla Barber et al., 2015), there is still a lack of empirical studies on the role and effects of springboard subsidiaries. Therefore, our contribution into the IB literature was to analyse how and why putting a springboard subsidiary in the midway between the HQ and the target region influences psychic distance between the two.

In order to address this objective we used a case study methodology and analysed a German MNC that expanded into Latin America through its Spanish subsidiary. The results of the study show how springboard subsidiaries shorten the perceived psychic distance between a HQ and a target region.

When we summed up the distances *HQ home country – springboard subsidiary country* (AB), and *springboard subsidiary country – target market country* (BC) (see the Conceptual Model in Fig. 1), in the majority of cases, these

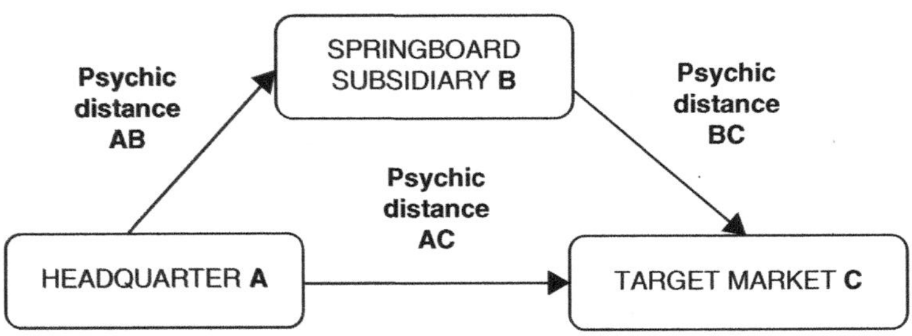

Fig. 1. Conceptual Model.
Source: Proper elaboration.

sums were less than the distance between *HQ home country – target market country* (AC).

Thus, using a springboard subsidiary as an intermediate-level unit contributes to a better understanding of the MNC's strategic goals in the target region and helped the springboard subsidiary to balance the interests of HQ in the target region. Specifically, our chapter shows that springboard subsidiaries find themselves in an intermediate position between HQ's home country and the target region in terms of psychic distance stimuli and MNC perception and are almost equally close to both the MNC's home country and the target market.

An important factor that helps springboard subsidiaries to perform their intermediate level duties is their 'outsidership' (Pla Barber & Camps, 2012), that is, their position outside the target region. Local-level subsidiaries are sometimes reluctant to collaborate with their neighbouring countries because of the intra-regional psychic distance intensified by political rivalry and international relations conflicts. On the contrary, springboard subsidiaries do not experience this intra-regional hostility and the collaboration with separate countries in the target region is more fluid. Thus, administering the region from the outside became more effective than it would be, if the intermediate-level unit were located inside the target region. This finding has important managerial implications. MNCs that decide to use a springboard intermediate unit will be able to use an indirect way of administering and opening psychically distant heterogeneous markets in a more effective manner.

The study has certain limitations. To begin with, the single case study methodology proposes the analysis of a peculiar phenomenon that can be unique for the particular inter-regional relationships of Europe–Spain–Latin America. More countries and industries should be analysed in order to explore how springboard subsidiaries behave in a different set of circumstances in terms of psychic distance. Additionally, we believe that these locations for springboard subsidiaries, or 'springboard countries' (Pla Barber & Camps, 2012) can be found in other geographical sites. Hence, further research is necessary to clarify the geographical location of potential springboards in other regional areas. Finally, the introduction of an intermediate level unit is able to decrease psychic distance unproportionally, which means that the arithmetic calculation of (country A – country B) + (country B – country C) < (country A – country C) is too simplified. This, and the unequal distribution of weight of distinct psychic distant stimuli can alter the results. Therefore, more mathematically sophisticated research should be done to explore this peculiar phenomenon.

NOTES

1. Beyond Hofstede's research on cultural dimensions (1980) currently exist several alternative new measures (see e.g. House, Hanges, Javidan, Dorfman, & Gupta, 2004; Gesteland, 2005; Trompenaars, 2003). Nevertheless, Hofstede's classical contribution remains the most influential one in the psychic distance literature.

2. According to Kogut & Singh (1988) index, the distance (CD_{XY}) between country X and Y is calculated as the average of differences of country scores adjusted by the variance (v_i) of the corresponding indicator:$D_{XY}=\Sigma\{(I_{ix} - I_{iy})/V_i\}/n$, where I_i stands from the index for the ith indicator, V_i is the variance of the index of the ith score, and n is the number of indicators.

REFERENCES

Agencia ISBN. (2016). *Agencia del ISBN en España*. Retrieved from http://agenciaisbn.es/web/index.php. Accessed on December 10, 2016.

Beckerman, W. (1956). Distance and the pattern of intra-European trade. *The Review of Economics and Statistics*, *38*(1), 31–40.

Bergström, G., Johansson, C., & Brundin, E. (2006). *Springboarding: A study of Swedish SMEs established in Singapore*. Jönköping: Jönköping International Business School.

Boersenverein des Deutschen Buchhandels (2016). Retrieved from http://www.boersenverein.de/buchmarkt2015. Accessed on December 10, 2016.

Berry, M. M., & Brock, J. K. U. (2004). Marketspace and the internationalisation process of the small firm. *Journal of International Entrepreneurship, 2*(3), 187–216.

Brewer, P. A. (2007). Operationalizing psychic distance: A revised approach. *Journal of International Marketing*, *15*(1), 44–66.

Brock, J. K, Johnson, J. E., & Zhou, J. Y. (2011). Does distance matter for internationally oriented small firms? *Industrial Marketing Management*, *40*(3), 384–394.

Caicedo Marulanda, C., Mora Rodriguez, J. J., Pla-Barber, J., & Leon Darder, F. (2015). A microeconometric analysis of the springboard subsidiary: The case of Spanish firms. *Economics Discussion Papers*, 2015-23.

Camara Colombiana del Libro (2016). *Estadisticas Swctor Editorial en Colombia años 2008–2015*. Retrieved from http://camlibro.com.co/historico-informes/. Accessed on December 10, 2016.

Camara del Libro de Chile. (2016). *Informe estadistico 2014 agencia chilena ISBN internacional standard book number*. Retrieved from https://camaradellibro.cl/agencia-isbn/estadisticas/. Accessed on December 10, 2016.

CANIEM. (2016). *Camara nacional de la industria editorial maxicana, estadñisticas de produccion y comercializacion del libro*. Retrived from http://www.caniem.com/es/content/actividad-editorial. Accessed on December 10, 2016.

Chan, C. M., Isobe, T., & Makino, S. (2008). Which country matters? Institutional development and foreign affiliate performance. *Strategic Management Journal*, *29*(11), 1179–1205.

Choi, K. S., Im, I., & Hofstede, G. J. (2016). A cross-cultural comparative analysis of small group collaboration using mobile twitter. *Computers in Human Behavior*, *65*, 308–318.

Creswell, J. W., & Plano Clark, V. L. (2011). *Designing and conducting mixed methods research* (2nd ed.). Thousand Oaks, CA: Sage.

Dikova, D. (2009). Performance of foreign subsidiaries: Does psychic distance matter? *International Business Review, 18*(1), 38–49.

Dow, D. (2000). A note on psychological distance and export market selection. *Journal of International Marketing, 8*(1), 51–64.

Dow, D., & Karunaratna, A. (2006). Developing a multidimensional instrument to measure psychic distance stimuli. *Journal of International Business Studies, 37*(5), 578–602.

Drogendijk, R., & Zander, L. (2010). Walking the cultural distance: In search of direction beyond friction. *Advances in International Management, 23*, 189–212.

Eisenhardt, K. M., & Graebner, M. E. (2007). Theory building from cases: Opportunities and challenges. *Academy of Management Journal, 50*(1), 25–32.

Evans, J., & Mavondo, F. T. (2002). Psychic distance and organizational performance: An empirical examination of international retailing operations. *Journal of International Business Studies, 33*(3), 515–532.

Evans, J., Treadgold, A., & Mavondo, F. T. (2000). Psychic distance and the performance of international retailers. *International Marketing Review, 17*(4/5), 373–391.

Forsgren, M., Johanson, J., & Sharma, D. (2000). Development of MNC centres of excellence.

Fletcher, R., & Bohn, J. (1998). The impact of psychic distance on the internationalization of the Australian firm. *Journal of Global Marketing, 12*(2), 47–68.

Gammelgaard, J., McDonald, F., Stephan, A., Tüselmann, H., & Dörrenbächer, C. (2012). The impact of increases in subsidiary autonomy and network relationships on performance. *International Business Review, 21*(6), 1158–1172.

Gesteland, R. R. (2005). *Cross-cultural business behavior: Negotiating, selling, sourcing and managing across cultures*. Copenhagen: Copenhagen Business School Pr.

Globerman, S., & Shapiro, D. (2003). Governance infrastructure and US foreign direct investment. *Journal of International Business Studies, 34*(1), 19–39.

Gordon, R.G., Jr. (Ed.). (2005). *Ethnologue: Languages of the World* (15th ed.). Dallas, TX: SIL International.

Hakanson, L. (2014). The role of psychic distance in international trade: A longitudinal analysis. *International Marketing Review, 31*(3), 210–236.

Hakanson, L., & Ambos, B. (2010). The antecedents of psychic distance. *Journal of International Management, 16*(3), 195–210.

Hakanson, L., Ambos, B., Schuster, A., & Leicht-Deobald, U. (2016). The psychology of psychic distance: Antecedents of asymmetric perceptions. *Journal of World Business, 51*, 308–318.

Hofstede, G. (1980), *Culture's consequences: International differences in work-related values*. Beverly Hills, CA: Sage.

House, R. J., Hanges, P. J., Javidan, M., Dorfman, P. W., & Gupta, V. (Eds.). (2004). *Culture, leadership, and organizations: The GLOBE study of 62 societies*. Beverly Hills, CA: Sage Publications.

Hutzschenreuter, T., Kleindienst, I., & Lange, S. (2014). Added psychic distance stimuli and MNE performance. Performance effect of added culture, governance, geographic and economic distance in MNEs' International expansion. *Journal of International Management, 20*(1), 38–54.

INFOARTES (2016). *Boletín Infoartes No. 1. Especial sector del libro.* Retrieved from http://www.infoartes.pe/boletin-infoartes-n1-especial-sector-del-libro/. Accessed on December 10, 2016.

IPA. (2014). *International Publishers Association Annual Report October 2013 – October 2014*, Switzerland.

Johanson, J., & Vahlne, J.-E. (1977). The internationalization process of the firm – A model of knowledge development and increasing foreign market commitments. *Journal of International Business Studies*, *8*(1), 25–34.

Johanson, J., & Vahlne, J.-E. (1990). The mechanism of internationalisation. *International Marketing Review*, *7*(4), 11–24.

Johanson, J., & Vahlne, J. E. (2009). The Uppsala internationalization process model revisited: From liability of foreignness to liability of outsidership. *Journal of international business studies*, *40*(9), 1411–1431.

Johanson, J. & Wiedersheim-Paul, F. (1975). The internationalization of the firm: Four Swedish cases. *Journal of Management Studies*, *12*(3), 305–322.

Kaufmann, D., Kraay, A., & Mastruzzi, M. (2009). *Governance matters VIII: Aggregate and individual governance indicators 1996–2008*. World Bank Policy Research Working Paper No. 4978.

Kedia, B. L., & Reddy, R. K. (2016). Language and cross-border acquisitions: An exploratory study. *International Business Review*, *25*(6), 1321–1332.

Klitmoller, A., & Lauring, J. (2013). When global virtual teams share knowledge: Media richness, cultural difference and language commonality. *Journal of World Business*, *48*(3), 398–406.

Kogut, B., & Singh, H. (1988). The effect of national culture on the choice of entry mode. *Journal of International Business Studies*, *19*(3), 411–432.

Kostova, T. (1997). Country institutional profiles: Concept and measurement. *Academy of Management Proceedings*, *1997*(1), 180–184.

Kostova, T., & Zaheer, S. (1999). Organizational legitimacy under conditions of complexity: The case of the multinational enterprise. *Academy of Management Review*, *24*(1), 64–81.

López-Duarte, C., & Vidal-Suárez, M. M. (2013). Cultural distance and the choice between wholly owned subsidiaries and joint ventures. *Journal of Business Research*, *66*(11), 2252–2261.

Malhotra, S., Sivakumar, K., & Zhu, P. C. (2009). Distance factors and target market selection: The moderating effect of market potential. *International Marketing Review*, *26*(6), 561–673.

Mariotto, F. L., Zanni, P. P., & Moraes, G. H. S. (2014). What is the use of a single-case study in management research? *Revista de Administração de Empresas*, *54*(4), 358–369.

Minkov, M., & Hofstede, G. (2011). The evolution of Hofstede's doctrine. *Cross Cultural Management: An International Journal*, *18*(1), 10–20.

Morosini, P., Shane, S., & Singh, H. (1998). National cultural distance and cross-border acquisition performance. *Journal of International Business Studies*, *29*(1), 137–158.

Nebus, J., & Chai, K. H. (2014). Putting the "psychic" back in psychic distance: Awareness, perceptions, and understanding as dimensions of psychic distance. *Journal of International Management*, *20*(1), 8–24.

Noorderhaven, N., & Harzing, A. W. (2009). Knowledge-sharing and social interaction within MNEs. *Journal of International Business Studies*, *40*(5), 719–741.

Nickerson, C. (2005). English as a lingua franca in international business contexts. *English for Specific Purposes*, *24*(4), 367–380.

Nordstrom, K. A., & Vahlne, J.-E. (1994). Is the globe shrinking? Psychic distance and the establishment of Swedish sales subsidiaries during the last 100 years. In M. Landeck (Ed.),

International trade: Regional and global issues (pp. 41–56). New York, NY: St Martin's Press.

Patton, M. Q. (2002). *Qualitative research and evaluation methods* (3rd ed.). Thousand Oaks, CA: Sage

Pla Barber, J., & Camps, J. (2012). Springboarding: A new geographical landscape for European foreign investment in Latin America. *Journal of Economic Geography*, *12*(2), 519–538.

Pla Barber, J., Villar, C., & Silva Domingo, L. (2015). *Parenting MNC networks through springboard subsidiaries: A dynamic model of evolution*. Uruguay: Universidad ORT Uruguay.

Reiche, B. S., Harzing, A. W., & Pudelko, M. (2015). Why and how does shared language affect subsidiary knowledge inflows? A social identity perspective. *Journal of International Business Studies*, *46*(5), 528–551.

Selmier, W. T., & Oh, C. H. (2012). International business complexity and the internationalization of languages. *Business Horizons*, *55*(2), 189–200.

Shenkar, O., Luo, Y., & Yeheskel, O. (2008). From "distance" to "friction": Substituting metaphors and redirecting intercultural research. *Academy of Management Review*, *33*(4), 905–923.

Reuss, T., & Lamont, B. (2009). The double edged sword of cultural distance in international acquisitions. *Journal of International Business*, *40*, 1298–1316.

The Hofstede Centre. (2017). Retrieved from https://geert-hofstede.com/countries.html. Accessed on January 10, 2017.

Tihanyi, L., Griffith, D. A., & Russell, C. J. (2005). The effect of cultural distance on entry mode choice, international diversification, and MNE performance: A meta-analysis. *Journal of International Business Studies*, *36*(3), 270–283.

TOEFL (2015). Test and score data summary for the TEFP ITP test, January–December 2014. *Education Testing Service*, Princeton, NJ, USA.

Trompenaars, F. (2003). *Did the pedestrian die: Insights from the world's greatest culture guru*. Oxford: Capstone.

Tsoukas, H. (2009). Craving for generality and small-N studies: The Wittgesteinian approach towards the epistemology of the particular in organization and management studies. In D. A. Buchanan & A. Bryman (Eds.), *Organizational research methods* (pp.285–301). London: Sage

UNCTAD (2016). *World investment report 2016. Global value chains: Investment and trade for development*. New York, NY and Geneva: UNCTAD.

UN Statistical Yearbook. (2014). *Department of Economic and Social Affairs, statistical division. Statistical Yearbook 2014 edition*. New York, NY: United Nations.

van Veen, K., Sahib, P. R., & Aangeenbrug, E. (2014). Where do international board members come from? Country-level antecedents of international board member selection in European boards. *International Business Review*, *23*(2), 407–417.

World Bank. (2014). *The world bank annual report 2014*. Washington, DC: World Bank.

Yin, R. K. (1989). Case study research: Design and methods, revised edition. *Applied Social Research Methods Series*, *5*. https://books.google.es/books/about/Case_study_research.html?id=gxy2AAAAIAAJ&redir_esc=y.

Yin, R. K. (2009). *Case study research: Design and methods* (4th ed.). Thousand Oaks, CA: Sage.

Zaheer, S. (1995). Overcoming the liability of foreignness. *Academy of Management Journal*, *38*(2), 341–363.

CHAPTER 21

CULTURAL DISTANCE, REPUTATION TRANSFERABILITY AND CROSS-BORDER ACQUISITIONS: A CONSUMER PERSPECTIVE

Michela Matarazzo, Federica De Vanna, Giulia Lanzilli and Riccardo Resciniti

ABSTRACT

The aim of the study is to investigate the effect of cultural distance on the reputation transferability from a made in Italy target firm to a foreign acquirer by analyzing local country consumers. The work compares two foreign acquiring firms a Chinese firm (large cultural distance to Italy) and a Spanish firm (small cultural distance to Italy). The findings show that Italian consumers have more negative attitudes toward the acquired firm and lower intentions to repurchase its products if the acquirer has large cultural distance rather than it has small cultural distance. Furthermore, the study aims at verifying that the case of small cultural distance fosters the reputation transferability more than the opposite case of large cultural

Distance in International Business: Concept, Cost and Value
Progress in International Business Research, Volume 12, 495–515

ISSN: 1745-8862/doi:10.1108/S1745-886220170000012025

distance. The work may be of value and interest because little has been studied dealing with the acquisition process in relation to market-based performance, particularly analyzing the consumer behavior toward a post-acquisition target.

Keywords: Cross-border acquisitions; cultural distance; corporate reputation; reputation transferability; consumer behavior; made in Italy

1. INTRODUCTION

Cross-border mergers and acquisitions (M&As) have become increasingly popular over the last decade and represent an important alternative for strategic expansion. A large part of scholars has focused on cross-border M&As performances in order to define and suggest good practices and reduce the failure number of such operations (Perry & Herd, 2004; Teerikangas & Very, 2006; Weber, Shenkar, & Raveh, 1996). However, few studies have focused on consumers' perspective after an acquisition (Fong, Lee, & Du, 2013; Thorbjørnsen and Dahlén, 2011). Another factor that has been mentioned but remains relatively unexplored, theoretically and empirically, is the impact of cultural distance on the reputation transferability in the acquisition process. Cultural distance plays a considerable and complex role in acquisitions because of its impact on the reputation transferability. The aim of the research is to fill this gap by investigating cross-border acquisitions in relation to market-based performance by analyzing the consumer's behavior. The literature concerning consumer behavior argues that consumer attitude is a determinant key of product or brand performance, and helps to predict future earnings (Aaker & Jacobson, 2001; Chaudhuri & Holbrook, 2001). Post-acquisition performance is also determined by purchasing behaviors of local consumers, therefore a direct investigation of consumer responses toward a cross-border acquisition can enhance knowledge of market-related post-acquisition performance. The study investigates how cultural distance affects local consumer responses toward cross-border acquisitions of a local firm.

To this aim, it firstly examines consumers' reactions toward a cross-border acquisition characterized by a large cultural distance, compared to the case of small cultural distance. Secondly, it examines how cultural distance affects reputation transferability of local targets in cross-border acquisitions. Specifically, the work analyzes the reputation transferability from the local target to the acquirer both in case of large and small cultural distances. It posits that reputation transferability of a local target is stronger in presence of small cultural distance between the local target and the acquirer.

The firms involved in the study are an Italian target firm, a Chinese firm (large cultural distance from the local target country) and a Spanish firm (small cultural distance from the local target; Hofstede, 1980), all of them belonging to the food sector (one of the sectors of made in Italy).

The study contributes to the cross-border acquisition literature in several manners. First, it investigates cross-border acquisitions in relation to market-based performance. Previous studies put more emphasis on objective data stressing managerial, organizational, and financial aspects (Akben-Selçuk, 2008; Balsvik & Haller, 2010; Bandick, 2011; Conyon, Girma, Thompson, & Wright, 2002) and ignoring the influence that cross-border acquisitions could have on consumers' responses. Second, the study analyzes the impact of cultural distance on consumers' choices. Existing literature is mainly based on the impact of cultural distance on organizational aspects in the post-acquisition process rather than the consumers' behavior (Datta, 1991; Haspeslagh & Jemison, 1991). Third, for the first time reputation transferability and cultural distance between firms involved in the acquisition process are linked in the same interpretative model in order to analyze the acquisitions success.

In the following section, a review of the relevant literature on the three topics analyzed is presented. Then the work describes the methodology adopted and the results (sections 3 and 4). The last section provides some comments on the authors' findings and discusses future research areas.

2. THEORETICAL BACKGROUND AND HYPOTHESES

2.1. Corporate Reputation

A commonly accepted definition of corporate reputation is "a perceptual representation of a firm's past actions and future prospects that describe the firm's overall appeal to all its key constituents when compared to other leading rivals" (Fombrun, 1996, p. 72). The three key attributes emphasized in previous definition are: reputation is based on perceptions; it is the aggregate perception of all stakeholders; and it is comparative. In addition to these three attributes, two additional ones are often mentioned in the sample to define corporate reputation: it can be positive or negative, and it is stable and enduring.

Corporate reputation is differentiated from the related concepts of organizational identity and corporate image (Barnett, Jermier, & Lafferty, 2006). There is a clear tendency for organizational identity to refer to internal stakeholders alone, for organizational image to refer to external stakeholders alone, and for corporate reputation to refer to both internal and external stakeholders.

Given that corporate reputation represents what is actually known (by both internal and external stakeholders), it can be positive or negative. Time is also an important distinction between image and reputation. Different scholars have discussed how to build a reputation takes time (Mahon, 2002; Rhee & Haunschild, 2006; Roberts & Dowling, 2002). On the other hand, images change frequently and may result in quickly attained perceptions of a firm. A positive reputation increases the likelihood that stakeholders will contract with a given firm (Deephouse, 2000; Rhee & Haunschild, 2006).

Corporate reputation should be measured as stakeholders' perceptions, not as factual representation (Wartick, 2002). Lewellyn (2002) takes into account three important issues for measuring corporate reputation: reputation "for what," reputation according "to whom," and use of the measure. These three issues will determine the appropriate reference group, the evaluators, and the appropriate measure and data set.

According to Fombrun (1996) measure can derive from sampling a representative set of stakeholders on a conceptually relevant set of criteria.

A number of measurement approaches are available reflecting the number of possible strategies toward measuring corporate reputation. Respondents can be asked to rate the reputation of a firm from poor to good (Goldberg & Hartwick, 1990). One of the most established measures of reputation derives from Fortune's AMAC survey based on eight attributes: financial soundness; long-term investment value; use of corporate assets; innovativeness; quality of the firm's management; quality of its products and services; ability to attract, develop, and keep talented people; and acknowledgement of social responsibility.

The brand equity scales (Aaker, 1991; Keller, 1993) are also popularly applied. For example, Keller and Aaker (1998) use Keller's three dimensions of "corporate credibility": corporate expertise, trustworthiness, and likability, in order to establish a link with successful brand extensions. Caruana and Chircop (2000) claim that corporate reputation is closely related to brand equity and developed 12 items for a corporate reputation scale based upon the five elements of "brand equity" from Aaker (1991) in order to measure the reputation of a beverage firm in Malta.

Brown and Dacin (1997) specify two dimensions of corporate image (referred to as "association"): corporate ability (CA) and corporate social responsibility (CSR). They argue that there is a need to develop and validate measures of corporate image that capture the full dimensionality of the concept.

The empirical measurement of identity has received less attention than its conceptual underpinnings (Hatch & Schultz, 2003). For example, Balmer and Soenen (1999) have developed a tool called the "Acid" (Actual, Communicated, Ideal, Desired Identity) Test of Corporate Identity Management and Davies (2003) have created the Corporate Character Scale. Through this instrument, they can measure a firm's reputation from both internal and external points of view simultaneously, and therefore measure any gaps between various stakeholders' views of a firm (Chun & Davies, 2006). Fombrun, Gardberg, and Sever (2000) have developed the RQ (Reputation Quotient) model that is based on six dimensions: emotional appeal, products and services, financial performance, vision and leadership, workplace environment, and social responsibility.

This study considers Fombrun's dimensions as criteria to evaluate corporate reputation. This method has been chosen to overcome the financial bias of the approach taken by Fortune (Fombrun & Shanley, 1990). Fombrun et al. (2000) rely on rating by the general public in order to overcome the above mentioned bias. Moreover, strong reputations occur when companies own a distinctive position in the minds of resource holders (Fombrun et al., 2000). In this context, the made in Italy in the food sector contributes to strengthen the corporate reputation of a firm, because the origin of a product affects the quality of the product concerned and has a remarkable impact in the consumer's mind. Additionally, according to Lafferty and Goldsmith (1999) corporate reputation has a significant influence on consumers' attitudes and purchase intentions.

2.2. Cultural Distance and Cross-Border Acquisitions

Ever since firms first started foreign operations, the question of whether and how the degree of internationalization fosters firm performance has been one of the most important in international business research (Buckley & Casson, 2003; Johanson & Vahlne, 1977). Despite all efforts, however, the internationalization–performance relationship is still the subject of ongoing debate following mixed empirical findings (Hennart, 2007, 2011).

Hofstede defines the concept of culture as the "collective programming of the human mind" which he operationalizes by means of five dimensions (Hofstede, Hofstede, & Minkov, 1991, p. 5): individualism/collectivism, masculinity/femininity, uncertainty avoidance, power distance, and long-/short-term orientation.

Individualism, contrasting collectivism, corresponds to the degree to which people in a country prefer to act as individuals rather than as members of a group. Masculinity, as opposed to femininity, refers to the way in which different cultures deal with the difference between the sexes. Uncertainty avoidance relates to the attitude against the risk and uncertain future. Power distance is defined as the extent to which the less powerful individuals in an organization accept that power is distributed unequally inside. Hofstede developed his original model proposing only the first four dimensions along which cultural values could be analyzed. Further research led him to add a fifth (long-term orientation), and then a sixth dimension (indulgence versus self-restraint).

The relative positions of 76 countries on these dimensions were expressed in a score on a 0–100 point scale. Exploring the Italian culture through the lens of the 6-D Model, it is possible to get the differences between this country and the others. In this study, the choice of foreign countries involved in the acquisition process is based on the previous cited model.

Numerous scholars have considered the effect of culture on cross-border acquisitions, but empirical evidence on the role of cultural differences on post-acquisition performance is inconclusive (Stahl & Voigt, 2008). One group of studies suggests a negative relation between cultural distance and acquisition performance due to increased costs of integration (Stahl & Voigt, 2005) and cultural collisions during the post-acquisition period (Buono, Bowditch, & Lewis, 1985). Another group of studies proposes that cultural distance brings forth perceptions of attraction rather than stress (Very, Lubatkin, & Calori, 1996). The latter line of research shows that cultural distances enhance performance by providing the acquirer with a diverse set of new routines and repertoires necessary to operate successfully in a new environment (Chakrabarti, Gupta-Mukherjee, & Jayaraman, 2009; Morosini, Shane, & Singh, 1998).

Some authors propose a reconciliation of the two conflicting literature streams. Reus and Lamont (2009) argue that cultural distance is not linearly and positively associated with acquisition performance because the integration capabilities of the acquirer play a mediating and a moderating role. Along similar lines, Slangen (2006) suggests that cultural distance should be taken into consideration but it is not the main factor affecting post-acquisition performance since it depends on the degree of integration the acquirer is able to gain. Cultural distance is beneficial for the acquisition performance in case of low degrees of post-acquisition integration whereas in case of high levels of integration cultural distance inhibits performance.

Acquirers showing more cross-border acquisition experience recognize cultural differences and have greater cultural sensitivity and ways of resolving organizational incompatibilities (Morosini et al., 1998; Very, Lubatkin, Calori, & Veiga, 1997).

Efforts to measure the organizational culture–performance relationship in M&As through survey-based research have surfaced. Datta (1991) finds differences in top-management styles, but not in reward and evaluation systems, to have a negative performance impact. Weber et al. (1996) investigate the role of corporate culture fit, autonomy removal and commitment of managers related to the performance of US mergers across different industries. The relationships between the variables were found to be complex, varying across industries and providing different results with different measures of performance. Differences have also been found to provide potential for value creation. Krishnan, Sahay, and Walsham (2004) examine the impact of top-management team complementarity on the performance of US acquisitions. Larsson and Finkelstein (1999) argue that complementarity of operations is a useful way of explaining M&As success, as it represents the potential for synergy realization in a deal.

2.3. Reputation Transferability and Cultural Distance

Little of the research on corporate reputation has paid adequate attention to link reputational transferability and cultural distance among firms involved in cross border acquisitions. Doney, Cannon, and Mullen (1998) suggest that norms and values linked to Hofstede's dimensions will influence the extent and manner in which the transfer of reputation to the corporate level can take place. Other authors analyzes the impact of distance on a single cue, like CSR. For example, Campbell, Eden, and Miller (2012) focus on the ways distance affects the MNE's willingness and ability to engage in CSR abroad. They argue that foreign affiliates from more distant home countries are less likely to engage in host country CSR.

Reputation is an intangible resource offering considerable potential as a rare, valuable, inimitable, and non-substitutable resource as described in the resource-based view of the firm (Barney, 1986; Wernerfelt, 1984). Asset redeployment following an acquisition should depend to some degree on the quality of the assets acquired (Capron, Dussauge, & Mitchell, 1998; Capron, Mitchell, & Swaminathan, 2001).

Saxton (2004) identifies in his work two characteristics of reputation as an intangible firm resource: mobility and transferability. Reputation transferability is the degree to which an acquiring firm may realize benefits from the positive perceptions of the target firm among its key constituents after the transaction. Saxton and Dollinger (2004) find that acquisition of targets with a better reputation results in higher acquirer satisfaction. However, it is not just the reputation of the acquired firm, but also how similar its reputation is to that of the acquiring firm.

As regards to reputation transferability, it is critical to consider the perceptions of the stakeholders who are assessing the target and acquirer's reputation pre- and post-transaction. Acquisitions can create a great deal of uncertainty for stakeholders such as customers and employees. When the relative standing of the target and acquirer differs, the result of an acquisition is likely to be cognitive dissonance in the mind of key stakeholders. Their willingness to act in a manner consistent with past behavior may be jeopardized by an acquisition, and the nature of the relationship with key stakeholders may undergo a transition approach to determining if the combined firm's behavior is consistent with that separate past actions. Different studies (Andreassen, 1994; Andreassen & Lindestad, 1998) have demonstrated that reputation is positively correlated with satisfaction and loyalty, with benefits for acquisitions of good-reputation targets. Doney et al. (1998) and Schweizer and Wijnberg (1999) highlight how significantly cultural differences on the side of the corporate audience can shape perception and create conditions which either support or inhibit transference of reputation.

Reputation mobility is the degree to which intangible assets of the target firm are detachable from the organization and may leave after a transaction. Examples of highly mobile intangible assets include key employees and process knowledge embedded in individuals (Coff, 1997). Immobile assets, in contrast, might include patented technologies where the firm holds the patent rights and brand or corporate loyalty in the marketplace with consumers. The benefits of acquiring a target with a good reputation may depend on the degree to which the acquired reputation assets can leave. While the relationships above may be present as main effects, it is important to identify other boundary variables that potentially have an impact on these relationships (Fromkin & Streufert, 1983). Three variables of particular interest are the acquisition experience of the acquirer, the hubris of the acquiring CEO, and cultural differences between target and acquirer. Particularly, cultural differences, or differences in organizational processes and beliefs that make cooperation and combining resources problematic, are a common source of blame for alliance and acquisition failure. This phenomenon has received much anecdotal attention in the popular press as well as some empirical efforts, though results have been inconsistent (Gomez-Mejia & Palich, 1997; Larsson & Finkelstein, 1999; Morosini et al., 1998). Cultural differences are likely to further exacerbate problems with reputation transferability. Acquiring firms are less able to appreciate the relationships a target has with key stakeholders when its value structures differ significantly (Larsson & Lubatkin, 2001). Further, mobile reputation assets are much more likely to depart when acquired by a firm that "just doesn't understand." For these reasons, it is reasonable to expect that intangible assets are even less likely to accrue to an acquirer when cultural differences are large (Saxton, 2004, p. 185).

Thus, we expect that the larger is cultural distance the lower is the reputation transferability. Consequently, consumers have more negative attitude toward a post-acquisition target and lower intentions to repurchase products of the post-acquisition target when the foreign acquirer has large cultural distance. The research has considered China and Spain to investigate this phenomenon. According to Hofstede's 6-D Model, China shows large cultural distance to Italy, whereas Spain has small cultural distance to it. The above discussion leads to the following hypotheses:

H1. Consumers have more positive attitude toward a post-acquisition target with high reputation when the foreign acquirer is a Spanish firm (large cultural distance) than they do when the foreign acquirer is a Chinese firm.

H2. Consumers have higher intentions to repurchase products of a post-acquisition target with high reputation when the foreign acquirer is a Spanish firm (small cultural distance) than they do when the foreign acquirer is a Chinese firm (see Fig. 1).

3. METHODOLOGY

In order to test the abovementioned hypotheses, the following assumptions were made (Fong et al., 2013):

1. The foreign firm acquires all shares of a local firm.
2. The corporate name of the acquired target remains unchanged.
3. The foreign acquirer assigned a new CEO and key positions in the firm.
4. The foreign acquirer firm has high reputation.
5. The respondents are habitual customers of the acquired firm.

The current study takes into account a cross-border acquisition of a made in Italy firm, which operates in the food sector and is characterized by a high

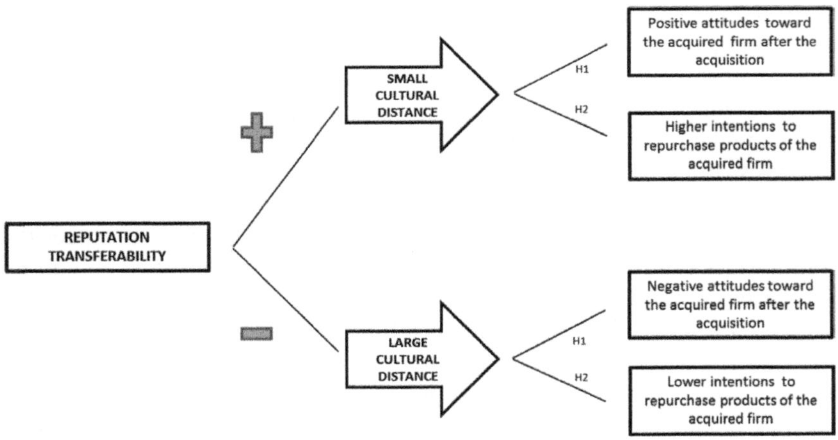

Fig. 1. The Research Model. *Source*: Our elaboration.

reputation. It is a real firm but with disguised brand name. It is the market leader in Italy for cured meats (ham, mortadella, salami, sausages, etc.), which are completely manufactured and packaged in the home country. Moreover, the study considers two acquirers: the first with large cultural distance (Chinese firm) and the second with small cultural distance to Italy (Spanish firm). The choice of countries was based on the Kogut and Singh's index (1988), a composite measure of Hofstede's dimensions of national cultures.

Then, we examined the behavior of participants for each of the two cases considered.

3.1. Subjects

The survey was conducted on Italian consumers through a questionnaire built on validated scales in the literature.

The questionnaires were administered to 424 individuals. All participants were students. The use of students as respondents is a common practice in consumer behavior studies (Chaudhuri & Holbrook, 2001; Fong et al., 2013) considering that they are a more homogeneous group than ordinary individuals are (Sternthal, Tybout, & Calder, 1994). All participants were university students from all over Italy. Specifically, there were 49% coming from faculties of economics.

Of the 424 students who participated in this study, 216 replied to the first type of questionnaire (local target acquisition from a Chinese firm) and 208 replied to the second type of questionnaire (local target acquisition from a Spanish firm).

3.2. Pretests

A pretest was developed before administering the main questionnaires with the aim of ensuring that consumer reaction to the cross-border acquisition depends mainly on the acquirer cultural distance rather than ethnocentrism.

The pretest was conducted on 60 university students, who were asked to indicate their agreement (on a 1 = "disagree very much" to 7 = "agree very much" scale) with statements regarding consumer ethnocentrism by four items (Fong et al., 2013; Funk, Arthurs, Treviño, & Joireman, 2010; Klein, Ettenson, & Morris, 1998; Ouellet, 2007; Shimp & Sharma, 1987): (1) purchasing foreign-made products is un-Italian; (2) it is not right to purchase foreign products, because it puts Italians out of jobs; (3) we should purchase products manufactured in Italy instead of allowing other countries to get rich off of us; and (4) we should buy from foreign countries only those products that we cannot obtain within our own country.

The 1–7 scale was converted in a 1–10 scale through the Thurstone method. Acting in this way we were able to undertake some quantitative estimations by transforming the judgments recorded in a metric scale.

The Cronbach *alpha* value of consumer ethnocentrism was 0.92 and the mean score was 2.94. The indicated mean was less than the neutral point (5). In addition, this neutral point was not included in the same confidence interval of the mean ($2.49 < 2.94 < 3.39$). This means that the differences perceived by the respondents on the dependent variables can be attributed to cultural distance.

3.3. Stimulus Materials and Procedure

In order to allow participants to better understand the relevant points of our research, both the acquired and the acquirer firm profile were described. The history, product lines, capabilities, and reputation were described in the first section of the questionnaire. The participants were also provided with a description of the acquisition and the underlying assumptions. They were also informed that the firms in the booklet were real, but with disguised names. This study used one disguised local firm (Alfa) and two disguised foreign firms (Delta and Gamma, the former with large cultural distance to Italy and the latter with a small cultural distance). Two versions of the booklet were prepared: one in which the acquirer had large cultural distance (Chinese firm) and the other in which the acquirer had small cultural distance (Spanish firm). Each participant was given a version of the booklet. It took approximately 10 minutes to complete. Participants were then debriefed and thanked.

3.4. Independent Variables

In the description of firms participants were informed about the high corporate reputation of the firms involved. The firm profile included firm introduction and information on six corporate reputation attributes (Fombrun et al., 2000): emotional appeal, products & services, financial performance, vision & leadership, workplace environment, and social responsibility.

The valence was manipulated using a number of stars (*) on six corporate attributes considered. The greater the number of stars, the higher the reputation status.

Participants were provided with a single version of questionnaire (with a combination of high reputation/large cultural distance or high reputation/small cultural distance), suggesting that both the acquired and the acquirer firms were highly capable of producing innovative and quality products and highly socially responsible. Moreover, respondents received information from the acquired firm report table about the goodness of the six attributes considered (i.e., **** or *****).

After reading the profiles of the different pairings of the high reputation/cultural distance, participants were asked to respond to a manipulation check in order to ensure that they had understood the instructions.

Following the description of the acquisition, participants then responded to the dependent measures.

3.5. Dependent Variables

Respondents were asked to express their attitudes toward the post-acquisition target on nine, 7-point bi-polar scales, anchored as "disagree very much" and "agree very much" (Gremler, 1995; Javalgi, Traylor, Gross, & Lampman, 1994; Mathwick & Rigdon, 2004; Pope, Voges, & Brown, 2004).

Later, participants were asked if they would consider repurchasing products of the acquired firm after the acquisition. Participants were asked to indicate their agreement on four 9-point scales, anchored at "disagree very much" and "agree very much" (Heitmann, Lehmann, & Herrmann, 2007).

Each measure demonstrated a relatively high internal consistency (Cronbach's $\alpha = 0.98$ and $\alpha = 0\ 95$), thus items measuring the same construct were averaged to form an index for that construct. The last page contained questions related to demographic information.

4. RESULTS

4.1. Manipulation Check

The manipulation check for the valence of the reputation of the local firm acquired was successful. The 1–7 scale was converted in a 1–10 scale through the Thurstone method. The means for the reputation of the local acquired were all above 5 for both the cases considered ($M_c = 7.72$ and $M_s = 7.84$).

Therefore, the local firm acquired was considered a high reputation firm.

4.2. Hypothesis Testing

Hypotheses were assessed using an analysis of variance (ANOVA). Before conducting ANOVA, the 1–7 scale and the 1–9 scale were converted in a 1–10 scale through the Thurstone method. **H1** predicts that Italian consumers have more negative attitudes toward the post-acquisition target when the acquirer firm is Chinese rather than Spanish. As expected, for attitudes toward the post-acquisition target, the main effect of cultural distance was significant ($F = 235.643$, $p < 0.001$; see Table 1).

Italian respondents evaluated the post-acquisition target more negatively if the acquiring firm has large cultural distance rather than the acquiring firm has small cultural distance (M_c = 2.83 versus M_s2 = 6.40. See Fig. 2). The results, therefore, are in line with the hypothesis.

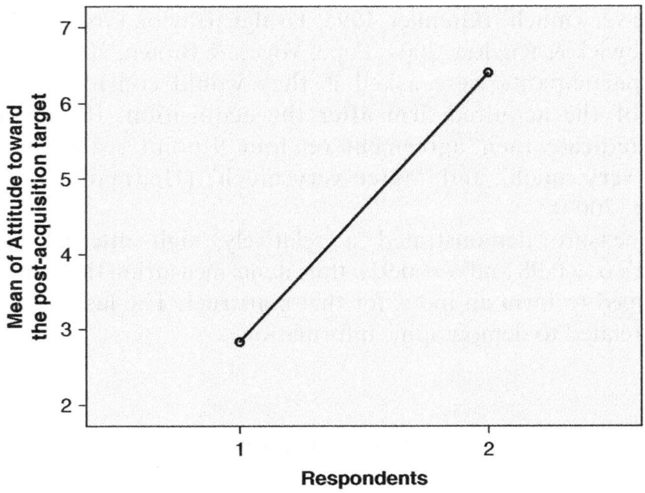

Fig. 2. Attitude toward the Post-Acquisition Target–Means Plot.

Table 1. Results of H1 and H2.

	Means		Std. Deviation		*F*-Value	Sig.
	Large CD	Small CD	Large CD	Small CD		
Attitude toward the post-acquisition target	2.8306	6.4006	2.0123	2.7341	235.643	0.000***
Repurchase intention toward the post-acquisition target	2.3958	5.7464	1.8 657	2.3961	259.2	0.000***

Note: $^{***}p < 0.001$.

In a similar manner, **H2** predicts that Italian consumers have lower intentions to repurchase products of the post-acquisition target if the acquiring firm is Chinese rather than Spanish. As expected, the main effect was significant ($F = 259.2$, $p < 0.001$; see Table 1).

Italian participants were found to have lower intentions to repurchase products of the post-acquisition target if the acquiring firm has large cultural distance rather than small cultural distance ($M_c1 = 2.40$ versus $M_s2 = 5.75$; see Fig. 3). The findings support the abovementioned hypotheses.

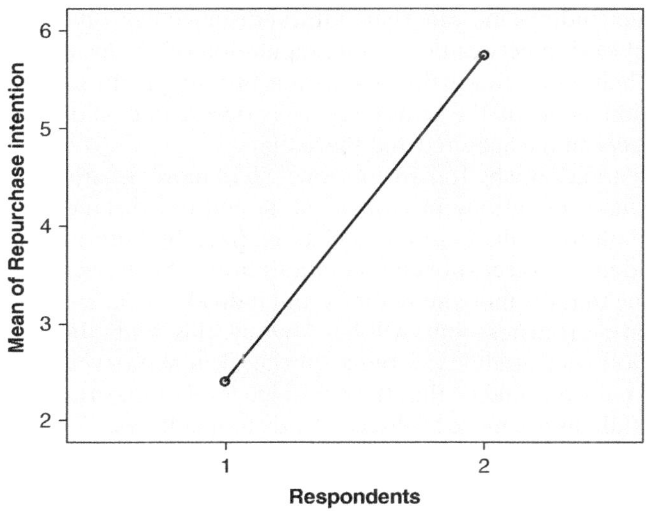

Fig. 3. Repurchase Intentions toward the Post-Acquisition Target–Means Plot.

5. DISCUSSION

Acquiring local firms is one of the most used mode of entry by foreign firms. The majority of literature has dealt with the effect of this phenomenon on performance of firms involved in the cross-border acquisitions ignoring the influence that they could have on consumers' responses. The theoretical reason why the cultural distance between the contry of the acquiring firm and that of the acquired firm should affect consumer's behavior toward the post-acquisition target is that consumer's choices are based on firm's reputation. According to Fombrun et al. (2000) reputation is based on dimensions which affect perceived organizational identity and image. As we assume that the foreign acquirer assigned a new CEO and key positions in the firm, these changes in the firm's management could lead to a different reputation perceived by consumers. The study aims to valuate cross-border acquisitions in relation to market-based performance by analyzing the Italian consumer behavior. Two indicators with significant performance impacts on cross-border acquisitions were studied: the attitude toward the post-acquisition target and the intention to repurchase its products. From the comparison between two acquiring firms the first with large cultural distance and the second one with small cultural distance, the results show more negative attitudes toward the post-acquisition target and lower intentions to repurchase its products in case of large cultural distance.

Thus, our findings indicate that cultural distance has a moderating effect on the relationship between corporate reputation of the local target and the consumer behavior toward the post-acquisition target. In fact, the transfer of reputation assets of the local target only occurs in case of small cultural distance between the acquired and the acquirer.

Perhaps a reason why Italian consumers had more negative attitudes and lower purchase intentions in case of large cultural distance is relative to their own culture. Italian culture is characterized by both high masculinity and individualism (geert-hofstede.com/italy.html). Schweizer and Wijnberg (1999) argue that the more masculinity and individualism, are the less corporate reputation transferability will be. Anyway, this study provides evidence of reputation transferability if the acquiring firm shows small cultural distance. The reason would be that Italy has high level of uncertainty avoidance; therefore, Italians are more frightened by distant cultures.

These results provide important evidences that the cultural distance directly affects consumers' attitudes and purchase intentions toward the post-acquisition target. Moreover, cultural distance could hinder the reputation transferability from the local target to the acquiring firm.

6. MANAGERIAL IMPLICATIONS

The managerial implications of the study are referred to firms engaging cross-border acquisitions. In order to get the intangible benefits of a faithful custom, a well-established brand and a good reputation, firms should carefully analyze the reactions of host consumers. When the cultural distance between the acquiring and the acquired firm is large, the host acquiring firm can't reap the benefits of the reputational capital and of the customer target. Differently, when cultural distance between the two entities is small, the acquiring firm can obtain the advantages of the reputational capital and of the base of custom. However, when the cultural distance seems to hamper the reputational transferability and the acquisition benefits, managers could consider other entry modes such as Joint ventures, due to the equality between the two parties.

Cultural distance represents a type of foreign liability resulting from different habits, histories, and traditions.

Prior research suggests that to enhance consumers' adaptability to a cross-border acquisition, it is necessary for the multinational to increase its legitimacy in order to be taken as a national firm (Luo & Mezias, 2002;

Zaheer, 1995) and to involve customers in the operations with their opinions (Thorbjørnsen & Dahlén, 2011).

If a Chinese firm wants to acquire an Italian firm, the acquirer should consider administering market surveys to investigate the influence of cultural distance.

This research also finds that in case of small cultural distance, local target reputation could be transferred to the post-acquisition target. Thus, an acquiring firm with similar characteristic can acquire an Italian firm and benefit from the advantages of its high reputation, customer base, and market resources. Taking into account all factors, foreign firms with small cultural distance to Italy may benefit from the local target reputation transferability. Italian will continue to consider the products of the post-acquisition target as made in Italy ones, and they will have a positive attitude toward them. Firms with small cultural distance to Italy can pursue successfully growth strategies by acquiring local firms holding relevant reputation assets.

7. LIMITATIONS AND FUTURE RESEARCH

The study has some limitations, and the recognition of these represent opportunities for future research. The findings are limited to the product tested. Future research with other products or services not belonging to sector of made in Italy could shed light on limits of these findings. Second, the study only considers acquirers with high reputation; however, considering a foreign acquirer with poor reputation may lead to different results despite the presence of small cultural distance Thus, future research could consider a poor reputation foreign acquirer in order to extend this line of research.

Third, as our sample solely consists of Italian consumers, we recommend future studies to replicate our test in other settings, analyzing the reaction of consumers from other countries in order to contribute to the generalizability of our findings.

REFERENCES

Aaker, D. A. (1991). Management brand equity. Free Press New York, NY

Aaker, D. A., & Jacobson, R. (2001). The value relevance of brand attitude in high-technology markets. *Journal of Marketing Research*, *38*(4), 485–493.

Akben-Selçuk, E. (2008). The impact of cross-border mon target company performance: Evidence from Turkey. *Economics Bulletin*, *13*(5), 1–9.

Andreassen, T. W. (1994). Satisfaction, loyalty and reputation as indicators of customer orientation in the public sector. *International Journal of Public Sector Management*, *7*(2), 16–34.

Andreassen, T. W., & Lindestad, B. (1998). The effect of corporate image in the formation of customer loyalty. *Journal of Service Research*, *1*(1), 82–92.

Balmer, J. M., & Soenen, G. B. (1999). The acid test of corporate identity management™. *Journal of Marketing Management*, *15*(1–3), 69–92.

Balsvik, R., & Haller, A. S. (2010). Picking "lemons" or picking "cherries"? Domestic and foreign acquisitions in Norwegian manufacturing. *The Scandinavian Journal of Economics*, *112*(2), 361–387.

Bandick, R. (2011). Foreign acquisition, wages and productivity. *The World Economy*, *34*(6), 931–951.

Barnett, M. L., Jermier, J. M., & Lafferty, B. A. (2006). Corporate reputation: The definitional landscape. *Corporate Reputation Review*, *9*(1), 26–38.

Barney, J. B. (1986). Strategic factor markets: Expectations, luck, and business strategy. *Management Science*, *32*(10), 1231–1241.

Brown, T. J., & Dacin, P. A. (1997). The company and the product: Corporate associations and consumer product responses. *The Journal of Marketing*, *61*(1), 68–84.

Buckley, P. J., & Casson, M. (2003). The future of the multinational enterprise in retrospect and in prospect. *Journal of International Business Studies, 34*(2), 219–222.

Buono, A. F., Bowditch, J. L., & Lewis, J. W. (1985). When cultures collide: The anatomy of a merger. *Human Relations*, *38*(5), 477–500.

Campbell, J. T., Eden, L., & Miller, S. R. (2012). Multinationals and corporate social responsibility in host countries: Does distance matter? *Journal of International Business Studies*, *43*(1), 84–106.

Capron, L., Dussauge, P., & Mitchell, W. (1998). Resource redeployment following horizontal acquisitions in Europe and North America, 1988–1992. *Strategic Management Journal*, *19*(7), 631–661.

Capron, L., Mitchell, W., & Swaminathan, A. (2001). Asset divestiture following horizontal acquisitions: A dynamic view. *Strategic Management Journal*, *22*(9), 817–844.

Caruana, A., & Chircop, S. (2000). Measuring corporate reputation: A case example. *Corporate Reputation Review*, *3*(1), 43–57.

Chakrabarti, R., Gupta-Mukherjee, S., & Jayaraman, N. (2009). Mars–Venus marriages: Culture and cross-border M&A. *Journal of International Business Studies*, *40*(2), 216–236.

Chaudhuri, A., & Holbrook, M. B. (2001). The chain of effects from brand trust and brand affect to brand performance: The role of brand loyalty. *Journal of Marketing*, *65*(2), 81–93.

Chun, R., & Davies, G. (2006). The influence of corporate character on customers and employees: Exploring similarities and differences. *Journal of the Academy of Marketing Science*, *34*(2), 138–146.

Coff, R. W. (1997). Human assets and management dilemmas: Coping with hazards on the road to resource-based theory. *Academy of Management Review*, *22*(2), 374–402.

Conyon, M. J., Girma, S., Thompson, S., & Wright, P. W. (2002). The productivity and wage effects of foreign acquisition in the United Kingdom. *The Journal of Industrial Economics*, *50*(1), 85–102.

Datta, D. K. (1991). Organizational fit and acquisition performance: Effects of post-acquisition integration. *Strategic Management Journal*, *12*(4), 281–297.

Davies, G. (2003). *Corporate reputation and competitiveness*. Psychology Press. Hove, United Kingdom

Deephouse, D. L. (2000). Media reputation as a strategic resource: An integration of mass communication and resource-based theories. *Journal of Management*, *26*(6), 1091–1112.

Doney, P. M., Cannon, J. P., & Mullen, M. R. (1998). Understanding the influence of national culture on the development of trust. *Academy of Management Review*, *23*(3), 601–620.

Fombrun, C. J. (1996). Reputation: Realising value from the corporate image, Boston, Massachusetts, Harvard Business School Press.

Fombrun, C. J., Gardberg, N. A., & Sever, J. M. (2000). The reputation quotient SM: A multi-stakeholder measure of corporate reputation. *Journal of Brand Management*, *7*(4), 241–255.

Fombrun, C. J., & Shanley, M. (1990). What's in a name? Reputation building and corporate strategy. *Academy of Management Journal*, *33*(2), 233–258.

Fong, C. M., Lee, C. L., & Du, Y. (2013). Target reputation transferability, consumer animosity, and cross-border acquisition success: A comparison between China and Taiwan. *International Business Review*, *22*(1), 174–186.

Fromkin, H. L., & Streufert, S. (1983). Laboratory experimentation. In: M. D. Dunnette (Ed.), *Handbook of industrial and organizational psychology* (pp. 415–466). New York, NY: Wiley.

Funk, C. A., Arthurs, J. D., Treviño, L. J., & Joireman, J. (2010). Consumer animosity in the global value chain: The effect of international production shifts on willingness to purchase hybrid products. *Journal of International Business Studies*, *41*(4), 639–651.

Goldberg, M. E., & Hartwick, J. (1990). The effects of advertiser reputation and extremity of advertising claim on advertising effectiveness. *Journal of Consumer Research*, *17*(2), 172–179.

Gomez-Mejia, L. R., & Palich, L. E. (1997). Cultural diversity and the performance of multinational firms. *Journal of International Business Studies*, *28*(2), 309–335.

Gremler, D. D. (1995). *The effect of satisfaction, switching costs, and interpersonal bonds on service loyalty*. Unpublished Doctoral Dissertation, Marketing Department, Arizona State University.

Haspeslagh, P., & Jemison, D. B. (1991) *Managing acquisitions: Creating value through corporate renewal*. New York, NY: Free Press.

Hatch, J. M., & Schultz, M. (2003). Bringing the corporation into corporate branding. *European Journal Of marketing*, *37*(7/8), 1041–1064.

Heitmann, M., Lehmann, D. R., & Herrmann, A. (2007). Choice goal attainment and decision and consumption satisfaction. *Journal of Marketing Research*, *44*(2), 234–250.

Hennart, J. F. (2007). The theoretical rationale for a multinationality-performance relationship. *Management International Review*, *47*(3), 423–452.

Hennart, J. F. (2011). A theoretical assessment of the empirical literature on the impact of multinationality on performance. *Global Strategy Journal*, *1*(1–2), 135–151.

Hofstede, G. (1980). *Culture's consequences: International differences in work-related values*. Beverly Hills: Sage.

Hofstede, G., Hofstede, G. J., & Minkov, M. (1991). *Cultures and organizations: Software of the mind* (Vol. 2). London: McGraw-Hill.

Javalgi, R. G., Traylor, M. B., Gross, A. C., & Lampman, E. (1994). Awareness of sponsorship and corporate image: An empirical investigation. *Journal of Advertising*, *23*(4), 47–58.

Johanson, J., & Vahlne, J. E. (1977). The internationalization process of the firm—A model of knowledge development and increasing foreign market commitments. *Journal of International Business Studies*, *8*(1), 23–32.

Keller, K. L. (1993). Conceptualizing, measuring, and managing customer-based brand equity. *The Journal of Marketing*, *57*(1), 1–22.

Keller, K. L., & Aaker, D. A. (1998). The impact of corporate marketing on a company's brand extensions. *Corporate Reputation Review*, *1*(4), 356–378.

Klein, J. G., Ettenson, R., & Morris, M. D. (1998). The animosity model of foreign product purchase: An empirical test in the People's Republic of China. *Journal of Marketing*, *62*(1), 89–100.

Kogut, B., & Singh, H. (1988). The effect of national culture on the choice of entry mode. *Journal of international business studies*, *19*(3), 411–432.

Krishnan, S., Sahay, S., & Walsham, G. (2004). Managing crosscultural issues in global software outsourcing. *Communication of the ACM*, *47*(4), 62–66.

Lafferty, B. A., & Goldsmith, R. E. (1999). Corporate credibility's role in consumers' attitudes and purchase intentions when a high versus a low credibility endorser is used in the ad. *Journal of Business Research*, *44*(2), 109–116.

Larsson, R., & Finkelstein, S. (1999). Integrating strategic, organizational, and human resource perspectives on mergers and acquisitions: A case survey of synergy realization. *Organization Science*, *10*(1), 1–26.

Larsson, R., & Lubatkin, M. (2001). Achieving acculturation in mergers and acquisitions: An international case survey. *Human Relations*, *54*(12), 1573–1607.

Lewellyn, P. G. (2002). Corporate reputation focusing the Zeitgeist. *Business & Society*, *41*(4), 446–455.

Luo, Y., & Mezias, J. M. (2002). Liabilities of foreignness: Concepts, constructs, and consequences. *Journal of International Management*, *8*(3), 217–221.

Mahon, J. F. (2002). Corporate reputation: Research agenda using strategy and stakeholder literature. *Business & Society*, *41*(4), 415–445.

Mathwick, C., & Rigdon, E. (2004). Play, flow, and the online search experience. *Journal of Consumer Research*, *31*(2), 324–332.

Morosini, P., Shane, S., & Singh, H. (1998). National cultural distance and cross-border acquisition performance. *Journal of International Business Studies*, *29*(1), 137–158.

Ouellet, J. F. (2007). Consumer racism and its effects on domestic crossethnic product purchase: An empirical test in the United States, Canada, and France. *Journal of Marketing*, *71*(1), 113–128.

Perry, J. S., & Herd, T. J. (2004). Reducing M&A risk through improved due diligence. *Strategy & Leadership*, *32*(2), 12–19.

Pope, N. K. L., Voges, K. E., & Brown, M. R. (2004). The effect of provocation in the form of mild erotica on attitude to the ad and corporate image. *Journal of Advertising*, *33*(1), 69–82.

Reus, T. H., & Lamont, B. T. (2009). The double-edged sword of cultural distance in international acquisitions. *Journal of International Business Studies*, *40*(8), 1298–1316.

Rhee, M., & Haunschild, P. R. (2006). The liability of good reputation: A study of product recalls in the US automobile industry. *Organization Science*, *17*(1), 101–117.

Roberts, P. W., & Dowling, G. R. (2002). Corporate reputation and sustained superior financial performance. *Strategic Management Journal*, *23*(12), 1077–1093.

Saxton, T. (2004). Acquisitions and intangible resources: Reputations as a mobile and transferable asset. *Advances in Mergers and Acquisition*, *3*, 177–191.

Saxton, T,. & Dollinger, M. (2004). Target reputation and appropriability: Picking and deploying resources in acquisitions. *Journal of Management*, *30*(1), 123–147.

Schweizer, T. S., & Wijnberg, N. M. (1999). Transferring reputation to the corporation in different cultures: Individuals, collectives, systems and the strategic management of corporate reputation. *Corporate Reputation Review*, *2*(3), 249–266.

Shimp, T. & Sharma, S. (1987). Consumer ethnocentrism: Construction and validation of the CETSCALE. *Journal of Marketing Research*, *24*(3), 280–289.

Slangen, A. H. (2006). National cultural distance and initial foreign acquisition performance: The moderating effect of integration. *Journal of World Business*, *41*(2), 161–170.

Stahl, G. K., & Voigt, A. (2005). Impact of cultural differences on merger and acquisition performance: A critical research review and an integrative model. *Advances in Mergers and Acquisitions*, *4*, 51–82.

Stahl, G. K., & Voigt, A. (2008). Do cultural differences matter in mergers and acquisitions? A tentative model and examination. *Organization Science*, *19*(1), 160–176.

Sternthal, B., Tybout, A. M., & Calder, B. J. (1994). Experimental design: Generalization and theoretical explanation. In R. Bagozzi (Ed.), *Principles of marketing research* (pp. 195–223). Cambridge, MA: Blackwell Publishers.

Teerikangas, S., & Very, P. (2006). The culture–performance relationship in M&A: From yes/no to how. *British Journal of Management*, *17*(S1), S31–S48.

Thorbjørnsen, H., & Dahlén, M. (2011). Customer reactions to acquirer-dominant mergers and acquisitions. *International journal of Research in Marketing*, *28*(4), 332–341.

Very, P., Lubatkin, M., & Calori, R. (1996). A cross-national assessment of acculturative stress in recent European mergers. *International Studies of Management and Organization*, *26*(1), 59–86.

Very, P., Lubatkin, M., Calori, R., & Veiga, J. (1997). Relative standing and the performance of recently acquired European firms. *Strategic Management Journal*, *18*(8), 593–614.

Wartick, S. L. (2002). Measuring corporate reputation: Definition and data. *Business & Society*, *41*(4), 371–392.

Weber, Y., Shenkar, O., & Raveh, A. (1996). National and corporate cultural fit in mergers/acquisitions: An exploratory study. *Management Science*, *42*(8), 1215–1227.

Wernerfelt, B. (1984). A resource-based view of the firm. *Strategic Management Journal*, *5*(2), 171–180.

Zaheer, S. (1995). Overcoming the liability of foreignness. *Academy of Management Journal*, *38*(2), 341–363.

CHAPTER 22

DOMESTIC ALLIANCE FORMATION AND THE FOREIGN DIVESTMENT DECISIONS OF FIRMS

Viacheslav Iurkov and Gabriel R.G. Benito

ABSTRACT

This study examines the effect of domestic alliances on firms' foreign divestment decisions. We argue that foreign subsidiaries face a higher risk of being divested when firms form new alliances with other firms in their home country. Alliances at home involve resources and may divert attention away from international operations. Also, opportunities emerging from entering into new relationships with other firms domestically may lead firms to reconfigure their value chain activities and resources across locations, thereby increasing the probability of foreign divestment. Using data from the electronic and electrical equipment industries in the USA over the period 2001–2008, we empirically investigate the link between domestic alliances and foreign divestment. We find that increases in domestic inter-firm collaboration indeed significantly affect firms' propensity to divest foreign operations.

Keywords: Foreign divestment; multinational firms; domestic alliances

Distance in International Business: Concept, Cost and Value
Progress in International Business Research, Volume 12, 517–538

ISSN: 1745-8862/doi:10.1108/S1745-886220170000012004

INTRODUCTION

Divestment decisions have significant implications for individual firms as well as for other stakeholders such as employees and local communities. Yet, studies about the drivers of foreign divestment remain relatively scarce. Although divestments and relocations are common aspects of firms' international activities, the vast majority of studies about the international operations of firms has focused on the expansion or positive development of international business operations, not on their contraction (Benito & Welch, 1997). The focus is on decisions to enter new markets and to make foreign direct investments (FDIs), rather than on decisions to exit markets and to divest operations abroad (McDermott, 2010; Turcan, 2013).

Which factors influence firms' propensity to divest foreign operations? Existing research on factors influencing firms' divestment decisions highlights the effects of corporate (parent company) and business unit performance (Duhaime & Grant, 1984; Engel, Procher, & Schmidt, 2013), industrial diversification of firms' operations (Chang & Singh, 1999), the type of ownership of foreign business units and their modes of entry and establishment (Benito, 1997a; Dhanaraj & Beamish, 2004; Mata & Portugal, 2000), international experience (Benito, 1997a), resource endowments (Mata & Portugal, 2000), age of a corporate parent (Mata & Freitas, 2012), better opportunities for firm resources (Berry, 2010), and market growth, policy stability, and exchange rate volatility (Belderbos & Zou, 2006; Benito, 1997a; Berry, 2013; Blake & Moschieri, 2017; Song, 2014, 2015). All in all, previous studies of foreign divestment have mostly focus on either the role of intra-firm characteristics or on factors that are external to firms or largely out of their control. We know very little about possible triggers of divestment activity that emerge from strategic tradeoffs in a firm's overall resource deployment strategy.

In this study, we extend the current knowledge about drivers of firm foreign divestment decisions by examining whether such decisions depend on the availability of strategic alternatives within firms' domestic (home country) environment. The emergence of such alternatives may render FDI more transient than commonly assumed. Changes in the home country environment can make existing foreign activities less attractive and ultimately even result in their divestment. Some previous studies demonstrate that firms are sensitive to favorable changes in domestic conditions, which could lead them to relocate activities back home (Fratocchi, Di Mauro, Barbieri, Nassimbeni, & Zanoni, 2014), and that they may lock some of their investment activities within the home location, thus setting thresholds for the types and size of activities conducted abroad (Benito, Lunnan, & Tomassen, 2011; Mudambi & Swift, 2012; Narula, 2002).

Embeddedness within domestic networks of interfirm collaborations (e.g., Ahuja, 2000; Gulati, 1998; Powell, Koput, & Smith-Doerr, 1996) is an important aspect of the domestic environment. We argue that divestment of foreign operations becomes more likely as firms become more embedded within such networks, that is, initiate new interfirm collaborations with the scope of activities being bounded to home country. Interfirm collaborations can alternatively be termed strategic alliances, that is, "voluntary arrangements between firms involving exchange, sharing, or co-development of products, technologies, or services" (Gulati, 1998, p. 293). Networks of strategic alliances play a significant role in providing opportunities for improving firm competitive advantage and hence generating additional rents. Such opportunities can include reaching multiple knowledge pools, developing firm absorptive capacity, and lowering corporate strategic risk. At the same time, leveraging network resources increases coordination costs and demands on managerial attention (Rothaermel, 2001). Firms continuously shape the composition of their resource portfolios (Helfat & Eisenhardt, 2004). Because foreign operations are particularly resource-consuming (Hitt, Hoskisson, & Kim, 1997) and bring additional risks (Kwok & Reeb, 2000; Reeb, Kwok, & Baek, 1998), firms may specifically choose to reduce them to allow increased domestic collaboration.

Our empirical setting is the US electronic and electrical equipment industry. The industry is characterized by liberal FDI policies across all economic regions (Sun & Lee, 2013), short product life cycles, dynamic competitive environment and increasing capital expenditure (West, 2002), high technological dynamism, and intensive alliance formation (Rosenkopf & Schilling, 2007). Given the importance of technological know-how, firms in the electronic and electrical equipment industry are likely to be concerned with know-how regeneration and continuously attempt to upgrade their knowledge bases by tapping into internal as well as external sources (Narasimhan, Rajiv, & Dutta, 2006). In all, the industry provides a highly suitable context to test our hypothesis.

Broadly, our study contributes to the corporate strategy literature on intertemporal economies of scope that firms achieve by redeploying resources and capabilities between business and geographic segments over time (Helfat & Eisenhardt, 2004). Specifically, we contribute to the perspective that firms' investment and divestment decisions are driven by efficiency motives (e.g., Berry, 2010; Bertrand & Capron, 2015; Blonigen, 2001). Because domestic and foreign investments of the firm compete for the same resources at its disposal, a firm's domestic interfirm collaboration activity can lead to relocation of its assets across geographic markets. To our best knowledge, this is the first study that investigates the impact of domestic interfirm collaboration on firms' foreign divestment decisions. As noted by Brauer (2006, p. 779): "Although the benefits of entering a market via M&A or alliances have been thoroughly researched, the choice and relationship between divestitures and alliances and networks have remained widely unexplored." With this study we aim to improve the understanding of how divestment decisions fit into a broader perspective on firms' strategies, especially as they involve multiple tradeoffs that top management teams face in dynamic competitive environments.

THEORY AND HYPOTHESES

Foreign Divestment as a Means to Opportunities

FDI is a long-term commitment to foreign operations. Dunning's (1980) eclectic framework states that firms are likely to engage in FDI when they possess ownership advantages, which they can most profitably exploit outside their national boundaries when internalized within the firm. Nevertheless, FDIs do not last forever, and the antecedents of foreign divestment are not simply the reverse of foreign investment. While all these conditions should be simultaneously satisfied for FDI to occur (Dunning, 1980), the violation of only one of them is sufficient for foreign divestment to take place (Boddewyn, 1983). As noted by Boddewyn (1983, p. 348): "the interrelatedness among the three factors [FDI pre-conditions] remains present in both the investment and divestment cases: without ownership advantages, investment does not happen in the first place, and divestment must ensue if an investment has already taken place and the advantage has disappeared. However, divestment can still take place when ownership advantages remain in existence, while investment cannot happen without them. In that sense, divestment theory can say "or" rather than "and" in connecting the three conditions of Dunning's theory." Being an essential condition for FDI, sufficient ownership advantages often develop as a result of engaging into a variety of value adding activities domestically, but they may not assure better chances of FDI survival. As emphasized in the conceptual framework developed by Benito (1997b), the propensity to divest on-going operations is a function of incentives to exit a well as barriers to exit. The former are a function of current to expected operations performance, while the latter depend upon the existence of tangible and intangible assets whose current value is contrasted with their best alternative use. Firms are prone to divest operations once incentives to exit exceed barriers to exit (Benito, 1997b).

In addition to the set of pure economic conditions behind foreign divestment decisions (Belderbos & Zou, 2006, 2009; Berry, 2013; Fisch & Zschoche, 2012), firms can cease their operations as a result of poor pre-investment analysis, organizational changes, adverse environmental conditions and external pressures, inability to gain a certain market share or achieve a desirable level of return on investment, the absence of strategic fit with other businesses, or due to cognitive limits to coordinate and integrate numerous operations; see Brauer (2006) for the extensive literature review on the determinants of divestitures. The drivers of foreign divestment are then those attributable to the non-achievement of certain objectives as well as those based on the detection of better alternatives to achieve the objectives. Finding alternative means to (re-)investing resources elsewhere may ease the position of a decision maker who has to tackle the impending (and sometimes unpleasant) withdrawal from an operation.

Broadly speaking, firms obtain efficiencies in the form of so-called inter-temporal economies of scope by redeploying capabilities and resources between their businesses over time, that is, as they exit some markets while entering others, particularly those where technologies and demand are in flux (Helfat & Eisenhardt, 2004). "Inter-temporal economies of scope point to the advantages of timely market exit. In redeploying resources, firms may benefit when they exit markets with declining opportunities in order to take advantage of new opportunities in other markets" (Helfat & Eisenhardt, 2004, p. 1230). Inability to conduct in-depth and timely portfolio reviews may result in failure to achieve intended outcomes. Yet, Ernst & Young's 2016 Global Corporate Divestment Study concludes that more than half of the studied companies hold on to assets too long when they should instead have divested them.

Alliances, Networks, and Strategic Tradeoffs

Strategic alliances provide access to complementary assets that are located outside the boundaries of a firm (Rothaermel, 2001). Combined with internal resources and capabilities, external knowledge and resources stemming from strategic alliances influence innovation performance (Ahuja, 2000; Sytch & Tatarynowicz, 2014) and allow firms to appropriate additional rents on top of the rents (Ricardian as well as quasi-rents) solely generated within the firm (Lavie, 2006). Strategic alliances are a widespread mode of operation, especially in technologically dynamic industries where overcoming technological change and volatility and demand uncertainty alone can be challenging (Uzzi, 1996). Many firms have several alliances or have alliances with multiple partners, so beyond having individual alliances, firms are often embedded in a network of alliances, which then shape firms' behavior and the outcomes of their chosen strategies (Gulati, 1998). By initiating alliances, firms may also improve their status and perceived attractiveness in alliance networks (Ahuja, Polidoro, & Mitchell, 2009).

Despite the recognized benefits, strategic alliances and networks may also lock firms into situations that limit strategic choices. An evident lock-in effect arises from resource constraints (Gulati, Nohria, & Zaheer, 2000). Firms have limited resources (both managerial and financial) to maintain a set of ongoing activities, and hence face dilemmas regarding effective allocation of their resources. Given bounded rationality, new collaborations could oversupply a firm with information thereby straining its information processing capacity and increasing the costs of coordinating across activities (Simsek, 2009). As pointed out by several studies, there may be diminishing returns to interfirm collaboration (Deeds & Hill, 1996; Lahiri & Narayanan, 2013; Rothaermel, 2001). To maximize managerial effectiveness in exploiting increased access to external resources and minimize coordination costs, firms have to narrow down the portfolio of existing options (Lee & Madhavan, 2010).

Another lock-in effect is related to the possibility to extract additional rents in a given period of time. While firms form strategic alliances to pursue new business opportunities, alliances often suffer from a short-term orientation (Das & Teng, 2000). Strategic alliances are known to be risky and their duration is often uncertain (Kogut, 1991). In addition, parties may prefer to exploit the alliance judiciously, before escalating commitment (Das & Teng, 2000). As a result, firms can become locked into their current choices while, and at the same time, becoming less committed to certain choices made previously.

Lock-in effects can also involve the location dimension. If firms start appropriating network rents in a specific location, they may subsequently reconfigure their value chain activities and resources in its favor. The literature emphasizes the role of a domestic network context. Domestic alliances and interfirm networks are characterized by relatively low levels of uncertainty, high confidence of cooperation, high trust, and ease of knowledge flows (Bell & Zaheer, 2007). Managers operating in the same geographic area will better understand and interpret the transferred knowledge (Paniccia, 1998). Thus, domestic collaboration networks provide firms with the means and mechanisms by which they can establish credibility and legitimacy (Gould, 2002), enhance efficiency, and provide better access to information, knowledge, and other resources (Zaheer & Bell, 2005). As noted by Chen, Chen, and Ku (2004): "New relationships to be sought in the foreign network are those that reinforce the flexibility of the domestic network" (p. 323). The organizational preference to form ties with geographically proximate partners is inherent in firms from locations with stable (Guillén, 2002; Vasudeva, Zaheer, & Hernandez, 2013) as well as dynamic institutional environments (Kiss & Danis, 2010). Studies suggest firms that are highly integrated with their domestic systems of innovation may become biased toward domestic activities (Narula, 2002; Narula & Santangelo, 2012). As noted by Narula (2002, p. 795): "Lock-in can be efficient when technologies and institutions maintain the competitiveness of firms." Hence, performance expectations related to current choices can trigger firms to reconsider their past choices.

The Effect of Domestic Alliance Formation on Foreign Subsidiary Divestment

Depending on whether or not the scope of alliance activities is limited to firms' home country, initiating an alliance may have distinct implications for foreign divestment decisions. Forming an alliance internationally may reinforce a firm's commitment to its international expansion strategy (Johanson & Vahlne, 2009) thus motivating it to retain its foreign operations. While alliances with an international focus allow firms to enter new markets, share costs and supplement capabilities (Hitt, Dacin, Levitas, Arregle, & Borza, 2000), they also bring challenges of not sharing mental models, and issues related to cultural differences (Bell & Zaheer, 2007), which may ultimately destroy firm value (Sirmon & Lane, 2004). New domestic interfirm collaborations also provide opportunities to bundle resources, develop capabilities, and leverage them to achieve a competitive advantage, but are typically easier to handle than international ones. Such collaborations may also serve a different purpose. Whereas international alliances are often given defined tasks such as marketing, domestic partnerships are frequently used for the riskier open-ended, non-routine projects like R&D and technology development activities (Duysters & Hagedoorn, 1996). Given the choice, firms are more likely to prefer a domestic rather than a foreign setting to transfer highly tacit knowledge and competencies (Martin & Salomon, 2003).

Since new domestic alliances are often formed to acquire, create, or augment higher order capabilities, their formation may trigger resource recombination and re-concentration of production capacities (Kinkel & Maloca, 2009). Moreover, to get the most benefits from new domestic alliances, resources typically have to be redeployed within a short time period: "If resource transfer occurs slowly, the time period during which the firm can obtain intertemporal economies of scope is shortened" (Helfat & Eisenhardt, 2004, p. 1223). Time pressure may therefore push firms to consider making corporate divestitures as short-term corrections of prior underestimates in investment decisions (Kinkel & Maloca, 2009). As noted by Brauer (2006, p. 776): "Most companies pursue divestiture programs involving the divestiture of multiple units within a relatively short period of time."

New domestic alliances may also trigger additional bounded rationality and bounded reliability challenges, which amplify with the presence of foreign operations (Kano & Verbeke, 2015; Verbeke & Greidanus, 2009). Developing and maintaining foreign operations is resource-consuming (Hitt et al., 1997), brings additional risks (Kwok & Reeb, 2000; Reeb et al., 1998), and the extent of regular and efficient knowledge flows between multinational firms and their foreign subsidiaries tends to shrink as resources become more scarce (Narula, 2014). Many firms experience decreasing returns to geographic spread. Hence, they may choose to reduce their bandwidth with foreign subsidiaries and perhaps even divest them to more fully obtain the potential benefits from new strategic alliances at home.

Based on the abovementioned arguments, we hypothesize the following relationship between a firm's propensity to divest it foreign subsidiaries and forming new domestic alliances:

Hypothesis 1. *Ceteris paribus*, firms are more likely to divest foreign operations if they have recently formed new domestic strategic alliances.

RESEARCH METHODOLOGY

Research Context

The research setting for this study is the US electronic and electrical equipment industry, which covers three three-digit SIC codes: 357 (computer and office equipment), 366 (communications equipment), and 367 (electronic components and accessories). We select the electronic and electrical equipment industry for a number of reasons. First, this allows us to control for the relative homogeneity in FDI and divestment motives. Second, FDI liberalization in these industries and stable FDI flows significantly reduce noise due to countries' policy-specific barriers to investment and divestment (Sun & Lee, 2013). Third, prior research shows that the industry is characterized by intensive alliance formation, which enhances the variance, reliability, and meaningfulness of alliance network variables and their implication for firm behavior (Gulati, Sytch, & Tatarynowicz, 2012; Rosenkopf & Schilling, 2007; Sytch & Tatarynowicz, 2014). Finally, the industry is characterized by significant technological dynamism (Rosenkopf & Schilling, 2007). Technological dynamism increases the proportion of the firms in the industry that engages in alliances (Rosenkopf & Schilling, 2007), which increases the likelihood that firm-specific advantages originate from alliance network embeddedness. Given the importance of technological know-how, dynamic competitive environment, short product life cycle, and increasing capital expenditure (West, 2002), firms in the electronic and electrical equipment industry are likely to be concerned with know-how regeneration, would try to upgrade their knowledge bases either with the use of internal or external sources (Narasimhan et al., 2006), and redistribute resources accordingly.

Data and Measures

To test the hypotheses, we collected data for the period of 2000–2008 on the population of the electronic and electrical equipment US firms that were publicly traded in US stock exchanges and had a consistent set of financial firm-level data during this period. To be included, firms must have had consistently reported their subsidiaries in 10-K fillings available in the EDGAR database and had at least one foreign subsidiary (excluding subsidiaries in tax heavens)[1] throughout the whole period. By a subsidiary we refer to an entity with at least 10% of the equity by a focal firm. Because we collected the data on companies' foreign subsidiaries from the EDGAR database, our definition of a subsidiary coincides with the definition of a "significant subsidiary" provided by the US Securities and Exchange Commission as of 2008. Following the prior literature (e.g., McGahan & Porter, 1997), we focus on firms with sales and/or assets of more than $10 million to assure that firms have sufficient resources for sustainable activities. As a result, our final sample included 159 firms observed over 9 consistent years.

Our main *dependent variable* is a dummy variable indicating whether a firm divested one or more its foreign subsidiaries in a given year. In additional analyses, we also use a count variable, that is, the number of divested foreign subsidiaries in a given year. Our data cover foreign divestitures over the period 2001–2008, a period considered as stable regarding global inflows and outflows of FDI and firm alliance activity. That allows us to reduce the undesirable noise that could otherwise be endemic to our data if shifting the year interval backward (the information technology bubble) or forward (the global financial crisis).

Our *independent variable* is a dummy variable indicating whether the firm engaged into a new strategic alliance domestically, that is, an alliance with the scope of activities being bounded to the United States. We define a strategic alliance as a "voluntary arrangement between firms involving exchange, sharing, or co-development of products, technologies, or services" (Gulati, 1998, p. 293). An example of a domestic strategic alliance is the alliance between Sun Microsystems and Intel formed to provide computer integrated systems services in the United States: "The scope of the agreement spans Solaris, Java and NetBeans software and Intel Xeon microprocessors, as well as other Intel and Sun enterprise-class technologies. The alliance also includes joint engineering, design and marketing efforts" (Intel News Release).[2] For the selected firms, we obtained data on their alliance activities from the SDC Platinum database. Generally considered as reliable, SDC Platinum provides a comprehensive database for analyzing investment banking and deal trends, identifying comparable deals, monitoring deal activity, and generating industry-leading league tables and market share analysis.

We introduce a number of firm-level *control variables*. They include R&D intensity (the ratio of R&D expenditures to total sales), marketing intensity (the ratio of selling, general, administrative expenses to total sales), export intensity (the ratio of foreign sales to total sales), age (number of years since incorporation), size (total sales, $bn), and performance (the ratio of earnings before interest and taxes to total assets). We used the Compustat database to construct these variables. We also account for the total number of alliances (adjusted by total assets), the proportion of non-domestic alliances in a firm's overall alliance portfolio, and new non-domestic alliances (a dummy indicating whether the firm engaged into a new strategic alliance with activities not bounded to the USA). An example of a non-domestic alliance is the agreement between SAP AG and Cisco Systems formed to "to develop business and network application solutions and services globally. The partners were expected to deliver a high levels of visibility, control and responsiveness across the extended enterprise of information technology" (SAP News Center).[3] We extracted these controls from the SDC Platinum database. Lastly, we control for the total number of foreign subsidiaries (adjusted by total assets), which we obtained from firms' 10-K fillings.

We lagged all of our independent and control variables one year with respect to the dependent variable to facilitate the direction of causality.

RESULTS

Table 1 provides descriptive statistics and the correlation matrix. We observe a positive and significant correlation ($r = 0.09$, $p < 0.01$) between firms' propensity to divest foreign operations and new domestic alliance formation, which points to preliminary support for our hypothesis. To examine the effect of one dichotomous variable on another dichotomous variable more rigorously, we rely on matching techniques. Our primary analysis utilizes the *nearest neighbor matching* (NNM) estimator for average treatment effects (ATE; *teffects nnmatch*, Stata 14). This technique implies matching on covariates thus making more explicitly the comparison of treated (i.e., engaged in new domestic alliances) and control firms (i.e., not engaged in new domestic alliances) on their propensity to divest foreign operations. Similarity between firms is based on a weighted function of the covariates for each observation (Abadie & Imbens, 2006). NNM is nonparametric, which means that no explicit functional form for the model is needed (Abadie & Imbens, 2006). In general, matching is preferred when the correct specification for the regression is unknown. In case of foreign divestments, they can be influenced by a myriad of factors (Brauer, 2006).

In additional analyses and robustness checks we also use other matching techniques; regression adjustment (RA), propensity score matching (PSM), and probit regression with cluster-robust standard errors. RA estimators use the contrasts of the averages of the treatment-specific predicted outcomes to estimate treatment effects (Freedman, 2008). The estimators use a two-step approach to estimating treatment effects. First, they fit separate regression models of the outcome on a set of covariates for each treatment level, and then compute the averages of the predicted outcomes for each subject and treatment level. The averages reflect the potential-outcome means. The contrasts of these averages provide estimates of ATE. RA estimators are preferred when the determinants of outcomes are known. PSM is used to estimate the probability of being treated – the propensity score – given the observed characteristics (Li, 2013). Based on propensity scores, firms are matched to the specified number of potential matching partners; that is, untreated firms with similar or even identical propensity scores. PSM is the preferred estimator when we know what determined the treatment status. Given a correct model specification, all matching techniques should produce similar results (StataCorp, 2015). Finally, we complement our matching analyses with results from estimating a probit regression model. We use a probit model because our dependent variable is dichotomous (Wooldridge, 2002). Compared to matching, the regression-based estimators are more

Table 1. Descriptive Statistics and Correlations.

	Mean	SD	1	2	3	4	5	6	7	8	9	10	11
1. New divestment (dummy)$_t$	0.20	0.40											
2. New domestic alliance (dummy)$_{t-1}$	0.14	0.34	0.09**										
3. R&D intensity$_{t-1}$	0.16	0.16	0.04	−0.01									
4. Marketing intensity$_{t-1}$	0.38	0.26	−0.02	−0.03	0.86***								
5. Export intensity$_{t-1}$	0.50	0.25	0.04	0.05†	0.10***	−0.01							
6. Age$_{t-1}$	30.00	26.80	0.07*	0.07*	−0.31***	−0.32***	−0.07*						
7. Size$_{t-1}$	1.91	7.41	0.12***	0.41***	−0.08**	−0.11***	0.10***	0.16***					
8. Performance$_{t-1}$	0.01	0.15	−0.04	0.07*	−0.40***	−0.56***	0.10***	0.18***	0.12***				
9. Number of alliances (asset-adjusted)$_{t-1}$	0.00	0.01	−0.07*	0.06*	0.03	0.14***	−0.07*	−0.09**	−0.05†	−0.22***			
10. % non-domestic alliances$_{t-1}$	0.22	0.35	0.09**	0.12***	−0.03	−0.02	0.11***	0.08**	0.16***	0.05†	0.21***		
11. New non-domestic alliance (dummy)$_{t-1}$	0.14	0.34	0.07*	0.36***	−0.01	−0.03	0.11***	0.06*	0.39***	0.07*	0.07*	0.48***	
12. Number of foreign subsidiaries (asset-adjusted)$_{t-1}$	0.04	0.06	−0.08**	−0.12***	−0.11***	0.09**	−0.01	0.00	−0.13***	−0.15***	0.25***	−0.06*	−0.12***

Notes: $N = 1{,}272$.
† $p < 0.10$, * $p < 0.05$, ** $p < 0.01$, *** $p < 0.001$.

efficient when we know the correct functional form, which is, however, rarely the case.

We use all of our control variables to match observations in our treatment and control groups. To correct for imperfect matching on multiple covariates, we use the *bias-corrected* NNM estimator developed by Abadie and Imbens (2011). The method is essentially based on a combination of matching and regression techniques, where the difference within the matches is regression-adjusted for the difference in covariate values. In addition, we specify *exact matching* on year to account for the panel structure of the data. In other words, we estimate the ATE by comparing firms with similar characteristics from treatment and control groups in the same year. Lastly, our primary analysis sets the number of *matching partners* to one. It should be noted that choosing a low number of matches has the possible disadvantage of including too little information, and therefore to provide conservative estimates of treatment effects (Abadie, Drukker, Herr, & Imbens, 2004). Conversely, using a higher number of matching partners leads to incorporating observations that may not be sufficiently similar. Abadie et al. (2004) recommend using up to four matching partners. We estimate and discuss results for two to four matching partners in the "Robustness checks" section.

Table 2 contains the results of different estimation techniques, namely NNM, PSM, RA, and probit regression. We also supplement our analysis with the effects of having a non-domestic alliance on firm's propensity to divest its foreign operations to see whether the effects of domestic versus foreign alliance networks differ. As shown in Table 2, the effect of forming new domestic interfirm alliances on foreign divestment is consistently positive and significant in all models. However, the magnitude of the effects varies across models. The estimated ATE from NNM implies that firms forming a new domestic alliance are 17% more likely to divest foreign subsidiaries in the subsequent year than firms without new domestic collaborations. The effects produced by PSM and RA are similar at 21.6%. The marginal effects of probit regression are lower compared to any of the matching techniques, resulting in a 6.4% increase (significant at the 10% level) in firms' probability to divest foreign operations given a new domestic alliance. Overall, we find support for our hypothesis that firms are more likely to divest foreign operations as they increase interfirm collaboration in their home country.

Contrary to the effects of a new domestic alliance on foreign divestment, we do not find consistent results for the effect of engaging in a new international alliance. Only PSM yields negative and significant results; firms that have formed a new international alliance are 14.4% less likely to divest their foreign subsidiaries. This indicates that firms may support their international

Table 2. Results of Different Estimation Techniques.

	NNM[c]	PSM[d]	RA[d]	Probit (Marginal Effects)[d]
	Foreign divestment (dummy)$_t$			
New domestic alliance (dummy)$_{t-1}$	0.170**	0.216***	0.216***	0.064†
	(0.064)	(0.063)	(0.048)	(0.039)
New international alliance[a] (dummy)$_{t-1}$	0.011	−0.144***	0.071	−0.011
	(0.070)	(0.021)	(0.099)	(0.045)
Number of observations[b]	1,272	1,257	1,272	1,272

Notes: Robust standard errors are included in parentheses.

[a] Model includes new domestic alliance dummy as a control variable (except for probit regression).

[b] Number of observations for model with new domestic alliance dummy as an independent variable.

[c] Exact matching by year.

[d] Year fixed effects.

† $p < 0.10$, *$p < 0.05$, **$p < 0.01$, ***$p < 0.001$

expansion strategies by entering into international alliances, and thereby avoid reducing foreign operations. However, neither the other matching techniques (NNM and RA) nor the probit regression provide significant estimates for the effect of a new international alliance. We therefore conclude that domestic and international alliance networks have distinctly different effects on firms' propensity to divest foreign operation and, more broadly, on their overall resource deployment strategies.

Robustness Checks

We performed several robustness checks. First, we checked whether results are sensitive to the number of matching partners. From Table 3, we observe that the estimates do not change dramatically by including more matching partners. Using NNM to estimate the effect of new domestic collaborations on foreign divestment, the analysis shows that increasing the number of matching partners amplifies effect sizes and decreases standard errors. For PSM, the effect size drops with the inclusion of more matching partners, and so do standard errors. For the effect of new international collaborations, the results are similar to those produced by matching to only one partner.

Table 3. NNM and PSM Estimations with Two and Four Matching Partners.

	NNM[c]		PSM[d]	
	2 Neighbors	4 Neighbors	2 Neighbors	4 Neighbors
	Foreign divestment (dummy)$_t$			
New domestic alliance	0.189**	0.201***	0.173**	0.167**
(dummy)$_{t-1}$	(0.061)	(0.058)	(0.057)	(0.057)
New international alliance[a]	−0.025	0.059	−0.137***	−0.118***
(dummy)$_{t-1}$	(0.060)	(0.055)	(0.023)	(0.021)
Number of observations[b]	1,272	1,272	1,257	1,257

Notes: Robust standard errors are included in parentheses.
[a] Model includes new domestic alliance dummy as a control variable (except for probit regression).
[b] Number of observations for model with new domestic alliance dummy as an independent variable.
[c] Exact matching by year.
[d] Year fixed effects.
$^{\dagger}p < 0.10$, $^{*}p < 0.05$, $^{**}p < 0.01$, $^{***}p < 0.001$

Additionally, we changed the operationalization of our dependent variable from a dummy to a count variable, that is, the number of divested foreign subsidiaries. To minimize outlier bias due to exceptional corporate restructurings, we excluded observations with foreign divestment being equal to four standard deviations above the mean. The results are reported in Table 4. Because the dependent variable is a count, estimation was done with a negative binomial model instead of probit. Except for PSM, having a new domestic alliance is found to have a strong positive effect on foreign divestment. Based on NNM and RA estimates, we can conclude that firms are more likely to divest foreign subsidiaries if they had formed a new domestic collaboration one year earlier. The corresponding effects for a new international alliance are negative and significant in PSM, while NNM, RA, and negative binomial regression all produced statistically insignificant results.

DISCUSSION AND CONCLUSIONS

The general premise of this chapter is that home country factors influence corporate strategic decisions, including those dealing with the international footprint of the firm. Specifically, we study whether forming new domestic

Table 4. Results of Different Estimation Techniques for Count of Foreign Divestment.

	NNM[c]	PSM[d]	RA[d,e]	Negative Binomial (Marginal Effects)[b]
	Foreign divestment (count)$_t$			
New domestic alliance	0.818*	0.791	1.000*	0.436**
(dummy)$_{t-1}$	(0.352)	(0.965)	(0.439)	(0.160)
New international alliance[a]	0.142	−0.283***	0.275	0.120
(dummy)$_{t-1}$	(0.184)	(0.085)	(0.382)	(0.163)
Number of observations[b]	1,262	1,246	1,262	1,262

Notes: Robust standard errors are included in parentheses.
[a] Model includes new domestic alliance dummy as a control variable (except for probit regression).
[b] Number of observations for model with new domestic alliance dummy as an independent variable.
[c] Exact matching by year.
[d] Year fixed effects.
[e] Linear model for the dependent variable.
$^{\dagger}p < 0.10$, $^{*}p < 0.05$, $^{**}p < 0.01$, $^{***}p < 0.001$.

strategic alliances has an effect on the divestment of foreign subsidiaries. Our arguments build on the idea that such decisions have to be analyzed within the wider context of a firm's overall strategy, taking into account and consolidating the multiple environments in which a firm operates (e.g., Berry, 2010; Bertrand & Capron, 2015; Blonigen, 2001). Because the domestic and foreign investments of a firm compete for the same resources at its disposal, inter-firm collaboration activity in its home country could lead to relocation of the firm's assets across geographic markets. Reducing the geographic spread while increasing access to network resources domestically could be beneficial for firms and help their top-management teams in facing dynamic competitive environments.

Our study supports the notion that better opportunities from improved access to external resources in their home country have an impact on firms' divestment decisions regarding their foreign operations. Although the geographic distribution of activities may provide benefits for a firm in the form of access to markets and resources, and potentially valuable external knowledge, cross-border activities increase firm risk (Kwok & Reeb, 2000; Reeb et al., 1998) and are resource-consuming (Hitt et al., 1997). In particular, the costs of accessing and utilizing knowledge across broadly distributed knowledge sources often times outweigh such benefits (Feinberg & Gupta, 2004; Lahiri,

2010; Narula, 2002, 2014), especially when firms initiate new activities, such as strategic alliances.

Our findings have implications for the internationalization process model. Johanson and Vahlne (2009) conceptualize firms' propensity to go abroad as a function of their relationships and networks, either domestic or foreign: To the extent that relationships offer potential for learning, building trust and commitment, they enhance firms' capabilities and help them to overcome resource deficiencies, thus decreasing the liability of foreignness and outsidership. The results from this study qualify that line of reasoning by showing that interfirm partnerships do not always positively contribute to international growth and that the location of partnerships matters.

Our results also suggest that firms' subsidiaries and strategic alliances should be jointly considered as part of a firm's overall portfolio of options. The study shows that firms can divest foreign subsidiaries as a result of engaging in new domestic collaborations. Despite a number of studies pointing to operation mode dynamics (e.g., Benito, Pedersen, & Petersen, 2005; Benito, Petersen, & Welch, 2009; Puck, Holtbrugge, & Mohr, 2009), previous research has typically looked at withdrawal from a given mode of operation as a result of the options available within the specific mode. For example, Belderbos and Zou (2009) and Fisch and Zschoche (2012) find that the configuration of firm's portfolio of manufacturing subsidiaries affects the probability of subsidiary divestment, and Berry (2010) examines how investment in lower-cost production subsidiaries triggers divestment of higher-cost production subsidiaries. Likewise, Vassolo, Anand, and Folta (2004) demonstrate that alliances are more likely to be divested if their technological performance characteristics overlap with the portfolio of other alliances. Conversely, our study suggests that divestment decisions can be induced by interrelations between several modes of operation.

While our key findings seem to be robust across different measures and estimation methods, the study has some limitations, which offer opportunities for future research. First, because we collect our data from subsidiaries from companies' 10-K forms (Annual Reports), the data do not allow us to distinguish between different types of divestitures. These limitations also prevent us from introducing subsidiary-level variables and analyzing data in alternative ways, such as conducting survival analysis (Berry, 2013; Norbäck, Tekin-Koru, & Waldkirch, 2015). Future research may attempt to address these limitations, especially on how to capture the motivations for foreign divestitures. Second, we consider a sample of US multinational firms within the electronic and electrical equipment industry. Further research could investigate whether the hypothesized relationships also hold for other contexts, such as European or Asian multinationals and for different industry contexts. The electronic and electrical equipment industry is characterized by dynamic competitive environments where a competitive advantage gained by a firm at some point in time may quickly disappear. Together with other high-tech industries, such as biotechnology and software, these industries have high proportions of firms engaging in interfirm collaborations and strong technological underpinnings of interfirm ties (Gulati et al., 2012; Rosenkopf & Schilling, 2007). While the choice of the context fits into our theoretical arguments, locational tradeoffs and divestment rationales within other contexts, especially less technologically intense industries, should also be analyzed. Third, we focus on divestitures of foreign assets. Other market exit strategies, such as exiting from a foreign market (but without implying divestment) could also be studied. Finally, further research should seek to shed more light on the contingencies that influence the relationship between interfirm networks and divestment of foreign operations. In particular, future research could examine the influence of relational network attributes on survival of foreign operations.

NOTES

1. We excluded divestments from tax heavens defined with respect to the OECD list from our analysis (OECD, 2006).
2. Available at http://www.intel.com/pressroom/archive/releases/2007/20070122corp.htm
3. Available at http://global.sap.com/news-reader/index.epx?pressid=7588

REFERENCES

Abadie, A., & Imbens, G. W. (2006). Large sample properties of matching estimators for average treatment effects. *Econometrica*, *74*(1), 235–267.

Abadie, A., & Imbens, G. W. (2011). Bias-corrected matching estimators for average treatment effects. *Journal of Business & Economic Statistics*, *29*(1), 1–11.

Abadie, A., Drukker, D., Herr, J. L., & Imbens, G. W. (2004). Implementing matching estimators for average treatment effects in Stata. *Stata Journal*, *4*(3), 290–311.

Ahuja, G. (2000). Collaboration networks, structural holes, and innovation: A longitudinal study. *Administrative Science Quarterly*, *45*(3), 425–455.

Ahuja, G., Polidoro, F., & Mitchell, W. (2009). Structural homophily or social asymmetry? The formation of alliances by poorly embedded firms. *Strategic Management Journal*, *30*(9), 941–958.

Belderbos, R., & Zou, J. L. (2006). Foreign investment, divestment and relocation by Japanese electronics firms in East Asia. *Asian Economic Journal*, *20*(1), 1–27.

Belderbos, R., & Zou, J. L. (2009). Real options and foreign affiliate divestments: A portfolio perspective. *Journal of International Business Studies*, *40*(4), 600–620.

Bell, G. G., & Zaheer, A. (2007). Geography, networks, and knowledge flow. *Organization Science*, *18*(6), 955–972.

Benito, G. R. G. (1997a). Divestment of foreign production operations. *Applied Economics*, *29*(10), 1365–1377.

Benito, G. R. G. (1997b). Why are foreign subsidiaries divested? A conceptual framework. In I. Björkman & M. Forsgren (Eds.), *The nature of the international firm: Nordic contributions to international business research* (pp. 309–344). Copenhagen: Copenhagen Business School Press.

Benito, G. R. G., & Welch, L. S (1997). De-internationalization. *Management International Review*, *37*(2), 7–25.

Benito, G. R. G., Lunnan, R., & Tomassen, S. (2011). Distant encounters of the third kind: Multinational companies locating divisional headquarters abroad. *Journal of Management Studies*, *48*(2), 373–394.

Benito, G. R. G., Pedersen, T., & Petersen, B. (2005). Export channel dynamics: An empirical investigation. *Managerial and Decision Economics*, *26*(3), 159–173.

Benito, G. R. G., Petersen, B., & Welch, L. S. (2009). Towards more realistic conceptualisations of foreign operation modes. *Journal of International Business Studies*, *40*(9), 1455–1470.

Berry, H. (2010). Why do firms divest? *Organization Science*, *21*(2), 380–396.

Berry, H. (2013). When do firms divest foreign operations? *Organization Science*, *24*(1), 246–261.

Bertrand, O., & Capron, L. (2015). Productivity enhancement at home via cross-border acquisitions: The roles of learning and contemporaneous domestic investments. *Strategic Management Journal*, *36*(5), 640–658.

Blake, D. J., & Moschieri, C. (2017). Policy risk, strategic decisions and contagion effects: Firm-specific considerations. *Strategic Management Journal*, *38*(3), 732–750.

Blonigen, B. A. (2001). In search of substitution between foreign production and exports. *Journal of International Economics*. *53*(1), 81–104.

Boddewyn, J. J. (1983). Foreign direct divestment theory: Is it the reverse of FDI theory? *Review of World Economics*, *119*(2), 345–355.

Brauer, M. (2006). What have we acquired and what should we acquire in divestiture research? A review and research agenda. *Journal of Management*, *32*(6), 751–785.

Chang, S. J., & Singh, H. (1999). The impact of modes of entry and resource fit on modes of exit by multibusiness firms. *Strategic Management Journal*, *20*(11), 1019–1035.

Chen, T. J., Chen, H. M., & Ku, Y. H. (2004). Foreign direct investment and local linkages. *Journal of International Business Studies*, *35*(4), 320–333.

Das, T. K., & Teng, B. S. (2000). Instabilities of strategic alliances: An internal tensions perspective. *Organization Science*, *11*(1), 77–101.

Deeds, D. L., & Hill, C. W. L. (1996). Strategic alliances and the rate of new product development: An empirical study of entrepreneurial biotechnology firms. *Journal of Business Venturing*, *11*(1), 41–55.

Dhanaraj, C., & Beamish, P. W. (2004). Effect of equity ownership on the survival of international joint ventures. *Strategic Management Journal*, *25*(3), 295–305.

Duhaime, I. M., & Grant, J. H. (1984). Factors influencing divestment decision-making: Evidence from a field study. *Strategic Management Journal*, *5*(4), 301–318.

Dunning, J. H. (1980). Towards an eclectic theory of international production: Some empirical tests. *Journal of International Business Studies*, *11*(1), 9–31.

Duysters, G., & Hagedoorn, J. (1996). Internationalization of corporate technology through strategic partnering: An empirical investigation. *Research Policy*, *25*(1), 1–12.

Engel, D., Procher, V., & Schmidt, C. M. (2013). Does firm heterogeneity affect foreign market entry and exit symmetrically? Empirical evidence for French firms. *Journal of Economic Behavior & Organization*, *85*, 35–47.

Feinberg, S. E., & Gupta, A. K. (2004). Knowledge spillovers and the assignment of R&D responsibilities to foreign subsidiaries. *Strategic Management Journal*, *25*(8–9), 823–845.

Fisch, J. H., & Zschoche, M. (2012). The effect of operational flexibility on decisions to withdraw from foreign production locations. *International Business Review*, *21*(5), 806–816.

Fratocchi, L., Di Mauro, C., Barbieri, P., Nassimbeni, G., & Zanoni, A. (2014). When manufacturing moves back: Concepts and questions. *Journal of Purchasing and Supply Management*, *20*(1), 54–59.

Freedman, D. A. (2008). On regression adjustments to experimental data. *Advances in Applied Mathematics*, *40*(2), 180–193.

Gould, R. V. (2002). The origins of status hierarchies: A formal theory and empirical test. *American Journal of Sociology*, *107*(5), 1143–1178.

Guillén, M. F. (2002). Structural inertia, imitation, and foreign expansion: South Korean firms and business groups in China, 1987–95. *Academy of Management Journal*, *45*(3), 509–525.

Gulati, R. (1998). Alliances and networks. *Strategic Management Journal*, *19*(4), 293–317.

Gulati, R., Nohria, N., & Zaheer, A. (2000). Strategic networks. *Strategic Management Journal*, *21*(3), 203–215.

Gulati, R., Sytch, M., & Tatarynowicz, A. (2012). The rise and fall of small worlds: Exploring the dynamics of social structure. *Organization Science*, *23*(2), 449–471.

Helfat, C. E., & Eisenhardt, K.M. (2004). Inter-temporal economies of scope, organizational modularity, and the dynamics of diversification. *Strategic Management Journal*, *25*(13), 1217–1232.

Hitt, M. A., Hoskisson, R. E., & Kim, H. (1997). International diversification: Effects on innovation and firm performance in product-diversified firms. *Academy of Management Journal*, *40*(4), 767–798.

Hitt, M. A., Dacin, M. T., Levitas, E., Arregle, J. L., & Borza, A. (2000). Partner selection in emerging and developed market contexts: Resource-based and organizational learning perspectives. *Academy of Management Journal*, *43*(3), 449–467.

Johanson, J., & Vahlne, J. E. (2009). The Uppsala internationalization process model revisited: From liability of foreignness to liability of outsidership. *Journal of International Business Studies*, *40*(9), 1411–1431.

Kano, L., & Verbeke, A. (2015). The three faces of bounded reliability: Alfred Chandler and the micro-foundations of management strategy. *California Management Review*, *58*(1), 97–122.

Kinkel, S., & Maloca, S. (2009). Drivers and antecedents of manufacturing offshoring and backshoring – A German perspective. *Journal of Purchasing and Supply Management*, *15*(3), 154–165.

Kiss, A. N., & Danis, W. M. (2010). Social networks and speed of new venture internationalization during institutional transition: A conceptual model. *Journal of International Entrepreneurship*, *8*(3), 273–287.

Kogut, B. (1991). Joint ventures and the option to expand and acquire. *Management Science*, *37*(1), 19–33.

Kwok, C. C. Y., & Reeb, D. M. (2000). Internationalization and firm risk: An upstream-downstream hypothesis. *Journal of International Business Studies*, *31*(4), 611–629.

Lahiri, N. (2010). Geographic distribution of R&D activity: How does it affect innovation quality? *Academy of Management Journal*, *53*(5), 1194–1209.

Lahiri, N., & Narayanan, S. (2013). Vertical integration, innovation, and alliance portfolio size: Implications for firm performance. *Strategic Management Journal*, *34*(9), 1042–1064.

Lavie, D. (2006). The competitive advantage of interconnected firms: An extension of the resource-based view. *Academy of Management Review*, *31*(3), 638–658.

Lee, D., & Madhavan, R. (2010). Divestiture and firm performance: A meta-analysis. *Journal of Management*, *36*(6), 1345–1371.

Li, M. X. (2013). Using the propensity score method to estimate causal effects: A review and practical guide. *Organizational Research Methods*, *16*(2), 188–226.

Martin, X., & Salomon, R. (2003). Tacitness, learning, and international expansion: A study of foreign direct investment in a knowledge-intensive industry. *Organization Science*, *14*(3), 297–311.

Mata, J., & Freitas, E. (2012). Foreignness and exit over the life cycle of firms. *Journal of International Business Studies*, *43*(7), 615–630.

Mata, J., & Portugal, P. (2000). Closure and divestiture by foreign entrants: The impact of entry and post-entry strategies. *Strategic Management Journal*, *21*(5), 549–562.

McDermott, M. C. (2010). Foreign divestment: The neglected area of international business? *International Studies of Management & Organization*, *40*(4), 37–53.

McGahan, A. M., & Porter, M. E. (1997). How much does industry matter, really? *Strategic Management Journal*, *18*(S1), 15–30.

Mudambi, R., & Swift, T. (2012). Multinational enterprises and the geographical clustering of innovation. *Industry and Innovation*, *19*(1), 1–21.

Narasimhan, O., Rajiv, S., & Dutta, S. (2006). Absorptive capacity in high-technology markets: The competitive advantage of the haves. *Marketing Science*, *25*(5), 510–524.

Narula, R. (2002). Innovation systems and 'inertia' in R&D location: Norwegian firms and the role of systemic lock-in. *Research Policy*, *31*(5), 795–816.

Narula, R. (2014). Exploring the paradox of competence-creating subsidiaries: Balancing bandwidth and dispersion in MNEs. *Long Range Planning*, *47*(1–2), 4–15.

Narula, R., & Santangelo, G. D. (2012). New insights on the role of location advantages in international innovation. In A. Verbeke & H. Merchant (Eds.), *Handbook of research on international strategic management* (pp. 291–309). Cheltenham: Edward Elgar.

Norbäck, P. J., Tekin-Koru, A., & Waldkirch, A. (2015). Multinational firms and plant divestiture. *Review of International Economics*, *23*(5), 811–845.

OECD. (2006). *The OECD's project on harmful tax practices: 2006 update on progress in member countries*. Paris: Organization for Economic Cooperation and Development.

Paniccia, I. (1998). One, a hundred, thousands of industrial districts. Organizational variety in local networks of small and medium-sized enterprises. *Organization Studies*, *19*(4), 667–699.

Powell, W. W., Koput, K. W., & Smith-Doerr, L. (1996). Interorganizational collaboration and the locus of innovation: Networks of learning in biotechnology. *Administrative Science Quarterly*, *41*(1), 116–145.

Puck, J. F., Holtbrugge, D., & Mohr, A. T. (2009). Beyond entry mode choice: Explaining the conversion of joint ventures into wholly owned subsidiaries in the People's Republic of China. *Journal of International Business Studies*, *40*(3), 388–404.

Reeb, D. N., Kwok, C. C. Y., & Baek, H. Y. (1998). Systematic risk of the multinational corporation. *Journal of International Business Studies*, *29*(2), 263–279.

Rosenkopf, L., & Schilling, M. A. (2007). Comparing alliance network structure across industries: Observations and explanations. *Strategic Entrepreneurship Journal*, *1*(3–4), 191–209.

Rothaermel, F. T. (2001). Incumbent's advantage through exploiting complementary assets via interfirm cooperation. *Strategic Management Journal*, *22*(6–7), 687–699.

Simsek, Z. (2009). Organizational ambidexterity: Towards a multilevel understanding. *Journal of Management Studies*, *46*(4), 597–624.

Sirmon, D. G., & Lane, P. J. (2004). A model of cultural differences and international alliance performance. *Journal of International Business Studies*, *35*(4), 306–319.

Song, S. (2014). Unfavorable market conditions, institutional and financial development, and exits of foreign subsidiaries. *Journal of International Management*, *20*(3), 279–289.

Song, S. (2015). Exchange rate challenges, flexible intra-firm adjustments, and subsidiary longevity. *Journal of World Business*, *50*(1), 36–45.

StataCorp. (2015). *Stata: Release 14. Statistical Software*. College Station, TX: StataCorp LP.

Sun, S. L., & Lee, R. P. (2013). Enhancing innovation through international joint venture portfolios: From the emerging firm perspective. *Journal of International Marketing*, *21*(3), 1–21.

Sytch, M., & Tatarynowicz, A. (2014). Exploring the locus of invention: The dynamics of network communities and firms' invention productivity. *Academy of Management Journal*, *57*(1), 249–279.

Turcan, R. V. (2013). The philosophy of turning points: A case of de-internationalization. *Advances in International Management*, *26*, 219–235.

Uzzi, B. (1996). The sources and consequences of embeddedness for the economic performance of organizations: The network effect. *American Sociological Review*, *61*(4), 674–698.

Vassolo, R. S., Anand, J., & Folta, T. B. (2004). Non-additivity in portfolios of exploration activities: A real options-based analysis of equity alliances in biotechnology. *Strategic Management Journal*, *25*(11), 1045–1061.

Vasudeva, G., Zaheer, A., & Hernandez, E. (2013). The embeddedness of networks: Institutions, structural holes, and innovativeness in the fuel cell industry. *Organization Science*, *24*(3), 645–663.

Verbeke, A., & Greidanus, N. S. (2009). The end of the opportunism vs trust debate: Bounded reliability as a new envelope concept in research on MNE governance. *Journal of International Business Studies*, *40*(9), 1471–1495.

West, J. (2002). Limits to globalization: Organizational homogeneity and diversity in the semiconductor industry. *Industrial and Corporate Change*, *11*(1), 159–188.

Wooldridge, J. M. (2002). *Econometric analysis of cross section and panel data*. Cambridge, MA: MIT Press.

Zaheer, A., & Bell, G. G. (2005). Benefiting from network position: Firm capabilities, structural holes, and performance. *Strategic Management Journal*, *26*(9), 809–825.

INDEX

Printed and bound by CPI Group (UK) Ltd, Croydon, CR0 4YY

13/09/2026

14961059-0008